The Cold War

The Cold War

A History in Documents
and Eyewitness Accounts

**Jussi Hanhimäki and
Odd Arne Westad**

OXFORD
UNIVERSITY PRESS

OXFORD

UNIVERSITY PRESS

Great Clarendon Street, Oxford OX2 6DP

Oxford University Press is a department of the University of Oxford.
It furthers the University's objective of excellence in research, scholarship,
and education by publishing worldwide in

Oxford New York

Auckland Cape Town Dar es Salaam Hong Kong Karachi Kuala Lumpur
Madrid Melbourne Mexico City Nairobi New Delhi Taipei Toronto
Shanghai

With offices in

Argentina Austria Brazil Chile Czech Republic France Greece
Guatemala Hungary Italy Japan South Korea Poland Portugal
Singapore Switzerland Thailand Turkey Ukraine Vietnam

Oxford is a registered trade mark of Oxford University Press
in the UK and in certain other countries

Published in the United States
by Oxford University Press Inc., New York

© Jussi Hanhimäki & Odd Arne Westad 2003

The moral rights of the author have been asserted
Database right Oxford University Press (maker)

First published 2003

First published in paperback 2004

British Library Cataloguing in Publication Data

Data available

Library of Congress Cataloging in Publication Data

Data available

ISBN 0-19-820862-6
ISBN 0-19-927280-8 (pbk.)

10 9 8 7 6 5 4 3 2

Typeset by SNP Best-set Typesetter Ltd., Hong Kong
Printed in Great Britain
on acid-free paper by
Ashford Colour Press Limited
Gosport, Hampshire

To our students; past, present, and future

Contents

List of Illustrations

Introduction: Studying the Cold War

This book contains a small selection of documents which the editors consider important for understanding the Cold War as a global conflict. It is not a compilation of diplomatic papers—there are many such already, and none of them, in our opinion, gives a satisfactory picture of the conflict. Nor is it an attempt at presenting the latest findings from secret archives—indeed, the majority of these documents have been published before. Rather, the purpose is to bring forward the different kinds of materials that are necessary to use in order to understand what the Cold War was about and how it was fought. By showing the experiences of East Berlin housewives and South African students as well those of political leaders from Europe and the Third World, we aim at a differentiation of the views of the conflict and of its significance. Emphasizing differences is perhaps the most important aspect of studying the Cold War (or any political conflict, for that matter), because it helps the student realize that the causes of the clash may have looked very different in Santiago from the way they looked in Seoul, not to mention in New York, Moscow, or Beijing. The variety of experience and opinion is therefore much of what this book is about.

Views of the Cold War

Throughout most of its duration the study of the Cold War was a heavily politicized field. Indeed, until the 1970s (and to some extent even today) questions over the responsibility for the East–West conflict dominated the scholarship on the Cold War. Whether one points the finger at the Soviet Union or the United States, the early explanations for the origins of the conflict were essentially extensions of the political atmosphere of their time. Given that American historians dominated Cold War scholarship, the application of blame reflected the political debates within the United States. While the so-called 'orthodox' scholars explained the Cold War as essentially a result of the Western need to defend itself against the onslaught of Soviet aggression, the 'revisionists' turned the argument on its head, maintaining that it was the American drive for hegemony that forced the Soviets to establish tight control over its neighbouring states. It was hardly an accident that the 'orthodox' view tended to dominate scholarly debate during the 1950s and most of the 1960s, when a broad consensus over the correctness of American policy prevailed in the United States. In contrast, the 'revisionists' had their heyday in the late 1960s and early 1970s, when the debacle of the Vietnam War split the Cold War consensus apart.[1]

Starting in the 1970s, however, the study of the Cold War also began to move beyond the simple application of blame and responsibility. While still focusing mainly on the diplomatic and military aspects of the Cold War, scholars started to view the conflict as a result of a complex interaction between all the various parties involved. Effectively this meant that Cold War historians—still a group dominated by Americans, but increasingly drawing on studies from Britain and other West European countries—explained the Cold War as a process in which geopolitical calculations, the imbalance of military and economic power, and numerous other factors contributed to the East–West tension. Some historians—with John Lewis Gaddis as the most prominent—saw an emerging synthesis between the orthodox and revisionist views and dubbed it the 'post-revisionist' school. As befits a general international atmosphere of detente, most post-revisionists de-emphasized the role of ideas and ideologies and instead explained the Cold War increasingly in a Realist manner: decision-makers on all sides became, in effect, rational geopolitical calculators advancing their respective national interests in the unique context of the post-war world.[2]

Out of this shift came much debate, but no broadly accepted synthesis. Aided by the increasing availability of primary sources (though still almost exclusively from Western archives), and influenced by new directions in the social sciences as well as in history, the study of the Cold War became more diversified. Not only did a growing number of scholars reassess the diplomatic record of the conflict, but—especially from 1980 on—the economic, social, and cultural history of the Cold War started to emerge. Some scholars—often referred to as 'corporatists'—would, for instance, examine the importance of co-operation between American political and business elites. In brief, while the debate about responsibility for the Cold War hardly disappeared, there was a growing interest in exploring the impact that the East–West division had on the people who were influenced by it.

Moreover, the global nature of the Cold War meant that anyone hoping to

---

[1] Some of the more influential practitioners in the orthodox tradition included Herbert Feis and Arthur Schlesinger; the 'Godfather' of the revisionists was William A. Williams, whose 'star students', Lloyd Gardner, Walter LaFeber, and Thomas McCormick, were particularly influential in the 1970s. For a series of essays on the changing views of the Cold War, see Odd Arne Westad, ed., *Reviewing the Cold War: Approaches, Interpretations, Theory* (2000).

[2] The best place to look for a summary of the post-revisionist argument is John Gaddis, 'The Emerging Post-Revisionist Synthesis on the Origins of the Cold War', *Diplomatic History*, 7: 3 (1983). While maintaining that Soviet expansionism was at the root of post-war tensions, Gaddis downplayed the role of ideology as a root cause of this expansionism. In some ways the original 'post-revisionist' was, in fact, Louis J. Halle, whose 1967 book *Cold War as History* was decidedly devoid of the emotional debates of its time and instead emphasized the 'geopolitical vacuum' that Germany's defeat had created as a 'natural' cause for the Cold War.

study a specific Cold War conflict in any detail needed to have at least a passing expertise in his/her chosen geographical area. For example, to understand the Vietnam War's impact in Southeast Asia required a certain amount of knowledge about the region, its history, its languages and cultures. All in all, even before the Cold War came to an end, the study of this global conflict had become a vast discipline that embraced the numerous ways of approaching the study of the past. Consequently, as the Cold War itself came to an end, the wealth of impressive and often cross-disciplinary scholarship, practiced by an increasingly international group of scholars, was already evident. By the early 1990s Cold War history had become, in the broadest possible sense, 'international history' (as opposed to the history of international relations or diplomatic history).[3]

Yet, until the late 1980s and early 1990s our understanding of the Cold War was still limited by the paucity of sources allowing historians to assess the policies and the social, economic, and political structures of all sides of the conflict with equal vigour. Only the collapse of the Cold War order could make possible such a shift, through increased access to the needed archival resources. At the same time, the collapse of the Soviet Union provided an end to the narrative known as the Cold War. The period could finally be treated as history rather than as an ongoing process in which the scholars themselves were, if in a limited way, participants.

The first, virtually inevitable, outcome of the Soviet collapse in the West was the rise of certain degree of triumphalism. The West had 'won', hence its opposition to Communism—however much it may have been criticized at various points during the Cold War—was vindicated. Indeed, there was even talk about the 'End of History' and the inevitable march of liberal capitalism now that it had defeated its 'totalitarian' enemy. To their credit, most Cold War historians resisted the temptation to join in such premature celebrations. Instead, the process of examining the Cold War 'as history'—with the help of sources from all, or most, of the countries that participated in the conflict—finally began.[4]

It was hardly a surprise that in the 1990s there was a shift in the emphasis of the study of the Cold War: if scholars had previously relied heavily on massive amounts of American, British, and other Western documentation, they now rushed to use the newly available former Soviet bloc materials to 'prove' what had made the other side tick. In the 1990s a new Cold War history began to take shape as scholars assessed and reassessed such issues as the fall of the Iron Curtain and

---

[3] Throughout the 1980s and early 1990s the need to 'broaden the horizons' was, in fact, a continuous theme in one of the key journals devoted to the study of US foreign relations, *Diplomatic History*.

[4] The debate about 'The End of History' took place already in 1989 when Francis Fukuyama published an article with that title in the American journal *The National Interest*. For an early collection of essays by historians trying to assess the end of the Cold War, see Michael J. Hogan, ed., *The End of the Cold War* (1992).

the origins of the Korean War. Some of the findings were hardly surprising: Josef Stalin, for example, remained by most accounts the chief 'villain' of the early Cold War; Mao Zedong maintained his place as the Soviet leader's chief rival. In other areas, however, the new scholarship—which is still in its early stages—has made some conceptual leaps.[5]

One of these is the general point that ideology and perceptions mattered inside the Soviet bloc and—at least in the view of some scholars—in the United States, much more than most historians had previously assumed. Or to put it another way: while ideology had been viewed by many as simply a convenient mask of 'real interests', one of the tentative conclusions of new Cold War history is that ideology was, in itself, a fundamental 'interest'. This general point is worth stressing, simply because it underlines one central fact that made the Cold War a unique confrontation: ideas, values, and belief systems were at the heart of the struggle that defined the second half of the twentieth century.

To acknowledge the role of ideologies is not to say that geopolitical, economic, or military assessments of the Cold War—or some its aspects—are irrelevant. Quite the contrary. Without taking into account the geopolitical interests of certain key powers in such areas as, say, Eastern Europe (the Soviet Union), without the relative and real economic power of the United States, and without the advances in military technology (especially in the field of nuclear weapons), it is impossible to truly understand the Cold War. At the same time, if one ignores the existence of a deep-seated—and evidently irreconcilable—ideological conflict, one can hardly understand why, for example, the Soviet determination to protect its geopolitical interests in Eastern Europe would have mattered as much as it did to the United States or would have garnered any support within Eastern (and even in Western) Europe. Nor can one easily explain the often self-defeating determination of both the United States and the Soviet Union to engage in foreign interventions around the globe, without considering the ideological underpinnings of such excursions.

The most significant impact of the end of the Cold War on our views about the conflict is simple: the collapse of the Soviet Union meant that the Cold War was, like the wars that preceded it, finally history. The conflict now has a beginning, a middle, and an end. Knowing that the West 'won' and the Soviet Union 'lost' almost automatically invites a certain degree of certainty about the superiority of the values and the system that prevailed. To succumb to such triumphalism, however, would be to miss the point of understanding the Cold War as history; as

---

[5] The list of important studies produced in the 1990s is far too long to be cited here, but the recommended Readings for each chapter does give some direction. For a (by now somewhat dated) synthesis of the first stage of the new Cold War history, see John L. Gaddis, *We Now Know: Rethinking Cold War History* (1997).

in any past event, it is ultimately more important to grasp what motivated the actors in their particular contexts than to judge them for their achievements. For, as the documents in this volume will show, participants' views of the meanings of the Cold War varied at least as much as do the present historical interpretations of the era.

Source Materials

Over the past ten years there has been a revolution in historians' access to Cold War historical sources. While up to 1990 few countries but the United States and Great Britain had instituted regularized and mandatory declassification of their documents on foreign affairs, now more than eighty-five countries have such laws or regulations, including Russia, all of Europe, many Asian states, and some in Latin America and Africa. For students of contemporary history, the revolution in source access has meant that key aspects of the Cold War could be re-evaluated, and that new and stronger interpretations could be developed.

It is important to note, however, that while access to new sources is of crucial importance to the historians, it is the accumulation of historical evidence that makes a breakthrough in terms of understanding possible. There has been, and still is, a danger that while we rush to study newly opened archival collections, we fail to put enough emphasis on crucial materials that have been available for decades. Some of these sources include non-archival evidence, and evidence that does *not* come from levels of high diplomacy but rather documents how people in other positions thought, felt, and acted with regard to the Cold War.

In putting together this volume, we have used three main types of quarries: archives and document depositories; electronic archives and source collections; and published source collections, including contemporary periodicals. A few words on each of these categories may be in order here.

Archives and Depositories

The most important collections of historical source materials to Cold War history are generally found in archives and document depositories. The reason for that is not that archives *always* provide the most important sources for historians—although students can easily be led to believe this, when listening to their teachers' rapt descriptions of their own archival discoveries. Rather, it is that many of the key events of the Cold War took place behind closed doors, and that decision-makers, East and West, often took great care to prevent the public from knowing how they arrived at their decisions.

Some of the great archives for students of the Cold War—such as the US National Archives and presidential libraries, or the Public Record Office in London, are open to all researchers. Others, such as the Foreign Policy Archives of the Russian Federation in Moscow, or the Archives of the South African Department of Foreign Affairs in Pretoria, expect you to apply for access first. In addition to public papers of institutions, there is also an increasing number of collections of private papers available worldwide.

Many public archives operate a twenty- or thirty-year rule for access, meaning that the more recent materials are, the more difficult they are to get access to. This is changing, however, as more and more governments realize that the Cold War is indeed a thing of the past, and that the public's access to information about its past should take precedence over the natural official instincts for secrecy.

Electronic Archives

The Internet is an increasingly important source for information on Cold War history. No other historical area of research has been so quick in taking up the possibilities offered by electronic communication, probably because the end of the Cold War and the rise of the worldwide web coincided almost precisely in time. Among the key collections available on the internet are the *Cold War International History Project* and the *National Security Archive* (both based in Washington, DC), the *Harvard Project on Cold War Studies*, and the London-based *Cold War Studies Centre*. All of these are private research institutions, which get their documentation from archives or other sources, public and private, and post them on the Web. In many cases the documents have to be translated first, and they are usually accompanied by brief commentaries by leading historians.

As with all Web-based research, students have to be very careful when verifying the authenticity of Cold War documents on the Internet. The Cold War still gives rise to much political passion, and one cannot be careful enough when making sure that the documentation one uses is accurate.

Published Source Collections

Many aspects of the Cold War are now covered in different forms of published source collections. One form is the published official archival document series, such as the *Documents Diplomatiques Français* or the *Foreign Relations of the United States*. Another is the privately compiled volume of official documents, such as those by Chen Jian and Shu Guang Zhang, eds., *Chinese Communist Foreign Policy and the Cold War in Asia: New Documentary Evidence, 1944–1950* (Chicago: Imprint, 1996), or William Burr, ed., *The Kissinger Transcripts: The Top Secret Talks in Beijing and Macau* (New York: Free Press, 1998). A third form is the collection of interviews, reminiscences, leaflets, speeches, or transcripts of meetings from non-officials sources—trade unions, political parties, protest movements, or individuals at all levels. The latter are especially important, since they tend to reflect information that often cannot be easily had from official documents.

A particular category of sources are contemporary periodicals—newspapers, journals—and radio or television broadcasts. Journalists are invariably among the best observers there are, and their reports serve both as eyewitness accounts and as critical commentaries on official sources. In many cases—and especially for the later years of the Cold War, when archives are still not fully available— news and media sources are invaluable, although their accuracy should always be checked against other available material.

In compiling this volume, we have found that literary sources—novels, short stories, poems—can sometimes provide rich insights into Cold War issues and mindsets. They may help us understand some of those aspects of the conflict that are mostly absent from the writings of politicians or journalists. But they should be used with care, always bearing in mind the sharp dividing-line there is between fact and fiction: however representative we may think a literary description is, it cannot be used as historical *evidence* for anything beyond the way a given author would like to represent a situation at a given moment.

Lastly, there is the work of historians, bound by the profession's rules of argument and evidence, and still ultimately a product of the interpretative abilities of each practitioner. We have chosen to use a few accounts by major historians writing today, both as a way of introducing their work and because they present key moments not easily reflected through other texts.

The Selection

Creating a source collection that portrays a fifty-year global conflict is necessarily an exercise in limitation. We have chosen a mixture of chronological and topical chapters that focus on significant Cold War issues which today's students need to understand. The content of the volume is in no way expected to be comprehensive—out of around fifty chapters considered we chose nineteen, based on the twin principles of relevance and coherence. That there is, for instance, no chapter on the Middle East conflict is not because the Arab–Israeli relationship was unimportant to the Cold War, but simply because its direct relevance—both in terms of causes and effects—is less obvious than that of some other regional conflicts.

What holds for the selection of chapters is even more painfully true for the selection of texts. In choosing among the myriad of texts considered, we tried to get a selection that is as stimulating and as representative as possible. In particular, we have made sure that this is an *international* textbook, sometimes opting for translations of foreign-language texts even when there are decent English-language documents available. We have also tried to introduce to students the many different forms of texts that are available for the study of the Cold War. Lastly, we have wanted to publish excerpts that can easily be discussed in class, both in terms of contrast and because of the views they contain.

Excerpting a document is always a difficult process. Through only presenting parts of a text, there is a danger that we unintentionally alter the significance or the meaning of the original, even though we have been as careful as possible in making excerpts. We are therefore very grateful that Oxford University Press will be setting up a website on which we can publish full-text versions of some of the documents in the printed collection. In addition, the source for a text is always cited (except for public treaties).

The *questions* following each chapter are meant as starting-points for discussion. In most cases they invite the reader to reflect on the content of the documents in conjunction with more general readings on Cold War history.

To avoid making this volume even heavier to carry, we have suggested only a few readings for each chapter, and the index at the end also serves as a glossary for the texts.

A work of this size and scope could never have been completed without the help and advice of others. First, we need to acknowledge two invaluable sources for documentation on the Cold War: the Cold War International History Project at the Woodrow Wilson Center, and the National Security Archive at George Washington University, both located in Washington, DC. Their help with this volume is deeply appreciated.

For specific advice on document selection we can only offer thanks to a selected few. The editors would like to acknowledge the following: Czaba Bekes, Antony Best, William Burr, Chen Jian, Alexander O. Chubarian, John Lewis Gaddis, Jonathan Haslam, James Hershberg, Anne Kjelling, Mark Kramer, Hanns-Jürgen Küesters, N. Piers Ludlow, Christian Ostermann, Kimmo Rentola, David Reynolds, and Nguyen Vu Tung.

We would further like to thank Laura Schmidt for translations from German and French, and Jerome Elie for translations from French. Candace Sobers's expert assistance with copyright and general editing was invaluable. Goran Jovanovic provided knowledgeable help—beyond the call of duty—with scanning some material. For a superb job with indexing we would like to thank Rodolfo Neirotti and Jonathan White at the Woodrow Wilson Center.

At OUP we are first and foremost indebted to Ruth Parr for taking on this project and tolerating several delays as it grew in scope and was complicated by the continued escalation of available Cold War related materials. Our heartfelt thanks go to Ruth and her wonderfully helpful staff.

For their help with illustrations we would like to acknowledge the Centre for the Study of Cartoons and Caricature at the University of Kent at Canterbury. A special thanks goes to Jane Newton at the Centre.

Last but not least, the editors would like to thank those students at the London School of Economics and the Graduate Institute of International Studies who tested some of the chapters as teaching materials. This book is dedicated to them and their successors.

JMH
OAW

1

Origins, 1917–1945

In 1917 the combined effect of the American entry into World War I and the Russian Revolution set in place much of the dynamics that would cloud the history of international relations for the remainder of the twentieth century. With the coming into power of the Bolsheviks in Russia, the foundation of the USSR, and the securing of the success of the Communist revolution, the Soviet Union came to represent a formidable challenge to prevailing assumptions about power and legitimacy. In Europe, the final collapse of the Central Powers was made possible by the belated US entry into the war that signalled the abandonment of America's splendid isolation from the old continent. While it was hardly evident at the time, moreover, the Russian Revolution and the American entry into the war were harbingers of a long twilight struggle, pitting against each other not just two of the largest countries in the world—the United States and the Soviet Union—but also liberal capitalism and totalitarian socialism.

The enmity between the United States and the Soviet Union was particularly fierce at the closing stages of World War I. In part, this was due to a sense of betrayal amongst the Western allies. While the Bolsheviks struggled to establish control of Russian territory, they negotiated a separate peace treaty with Germany at Brest-Litovsk in the spring of 1918 and thus allowed Germans to concentrate on the western front of the war. Given the foreign intervention in the Russian Civil War (including US, British, Japanese, French, and other troops) in 1918–20, Lenin and other Bolshevik leaders were also justified in their argument that the Western capitalists and imperialists were trying to strangle the Soviet baby in its cradle. The outpouring of anti-Communist feelings in the United States during the first Red Scare in 1919–20 was further evidence of the deep ideological conflict that would have a profound impact on international affairs over the remainder of the twentieth century.

Although some historians have argued otherwise, neither the United States nor the Soviet Union retreated entirely from the international arena during the interwar years. As the most prosperous nation on earth the United States was particularly active during the 1920s in international economics, playing a key role in various plans aimed at boosting European recovery, while expanding its trade

connections and cultural influence. Meanwhile the Soviet Union played a leading role as the 'motherland of the international proletariat', using the Comintern
as a tool of its international influence that was felt, among other places, in China.
Moreover, while the two countries failed to establish diplomatic relations until
1933, Americans were among the most active foreign investors in the Soviet
Union already in the late 1920s. It is one of the ironies of the period that this
investment actually declined after official recognition was acheived.

From the late 1920s until the summer of 1941 Communism remained a threat
in the eyes of many Americans and West Europeans. But it was gradually being
transplanted as the foremost threat to international stability by the emergence
of the Nazi regime in Germany and the increasingly aggressive policies of the
empire of Japan. The onset of the Great Depression after 1929 also raised
isolationist sentiment within the United States and sowed doubts about the survival of capitalism. Undoubtedly, Stalin's consolidation of his power and the new
Soviet slogan of 'socialism in one country' made the Soviet threat appear less
imminent. News of the Nazi–Soviet Pact of August 1939, however, raised
the unexpected spectre of a truly 'unholy alliance'—followed by Germany's successes in Western Europe in 1940—that threatened to destroy the last semblance
of the liberal world order that Woodrow Wilson had propagated at the end of
World War I.

When Nazi Germany launched a massive attack on the Soviet Union in June
1941, the United States and the Soviet Union were quickly transformed from
distant enemies to allies. Along with Great Britain, the United States offered
material support and, following American entry into the war in December 1941,
the wartime Grand Alliance was consolidated. For the next four years the Big
Three co-operated in defeating the Axis powers. The wartime co-operation
included massive US military assistance, several wartime conferences, and the
co-ordination of military strategies to bring about the unconditional surrender of
Germany (in May 1945) and Japan (in September 1945).

The Grand Alliance was, though, far from a harmonious one, as is evidenced
by the Big Three's shared mistrust of each others' motives. The Soviets, who had
to bear the brunt of the German onslaught, continuously complained about
delays in the opening of a second front in Europe. Stalin's suspicions of Western
aims were undoubtedly further fed by his knowledge of the secret Anglo-
American project to build an atomic bomb. As the Allies began to contemplate
the structure of the post-war settlement, moreover, their different perceptions
began to gnaw away the façade of wartime comradeship. Neither the Americans
nor the Soviets, for example, had much interest in the perpetuation of the British
Empire. To the British and the Americans, the uncompromising Soviet stand
on the future of Eastern Europe appeared potentially menacing. Franklin
Roosevelt's death in April 1945 and Harry S. Truman's ascendancy to the

presidency seemed to usher in a new, more uncompromising and moralistic American policy. In the end, the surrender of Germany and Japan brought to an end an exceptional period of co-operation between the United States and the Soviet Union. Moreover, as the most destructive war in human history came to an end, the leaders in Moscow and Washington—as well as their counterparts in Britain, China, and elsewhere—had not come to an agreement about the shape of the post-war world. In the new international context of 1945, the contest between the United States and the Soviet Union, between liberal capitalist internationalism and totalitarian socialist internationalism, seemed ready to be fought again, with similar vigour but with far greater global consequences than had occurred at the closing stages of World War I.

Readings

Thomas Knock, *To End All Wars: Woodrow Wilson and the Quest for a New World Order* (1992). A thorough overview of the US president's post-World War I plans and their fate.

John Lewis Gaddis, *Russia, the Soviet Union and the United States* (1990). Probably the most readable succinct account of the overall relationship, with an insightful overview of the period of the Russian Revolution and its aftermath.

Kevin McDermott and Jeremy Agnew, *The Comintern: A History of International Communism from Lenin to Stalin* (1996). A brief history of the international Communist movement from the Russian Revolution to World War II.

David Reynolds, Warren F. Kimball, and Alexander O. Chubarian, (eds.), *Allies at War: The Soviet, American and British Experience* (1994). A collection of essays analysing the different wartime experiences of the 'Big Three'.

Robert C. Tucker, *Stalin in Power: The Revolution from Above, 1928–1941* (1992). One of the many studies on Stalin, focusing on the years prior to the German invasion.

1.1 Lenin to American Workers, 22 August 1918

In the aftermath of the Western allies' decision to intervene in the Russian Civil War, Lenin sent an open letter—addressed to 'American workers'—in which he pleaded for their support and rationalized the 'inevitable' victory of the world proletarian revolution. These are excerpts from the letter.

Comrades!
(...) at the present time the American revolutionary workers have to play an exceptionally important role as confrontational enemies of American imperialism—the freshest, strongest and latest in joining in the world-wide slaughter of

nations for the division of capitalist profits. At this very moment, the American multimillionaires, these modern slaveowners, have turned an exceptionally tragic page in the bloody history of bloody imperialism by giving their approval—whether direct or indirect, open or hypocritically concealed, makes no difference—to the armed expedition launched by the brutal Anglo-Japanese imperialists for the purpose of throttling the first socialist republic.

(...) The results of the four years of war have revealed the general law of capitalism as applied to war between robbers for the division of spoils: the richest and strongest profited and grabbed most, while the weakest were utterly robbed, tormented, crushed and strangled. The British imperialist robbers were the strongest in number of 'colonial slaves'. The British capitalists have not lost an inch of 'their' territory (i.e., territory they have grabbed over the centuries), but they have grabbed all the German colonies in Africa, they have grabbed Mesopotamia and Palestine, they have throttled Greece, and have begun to plunder Russia (...)

The American multimillionaires were, perhaps, richest of all, and geographically the most secure. They have profited more than all the rest. They have converted all, even the richest, countries into their tributaries. They have grabbed hundreds of billions of dollars. And every dollar is sullied with filth: the filth of the secret treaties between Britain and her 'allies', between Germany and her vassals, treaties for the division of the spoils, treaties of mutual 'aid' for oppressing the workers and persecuting the internationalist socialists. Every dollar is sullied with the filth of 'profitable' war contracts, which in every country made the rich richer and the poor poorer. And every dollar is stained with blood—from that ocean of blood that has been shed by the ten million killed and twenty million maimed in the great, noble, liberating and holy war to decide whether the British or the German robbers are to get most of the spoils, whether the British or the German thugs are to be foremost in throttling the weak nations all over the world (...)

The old bourgeois-democratic constitutions waxed eloquent about formal equality and right of assembly; but our proletarian and peasant Soviet Constitution casts aside the hypocrisy of formal equality. When the bourgeois republicans overturned thrones they did not worry about formal equality between monarchists and republicans. When it is a matter of overthrowing the bourgeoisie, only traitors or idiots can demand formal equality of rights for the bourgeoisie. 'Freedom of assembly' for workers and peasants is not worth a farthing when the best buildings belong to the bourgeoisie. Our Soviets have confiscated all the good buildings in town and country from the rich and have transferred all of them to the workers and peasants for their unions and meetings. This is our freedom of assembly—for the working people! This is the meaning and content of our Soviet, our socialist Constitution!

That is why we are all so firmly convinced that no matter what misfortunes may still be in store for it, our Republic of Soviets is invincible (…)

We know that help from you will probably not come soon, comrade American workers, for the revolution is developing in different countries in different forms and at different tempos (and it cannot be otherwise). We know that although the European proletarian revolution has been maturing very rapidly lately, it may, after all, not flare up within the next few weeks. We are banking on the inevitability of the world revolution, but this does not mean that we are such fools as to bank on the revolution inevitably coming on a definite and early date. We have seen two great revolutions in our country, 1905 and 1917, and we know revolutions are not made to order, or by agreement. We know that circumstances brought our Russian detachment of the socialist proletariat to the fore not because of our merits, but because of the exceptional backwardness of Russia, and that before the world revolution breaks out a number of separate revolutions may be defeated.

In spite of this, we are firmly convinced that we are invincible, because the spirit of mankind will not be broken by the imperialist slaughter. Mankind will vanquish it. And the first country to break the convict chains of the imperialist war was our country. We sustained enormously heavy casualties in the struggle to break these chains, but we broke them. We are free from imperialist dependence, we have raised the banner of struggle for the complete overthrow of imperialism for the whole world to see.

We are now, as it were, in a besieged fortress, waiting for the other detachments of the world socialist revolution to come to our relief. These detachments exist, they are more numerous than ours, they are maturing, growing, gaining more strength the longer the brutalities of imperialism continue. The workers are breaking away from their social traitors (…) Slowly but surely the workers are adopting Communist, Bolshevik tactics and are marching towards the proletarian revolution, which alone is capable of saving dying culture and dying mankind.

In short, we are invincible, because the world proletarian revolution is invincible.

US Atty. Gen.

1.2 A. Mitchell Palmer on Eradicating Bolshevism in the United States, April 1920

In part as a response to Lenin's 'courting' of American workers, a powerful reaction against 'radicalism' in various forms swept the United States immediately after the end of World War I. In 1920 the attorney-general of the United States, A. Mitchell Palmer,

*directed the FBI to round up hundreds of suspected radicals. While many were soon
released, others arrested during the 'Palmer raids' faced prison sentences. Those who did
not enjoy US citizenship were deported. In the article below, Palmer summarizes his fears
of Bolshevism and his methods of extirpating it.*

(…) Like a prairie-fire, the blaze of revolution was sweeping over every American
institution of law and order a year ago. It was eating its way into the homes of
the American workmen, its sharp tongues of revolutionary heat were licking the
altars of the churches, leaping into the belfry of the school bell, crawling into the
sacred corners of American homes, seeking to replace marriage vows with liber-
tine laws, burning up the foundations of society.

Robbery, not war, is the ideal of Communism. This has been demonstrated in
Russia, Germany, and in America. As a foe, the anarchist is fearless of his own life,
for his creed is a fanaticism that admits no respect of any other creed. Obviously
it is the creed of any criminal mind, which reasons always from motives impossible to clean thought. Crime is the degenerate factor in society.

Upon these two basic certainties, first that the 'Reds' were criminal aliens and
secondly that the American Government must prevent crime, it was decided that
there could be no nice distinctions drawn between the theoretical ideals of the
radicals and their actual violations of our national laws. An assassin may have brilliant intellectuality, he may be able to excuse his murder or robbery with fine
oratory, but any theory which excuses crime is not wanted in America. This is
no place for the criminal to flourish, nor will he do so, as long as the rights of
common citizenship can be exerted to prevent him (…)

It has always been plain to me that when American citizens unite upon any
national issue they are generally right, but it is sometimes difficult to make the
issue clear to them. If the Department of Justice could succeed in attracting the
attention of our optimistic citizens to the issue of internal revolution in this country, we felt sure there would be no revolution. The Government was in jeopardy;
our private information of what was being done by the organization known as the
Communist Party of America, with headquarters in Chicago, of what was being
done by the Communist Internationale under their manifesto planned at
Moscow last March by Trotzky, Lenin and others addressed 'To the Proletariats
of All Countries,' of what strides the Communist Labor Party was making,
removed all doubt. In this conclusion we did not ignore the definite standards of
personal liberty, of free speech, which is the very temperament and heart of the
people. The evidence was examined with the utmost care, with a personal leaning
toward freedom of thought and word on all questions.

The whole mass of evidence, accumulated from all parts of the country,
was scrupulously scanned, not merely for the written or spoken differences of

viewpoint as to the Government of the United States, but, in spite of these things, to see if the hostile declarations might not be sincere in their announced motive to improve our social order. There was no hope of such a thing (…)

My information showed that Communism in this country was an organization of thousands of aliens who were direct allies of Trotzky. Aliens of the same misshapen caste of mind and indecencies of character, and it showed that they were making the same glittering promises of lawlessness, of criminal autocracy to Americans, that they had made to the Russian peasants.

How the Department of Justice discovered upwards of 60,000 of these organized agitators of the Trotzky doctrine in the United States is the confidential information upon which the Government is now sweeping the nation clean of such alien filth (…)

Behind, and underneath, my own determination to drive from our midst the agents of Bolshevism with increasing vigor and with greater speed, until there are no more of them left among us, so long as I have the responsible duty of that task, I have discovered the hysterical methods of these revolutionary humans with increasing amazement and suspicion. In the confused information that sometimes reaches the people they are compelled to ask questions which involve the reasons for my acts against the 'Reds.' I have been asked, for instance, to what extent deportation will check radicalism in this country. Why not ask what will become of the United States Government if these alien radicals are permitted to carry out the principles of the Communist Party as embodied in its so-called laws, aims and regulations?

There wouldn't be any such thing left. In place of the United States Government we should have the horror and terrorism of bolsheviki tyranny such as is destroying Russia now. Every scrap of radical literature demands the overthrow of our existing government. All of it demands obedience to the instincts of criminal minds, that is, to the lower appetites, material and moral. The whole purpose of Communism appears to be a mass formation of the criminals of the world to overthrow the decencies of private life, to usurp property that they have not earned, to disrupt the present order of life regardless of health, sex or religious rights (…)

It has been inferred by the 'Reds' that the United States Government, by arresting and deporting them, is returning to the autocracy of Czardom, adopting the system that created the severity of Siberian banishment. My reply to such charges is that in our determination to maintain our government we are treating our alien enemies with extreme consideration. To deny them the privilege of remaining in a country which they have openly deplored as an unenlightened community, unfit for those who prefer the privileges of Bolshevism, should be no hardship. It strikes me as an odd form of reasoning that these Russian Bolsheviks who extol the Bolshevik rule should be so unwilling to return to Russia. The nationality of most of the alien 'Reds' is Russian and German. There is almost no other nationality represented among them.

(…) The Department of Justice will pursue the attack of these 'Reds' upon the Government of the United States with vigilance, and no alien, advocating the overthrow of existing law and order in this country, shall escape arrest and prompt deportation.

It is my belief that while they have stirred discontent in our midst, while they have caused irritating strikes, and while they have infected our social ideas with the disease of their own minds and their unclean morals we can get rid of them! and not until we have done so shall we have removed the menace of Bolshevism for good.

1.3 The Wilson Administration on Non-Recognition of Russia, August 1920

As it became clear that the allied intervention was unlikely to succeed in preventing the Bolsheviks from holding on to power, the Wilson government agonized over the proper course of action to take towards the new rulers of Russia. This note, drafted by Woodrow Wilson's close aide Bainbridge Colby in August 1920, sums up the policy of the US government until the 1930s. Wilson wrote at the top of this note: 'Thank you. This seems to me excellent and sufficient.'

This Government (…) would not, at least for the present, participate in any plan for the expansion of the armistice negotiations into a general European conference which would in all probability involve two results, from both of which this country strongly recoils, viz. the recognition of the Bolshevist regime and a settlement of Russian problems almost inevitably upon the basis of a dismemberment of Russia (…)

The United States maintains unimpaired its faith in the Russian people, in their high character and their future. That they will overcome the existing anarchy, suffering and destitution we do not entertain the slightest doubt. The distressing character of Russia's transition has many historical parallels, and the United States is confident that restored, free and united Russia will again take a leading place in the world, joining with the other free nations in upholding peace and orderly justice.

Until that time shall arrive the United States feels that friendship and honor require that Russia's interests must be generously protected, and that, as far as possible, all decisions of vital importance to it, and especially those concerning its sovereignty over the territory of the former Russian Empire, be held in abeyance (…)

That the present rulers of Russia do not rule by the will or the consent of any considerable proportion of the Russian people is an incontestable fact. Although nearly two and a half years have passed since they seized the machinery of government, promising to protect the Constituent Assembly against alleged conspiracies against it, they have not yet permitted anything in the nature of a popular election. At the moment when the work of creating a democratic representative government based upon universal suffrage was nearing completion the Bolsheviki, although, in number, an inconsiderable minority of the people, by force and cunning seized the powers and machinery of government and have continued to use them with savage oppression to maintain themselves in power.

Without any desire to interfere in the internal affairs of the Russian people, *asserts* or to suggest what kind of government they should have, the Government of *non-* the United States does express the hope that they will soon find a way to set up a *interference* government representing their free will and purpose. When that time comes, the United States will consider the measures of practical assistance which can be taken to promote the restoration of Russia (…)

It is not possible for the Government of the United States to recognize the present rulers of Russia as a government with which the relations common to friendly governments can be maintained. This conviction has nothing to do with any particular political or social structure which the Russian people themselves may see fit to embrace. It rests upon a wholly different set of facts. These facts, which none disputes, have convinced the Government of the United States, against its will, that the existing regime in Russia is based upon the negation of every principle of honor and good faith, and every usage and convention, underlying the whole structure of international law; the negation, in short, of every principle upon which it is possible to base harmonious and trustful relations, whether of nations or of individuals. The responsible leaders of the regime have frequently and openly boasted that they are willing to sign agreements and undertakings with foreign Powers while not having the slightest intention of observing such undertakings or carrying out such agreements. This attitude of disregard of obligations voluntarily entered into, they base upon the theory that no compact or agreement made with a non-Bolshevist government can have any moral force for them. They have not only avowed this as a doctrine, but have exemplified it in practice. Indeed, upon numerous occasions the responsible spokesmen of this Power, and its official agencies, have declared that it is their understanding that the very existence of Bolshevism in Russia, the maintenance of their own rule, depends, and must continue to depend, upon the occurrence of revolutions in all other great civilized nations, including the United States, which will overthrow and destroy their governments and set up Bolshevist rule in their stead. They have made it quite plain that they intend to use every means, including, of course, diplomatic agencies, to promote such revolutionary movements in other countries.

It is true that they have in various ways expressed their willingness to give 'assurances' and 'guarantees' that they will not abuse the privileges and immunities of diplomatic agencies by using them for this purpose. In view of their own declarations, already referred to, such assurances and guarantees cannot be very seriously regarded. Moreover, it is within the knowledge of the Government of the United States that the Bolshevist Government is itself subject to the control of a political faction, with extensive international ramifications through the Third Internationale, and that this body, which is heavily subsidized by the Bolshevist Government from the public revenues of Russia, has for its openly avowed aim the promotion of Bolshevist revolutions throughout the world. The leaders of the Bolsheviki have boasted that their promises of non-interference with other nations would in no wise bind the agents of this body. There is no room for reasonable doubt that such agents would receive the support and protection of any diplomatic agencies the Bolsheviki might have in other countries. Inevitably, therefore, the diplomatic service of the Bolshevist Government would become a channel for intrigues and the propaganda of revolt against the institutions and laws of countries, with whom it was at peace, which would be an abuse of friendship to which enlightened governments cannot subject themselves.

In the view of this Government, there cannot be any common ground upon which it can stand with a Power whose conceptions of international relations are so entirely alien to its own, so utterly repugnant to its moral sense. There can be no mutual confidence or trust, no respect even, if pledges are to be given and agreements made with a cynical repudiation of their obligations already in the mind of one of the parties. We cannot recognize, hold official relations with, or give friendly reception to the agents of, a government which is determined and bound to conspire against our institutions; whose diplomats will be the agitators of dangerous revolt; whose spokesmen say that they sign agreements with no intention of keeping them.

1.4 Stalin on International Communism, March 1925

Lenin died in 1924, sparking the first of several succession struggles within the Soviet leadership. By the late 1920s Josef Stalin had emerged as the clear supreme leader, a position he would hold until his death in 1953. In this message from 1925 Stalin sums up his views of the international situation in the 1920s and the necessity of the international Communist movement to prepare for a long-term struggle against capitalism.

(...) Undoubtedly, capital has succeeded in extricating itself from the quagmire of the post-war crisis (...) It is also beyond doubt that in Germany, in the centre of Europe, the period of revolutionary upsurge has come to an end (...) The working class movement in Germany has passed from the period of assault to the period of accumulating forces, to the period of forming and training a proletarian army under the banner of Communism. It scarcely needs proof that this circumstance is bound to be of great importance. All the more definitely, therefore, must this be said, in order to be able quickly to find our bearings in the new situation and to start the work of preparing the revolution on new lines (...)

Undoubtedly, side by side with the strengthening of capitalism, there is a growth of the contradictions between the capitalist groups, a growth of the forces which weaken and disintegrate capitalism. The struggle between Britain and America for oil, for Canada, for markets, etc.; the struggle between the Anglo-American bloc and Japan for Eastern markets; the struggle between Britain and France for influence in Europe; and, lastly, the struggle between enslaved Germany and the dominant Entente (...) the growth and consolidation of the national-liberation movement in India, China, Egypt, Indonesia, North Africa, etc., which are undermining capitalism's rear (...)

There is no doubt that the stories of the bourgeois hack writers about the Soviets being incapable of organising industry have been completely refuted. There is no doubt that during the past two years, after intervention and the blockade ceased, the industry of the Soviet Union has revived and gained strength. There is no doubt that the material and cultural conditions of the workers have substantially improved during this short period (...) All these circumstances are now of decisive importance for revolutionising the workers in the capitalist countries (...) And when the Western workers become convinced that every step in the development of industry in Russia also means a step in the improvement of the conditions of the workers, and not the deterioration of these conditions, as usually happens in the capitalist countries, they will realize that it is high time for them, the Western workers, to set up workers' states in their own countries. That is why the very existence of the Soviet state is a deadly menace to imperialism. That is why no successes that imperialism achieves can be durable as long as the Soviet state exists and develops (...)

There can be no doubt that in time the trends that are unfavorable for capitalism and favorable for the revolution must triumph, for imperialism is incapable of resolving the contradictions that are corroding it, for it is capable only of alleviating them for a time with the result that they break out again later on and manifest themselves with fresh destructive force. It is also beyond doubt, however, that at the present time the positive trends, that are favorable for capitalism, are gaining the upper hand (…)

As a result we have a sort of lull in Europe and America, 'disturbed' by the national revolutionary movement in the colonies and 'marred' by the existence, development and growing strength of the Soviet Union.

For the bourgeoisie it means a respite, increased exports of capital, increased wealth, increased oppression and exploitation in the colonies, increased pressure on the Soviet Union, the concentration of all the counter-revolutionist forces around Anglo-American capital.

For the proletariat in the capitalist countries it means the opening of a period of accumulating forces, the opening of a period of forming and training the proletarian armies under the banner of Communism in the conditions of a system of repression alternating with a system of 'liberties.'

For the colonies it means an intensification of the struggle against national oppression and exploitation, an intensification of the struggle for liberation from imperialism.

For the Soviet Union it means the exertion of all efforts to develop industry further, to strengthen the country's defensive capacity, to concentrate the revolutionary forces of all countries against imperialism.

Hence the tasks of the Communist Parties:

1. To utilize to the utmost all contradictions in the camp of the bourgeoisie with the object of disintegrating and weakening its forces and of strengthening the positions of the proletariat.

2. To devise concrete forms and methods of drawing the working class in the advanced countries closer to the national revolutionary movement in the colonies and dependent countries with the object of rendering all possible support to this movement against the common enemy, against imperialism.

3. To promote the fight for trade-union unity and to carry it to a successful conclusion, bearing in mind that this is the surest means of winning over the vast working class masses; for it is impossible to win over the vast proletarian masses unless the trade unions are won over; and it is impossible to win over the trade unions unless work is conducted in them and unless the confidence of the masses of the workers is won in the trade unions month by month and year by year. Failing this, it is out of the question even to think of achieving the dictatorship of the proletariat.

4. To devise concrete forms and methods of drawing the working class closer to the small peasantry, who are crushed by the bureaucratic machine of the bourgeois state and by the extortionate prices of the all-powerful trusts, bearing in mind that the struggle to win over the small peasantry is the immediate task of a party that is advancing towards the dictatorship of the proletariat.

5. To support the Soviet regime and to frustrate the interventionist machina-

tions of imperialism against the Soviet Union, bearing in mind that the Soviet Union is the bulwark of the revolutionary movement in all countries, and that to preserve and strengthen the Soviet Union means to accelerate the victory of the working class over the world bourgeoisie.

1.5 Mao Zedong's Report on the Peasant Movement in Hunan, March 1927

diff. than Lenin

Mao was a Hunanese peasant who became one of the founding members of the Chinese Communist Party in 1921. A 'home-grown' Marxist, Mao was particularly interested in mobilizing the rural peasantry, rather than the (in China relatively small) industrial working class. Mao became an active rural organizer and promoted the idea that peasants rather than workers create revolution. Below are some excerpts from an early report.

During my recent visit to Hunan I made a first-hand investigation of conditions in the five counties of Xiangtan, Xiangxiang, Hengshan, Liling and Changsha. In the thirty-two days from January 4 to February 5 [1927], I called together fact-finding conferences in villages and country towns, which were attended by experienced peasants and by comrades working in the peasant movement, and I listened attentively to their reports and collected a great deal of material. Many of the hows and whys of the peasant movement were the exact opposite of what the gentry in Hankou and Changsha are saying. I saw and heard of many strange things of which I had hitherto been unaware. I believe the same is true of many other places, too. All talk directed against the peasant movement must be speedily set right. All the wrong measures taken by the revolutionary authorities concerning the peasant movement must be speedily changed. Only thus can the future of the revolution be benefited. For the present upsurge of the peasant movement is a colossal event. In a very short time, in China's central, southern and northern provinces, several hundred million peasants will rise like a mighty storm (…) They will smash all the trammels that bind them and rush forward along the road to liberation. They will sweep all the imperialists, warlords, corrupt officials, local tyrants and evil gentry into their graves. Every revolutionary party and every revolutionary comrade will be put to the test, to be accepted or rejected as they decide. There are three alternatives. To march at their head and lead them? To trail behind them, gesticulating and criticizing? Or to stand in their way and oppose them? Every Chinese is free to choose, but events will force you to make the choice quickly (…)

The main targets of attack by the peasants are the local tyrants, the evil gentry and the lawless landlords, but in passing they also hit out against patriarchal ideas and institutions, against the corrupt officials in the cities and against bad practices and customs in the rural areas. In force and momentum the attack is tempestuous; those who bow before it survive and those who resist perish. As a result, the privileges which the feudal landlords enjoyed for thousands of years are being shattered to pieces. Every bit of the dignity and prestige built up by the landlords is being swept into the dust. With the collapse of the power of the landlords, the peasant associations have now become the sole organs of authority and the popular slogan 'all power to the peasant associations' has become a reality. Even trifles such as a quarrel between husband and wife are brought to the peasant association. Nothing can be settled unless someone from the peasant association is present. The association actually dictates all rural affairs, and, quite literally, 'whatever it says, goes.' Those who are outside the associations can only speak well of them and cannot say anything against them. The local tyrants, evil gentry and lawless landlords have been deprived of all right to speak, and none of them dares even mutter dissent. In the face of the peasant associations' power and pressure, the top local tyrants and evil gentry have fled (…)

(…) what was looked down upon four months ago as a 'gang of peasants' has now become a most honorable institution. Those who formerly prostrated themselves before the power of the gentry now bow before the power of the peasants. No matter what their identity, all admit that the world since last October is a different one (…) The patriarchal-feudal class of local tyrants, evil gentry and lawless landlords has formed the basis of autocratic government for thousands of years and is the cornerstone of imperialism, warlordism and corrupt officialdom.

To overthrow these feudal forces is the real objective of the national revolution. In a few months the peasants have accomplished what Dr. Sun Yat-sen[3] wanted, but failed, to accomplish in the forty years he devoted to the national revolution. This is a marvelous feat never before achieved, not just in forty, but in thousands of years (…) Every revolutionary comrade should know that the national revolution requires a great change in the countryside. The Revolution of 1911 did not bring about this change, hence its failure. This change is now taking place, and it is an important factor for the completion of the revolution. Every revolutionary comrade must support it, or he will be taking the stand of counter-revolution (…)

(…) The peasants are clear-sighted. Who is bad and who is not, who is the worst and who is not quite so vicious, who deserves severe punishment and who deserves to be let off lightly—the peasants keep clear accounts, and very seldom has the punishment exceeded the crime. Secondly, a revolution is not a dinner party, or writing an essay, or painting a picture, or doing embroidery; it cannot be so refined, so leisurely and gentle, so temperate, kind, courteous, restrained and magnanimous. A revolution is an insurrection, an act of violence by which one class overthrows another. A rural revolution is a revolution by which the peasantry overthrows the power of the feudal landlord class. Without using the greatest force, the peasants cannot possibly overthrow the deep-rooted authority of the landlords which has lasted for thousands of years. The rural areas need a mighty revolutionary upsurge, for it alone can rouse the people in their millions to become a powerful force (…)

(…) To put it bluntly, it is necessary to create terror for a while in every rural area, or otherwise it would be impossible to suppress the activities of the counter-revolutionaries in the countryside or overthrow the authority of the gentry. Proper limits have to be exceeded in order to right a wrong, or else the wrong cannot be righted. Those who talk about the peasants 'going too far' seem at first sight to be different from those who say 'It's terrible!' as mentioned earlier, but in essence they proceed from the same standpoint and likewise voice a landlord theory that upholds the interests of the privileged classes. Since this theory impedes the rise of the peasant movement and so disrupts the revolution, we must firmly oppose it.

[handwritten margin note: promotes use of terror]

1.6 Two US opinions on Recognizing the Soviet Union, October 1933

Prior to the formal decision to recognize the Soviet Union Franklin Roosevelt and his secretary of state, Cordell Hull, enlisted numerous views on the subject. Below are two samples: by Walton Moore, assistant secretary of state (for Legal Affairs) and William Bullitt, about to become the first US ambassador to the USSR.

A. Memorandum by the Assistant Secretary of State (Walton Moore)

[handwritten margin note: pro-recognition (with reservations, limitations)]

(…) Impressions relative to the recognition of the Russian Government derived from the data furnished me by the Secretary and other data available at this moment:

(1) It seems clear that there should and must be recognition eventually and without undue delay, provided there is assurance that the Russian Government will not directly or indirectly make any effort to affect the political institutions or integrity of the United States and that certain other major matters can be satisfactorily disposed of.

(2) (…) as illustrated by the experience of Great Britain, Russia is (a) inclined to a more reasonable attitude towards nations that have not accorded the recognition she seeks than towards those that have, and (b) after eagerly seeking and

obtaining recognition she becomes more indifferent to her obligations than theretofore.

(3) If what is said in the last paragraph can be assumed as a correct premise, it may be thought best in advance of actual recognition to (…) explore the entire situation and endeavor to reach a full agreement between the two governments to be embodied in a treaty, pertaining to all or most of the very large number of important questions that sooner or later will call for consideration, e.g. as to the alleged desire of Russia to undermine our system of government; as to the personal, religious and property status and rights of our nationals in Russia and the ports of that country; as to the claims of Americans for the repayment of loans or for damages, and the claims that may be asserted against our Government by the Russian Government in its own behalf or in behalf of its subjects; as to the basis and character in various aspects of the commercial dealings between the two nations, etc., etc.

(4) An act of recognition is not revocable and it is certainly retroactive unless otherwise limited. Should the President extend recognition without the situation being dealt with in advance as suggested, then for the purpose of eliminating disputable questions as far as possible it might be accompanied by such conditions as may be agreed upon.

A restricted representation of each country, in the other until otherwise mutually determined, might well be specified and in such manner as to encourage the performance of the conditions accompanying recognition (…).

It would seem that immediate and unconditional recognition would not be of any special moral or material advantage and, on the other hand, might be attended by very widespread adverse criticism.

B. Memorandum by the Special Assistant to the Secretary of State (William Bullitt)

(…) Whatever method may be used to enter into negotiations with the Soviet Government, it seems essential that formal recognition should not be accorded except as the final act of an agreement covering a number of questions in dispute. Before recognition and before loans, we shall find the Soviet Government relatively amenable. After recognition or loans, we should find the Soviet Government adamant. Among the chief agreements which, in my opinion, must be reached before recognition are the following:

1. Prohibition of Communist propaganda in the United States by the Soviet Government and by the Comintern.

2. Protection of the civil and religious rights of Americans in Russia which are inadequately protected under current Russian practice (e.g. 'economic espionage').

3. Agreement by the Soviet Government that the act of recognition shall not be retroactive to the foundation of that government (which is the usual practice), but shall take effect only from the day on which it may be accorded. This is essential to protect both our Government and many citizens and corporations from suits for damages.

(…) before recognition, we should also attempt to obtain an agreement in regard to the repayment of the loans of the Government of the United States to the Kerensky Government, a waiver of Russian counter claims based upon our Vladivostok, Archangel and Murmansk expeditions; also some sort of provision for the settlement of claims of American nationals and corporations for property, goods and cash seized by the Soviet Government.

(…) Our position would be strongest, I believe, if all these questions, whether of a legal, economic or financial nature, should be handled as a unit in one global negotiation, the end of which would be signature of the agreements and simultaneous recognition.

1.7 An American impression of the USSR in the 1930s

In the midst of the Great Depression a number of Americans found work in the Soviet Union. Below, an American 'guest worker' recounts his experiences in the Soviet Union during the 1930s.

(…) I left the University of Wisconsin in 1931 to find myself in an America sadly dislocated, an America offering few opportunities for young energy and enthusiasm (…) Something seemed to be wrong with America. I began to read extensively about the Soviet Union, and gradually came to the conclusion that the Bolsheviks had found answers to at least some of the questions Americans were asking each other. I decided to go to Russia to work, study, and to lend a hand in the construction of a society which seemed to be at least one step ahead of the American (…) Finally arrangements were completed, and I started out on the four-day train trip to a place called Magnitogorsk on the eastern slopes of the Ural Mountains.

I was very happy. There was no unemployment in the Soviet Union. The Bolsheviks planned their economy and gave opportunities to young men and women. Furthermore, they had got away from the fetishization of material possessions, which, my good parents had taught me, was one of the basic ills of our American civilization. I saw that most Russians ate only black bread, wore one suit until it disintegrated, and used old newspapers for writing letters and office memoranda, rolling cigarettes, making envelopes, and for various personal functions.

I was about to participate in the construction of this society. I was going to be one of many who cared not to own a second pair of shoes, but who built blast furnaces which were their own. It was September, 1932, and I was twenty years old (…)

In 1940, Winston Churchill told the British people that they could expect nothing but blood, sweat, and tears. The country was at war. The British people did not like it, but most of them accepted it.

Ever since 1931 or thereabouts the Soviet Union has been at war, and the people have been sweating, shedding blood and tears. People were wounded and killed, women and children froze to death, millions starved, thousands were court-martialed and shot in the campaigns of collectivization and industrialization. I would wager that Russia's battle of ferrous metallurgy alone involved more casualties than the battle of the Marne. All during the thirties the Russian people were at war.

It did not take me long to realize that they ate black bread principally because there was no other to be had, wore rags because they could not be replaced.

In Magnitogorsk I was precipitated into a battle. I was deployed on the iron and steel front. Tens of thousands of people were enduring the most intense hardships in order to build blast furnaces, and many of them did it willingly, with boundless enthusiasm, which infected me from the day of my arrival.

I plunged into the life of the town with the energy of youth. I literally wore out my Russian grammar, and in three months I was making myself understood. I gave away many of the clothes I had brought with me, and dressed more or less like the other workers on the job. I worked as hard and as well as my comparatively limited experience and training permitted.

I was liberally rewarded. My fellow workers accepted me as one of themselves. The local authorities urged me to study, and arranged for me to be accepted into the 'Komvuz,' or Communist University, to which only Communist Party members were usually admitted. They helped me to make arrangements to go on trips around the country.

While political leaders in Moscow were scheming and intriguing, planning and organizing, I worked in Magnitogorsk with the common soldiers, the steel workers, the simple people who sweated and shed tears and blood.

For five years I worked in Magnitogorsk. I saw a magnificent plant built. I saw much sweat and blood, many tears (…)

(…) In 1940 I saw Syemichkin for a few minutes in Moscow. He was on his way to the Ukraine for a vacation, his first in three years. Things looked good in the mills in Magnitogorsk, he told me, and rather grim in people's homes. People worked eight hours instead of seven, and everyone put in overtime as well. Stores were empty.

I mentioned the Soviet–German pact. Syemichkin shrugged his shoulders. 'Stalin did it,' he said. 'Yemu Vidnyei—He knows what he is doing.' He did not say this for effect. He felt that way. He was a Soviet engineer, and had become a very good technician and administrator. He knew his business. He made mistakes sometimes, but by and large he knew how to run a coke by-products plant. Stalin had worked his way to the top of the complicated Soviet State apparatus. He had done well in steering the Soviet Ship of State through the stormy seas of recent European politics. He might make mistakes sometimes, but by and large he knew his business.

Soviets trust Stalin in 1939 pact

This typified the attitude of the Soviet people.

I went to a workers' meeting in a large Moscow factory in 1940. I saw workers get up and criticize the plant director, make suggestions as to how to increase production, improve quality, and lower costs. They were exercising their rights of freedom of speech as Soviet citizens. Then the question of the new Soviet–German trade pact came up. The workers unanimously passed a previously prepared resolution approving the Soviet foreign policy. There was no discussion. The Soviet workers had learned what was their business and what was not.

Many Soviet workers had become competent technicians. They made planes which flew well, and their pilots operated them with great skill. I know, I flew in them on several occasions. The Soviet railroad system carried more freight and more passengers per mile of track and per unit of rolling stock than any other railroad system in the world including the American.

The purge liquidated many workers and technicians, but Russia was a very large country. Most of the population stayed in their shops and factories, worked and produced. They were a little worried, perhaps, but they continued to turn out tanks, to read *Pravda*, and to practice air-raid alarms on their free days.

Life was hard for the Russian people in 1940 and 1941, and, of course, much harder after the German attack, but the Russian people were used to hard lives. They had never been softened by easy living. The papers told them every day that they were the luckiest people in the world, and they believed it. They had work and bread.

Millions of Syemichkins and Kolyas had been preparing for war for a decade, industrially, personally, and ideologically (…)

Here, then, lies the answer to the question so many people in America have been asking themselves since June 22, 1941: 'How are the Russians able to do so well? What makes Russia click?'

Russia has always had masses of men and incalculable natural resources.

During the last ten years the Russian people shed blood, sweat, and tears to create something else, a modern industrial base outside the reach of an invader—Stalin's Ural Stronghold—and a modern mechanized army. In the process millions of Russians and Ukrainians, Tartars and Jews, became competent technicians and efficient soldiers.

At the same time the population was taught by a painful and expensive process to work efficiently, to obey orders, to mind their own business, and to take it on the chin when necessary with a minimum of complaint.

These are the things that it takes to fight a modern war.

1.8 The Nazi–Soviet Pact, August 1939

The signing of the Nazi–Soviet pact in August 1939 is widely seen as the act that gave Germany the green light to attack Poland. In the first excerpt below Soviet foreign minister Vyacheslav Molotov gives the Soviet Government's explanation for the necessity of the pact. The second excerpt is from the secret protocols attached to the Nazi–Soviet Pact.

A. Molotov's Speech, 31 August 1939

(…) the conclusion of a pact of non-aggression between the U.S.S.R. and Germany is of tremendous positive value, eliminating the danger of war between Germany and the Soviet Union (…)

As you are aware, Anglo-French-Soviet negotiations for the conclusion of a pact of mutual assistance against aggression in Europe began as far back as April (…) The Anglo-French-Soviet negotiations lasted for four months. They helped to clarify a number of questions. At the same time they made it clear to the representatives of Great Britain and France that the Soviet Union had to be seriously reckoned with in international affairs.

But these negotiations encountered insuperable obstacles (…) The conclusion of a pact of mutual assistance against aggression would have been of value only if Great Britain, France and the Soviet Union had arrived at an agreement as to definite military measures against the attack of an aggressor (…) However, nothing came of the military negotiations. They encountered the difficulty that Poland, who was to be jointly guaranteed by Great Britain, France, and the U.S.S.R., rejected military assistance on the part of the Soviet Union. Attempts to overcome the objections of Poland met with no success. More, the negotiations showed that Great Britain was not anxious to overcome these objections of Poland, but on the contrary encouraged them.

It is clear that, such being the attitude of the Polish Government and its principal ally towards military assistance by the Soviet Union in the event of aggression, the Anglo-French-Soviet negotiations could not bear fruit (…) the negotiations with Great Britain and France (…) have shown that the position of Great Britain and France is characterized throughout by crying contradictions (…)

On the one hand, Great Britain and France demanded that the U.S.S.R. should give military assistance to Poland in case of aggression. The U.S.S.R., as you know, was willing to meet this demand, provided the U.S.S.R. itself received like assistance from Great Britain and France. On the other hand, the same Great Britain and France brought Poland on to the scene, and the latter resolutely declined any military assistance on the part of the U.S.S.R. Just try in such circumstances to reach an agreement regarding mutual assistance—when assistance on the part of the U.S.S.R. is declared beforehand to be unnecessary and an intrusion!

Further, on the one hand, Great Britain and France offered a guarantee to the Soviet Union of military assistance against aggression, in return for like assistance on the part of the U.S.S.R. On the other hand they hedged round their assistance with such reservations regarding indirect aggression as might convert this assistance into a myth, and provided them with a formal legal excuse for evading assistance and placing the U.S.S.R. in a position of isolation in face of the aggressor. Just try and distinguish between such a 'pact of mutual assistance' and a pact of more or less camouflaged chicanery! (…)

Such were the intrinsic contradictions in the attitude of Great Britain and France which held to the breakdown of negotiations with the U.S.S.R. (…) On the one hand the British and French Governments fear aggression, and for that reason would like to have a pact of mutual assistance with the Soviet Union, in so far as it would strengthen them (…) But on the other hand the British and French Governments are afraid that the conclusion of a real pact of mutual assistance with the U.S.S.R. may strengthen our country—the Soviet Union—which it appears does not answer their purpose. One cannot but see that these fears outweighed other considerations. Only in this way can we understand the position of Poland, which has been acting on the instructions of Great Britain and France (…)

The decision to conclude a non-aggression pact between the U.S.S.R. and Germany was adopted after military negotiations with France and Great Britain had reached an impasse owing to the insuperable difficulties I have mentioned. As the negotiations had shown that the conclusion of a pact of mutual assistance could not be expected, we could not but explore other possibilities of ensuring peace and eliminating the danger of war between Germany and the U.S.S.R. If the British and French Governments refused to reckon with this, that is their affair. *It is our duty to think of the interests of the Soviet people, the interests of the Union of Soviet Socialist* Republics—all the more because we are firmly convinced that the interests of the U.S.S.R. coincide with the fundamental interests of the peoples of other countries.

(...) Another circumstance was required before the Soviet–German Non-Aggression Pact could come into existence. It was necessary that in her foreign policy Germany should make a turn towards good neighborly relations with the Soviet Union. Only when this second condition was fulfilled, only when it became clear to us that the German Government desired to change its foreign policy so as to secure an improvement of relations with the U.S.S.R., was a basis found for the conclusion of the Soviet–German Non-Aggression Pact. Everybody knows that during the last six years, ever since the National-Socialists came into power, political relations between Germany and the U.S.S.R. have been strained. Everybody also knows that, despite the differences of outlook and political systems, the Soviet Government has endeavored to maintain normal business and political relations with Germany (...)

It is true that, in the present case, we are dealing *not with a pact of mutual assistance*, as in the case of Anglo-French-Soviet negotiations, but *only with a non-aggression pact*. Nevertheless, conditions being what they are it is difficult to over-estimate the international importance of the Soviet–German pact (...)

August 23, 1939, the day the Soviet–German Non-Aggression Pact was signed, is to be regarded as a date of great historical importance. The non-aggression pact between the U.S.S.R. and Germany marks a turning point in the history of Europe, and not of Europe alone. Only yesterday German Fascists were pursuing a foreign policy hostile to us. Yes, only yesterday we were enemies in the sphere of foreign relations. Today, however, the situation has changed and we are enemies no longer.

The art of politics in the sphere of foreign relations does not consist in increasing the number of enemies for one's country. On the contrary, the art of politics in this sphere is to reduce the number of such enemies and make the enemies of yesterday good neighbors, maintaining peaceable relations one with the other. History has shown that enmity and wars between our country and Germany have been to the detriment of our countries, not to their benefit (...) The fact that our outlooks and political systems differ must not and cannot be an obstacle to the establishment of good political relations between both States (...)

The chief importance of the Soviet–German Non-Aggression pact lies in the fact that the two largest states of Europe have agreed to put an end to enmity between them, to eliminate the menace of war and to live at peace one with the other, making narrower thereby the zone of possible military conflicts in Europe (...)

B. Secret Protocols of the German–Soviet Non-Aggression Pact, August 1939

Article I: In the event of a territorial and political rearrangement in the areas belonging to the Baltic States (Finland, Estonia, Latvia, Lithuania), the northern boundary of Lithuania shall represent the boundary of the spheres of influence of Germany and U.S.S.R. In this connection the interest of Lithuania in the Vilna area is recognized by each party.

Article II: In the event of a territorial and political rearrangement of the areas belonging to the Polish state, the spheres of influence of Germany and the U.S.S.R. shall be bounded approximately by the line of the rivers Narev, Vistula and San. The question of whether the interests of both parties make desirable the maintenance of an independent Polish State and how such a state should be bounded can only be definitely determined in the course of further political developments. In any event both Governments will resolve this question by means of a friendly agreement.

Article III: With regard to Southeastern Europe attention is called by the Soviet side to its interest in Bessarabia. The German side declares its complete political disinterestedness in these areas (…)

1.9 American and British Offers of Support for the Soviets, July–August 1941

The German attack on the Soviet Union in June 1941 dramatically shifted the relationship between the United States, Great Britain, and the Soviet Union. The following extracts are from a memorandum by Harry Hopkins —President Roosevelt's special envoy —regarding his meeting with Stalin on 30 July; and a joint message from President Roosevelt and Prime Minister Churchill delivered to Stalin on 15 August 1941.

A. Hopkins and Stalin

I told Mr. Stalin that I came as personal representative of the President. The President considered Hitler the enemy of mankind and that he therefore wished to aid the Soviet Union in its fight against Germany. I told him that my mission was not a diplomatic one in the sense that I did not propose any formal understanding of any kind or character.

I expressed to him the President's belief that the most important thing to be done in the world today was to defeat Hitler and Hitlerism. I impressed upon him the determination of the President and our Government to extend all possible aid to the Soviet Union at the earliest possible time.

I told Mr. Stalin that I had certain personal messages from the President and explained my relationship to the Administration in Washington. I told him further that I just left Mr. Churchill in London who wished me to convey to him the sentiments which I had already expressed from the President.

Mr. Stalin said he welcomed me to the Soviet Union; that he had already been informed of my visit. Describing Hitler and Germany, Mr. Stalin spoke of the necessity of there being a minimum moral standard between all nations (...) He stated that the present leaders of Germany knew no such minimum moral standard and that, therefore, they represented an anti-social force in the present world. The Germans were a people, he said, who without a second's thought would sign a treaty today, break it tomorrow and sign a second one the following day. Nations must fulfill their treaty obligations, he said, or international society could not exist.

When he completed his general summary of the Soviet Union's attitude toward Germany he said 'therefore our views coincide'. I told Mr. Stalin that the question of aid to the Soviet Union was divided into two parts. First, what would Russia most require that the United States could deliver immediately and, second, what would be Russia's requirements on the basis of a long war?

Stalin listed in the first category the immediate need of, first, anti-aircraft guns of medium calibre, of from 20 to 37 mm., together with ammunition (...) Second, he asked for large size machine guns for the defense of his cities. Third, he said he heard there were many rifles available in the United States and he believed their calibre corresponded to the calibre used in his Army. He stated that he needed one million or more such rifles. I asked Mr. Stalin if he needed ammunition for these rifles and he replied that if the calibre was the same as the one used by the Red Army 'we have plenty'.

In the second category, namely, the supplies needed for a long range war, he mentioned first high octane aviation gasoline, second, aluminum for the construction of airplanes and, third, the other items already mentioned in the list presented to our Government in Washington.

At this point in the conversation Mr. Stalin suddenly made the remark, 'Give us anti-aircraft guns and the aluminum and we can fight for three or four years (...)'

Mr. Stalin stated that he would be glad if we would send any technicians that we could to the Soviet Union to help train his own airmen in the use of these planes. He stated that his own airmen would show us everything about the Russian equipment, which he stated we would find very interesting.

He described at some length, but not in great detail as he did in the conference the next day, the planes which he had available. Mr. Stalin said the plane he needed particularly was the short-range bomber, capable of operating in a radius of 600 to 1,100 kilometres, or with a total range of 1,200 to 2,200 kilometres.

I asked Mr. Stalin what he thought was the best route to ship supplies from the United States to the Soviet Union. Mr. Stalin stated that the Persian Gulf–Iranian route was not good because of the limited capacity of the Iranian railways and highways. He stated, 'Furthermore we do not yet know the view of the Iranian Government on this subject'.

Mr. Stalin stated that the Vladivostok route was not a favorable one. I emphasized the danger of its being cut off by the Japanese and Mr. Stalin in turn emphasized the great distance from the scene of battle.

Mr. Stalin believed that the Archangel route was probably the most practicable. Both Mr. Stalin and Mr. Molotov stated that the Archangel harbor could be kept open in the winter by the aid of ice breakers. Mr. Stalin pointed out that the only two absolutely ice free ports in the north were Murmansk and Kaldalaksha (...)

I reiterated to Mr. Stalin the appreciation of the people of the United States of the splendid resistance of the Soviet Army and of the President's determination to do everything to assist the Soviet Union in its valiant struggle against the German invader. Mr. Stalin replied with an expression of gratitude of the Soviet Government.

B. Churchill and Roosevelt to Stalin   *15 Aug 1941*

We have taken the opportunity afforded by the consideration of the report of Mr. Harry Hopkins on his return from Moscow to consult together as to how best our two countries can help your country in the splendid defense that you are making against the Nazi attack. We are at the moment cooperating to provide you with the very maximum of supplies that you most urgently need. Already many shiploads have left our shores and more will leave in the immediate future.

We must now turn our minds to the consideration of a more long term policy, since there is still a long and hard path to be traversed before there can be won that complete victory without which our efforts and sacrifices would be wasted.

The war goes on upon many fronts and before it is over there may be further fighting fronts that will be developed. Our resources though immense are limited, and it must become a question as to where and when those resources can best be used to further to the greatest extent our common effort. This applies equally to manufactured war supplies and to raw materials.

The needs and demands of your and our armed services can only be determined in the light of the full knowledge of the many factors which must be taken into consideration in the decisions that we make. In order that all of us may be in a position to arrive at speedy decisions as to the apportionment of our joint resources, we suggest that we prepare for a meeting to be held at Moscow, to which we would send high representatives who could discuss these matters directly with you. If this conference appeals to you, we want you to know that pending the decisions of that conference we shall continue to send supplies and material as rapidly as possible.

We realize fully how vitally important to the defeat of Hitlerism is the brave and steadfast resistance of the Soviet Union and we feel therefore that we must not in any circumstances fail to act quickly and immediately in this matter on planning the program for the future allocation of our joint resources.

1.10 Stalin, Roosevelt, and Churchill on the Future of Europe, December 1943

The first Big Three meeting—between President Roosevelt, Marshall Stalin, and Prime Minister Churchill—took place in late November–early December 1943 in Teheran. Below are excerpts from one of the meetings. As would be the case on numerous future occasions, the leaders focused particularly on two European countries, Germany and Poland.

THE PRESIDENT, turning to the subject of Poland, said it was his hope that negotiations could be started for the re-establishment of relations between the Polish and Soviet Governments. He felt that the re-establishment of relations would facilitate any decision made in regard to the questions at issue. He said he recognized the difficulties which lay in the way.

MARSHAL STALIN replied that the Polish Government in exile were closely connected with the Germans and their agents in Poland were killing partisans. He said it is impossible to imagine what is going on in Poland.

THE PRIME MINISTER said the great question before the English was the fact that they had declared war because of the German invasion of Poland. He said he personally had been astonished when Chamberlain had given the guarantee in April, 1939 to Poland when he had refused to fight for the Czechs. He had been astonished and glad.

He said that England and France had gone to war in pursuance of this guarantee and it was not that he regretted it, but still it would be difficult not to take cognizance of the fact that the British people had gone to war because of Poland. He said he had used the illustration of the three matches the other evening in order to demonstrate one possible solution of the questions.

He said the British Government was first of all interested in seeing absolute security for the Western frontiers of the Soviet Union against any surprise assault in the future from Germany.

MARSHAL STALIN replied that Russia, probably more than any other country was interested in having friendly relations with Poland, since the security of Soviet frontiers was involved.

He said the Russians were in favor of the reconstitution and expansion of Poland at the expense of Germany and that they make distinction between the Polish Government in exile and Poland.

He added that they broke relations with Poland not because of a whim but because the Polish had joined in slanderous propaganda with the Nazis.

He inquired what guarantee could there be that this would not be repeated. He said they would like to have a guarantee that the Polish Government in exile would cease the killing of partisans in Poland and secondly to urge the people to fight against the Germans and not to indulge in intrigues.

The Russians would welcome relations with a Polish Government that led its people in the common struggle but it was not sure that the Polish Government in exile could be such a government. However, he added, if the government in exile would go along with the partisans and sever all connections with the German agents in Poland, then the Russians would be prepared to negotiate with them.

THE PRIME MINISTER said he would like to obtain the views of the Soviet Government in regard to the frontier question, and if some reasonable formula could be devised, he was prepared to take it up with the Polish Government in exile, and without telling them that the Soviet Government would accept such a solution, would offer it to them as probably the best they could obtain. If the Polish Government refused this, then Great Britain would be through with them and certainly would not oppose the Soviet Government under any condition at the peace table.

He said the British Government wished to see a Poland strong and friendly to Russia.

MARSHAL STALIN replied this was desirable, but it was not just for the Poles to try and get back the Ukraine and White Russia; that the frontiers of 1939 had returned the Ukrainian soil to the Ukraine and White Russian soil to White Russia. The Soviet Government adheres to the 1939 line and considers it just and right.

MR. EDEN said that was the line known as the Ribbentrop–Molotov Line.

MARSHAL STALIN said call it what you will, we still consider it just and right.

MR. MOLOTOV interjected to say that the 1939 frontier was the Curzon Line.

MR. EDEN said there were differences.

MR. MOLOTOV replied in no essential points.

There was then an examination of maps as to the exact location of the Curzon Line, and its location was finally established.

THE PRESIDENT inquired whether in the opinion of Marshal Stalin, East Prussia and the area between the old Polish frontier and the Oder was approximately equal to the former Polish territory acquired by the Soviet Union.

MARSHAL STALIN replied he did *not* know.

THE PRIME MINISTER said that if it was possible to work out some fair solution that it would be up to the Polish to accept it.

MARSHAL STALIN replied that the Soviet Union did not wish to retain any regions primarily occupied by Poles even though they were inside the 1939 Line.

THE PRESIDENT inquired whether a voluntary transfer of peoples from the mixed areas was possible.

MARSHAL STALIN said that such a transfer was entirely possible. Turning to the question of Germany, THE PRESIDENT said that the question was whether or not to split up Germany.

MARSHAL STALIN replied that they preferred the dismemberment of Germany.

THE PRIME MINISTER said he was all for it but that he was primarily more interested in seeing Prussia, the evil core of German militarism, separated from the rest of Germany.

THE PRESIDENT said he had a plan that he had thought up some months ago for the division of Germany in five parts. These five parts were:

1. All Prussia to be rendered as small and weak as possible.
2. Hanover and Northwest section.
3. Saxony and Leipzig area.
4. Hesse–Darmstadt.
   Hesse–Kassel and the area South of the Rhine.
5. Bavaria, Baden, and Wurtemburg.

He proposed that these five areas should be self-governed and that there should be two regions under United Nations or some form of International control. These were:

1. The area of the Kiel Canal and the City of Hamburg.
2. The Ruhr and the Saar, the latter to be used for the benefit of all Europe.

THE PRIME MINISTER said, to use an American expression, 'The President had said a mouthful.'

He went on to say that in his mind there were two considerations, one destructive and the other constructive.

1. The separation of Prussia from the rest of the Reich.
2. To detach Bavaria, Baden, Wurtemburg and the Palatinate from the rest of Germany and make them part of the Confederation of the Danube.

MARSHAL STALIN said he felt if Germany was to be dismembered, it should really be dismembered, and it was neither a question of the division of Germany in five or six states and two areas as the President suggested. However, he said he preferred the President's plan to the suggestion of Mr. Churchill.

He felt that to include German areas within the framework of large confederations would merely offer an opportunity to the German elements to revive a great State.

He went on to say that he did not believe there was a difference among Germans; that all German soldiers fought like devils and the only exception was the Austrians.

He said that the Prussian Officers and Staffs should be eliminated, but as to the inhabitants, he saw little difference between one part of Germany and another.

He said he was against the idea of confederation as artificial and one that would not last in that area, and in addition would provide opportunity for the German elements to control.

Austria, for example, had existed as an independent state and should again. Hungary, Rumania, and Bulgaria likewise.

THE PRESIDENT said he agreed with the Marshal, particularly in regard to the absence of differences between Germans. He said fifty years ago there had been a difference but since the last war it was no longer so.

He said the only difference was that in Bavaria and the Southern part of Germany there was no officer cast[e] as there had been in Prussia. He agreed with Marshal Stalin that the Austrians were an exception.

THE PRIME MINISTER said he did not wish to be considered as against the dismemberment of Germany—quite the contrary, but he felt to separate the parts above would merely mean that sooner or later they will reunite into one nation and that the main thing was to keep Germany divided if only for fifty years.

MARSHAL STALIN repeated what he had said as to the danger of the reunification of Germany. He said no matter what measures were adopted there would always be a strong urge on the part of the Germans to unite.

He said it was a great mistake to unite Hungary with Germans since the Germans would merely control the Hungarians and to create large frameworks within which the Germans could operate would be very dangerous.

He felt the whole purpose of any international organization to preserve peace would be to neutralize this tendency on the part of the Germans and apply against them economic and other measures and if necessary, force, to prevent their unification and revival. He said the victorious nations must have the strength to beat the Germans if they ever start on the path of a new war.

THE PRIME MINISTER inquired whether Marshal Stalin contemplated a Europe composed of little states, disjoined, separated and weak.

MARSHAL STALIN replied not Europe but Germany. He supposed for example that Poland would be a strong country, and France, and Italy likewise; that Rumania and Bulgaria would remain as they always had; small States.

THE PRESIDENT remarked Germany had been less dangerous to civilization when in 107 provinces.

THE PRIME MINISTER said he hoped for larger units.

THE PRIME MINISTER then returned to the question of Poland and said he was not asking for any agreement nor was he set on the matter but he had a statement which he would like to have the Marshal examine.

This statement suggested that Poland should obtain equal compensation in the West, including Eastern Prussia and frontiers on the Oder to compensate for the areas which would be in the Soviet Union.

THE PRESIDENT interjected to say that one question in regard to Germany remained to be settled and that was what body should be empowered to study carefully the question of dismemberment of Germany.

It was agreed that the European Advisory Committee [*Commission*] would undertake this task.

THE PRIME MINISTER said in his opinion the Polish question was urgent.

He repeated if it would be possible to work out a formula here, and then [*sic*] he could go back to the Polish Government in London and urge on them the desirability of at least attempting to reach a settlement along those lines, without however indicating any commitment on the part of the Soviet Government.

MARSHAL STALIN said that if the Russians would be given the northern part of East Prussia, running along the left bank of the Niemen and include Tils[i]t and the City of Königsberg, he would be prepared to accept the Curzon Line as the frontier between the Soviet Union and Poland.

He said the acquisition of that part of Eastern Prussia would not only afford the Soviet Union an ice-free port but would also give to Russia a small piece of German territory which he felt was deserved.

Although nothing definitely was stated, it was apparent that the British were going to take this suggestion back to London to the Poles.

1.11 British View of Post-war Soviet Aims, March 1945

In this 12 March 1945 message to the Foreign Office, the British minister in Moscow, Sir John Balfour, sums up his views on Soviet policy, paying particular attention to events in the Balkans and their potential long-term significance in understanding the USSR's major goals.

(...) there is most certainly a long-term element in what the Russians are doing in the Balkans. Security writ large is the first and paramount factor there in relation to other neighbouring territories of the U.S.S.R (...) the Soviet Union looks upon the South-Eastern European area, no less than on Poland, as a security zone in which it is to her peculiar interest to see that there is no renewal of the German *Drang nach Osten*.

No plans for world organisation or pacts with the Western Powers will deflect the U.S.S.R. from buttressing up her security system in this region as a first line of defence. All-Slavism (...) is one important instrument of this insurance policy which demands as a corollary that the interests and influence of other Great Powers in the Soviet security zone should be strictly subordinated to those of the U.S.S.R. It would, for example, be unthinkable—in this setting that Czechoslovakia and Yugoslavia should look as they did after the last war to the West for the main guarantee of their security rather than to Mother Russia in the East (...) as Molotov has more than once clearly implied (...) the U.S.S.R. has suffered too much during the war to allow her great Allies to play more than a secondary part in dictating the treatment of ex-German satellites whom the Red army has defeated.

In all this there is a well-defined long-term policy which, so far as can at present be foreseen is summed up in the word 'Security.' I say 'at present' because the self-confidence of the Soviet Union, which victory has immeasurably increased, combined with a love of power for its own sake which has distinguished Russia's outstanding rulers throughout the ages, might cause this policy as it unfolds itself to assume dangerous forms (...) So far as the Balkans are concerned we can at any rate take heart of grace from the wholly correct attitude which the Soviet Government have so far adopted towards the Greek imbrogilo (...)

Whilst the determination of the Soviet Government to maintain and develop a position of paramount influence in Balkan countries other than Greece can thus, I think, be taken for granted as a matter of well-defined long-term policy, there still remains, within that overriding framework, good reason for arguing (...) that Russian actions to which we object are the result of minds automatically working along old lines. We must at all times make allowance for the Bolshevik mentality, which, if it has repudiated the idea of world revolution as a fixed aim, is still infected with suspicion of the bourgeois world, Marxist in outlook, and imbued with a rough and ready disposition indiscriminately to lump together as 'Fascist beasts' all those who criticise or appear to obstruct the will of the Soviet Union.

In addition to this state of mind must be set, so far as defeated enemies are concerned, and particularly Germany, something of the Old Testament adage of 'An eye for an eye and a tooth for a tooth.' (...) it does imply on present showing the mass deportation for forced labour in the Soviet Union of able-bodied Germans, including Germans belonging to minority groups in satellite States, a tight squeeze of ex-enemy Governments in the matter of reparation deliveries and a ruthless attitude towards all elements in neighbouring countries suspected of collaborationism. By the same token resistance groups, wherever situated, will receive the utmost encouragement, without too nice a regard for adjusting excessive claims on their part for post-war recognition to the principles of democracy as understood in the West.

(…) It would be a mistake to set store on the persuasive powers of the Allies to eradicate them from the minds of the men who rule Russia to-day, beginning with Stalin himself, who, as an old-time revolutionary and the chief of his people in repelling the barbarian invader, shares the prevailing outlook in full measure.

On the other hand, as a shrewd realist, Stalin, so far as can be judged, has no wish to overreach the limits within which he can prudently exercise autocratic power. Although 'deathly proud' and quick to react against the slightest suggestion of Soviet inferiority or bad faith, Stalin and the more sensible of his followers are no less imbued with a jealous wish to raise the reputation of the U.S.S.R. in the eyes of the world. It follows that where, but only where, the Allies have just cause for complaint that their legitimate interests are being set at nought, a restraining influence can be brought to bear by appeals to Stalin himself on matters of real importance. The centralised character of the Soviet machine unfortunately multiplies the number of such matters beyond what would be normal in our dealings with régimes of another character. But I see no remedy for this (…)

1.12 Henry L. Stimson on Sharing the Atomic Bomb, September 1945

One of the issues that raised the level of distrust between the United States and the Soviet Union was the American monopoly of the atomic bomb. One of those who suggested sharing the secret with the Soviets as a way of gaining co-operation was the US secretary of war, Henry L. Stimson. Below he sums up the rationale for such a plan to President Truman, who had only learned about the atomic bomb project (the Manhattan Project) upon assuming office after President Roosevelt's death in April 1945.

(…) The advent of the atomic bomb has stimulated great military and probably even greater political interest throughout the civilized world. In a world atmosphere already extremely sensitive to power, the introduction of this weapon has profoundly affected political considerations in all sections of the globe.

In many quarters it has been interpreted as a substantial offset to the growth of Russian influence on the continent. We can be certain that the Soviet government has sensed this tendency and the temptation will be strong for the Soviet political and military leaders to acquire this weapon in the shortest possible time.

Britain in effect already has the status of a partner with us in the development of this weapon. Accordingly, unless the Soviets are voluntarily invited into the partnership upon a basis of cooperation and trust, we are going to maintain the Anglo-Saxon bloc over against the Soviet in the possession of this weapon. Such a condition will almost certainly stimulate feverish activity on the part of the Soviet toward the development of this bomb in what will in effect be a secret armament race of a rather desperate character (…)

If we feel, as I assume we must, that civilization demands that some day we shall arrive at a satisfactory international arrangement respecting the control of this new force, the question then is how long we can afford to enjoy our momentary superiority in the hope of achieving our immediate peace council objectives.

Whether Russia gets control of the necessary secrets of production in a minimum of say four years or a maximum of twenty years is not nearly as important to the world and civilization as to make sure that when they do get it they are willing and cooperative partners among the peace-loving nations of the world. It is true that if we approach them now, as I would propose, we may be gambling on their good faith and risk their getting into production of bombs a little sooner than they would otherwise.

To put the matter concisely, I consider the problem of our satisfactory relations with Russia as not merely connected with but as virtually dominated by the problem of the atomic bomb. Except for the problem of the control of that bomb, those relations, while vitally important, might not be immediately pressing. The establishment of relations of mutual confidence between her and us could afford to await the slow progress of time. But with the discovery of the bomb, they become immediately emergent. Those relations may be perhaps irretrievably embittered by the way in which we approach the solution of the bomb with Russia. For if we fail to approach them now and merely continue to negotiate with them, having this weapon rather ostentatiously on our hip, their suspicions and their distrust of our purposes and motives will increase. It will inspire them to greater efforts in an all out effort to solve the problem. If the solution is achieved in that spirit, it is much less likely that we will ever get the kind of covenant we may desperately need in the future (…) The chief lesson I have learned in a long life is that the only way you can make a man trustworthy is to trust him; and the surest way to make him untrustworthy is to distrust him and show your distrust.

If the atomic bomb were merely another though more devastating military weapon to be assimilated into our pattern of international relations, it would be one thing. We could then follow the old custom of secrecy and nationalistic military superiority relying on international caution to prescribe [*proscribe*] the future use of the weapon as we did with gas. But I think the bomb instead constitutes merely a first step in a new control by man over the forces of nature too revolutionary and dangerous to fit into the old concepts. I think it really caps the climax of the race between man's growing technical power for destructiveness and his psychological power of self-control and group control—his moral power. If so, our method of approach to the Russians is a question of the most vital importance in the evolution of human progress.

Since the crux of the problem is Russia, any contemplated action leading to the control of this weapon should be primarily directed to Russia. It is my judgment that the Soviet would be more apt to respond sincerely to a direct and forthright approach made by the United States on this subject than would be the case if the approach were made as a part of a general international scheme, or if the approach were made after a succession of express or implied threats or near threats in our peace negotiations.

My idea of an approach to the Soviets would be a direct proposal after discussion with the British that we would be prepared in effect to enter an arrangement with the Russians, the general purpose of which would be to control and limit the use of the atomic bomb as an instrument of war and so far as possible to direct and encourage the development of atomic power for peaceful and humanitarian purposes (…) We might also consider including in the arrangement a covenant with the U.K. and the Soviets providing for the exchange of benefits of future developments whereby atomic energy may be applied on a mutually satisfactory basis for commercial or humanitarian purposes.

I would make such an approach just as soon as our immediate political considerations make it appropriate.

I emphasize perhaps beyond all other considerations the importance of taking this action with Russia as a proposal of the United States—backed by Great Britain—but peculiarly the proposal of the United States. Action of any international group of nations, including many small nations who have not demonstrated their potential power or responsibility in this war would not, in my opinion, be taken seriously by the Soviets. The loose debates which would surround such proposal, if put before a conference of nations, would provoke but scant favor from the Soviet (…)

After the nations which have won this war have agreed to it, there will be ample time to introduce France and China into the covenants and finally to incorporate the agreement into the scheme of the United Nations. The use of this bomb has been accepted by the world as the result of the initiative and productive capacity of the United States, and I think this factor is a most potent lever toward having our proposals accepted by the Soviets, whereas I am most skeptical of obtaining any tangible results by way of any international debate. I urge this method as the most realistic means of accomplishing this vitally important step in the history of the world.

Questions

What was Lenin's message to 'American workers'?

Why did A. Mitchell Palmer consider Communism a mortal threat to the United States?

Aside from the ideological antipathy towards the Bolsheviks, did the Wilson Administration have other reasons for its hostility towards the new Soviet state?

What differences can you detect between Stalin's and Mao's views?

What were the arguments for and against the United States recognition of the USSR in 1933?

What concerns did the Americans have about the new relationship?

What attracted foreign workers to the Soviet Union in the 1930s?

What were the positive and negative features that the American 'guest worker' detected during his time in the USSR?

Why did the Soviet Union conclude a pact with Nazi Germany in 1939?

Why did the United Stated and Great Britain decide to support the USSR in 1941?

What were the major points of agreement and conflict between the Big Three at the Tehran Conference in 1943?

Were the British suspicious of Stalin's post-war aims in the spring of 1945?

Were there any differences in American and British perceptions of the Soviet Union at the end of the war?

Why did US Secretary of War Henry L. Stimson wish to share nuclear weapons with the Soviets?

The Iron Curtain

Aside from Germany, the area that came to symbolize the onset of the Cold War was East-Central Europe. For many in the West, the Communist takeovers in this region between 1944 and 1948 were easily seen as a frightening and gradually escalating sign of Stalin's true intentions. In October 1944, for example, Winston Churchill had been willing to divide East-Central Europe into British and Soviet spheres of influence, with the so-called percentage agreement. A year and a half later, however, Churchill—who had been defeated in late July 1945 in the British general election—had changed his mind. In March 1946 the former prime minister declared in a speech in Fulton, Missouri, that an Iron Curtain had descended from the Baltic to the Adriatic. Calling for the Anglo-Americans to resist the expansion of Soviet-Communist power, Churchill not only sounded the alarm about Soviet intentions but also expressed the public rationale for much of Western policy that was to follow.

While Churchill gave a straightforward (and widely accepted) explanation for the events in East-Central Europe, Soviet policies were, in all likelihood, driven by a complex set of motives. Ideology, security, and historical memory each played a role. Similarly, it would be naive to assume that Soviet leadership was not affected by Western rhetoric and policy. An additional point to stress is that the imposition of Soviet and/or Communist hegemony in Eastern Europe did not take place overnight. Much depended on local conditions in the various East European countries; the strength of its local Communist party, the presence or lack thereof of the Red Army, the strength of the anti-Russian sentiments, the presence (or lack thereof) of an Allied Control Commission (ACC). In addition, geographic location made a difference—while Poland, given its location between Germany and the USSR, was central in the post-war Soviet quest for security and had little chance of escaping Soviet hegemony in the post-war years, Finland, which shared a long border with the USSR but lacked Poland's strategic significance, managed to avoid the fate of East-Central European nations.

The importance of local conditions was highlighted by the first two East European Communist takeovers. In Yugoslavia and Albania the local Communists established their rule in 1944–5 as patriots who had, often heroically, fought against the German invaders. In Albania, Enver Hoxha's National Liberation Movement faced little resistance when it deposed King Zog in May 1944 and established its rule firmly after the Germans left the country in the fall of 1944. Perhaps ironically, in the years to come the major threat to Hoxha's rule would come from neighbouring Yugoslavia, where Tito manoeuvred himself and his partisans into a powerful position at the end of the war. After a brief coalition with the royalists, Tito's Popular Front quickly organized an election in November 1945 and proclaimed the creation of the Federative People's Republic of Yugoslavia on 31 January 1946. To the increasing fury of Stalin and the growing concern of his neighbours, however, Tito harboured dreams of creating a larger Balkan Federation, which would include the neighbouring countries to the south and east.

While Tito's independent actions would later spark the first serious internal post-war crisis of the Communist movement, his path to power was in many ways an exception. In Poland, for example, the Communists' takeover was prompted by much greater Soviet involvement. The Soviets recognized the Polish Workers Party's (PWP) major political organization, the Lublin Committee, in late 1944 as the provisional government. As a precondition to British and American recognition, however, the Lublin government was enlarged in the spring of 1945 to include some token representatives of other parties, most significantly from the Polish Peasants Party (PPS). In the next two years, bolstered by Soviet support and headed by Wladislaw Gomulka and Boleslaw Bierut, the Communists gradually marginalized other political parties.

The priority accorded to securing socialist control in Poland affected Soviet policy in other countries. In Hungary, for example, Stalin felt compelled to hold back the local Communists from seizing power immediately after the war. It was only after the conclusion of the Hungarian Peace Treaty and the exit of the Allied Control Commission from Hungary in 1947 that the Communists moved to establish complete supremacy. Elections in April 1949 were held without opposing candidates, and were followed by the adoption of a new Soviet-style constitution. By this time Bulgaria and Romania had also become socialist republics. In Bulgaria, the local Communist leaders had, in fact, been a respectable party prior to World War II and were included in a coalition government that was formed in September 1944. Still, as in Hungary, the takeover was gradual, in part due to the presence of the ACC and the anticipation of a peace treaty. In September 1946 Bulgaria formally became a republic (11-year-old King Simeon II was sent into exile). In the following month the Bulgarian Communist Party's (BCP) leader Gheorghi Dimitrov—who had spent the war in Moscow—became the head of a coalition government. From there on the BCP moved quickly: in the summer and fall of 1947 it removed major opposition figures and destroyed their organizations; in December 1947 it introduced a new constitution.

The last European country to fall under Communist rule was Czechoslovakia. Indeed, for quite some time after the return of the pre-war president Eduard Benes in April 1945 Czechoslovakia appeared likely to remain a liberal democracy. To be sure, the Czech Communists, under the leadership of Klement Gottwald, won 38 per cent of the popular vote in the May 1946 elections and occupied key posts—with Gottwald as premier—in the post-war coalition cabinet. But the lack of a Red Army presence after December 1945 and the existence of a friendship treaty with the USSR seemed to make Czechoslovakia a special case, as Czech Communists did not resort to the strong-arm strategies or salami tactics of some of their East European counterparts. In the second half of 1947, however, the picture began to change. Under Soviet pressure the Czech government declined to participate in the Marshall Plan, sending the Czech Communists' already declining popularity into a severe downward spiral. In response, while the Red Army amassed troops on the Czech borders, Gottwald and his party staged a *coup d'état* in February 1948. Between 12 and 22 February President Benes, probably assuming that no Western help was forthcoming, failed to take advantage of obvious popular anti-Communist sentiment and effectively allowed the Communists to take control of the state apparatus. Jan Masaryk, the non-Communist foreign minister, was soon found dead; Benes was forced into permanent house arrest (until his death in September 1948); and Gottwald became president.

The Prague coup of February 1948 was the last addition to what would for four decades be known as the Soviet bloc. Rumours that a similar coup was under way in Finland proved false. Instead of further expansion of the bloc, the Soviet Union moved to press for conformity within Eastern Europe. In practice this meant that the Soviet bloc underwent a series of purges and show trials during which a number of national Communist leaders—accused of Western sympathies or 'national deviation'—were sent to their deaths or removed from office. Between 1948 and 1952 such national Communist leaders as Rajk in Hungary, Kostov in Bulgaria, and Slansky in Czechoslovakia were executed; others, including Gomulka in Poland and Patrascanu in Romania, were 'merely' purged. East European economies were subjugated to the Soviet economy through a series of joint Soviet–East European companies and by the imposition of Soviet-style five-year plans that were to promote the development of heavy industry. All in all, the late 1940s and early 1950s saw a clear move towards conformity inside the Iron Curtain.

Readings

Sheldon Anderson, *A Cold War in the Soviet Bloc: Polish–East German Relations, 1945–1962* (2000). An account of a difficult relationship between two Soviet bloc countries.

Ivo Banac, *With Stalin Against Tito* (1988). An account of the Tito–Stalin split and its impact, with specific focus on Yugoslav politics.

Vojtech Mastny, *The Cold War and Soviet Insecurity* (1996). A balanced account of Stalin's foreign policy after World War II.

Krystyna Kersten, *The Establishment of Communist Rule in Poland, 1943–1948* (1991). A well-researched account of the Communist takeover in Poland.

Vladislav Zubok and Constantin Pleshakov, *Inside the Kremlin's Cold War* (1996). A highly readable accounting of foreign policy decision-making inside the USSR from Stalin to Khrushchev.

2.1 Churchill on Meeting Stalin, October 1944

One of the most controversial wartime documents is the so-called percentage agreement between Stalin and Churchill in Moscow on 9 October 1944. While it is clear that the British prime minister thought some sort of deal had been reached, there is much less evidence that Stalin took the incident seriously. Below, Winston Churchill recounts how he and the Soviet leader concluded this agreement during the British prime minister's visit to the Soviet capital.

We alighted at Moscow on the afternoon of October 9, and were received very heartily and with full ceremonial by Molotov and many high Russian personages. This time we were lodged in Moscow itself, with every care and comfort. I had one small, perfectly appointed house, and Anthony [Eden] another near by. We were glad to dine alone together and rest. At ten o'clock that night we held our first important meeting in the Kremlin. There were only Stalin, Molotov, Eden, and I, with Major Birse and Pavlov as interpreters. It was agreed to invite the Polish Prime Minister, M. Romer, the Foreign Minister, and M. Grabski, a grey-bearded and aged academician of much charm and quality, to Moscow at once. I telegraphed accordingly to M. Mikolajczyk that we were expecting him and his friends for discussions with the Soviet Government and ourselves, as well as with the Lublin Polish Committee. I made it clear that refusal to come to take part in the conversations would amount to a definite rejection of our advice and would relieve us from further responsibility towards the London Polish Government.

The moment was apt for business, so I said, 'Let us settle about our affair in the Balkans. Your armies are in Roumania and Bulgaria. We have interests, missions, and agents there. Don't let us get at cross-purposes in small ways. So far as Britain and Russia are concerned, how would it do for you to have ninety per cent. predominance in Roumania, for us to have ninety per cent. of the say in Greece, and go fifty-fifty about Yugoslavia?' While this was being translated I wrote out on a half-sheet of paper:

Roumania
  Russia 90%
  The others 10%

Greece
  Great Britain 90% (in accord with U.S.A.)
  Russia 10%

Yugoslavia 50–50%

Hungary 50–50%

Bulgaria
  Russia 75%
  The others 25%

I pushed this across to Stalin, who had by then heard the translation. There was a slight pause. Then he took his blue pencil and made a large tick upon it, and passed it back to us. It was all settled in no more time than it takes to set down.

Of course we had long and anxiously considered our point, and were only dealing with immediate war-time arrangements. All larger questions were reserved on both sides for what we then hoped would be a peace table when the war was won.

After this there was a long silence. The pencilled paper lay in the centre of the table. At length I said, 'Might it not be thought rather cynical if it seemed we had disposed of these issues, so fateful to millions of people, in such an offhand manner? Let us burn the paper.' 'No, you keep it,' said Stalin.

2.2 The Issue of Poland, 1944–1945

For much of 1944–1945 Poland was the country that preoccupied the minds of Soviet, American, and British leaders. One of the key issues was over which Polish government— the Soviet-supported 'Lublin Poles' or the British-backed 'London Poles'—should be recognized as the legitimate Polish post-war cabinet. US President Roosevelt ended up pressing for a coalition that was, in the end, heavliy in favour of the 'Lublin Poles'. The three excerpts below include Stalin's letter to Roosevelt in late 1944, the Churchill– Stalin–Roosevelt discussion about Poland at the Yalta Conference in February 1945, and Roosevelt's letter to Stalin, written soon after the tripartite meeting.

A. Stalin to Roosevelt, 27 December 1944

(…) proves that the negotiations of Mr. Mikolajczyk with the Polish National Committee served as a screen for those elements who conducted from behind Mikolajczyk's back criminal terrorist work against Soviet officers and soldiers on

the territory of Poland. We cannot reconcile with such a situation when terrorists instigated by Polish emigrants kill in Poland soldiers and officers of the Red
Army, lead a criminal fight against Soviet troops which are liberating Poland, and
directly aid our enemies, whose allies they in fact are (…)

Meanwhile the Polish National Committee has made serious achievements in
the strengthening of the Polish state and the apparatus of governmental power on
the territory of Poland, in the expansion and strengthening of the Polish army, in
carrying into practice of a number of important governmental measures and,
in the first place, of the agrarian reform in favor of the peasants. All this has led to
consolidation of democratic powers of Poland and to powerful strengthening of
authority of the National Committee among the wide masses in Poland and
among wide social Polish circles abroad.

It seems to me that now we should be interested in the support of the Polish
National Committee and all those who want and are capable to work together
with it and that is especially important for the Allies and for the solution of our
common task—the speeding of the defeat of Hitlerite Germany (…)

I have to say frankly that if the Polish Committee of National Liberation will
transform itself into a Provisional Polish Government then (…) the Soviet
Government will not have any serious ground for postponement of the question
of its recognition. It is necessary to bear in mind that in the strengthening of a
pro-Allied and democratic Poland the Soviet Union is interested more than any
other power not only because the Soviet Union is bearing the main brunt of the
battle for liberation of Poland but also because Poland is a border state with the
Soviet Union and the problem of Poland is inseparable from the problem of security of the Soviet Union. To this we have to add that the successes of the Red
Army in Poland in the fight against the Germans are to a great degree dependent
on the presence of peaceful and trustworthy rear in Poland, and the Polish
National Committee fully takes into account this circumstance while the émigré
government and its underground agents by their terroristic actions are creating a
threat of civil war in the rear of the Red Army and counteract the success of the
latter. On the other hand, under the conditions which exist in Poland at the present time there are no reasons for the continuation of the policy of support of the
émigré government, which has lost all confidence of the Polish population in the
country and besides creates a threat of civil war in the rear of the Red Army, violating thus our common interests of a successful fight against the Germans. I
think that it would be natural, just and profitable for our common cause if the
governments of the Allied countries as the first step have agreed on an immediate
exchange of representatives with the Polish National Committee so that after a
certain time it would be recognized as the lawful government of Poland after the
transformation of the National Committee into a provisional government of
Poland. Otherwise I am afraid that the confidence of the Polish People in the

Allied powers may weaken. I think that we cannot allow the Polish people to say that we are sacrificing the interests of Poland in favor of the interests of a handful of Polish emigrants in London.

B. Churchill, Roosevelt, and Stalin at Yalta, 6 February 1945

PRESIDENT: I should like to bring up Poland. I come from a great distance and therefore have the advantage of a more distant point of view of the problem. There are six or seven million Poles in the United States. As I said in Tehran, in general I am in favor of the Curzon line. Most Poles, like the Chinese, want to save face.

STALIN: Who will save face, the Poles in Poland or the émigré Poles?

PRESIDENT: The Poles would like East Prussia and part of Germany. It would make it easier for me at home if the Soviet Government could give something to Poland. I raised the question of giving them Lvov at Tehran. It has now been suggested that the oil lands in the southwest of Lvov might be given them. I am not making a definite statement but I hope that Marshal Stalin can make a gesture in this direction.

But the most important matter is that of a permanent government for Poland. Opinion in the United States is against recognition of the Lublin government on the ground that it represents a small portion of the Polish people. What people want is the creation of a government of national unity to settle their internal differences (…)

The main suggestion I want to make is that there be created an ad interim government which will have the support of the majority of the Polish people. There are many ways of creating such a government. One of the many suggestions is the possibility of creating a presidency council made up of a small number of men who would be the controlling force ad interim to set up a more permanent government. I make this suggestion as from the distance of three thousand miles. Sometimes distance is an advantage. We want a Poland that will be thoroughly friendly to the Soviet for years to come. This is essential.

STALIN: Friendly not only to the Soviet but all three allies.

PRESIDENT: This is my only suggestion. If we can work out some solution of this problem it will make peace much easier.

PRIME MINISTER: I have made repeated declarations in Parliament in support of the Soviet claims to the Curzon line, that is to say, leaving Lvov with Soviet Russia. I have been much criticized and so has Mr Eden especially by the party which I represent. But I have always considered that after all Russia has suffered in fighting Germany and after all her efforts in liberating Poland her claim is one founded not on force but on right. In that position I abide. But of course if the mighty power, the Soviet Union, made a gesture of magnanimity to a much weaker power and made the gesture suggested by the President we would heartily acclaim such action.

However, I am more interested in the question of Poland's sovereign independence and freedom than in particular frontier lines. I want the Poles to have a home in Europe and to be free to live their own life there (...) Never could I be content with any solution that would not leave Poland as a free and independent state. However, I have one qualification: I do not think that the freedom of Poland could be made to cover hostile designs by any Polish government, perhaps by intrigue with Germany, against the Soviet (...) At the present time there are two governments about which we differ (...) Can we not make a government here in Poland? A provisional or interim government, as the President said, pending free elections so that all three of us can extend recognition as well as the other United Nations. Can we not pave the way for a free future on the future constitution and administration of Poland? If we could do that we should leave the table with one great step accomplished toward future peace and the prosperity of Central Europe (...)

STALIN: The Prime Minister has said that for Great Britain the question of Poland is a question of honor. For Russia it is not only a question of honor but also of security. It is a question of honor for Russia for we shall have to eliminate many things from the books. But it is also a question of security of the state not only because we are on Poland's frontier but also because throughout history Poland has always been a corridor for attack on Russia. It is sufficient that during the last thirty years our German enemy has passed through this corridor twice. This is because Poland was weak. It is in the Russian interest as well as that of Poland that Poland be strong and powerful and in a position in her own and in our interests to shut the corridor by her own forces. The corridor cannot be mechanically shut from outside by Russia. It could be shut from inside only by Poland. It is necessary that Poland be free, independent and powerful (...)

I refer now to our allies' appeal with regard to the Curzon line. The President has suggested modification giving Poland Lvov and Lvov Province. The Prime Minister thinks that we should make a gesture of magnanimity. But I must remind you that the Curzon line was invented not by Russians but by foreigners. The Curzon line (...) was made by Curzon, Clemenceau and the Americans in 1918–1919. Russia was not invited and did not participate. This line was accepted against the will of the Russians on the basis of ethnological data. Lenin opposed it. He did not want to give Bialystok and Bialystok Provinces to Poland but the Curzon line gives them to Poland. We have retreated from Lenin's position. Some want us to be less Russian than Curzon and Cleamenceau. What will the Russians say at Moscow and the Ukrainians? They will say that Stalin and Molotov are far less defenders of Russia than Curzon and Clemenceau. I cannot take such a position and return to Moscow. I prefer that the war continue a little longer and give Poland compensation in the west at the expense of Germany. I asked Mikolajczyk what frontier he wanted. Mikolajczyk was delighted to hear of a western frontier to the river Neisse. I must say that I will maintain this line and ask this conference to support it. There are two Neisse rivers. The east and the west. I favor the west.

Now about the government. The Prime Minister has said that he wants to create a Polish government here. I am afraid that was a slip of the tongue. Without the participation of Poles we can create no Polish government. They all say that I am a dictator but I have enough democratic feeling not to set up a Polish government without Poles. It must be with participation of Poles. We had the opportunity in Moscow to create a Polish government with Poles. Both London and Lublin groups met in Moscow and certain points of agreement were reached. Mikolajczyk returned to London and was kicked out of the government. The present London government (…) called the Lublin government 'bandits' and 'traitors.' Naturally the Lublin government paid the same coin to the London government. It is difficult to bring them together (…) I am prepared to call the Warsaw Poles here or better to see them in Moscow. But frankly, the Warsaw government has as great a democratic basis in Poland as de Gaulle has in France.

Now as a military man I must say what I demand of a country liberated by the Red Army. First there should be peace and quiet in the wake of the army. The men of the Red Army are indifferent as to what kind of government there is in Poland but they do want one that will maintain order behind the lines (…) When I compare the agents of both governments I find that the Lublin ones are useful and the others the contrary. The military must have peace and quiet. The military will support such a government and I cannot do otherwise. Such is the situation (…)

PRIME MINISTER: I must put on record that both the British and Soviet governments have different sources of information in Poland and get different facts. Perhaps we are mistaken but I do not feel that the Lublin government represents even one third of the Polish people. This is my honest opinion and I may be wrong. Still, I have felt that the underground might have collisions with the Lublin government. I have feared bloodshed, arrests, deportation, and I fear the effect on the whole Polish question. Anyone who attacks the Red Army should be punished but I cannot feel that the Lublin government has any right to represent the Polish nation.

C. Roosevelt to Stalin, 6 February 1945

I have been giving a great deal of thought to our meeting this afternoon, and I want to tell you in all frankness what is on my mind.

In so far as the Polish Government is concerned, I am greatly disturbed that the three great powers do not have a meeting of minds about the political setup in

Poland. It seems to me that it puts all of us in a bad light throughout the world to have you recognizing one government while we and the British are recognizing another in London. I am sure this state of affairs should not continue and that if it does it can only lead our people to think there is a breach between us, which is not the case. I am determined that there shall be no breach between ourselves and the Soviet Union. Surely there is a way to reconcile our differences (…)

I was very much impressed with some of the things you said today, particularly your determination that your rear must be safeguarded as your army moves into Berlin. You cannot, and we must not, tolerate any temporary government which will give your armed forces any trouble of this sort. I want you to know that I am fully mindful of this.

You must believe me when I tell you that our people at home look with a critical eye on what they consider a disagreement between us at this vital stage of the war. They, in effect, say that if we cannot get a meeting of minds now when our armies are converging on the common enemy, how can we get an understanding on even more vital things in the future (…) You said today that you would be prepared to support any suggestions for the solution of this problem which offered a fair chance of success, and you also mentioned the possibility of bringing some members of the Lublin government here.

Realizing that we all have the same anxiety in getting the matter settled, I would like to develop your proposal a little and suggest that we invite here to Yalta at once Mr. Beirut [Bierut] and Mr. Osubka [Osóbka] Morawski from the Lublin government and also two or three from the following list of Poles, which according to our information would be desirable as representatives of the other elements of the Polish people in development of a new temporary government which all three of us could recognize and support: Bishop Sapieha of Cracow, Vincente [Wincenty] Witos, Mr. Zurlowski [Zulawski], Professor Buyak [Bujak], and Professor Kutzeva [Kutzeba]. If, as a result of the presence of these Polish leaders from abroad such as Mr. Mikolajczyk, Mr. Grabski, and Mr. Romer, the United States Government, and I feel sure the British government as well, would be prepared to examine with you conditions in which they would dissociate themselves from the London government and transfer their recognition to the new provisional government.

I hope that I do not have to assure you that the United States will never lend its support in any way to any provisional government in Poland that would be inimical to your interest.

It goes without saying that any interim government could be formed as a result of our conference with the Poles here would be pledged to the holding of free elections in Poland at the earliest possible date. I know this is completely consistent with your desire to see a new free and democratic Poland emerge from the welter of this war.

2.3 Stalin on the Situation in Poland, 14 November 1945

By November 1945 Soviet control over Poland had by and large been established. In the excerpts below Stalin himself describes a meeting with two Polish leaders, W. Gomulka and G. Mintz, that indicate a heavy dose of subservience to the Soviet leader as well as a heavy degree of co-ordination in moves against remaining opposition.

(...) The discussion was not being transcribed (the Poles deemed it unnecessary to make a record of conversation), thus I am sending you the contents of the discussion in the form of questions and answers.

QUESTION FROM POLES. Has there been a change in the Soviet leaders' attitude toward Poland and, in particular, toward [the] Polish Communists?

ANSWER FROM COM. STALIN. It has not changed and could not change. Our attitude toward Poles and Polish Communists is as friendly as before.

QUESTION. Should we adopt a law for nationalizing large industry and banks?

ANSWER. Following [Czechoslovak President Eduard] Benes's adoption of such a law, the time has come when such a law should be adopted in Poland as well (...)

QUESTION. Would I object if the Poles accepted a loan from the Americans or the English, and would I allow this loan to be accepted under the conditions that would more or less limit Poland's utilization of the loan?

ANSWER. The loan can be accepted, but without any types of conditions that would limit Poland's rights in the utilization of the loan.

QUESTION. Can we conclude a pact of mutual assistance with France?

ANSWER. You can, but it must fully conform to the spirit of the mutual assistance pact concluded between Poland and the USSR.

QUESTION. Should we pursue further the question of Teshin [Cieszyn] and can the USSR support Poland in the negotiations on Teshin with Czechoslovakia?

ANSWER. I don't advise you to pursue this question further, since, after receiving Silesian coking coal, Poland no longer has an argument for the transfer of Teshin to the Poles, in light of which the USSR cannot support the Poles in this matter. It would be better to eliminate quickly this contentious issue with Czechoslovakia, limit the matter to the resettlement of Teshin Poles in Poland, and re-establish good relations with Czechoslovakia. On the question of resettling Teshin Poles in Poland, the USSR can support the Poles in the negotiations with Czechoslovakia (...)

QUESTION. Can we announce at the PPR Congress that the PPR is a successor of the line and tradition of the Polish Communist Party, which had been liquidated even prior to the war?

ANSWER. This should not be done because the Polish Communist Party has in actuality become [the] agents of Pilsudchiks (...) It would be better to announce at the PPR Congress that the PPR is a new party and that it is not tied to the line and traditions of the Polish Communist Party.

QUESTION. Are we correct in thinking that it would be expedient to postpone general elections in Poland for another year?

ANSWER. I think that it would be better to hold elections no later than spring of 1946, since further postponement of elections would be very difficult both due to internal and international reasons.

QUESTION. Osóbka-Morawski is acting badly. If he does not improve in the near future, we would like to replace him prior to the organization of the elections with Mr. Lange (the current Polish ambassador to the USA, a moderate PPS-ist, and well disposed, in the Poles' opinion, toward Communists). What can you suggest?

ANSWER. If you have no other option and if it is impossible at present to put forth the candidacy of Bierut (the Poles believe this combination to be inexpedient), then you can make an attempt with Lange, with the goal of using Lange to dismantle the PPS. Consult with Wanda Lvovna, who is closely familiar with Lange.

2.4 Churchill's Iron Curtain Speech and Stalin's Reply, March 1946

One of the seminal documents of the early Cold War is undoubtedly Winston Churchill's Iron Curtain speech. At Fulton, Missouri, on 6 March 1946, with President Truman in attendance and aware of the speech's content, Churchill launched into a sharp criticism of Soviet policy in Eastern Europe that helped to galvanize public opinion in the United States (and Great Britain) in favour of a strong anti-Soviet policy. The Soviets were, not unexpectedly, unhappy with Churchill's Iron Curtain speech. Ten days later the Soviet daily Pravda published an interview in which Stalin criticized the former prime minister's tough rhetoric and criticism of the events unfolding in Eastern Europe.

A. Churchill

(…) I have a strong admiration and regard for the valiant Russian people and for my wartime comrade, Marshal Stalin. There is deep sympathy and goodwill in Britain—and I doubt not here also—towards the peoples of all the Russias and a resolve to persevere through many differences and rebuffs in establishing lasting friendships (…) It is my duty however, for I am sure you would wish me to state the facts as I see them to you, to place before you certain facts about the present position in Europe.

From Stettin in the Baltic to Trieste in the Adriatic, an iron curtain has descended across the Continent. Behind that line lie all the capitals of the ancient states of Central and Eastern Europe. Warsaw, Berlin, Prague, Vienna, Budapest, Belgrade, Bucharest and Sofia, all these famous cities and the populations around them lie in what I must call the Soviet sphere, and all are subject in one form or another, not only to Soviet influence but to a very high and, in many cases, increasing measure of control from Moscow (...) The Communist parties, which were very small in all these Eastern States of Europe, have been raised to pre-eminence and power far beyond their numbers and are seeking everywhere to obtain totalitarian control. Police governments are prevailing in nearly every case, and so far, except in Czechoslovakia, there is no true democracy (...) Whatever conclusions may be drawn from these facts—and facts they are—this is certainly not the Liberated Europe we fought to build up. Nor is it one which contains the essentials of permanent peace.

(...) I do not believe that Soviet Russia desires war. What they desire is the fruits of war and the indefinite expansion of their power and doctrines. But what we have to consider here today, while time remains, is the permanent prevention of war and the establishment of conditions of freedom and democracy as rapidly as possible in all countries. Our difficulties and dangers will not be removed by closing our eyes to them. They will not be removed by mere waiting to see what happens; nor will they be removed by a policy of appeasement. What is needed is a settlement, and the longer this is delayed, the more difficult it will be and the greater our dangers will become.

From what I have seen of our Russian friends and Allies during the war, I am convinced that there is nothing they admire so much as strength, and there is nothing for which they have less respect than for weakness, especially military weakness. For that reason the old doctrine of a balance of power is unsound. We cannot afford, if we can help it, to work on narrow margins, offering temptations to a trial of strength. If the Western Democracies stand together in strict adherence to the principles of the United Nations Charter, their influence for furthering those principles will be immense and no one is likely to molest them. If however they become divided or falter in their duty and if these all-important years are allowed to slip away, then indeed catastrophe may overwhelm us all (...)

B. Stalin

(...) In substance, Mr. Churchill now stands in the position of a firebrand of war. And Mr. Churchill is not alone here. He has friends not only in England but also in the United States of America.

In this respect, one is reminded remarkably of Hitler and his friends. Hitler began to set war loose by announcing his racial theory, declaring that only people

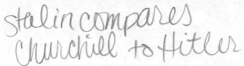
stalin compares Churchill to Hitler

speaking the German language represent a fully valuable nation. Mr. Churchill begins to set war loose, also by a racial theory, maintaining that only nations speaking the English language are fully valuable nations, called upon to decide the destinies of the entire world.

The German racial theory brought Hitler and his friends to the conclusion that the Germans, as the only fully valuable nation, must rule over other nations. The English racial theory brings Mr. Churchill and his friends to the conclusion that nations speaking the English language, being the only fully valuable nations, should rule over the remaining nations of the world (…)

As a result of the German invasion, the Soviet Union has irrevocably lost in battles with the Germans, and also during the German occupation and through the expulsion of Soviet citizens to German slave labor camps, about 7,000,000 people. In other words, the Soviet Union has lost in men several times more than Britain and the United States together.

It may be that some quarters are trying to push into oblivion these sacrifices of the Soviet people which insured the liberation of Europe from the Hitlerite yoke.

But the Soviet Union cannot forget them. One can ask therefore, what can be surprising in the fact that the Soviet Union, in a desire to ensure its security for the future, tries to achieve that these countries should have governments whose relations to the Soviet Union are loyal? How can one, without having lost one's reason, qualify these peaceful aspirations of the Soviet Union as 'expansionist tendencies' of our Government?

(…) Mr. Churchill wanders around the truth when he speaks of the growth of the influence of the Communist parties in Eastern Europe (…) The growth of the influence of Communism cannot be considered accidental. It is a normal function. The influence of the Communists grew because during the hard years of the mastery of fascism in Europe, Communists showed themselves to be reliable, daring and self-sacrificing fighters against fascist regimes for the liberty of peoples.

2.5 Co-ordination Among Communist Parties, May 1946

After the dissolution of the Comintern in 1943, the international Communist movement lacked a comprehensive umbrella organization. In the aftermath of World War II, however, the idea of resuscitating the Comintern began to gain ground. In the excerpt below Hungarian Communist Party leader Matyas Rakosi foreshadows the subsequent (September 1947) formation of the Cominform in a speech to a meeting of the Hungarian Communist Party on 17 May 1946.

(...) Finally I would like to raise another question, which, like socialism, we have not spoken much about so far. This refers to the creation of a new International. The comrades know that the third International had to be dissolved, because progress proved that it damaged rather than benefited the growth of the Communist parties (...)

(...) I should immediately say that as far as this is concerned, the new International cannot be compared to the previous ones. This will not be an organizing body; its task will be to compose, to help in making objections, to communicate the good or bad experiences of one country's Communist party to that of another country, that they should learn from their neighbors' experiences and losses (...) It is such an International that we now intend to establish, and this International will help rather than hinder the international Communist movement. On the same note, the view will change that was widely spread at the third International, for example, that we have to wait for the conditions for revolution to appear in at least a bunch of countries, and only then can we instigate the revolution (...) History has shown that that was wrong. Now we are going to follow another route (...)

Now that Communist parties have everywhere become stronger and come to the fore, there should be pressure for the institution of the Communist International or some other international Communist body. At the moment this is being disturbed by the whole list of parties preparing for elections. The comrades know that they are preparing for elections in France, Czechoslovakia and Romania, and that our comrades there are otherwise occupied. They are also occupied with the question of peace. But as soon as the elections die down and peace is agreed, at that moment this will come to the fore and then we will establish some kind of international body. One part of this conception is that in these changed circumstances, whenever a country achieves the conditions for the liberation of the proletariat or for socialism, this will be carried out, with no regard for whether the respective country is in a capitalist environment or not. This is also a new perspective, which simply means that in a country where as a result of the work of the Communist party these conditions are present, it has to be realized. This is fresh encouragement for all Communist parties, because now it will principally be dependent on their work whether or not the conditions for the liberation of the proletariat are created in their own country.

2.6 Zhdanov on the Founding of the Cominform, September 1947

In September 1947 Communist party leaders from around the world gathered in Warsaw to form the Communist Information Bureau (Cominform). The excerpts below—

taken from Soviet leader Andrei Zhdanov's speech at the meeting—provide a sample of the tough and uncompromising rhetoric that had by this time come to characterize Soviet views of US policy in Europe.

(…) the crusade against Communism proclaimed by America's ruling circle with the backing of the capitalist monopolies, leads as a logical consequence to the attacks on the fundamental rights and interests of the American working people (…) to adventures abroad in poisoning the minds of the politically backward and unenlightened American masses with virus of chauvinism and militarism, and in stultifying the average American with the help of all the diverse means of anti-Soviet and anti-Communist propaganda—the cinema, the radio, the church and the press.

(…) The strategic plans of the United States envisage the creation in peacetime of numerous bases and vantage grounds situated at great distances from the American continent against the USSR and the countries of the new democracy. America has built, or is building, air and naval bases in Alaska, Japan, Italy, South Korea, China, Egypt, Iran, Turkey, Greece, Austria and Western Germany. There are American military missions in Afghanistan and even in Nepal. Feverish preparation are being made to use the Arctic for purposes of military aggression.

(…) Economic expansion is an important supplement to the realization of America's strategical plan. American imperialism is endeavoring (…) to take advantage of the post-war difficulties of the European countries, in particular the shortage of raw materials, fuel and food in the Allied countries that suffered most from the war, to dictate to them extortionate terms for any assistance rendered. With an eye to the impeding economic crisis, the Unites States is in a hurry to find new monopoly spheres of capital investment and markets for its goods. American economic 'assistance' pursues the broad aim of bringing Europe into bondage to American capital (…)

In their ideological struggle against the USSR, the American imperialists (…) demonstrate their ignorance by laying primary stress on the allegation that the Soviet Union is undemocratic and totalitarian, while the United States and Great Britain and the whole capitalist world are democratic (…)

One of the lines taken (…) is an attack on national sovereignty, an appeal for the renouncement of the sovereign rights of nations, to which is opposed the idea of a 'world government'. The purpose of this campaign to import the unbridled expansion of American imperialism, which is ruthlessly violating the sovereign rights of nations, to represent the United States as a champion of universal laws, and those who resist American penetration as believers in an obsolete and 'selfish' nationalism. The idea of 'world government' has been taken up by bourgeois intellectual cranks and pacifists (…) also as a slogan specially directed at the Soviet Union, which indefatigably and consistently upholds the principle of real equality and protection of the sovereign rights of all nations, big and small (...)

(...) Soviet foreign policy and, in particular, Soviet economic relations with foreign countries, are based on the principle of equality, on the principle that agreements must be of advantage to both parties (...) This fundamental feature of the agreements with the USSR with other states stands out particularly vividly just now, in the light of the unfair and unequal treaties concluded or planned by the United States. Unequal agreements are alien to Soviet foreign trade policy. More, the development of the Soviet Union's economic relation with all countries interested in such relation demonstrates on what principles normal relations between states should be built. Suffice it to recall the treaties recently concluded by the USSR with Poland, Yugoslavia, Czechoslovakia, Hungary, Bulgaria and Finland. In this way the USSR has clearly shown along what lines Europe may find the way out of its present economic plight (...)

(...) In the course of the four years that have elapsed since the dissolving of the Comintern, the Communist Parties have grown considerably in strength and influence in nearly all the countries of Europe and Asia. The influence of the Communist Parties has increased not only in Eastern Europe, but in practically all European countries where fascism held sway, as well as in those which were occupied by the German fascists—France, Belgium, Holland, Norway, Denmark, Finland, etc. (...) But the present position of the Communist Parties has its shortcomings. Some comrades understood the dissolution of the Comintern to imply the elimination of all ties, of all contact, between the fraternal Communist parties. But the experience has shown that such mutual isolation of the Communist Parties is wrong, harmful and, in point of fact, unnatural (...) The need for mutual consultation (...) has become particularly urgent at the present juncture when continued isolation may lead to a slackening of mutual understanding, and at times, even to serious blunders.

In view of the fact that the majority of the leaders of the Soviet parties (especially the British Labourites and the French Socialists) are acting as agents of the United States imperialist circles, there has developed upon the Communists the special historical task of leading the resistance to the American plan for the enthrallment of Europe, and of boldly denouncing all coadjutors of American imperialism in their own countries. At the same time, Communists must support all the really patriotic elements who do not want their countries to be imposed upon, who want to resist enthrallment of their countries to foreign capital, and to uphold their national sovereignty (...)

Just as in the past the Munich policy untied the hands of the Nazi aggressors, so today the concessions to the new course of the United States and the imperialist camp may encourage its inspirers to be even more insolent and aggressive (...)

2.7 The Beginnings of the Soviet–Yugoslav Split, 10 February 1948

In 1948 the conflict between the Soviet Union and Yugoslavia over its independent course under Tito flared up. This extract from the Yugoslav leader Milovan Djilas's report of a meeting in Moscow between Soviet, Bulgarian, and Yugoslav representatives foreshadowed the subsequent expelling of the Yugoslav 'heretics' from the Comintern and illustrates Soviet dislike of the independent-minded policies adopted in Belgrade. The particular focus of the meeting is on the plan to create a Yugoslav–Bulgarian federation in the Balkans.

Molotov (…) stressed that (…) [t]hese disagreements were inadmissible both from the party and the state point of view. As examples of the serious discord he gave three: firstly, the conclusion of the Yugoslav–Bulgarian Treaty of Union— lack of coordination between the USSR, on one hand, and Bulgaria and Yugoslavia, on the other hand; secondly, the declaration of Dimitrov about a Federation of East European and Balkan countries, including Greece—lack of coordination between the USSR, on one side, and Bulgaria, on the other; thirdly, the introduction of a Yugoslav division into Southern Albania (Korcha)—lack of coordination between the USSR, on one hand, and Yugoslavia, on the other. As to the first point, he stresses that the Soviet government informed the Yugoslav and Bulgarian governments—and they agreed to this—that one should not conclude a treaty with Bulgaria until the expiration of limitations imposed by the Peace Treaty [with Bulgaria in 1946]. However, the Yugoslav and Bulgarian governments concluded the treaty, and the Soviet government learned about it from the newspapers (…)

At this moment, Stalin cut in to remind [us] that the Poles who were in Moscow in those days, spoke against [the Federation]. That means that the Soviet representatives first asked them what they thought of Dimitrov's declaration. And they said that they agreed, but when Stalin told them that the Soviet Union was against it, they also said that they were against, but they had previously believed that this was a position and request of Moscow. Stalin adds that the subsequent clarification by Dimitrov (he probably had in mind the announcement of the Bulgarian telegraph agency) explained nothing. Stalin quotes from this announcement that says how Austria-Hungary had thwarted a customs union between Bulgaria and Serbia, and adds that it means—the Germans had worked against a customs union, and now we do (i.e. the Soviet Union). Stalin adds that Dimitrov diverts attention from domestic issues to foreign affairs—Federation, etc.

Then Molotov (…) stresses (…) that they [in Moscow] accidentally learned about the entry of the Yugoslav troops into Albania. The Albanians told the Russians that they thought that the entry of the Yugoslav troops had been coordinated with the Soviet Union, and meanwhile it was not so. At that moment Molotov began citing some sort of dispatches, and Stalin told him to read them aloud. He asks Stalin which message he should read. Stalin leans [over] and points out [one]. Molotov reads a message from [Soviet ambassador in Yugoslavia] Lavrent'ev about his meeting with Tito. From this reading, it becomes clear that the message is an answer to the question of the Soviet government if there is a decision about the entry of Yugoslav troops into Albania, and it says that such a decision—coordinated with Hoxha—really exists, that the motive comes from the notification about a probable attack against Albania; then the message points out that Tito said that he does not agree with Moscow that in case of an entry of Yugoslav troops into Albania, the Anglo-Americans would intervene beyond a campaign in the press (…) At the end, Molotov points out that Tito did not inform them about his disagreement with Moscow. He stresses that disagreements are inadmissible both from the party and state viewpoint and that disagreements should be taken out [for discussion], and not concealed, and that it is necessary to inform and consult. One must be cautious with regard to press conferences.

Following Molotov, Dimitrov spoke. He, as well as the other Bulgarians and Kardelj (he was the only one among the Yugoslavs who spoke), did not give his reasons coherently, because Stalin kept interrupting him. He said that what Yugoslavia and Bulgaria publicized at Bled was not a treaty, but only a statement that a future treaty had been agreed upon. Soviet representatives affirm that they learned about this affair from newspapers, etc. Dimitrov stresses that Bulgaria's economic difficulties are so serious that it cannot develop without cooperation with other countries. It is true that he got carried away at a press conference. Stalin interrupts and tells him that he wanted to shine with a new word, and that is wrong, and it is a mistake because such a Federation is not feasible. Dimitrov says that he did not target the USSR by his assertion that Austria-Hungary had blocked a Bulgarian–Serb customs union. He stresses, at last, that there are essentially no disagreements between the foreign policies of Bulgaria and the Soviet Union.

Stalin interrupts and asserts that there are substantial differences and there is a practice of the Leninists—to recognize differences and mistakes and to liquidate them. Dimitrov says that they make mistakes because they are only learning foreign policy, but Stalin replies to this that he [Dimitrov] is a senior political figure who had been engaged in politics for forty years, and in his case it is not mistakes, but a different perception [than the USSR's] (he [Stalin] said it two or three times during the meeting, addressing Dimitrov). As to the repeated emphasis by Dimitrov on the fact that Bulgaria must get closer with other countries for economic reasons, Stalin says that he agrees if one speaks of a customs union between Yugoslavia and Bulgaria, but if one speaks of Romania (later, as I recall, he also mentioned Hungary), then he is against it. In general, when he spoke about such ties of Bulgaria with which the Soviet Union disagreed, most often [he] cited Romania as an example (…)

Then Kolarov began to speak. He says about this part from the Bulgarian announcement regarding a customs union between Serbia and Bulgaria, where nobody meant to hint at the USSR, and as to the customs union between Romania and Bulgaria, the Romanians are also all for it. Besides, the Romanian–Bulgarian treaty had been earlier sent to the Soviet government and it already made only one amendment so that an article [on the joint defense] against any aggressor would be replaced by an article against Germany or a power that could be in alliance with it, and there were no comments on the Bulgarian–Romanian customs union. Then a brief exchange between Stalin and Molotov occurs. Molotov confirms what Kolarov says. Stalin stresses again that he is against the Bulgarian–Romanian customs union, although Bulgarians have a reason to think otherwise, on the basis of dispatches. He stresses that he did not know that there was an article about a customs union in the Romanian–Bulgarian treaty that had been previously sent to the Soviet government. Dimitrov says that that it was the very cause why in his statement he went further than necessary.

Stalin says to him that he [Dimitrov] wanted to surprise the whole world and adds that it looked like the secretary of the Comintern was explaining tediously and meticulously what should be done and how (…) that this gives food to American reactionaries (…) He then speaks about the significance of the American elections and [says] that one should be careful to do nothing to give the reactionaries arguments that could facilitate their victory (…) The reactionaries in America, when they hear such statements, say that in Eastern Europe there is not only a bloc in the making, but [the countries] are merging into common states. He tells Dimitrov and the others that they are overdoing it (…) Then he makes a linkage to the issue of Albania. The three world powers—the USSR, England, and America—guaranteed Albania's independence by a special agreement. Albania is our weakest spot, because other states are either members of the United Nations, or recognized, etc., but Albania is not (…) If Yugoslav troops entered Albania, the reactionaries in England and America would be able to use it and step forward as defenders of Albanian independence. Instead of sending troops we should work intensely to build up the Albanian army, we should teach the Albanians, and then, if they are attacked, let the Albanian Skupcina [parliament] appeal to Yugoslavia for help (…)

(…) Stalin said half-jokingly that the Yugoslavs are afraid of having Russians in Albania and because of this are in a hurry to send their troops. He also said that the Bulgarians and Yugoslavs think that the USSR stands against a unification of Bulgaria and Yugoslavia, but it does not want to admit it. Molotov raised some kind of a point from the Bulgarian–Romanian communiqué about the coordination of plans and mentioned that it would have been essentially a merger of these states. Stalin is categorical that this is inconceivable and that Dimitrov would soon see for himself that it is nonsense, and instead of cooperation it would bring about a quarrel between the Romanians and Bulgarians. Therefore mutual relations should be limited to trade agreements. Then Stalin laid out a Soviet view that in Eastern Europe one should create three federations—Polish–Czechoslovak, Romanian–Hungarian and Yugoslav–Bulgarian–Albanian. Bulgaria and Yugoslavia [he said] may unite tomorrow if they wish, there are no constraints on this, since Bulgaria today is a sovereign state.

Kardelj says that we were not in a hurry to unify with Bulgaria and Albania, in view of international and domestic moments, but Stalin reacts to it by saying that it should not come too late, and that the conditions for that are ripe. At first, Yugoslavia and Bulgaria must unite, and then let Albania join them. This should be agreed upon through People's Skupcina [parliaments], by the will of the peoples. Stalin thinks that one should begin with political unification and then it would be difficult [for the West] to attack Albania. As to a Bulgarian–Yugoslav unification, Stalin repeatedly stressed that this question has ripened, and one even began a discussion about the name of [a united] state.

Then Kardelj returned to the issue about what after all one should do in Albania, but [Stalin's] answer boiled down to what Stalin said earlier, i.e., the Albanian army ought to be taught, and that Albania should ask for assistance in case of aggression (…) Then Kardelj says that he does not see any big differences between Yugoslavia and the USSR in foreign policy (…) says it was a mistake that we [the Yugoslavs] failed to inform them. Stalin interrupts him and says that it was not a mistake, it was a system [a policy] and that we do not inform them on anything.

Then Stalin and Molotov propose a protocol on mutual coordination of foreign affairs. Kardelj agrees with that. Stalin proposes that we inquire of them [the Soviets] on all questions of interest to us, and that they would also inform us about everything (…)

(…) Dimitrov raised the issue about the conclusion of a treaty on mutual assistance between the USSR and Bulgaria. He stressed that it would be of great significance for Bulgaria. Stalin agreed with this, but added that among the Quisling countries [the USSR] would first conclude treaties with neighbors: with Romania—this treaty is almost ready, with Hungary and Finland.

2.8 The West Europeans and the Czech Coup, February 1948

After the February 1948 Communist coup d'état in Czechoslovakia, Finland and Norway remained the only countries bordering the Soviet Union that had not become people's

" WHO'S NEXT TO BE LIBERATED FROM FREEDOM, COMRADE ?"

1. Stalin to Molotov: 'Who's next to be liberated from freedom, comrade?' (David Low, *Evening Standard*, March 1948). Reprinted by permission. Photo supplied by The Centre for the Study of Cartoons and Caricature, University of Kent.

democracies. Yet, soon after the Czech coup, both countries felt under imminent pressure. The Soviets demanded that Finland negotiate a 'friendship treaty' with the USSR, and rumours of similar demands on Norway circulated. The Finns concluded a 'friendship' treaty with the USSR in April 1948 without a subsequent coup d'état. *In Norway, however, the left-leaning Social Democrat prime minister, Einar Gerhardsen, who had attempted to co-operate with the Communists after the war, turned decisively against them. The first extract is from Gerhardsen's speech on 29 February 1948, in which he attacked the Communists. The second excerpt—from the Finnish president J. K. Paasikivi's diaries—lays down the Finnish rationalization for the lack of a Communist takeover.*

A. Einar Gerhardsen Attacks the Norwegian Communists, February 1948

We see the Czechoslovak people as a freedom-loving people, who have fought bravely against aggressors and oppressors of all kinds. We have felt a strange form of kinship with this people, we have sympathized with it and admired it. Because of this, it hurts us to see what is happening today. The Communists must be the only ones who take pleasure. They tell us that it is the popular will and the people who have now won. The rest of us have trouble understanding why it would then be necessary to exclude the parliament that the people itself has elected. And we have trouble understanding that the Communists could not have waited for the results of the election that should have taken place within a couple of months. Under these circumstances, we must be forgiven for only finding one possible explanation: that the Communists did not dare to wait for the people to decide in a free election.

The events in Czechoslovakia have not only aroused sorrow and anger among most Norwegians, but also fear and alarm. Norway's problem is, as far as I can see, primarily a domestic problem. What could threaten the freedom and democracy of the Norwegian people is the danger that the Norwegian Communist Party represents at any given time.

The most important task in the struggle for Norway's independence, for democracy and law, is to reduce the influence of the Communist Party and the Communists as much as possible.

We must not create a climate of harassment against them. We will not fight them with the same methods which their Czechoslovak party-comrades use to fight their political opponents. The Norwegian Communists will still be able to make use of their full democratic rights. They will be able to speak and write in freedom. No action committees from other parties will be purging *their* editorial boards or *their* leaders. Their representatives in the *Storting* [Parliament] and in county councils will be able to continue their work, until the voters replace them in free elections. And they will be able to continue their attempts at gaining influence in the trade unions, and use their influence there to create difficulties for our social economy.

We will fight the Communists by democratic means and spiritual weapons.

We will try to convince the many who joined them during the war in good faith, because they believed that the Communist Party was patriotic and democratic. Today nobody can claim good faith. Those who head the Communist Party in Norway are Comintern and Cominform Communists. Like their comrades-in-arms in other countries they are, in their hearts, supporters of terror and dictatorship. Today no pretty declarations must prevent people from facing up to the brutal truth—even if for many it will be a terrible discovery. The only ones who can disprove this stern judgement are the Norwegian Communists themselves (…)

B. J. K. Paasikivi and Finland's position, June 1948

2.6.1948
A discussion with Dr. Kihlberg.
(…) Then I spoke of our situation and policy. I first said that I was gratified that

Dagens Nyheter ['The Daily News'] and all the media in Sweden was interested in our affairs. I hoped that this would continue to be the case. I said that the Swedes are more worried about our situation than we are. The events in Czechoslovakia were not likely to be repeated in Finland. There were great many differences between Czechoslovakia and Finland:

1) Czechoslovakia is dependent on the Soviet Union for its security, because it is only with the aid of the USSR that the Czechs can defend themselves against East Germany. Because Germany will never forget that the Czechs forced 3.5 million Sudeten Germans to leave and confiscated their property and their lands. Because of this the entire Czech population is convinced that Soviet military support is necessary and therefore pro-Russian sentiments are commonplace in Czechoslovakia. Finland is not dependent on the Soviets in this way. We do not need military aid from the Soviet Union nor do we expect it. No one threatens Finland, assuming that Russia does not. Therefore the Finnish popular opinion is not favorable to the Soviet Union in the same way as it is in Czechoslovakia.

2) The Communists in Czechoslovakia were in a different position than those in Finland. By nationalising the property of the industries of the Sudeten Germans the majority of Czech industries had become property of the state. Marxism was as a result in a strong position.

3) Czechs were a Slavic people. In 1938 when Hitler and the Nazis attacked not one shot was fired despite the fact that the Czechs had a large army and good weapons (Skoda) and fortifications. The Finns would not have acted this way. In his recently published wartime memoirs Churchill writes that should the Czechs have resisted back then the war would have started earlier than it did.

4) The Social Democrats in Czechoslovakia appear to be of a different sort than the ones in Finland. Our Social Democrats are reliable. They would not give in like the Czech ones.

In this connection I asked what he knew about opposition in Czechoslovakia and the other 'new democracies'. Kihlberg replied that the information is depressing. Then I spoke about our relationship with the Soviets. I told him about the talks I and Mannerheim had with Zhdanov in January–May 1945.—I said that General Heinrichs and [Foreign] Minister Enckell had thought about this matter a lot. The [Soviet Treaty] is based on our proposal. We do not think that it is dangerous. No more so than if we had no treaty at all. The Russians accepted our proposal due to the following reasons: 1) It satisfied Russia's general concerns; 2) the Russians knew that we would not go any further but would rather have chosen an open conflict. I told as much to our Communists; 3) the conflict would have drawn attention from the entire world, especially from Scandinavia, a world wide scandal, and the Soviet Union would have faced severe problems in Finland without gaining anything substantial (…) I said that the men in the Kremlin would naturally be happy to see the Communists in Finland take over. But it is not a major goal and they are unwilling face a great amount of difficulties in search of that goal. Lenin always said that it was important to bring about Communism in one or two of the great powers in Europe but Finland's significance is very small in this context (…)

2.9 A Meeting with President Beneš, August 1948

Perhaps the last Westerner to meet with former Czechoslovak president Eduard Beneš was the Swedish journalist Amelie Pose, on 19 August 1948. Beneš, who was in internal exile at his country house in Sezimovo Usti, agonized over his memories from the Communist coup d'état that had taken place six months prior to their meeting.

(…) I told him about the concert at the National Museum in Stockholm where no one spoke with the current [Czechoslovak] regime's representatives—and this amused him a lot. 'It feels like a fresh breath of air from another and better world where people feel free to show their feelings—we easily forget that such places still exist!' (…) He called Gottwald a figurehead, a spineless tool for the Russians—and that he is losing more and more of his influence. 'I believed for a long time that at least he would not lie to me, but have now seen that they all do it without exception. My biggest mistake was that for a long time I could not believe that even Stalin cold bloodedly and cynically lied to me—both in 1935 and later, and that his guarantees to myself and Masaryk were an intentional and purposeful swindle (…) the only time that I allowed myself to be jerked around without being able to withstand personal charm was exactly with Stalin—and now you see how wrong I was.' I asked if Zorin had tried to make contact with him in February and he denied it. He described instead that Gottwald and others had told him that the Russians stood in full 'readiness' along the borders, ready to come in if the Communists sent an SOS, and that they had also pointed out that the Americans had far too few divisions on the Continent, that neither they nor their allies were ready to respond with violence should the Russians march into Czechoslovakia. Benes's own information confirmed this, 'also Steinhardt's' (US ambassador to Prague). Benes said that it was at that time he began sending an SOS to the various party leaders (…) and even to some generals he thought could be trusted. But these had later been placed on house arrest and were unreachable. 'They blame me for having failed them, I blame them for having failed me at the fateful hour. Without their support I was powerless (…) when no-one stood up I could not allow Gottwald's hordes to massacre Prague's innocent populace. There were no limits to what they threatened to do.'

(...) When I told him straight out that all of us abroad hoped for, indeed demanded to hear from him in order to find encouragement and strength in this politically dark age to continue our resistance movement, the purpose which we were unable to formulate or even distinguish—he said with truly solemn voice 'yes—tell them that I give them my blessing and that every time I think about their work it gives me comfort in these difficult times. Tell them that at the moment there are so many experienced and sensible Czechs outside the borders that, despite their different party affiliations, they must unite behind some broad common ideas, particularly when it comes down to influencing the governments and politicians of the various countries in which the emigrants live. They must try to open their eyes and see the fact that Czechoslovakia has once again become a European affair—there will not be a lasting peace before this country is free again. Tell them that logically, psychologically, and historically there is no possibility that the situation here can remain as it is indefinitely—it is built upon a false basis, a colossus with clay feet that will soon collapse. Dissatisfaction grows like an avalanche throughout the entire country—not least among the industrial workers, particularly in Morava and Slovakia—and even amongst the old committed pre-war Communists' (...)

I spoke very warmly about his possible trip to Switzerland—and said that it was his duty to his people and to humanity. 'All the mistakes that the Czech people and you yourself may have committed could in this way be reconciled and cleared, you should be rehabilitated for the sake of the present, the future and history. Masaryk was murdered or killed himself. (Benes is no longer sure which was the case) (...)—but Benes must in some other, equally definitive way show the world that he distances himself from what has and is still happening here. He does not need to jump out of some window—just over the border.' 'No—I don't believe that suicide is a solution', he intervened (...) I explained that (...) we wanted only to have him outside the country's borders alive—as a vital symbol of the democracy that he and Masaryk had fought for and as a protest against those who had brought it down. If he merely sat in Switzerland and by doing so gave his authoritative and moral support for the cause, all the others would carry out the work he clearly no longer was capable of doing. 'We are a group of nobodies who alone cannot make the great powers listen to our words and accept that Czechoslovakia's return to the group of independent democracies is a necessary condition for the peaceful resolution of her disputes with Russia—but if we can have you as the front for us nobodies, our combined strength can become unimaginably large and significant' (...) I said that I was quite happy about his illness, which instead of being used as a weapon against him could become an effective weapon against them—and in the service of the good cause. (...)

And then I told him about spontaneous demonstrations that were being prepared for October and about all the proclamations regarding the 'Anschluss' to Russia which I had heard would be displayed on billboards and flags. I had learned about this from eyewitnesses. Before something like that takes place he must be out of the country—because afterwards the curtain will fall completely over Czechoslovakia, at least for some time to come (...)

2.10 The Cominform Expels Yugoslavia

In the summer of 1948 the conflict between Tito and Stalin broke out into the open as the Cominform expelled Yugoslavia from its ranks. The Cominform's explanation for the action is printed below.

7. The Information Bureau notes that characteristic of the leaders of the Yugoslav Communist Party is not only their departure from Marxism-Leninism and slippage into anti-Party positions but also widespread use, in the style and methods of their political activity, of the procedures of intrigue and petty cheating (fraud), discreditable to their honour and dignity. This identification of politics with intrigue and cheating by the leaders of Yugoslavia was shown, for example, in Yugoslavia's negotiations (...) in connection with the claims put forward by Yugoslavia regarding the Yugoslav–Austrian frontier. After having at first advanced more extensive demands for territorial concessions to Yugoslavia to be made by Austria, the Yugoslavs later told the British that they would make territorial concessions. However, the Yugoslavs made no official announcement of these back-stage concessions to the Anglo-Americans, nor did they inform the USSR, thus giving the latter to understand that it must uphold Yugoslavia's original demands. In this way the Yugoslavs urged the USSR to uphold the Yugoslavs' position more resolutely than they were doing themselves and, by making at the same time back-stage concessions to the British, they not only tried to put the USSR in a false position, but also made it possible for themselves, having made concessions to the Anglo-Americans, to put the onus of their failure on the USSR, blaming the latter for their inability to obtain their demands (...)

A second point. By agreement between the USSR and Yugoslavia the governments of the two countries were obliged to consult each other on the more important questions of international relations. The Yugoslav government, however, almost always violates this agreement and thereby creates difficulties for the USSR, in its foreign political activity and worsens its own position for the sake of petty intrigue. This happened, for example, with regard to the Trieste question, when the Anglo-Americans proposed unilaterally to violate the international agreement and return Trieste to Italy. Despite the best efforts of the USSR, and the democratic states, which obtained at one time the well-known decision on the status of Trieste, the Yugoslav government hastened, without informing or consulting the USSR, to declare its agreement to unilateral negotiations with Italy on changing the status of Trieste and handing it over to Italy, which strengthened the position of the Anglo-Americans and Italian reactionaries (…)

A third point. At the beginning of 1948, without informing or consulting the USSR, Yugoslavia decided to send one of its divisions into Albania, which could have endangered the security of Albania, since the Anglo-Americans might have seen this step taken by the Yugoslavs as an attempt to violate the independence of Albania and, on those grounds, might have launched an armed intervention in Albania, with the threat of creating a focus of war in the Balkans. For this reason the government of the USSR, having by chance learnt of the Yugoslavs' intentions, pronounced a categorical protest against both the content and the method of the deciding of this question without consultation with the USSR. The Yugoslav government revoked the despatch into Albania of a Yugoslav division, but without even informing the Soviet government that it had taken this step (…)

The Information Bureau considers that these and similar facts testify not only to errors in relation to Marxism by the leaders of the Yugoslav CP but also to their low moral-political level, their ability to slip from the rails of honest, principled politics on to the rails of petty intrigue and unworthy betrayal of their allies.

2.11 The Purges in Eastern Europe, 1949

Following the announcement of Yugoslavia's expulsion from the Comintern the Soviet Union launched a series of measures to purge any elements of 'nationalist deviation' from the ranks of East European Communist parties. By using fabricated charges, such leaders as Hungarian foreign minister László Rajk were demoted, tried, and either imprisoned or executed in the most intense period of 'Stalinization' during the late 1940s. Below is an excerpt from Rajk's indictment.

(…) At the end of May, 1945, Laszlo Rajk returned to Hungary. He succeeded in concealing his past and playing the part of a much-persecuted Communist, steeled in the Spanish struggle. He rose to be the secretary of the Greater Budapest district of the Hungarian Communist Party, a member of the National Assembly, Minister of Home Affairs and finally Minister of Foreign Affairs. Naturally he continued his old activities. About this he admitted in his statement:

'I regularly and constantly informed the American intelligence agents of every question that cropped up in the Ministry of Home Affairs and later in the Ministry of Foreign Affairs.'

American intelligence in Hungary gave increasing prominence to the Yugoslav spies of the foreign espionage services, the envoys of Tito. Foully abusing the fraternal sympathy of Hungarian democracy with the working people of Yugoslavia, Tito's diplomatic representatives and other official envoys built up their net of espionage with the greatest effrontery from the moment they first set foot on Hungarian soil at the beginning of 1945. First of all they recruited Laszlo Rajk for their service, as they were acquainted with his past as police informer and spy. Rajk readily (…) handed over to Yugoslav spies confidential information about Hungarian conditions, about the Soviet Army, about the Soviet diplomatic corps, etc. (…)

Laszlo Rajk, as cabinet minister and member of the National Assembly, that is, as a public servant, grossly abusing his official position, gave secrets to foreign powers which seriously endangered the interests of the Hungarian state; by so doing he committed the crimes of espionage and sedition.

The coming into prominence of the Yugoslav spies was connected with the fact that American spies, agents provocateurs, and Trotskyists like Rajk himself had come into power in liberated Yugoslavia. The Gestapo had sent, from French internment camps alone, 150 of these people to Yugoslavia for espionage work at the same time as Rajk himself had been sent home. These spies formed the bulk of the circle around Tito and they systematically forced back the honest elements among the Yugoslav partisans, those who were true to their people. Encouraged by this success, the American imperialists set themselves no smaller target than, with the assistance of Tito and company, to attempt to bring the countries of the people's democracies over to their side (…) In pursuit of this aim the Yugoslav, American and other intelligence services gave every support in their power to Rajk (…) Rajk established a fairly widespread organisation. Wherever possible he appointed the agents of the imperialists, especially former Trotskyists, agent provocateurs and spies to high positions (…) The adherents of the people's democracy, especially workers and peasants, were systematically squeezed out of the police, the army and the civil service by Rajk and his spy ring; at the same time, the spies and agents provocateurs were released from internment camps (…)

In addition to the Rajk organisation, the Yugoslavs built up their own separate spy rings. Abusing the confidence accorded them by the Hungarian people's democracy, they infiltrated not only into state organisations, but into political parties, economic institutions and social organisations as well. Their network of organisation seemed so comprehensive that, relying on Rajk and his gang, in the autumn of 1947 they set out to overthrow the Hungarian people's democracy (…) It was to advance the preparations for the execution of this plan that Tito visited Hungary in December 1947. This visit—which in many ways resembled the triumphant entry of a conqueror into Budapest—was made according to the carefully prepared plans of the Yugoslav leaders and had the purpose of increasing the prestige of Tito and Yugoslavia in Hungary, just as Rajk and his circle and their

Yugoslav accomplices regularly attempted to popularise Tito artificially and reduce the great popularity of the Soviet Union (…)

Since March, 1948, however, there was an increasing number of signs indicating that the Yugoslav–American plans were beginning to be exposed. As a member of the Political Committee of the Communist Party Rajk came to know that the Information Bureau was about to unmask the treachery of Tito and his followers (…) Tito and his circle now informed Rajk that new tactics would have to be worked out to deal with the altered situation, and that Rajk must therefore arrange a secret meeting with Rankovich, the Yugoslav Minister of Home Affairs (…) Rankovich informed Rajk of the new plan, emphasising that it was the result of Tito's own work and that besides him only Djilas and Kardelj knew of it (…) He spoke of Tito's 'brilliant' scheme for turning the Yugoslav people gradually against the Soviet Union and leading them into the camp of the Western imperialists. He also explained how Tito intended to increase the reactionary forces in the people's democracies, ensure their organisational co-operation and put them on the side of the imperialists against the Soviet Union (…) The political directives also prescribed that Rajk should seek the support of the followers of Horthy and Szalasi, the Catholic reactionaries, and the kulaks. In connection with the latter he should emphasise the Yugoslav example, where 'Tito does not fight against the kulaks'. Finally Rankovich said that for the armed overthrow of the government he would make the services of his own military expert available to Rajk.

Laszlo Rajk undertook to carry out these directives of Tito. After his arrival in Budapest he commissioned Gyorgy Palffy to make the necessary armed preparations within the Army for the overthrow of the Republic. Palffy, who had already been informed through his own channels of the plan transmitted by Rankovich, reported to Rajk that he had already commenced preparations, and informed him of the details of the plan for an armed putsch.

(…) All these plans were foiled by the measures taken against reactionary elements and spies, as a result of which a significant proportion of Rajk's followers were removed from the Army, the Police, and the Civil Service. In the middle of May the arrest of the conspirators began (…)

2.12 United States Policy Towards Eastern Europe, 1953

This document outlines the American view of Eastern Europe in the aftermath of Stalin's death and the riots that took place in Eastern Germany in the summer of 1953.

1. Soviet Control over the Soviet satellites in Eastern Europe (Poland, Czechoslovakia, Hungary, Romania, Bulgaria, Albania and East Germany) has

not just about pwr. in Europe

contributed importantly to the power disequilibrium in Europe and to the threat to the security of the United States. (…)

3. Despite the widespread popular opposition to Communism in each of the satellites, known underground groups capable of armed resistance have survived only as scattered remnants in a few areas, and are now generally inactive (…) the ability of the USSR to exercise effective control over, and to exploit the resources of, the European satellites has not been appreciably reduced, and is not likely to be, so long as the USSR maintains adequate military forces in the area.

4. The death of Stalin created for Soviet dominion over the satellites new problems which may lend themselves to exploitation. Although there is as yet no evidence that Soviet capability to dominate the satellites has been impaired since the death of Stalin, the possibility nevertheless exists that a greater concentration of effort may be required to maintain control and that the new Soviet leaders may have to moderate the pace and scope of their programs in the satellites (…)

5. Although nationalist opposition to Soviet domination is a disruptive force within the Soviet orbit, and even within the Communist movement itself, it does not appear likely that a non-Soviet regime on the Tito model will emerge in any of the satellites under existing circumstances. The combination of basic factors which made possible the successful Yugoslav defection from Moscow is lacking in any of the satellites. In addition the Kremlin has taken drastic measures since the Yugoslav defection to guard against further defections.

6. Tito's establishment of an independent Communist regime, nevertheless, has brought valuable assets to the free world in the struggle against aggressive Soviet power. It provides a standing example of successful defiance of the Kremlin and is proof that there is a practical alternative for nationalist Communist leaders to submission to Soviet control. There are further advantages flowing from Yugoslavia's political and military cooperation with the West, its association with Greece and Turkey in a Balkan entente, and its role as a vigorous propaganda weapon against Soviet Communism.

7. East Germany poses special and more difficult problems of control for the USSR than do the other satellites (…)

8. The detachment of any major European satellite from the Soviet bloc does not now appear feasible except by Soviet acquiescence or by war. Such a detachment would not decisively affect the Soviet military capability either in delivery of weapons of mass destruction or in conventional forces, but would be a considerable blow to Soviet prestige and would impair in some degree Soviet conventional military capabilities in Europe.

Policy Conclusions

9. It is in the national security interests of the United States to pursue a policy of determined resistance to dominant Soviet influence over the satellites in East-

ern Europe and to seek the eventual elimination of that influence. Accordingly, feasible political, economic, propaganda and covert measures are required to create and exploit troublesome problems for the USSR, complicate control in the satellites, and retard the growth of the military and economic potential of the Soviet bloc (...)

Basic Objectives

10. Long-range: The eventual fulfillment of the rights of the peoples in the Soviet satellites to enjoy governments of their own choosing, free of Soviet domination and participating as peaceful members in the free world community.

11. Current:

a. To disrupt the Soviet-satellite relationship, minimize satellite contributions to Soviet power, and deter aggressive world policies on the part of the USSR by diverting Soviet attention and energies to problems and difficulties within the Soviet bloc.

b. To undermine the Satellite regimes and promote conditions favorable to the eventual liberation of the satellite peoples.

c. To conserve and strengthen the assets within the satellites, and among their nationals outside, which may contribute to U.S. interests in peace or war, and to the ultimate freedom of the satellites.

d. To lay the groundwork, as feasible with reasonable risk, for resistance to the Soviets in the event of war.

Courses of Action

12. Use appropriate means short of military force to oppose, and to contribute to the eventual elimination of, Soviet domination over the satellites; including, when appropriate, concert with NATO or other friendly powers, resort to UN procedures, and, if possible, negotiation with the USSR.

13. Encourage and assist the satellite peoples in resistance to their Soviet-dominated regimes, maintaining their hopes of eventual freedom from Soviet domination, while avoiding:

a. Incitement to premature revolt.

b. Commitments on the nature and timing of any U.S. action to bring about liberation.

c. Incitement to action when the probable reprisals or other results would yield a net loss in terms of U.S. objectives.

14. Develop and encourage, as appropriate, increased use of passive resistance by the peoples of the satellites.

15. Be prepared to exploit any future disturbances similar to the East German

riots of 1953 by planning courses of action which would best serve U.S. interests in such events.

16. Foster satellite nationalism as a force against Soviet imperialism, while avoiding commitments to national ambitions which would interfere with U.S. post-liberation objectives.

17. Cooperate with other forces—such as religious, cultural, social—which are natural allies in the struggle against Soviet imperialism.

18. Stimulate and exploit conflicts within the Communist ruling groups in each satellite, among such groups, and between them and the Kremlin.

19. Foster disaffection in satellite armed forces and police, to diminish their reliability in suppressing domestic disturbances and their will to fight in the event of war.

20. Encourage democratic, anti-Communist elements in the satellites; but at the same time be prepared to exploit any Titoist tendencies, and to assist 'national Communist' movements under favorable conditions, making clear, as appropriate, that opportunities for survival exist outside the Soviet bloc.

21. Exploit the developing organizations of Western unity (NATO, OEEC, ECSC, etc.) as a force of attraction for the satellites.

22. Encourage defection of key satellite personnel and possible VFC recruits, but not mass defection; and assist in the resettlement and rehabilitation of refugees who do escape.

23. Support or make use of refugees or exile organizations which can contribute to the attainment of U.S. objectives, but do not recognize governments-in-exile.

24. Strengthen covert activities in support of the objectives in paras. 10 and 11 above.

25. Maintain flexibility in U.S. economic policies toward the Soviet bloc, and toward individual satellites, in order to gain maximum advantage with the limited economic weapons at hand (both restrictions and incentives).

26. Continue U.S. diplomatic missions in Poland, Czechoslovakia, Hungary, and Rumania as long as may be in the U.S. interest, and keep under review the possibility of resuming diplomatic relations with Bulgaria.

27. Exploit the existence, and encourage the development, of the Yugoslav–Greek–Turkish entente as a means of weakening Soviet power in the Balkan satellites and as an example of free association of independent Balkan nations serving as a potential alternative to Soviet rule.

28. Keep the situation with respect to Albania under continuing surveillance with a view to the possibility of detachment of that country from the Soviet bloc at such time as its detachment might be judged to serve the over-all U.S. interest.

29. Exploit, to the fullest extent compatible with the policies regarding Germany as a whole and Berlin, the special opportunities offered by West Berlin

and the facilities of the Federal Republic to undermine Soviet power in East Germany. Place the Soviets in East Germany on the defensive by such measures as may be taken to keep alive the hope of German reunification.

30. Emphasize (a) the right of the peoples of Eastern Europe to independent governments of their own choosing and (b) the violation of international agreements by the Soviet and satellite Governments, whereby they have been deprived of that right, particularly the Yalta Declaration on Liberated Europe and the Treaties of Peace with Bulgaria, Hungary and Rumania.

Questions

What do you think was the significance of the Stalin–Churchill 'October Agreements'?

Did the Big Three have specific agreements on the future of Poland? What were their major sources of disagreement?

Did Stalin have a convincing answer to the accusations in Churchill's Iron Curtain speech?

What was the purpose of the COMINFORM when it was founded in September 1947?

What were the sources of disagreement and tension between the Soviets, the Yugoslavs, and the Bulgarians?

What explains the different Norwegian and Finnish reactions to the February 1948 coup in Czechoslovakia?

Why did the COMINFORM expel Yugoslavia?

Is there a link between the Tito–Stalin split and the purges of such national Communist leaders as Laszlo Rajk in Hungary?

What was the long-term American strategy in Eastern Europe in 1953?

3

The Division of Germany

The future of Germany was undoubtedly the most contentious issue in post-war Europe. After the surrender of Germany in the spring of 1945, the clashes between the four occupying powers—Britain, France, the Soviet Union, and the United States—over such issues as as the redrawing of the German–Polish border, reparations, and political power became endemic. By 1949 the differences between the former allies had helped to create the basis of the four-decade-long division of Germany and the bizarre division of Berlin into eastern and western zones.

Most historians would agree that the creation of the German Democratic Republic (or East Germany) and the Federal Republic of Germany (or West Germany) in 1949 was both a symptom and a cause of the Cold War. On the one hand, the inability of the four occupying powers to reach a settlement that would allow a unified post-war Germany to exist reflected the growing suspicions that the Soviet Union and the Western allies held of each others aims and goals in the immediate aftermath of the war. On the other hand, the discussions over Germany in the Big Three meetings at Yalta and Potsdam, and later at several sessions of the Council of Foreign Ministers, hardened the confrontational approach that ultimately made a mutually agreeable settlement on Germany impossible.

Historians disagree, though, on the timing and process of the division. Some would argue that the division was, in fact, determined already in the summer of 1945, when the zonal division was established. Although the general agreement, at Potsdam, was to treat Germany as one single economic unit, the Potsdam Protocol gave each of the four military governors supreme authority in his respective zone. The Allied Control Commission, that was to co-ordinate the exercise of power in all of Germany, was hindered by the principle of unanimity which, as differences became more marked between the occupiers, was at best a noble dream.

But other historians dispute the argument that Germany's future division was somehow preordained by the decisions made in the summer of 1945. They would argue that even with the existence of separate zones, Germany could still have emerged as one single unit if an acceptable political formula had been found. One possibility, many would argue, was that if Germany had been neutralized and demilitarized it could have been unified in the first few post-war years. But the emergence of the Cold War, particularly in 1947–8, made any compromise over the future of such a strategically and economically important European country as Germany impossible. The Berlin Blockade, that lasted from June 1948 to May 1949, and the subsequent creation of the FRG and the GDR were thus culminations of a gradual process rather than an inevitable result of Germany's defeat in World War II. In fact, some historians would go as far as to argue that even after the formal creation of the two states, and certainly until 1952 when Stalin's proposal to create a unified-neutralized Germany was rebuffed by the Western powers, the division was not final.

In addition to questions about the timing and inevitability of the division, the other major debate has focused on the question of responsibility. Which power, or even individual, should bear the brunt of the blame for the division of Germany? While the easy answer—and one most would probably agree with—is 'Hitler', historians have generally focused on the nature and substance of decision-making on the Soviet and Western sides. Hence, for a long time, the debate was extremely politicized, with the Soviets (and Stalin) emerging most often as the major villains. In the last two decades, though, the divergent interests and needs of the three Western powers have received further attention as well. As a result, most historians today present a far more complex picture of the process that created two Germanies and a divided Berlin in the years following the defeat of Nazi Germany.

At the basis of the problem lay the destruction of any cohesive political power structure in Germany, that left its enormous economic potential open for penetration. As Germany had been the major threat to and the primary enemy of the four occupying powers during the war, so the question of its future was hence laden with questions of insecurity made more complex by the four powers' varied economic needs and political preferences. The Americans and the British, for example, moved rather quickly from emphasizing the punitive aspects of their post-war policies to preferring the reconstruction of a Germany that could become part of an integrated Europe. While the Americans came to this conclusion largely out of fear that a depressed Germany would be easy prey for Soviet-Communist penetration, the British found the costs of a separate occupation regime prohibitively expensive. Hence, the creation of Bizonia in late 1946 was followed by an eventual influx of Marshall Plan aid. In June 1948 the introduction of currency reform and the subsequent Berlin Blockade by the USSR only hardened the determination to link the western part of Germany with the 'free world'. Yet it was only in April 1949 that France agreed to abandon its quest for maximum reparations and join what first became 'Trizonia' and, soon afterwards, the Federal Republic of Germany.

In fact, of the four countries participating in the occupation, the Soviets seem to have acted in the most consistent manner throughout this period. Virtually from the outset, the eastern zone of Germany was being transformed along the Soviet model: local Communists, many of them Moscow-trained, took up key positions and, with the help of Soviet authorities, launched into radical land reform and nationalization. At the same time, however, Stalin appeared less interested in building a stable socialist German state than in shipping East German economic assets to the USSR as reparations. That the Western powers ultimately refused to entertain Soviet demands for reparations from the other zones only served to exacerbate such efforts. A number of scholars, indeed, argue that the Soviet policies in their zone were relatively flexible and only hardened as a response to Western initiatives.

The formal creation of the two German states in 1949 thus resulted from a web of divergent interests and priorities. Whether inevitable or ad hoc, whether initiated by one or more of the key players, the division was bound to remain as a symbol of the Cold War in Europe for the next four decades. Because of this, the sources of the division, however complex, remain central to our understanding of the origins of the Cold War in general.

Readings

Anne Deighton, *The Impossible Peace: Britain, the Division of Germany and the Origins of the Cold War* (1990). An insightful account of British policy towards Germany.

Carol Eisenberg, *Drawing the Line: The American Decision to Divide Germany, 1944–1949* (1996). A critical assessment of US policy and its role in the division of Germany.

Thomas A. Schwartz, *America's Germany: John J. McCloy and the Federal Republic of Germany* (1991). A more positive account of the United States's German policy.

Norman Naimark, *Russians in Germany: A History of the Soviet Zone of Occupation* (1995). The best available study of Soviet policy in Eastern Germany.

Marc Trachtenberg, *A Constructed Peace* (2001). Venturing far beyond the immediate post-war issue of Germany, this well-researched book places the division in a broader context.

3.1 Roosevelt on the Treatment of Germany, September 1944

As the war in Europe began to move towards its final stages, various plans for the future of Germany preoccupied the leaders of the Allies. In the United States Hans Morgenthau, secretary of the Treasury, recommended the 'pastoralization' of the German state so as to prevent it from emerging as a threat to its neighbours in the future. But President Roosevelt, concerned over the reconstruction of Europe and its general stability, was not

(pastoralization)

so clear on this. Here the president is writing to his secretary of state, Cordell Hull, on 29 September 1944.

I do not think that in the present stage any good purpose would be served by having the State Department or any other department sound out the British and Russian views on the treatment of German industry. Most certainly it should not be taken up with the European Advisory Commission which, in a case like this, is on a tertiary and not even a secondary level.

The real nub of the situation is to keep Britain from going into complete bankruptcy at the end of the war (...)

No one wants to make Germany a wholly agricultural nation again, and yet somebody down the line has handed this out to the press. I wish we could catch and chastise him. You know that before the war Germany was not only building up war manufacture, but was also building up enough of a foreign trade to finance re-arming sufficiently and still maintain enough international credit to keep out of international bankruptcy.

I just can not go along with the idea of seeing the British empire collapse financially, and Germany at the same time building up a potential re-armament machine to make another war possible in twenty years. Mere inspection of plants will not prevent that.

But no one wants 'complete eradication of Germany's industrial productive capacity in the Ruhr and Saar'.

It is possible, however, in those two particular areas to enforce rather complete controls. Also, it must not be forgotten that outside of the Ruhr and Saar, Germany has many other areas and facilities for turning out large exports.

on Soviets

In regard to the Soviet government, it is true that we have no idea as yet what they have in mind, but we have to remember that in their occupied territory they will do more or less what they wish. We cannot afford to get into a position of merely recording protests on our part unless there is some chance of some of the protests being heeded.

I do not intend by this to break off or delay negotiations with the Soviet government over lend-lease either on the contract basis or on the proposed Fourth Protocol basis. This, however, does not immediately concern the German industrial future.

3.2 Hitler on the Future of Germany and Europe, April 1945 *from H's "last testament"*

With the Allies approaching Berlin and German defeat appearing inevitable, Adolf Hitler spent his last days holed up in a heavily fortified bunker in the German capital.

Before committing suicide he wrote his 'last testament'. As the excerpts show, Hitler exhibited little remorse for his policies and provided a gloomy prognosis of the future.

If we are destined to be beaten in this war, our defeat will be utter and complete. Our enemies have proclaimed their objectives in a manner which leaves us no illusions as to their intentions (…) In a ghastly conflict like this, in a war in which two so completely irreconcilable ideologies confront one another, the issue can inevitably only be settled by the total destruction of one side or the other. It is a fight which must be waged, by both sides, until they are utterly exhausted; and for our part, we know that we shall fight on until victory is achieved or until our last drop of blood has been shed.

It is a cruel thought. It fills me with horror to think of our Reich hacked to pieces by the victors, our peoples exposed to the savage excesses of the Bolsheviks and the American gangsters (…) as far as I personally am concerned I could not bear to live in Germany during the transition period that would follow the defeat of the Third Reich. The ignominies and the treachery we experienced in 1918 will be as nothing in comparison with what we may now expect (…)

What advice can we give, then, what rules of conduct can we recommend to those who survive, with their souls untarnished and their hearts unshaken? Battered, left alone to work out its own salvation, existing solely as a custodian during the grim darkness of the night, the German people must strive its very utmost spontaneously to respect those racial laws which we laid down for it (…)

Post-war Germany's second preoccupation should be to preserve indissoluble the union of all the German races. It is only when we are united that our qualities expand to their full stature; only when we cease to be Prussians, Bavarians, Austrians, Rhinelanders and become just Germans. The Prussians were the first to gather the Germans into one Reich under Bismarck, and by so doing gave the German people their opportunity to show that they were the premier people in Europe. I myself, by uniting them all in the Third Reich, set them on the path to become the architects of a new Europe. Whatever the future holds, the German peoples must remember that it is essential that they should cast out all elements that make for discord among them and should indefatigably pursue every measure which contributes to the maintenance of their unity.

As far as foreign countries are concerned, it is not possible to lay down rigid rules, for the situation is in a constant state of change. Twenty years ago, I wrote that there were only two possible allies in Europe for Germany—Britain and Italy. The course of events during this period has not been such as to permit the implementation of a policy which would have been the logical sequence to my statement. The British, admittedly, still wielded imperial power, but they no longer possessed the moral qualities requisite for the preservation of their empire (…)

There remains France. Twenty years ago I wrote what I thought of France. She was and is the mortal enemy of the German people. Her steady degeneration and her frequent *crises de nerfs* have sometimes led us to minimize the importance of her actions. Should she continue to become more feeble, as seems probable, that will be no reason for us to become less distrustful of her. The military might of France is now nothing but a memory, and purely from that point of view you may be quite sure that she will never again cause us a moment's anxiety. Whatever may be the issue of it, this war has at least put France in the category to which she belongs—that of a fifth-class Power. Even so, thanks to her unlimited powers of corruption and her inimitable skill in the art of blackmail, she can still be a source of danger to us. Our watchwords therefore must be: mistrust and vigilance. Let the Germans take care never to allow themselves to be lulled by the voice of this syren!

While, therefore, it is not possible to adhere to rigid principles in dealing with foreign countries and one must always be prepared to adapt one's policy to the changing conditions, it can nevertheless be asserted with confidence that Germany will always recruit her staunchest friends from among those peoples who are actively resistant to Jewish contagion. I am sure that the Japanese, the Chinese for example, and the peoples of Islam will always be closer to us than, for example, France, in spite of the fact that we are related by blood (…)

With the defeat of the Reich and pending the emergence of the Asiatic, the African and, perhaps, the South American nationalisms, there will remain in the world only two Great Powers capable of confronting each other—the United States and Soviet Russia. The laws of both history and geography will compel these two Powers to a trial of strength, either military or in the fields of economics and ideology. These same laws make it inevitable that both Powers should become enemies of Europe. And it is equally certain that both these Powers will sooner or later find it desirable to seek the support of the sole surviving great nation in Europe, the German people. I say with all the emphasis at my command that the Germans must at all costs avoid playing the role of pawn in either camp.

At this juncture it is difficult to say which, from the ideological point of view, would prove to be the more injurious to us—Jew-ridden Americanism or Bolshevism. It is possible that under the pressure of events, the Russians will rid themselves completely of Jewish Marxism, only to re-incarnate pan-slavism in its most fierce and ferocious form. As for the Americans, if they do not swiftly succeed in casting off the yoke of New York Jewry (which has the same intelligence as a monkey that saws through the branch on which it is perching), well—it won't be long before they go under, before even having reached the age of maturity. The fact that they combine the possession of such vast material power with so vast a lack of intelligence evokes the image of some child stricken with elephantiasis. It may well be asked whether this is not simply a case of a mushroom civilization, destined to vanish as quickly as it sprang up (…)

And so, in this cruel world into which two great wars have plunged us again, it is obvious that the only white peoples who have any chance of survival and prosperity are those who know how to suffer and who still retain the courage to fight, even when things are hopeless, to the death (…)

3.3 Soviet and American Troops Meet at the Elbe, April 1945

In April 1945 American and Soviet troops met along the Elbe river in Germany, greeting each other with mutual enthusiasm. Below a former US rifleman reminisces about these historic meetings and the atmosphere surrounding them.

We were in a quiet area along the Mulde River, a tributary of the Elbe. A town called Trebsen, twenty miles west of the Elbe. This was April 24 [1945].

I was called into company headquarters. They were checking on documents of Germans, suspects and former Nazis and those who wanted to be officials. I was the only man in the company who had a good working knowledge of German.

A phone call comes in from battalion headquarters. They want a patrol to be formed immediately, seven jeeps, twenty-eight men, to go about five miles in front of the lines to see if they could get some signs of the Russians. They were supposed to be anywhere from twenty to thirty miles in front of us.

The best platoon leader in our company, by general consensus, was Lieutenant Kotzebue. He was quiet, young, and about twenty-two years old. I was twenty-six. He quickly assembled the jeeps and the men. He took a map of the area. I was in the lead jeep with him, because I spoke German. We were warned before we left that platoons from other companies had been badly shot up by the Germans in this region.

It was seventy miles from Berlin, directly south. The Battle of Berlin was being waged north of us. Every available German soldier was called up to the defense of Berlin. There were many deserters, however, that we ran into. A continual stream. Some of 'em actually dressed up in women's clothing. The great mass was the German civilian refugees, fleeing the Russians. They were continually blocking the road. Mostly women, children, and old men.

To show you how slowly we proceeded, we had just managed to get about seven miles and we'd started about noon. We holed up in a little town called Kübren. Kotzebue pored over the maps all evening. We interrogated anybody who had any idea where the Russians might be.

Actually, we weren't supposed to meet the Russians. If we met them, we were gonna take the consequences in case anything was fouled up. At Eisenhower's headquarters, they were making detailed plans to meet the Russians. We were just on patrol. We were told that after five miles, we were going at our own risk. If anything went awry, instead of being heroes, we might wind up being court-martialed.

They were afraid if the two armies met at full speed, there would be casualties. Two armies, even friendly armies, going hellbent toward each other, there would be some guys who would be hurt. So Eisenhower and Zhukov decided that the two armies would stop about twenty-five miles short of each other. That's why we stopped at the Mulde and they at the Elbe.

When we holed up for the night, we'd gone only a third of the way. As dawn broke, Kotzeue made a decision: we're going ahead. There was a tremendous cheer. We all hopped in the jeeps and proceeded. We didn't know what faced us. At noon, we also saw long streams of liberated civilians from concentration camps, slave laborers, Allied soldiers who were freed.

Would you believe it? There was a tremendous burst of lilacs as we approached the Elbe River. This exaltation of being alive, after all those days trapped in a trench war. There was even jokes that we were approaching the River Jordan, crossing into Canaan. Of course, we were saddened to learn that President Roosevelt had died about two weeks earlier. We also knew that the United Nations was being born in San Francisco on the very same day, twenty-fifth of April. Can you imagine? The very day we linked up with the Russians at the Elbe River.

It was a tremendous feeling to see the Elbe. This was about eleven-thirty in the morning. The Elbe is a swift-running river, about 175 yards wide. Kotzebue shot up two green flares. After about ten minutes, with shouts and the wind blowing towards the east, our voices were able to carry across the river. The Russians waved at us and gave the signal to approach their lines. The problem was getting across the river. The Germans in retreat, the Allied forces dropping bombs along the bridges, the Russian artillery blowing up bridges: between the three, there was no bridge to cross. We were at Strehla, about sixteen miles south of Torgau.

At the far side of the Elbe, the Russian side, there was the remains of a steel bridge which jutted out maybe fifty yards into the river. On our side, there was a heavy chain attached to a barge and two sailboats. With a hand grenade, Kotzebue exploded the chain. About six of us piled into the sailboat. There were makeshift paddles. With tremendous effort, we managed to guide that boat into the girders protruding from the opposite side. As we climbed up, there were three Russian soldiers approaching the bank. Why were there only three? On the road ahead, we saw many Russian soldiers.

What happened was this. That bridge had been blown up at least three days. A tremendous wave of civilians, mostly Germans, a great mass, had approached the bridge, fleeing the Russians to go west. So they were piled like lumber at the bridge, along the whole bank. Fifty yards on each side was literally covered with bodies of women, old men, children. I still remember seeing a little girl clutching a doll in one hand—it was right there. She couldn't have been more than five or six years old. And her mother's hand in the other. They were all piled up like cordwood at the bank.

How had it happened? Who knows? Part of it was German fire, maybe Allied planes bombing the bridgehead. Probably the Russian artillery from a distance of several miles. It was a depressed area, impossible to see. It was an accident. There were so many in the war.

Actually, it was difficult for the Russians to pierce their way into meeting us. Because of the bodies. Here we are, tremendously exhilarated, and there's a sea of dead. Kotzebue, who is a very religious man, was much moved. He couldn't talk Russian. The Russians couldn't talk English. He said, 'Joe, Let's make a resolution with these Russians here and also the ones on the bank: this would be an important day in the lives of the two countries and the symbolism of all the civilian dead. Talk to them in German.' As I was translating to Kotzebue in English, one of the Russians who knew German was translating to the other Russians. It was very informal, but it was a solemn moment. There were tears I the eyes of most of us. Perhaps a sense of foreboding that things might not be as perfect in the future as we anticipated. We embraced. We swore never to forget.

When we got to the top of the embankment, there was Lieutenant Colonel Gardead. He greeted us, and again we took an oath. Kotzebue's main mission was to immediately contact the Americans. Our radios were in the jeeps on the other side of the Elbe. So Gardead said to and come back. We'd been drinking and embracing and toasting. The Russians had brought some vodka and some German wine and beer. We were real drunk, but not because of the liqor. Gardead said, 'It's important you tell the others. After you've done that, pile into your jeeps, cross onto a ferry, and we'll continue our celebration here.' He sent a couple of Russians to accompany us.

As soon as we got across, Kotzebue gets in touch with headquarters. He gave them readings where we were at Strehla. But there was radio interference. As often happens, radio communications in combat rarely work perfectly. An hour passed. We're getting impatient. He wants to make firm contact with the American forces. To either bring the Russians back to the American lines or Americans to come up.

After we made the communications, we piled into the jeeps with the two Russian guys. We went about three, four miles north into this hand ferry and we all crossed again into the Russian lines. As we crossed the bank, Kotzebue tossed me the map. He said, 'You've done a good job, here's a little present for you.' I kept it as a souvenir. I was actually offered a very considerable sum of money for it. Of course, I wouldn't dream of givin' it up. It's not for sale.

As we learned later, there were mixed feelings on the part of the American headquarters. We weren't supposed to meet the Russians. They were, of course, secretly glad that we met them without casualties. They really dispatched a helicopter to Strehla, but there were no seven jeeps. Something had been fouled up. Meanwhile, there are tremendous celebrations in the Russian lines.

We drank and there were accordions and balalaikas and music and dancing. They played American songs. Some of the other guys could play the guitar. And there were some from slave-labor camps. Russian girls dancing. It was a strange sight. I was so captivated by the event, that it took possession of me for the rest of my life. It has colored my life, in spite of difficulties I've run into—general indifference. It has become a nonevent.

I always felt that American–Russian relations were plagued by bad luck right from the beginning. If we had gotten publicity with the Oath of the Elbe, there would have been a certain depth in the feelings. Just think of the millions who died on the Russian side and the tremendous effort of the American side, amidst all those dead women and children and that little girl clutching the doll in her hand. Nothing (…)

3.4 Soviet Soldiers in Occupied Berlin, 1945

Soviet policy towards occupied Germany was influenced by feelings of revenge, often sanctioned by the Soviet leadership. One specific 'policy' was the systematic raping of German women in the Soviet-occupied zone. Here the historian Norman Naimark discusses the problem of rape in Berlin immediately after the Red Army conquered Berlin.

(…) 'Of course (…) a lot of nasty things have happened,' commented Lieutenant General (later Marshal) V. D. Sokolovskii to Alexander Werth in a June 5 interview. 'But what do you expect? (…) In the first flush of victory our fellows no doubt derived a certain satisfaction from making it hot for those Herrenvolk women. However, that stage is over (…) Our main worry,' he grinned, 'is the awful spread of clap among our troops.'

But Sokolovskii was wrong to give the impression that the raping would cease after the establishment of the military government. At least until the end of June and the beginning of July, when many military and civilian administrations were removed from the hands of battle-worn officers, hundreds of local commandants, each with his own policies and preferences, set the tone for the treatment of the German population. The commandants treated the regions as personal fiefdoms complained one Soviet report, and they simply didn't bother reporting the 'excesses' of their troops. Sometimes rape and pillage were severely punished, by death or a severe whipping. But too often local commandants sympathized with their soldiers' anger and frustration and ignored their nightly rampages, which were now almost always exacerbated by the influence of alcohol. Adding to the problem in the first few weeks of the occupation were the terrifying attacks by released Russian POWs and forced labourers, who also engaged in rape and pillage (…)

The taking of Berlin was accompanied by an unrestrained explosion of sexual violence by Soviet soldiers. Ambassador Robert Murphy concluded in a memorandum of July 19, 1945, that 'according to trustworthy estimates (…) the majority of the eligible female population' was reported to have been violated. Murphy's estimate is probably exaggerated; some intelligence reports indicated, for example, that although rape was quite common in those days, 'it was not as widespread as some sources would have made it.' In any case, there are so many reports that indicate a systematic carrying out of violence against Berlin's women that it is hard to dismiss the seriousness of the problem. Even as they entered bunkers and cellars where Germans hid from the fierce fighting, Soviet soldiers brandished weapons and raped women in the presence of children and men. In some cases, soldiers divided up women according to their tastes. In others, women were gang-raped. Generally, the soldiers raped indiscriminately, not excluding old women in their seventies or young girls. The first antifascist mayor of Charlottenburg wrote: 'In the beginning, the Russians looted on a grand scale; they stole from individuals, warehouses, stores, homes. Innumerable cases of rape occurred daily. A woman could not escape being raped unless she kept in hiding (…) It is difficult to grasp the full extent to which rape is practised.'

Rape in the bunkers was followed by restless pillaging and rape in apartments and homes throughout Berlin. Countless reports were filed by Germans complaining to their local government. Typical was the following police report sent to Rathaus Spandau and passed on to the Soviet commandant of Spandau. (The names are blacked out in the archive files.)

'On the night of May 6, 1945, at 2:30 in the morning, three Russian soldiers broke through the window in the hallway. A tenant was hauled out to open the door. At this point, all of the apartments of the house were to be searched by soldiers, supposedly on the orders of the kommandantura, and the three soldiers searched the house. They got as far as the second floor when they returned to where two young women were sleeping with a baby. The two soldiers then sat down on the bed with Frau [A] and Frau [B], both twenty-four years old, with a child of six months on the bed, smoking cigarettes and demanding then that they should sleep with them. At the moment the two women wanted to scream [the soldiers] threatened them with a pistol. Frau [A] called her mother, and the third soldier stood guard when she came and forced her into another room where he held her back with a machine gun. There he went through all the suitcases, from which he took just a pen holder. In the meanwhile, the other two soldiers raped the two young women. Shortly after a quarter to four in the morning, they left the apartment. In addition they took an accordian from the apartment of family [C].' (Signed by the petitioner and four witnesses).

Sometimes, the cases were more violent, as in a June 28, 1945, petition from Berlin-Reinickendorf.

'In the night of the 4th to 5th of May of this year, the married couple [A] and Frau [B] were attacked by two drunken Russians in our apartment. During this [attack], I—a 62-year-old wife—was violated by both [soldiers] and my husband, 66 years old, was shot [to death] without reason. Then in a half an hour a third Russian also came, after the others were gone, and I was abused again, and this act in the apartment of a renter who had in the meantime taken me in (...) As a note: my husband belonged to no Nazi organizations and I ask the Herr Commandant for a hearing.' (Signed by petitioner and four witnesses).

The garden-house settlements on the outskirts of Berlin were frequently the targets of nightly raids, plundering, and rape. At one of them, Mächeritzwiesen in Tegel-South, local Communist Party activists tried to get weapons to protect themselves against the marauders. In their appeals to the KPD central, they noted: 'The occupation by the Red Army has unfolded into a real plague on the land. No day or night goes by that the bandits in Red Army uniform, even in attack formation, engage in plunder and rape against the garden colony settlers.'

Monsignor G. B. Montini, the Vatican representative in Berlin, also reported the ubiquitous nature of rape, though one suspects—as in the case of Robert Murphy—that he may be exaggerating the extent of the terror. Still, his report of October 1945 is chilling:

'Women from 10 to 70 and 75 years of age have been ravished; consequently, there have been pregnancies, abortions, and 80% of the women have become infected by venereal disease (...) The worst crimes have been committed in the district of the Kurfürstendamm in the presence of their parties (husbands, fathers, mothers, brothers). Nuns were raped in the Franziskus Sanatorium, even though they were wearing their religious habits (...) Professor Schüler of the Rutberg-Krankenhaus in Lichterfelde killed his wife and daughters and then himself not to have to bear the anguish [of their rape]. Many women lived on rooftops for weeks to escape Russian violence.'

The Swiss journalist Max Schnetzer notes in his diaries that one could not condemn all the Russian soldiers for rape; still, in his collection of eyewitness accounts of the first days of the Russian occupation of Berlin, he made clear the extent of the violence. How did the Russians behave, Schnetzer asked a journalist colleague, who described the fighting in Wannsee: 'In part like pigs, in part like angels (…) In single apartments it often came to wild scenes with women and girls. One woman died from being misused by the soldiers. In other houses, the Russians acted more like friends (…) They are like a hailstorm that only destroys part of the harvest.'

(…) Ellen Gräfin Poninski kept a diary of the first weeks and months of the Russian occupation, from the vantage point of her family home in Potsdam. Like Schnetzer, she emphasized the extremes in the behavior of Russian soldiers toward the defeated Germans, from the most brutal and inhuman to the unbelievably generous and kind. Still, she wrote:

'Almost no evening went by, no night, in which we did not hear the pitiful cries for help from women who were attacked on the streets or in the always open houses. All of these abominations are well known. Perhaps in the more lucky zones [of occupation] one thought that the descriptions were exaggerated. But unfortunately the reality was actually even much worse, and I don't have to repeat here the tortures that women and girls, from 10 to 80 years of age, were forced to endure.'

(…) The Soviets certainly knew that the Germans were afraid of them in Berlin. Major General I. V. Shikin, commander of GlavPURKKA, noted that when German women met up with Soviet soldiers, they would 'raise their hands, cry and shake all over from fear.' According to Shikin, though, once the women realized that nothing would happen to them and that the Nazis had lied about the true nature of the Soviet soldiers, everything was fine. In a post-perestroika interview, Shikin's deputy, Major General M. I. Burtsev, former head of the Seventh Section of Glav-PURKKA, claimed that stories of rape had been much overdone. Besides, he chuckled, most of the cases of rape were like the woman who had complained to him about having been raped on the floor instead of in the bedroom.

3.5 Potsdam Protocol on Germany, August 1945

At the Potsdam Conference on the outskirts of Berlin the leaders of the Grand Alliance agreed to a number of general principles on the future of Germany. Below is an excerpt from the Potsdam Protocol that was signed by Stalin, US president Harry S. Truman (who had replaced Roosevelt after his death in April 1945), and Clement Attlee (who took over as British prime minister after Churchill's Conservative Party suffered a surprise defeat at the start of the Potsdam proceedings).

1. In accordance with the Agreement on Control Machinery in Germany, supreme authority in Germany is exercised, on instructions from their respective

Governments, by the Commanders-in-Chief of the armed forces of the United
States of America, the United Kingdom, the Union of Soviet Socialist Republics
and the French Republic, each in his own zone of occupation, and also jointly, in
matters affecting Germany as a whole, in their capacity as members of the Control Council.

2. So far as is practicable, there shall be uniformity of treatment of the German
population throughout Germany.

3. The purposes of the occupation of Germany by which the Control Council
shall be guided are:

(i) The complete disarmament and demilitarisation of Germany and the
elimination or control of all German industry that could be used for
military production (...)

(ii) To convince the German people that they have suffered a total military
defeat and that they cannot escape responsibility for what they have
brought upon themselves, since their own ruthless warfare and the fanatical Nazi resistance have destroyed the German economy and made chaos
and suffering inevitable.

(iii) To destroy the National Socialist Party and its affiliated and supervised
organisations, to dissolve all Nazi institutions, to ensure that they are
not revived in any form, and to prevent all Nazi and militarist activity or
propaganda.

(iv) To prepare for the eventual reconstruction of German political life on a
democratic basis and for eventual peaceful co-operation in international
life by Germany.

4. All Nazi laws which provided the basis of the Hitler régime or established
discrimination on grounds of race, creed, or political opinion shall be abolished.
No such discriminations, whether legal, administrative or otherwise, shall be
tolerated.

5. War criminals and those who have participated in planning or carrying out
Nazi enterprises involving or resulting in atrocities or war crimes shall be arrested and brought to judgment. Nazi leaders, influential Nazi supporters and high
officials of Nazi organisations and institutions and any other persons dangerous
to the occupation or its objectives shall be arrested and interned.

6. All members of the Nazi party who have been more than nominal participants in its activities and all other persons hostile to Allied purposes shall be
removed from public and semi-public office, and from positions of responsibility in important private undertakings. Such persons shall be replaced by persons
who, by their political and moral qualities are deemed capable of assisting in
developing genuine democratic institutions in Germany.

7. German education shall be so controlled as completely to eliminate Nazi

and militarist doctrines and to make possible the successful development of democratic ideas.

8. The judicial system will be reorganised in accordance with the principles of democracy, of justice under law, and of equal rights for all citizens without distinction of race, nationality or religion.

9. The administration in Germany should be directed towards the decentralisation of the political structure and the development of local responsibility (...)

10. Subject to the necessity for maintaining military security, freedom of speech, press and religion shall be permitted and religious institutions shall be respected. Subject likewise to the maintenance of military security, the formation of free trade unions shall be permitted (...)

11. In order to eliminate Germany's war potential, the production of arms, ammunition and implements of war as well as all types of aircraft and sea-going ships shall be prohibited and prevented. Production of metals, chemicals, machinery and other items that are directly necessary to a war economy, shall be rigidly controlled and restricted to Germany's approved post-war peacetime needs (...) Productive capacity not needed for permitted production shall be removed in accordance with the reparations plan recommended by the Allied Commission on reparations and approved by the Governments concerned or, if not removed, shall be destroyed.

12. At the earliest practicable date, the German economy shall be decentralised for the purpose of eliminating the present excessive concentration of economic power as exemplified in particular by cartels, syndicates, trusts and other monopolistic arrangements.

13. In organising the German economy, primary emphasis shall be given to the development of agriculture and peaceful domestic industries.

14. During the period of occupation Germany shall be treated as a single economic unit. To this end common policies shall be established in regard to:-

(a) mining and industrial production and its allocation;
(b) agriculture, forestry and fishing;
(c) wages, prices and rationing;
(d) import and export programmes for Germany as a whole;
(e) currency and banking, central taxation and customs;
(f) reparation and removal of industrial war potential;
(g) transportation and communications.

In applying these policies account shall be taken, where appropriate, of varying local conditions (...)

19. Payment of reparations should leave enough resources to enable the German people to subsist without external assistance. In working out the economic balance of Germany the necessary means must be provided to pay for

imports approved by the Control Council in Germany. The proceeds of exports from current production and stocks shall be available in the first place for payment for such imports (…)

1. Reparation claims of the U.S.S.R. shall be met by removals from the zone of Germany occupied by the U.S.S.R., and from appropriate German external assets.

2. The U.S.S.R. undertakes to settle the reparation claims of Poland from its own share of reparations.

3. The reparations claims of the United States, the United Kingdom and other countries entitled to reparations shall be met from the Western Zones and from appropriate German external assets.

4. In addition to the reparations to be taken by the U.S.S.R. from its own zone of occupation, the U.S.S.R. shall receive additionally from the Western Zones:

(a) 15 per cent of such usable and complete industrial capital equipment, in the first place from the metallurgical, chemical and machine manufacturing industries, as is unnecessary for the German peace economy and should be removed from the Western Zones of Germany, in exchange for an equivalent value of food, coal, potash, zinc, timber, clay products, petroleum products, and such other commodities as may be agreed upon.

(b) 10 per cent of such industrial capital equipment as is unnecessary for the German peace economy and should be removed from the Western Zones, to be transferred to the Soviet Government on reparations account without payment or exchange of any kind in return (…)

5. The amount of equipment to be removed from the Western Zones on account of reparations must be determined within six months from now at the latest.

6. Removals of industrial capital equipment shall begin as soon as possible and shall be completed within two years from the determination specified in paragraph 5. The delivery of products covered by 4(a) above shall begin as soon as possible and shall be made by the U.S.S.R. in agreed instalments within five years of the date hereof. The determination of the amount and character of the industrial capital equipment unnecessary for the German peace economy and therefore available for reparations shall be made by the Control Council under policies fixed by the Allied Commission on Reparations, with the participation of France, subject to the final approval of the Zone Commander in the Zone from which the equipment is to be removed.

7. Prior to the fixing of the total amount of equipment subject to removal, advance deliveries shall be made in respect of such equipment as will be determined to be eligible for delivery in accordance with the procedure set forth in the last sentence of paragraph 6.

8. The Soviet Government renounces all claims in respect of reparations to shares of German enterprises which are located in the Western Zones of occupation in Germany as well as to German foreign assets in all countries except those specified in paragraph 9 below.

9. The Governments of the United Kingdom and United States renounce all claims in respect of reparations to shares of German enterprises which are located in the Eastern Zone of occupation in Germany, as well as to German foreign assets in Bulgaria, Finland, Hungary, Roumania and Eastern Austria.

(...) Since the influx of a large number of Germans into Germany would increase the burden already resting on the occupying authorities, they consider that the Control Council in Germany should, in the first instance, examine the problem, with special regard to the question of the equitable distribution of these Germans among the several zones of occupation. They are accordingly instructing their respective representatives on the Control Council to report to their Governments as soon as possible the extent to which such persons have already entered Germany from Poland, Czechoslovakia and Hungary, and to submit an estimate of the time and rate at which further transfers could be carried out having regard to the present situation in Germany.

3.6 Marshall Zhukov on American Proposals for Germany, May 1946

In the following comments, sent to Stalin in May 1946, Marshall Zhukov, on 24 May 1946, comments on (and proposes the rejection of) the American secretary of state James F. Byrnes's proposals for the disarming and demilitarization of Germany and Japan.

Reporting my comments on the draft treaty of U.S. Secretary of State Byrnes on the disarmament and demilitarization of Germany, it is my opinion that the true purpose of the draft treaty is:

— the desire to end the occupation of Germany and to remove the armed forces of the Soviet Union from Germany as soon as possible. This is necessary to the Americans and British in order to raise the question of the withdrawal of our forces from Poland, and in the future also from the Balkan states;

— the desire to disrupt the export of equipment and manufactured goods as reparations from Germany to the Soviet Union;

— the desire to preserve military potential in Germany as the necessary base for fulfilling their aggressive objectives in the future;

— the desire to inhibit the growth of political activity of the masses and the growth of Communist party influence in Europe;

Everything that BYRNES proposes in the draft treaty for the disarmament and demilitarization of Germany is already contained in the German surrender and was announced in the proclamation of Germany's defeat. In the introductory section of the draft treaty, BYRNES states that the disarmament and demilitarization of Germany have already been accomplished for the most part and that all that remains to be done is ensure that Germany stays completely disarmed and demilitarized.

This assertion does not correspond to reality and is false. The actual state of affairs with respect to Germany's disarmament is quite different, especially in the British and American occupation zones. Consequently, instead of drafting and adopting a new treaty, what we should do now is ensure that the existing treaties are scrupulously enforced.

Byrnes's proposal to institute quadrilateral inspection and organize a control commission is unworthy of consideration, because even a Control Council based on the occupying powers has not managed to achieve any tangible results, except in the Soviet occupation zone, and a commission would be even less capable of completing the task of German disarmament.

A control commission to foil any attempts to revive German militarism and Germany's ability to wage war could be accepted only when the occupation authorities complete the task of disarmament and demilitarization.

I suggest: 1. Abstain from accepting the treaty. 2. Accept a coordinated document obliging the Control Council in Germany to issue a declaration on the defeat of Germany and the decision of the Potsdam Conference and to recognize that raising the issue of ending the occupation is premature (...)

advice to Stalin

3.7 S. Tiul'panov on the East German Communists, September 1946

In September 1946 local elections were held throughout the Soviet zone in Germany. This is an excerpt from Soviet adviser Colonel Sergei Tiul'panov's report reflecting on the situation in Soviet-occupied Germany five months after the unification of the Communist and Social Democratic (SPD) parties into the Communist-controlled socialist Unity Party (SED) and right after local elections were held in the Soviet zone.

(...) I believe that in no way should even the SED's victory in the district elections be overestimated. There are a number of obvious major shortcomings that threaten the worker, Marxist, and pro-Soviet nature of the SED, which it strove to attain at the outset and remain important in its work (...) There is a marked political passivity among the former members of the SPD, which will long be felt among members of the SED. The Social Democrats still feel frustrated by the attitudes of our apparat; the commandants have treated them with cautious distance; and they felt that they were not trusted completely and that they were treated inequitably. We have got past this by now to a certain extent, but not completely. Secondly, even the most farsighted Communists feel the need to discuss every issue with the Social Democrats in order not to offend them, [and this] has led to a lessening of flexibility within the party (...) Full attention has been given to the technical questions of the organization, but not to its political character. Organizational questions of the party were considered, while issues having to do with the apparat and with the masses, especially in Berlin, were obviously neglected (...)

Despite the merger of the parties, there is still a sense that two distinct groups exist. The results of the elections, which were discussed in the Saxon party organization, offer [only] the most recent example. The results of these elections prompted extremely heated debates. First of all, they [the Saxon party members] were disconcerted by the results because they had counted on a much higher percentage of the vote, reflecting the extent to which they overestimated their influence among the masses. They were overly complacent because they could count on our administrative support. They were reassured by the fact that they had more paper, posters and other resources, and, if necessary, there was always the possibility to put some pressure [on the population]. This led in Saxony to a major overestimation of their influence on the masses. It was immediately obvious at the Saxon party meeting (...) that there was a group of Social Democrats talking on the one hand and a group of earlier Communists on the other. One still notices this everywhere (...)

Organizationally the party is also still not fully formed, which can be seen in the fact that even the exchange of party membership cards has not yet been implemented, or, if it has been implemented it has been done in such a way that the individual's files are processed but they keep their old membership cards. Both Social Democrats and Communists keep their cards. And when you talk to them, they pull out their old membership cards and say: 'I am a former Communist and member of the SED.' This shows that the party is not fully accepted as a real Marxist party (...)

We have another dangerous problem here.—And I don't even know whether it is the more dangerous (...) and that is the presence of sectarianism among some former Communists. This sectarianism is expressed in conversations, which are held in private apartments and sometimes during the course of [party] meetings. [They say] that we [Communists] have forfeited our revolutionary positions, that we alone would have succeeded much better had there been no SED, and that the Social Democrats are not to be trusted. Here is an example for you: once one of my instructors came and said: 'I am a Communist, so it's not even worth talking to him [a Social Democrat], you can tell him by sight.' These are the words of the Secretary of the most powerful organization [in Berlin] and this kind of attitude is cultivated by [Hermann] Matern. This is not to mention [Waldemar] Schmidt, who has gone so far as to invent the existence of a spy apparatus among Communists [allegedly] to inform on Social Democrats [in the SED]. This is over now, but serious problems remain.

At the moment, it is hard to evaluate the strength of sectarianism among the [former] Communists, but one could estimate that in the Berlin organization approximately 10 percent [of the members] are so discontented that they are ready to join another group in order to break off with the SED. The problem is less serious in other regions. From the point of view of the Communists [in the SED] the party is considered to be more solid [than among former Social Democrats]. But there is the danger that these Social Democrats hold key positions, and their group has much more power (…) Therefore, there are two wings [in the party.] There is another major shortcoming of the Central Committee of the SED and its district committees. They do not seek out and develop new cadres who can work consistently with the party aktiv. In addition, the party is just beginning the theoretical elucidation of all of our earlier disagreements [with the Social Democrats] (…)

There still remains in the party a whole list of major [unanswered] questions (…) Deviations from Marxist positions pose a substantial danger for the party. There is a significant percentage of petit-bourgeois members [in the SED]; 40 percent to 51 percent workers. Still, neither the Communists nor the Social Democrats understand the new forms shaping the struggle for power, the movement towards socialism. They do not understand that the SED is not a tactical maneuver, but the situation by which they can achieve (…) that which was accomplished in our country by different means. They do not speak about the dictatorship of the proletariat, but about democracy (…) they have no understanding of the nature of the struggle after World War II. Then there is another issue; the party can very easily retreat into nationalist positions (…) Recently this issue was raised at the large party meeting in Chemnitz. They argued that they did not have to orient themselves either on the Soviet Union or on Great Britain. They should be oriented on Germany. They said that Russian workers live badly and that they, the Germans, should think only about the German working class.

(…) we run the danger of allowing the party to revert to extreme nationalism. Despite this, the SED's propaganda was unable to convince the population that the party is a real German party, and not simply the agents of the occupation authorities. There are still countless such shortcomings and failures of [the SED's] propaganda (…)

3.8 Lucius D. Clay on the Fusion of British and American Zones, November 1946

At Secretary of State James F. Byrnes's request Lucius D. Clay, the head of the American occupation forces, returned to the United States for discussions concerning the merger of the US and British zones in Germany. In this report he sums up his perspective on the problems in Germany at the time.

1. From a quadripartite viewpoint, the German problems which cannot be resolved in Berlin without inter-governmental decisions are: (a) the disarmament treaty, (b) the final fixing of boundaries, and (c) the peace treaty, which are beyond the competence of military government; and (d) the conditions which must be fulfilled for the economic unification of Germany which are largely internal and within the competence of military government.

2. Manifestly, the disarmament and peace treaties are inter-governmental problems on which it would be presumptuous for military government to comment or to offer suggestions except as specific information is requested.

3. However, the fixing of the Western boundaries is most important to the internal administration of Germany. The views of military government have been expressed in detail in a paper previously submitted to the War and State Departments.

Summarized they are:

a. The Ruhr is essential to the German economy and to the political stability of Germany. Some form of international control of its industry appears feasible and both the American and the British [elements] have submitted specific proposals for this purpose. Regardless of the control, the Ruhr must remain within the political and economic framework of a unified Germany if we do not wish to plunge Germany into economic chaos and continuing political unrest.

b. The Saar may be transferred to France without drastic effect on German economy but it must be recognized that it will create some continuing political unrest. Nevertheless, the transfer will not create undue economic dislocation in Germany. If this transfer is agreed, the territorial lines should be sharply defined to limit the area of transfer to the Saar proper.

c. Further transfers should be avoided as inconsistent with our policy as expressed at Stuttgart by the Secretary of State except for minor boundary rectifications. For instance, a recent request by the Dutch for such a boundary change would take in thirteen coal mines. Coal is Germany's principal raw material. The transfer of thirteen coal mines would increase the annual financial liability of the United States and the United Kingdom as a minimum by the value of the coal produced in these mines. Transfers of this type would hence be financed by ourselves and the United Kingdom, and this cost should be recognized if such transfers are approved.

4. The stalemate in Berlin in obtaining political and economic unity results from:

a. French opposition to any unification proposals until boundary claims have been settled.

b. Soviet opposition to a common utilization of German resources and to a common acceptance of responsibility for deficits. The French position is well known and requires little further comment. It would appear that only full agreement by the three other powers and a firm presentation of their agreed views would succeed in obtaining French cooperation. Even this would probably fail unless it is accompanied by Soviet acquiescence in the ceding of the Saar area to France.

The Soviet opposition appears now to rest primarily on its need and desire for current production as reparations. The Soviet representatives do not accept our interpretation that this was ruled out in the Potsdam Protocol. It must be admitted that the Potsdam Protocol is not specific on this point, although its intent seems clear.

5. Our studies indicate that reparations from current production is not possible within the agreed level of industry and that any real consideration of this kind of reparations must be based on an increase in the presently agreed level of industry. An increase in the level of industry, if not essential to the approved German standard of living, is of vital importance to the revival of European economy. If this increase is not essential to the approved German standard of living, the products therefrom could be utilized for reparations without adding to external costs for the support of German economy. Obviously, this is an over-statement, as the effort to obtain production for reparations would conflict in practice with the effort to obtain production for internal consumption and export. However, the psychological uplift to German morale would compensate to some extent. At least in theory, increasing the level of industry and utilizing the output for reparations would not increase our annual costs, provided raw materials not surplus within Germany were brought in by the recipient countries. It would tend to increase the period required to obtain economic balance.

6. Our economic studies indicate that an increase of 15% in the agreed level of

industry would gross seven and a half billion dollars over a ten-year period but would require the furnishing of two and one half billion dollars in raw materials, thereby netting five billion dollars for reparations for the Soviet Union and the Western allies. Of course, the yearly rate would be very low in the first year, rising steadily throughout the period. Moreover, this increase would still leave somewhat more than 50% of the plants previously considered as available for reparations, still available for that purpose. The plants to be utilized for manufacture of reparations items would be left in Germany permanently as an incentive for meeting the program.

The arguments in favor are:

a. An increase in the presently agreed level of industry is needed to hasten the revival of European economy.

b. An increase in the presently agreed level of industry is politically desirable in Germany. The Soviet representatives are now advocating such an increase and charging the opposition of the Western zones to a capitalistic desire to destroy possible future competition.

c. Failure to agree to an increase in the level of industry for this purpose would result either in several years of delay in effecting unification while the Soviet representatives continued to mine the industry of Eastern Germany or might even result in the partition of Germany with all that is implied thereby.

d. The increase in the level of industry and its utilization for reparations will not result in huge additional expenditures and might permit Germany to develop a production program which would help in part to repay past costs.

e. The acceptance of this principle would require as a condition the full political unification of Germany, thus extending Western liberalism to the borders of countries now under Communist influence.

The disadvantages are:

a. Production (which, under existing agreements, is not available for any purpose) would be authorized as reparations rather than as exports which would reduce occupation costs.

b. An increase in the level of industry as now agreed would have to be controlled to prevent Germany from re-developing a war potential, and such controls might be difficult to maintain effectively in the years ahead.

c. Soviet acceptance would not necessarily lead to real Soviet cooperation in political unification under democratic processes, as we define such processes.

d. The American and British tax payers would find it difficult to understand why any production should be utilized for reparations while American and British financial support is being extended to the German economy.

7. It is impossible to evaluate specifically the advantages and disadvantages until there is an agreed plan for the German economy in which the cost of reparations from current production is determined in dollars and cents in comparison with internal needs and an agreed import-export plan. The question is, therefore, whether or not such a proposal deserves full consideration and investigation by quadripartite military government. If, in fact, German unification is impossible unless this question is resolved, a *failure* to investigate it fully means the partition of Germany, with ultimate political and economic competition between Western Germany under allied controls and Eastern Germany under Soviet controls. Obviously, this establishes the frontier of Western democracy along the Elbe.

Certainly, no consideration should be given to a plan for economic unification in which production for reparations is authorized without complete understanding that political unification would be undertaken simultaneously, and that production for reparations would cease if political unification proved impossible along democratic lines.

If this condition is fulfilled, the gain for Western democracy is the right to contest for its philosophy throughout Germany and to extend its frontier to the borders of Poland and Czechoslovakia, thus encouraging any will for democracy in the peoples of these countries (...)

9. American objectives in Germany should not preclude serious consideration being given to the utilization of some current production for reparations in the interest of the European economy and in obtaining economic and political stability for Germany as a whole. Obviously, it is essential to define the controlling conditions which must be accepted by all of the occupying powers if we are to permit this deviation from the existing three-power agreement. If the conditions can be agreed it will still be necessary to determine the additional costs which would be incurred by the several occupying powers and whether or not these additional costs are warranted (...)

10. This question of reparations appears to be a basic problem which needs to be resolved before final decisions can be reached with respect to the disarmament treaty and a treaty of peace with Germany. However, its study in detail would not interfere with the work of designated deputies on these large questions and it need not interfere with the consideration of boundary questions by such deputies.

We have much at stake in gaining the opportunity to fight for democratic ideals in Eastern Germany and in Eastern Europe. This opportunity would result from the true unification of Germany under quadripartite control.

Therefore, it does appear worthwhile to investigate fully this possible solution to the internal German problem. How much we are willing to pay to achieve our objectives is unknown, but it is possible that the investigation may indicate that

2. Marshall and Molotov 'Sawing through a woman'. (David Low, *Evening Standard*, 13 April 1948). Reprinted by permission. Photo supplied by The Centre for the Study of Cartoons and Caricature, University of Kent.

the cost in dollars and cents is not too high, particularly when measured in terms of European stability and the possible contribution of such stability to world peace.

3.9 Ernest Bevin on the Significance of Germany, July 1948

The Berlin Blockade was seen by many as the gravest and most dangerous crisis in Europe since the end of World War II and as a significant test of the future of the Continent. In this excerpt, written at the start of the Blockade and the subsequent airlift, British foreign secretary Ernest Bevin presents an analysis of the significance of Germany and about Soviet intentions to Prime Minister Clement Attlee.

1. A prosperous and contented Germany, built on sound democratic principles, is the best guarantee for the safety of Europe. These conditions cannot at
present be secured in the Eastern Zone; it is therefore all the more important that
they should be secured in the West. If our policy suceeds, Western Germany,
forming part of the Western Defence System and contributing to the E.R.P
[Economic Recovery Programme] can become a most effective barrier against
the spread of Communism across Europe. On the other hand, if we fail, the only
alternative is Soviet control on the whole of Germany and therefore Europe (…)

2. By far the greater part of Germany's industrial wealth and two thirds of the
population are in the Western Zones. The Ruhr industries are essential to the
success of the E.R. Programme. While economic conditions in the West are
improving, the economy of the Eastern Zone has, as a result of wholesale
removals by the Soviet, become desperate. Control of the West German economy and in particular a controlling interest in the Ruhr is therefore a major
Soviet objective in Germany (…)

3. The Russians have two main objectives in Germany:

(a) To obtain a foothold in the Western Zones and the Ruhr, and, as indicated
in the Warsaw communique, ultimately communise the whole of Germany,
probably through an all-German Government established in Berlin.

(b) As a first step to evict the Western Allies from Berlin, where our presence
is an obstacle to their political and economic policies both in the Eastern Zone
and for Germany as a whole.

4. The presence of the Western Allies in Berlin is no doubt most unwelcome
to the Russians but in present conditions it cannot do them much direct damage.
We cannot attack Russia from Berlin and we have not been able to prevent the
economic exploitation and the political oppression in the Eastern Zone. On the
other hand the political and economic gains which the Russians would hope to
obtain from controlling Western Germany and the Ruhr are both for offensive,
and as they wrongly believe for defensive, reasons essential to them.

5. But our policy in Germany cannot be restricted to rehabilitating the
Western Zones and allowing the Russians to evict us from Berlin. Berlin is
regarded by the vast majority of Germans as the symbol of German unity and as
the only possible capital for a united Germany. The mere fact of our continuing
presence has so far prevented and shall continue to hinder the setting up in Berlin
of a Soviet controlled German Government. At the same time our struggle for
position in the city has made it in the eyes of the Germans and of Europe generally a test case between the Soviet and the Western Powers in which prestige of
both sides is heavily engaged. To retreat from Berlin, the last democratic island in
the Soviet sphere, would immensely increase Soviet prestige, win over the doubtful masses in Germany to their side and depress our friends in each of the free

countries in Europe. It would also encourage the Russians to hazard adventures in Vienna, Turkey or elsewhere. On the other hand, if we stand fast in Berlin we shall undoubtedly rally German opinion and gain the time which is so necessary to pursue the advantages we posses in the West.

6. We must however be clear in our minds that to stay in Berlin is a means to an end rather than an end in itself. In consequence it would be a mistake to buy a settlement in Berlin by concessions to the Russians which would give them influence in Eastern Germany and above all in the Ruhr. For their part the Russians are unlikely to make any concessions in Berlin unless they expect to obtain important advantages in Germany as a whole. We can therefore expect a progressive worsening of the position in Berlin as the winter approaches. It will indeed be difficult for us to meet all the Berliners' requirements from airborne attacks, but our policy should be to continue the air supply route to its maximum capacity. This may result in the Berliners going hungry and a complete standstill in industry resulting in unrest. The Russians are unlikely to agree to take on the responsibility of feeding the population of the Western sectors unless under conditions which are unacceptable to us. We should continue, however, to build up our airlink to the maximum and maintain our garrison until the only alternative for the Soviet is to eject us by force. Meanwhile efforts should be made through the diplomatic channel to ascertain whether the Russians are prepared to negotiate a settlement on tolerable terms.

3.10 Willy Brandt on the Berlin Blockade, 1948

Future West German Social Democrat chancellor Willy Brandt, who returned to Germany in 1946 from exile in Scandinavia, experienced the Berlin Blockade as an assistant to the mayor of West Berlin, Ernest Reuter. In this excerpt Brandt describes what life was like in the besieged city during the crisis.

The Soviets proclaimed the blockade of Berlin on the pretext that the streets were temporarily impassable and that near Magdeburg a bridge had to be repaired. Railway traffic, autobahn, highways, and waterways to and from the West were blocked. Only the three air corridors, each thirty kilometres wide, remained open (...) Even the supply of medicine for sick persons and milk for little babies was stopped. Two million West Berliners were to be starved into capitulation.

The efficiency of the airlift surpassed the highest expectations (...) The transport capacity increased from week to week. One had counted on a minimum requirement of 3,400–4,500 tons; in September, on a single day, approximately

7,000 tons were flown into Berlin. And on the 15th of April of the following year 1,400 planes landed in Berlin's airports—an aeroplane every sixty-three seconds. They transported 5,300 tons of coal, 1,850 tons of foodstuffs, 1,000 tons of raw material of different kinds—i.e., on a single day 8,000 tons of freight. That was the same quantity which prior to the blockade was brought to Berlin on all highways and waterways (…)

When the blockade was lifted by the Russians on May 12th, 1949, it had lasted exactly 322 days. In these eleven months more than two million tons had been flown into Berlin—a gigantic achievement which revolutionised all ideas regarding air transport, prevalent up to that time.

Over these figures, these miracles of technique, organisation and machines, we must not forget the victims. Thirty-nine Englishmen, thirty-one Americans, and nine Germans lost their lives on the front of the blockade (…)

At the beginning of the blockade the supplies in the west sectors were enough to guarantee the barely sufficient rations for approximately four weeks at maximum. In the first months just enough food was brought in by air to secure the further issue of the rations and to save the Berliners from starving to death—but hunger they could not be spared.

The stock of coal was supposed to last for thirty days but it was impossible to replenish it to the same extent as the urgently needed food. Apartments and the greater part of offices—even the administration buildings—could no longer be heated. Every family got for the whole winter an allotment of twenty-five pounds of coal and three boxes of wood. Some fuel was smuggled in by black-marketeers. Most of the families were glad when they could keep one room of their apartment moderately warm for a few hours of the day. Fortunately, the winter was not particularly severe.

Cooking in Berlin was done ninety per cent by gas. During the first five months of the blockade consumers were limited to half their previous gas consumption.

Electric current was only available for four hours daily, usually in two periods of two hours each. These periods came at different times of day in different sections of the city, and people had to rise at odd hours in order to take advantage of the available current. The preparation of a cup of hot 'Ersatz' coffee or of a bowl of soup gave the housewife a nearly insoluble problem (…)

One factory after the other had to shut down. Small businesses that required electric current for their operations had no choice but to operate when this was available, even at four o'clock in the morning. Most often their employees had to get to work on foot. The subway operated only from six o'clock in the morning to six o'clock in the evening; the street-car service was greatly curtailed; the buses ran only at rare intervals because of limited petrol stocks. Although 25,000 unemployed were occupied with the removal of the ruins, the figure of people out of work increased to more than 150,000.

In the meantime the Communists had changed their tactics. After threats and intimidations they suddenly made a tempting offer to the West Berliners. They asserted that the Soviet government had brought large quantities of foodstuffs into the east sector. All the West Berliners had to do if they wanted to get that food was to register with ration offices in the east sector. The answer was very impressive. The ration office in Treptow had sent out invitations to 285,000 persons. At first, only twenty persons from the west sectors registered. Sixteen persons registered in Prenzlauer Berg, and nineteen in Pankow. By the end of the year, out of two million Berliners 85,000 had accepted the Communist offer— four per cent of the population. And most of them were people who lived in the west sector, but who worked in the east sector and continued to buy their rations there as they had always done.

The Berliners did not waver, though in addition to hunger and cold—particularly in the first months of the blockade—they were subjected to a vicious fear propaganda. The Soviets had declared that all of Berlin was theirs, and their newspapers in German language didn't cease to foretell the realisation of that claim. They spread rumours of different kinds, they didn't spare threats and intimidations. Thus, here and there, doubts arose as to whether one would be able to resist the Russian pressure in the long run. The retaliation and vengeance in case of a defeat would be terrible.

In spite of Reuter's arousing appeals and in spite of General Clay's assurances, one couldn't close one's mind to the plain fact that, from the military point of view, Berlin's situation was hopeless. The United States had 3,000 troops in the city, the British 2,000, and the French 1,500, while the Soviets had 18,000 soldiers in East Berlin and a further 300,000 in the east zone. They could at any time overrun Berlin. And what would happen then? Would the Western democracies risk a world war in the interest of a few million Berliners?

The secret doubts were continually nourished by means of a sometimes skilful Communist propaganda. Their press and their radio brought up every day new 'revelations' regarding the imminent withdrawal of the Western Powers; the SED swamped West Berlin with pamphlets; at the borders of the sectors propaganda cars were placed, their loudspeakers announced the hopelessness of any further resistance. The 'front-town politicians' asked the Berliners to sacrifice their savings in favour of the Westmark, the workers were asked to leave the Communist Trade Union Federation, and thus lose their relief contributions, hunger and unemployment were their certain fate—and all for what? For the defence of a system the collapse of which was only a matter of weeks.

The Communists didn't limit themselves to mere propaganda by word and writing. The sessions of the Municipal Council were broken up by a Communist mob, Social Democratic city councillors and members of the Municipal Council were assaulted when they were leaving the hall, policemen who tried to come to their aid were arrested (…)

The cases of kidnapping and arbitrary arrests increased from month to month. Russian soldiers repeatedly invaded the American sector. Once they kidnapped five policemen, and confiscated their police car. That same day a city councillor was arrested in his office by the east sector police. The next day Soviet military police assaulted two Berliner policemen in the American sector. When they tried to resist the arrest they were knocked down, stabbed, and dragged into the Russian sector.

The blockade became tighter from week to week. Throughout the summer West Berliners were able to obtain a limited quantity of food and other supplies from the Soviet zone. Trucks drove out daily into the surrounding countryside and brought back vegetables; individuals went on 'hoarding expeditions' to the east zone and returned by boat, train, subway, or bicycle with wood, coal, briquettes, potatoes.

In the autumn the Soviets sealed these holes. German travellers were forbidden to bring food and supplies from the surrounding countryside into the west sectors. Controls were extended to the subway lines running between West and East Berlin. The Communist police not only confiscated food and other goods, but extended their searches to pocket-books and wallets and confiscated West-marks. Even the possession of a West Berlin newspaper made a person suspect—the police took his name down, he was a marked man.

The Berliners lived in a besieged fortress. To hunger and cold was added the paralysing feeling of complete isolation from the outside world.

On May 12th the 'traffic restrictions'—as the Soviets called their blockade—were lifted. As Reuter said, the Berliners could celebrate 'the most beautiful May since 1945' (…) Berlin was, as Reuter said, the shield behind which the consolidation in the free part of Germany could take place.

3.11 Andrei Gromyko on the Establishment of the Federal Republic, September 1949

In this note Soviet deputy foreign minister Andrei Gromyko comments on the establishment of the Federal Republic of Germany on 20 September 1949. The German Democratic Republic (GDR) was formed soon afterwards.

On September 20, 1949, a separate government was formed [in Bonn] for the western zones of Germany. In connection with this new step by the governments of the U.S.A., Great Britain and France, designed to deepen the division of Germany, we ought to react to these divisive actions by sending the appropriate notes to the governments of the three powers.

Sending notes to the governments of the U.S.A., Great Britain, and France is called for not only because of the need to react to the new step by the three powers to divide Germany, resulting in the establishment of a separate government in Bonn, but also by the impending formation of the Government of the German Democratic Republic in Berlin. These notes are part of a general plan of measures to be carried out in connection with the planned formation of a government in Berlin.

The Ministry of Foreign Affairs of the USSR also advises that the Soviet ambassadors to Poland, Czechoslovakia, Hungary, Romania, and Bulgaria and the envoy to Albania be instructed to visit the foreign ministries and inform them of the impending delivery of the aforementioned notes from the Soviet government. Furthermore, we should express our desire that the governments of Czechoslovakia and Poland, in light of the formation of the puppet government for the western zones of Germany, also send notes to the governments of the U.S.A., Great Britain, and France, and that the Romanian, Bulgarian, Albanian, and Hungarian ministries of foreign affairs issue appropriate statements on this matter. Being informed well in advance of the impending delivery of the notes to the three powers, the governments of these countries will be able to prepare themselves better to support the Soviet Union and its position on the German question.

3.12 The Stalin Note on the Neutralization of Germany, April 1952

One of the many intense controversies in Cold War historiography concerns the famous 'Stalin Note' of 10 March 1952, in which the Soviet leader offered to exchange German unification and the withdrawal of foreign armies for the country's neutrality. Debate continues on whether Stalin's proposals were seriously advanced in an attempt to reach a general settlement with the West, or whether they were simply part of a Kremlin propaganda campaign to hamper the West's efforts to integrate the Federal Republic of Germany into its military alliance. Western governments, including the United States, adopted the latter view, reflected in the State Department memorandum of 2 April. Following Western rejection of his proposals, Stalin met in the Kremlin with a visiting delegation of East German Communist leaders (Wilhelm Pieck, Walter Ulbricht, and Otto Grotewohl) to reassess strategy on 7 April 1952.

A. Soviet Draft for a German Peace Treaty, 10 March 1952

(...) The conclusion of a peace treaty with Germany has an important significance for strengthening the peace in Europe (...) The necessity of hastening the conclusion of peace treaty with Germany is required by the fact that the danger of a re-establishment of German militarism which has twice unleashed world wars has not been eliminated in as much as the appropriate provisions of Potsdam conference still remain unfilled. A peace treaty with Germany must guarantee the elimination of any possibility of a rebirth of German militarism and German aggression (…)

Political provisions

1. Germany is re-established as a unified state, thereby an end is put to the division of Germany and a unified Germany has the possibility of development as an independent democratic peace loving state.

2. All armed forces of occupying powers must be withdrawn from Germany not later than one year from the date of entry into force of the peace treaty. Simultaneously all foreign military bases on territory of Germany must be liquidated.

3. Democratic rights must be guaranteed to the German people to ensure that all persons under German jurisdiction without regard to race, sex, language or religion enjoy the rights of man (…)

4. The free activity of democratic parties and organizations must be guaranteed in Germany, with the right of freedom to decide their own internal affairs (…)

5. The existence of organizations inimical to democracy and to the maintenance of peace must not be permitted on the territory of Germany.

6. Civil and political rights equal to those of all other German citizens for participation in the building of a peace-loving democratic Germany must be made available to all former members of the German army, including officers and generals, all former Nazis, excluding those who are serving court sentences for committing crimes.

7. Germany guarantees that it will not enter into any kind of coalition or military alliance directed against any power which took part with its armed forces in the war against Germany (…)

Military provisions

1. Germany will be permitted to have its own national armed forces which are necessary for the defense of the country.

2. Germany is permitted to produce war materials and equipment, the quantity and type of which must not exceed the limitations set for its armed forces by the peace treaty (…)

B. US State Department on Potential German Unification, 2 April 1952

(…) On the question of whether we really want German unification there seemed to be very substantial differences of opinion, and also—at least in terms of our fundamental European objectives—considerable uncertainties of opinion. On the immediate question of whether we presently favor German unification, Nitze was clear that we had put ourselves on record in favor of free elections leading to a unified Germany, and that we could not withdraw from this position.

At the outset, Nitze and Bohlen were in agreement that the preferred U.S. solution of the German situation would be a unified Germany within the EDC [European Defence Community]. (Nitze and Bohlen were both very doubtful whether the French would buy such a solution; there was no discussion of how the French would feel about a unified Germany outside the EDC, but presumably they would have very grave reservations about this, too, unless very strict controls on German war potentials were maintained.)

Discussion of the abstract desirability of German unification produced less rather than more conviction that a unified Germany was a desirable goal. Bohlen, while not convinced one way or another, feels that a unified Germany in a Europe which is still divided presents certain very grave dangers of German domination of the Continent or rapprochement with the Soviet Union. Bohlen feels that the present Soviet bid for a unified Germany is really directed at the right-wing industrialists who support Adenauer rather than at the German Socialists; it is the industrialists whom the Soviet Union could tempt with markets stretching from Eastern Europe to the Pacific (including China)—markets which it would be very difficult for Germany to duplicate in the West.

b. There was also no clear agreement as to what the West Germans want—i.e., just how they are likely to respond to possible Soviet and Western moves (…) Nitze thinks it unlikely, however, that the West Germans would be confronted with a simple choice between integration and unification; he foresees a choice between unification in the near future and a present integration which would not preclude subsequent unification. Faced with that choice, the West Germans would, in the view of Nitze and also of Ger, take the latter course. Ferguson was very doubtful of this analysis; based on the intelligence reports which he has studied, Ferguson is pretty well convinced that the Germans want unity above all, and would buy what appeared to them a bona fide Soviet offer. Ferguson regards it as very difficult to pursue effectively the parallel propaganda course suggested by Jessup pursuant to the Nitze analysis—i.e., simultaneous emphasis on German unity and German integration with the West. Bohlen, on the other hand, is inclined to feel that we may be exaggerating the West German pressure for unity; put another way, Bohlen wonders whether the West Germans are not more skeptical of Soviet good faith on the unification issue than we have been inclined to believe.

c. Assuming German integration with the West now, it was not agreed whether such integration would continue after the establishment of a unified German government (…)

(...) a. With regard to the content of our next note on Germany, Bohlen suggested that the following two-point policy would most accurately reflect our objectives, would be the simplest of exposition, and would be the least likely to get us tripped up:

1. We are going ahead on integration.
2. If the Soviet Union is genuinely prepared to permit free elections and the consequent establishment of a unified Germany, we are prepared to let the ultimate all-German government decide whether it wishes to continue its adherence to the integration program.

b. On the question of possible talks with the Soviet Union about Germany, there was general agreement that they should be avoided if possible (...)

c. There was general agreement that we should step up our propaganda in Germany in accordance with whatever substantive objectives we agree upon. It was specifically suggested by Bohlen, pursuant to his analysis outlined above, that we lay increasing stress on the dangers to Germany of the Soviet armies and the need to counter those dangers by accelerating the integration program (...)

C. Stalin and the SED Leadership, 7 April 1952

Com[rade] Stalin said that the last time W. Pieck raised the question about the prospects for the development of Germany in connection with the Soviet proposals on a peace treaty and the policy of the Americans and British in Germany. Comrade Stalin considers that irrespective of any proposals that we can make on the German question the Western powers will not agree with them and will not withdraw from Germany in any case. It would be a mistake to think that a compromise might emerge or that the Americans will agree with the draft of the peace treaty. The Americans need their army in West Germany to hold Western Europe in their hands. They say that they have there their army [to defend] against us. But the real goal of this army is to control Europe. The Americans will draw West Germany into the Atlantic Pact. They will create West German troops. Adenauer is in the pocket of the Americans.

All ex-fascists and generals also are there. In reality there is an independent state being formed in West Germany. And you must organize your own state. The line of demarcation between East and West Germany must be seen as a frontier and not as a simple border but a dangerous one. One must strengthen the protection of this frontier.

Questions

Did Franklin D. Roosevelt have a clear idea on how to deal with post-war Germany in 1944?

How does the perspective of the 'foot soldier'—such as the Americans who met their Soviet counterparts on the Elbe in 1945—differ from those of the policy-maker?

What accounts for the brutality of Soviet soldiers towards German women?

What agreements were reached about the German question at he Potsdam Conference? Were there many unresolved issues?

Did the Soviets wish to create an independent East German state early on?

What were Sergei Tiul'panov's major concerns in East Germany in 1946?

Why did the Americans wish to fuse their occupation zone with the British?

What did the Berlin Blockade mean to those involved?

Did the Stalin Note of 1952 represent a 'lost chance' for German unification?

4

The Marshall Plan and NATO

There is no question that the enhanced American role in Western Europe was both a contributing source and an outcome of the tensions and divisions that characterized the origins of the Cold War in Europe. In retrospect it is easy to assume that US policy followed a straightforward logic whose major goals were to restore and strengthen capitalism, minimise left-wing influence, and prevent the Soviet Union from extending its power beyond the regions were the Red Army was stationed in the aftermath of World War II. Accordingly, the Western response grew gradually harsher and more comprehensive, eventually excluding any serious attempt at rapprochement with the USSR. By 1947, with the announcement of the Truman Doctrine and the launch of the Marshall Plan, the division of Europe accelerated; by 1949 it was confirmed with the creation of the North Atlantic Treaty Organization (NATO).

That the United States would eventually engage so deeply in Western Europe, however, was by no means inevitable in 1945–6. In fact, domestic pressures bearing on the Truman administration to disengage the United States from the Old Continent were strong. In the November 1946 congressional elections the Republicans, under the influential leadership of Senator Robert Taft, defeated the Democrats for the first time in decades; it was no secret that Taft and a large portion of the Republicans favoured a return to some form of American isolationism (although their more appealing message was probably the promise to cut down government expenditure by 20 per cent). President Truman, who lacked the unchallenged authority of his deceased predecessor, thus faced an uphill battle as he became more convinced of the need to forcefully oppose the USSR.

Inexperienced in foreign affairs, Truman relied on a number of advisors who, in turn, rarely agreed on the gravity of and the correct response to what was viewed as increasingly aggressive Soviet behaviour. To be sure, a strong anti-Soviet consensus was being formed among a number of key policy analysts who tended to agree with the ideas of George Kennan (quickly emerging as the most prominent Soviet specialist in the State Department). In his so-called Long Telegram of February 1946, Kennan presented an analysis of Soviet behaviour

that, over the year that followed, heavily influenced the Truman administration's
Cold War policies. Meanwhile, the American administration launched a campaign to publicize Soviet 'misbehaviour': leading Democratic senator Arthur
Vandenberg made fiery speeches about Soviet aggressiveness in the US Senate,
Secretary of State James F. Byrnes publicly articulated the Truman administration's tough stand against the Soviets. The latter was particularly clear in the
crisis over the continued presence of Soviet troops in northern Iran (Azerbaijan).
Faced with a tough stand from the United States and Britain, the Soviets did
eventually withdraw their troops in the late spring of 1946, thus seemingly confirming another principle of the policy of containment: if you are tough, the
Soviets will eventually step back. This trend became even clearer in early 1947,
when the central focus of the emerging Cold War shifted to the ongoing civil war
in Greece.

Since the evacuation of German forces from Greece in late 1944, the country
had experienced a brief period of relative calm. The British forces that subsequently entered the country managed to forge a truce between two Greek
factions: the Greek Communists and the royalists. In March 1946 Greece held
elections that were, however, boycotted by the Communists and thus resulted in
a royalist government that enjoyed Britain's support. A few months later the
Greek Civil War erupted and became immediately internationalized: the Greek
Communists received support from Yugoslavia, Albania, and Bulgaria; the
royalists continued to receive British assistance. In early 1947, however, Britain
proved unable to continue its assistance to the Greek government. As the Soviets,
meanwhile, vetoed any United Nations intervention in the Greek Civil War, the
British informed the United States in February 1947 of their inability to continue aiding the Greek royalists, and the Greek government specifically pleaded
for American assistance.

In March 1947 President Truman unveiled the so-called Truman Doctrine. It
amounted to a programme to provide US assistance to the non-Communist side
in the ongoing Greek Civil War and further aid to neighbouring Turkey. But
while the 'practical' side of Truman's message related to the requests made by the
Greek government for aid in their struggle against Communists, the Truman
Doctrine went a step further. Truman made references to the United States's mission to support 'free peoples who are resisting subjugation by armed minorities'
anywhere, and clearly stated that should such aid not be provided, the other
European countries would soon be under threat.

The Truman Doctrine was more than a response to a local conflict clothed in
universalistic terms, and American involvement in Western Europe soon reached
new heights with the announcement of the Marshall Plan. In June 1947 Secretary
of State George Marshall unveiled what was to become probably the most popular US policy initiative in the post-war years. The European Recovery Program

(ERP), as the Marshall Plan was formally known, eventually offered US aid to nearly all West European countries. From 1948 to mid-1952 more than $13 billion (approx. $90 billion in 2000 dollars) was distributed in the form of direct aid, loan guarantees, grants, and necessities from medicine to mules. With such aid the transatlantic link between the United States and Western Europe was confirmed. Indeed, the announcement of the Marshall Plan put the Soviets on the defensive and effectively served to push the onus for the commencement of the Cold War onto the Kremlin's shoulders. To be sure, the United States offered aid to all European countries, and the Soviets attended a meeting in Paris with the British and the French in late June and early July of 1947 to discuss the particulars of the American offer. The Soviets, headed by Foreign Minister Molotov, soon walked out of the meeting, denouncing the plan as a capitalist plot. While Americans insisted on controlling the plan, the Soviets rejected any external intrusion into East European, let alone Soviet, national economies. In particular, the Soviets rejected the idea that East European raw materials would be shipped to boost Western recovery. The Kremlin, as previously noted, thus pressed East Europeans to remain outside the ERP, effectively sealing the economic division of Europe.

The culmination of the early containment policy in Europe came approximately a year after the Marshall Plan became operational. On 4 April 1949 the United States, Canada, and ten West European countries formed the North Atlantic Treaty Organization. 'An alliance for peace', as the chairman of the Senate Foreign Relations Committee, Tom Connally, termed it, NATO in many ways symbolized the key role that the United States had come to play in Europe. And while there had been some initial reluctance to commit the United States in this manner—a streak of latent isolationism ran deep amongst American politicians—the pressure from Great Britain and a number of other European countries, as well as the need to create an institutional structure linking the United States permanently with Western Europe, had eventually forced the issue. Still, in the spring of 1949 it was clear that NATO was in large part created to send yet another message to the Soviet Union; a message that conveyed the United States's determination to object to any further expansion of Soviet influence in Europe. To a large extent NATO was at the time of its creation a political rather than a military alliance. Together with the Marshall Plan, it solidified the political and economic division of Europe by emphasizing the similarities between the participating countries' domestic systems and values. Soon after the formation of NATO, however, the nature of the Cold War confrontation began to change. While many in the Truman administration may have viewed the Cold War initially as a political and economic contest with a particularly European focus, developments in late 1949 and throughout the early 1950s served to both militarize and globalize the conflict.

Readings

Melvyn Leffler, *A Preponderance of Power* (1992). A detailed account of the Truman administration's foreign policy.

John L. Gaddis, *We Now Know: Re-thinking Cold War History* (1997). One of the first efforts at synthesizing the new documentary material from the former Soviet bloc.

Lawrence Kaplan, *NATO and the United States: The Enduring Alliance* (1994). The classic account of NATO, its origins, and its role in the Cold War.

William I. Hitchcock, *France Restored* (1998). Reassesses France's role in the early Cold War.

Michael Hogan, *The Marshall Plan* (1987). The most thorough account of the Marshall Plan, its origins and impact.

4.1 George Kennan's Long Telegram, February 1946

On 22 February 1946 George F. Kennan, the chargé d'affaires *at the US Embassy in Moscow, sent a long analysis of Soviet policy to his colleagues in Washington. This so-called Long Telegram—from which the excerpts below are taken—was widely circulated within the Truman administration and became one of the basic documents for the framing of US containment policy.*

It may be expected that the component parts of this far-flung [Soviet] apparatus will be utilized, in accordance with their individual suitability, as follows:

1. To undermine general political and strategic potential of major Western powers. Efforts will be made in such countries to disrupt national self-confidence, to hamstring measures of national defense, to increase social and industrial unrest, to stimulate all forms of disunity. All persons with grievances, whether economic or racial, will be urged to seek redress not in mediation and compromise, but in defiant violent struggle for destruction of other elements of society. Here poor will be set against rich, black against white, young against old, newcomers against established residents, etc.

2. On unofficial plane particularly violent efforts will be made to weaken power and influence of Western powers over colonial, backward, or dependent peoples. On this level, no holds will be barred. Mistakes and weaknesses of Western colonial administration will be mercilessly exposed and exploited. Liberal opinion in Western countries will be mobilized to weaken colonial policies. Resentment among dependent peoples will be stimulated. And while latter are being encouraged to seek independence of Western powers, Soviet-dominated puppet political machines will be undergoing preparation to take over domestic power in respective colonial areas when independence is achieved.

3. Where individual governments stand in path of Soviet purposes pressure will be brought for their removal from office. This can happen where governments directly oppose Soviet foreign policy aims (Turkey, Iran), where they seal their territories off against Communist penetration (Switzerland, Portugal), or where they compete too strongly, like Labor government in England, for moral domination among elements which it is important for Communists to dominate (…)

4. In foreign countries Communists will, as a rule, work toward destruction of all forms of personal independence, economic, political, or moral (…)

5. Everything possible will be done to set major Western powers against each other. Anti-British talk will be plugged among Americans, anti-American talk among British. Continentals, including Germans, will be taught to abhor both Anglo-Saxon powers. Where suspicions exist, they will be fanned; where not, ignited. No effort will be spared to discredit and combat all efforts which threaten to lead to any sort of unity or cohesion among others from which Russia might be excluded. Thus, all forms of international organization not amenable to Communist penetration and control, whether it be the Catholic Church, international economic concerns, or the international fraternity of royalty and aristocracy, must expect to find themselves under fire.

6. In general, all Soviet efforts on unofficial international plane will be negative and destructive in character, designed to tear down sources of strength beyond reach of Soviet control (…) The Soviet regime is a police regime par excellence, reared in the dim half-world of Tsarist police intrigue, accustomed to think primarily in terms of police power. This should never be lost sight of in gauging Soviet motives.

Practical deductions from standpoint of US policy

In summary, we have here a political force committed fanatically to the belief that with US there can be no permanent modus vivendi, that it is desirable and necessary that the internal harmony of our society be disrupted, our traditional way of life be destroyed, the international authority of our state be broken, if Soviet power is to be secure. This political force has complete power of disposition over energies of one of the world's greatest peoples and resources of the world's richest national territory, and is borne along by deep and powerful currents of Russian nationalism. In addition, it has an elaborate and far-flung apparatus for exertion of its influence in other countries, an apparatus of amazing flexibility and versatility, managed by people whose experience and skill in underground methods are presumably without parallel in history. Finally, it is seemingly inaccessible to considerations of reality in its basic reactions. For it, the vast fund of objective fact about human society is not, as with us, the measure against which outlook is constantly being tested and reformed, but a grab bag from which individual items are selected arbitrarily and tendentiously to bolster an outlook already preconceived. This is admittedly not a pleasant picture. Problem of how to cope with this force is undoubtedly greatest task our diplomacy has ever faced and probably the greatest it will ever have to face (...) But I would like to record my conviction that the problem is within our power to solve—and that without recourse to any general military conflict. And in support of this conviction there are certain observations of a more encouraging nature I should like to make:

(One) Soviet power, unlike that of Hitlerite Germany, is neither schematic nor adventuristic. It does not work by fixed plans. It does not take unnecessary risks. Impervious to logic of reason, and it is highly sensitive to logic of force. For this reason it can easily withdraw—and usually does—when strong resistance is encountered at any point. Thus, if the adversary has sufficient force and makes clear his readiness to use it, he rarely has to do so. If situations are properly handled there need be no prestige-engaging showdowns.

(Two) Gauged against Western world as a whole, Soviets are still by far the weaker force. Thus, their success will really depend on degree of cohesion, firmness, and vigor which Western world can muster. And this is factor which it is within our power to influence.

(Three) Success of Soviet system, as form of internal power, is not yet finally proven (...) We here are convinced that never since termination of the civil war have the mass of Russian people been emotionally farther removed from doctrines of Communist Party than they are today. In Russia, party has now become a great and—for the moment—highly successful apparatus of dictatorial administration, but it has ceased to be a source of emotional inspiration. Thus, internal soundness and permanence of movement need not yet be regarded as assured.

(Four) All Soviet propaganda beyond Soviet security sphere is basically negative and destructive. It should therefore be relatively easy to combat it by any intelligent and really constructive program.

For these reasons I think we may approach calmly and with good heart the problem of how to deal with Russia. As to how this approach should be made, I only wish to advance, by way of conclusion, the following comments:

1.   Our first step must be to apprehend, and recognize for what it is, the nature of the movement with which we are dealing (...)

2.   We must see that our public is educated to realities of Russian situation. I cannot overemphasize the importance of this. Press cannot do this alone. It must be done mainly by government, which is necessarily more experienced and better informed on practical problems involved. In this we need not be deterred by ugliness of the picture. I am convinced that there would be far less hysterical anti-Sovietism in our country today if the realities of this situation were better understood by our people. There is nothing as dangerous or as terrifying as the

unknown (…) Our stake in this country, even coming on the heels of tremendous demonstrations of our friendship for Russian people, is remarkably small. We have here no investments to guard, no actual trade to lose, virtually no citizens to protect, few cultural contacts to preserve. Our only stake lies in what we hope rather than what we have; and I am convinced we have a better chance of realizing those hopes if our public is enlightened and if our dealings with Russians are placed entirely on realistic and matter of fact basis.

3.   Much depends on health and vigor of our own society. World Communism is like malignant parasite which feeds only on diseased tissue. This is the point at which domestic and foreign policies meet. Every courageous and incisive measure to solve internal problems of our own society, to improve self-confidence, discipline, morale, and community spirit of our own people, is a diplomatic victory over Moscow worth a thousand diplomatic notes and joint communique's (…)

4.   We must formulate and put forward for other nations a much more positive and constructive picture of the sort of world we would like to see than we have put forward in the past. It is not enough to urge the people to develop political processes similar to our own. Many foreign peoples, in Europe at least, are tired and frightened by experiences of the past, and are less interested in abstract freedom than in security. They are seeking guidance rather than responsibilities. We should be better able than the Russians to give them this. And unless we do, the Russians certainly will.

5.   Finally, we must have courage and self-confidence to cling to our own methods and conceptions of human society. After all, the greatest danger that can befall us in coping with this problem of Soviet Communism is that we shall allow ourselves to become like those with whom we are coping (…)

4.2   The Soviet Ambassador to the United States on Post-war American Policy, 27 September 1946

These excerpts from the Soviet Ambassador Nikolai Novikov's analysis of US policy provide a summation of the Soviet interpretation of aggressive American post-war policy goals.

The foreign policy of the United States, which reflects the imperialist tendencies of American monopolistic capital, is characterized in the post-war period by a striving for world supremacy. This is the real meaning of the many statements by President Truman and other representatives of American ruling circles; that the United States has the right to lead the world. All the forces of American diplomacy—the army, the air force, the navy, industry, and science—are enlisted in the service of this foreign policy. For this purpose broad plans for expansion have been developed and are being implemented through diplomacy and the establishment of a system of naval and air bases stretching far beyond the boundaries of the United States, through the arms race, and through the creation of ever newer types of weapons.

(...) Europe has come out of the war with a completely dislocated economy, and the economic devastation that occurred in the course of the war cannot be overcome in a short time. All of the countries of Europe and Asia are experiencing a colossal need for consumer goods, industrial and transportation equipment, etc. Such a situation provides American monopolistic capital with prospects for enormous shipments of goods and the importation of capital into these countries —a circumstance that would permit it to infiltrate their national economies (...)

(...) On the other hand, we have seen a failure of calculations on the part of U.S. circles which assumed that the Soviet Union would be destroyed in the war or would come out of it so weakened that it would be forced to go begging to the United States for economic assistance (...) In actuality, despite all of the economic difficulties of the postwar period connected with the enormous losses inflicted by the war and the German fascist occupation, the Soviet Union continues to remain economically independent of the outside world and is rebuilding its national economy with its own forces.

At the same time the USSR's international position is currently stronger than it was in the prewar period. Thanks to the historical victories of Soviet weapons, the Soviet armed forces are located on the territory of Germany and other formerly hostile countries, thus guaranteeing that these countries will not be used again for an attack on the USSR. In formerly hostile countries, such as Bulgaria, Finland, Hungary, and Romania, democratic reconstruction has established regimes that have undertaken to strengthen and maintain friendly relations with the Soviet Union. In the Slavic countries that were liberated by the Red Army or with its assistance—Poland, Czechoslovakia, and Yugoslavia—democratic regimes have also been established that maintain relations with the Soviet Union on the basis of agreements on friendship and mutual assistance (...) Such a situation in Eastern and Southeastern Europe cannot help but be regarded by the American imperialists as an obstacle in the path of the expansionist policy of the United States.

3. Obvious indications of the U.S. effort to establish world dominance are also to be found in the increase in military potential in peacetime and in the establishment of a large number of naval and air bases both in the United States and beyond its borders.

In the summer of 1946, for the first time in the history of the country, Congress passed a law on the establishment of a peacetime army, not on a volunteer basis but on the basis of universal military service (...) Expenditures on the army and navy have risen colossally, amounting to $13 billion according to the budget for 1946–47 (about 40 percent of the total budget of $36 billion). This is more than 10 times greater than corresponding expenditures in the budget for 1938, which did not amount to even $1 billion.

Along with maintaining a large army, navy, and air force, the budget provides that these enormous amounts also will be spent on establishing a very extensive system of naval and air bases in the Atlantic and Pacific oceans. According to existing official plans, in the course of the next few years 228 bases, points of support, and radio stations are to be constructed in the Atlantic Ocean and 258 in the Pacific. A large number of these bases and points of support are located outside the boundaries of the United States (...) The establishment of American bases on islands that are often 10,000 to 12,000 kilometers from the territory of the United States and are on the other side of the Atlantic and Pacific oceans clearly indicates the offensive nature of the strategic concepts of the commands of the U.S. army and navy (...) All of these facts show clearly that a decisive role in the realization of plans for world dominance by the United States is played by its armed forces.

(...) It must be kept in mind (...) that incidents such as the visit by the American battleship Missouri to the Black Sea straits, the visit of the American fleet to Greece, and the great interest that U.S. diplomacy displays in the problem of the straits have a double meaning. On the one hand, they indicate that the United States has decided to consolidate its position in the Mediterranean basin to support its interests in the countries of the Near East and that it has selected the navy as the tool for this policy. On the other hand, these incidents constitute a political and military demonstration against the Soviet Union. The strengthening of U.S. positions in the Near East and the establishment of conditions for basing the American navy at one or more points on the Mediterranean Sea (Trieste, Palestine, Greece, Turkey) will therefore signify the emergence of a new threat to the security of the southern regions of the Soviet Union.

(...) The ruling circles of the United States obviously have a sympathetic attitude toward the idea of a military alliance with England, but at the present time the matter has not yet culminated in an official alliance. Churchill's speech in Fulton calling for the conclusion of an Anglo-American military alliance for the purpose of establishing joint domination over the world was therefore not supported officially by Truman or Byrnes, although Truman by his presence [during the 'Iron Curtain' speech] did indirectly sanction Churchill's appeal.

Even if the United States does not go so far as to conclude a military alliance with England just now, in practice they still maintain very close contact on military questions. The combined Anglo-American headquarters in Washington continues to exist, despite the fact that over a year has passed since the end of the war. Frequent personal contact continues among leading military figures of England and the United States (...)

(…) The present policy of the American government with regard to the USSR is also directed at limiting or dislodging the influence of the Soviet Union from neighboring countries. In implementing this policy in former enemy or Allied countries adjacent to the USSR, the United States attempts, at various international conferences or directly in these countries themselves, to support reactionary forces with the purpose of creating obstacles to the process of democratization of these countries. In so doing, it also attempts to secure positions for the penetration of American capital into their economies.

4.3 The British Government on its Inability to Continue Aiding Greece, February 1947

By early 1947 the British government was in severe financial trouble, that reduced its ability to carry out extensive external operations. In this excerpt from a 21 February 1947 aide-mémoire, the British Embassy in Washington asks for the United States to take over the British commitments in Greece and Turkey.

His Majesty's Government are giving most earnest and anxious consideration to the important problem that on strategic and political grounds Greece and Turkey should not be allowed to fall under Soviet influence.

2. It will be remembered that at the Paris Peace Conference Mr. Byrnes expressed full realisation of the great importance of this question and proposed that the United States Government should give active help in sustaining the economic and military position in those two countries, the United States Government in particular taking care of the economic side.

3. On various occasions subsequent to the meeting referred to above the United States Government have exchanged views with His Majesty's Government, indicating the acute interest of the United States Government in the future of Greece, and from these exchanges His Majesty's Government have understood that the United States Government does not exclude the possibility of helping Greece on the military side as well as the economic.

4. The State Department will recollect the conversation between Mr. Byrnes and the Minister of Defence which took place on the 15th October, 1946, subsequent to which the whole question of British military and economic help for Greece has been carefully examined by His Majesty's Government. On the economic side, the reports received by His Majesty's Government from their representatives in Greece show that the Greek economic situation is on the point of collapse, owing to the virtual exhaustion of Greece's foreign exchange reserves and the low level of industrial activity resulting from political instability.

5. The United States Government are as well aware as His Majesty's Government that unless Greece can obtain help from outside there is certain to be widespread starvation and consequent political disturbances during the present year (…) it is most urgent that the United States Government should be able to decide what economic help they will give to Greece and what form it will take.

7. On the military side, Greek needs have been very carefully considered by the British military authorities during the last few months (…) His Majesty's Government have agreed to pay the foreign exchange cost of the Greek armed forces, both in regard to maintenance and initial equipment, until the 31st March next (…) This, in view of H.M.G.'s financial difficulties, can be regarded as a very generous measure of assistance to Greek reconstruction. Hitherto the Greek armed forces have been built up on an establishment which allows for an army of 100,000 men, the total foreign exchange cost of which is estimated at about £16 million a year. In order to meet the present emergency caused by the bandits, the British service authorities consider that the Greek armed forces should now be reorganised to enable them to make an all-out assault on the bandits in the Spring (…)

(…) the total amount of assistance for civilian and military needs which Greece requires during 1947 appears to be between £60 million and £70 million. His Majesty's Government have already strained their resources to the utmost to help Greece and have granted, or undertaken to grant, assistance up to 31st March, 1947 to the amount of £40 million. The United States Government will readily understand that His Majesty's Government, in view of their own situation, find it impossible to grant further financial assistance to Greece. Since, however, the United States Government have indicated the very great importance which they attach to helping Greece, His Majesty's Government trust that the United States Government may find it possible to afford financial assistance to Greece on a scale sufficient to meet her minimum needs, both civil and military.

(…) His Majesty's Ambassador is instructed to express the earnest hope of His Majesty's Government that, if a joint policy of effective and practical support for Greece is to be maintained, the United States Government will agree to bear, as from the 1st of April, 1947, the financial burden, of which the major part has hitherto been borne by His Majesty's Government (…)

4.4 The Truman Doctrine, March 1947

The Truman Administration responded favourably to British and Greek requests for aid in the ongoing Civil War in Greece. In this address, that was soon dubbed the Truman Doctrine, the US president asks for Congress to support an aid package. Truman's use of language is notable for its emphasis on concepts such as 'survival' and 'freedom'.

(…) One aspect of the present situation, which I wish to present to you at this time for your consideration and decision, concerns Greece and Turkey.

The United States has received from the Greek Government an urgent appeal for financial and economic assistance. Preliminary reports from the American Economic Mission now in Greece and reports from the American Ambassador in Greece corroborate the statement of the Greek Government that assistance is imperative if Greece is to survive as a free nation (…)

Greece is today without funds to finance the importation of those goods which are essential to bare subsistence. Under these circumstances the people of Greece cannot make progress in solving their problems of reconstruction. Greece is in desperate need of financial and economic assistance to enable it to resume pur-chases of food, clothing, fuel and seeds. These are indispensable for the subsis-tence of its people and are obtainable only from abroad. Greece must have help to import the goods necessary to restore internal order and security, so essential for economic and political recovery (…)

The very existence of the Greek state is today threatened by the terrorist activities of several thousand armed men, led by Communists, who defy the government's authority at a number of points, particularly along the northern boundaries. A Commission appointed by the United Nations Security Council is at present investigating disturbed conditions in northern Greece and alleged border violations along the frontier between Greece on the one hand and Albania, Bulgaria, and Yugoslavia on the other.

Meanwhile, the Greek Government is unable to cope with the situation. The Greek army is small and poorly equipped. It needs supplies and equipment if it is to restore the authority of the government throughout Greek territory. Greece must have assistance if it is to become a self-supporting and self-respecting democracy.

The United States must supply that assistance. We have already extended to Greece certain types of relief and economic aid but these are inadequate. There is no other country to which democratic Greece can turn (…) The British Gov-ernment, which has been helping Greece, can give no further financial or eco-nomic aid after March 31 (…) We have considered how the United Nations might assist in this crisis. But the situation is an urgent one requiring immediate action and the United Nations and its related organizations are not in a position to extend help of the kind that is required (…)

No government is perfect. One of the chief virtues of a democracy, however, is that its defects are always visible and under democratic processes can be pointed out and corrected. The Government of Greece is not perfect. Nevertheless it represents eighty-five per cent of the members of the Greek Parliament who were chosen in an election last year. Foreign observers, including 692 Americans, considered this election to be a fair expression of the views of the Greek people.

The Greek Government has been operating in an atmosphere of chaos and extremism. It has made mistakes. The extension of aid by this country does not mean that the United States condones everything that the Greek Government has done or will do. We have condemned in the past, and we condemn now, extremist measures of the right or the left. We have in the past advised tolerance, and we advise tolerance now.

Greece's neighbor, Turkey, also deserves our attention.

The future of Turkey as an independent and economically sound state is clearly no less important to the freedom-loving peoples of the world than the future of Greece. The circumstances in which Turkey finds itself today are considerably different from those of Greece. Turkey has been spared the disasters that have beset Greece. And during the war, the United States and Great Britain furnished Turkey with material aid (...) Since the war Turkey has sought financial assistance from Great Britain and the United States for the purpose of effecting that modernization necessary for the maintenance of its national integrity. That integrity is essential to the preservation of order in the Middle East.

The British government has informed us that, owing to its own difficulties, it can no longer extend financial or economic aid to Turkey. As in the case of Greece, if Turkey is to have the assistance it needs, the United States must supply it. We are the only country able to provide that help.

(...) One of the primary objectives of the foreign policy of the United States is the creation of conditions in which we and other nations will be able to work out a way of life free from coercion. This was a fundamental issue in the war with Germany and Japan. Our victory was won over countries which sought to impose their will, and their way of life, upon other nations (...) We shall not realize our objectives, however, unless we are willing to help free peoples to maintain their free institutions and their national integrity against aggressive movements that seek to impose upon them totalitarian regimes. This is no more than a frank recognition that totalitarian regimes imposed on free peoples, by direct or indirect aggression, undermine the foundations of international peace and hence the security of the United States (...)

At the present moment in world history nearly every nation must choose between alternative ways of life (...) One way of life is based upon the will of the majority, and is distinguished by free institutions, representative government, free elections, guarantees of individual liberty, freedom of speech and religion, and freedom from political oppression. The second way of life is based upon the will of a minority forcibly imposed upon the majority. It relies upon terror and oppression, a controlled press and radio, fixed elections, and the suppression of personal freedoms.

I believe that it must be the policy of the United States to support free peoples who are resisting attempted subjugation by armed minorities or by outside pressures. I believe that we must assist free peoples to work out their own destinies in their own way. I believe that our help should be primarily through economic and financial aid which is essential to economic stability and orderly political processes (…)

It is necessary only to glance at a map to realize that the survival and integrity of the Greek nation are of grave importance in a much wider situation. If Greece should fall under the control of an armed minority, the effect upon its neighbor, Turkey, would be immediate and serious. Confusion and disorder might well spread throughout the entire Middle East. Moreover, the disappearance of Greece as an independent state would have a profound effect upon those countries in Europe whose peoples are struggling against great difficulties to maintain their freedoms and their independence while they repair the damages of war.

It would be an unspeakable tragedy if these countries, which have struggled so long against overwhelming odds, should lose that victory for which they sacrificed so much. Collapse of free institutions and loss of independence would be disastrous not only for them but for the world. Discouragement and possibly failure would quickly be the lot of neighboring peoples striving to maintain their freedom and independence.

Should we fail to aid Greece and Turkey in this fateful hour, the effect will be far reaching to the West as well as to the East. We must take immediate and resolute action. I therefore ask the Congress to provide authority for assistance to Greece and Turkey (…) In addition to funds, I ask the Congress to authorize the detail of American civilian and military personnel to Greece and Turkey, at the request of those countries, to assist in the tasks of reconstruction, and for the purpose of supervising the use of such financial and material assistance as may be furnished. I recommend that authority also be provided for the instruction and training of selected Greek and Turkish personnel. Finally, I ask that the Congress provide authority which will permit the speediest and most effective use, in terms of needed commodities, supplies, and equipment, of such funds as may be authorized (…) This is an investment in world freedom and world peace (…)

The seeds of totalitarian regimes are nurtured by misery and want. They spread and grow in the evil soil of poverty and strife. They reach their full growth when the hope of a people for a better life has died. We must keep that hope alive.

4.5 Janet Flanner on Life in Paris, 1946 and 1948

In her writings the American journalist Janet Flanner ('Genet') captured the mood on the streets of Paris during the 1940s. In the following two excerpts she describes the situation in early 1946 and in the spring of 1948.

A. 3 January 1946

On New Year's Day here this year there was more food on the plate, if less hope in the heart, than there was last year. A year ago there were still empty stomachs and heads were light not only with hunger but with desperate notions of a better world to come. The three most important things that have happened to France since last January 1st have been disillusion, devaluation, and the continued dominance of General Charles de Gaulle. All these happenings have been normal to the times. France today has little chance for the abnormal.

Achieving what amounted to a total surprise to the Paris population, the shops at Christmastime were suddenly filled with practically everything but the money to buy it with. Along with diamond bracelets, there were inelegant rabbit-skin moccasins—at the price of a midinette's weekly wage—for the icy, unheated home. There were grapefruit for the first time since 1939, at what a laboring man got then for four days' work. The butcher shops were crowded with the old-time, statuesque figures of sacrificial lambs, marble-white with fat and at such high, though legal, prices that the butchers have threatened to close up shop and hand the whole business back to the government, which has already taken back bread. Before the October elections, de Gaulle's government derationed bread, thus trading bread tickets for votes in a smart political move which elected its deputies, who are now faced once again with a wheat shortage. Under the new rationing, the government will give each person only three slices a day more than the Nazis gave in 1942, the worst of all years for those poorer French who practically live by bread alone. All over Europe, government has become a sort of harried, shabby, food-spotted maître d'hôtel fumbling over the menu of what its people will eat next and wondering who will pay the political and financial bill.

23 January 1946

The only flash of brightness that General de Gaulle's resignation brought was a political witticism which was not even true: 'What we now have is a de Gaulle government without de Gaulle.' Otherwise, his striding out of the Presidency left French morale in a state of empty gloom. This past fortnight has obviously been the worst here since the war ended. In Paris, the sense of crisis has been greater than in any other peacetime period since the February 6th riots of 1934, when there was at least the effervescence of fresh political hopes. The malaise is quieter but deeper now. There is no feverish surface reaction that might stir citizens into doing anything. The four years of occupation, the obedience to hundreds of orders, and the thousands of hours the French have spent in queues seem to have taken the old, violent, animated crowd spirit out of them. This is perhaps a good, perhaps a bad, thing; anyway, it is a new thing for Parisians. They act like people who know that there is nothing they can do except stand, as usual, and wait. The French are waiting to be governed.

B. 2 April 1948

On the surface, France has improved so much in the last six months that all that is lacking is the belief that the vital, invisible underpinnings of state and society can hold the improvements in place. The average Frenchman can now find in the shops nearly everything he wants except the means of paying for it. In midtown Paris shop windows, perfect taste, which is the supreme French luxury, has at last reappeared. On the farms, the hedges have been trimmed and the ditches have been cleaned out, the farmers having profited from what may be the last year of German-prisoner farm labor. By day, in the limpid spring sunshine, Paris looks her old, beautiful self, reclining full length in the greenery by the Seine. By night, the city is lighted but largely deserted; restaurants are half empty and cafés are closed for lack of clients. Parisians dine at home, on soup, and go to bed. The rise in the birthrate here may be accidentally patriotic, but it is also alarming, considering the world shortage of food. Since the recent freeing of the franc and of the prices of most edibles and other goods, the frantic black-market bustle for necessities to eat and wear has quieted down. Paris is hovering around a new norm; the new heavy tax increases, the special fiscal levies, and the seizure of five-thousand-franc notes have combined to produce an odd, un-Gallic stoicism that is a substitute for morality. The anti-inflationary government, still insisting that the sellers' margin of profit is too wide, is using pressure to hold retail prices down, and has made a first public example of the vegetable market-man. In the spinach basket in his grocery shop or on his lettuce cart by the curb, he is forced to placard his cost price as well as his selling price. The fixers and the middlemen in the gray market—the nibblers rather than the producers—are the only business groups making big money. Factory workers say that wages must go up; factory owners say that prices cannot come down any farther without economic suicide. For political reasons, both sides exaggerate their difficulties, which are nevertheless real, and which are opposite. It is this absolute diametricism that is cutting France into two bleeding, anemic, and perhaps impermanent parts.

Many important items are still rationed. Except for doctors, taxi-drivers, and other specialists, the French do not get a drop of gasoline. Because the government acutely needs tourist dollars, gasoline flows in fountains for American tourists, as well as for abashed American jounalists (French journalists get nearly none) for whom the liberated franc makes life nice and cheap anyway. The French operate on costly black-market gasoline coupons that trickle down from the Brittany fishing ports, where fishermen make more money by selling them than by putting out to sea in their motorboats and catching fish. The farmers also oblige, by selling their tractor gasoline coupons. Parisian adults have had no butter ration since Christmas and this month their quarter-pound monthly coffee ration is to be skipped, but they received a government Easter present—a rationed tin of sardines, at thirty times the prewar price. Wine is finally unrationed, but some of it is watered, or what the French call baptized, wine and spoils quickly. Compared with conditions a half year ago, there is more choice in everything and more comfort everywhere, except in the average French pocketbook. France is in a curious, momentarily excellent position of recovery. The goods are here, but the marts need faith and buyers with cash. There is a lot of intelligent skepticism as to what tomorrow and tomorrow will be in France, in Europe, and on this earth. France is like someone who has unexpectedly climbed a very high hill and stands breathless and poised on the crest.

4.6 The Marshall Plan Speech, 5 June 1947

After careful planning, and amid growing concern over the political effects of the continued economic difficulties in post-war Europe, the Truman administration launched the Marshall Plan (the European Recovery Program). It got its name from Secretary of State George Marshall, who unveiled the plan in a commencement address at Harvard University in June 1947.

(…) the people of this country are distant from the troubled areas of the earth and it is hard for them to comprehend the plight and consequent reactions of the long-suffering peoples, and the effect of those reactions on their governments in connection with our efforts to promote peace in the world.

In considering the requirements for the rehabilitation of Europe, the physical loss of life, the visible destruction of cities, factories, mines, and railroads was correctly estimated, but it has become obvious during recent months that this visible destruction was probably less serious than the dislocation of the entire fabric of European economy. For the past 10 years conditions have been highly abnormal. The feverish preparation for war and the more feverish maintenance of the war effort engulfed all aspects of national economies. Machinery has fallen into disrepair or is entirely obsolete. Under the arbitrary and destructive Nazi rule, virtually every possible enterprise was geared into the German war machine. Long-standing commercial ties, private institutions, banks, insurance companies, and shipping companies disappeared, through loss of capital, absorption through nationalization, or by simple destruction. In many countries, confidence in the local currency has been severely shaken. The breakdown of the business structure of Europe during the war was complete. Recovery has been seriously retarded by the fact that two years after the close of hostilities a peace settlement with Germany and Austria has not been agreed upon. But even given a more prompt solution of these difficult problems, the rehabilitation of the economic structure of Europe quite evidently will require a much longer time and greater effort than had been foreseen (…)

The truth of the matter is that Europe's requirements for the next three or four years of foreign food and other essential products—principally from America— are so much greater than her present ability to pay that she must have substantial additional help or face economic, social, and political deterioration of a very grave character (…)

Aside from the demoralizing effect on the world at large and the possibilities of disturbances arising as a result of the desperation of the people concerned, the consequences to the economy of the United States should be apparent to all. It is logical that the United States should do whatever it is able to do to assist in the return of normal economic health in the world, without which there can be no political stability and no assured peace.

Our policy is directed not against any country or doctrine but against hunger, poverty, desperation, and chaos. Its purpose should be the revival of a working economy in the world so as to permit the emergence of political and social conditions in which free institutions can exist. Such assistance, I am convinced, must not be on a piecemeal basis as various crises develop. Any assistance that this Government may render in the future should provide a cure rather than a mere palliative. Any government that is willing to assist in the task of recovery will find full cooperation, I am sure, on the part of the United States Government. Any government which maneuvers to block the recovery of other countries cannot expect help from us. Furthermore, governments, political parties, or groups which seek to perpetuate human misery in order to profit therefrom politically or otherwise will encounter the opposition of the United States.

It is already evident that, before the United States Government can proceed much further in its efforts to alleviate the situation and help start the European world on its way to recovery, there must be some agreement among the countries of Europe as to the requirements of the situation and the part those countries themselves will take in order to give proper effect to whatever action might be undertaken by this Government. It would be neither fitting nor efficacious for this Government to undertake to draw up unilaterally a program designed to place Europe on its feet economically. This is the business of the Europeans. The initiative, I think, must come from Europe. The role of this country should consist of friendly aid in the drafting of a European program and of later support of such a program so far as it may be practical for us to do so. The program should be a joint one, agreed to by a number, if not all, European nations (…)

4.7 Vincent Auriol on the Paris Meeting, July 1947

Soon after the Marshall Plan speech the planning for the ERP began. In its initial stages the Soviets were involved but, as French President Vincent Auriol's diary notes indicate, the Franco-British-Soviet conference soon led to disagreements over the structure of the aid programme. After a few meetings in Paris in July 1947 the Soviets walked out of the tripartite conference. A number of Eastern European countries quickly followed suit.

2nd of July [1947]

At the end of the afternoon, I learn that the Three Powers Conference has failed. Molotov bluntly ensured that the new French proposals were rejected and he did not come up with a counter-project. I am not surprised. The communiqué from the *Tass* agency that charged France and Britain with wanting to impose their domination over small countries had made me fear this failure. One more time, Molotov justified his attitude by declaring that the plan implied interference in internal affairs of each country, whereas Bevin, Bidault, and Marshall said the contrary. Moreover, Bidault's project well specified that it was not an empty promise but on the contrary that everything was organized so that the countries' independence would be safeguarded. Besides, to claim that the envisioned organization assured French and British domination is a proof of bad faith. One should read over the texts to see that France, Britain, but also the Soviet Union are *de jure* part of the commission. Three other European countries are representing the remaining states and consequently no one could prevail; it would be co-operation. In addition, he declared that European States would be controlled whereas in reality the purpose of the organization is to ensure their complete national independence. The new element is that Molotov put the German question forward and this is a quite insidious propaganda theme. It argues that with the use of pooled resources, Germany would avoid paying the reparations it owes to the nations it has ruined.

Lastly, a new argument, he (Molotov) claims that Bidault's project would divide Europe, when in reality it is clear that the actual aim is to unite Europe; but it may be exactly this that bothered Molotov and the Soviet Union. Had the United States wanted to impose their presence and run Europe, they would have resorted to bilateral negotiations with every State (...) But nothing of the kind. On the contrary the unfolding Europe would, by itself, divide up resources as well as the Marshall Plan. Concerning the idea of freeing Germany from reparations, this is an absurdity. Indeed, because there is no German government, Germany would not have been represented in the conferences, the commissions or the ad hoc committees. Moreover, this body would have included the nations Germany has devastated and occupied: how can one believe that they would have given up their reparations? The issue of German reparations is outside the

Marshall Plan framework. It is a matter of ensuring those countries' independence, their co-operation in order to solve all European problems. The truth is that from the very first day, the Soviet Union was hostile to the Marshall Plan. Conversations had been held at the Soviet Embassy with Communist party elected representatives, only to explain the USSR attitude; the Soviet Union did not want to shatter small nations' hopes because Poland, Czechoslovakia, and some other small Eastern States had agreed to the Marshall Plan and they reckoned on it to recover and to rebuild their ruined economy. It would have been impossible for the Soviet Union to exploit small satellite States' economies in the way it has already begun to; besides the Soviet Union fears Germany and is afraid of the external situation; it is obvious that that the USSR wants to barricade itself in its corner with a belt of satellites around and that is what determined its attitude; but it remains true that this terrible blow struck at men's hopes and at peace will be deeply resented. I know very well that the arguments Molotov presented are propaganda tools that will be used by the Communist party but those are bad faith arguments and it will be easy to discount them (…)

11ᵗʰ of July [1947]

Bidault informs the Cabinet about membership of the Marshall Plan. In Hungary, he says, every minister and public opinion is willing to accept (…) The obstacle comes from the Communist party (…) In Prague, Clementis, the Communist under-secretary of state, the true foreign policy decision-maker, said to the French and British ambassadors that his government had changed its mind after a number of allied States linked by common interests had expressed their opinion. He looked very embarrassed because he had received a phone call from Moscow ordering him to refuse in turn. He was obviously aware that his country had been humiliated and that national independence had suffered a heavy blow.

I read a telegram from our ambassador in Finland. The Finnish foreign minister appeared very nervous, it seems, when the invitations for the Paris Conference were issued. Finland needs Western help but is also willing to maintain good relationships with Moscow. Depending on the choice Finland will make, the consequences could be tragic for her. The peace treaty has not been ratified yet, the USSR holds this country in its hands. The Soviet control commission continues to present contradictory demands on every issue. Finland will have to yield to a Russian veto. The minister hopes there will be no veto. On the same day a press release announced (…) that the USSR would deliver to Finland 40,000 tons of cereals.

15ᵗʰ of July [1947]

Towards the end of the afternoon, Dejean, ambassador in Prague, comes to keep me informed about the events. Before coming here, he had a conversation with

Masaryk and Drtina. Here is the gist of it: before meeting with the Czech delegation, Stalin discussed with the prime minister, Mr Gottwald, and he obtained his firm promise that Czechoslovakia would not take part in the conference. They talked for one hour. Gottwald described the head of the Soviet government as a very irritated man, who insisted on cancelling immediately the decisions that had been taken. Then, confident about the result, he appeared serene and friendly at the meeting of 11:00 pm. He declared that after Molotov had returned, he thought for a while that countries such as Poland, Yugoslavia, and Czechoslovakia could participate in the Paris conference in spite of the Soviet abstention; but the Soviet government received from its ambassadors converging information indicating that the Paris conference was part of a larger plan that aimed at isolating Soviet Russia. He also said that one essential point of the plan was the priority given to the German economic recovery and especially to the recovery of the Ruhr Valley, which is destined to become the industrial basis of the Western bloc. In these circumstances Stalin said the Soviet government was led to think it impossible for Russia's friends to participate. Therefore, faced with this anti-Soviet crusade, Soviet friendship will be conditional on the attitude the Czechoslovak government will opt for. Masaryk tried to win acceptance for the idea that his government could be represented during the first part of the debate and could then withdraw. Drtina pointed out that 70 per cent of the Czechoslovak foreign trade was dependent on Western powers; Stalin brushed Masaryk's proposal aside and after a two-hour discussion, Beneš resigned himself while saying that both the USSR and Czechoslovakia were making a serious mistake.

Masaryk was particularly amazed by Stalin's insistence on the danger that could arise from a Germany back on its feet thanks to American credits, just as after World War I, and by his assertion that the Marshall Plan aimed at isolating the USSR just as had been done during the inter-war years. Dejean replied that France would never join in an effort to restore Germany's power and she proved that her deeds reflected her words.

1ˢᵗ of August [1947]

Lunch with Léon Blum.[2] I tell him about my misgivings. Europe and the world are more and more divided. I tell him what is happening confirms the opinion I expressed in my book *Hier–Demain* [Yesterday–Tomorrow] concerning the necessity we faced already during the war to make precise, using treaties between co-belligerents, what Europe and international relations would be after the war.

I remind him of our letters and the conversations we had at the beginning of the war and after. For me, the mistake that was made when the USSR entered the war comes to light; happy about the Russian contribution, we were forgetting the Russian aggression on Poland, on Finland, and the occupation of the Baltic

States. At this time the USSR needed all the Allies. In turn, they needed the USSR. It was the given moment to establish together just war aims and conditions for peace. The mistake got worse at Yalta where, by fear of a separate peace treaty between Germany and Russia, Roosevelt and Churchill gave in to Soviet demands concerning their Eastern borders up to the Oder; at the Potsdam Conference the situation worsened again. The partition of Germany into four zones, with the Big Two getting more than their fair share; the USSR reserved for itself the richest and neighbouring part, which is now being sovietized and integrated in its empire. The fact that France got the poorest part makes the situation even worse. We repeated the mistakes that had been made at Versailles. The price will be bitter and may even be bloody.

Léon Blum shares my pessimistic view. According to him, what is really serious is the fact that everyone considers his zone as his property and consequently, instead of uniting the Allies, they are being divided. A joint occupation should have taken place and thus the first international army planned by the UN could have been organized. As this army will never come into being, the UN will obviously be an ineffective instrument, a council lacking sanctions capability and power.

I entirely agree, but what is to be done now? To try to rebuild the lost unity? Because it is lost, there are two blocs, as the Marshall Plan controversy proved. Léon Blum said we have to go on with the option we have adopted. We have to fight until the end, even until despair, to prevent this situation from crystallizing, this Eastern bloc versus the Western bloc.

4.8 Vyshinsky Speech to the United Nations General Assembly, September 1947

In this speech to the UN General Assembly in September 1947, Soviet deputy foreign minister Andrei Vyshinsky outlined his government's interpretation of the Marshall Plan.

(…) The so-called Truman Doctrine and the Marshall Plan are particularly glaring examples of the manner in which the principles of the United Nations are violated, of the way in which the organization is ignored.

As the experience of the past few months has shown, the proclamation of this doctrine meant that the United States government has moved towards a direct renunciation of the principles of international collaboration and concerted action by the great powers and towards attempts to impose its will on other independent states, while at the same time obviously using the economic

3. Molotov pulls down the Marshall Plan. L'enfant terrible. 'He's done it again.' (Ernest H. Shepard, *Punch*, 9 July 1947). Reprinted by permission. Photo supplied by The Centre for the Study of Cartoons and Caricature, University of Kent.

resources distributed as relief to individual needy nations as an instrument of political pressure. This is clearly proved by the measures taken by the United States government with regard to Greece and Turkey which ignore and bypass the United Nations as well as by the measures proposed under the so-called Marshall Plan in Europe. This policy conflicts sharply with the principle expressed by the General Assembly in its resolution of 11 December 1946, which declares that relief supplies to other countries 'should (...) at no time be used as a political weapon.'

As is now clear, the Marshall Plan constitutes in essence merely a variant of the Truman Doctrine adapted to the conditions of postwar Europe. In bringing forward this plan, the United States government apparently counted on the cooperation of governments of the United Kingdom and France to confront the European countries in need of relief with the necessity of renouncing their inalienable right to dispose of their economic resources and to plan their national economy in their own way. The United States also counted on making all these countries directly dependent on the interests of American monopolies, which are striving to avert the approaching depression by an accelerated export of commodities and capital to Europe (...)

It is becoming more and more evident to everyone that the implementation of the Marshall Plan will mean placing European countries under the economic and political control of the United States and direct interference by the latter in the internal affairs of those countries.

Moreover, this plan is an attempt to split Europe into two camps and, with the help of the United Kingdom and France, to complete the formation of a bloc of several European countries hostile to the interests of the democratic countries of Eastern Europe and most particularly to the interests of the Soviet Union.

An important feature of this plan is the attempt to confront the countries of Eastern Europe with a bloc of Western European states including Western Germany. The intention is to make use of Western Germany and German heavy industry (the Ruhr) as one of the most important economic bases for American expansion in Europe, in disregard of the national interests of the countries which suffered from German aggression.

I need only recall these facts to show the utter incompatibility of this policy of the United States, and of the British and French governments which support it, with the fundamental principles of the United Nations.

4.9 The US State Department on NATO, 2 November 1948

In 1948 the United States became involved in the planning for a North Atlantic military alliance. Finally concluded in April 1949, NATO's significance raised a great deal of concern among American foreign-policy planners. Some of these concerns are summarized in this study, made under the auspices of the State Department's Policy Planning Staff (headed by George F. Kennan) in the fall of 1948.

1. *Misconceptions as to the significance of the pact*

There is danger that we will deceive ourselves, and permit misconceptions to exist among our own public and in Europe, concerning the significance of the conclusion of such a pact at this time.

It is particularly difficult to assess the role of such a pact in our foreign policy for the reason that there is valid long-term justification for a formalization, by international agreement, of the natural defense relationship among the countries of the North Atlantic community. Such a formalization could contribute to the general sense of security in the area; facilitate the development of defensive power throughout the area; and act as a deterrent to outside aggressive forces.

It is therefore desirable, quite aside from the situation of the moment in Europe, that we proceed deliberately, and with careful study to the elaboration and negotiation of such an agreement.

On the other hand, it is important to understand that the conclusion of such a pact is not the main answer to the present Soviet effort to dominate the European continent, and will not appreciably modify the nature or danger of Soviet policies.

A military danger, arising from possible incidents or from the prestige engagement of the Russians and the western powers in the Berlin situation, does exist, and is probably increasing rather than otherwise. But basic Russian intent still runs to the conquest of western Europe by political means. In this program, military force plays a major role only as a means of intimidation.

The danger of political conquest is still greater than the military danger. If a war comes in the foreseeable future, it will probably be one which Moscow did not desire but did not know how to avoid. The political war, on the other hand, is now in progress; and, if there should not be a shooting war, it is this political war which will be decisive.

A North Atlantic Security Pact will affect the political war only insofar as it operates to stiffen the self-confidence of the western Europeans in the face of Soviet pressures. Such a stiffening is needed and desirable. But it goes hand in hand with the danger of a general preoccupation with military affairs, to the detriment of economic recovery and of the necessity for seeking a peaceful solution to Europe's difficulties.

This preoccupation is already widespread, both in Europe and in this country. It is regrettable; because it addresses itself to what is not the main danger. We have to deal with it as a reality; and to a certain extent we have to indulge it, for to neglect it would be to encourage panic and uncertainty in western Europe and to play into the hands of the Communists. But in doing so, we should have clearly in mind that the need for military alliances and rearmament on the part of the western Europeans is primarily a subjective one, arising in their own minds as a result of their failure to understand correctly their own position. Their best and most hopeful course of action, if they are to save themselves from Communist pressures, remains the struggle for economic recovery and for internal political stability.

Compared to this, intensive rearmament constitutes an uneconomic and regrettable diversion of effort. A certain amount of rearmament can be subjectively beneficial to western Europe. But if this rearmament proceeds at any appreciable cost to European recovery, it can do more harm than good. The same will be true if concentration on the rearmament effort gradually encourages the assumption that war is inevitable and that therefore no further efforts are necessary toward the political weakening and defeat of the Communist power in central and eastern Europe.

2. *The territorial scope of the pact*

The Policy Planning Staff is of the opinion that the scope of a pact of this sort should be restricted to the North Atlantic area itself, and that attempts to go further afield and to include countries beyond that area might have undesirable consequences.

The possibility of a mistake in this respect is particularly acute because we ourselves showed uncertainty on this point in the preliminary discussions of the past summer, and the final record of the results of those discussions left open the possibility of the Pact's being extended beyond the North Atlantic area.

This point was included largely at the insistence of the United States group. While it might do no great harm to have this possibility left open in the final text of the Pact, the Policy Planning Staff did not then, and does not now, agree with the thinking that lay behind this insistence.

The Staff considers that a North Atlantic security pact might properly embrace any country whose homeland or insular territories are washed by the waters of the North Atlantic, or which form part of a close union of states which meets this description. Under this concept, for example, Luxembourg would properly come into such a pact through its membership in the Benelux group. But to go beyond this, and to take in individual continental countries which do not meet this description would, in the opinion of the Staff, be unsound, for the following reasons.

In the first place, the admission of any single country beyond the North Atlantic area would be taken by others as constituting a precedent, and would almost certainly lead to a series of demands from states still further afield that they be similarly treated. Failure on our part to satisfy these further demands would then be interpreted as lack of interest in the respective countries, and as evidence that we had 'written them off' to the Russians. Beyond the Atlantic area, which is a clean-cut concept, and which embraces a real community of defense interest firmly rooted in geography and tradition, there is no logical stopping point in the development of a system of anti-Russian alliances until that system has circled the globe and has embraced all the non-Communist countries of Europe, Asia and Africa.

To get carried into any such wide system of alliances would lead only to one of two results; either all these alliances become meaningless declarations, after the pattern of the Kellogg Pact, and join the long array of dead-letter pronouncements through which governments have professed their devotion to peace in the past; or this country becomes still further over-extended, politically and militarily. In the first case, we would have made light of our own word and damaged the future usefulness of Article 51 of the United Nations Charter. In addition, we would have weakened the integrity and significance of our own defense relationship with our neighbors of the north Atlantic community. In the second case, we would be flying in the face of the solemn warning recently given by the Joint Chiefs of Staff concerning the increasing discrepancy between our commitments and our military resources.

A particularly unfortunate effect of going beyond the North Atlantic area would be that we would thereby raise for every country in Europe the question: to belong or not to belong. An issue would thus be raised which would be in many cases unnecessary and potentially embarrassing, and in some cases outright dangerous. If individual countries rejected membership or were refused membership, the Russians could make political capital out of this, either way. If, on the other hand, most of the ERP countries were permitted to join, and did so, this would amount to a final militarization of the present dividing-line through Europe. Such a development would be particularly unfortunate, for it would create a situation in which no alteration, or obliteration, of that line could take place without having an accentuated military significance. This would reduce materially the chances for Austrian and German settlements, and would make it impossible for any of the satellite countries even to contemplate anything in the nature of a gradual withdrawal from Russian domination, since any move in that direction would take on the aspect of a provocative military move.

Unquestionably, there is already a strong tendency in this direction; and it may not be possible for us to prevent a progressive congealment of the present line of division. But our present policy is still directed (and in the opinion of the Staff, rightfully so) toward the eventual peaceful withdrawal of both the United States and the U.S.S.R. from the heart of Europe, and accordingly toward the encouragement of the growth of a third force which can absorb and take over the territory between the two.

Unless we are prepared consciously to depart from this policy, to renounce hope of a peaceful solution of Europe's difficulties, and to plan our foreign policy deliberately on the assumption of a coming military conflict, we should not do things which tend to fix, and make unchangeable by peaceful means, the present line of east–west division.

The Staff feels that, rather than extending membership in the pact to non-North Atlantic powers, a much sounder way of enhancing the sense of security of other European countries would be through the implementation of the suggestion, contained in Paragraph 9 of Part 11 of the record of the recent informal discussions, that the members of the pact jointly make known their interest in the security of the given country.

This view of the Staff is without prejudice to the question of the desirability of the United States associating itself with any further regional agreements, as for example a Mediterranean pact, which question lies outside the scope of this paper.

Recommendations

In the light of the above, the Policy Planning Staff recommends:
    a. That it be accepted as the view of this Government:

(1) That there is a long-term need for a permanent formalization of the defense relationship among the countries of the North Atlantic area;
(2) That the conclusion of a North Atlantic Security Pact just at this time will have a specific short-term value in so far as it may serve to increase the sense of security on the part of the members of the Brussels Pact and of other European countries; but
(3) That, nevertheless, the conclusion of the Pact is not the main answer to the Russian effort to achieve domination over western Europe, which still appears to be primarily political in nature. The conclusion and implementation of such a pact should therefore not be considered as a replacement for the other steps which are being taken and should be taken to meet the Russian challenge, nor should they be given priority over the latter.

    b. That steps be taken to see that this view of the significance of a possible North Atlantic Security Pact be made available for background to all higher officials of the Department, to Missions in the field, and to the informational organs of this Department and other Government Departments, with a view to keeping it before the public and to combatting opposite concepts.
    c. That it be the policy of this Government not to encourage adherence to a North Atlantic Security Pact of any country not properly a part of the North Atlantic community.

4.10 Togliatti Speech Against NATO, 12 March 1949

The creation of NATO was not uniformly popular in the member countries. It raised particularly strong objections from the West European Communists. Below, the Italian Communist Party leader Palmiro Togliatti expresses his reservations about the government's policy on the eve of the Italian National Assembly's vote that ratified the country's NATO membership.

(...) Let us make it clear, then, that we shall not recognise the vote that you will undoubtedly give to this pact. We shall appeal to the Italian people, telling them that they have the right and the duty not to recognise that vote.

To have military bases of a great foreign imperialist power on one's own territory means being a military objective from the moment war breaks out.

The Atlantic Pact which you are about to sign will ensure from the moment it is signed that Italy—whether she likes it or not—will be swept by the fever of propaganda for a new war.

The pact you are about to sign will ensure that Italy will be a military objective and a theatre of war if it breaks out, or, as I should say, wherever it breaks out. Italy is one of those countries which will be 'a carpet of atom bombs', as the American strategists so elegantly express it. This is your doing.

You say that in this way you are revising the Peace Treaty. No, you are revising nothing. To revise the Peace Treaty is only possible for a country like Italy, who has suffered from the evils and disasters brought by Fascism, by working with all our might for a policy of reducing tension and of agreement and collaboration between the great Powers, and not for a policy of splitting Europe and the world. But if you do sign the aggressive Atlantic Pact, from the moment you sign it there will always be an opposition party which will remind you of all the clauses of the Peace Treaty and force you to observe them to the letter, and will keep you to the U.N. policy. And it will be you who will have provoked this state of affairs.

Moreover, you are merely repeating what the former Italian capitalist governing classes did during several decades and on too many occasions. You are barring the road towards a policy of social reform, you are barring the road to a policy of reform in South Italy, and to that policy of lowering social tension which our country needs at the moment.

We want to avoid these troubles, we want to avoid this disaster. At the present time we have no illusions about you, you leaders of the government and of the Christian Democrat Parliament. We know indeed that for the most part you do not decide your own conduct. Forces stronger than you decide your policy and impose their will upon you. Here I do not speak of foreign influences or orders, for I do not want to arouse the faintest suspicion that I wish to offend anyone. I speak mainly of those capitalist forces which, in 1911, 1915, 1935 and since, have always tried to elude their difficulties through military blocs, war alliances and war itself. We have no illusions. We hope that one of you will open your eyes in time, that many of you, my colleagues in Parliament, will open your eyes. We hope so, but if we have no illusions about you, do not you either have any illusions about our proposal.

At present, however, it is a question of a particular war—a war against the Soviet Union. Yet there will be no such war, for the people will prevent you from starting it.

We want to unite in a single front for joint action, we partisans of peace here in Italy and friends and allies of the peace campaign in the capitalist and colonial world. All who want to preserve peace are ready to fight against your war policy. In this struggle we want to be more fearless, more prepared, more able to help those opposed to war and those who want to take concrete measures for avoiding war and fulfilling a positive peace policy.

In the name of such people, we say 'no' to the Atlantic Pact, 'no' because it is a pact of preparation for war. We say 'no' to your policy, a policy of hostility and aggression against the Soviet Union. We say 'no' to the imperialist intrigues which you are plotting to the harm of the Italian people, their independence and their liberty, and we shall do everything in our power to unmask this policy of yours and make it a failure.

4.11 Soviet Protest against the Formation of NATO, March 1949

The strongest objections to NATO came, not unexpectedly, from the Soviet Union. In this extract from his 31 March 1949 letter to the US secretary of state, the Soviet ambassador to the United States, A. Paniushkin, sums up Moscow's reaction.

(…) The text of the North Atlantic Treaty has fully confirmed what was said in the declaration of the Ministry of Foreign Affairs of the USSR of January 29 of this year, both as regards the aggressive aims of this Treaty and as regards the fact that the North Atlantic Treaty is in contradiction with the principles and aims of the United Nations Organization (…)

Among the great powers only the Soviet Union is excluded from the number of the parties to this treaty, which may only be explained by the fact that this Treaty is directed against the Soviet Union (…) To justify the conclusion of the North Atlantic Treaty, reference is made to the fact that the Soviet Union has defensive treaties with the countries of people's democracy. However, these references are completely untenable.

All the treaties of the Soviet Union on friendship and mutual assistance with the countries of people's democracy have a bilateral character and are directed solely against the possibility of a repetition of German aggression, the danger of which no peace-loving nation can forget. In this connection the possibilty of interpreting them as treaties in any degree directed against the allies of the USSR in the last war, against the United States or Great Britain or France, is entirely excluded.

Moreover the USSR has similar treaties against a repetition of German aggression, not only with the countries of people's democracy, but also with Great Britain and France.

In contradiction therewith the North Atlantic Treaty is not a bilateral but a multilateral treaty which creates a closed grouping of states and, what is particularly important, entirely ignores the possibility of a repetition of German aggression, not having consequently as its aim the prevention of a new German aggression (...) the North Atlantic Treaty must be regarded as a treaty directed against one of the chief Allies of the United States, Great Britain, and France in the last war—against the USSR.

(...) The carrying out under present peace-time conditions by the United States in cooperation with Great Britain and France of extensive military measures, including an increase in all types of armed forces, the drafting of a plan for the utilization of the atomic weapon, the stockpiling of atomic bombs, which are a purely offensive weapon, the construction of a network of military air and naval bases, and so forth—have by no means a defensive character.

The preservation of a Combined Anglo-American Military Staff in Washington, organized during the second World War, the recent establishment of a military staff of the so-called Western Union in Fontainebleau (France), as well as the intention to establish immediately a Defense Committee provided by the North Atlantic Treaty are by no means an indication of the peace-loving or defensive aims of the parties to the Treaty, but along with other numerous military preparations contribute to intensifying anxiety, alarm and the whipping up of war hysteria, in which all kinds of instigators of a new war are so interested.

The North Atlantic Treaty is designed to frighten states which do not agree to submit to the dictates of the Anglo-American grouping of powers, which aspire to world domination (...) At the same time one cannot but see the groundlessness of the anti-Soviet motives of the North Atlantic Treaty, since as everyone knows the Soviet Union does not intend to attack anyone and in no way threatens either the United States of America, Great Britain, France, or other parties to the Treaty.

The conclusion of the North Atlantic Treaty and the establishment of a new grouping of powers is motivated by the weakness of the United Nations Organization. It is quite evident however that the North Atlantic Treaty does not serve the cause of strengthening the United Nations Organization but on the contrary leads to undermining the very foundations of this international organization, as the establishment of the mentioned grouping of powers not only does not correspond to the aims and principles of the UNO but contradicts the Charter of this Organization (...) It is clear that references to Articles 51 and 52 of the UNO Charter are untenable and designed solely to cover up the real aggressive aims of the military grouping of states which is being established by the conclusion of the North Atlantic Treaty.

No one can deny that the North Atlantic Treaty and, first of all, Article 5 of this Treaty, is in direct contradiction with the Charter of the United Nations Organization. The text of Article 53 of the Charter which speaks of enforcement actions, in accordance with regional agreements, states directly that 'no enforcement action shall be taken under regional agreements or by regional agencies without the authorization of the Security Council' with the exception of measures specifically provided with regard to former enemy states. In spite of this, Article 5 of the North Atlantic Treaty envisages the application of armed force by parties to the treaty without any authority whatsoever from the Security Council (...)

Questions

What kind of similarities and differences can one detect in George Kennan and Nikolai Novikov's analyses of the respective Soviet and American post-war goals?

Why did the British have to abandon Greece in 1947?

What similarities and/or differences can you detect in the tone and focus of Truman and Marshall's speeches?

How would you describe everyday life in Paris after the war?

Did French President Vincent Auriol see the East–West division as an inevitable consequence of the Marshall Plan?

What accounts for the negative Soviet reaction to the Marshall Plan?

What considerations weighed on the US decision to form NATO?

What were the arguments for and against Italy's NATO membership?

5

The United States and Japan, 1945–1965

World War II had been a disaster for East Asia and for Japan, as it had been for Europe. For the Japanese, the war against the United States and its allies had led to the destruction through bombing of much of their economic superstructure, and many people had begun to lose faith in the authoritarian system of government, centred around the Emperor. The American nuclear bombing of Hiroshima and Nagasaki in August 1945, and the Soviet entry into the Pacific war immediately afterwards, made the Japanese elites decide that they would have to accept the US demand for unconditional surrender.

As it became clear to the Japanese authorities that the war was lost, they worried more about social instability and the Communist threat than about the effects of a foreign occupation. The US policy of keeping Soviet forces out of Japan suited the traditional power-holders in Tokyo well. Still, the initial insistence of the Allied occupation regime, headed by US General Douglas MacArthur, on basic social, economic, and political reform and the political exclusion of prominent members of the wartime regime led to fears that the occupiers would force radical change. In order to prevent such change, the Japanese authorities were willing to extend all possible favours to the occupying forces, as long as they themselves would be protected against a challenge from the left.

Already by late 1947 it had become clear that the United States was more concerned by the Cold War threat from the Soviet Union in East Asia than by the entrenchment of the Japanese conservatives. In a shift in policy, often referred to as the 'reverse course', the US occupation authorities began to assist the Japanese government to curtail the activities of left-wing politicians, student activists, and labour leaders. Japanese support would be essential, the Truman administration thought, to confront the threat from Moscow and the Chinese Communists, and such support could only be based on stability within Japan itself.

The North Korean attack on South Korea seemed to confirm the necessity of Japan as a Cold War ally. Talks on a peace settlement between Tokyo and the Western allies had already begun before the outbreak of war in Korea, but was speeded up, on US insistence, in 1951. A bilateral US–Japan Security Treaty was negotiated first, and after Yoshida Shigeru's government had removed the last obstacle by agreeing to a US Senate demand to recognize Chiang Kai-shek's Chinese government on Taiwan, the peace treaty was ratified in April 1952. Japan had regained its sovereignty, but only within the framework of a close alliance with the United States.

In spite of the best efforts of Japanese conservatives, such as Prime Minister Yoshida, to prevent it, Japan's had become a more culturally and politically open system under American tutelage. Economically, however, Japan remained closed to outsiders. By the mid-1950s the Japanese government, headed by the conservative Liberal Democratic Party (LDP), had instituted a vigorous policy of promoting export industries while discouraging imports from abroad. Well protected by the security relationship with the United States, the LDP governments showed no inclination to rearm, in spite of recurrent (but secret) American proposals for them to do so. The Eisenhower administration, therefore, found itself in the slightly ironic position of defending what was rapidly becoming a main international competitor, while being subject to intense criticism by the Japanese left for talks to revise the Security Treaty and the continued occupation of the island of Okinawa, used by the Americans as a military base. The president's 1960 cancellation of a visit to Japan, because Tokyo could not guarantee his safety in face of angry protests, marked a nadir in the US–Japanese diplomatic relationship.

The 1960 events forced the resignation of Prime Minister Kishi Nobusuke, a former indicted war criminal who for some time had been a US favourite. His successor, Ikeda Hayato, and other LDP leaders in the 1960s and 1970s, settled into a close alliance relationship with the United States, buying off American pressure to remilitarize with secret acceptance of US forces using Japanese territory as forward bases in the Cold War. Ikeda, the former director of the Ministry of International Trade and Industry, also began a limited liberalization of Japanese markets, while setting out a comprehensive plan for future export-led economic growth. As long as the Cold War was at its peak, Washington was willing to indirectly fund a gigantic Japanese economic resurgence.

Readings

John W. Dower, *Embracing Defeat: Japan in the Wake of World War II* (1999). A brilliant reinterpretation of the changes in Japan during the American occupation.

John W. Dower, *Empire and Aftermath: Yoshida Shigeru and the Japanese Experience* (1989). The career of a leading conservative politician, who served as prime minister 1946–7 and 1949–54.

Aaron Forsberg, *America and the Japanese Miracle: The Cold War Context of Japan's*

Postwar Economic Revival, 1950–1960 (2000). A new view of the American role in re-
creating the Japanese economy in the 1950s.

Sodei Rinjiro and John Junkerman (eds.), *Dear General MacArthur: Letters From
the Japanese During the American Occupation* (2001). An excellent look into how the
Japanese tried to live with the occupation.

Michael Schaller, *Altered States: The United States and Japan Since the Occupation* (1997).
The best overview of US–Japanese relations in the post-occupation period.

5.1 The Nuclear Bomb: Nagasaki, August 1945

*In August 1945 the United States used nuclear weapons in war for the first and so far only
time in history. The Japanese doctor Akizuki Tatsuichiro recorded the effects of the attack.*

On Thursday, 9 August, the boundless blue sky, the loud shrilling of cicadas,
promised another day as hot and as sultry as the day before.

At 8.30 I began the medical examination and treatment of out-patients.
Nearly thirty had turned up by ten o'clock. Some were patients requiring
artificial pneumo-thorax (the temporary collapsing of a lung); they had been
entrusted to us by Takahara Hospital, 5,000 meters away (…)

It was eleven o'clock. Father Ishikawa, who was Korean, aged about thirty-six
and the hospital chaplain, was listening in the hospital chapel to the confessions
of those Catholics who had gone to him to confess, one after the other, before the
great festival, on 15 August, of the Ascension of the Virgin Mary, which was only
a week away. Brother Joseph Iwanaga was toiling outside the hospital with some
farm workers, digging another air-raid shelter in the shrubbery in the center of
the hospital yard. Mr. Noguchi had just begun to repair the apparatus used to lift
water from the well. Other members of staff were busy providing a late breakfast.
Some were filling big bowls with miso soup; others were carrying them through
the corridors or up the stairs. The hospital was a hive of activity after the all-clear.

'Well, we'll soon be getting our breakfast,' I said to Miss Murai. 'The patients
must be hungry.'

So was I, but before we had our breakfast we would have to finish treating all
the out-patients.

I stuck the pneumo-thorax needle into the side of the chest of the patient lying
on the bed. It was just after 11 a.m.

I heard a low droning sound, like that of distant aeroplane engines.

'What's that?' I said. 'That all-clear has gone, hasn't it?'

At the same time the sound of the plane's engines, growing louder and louder,
seemed to swoop down over the hospital.

I shouted: 'It's an enemy plane! Look out—take cover!'

As I said so, I pulled the needle out of the patient and threw myself beside the bed.

There was a blinding white flash of light, and the next moment—*Bang! Crack!* A huge impact like a gigantic blow smote down upon our bodies, our heads and our hospital. I lay flat—I didn't know whether or not of my own volition. Then down came piles of debris, slamming into my back.

The hospital has been hit, I thought. I grew dizzy, and my ears sang.

Some minutes or so must have passed before I staggered to my feet and looked around. The air was heavy with yellow smoke; white flakes of powder drifted about; it was strangely dark.

Thank God, I thought—I'm not hurt! But what about the patients?

As it became brighter, little by little our situation grew clearer. Miss Murai, who had been assisting me with the pneumo-thorax, struggled to her feet beside me. She didn't seem to have been seriously injured, though she was completely covered with white dust. 'Hey, cheer up!' I said. 'We're not hurt, thank God!'

I helped her to her feet. Another nurse, who was also in the consulting room, and the patient, managed to stand up. The man, his face smeared white like a clown and streaked with blood, lurched towards the door, holding his bloody head with his hands and moaning.

I said to myself over and over again: Our hospital has suffered a direct hit— We've been bombed! Because the hospital stood on a hill and had walls of red brick, it must, I thought, have attracted the attention of enemy planes. I felt deeply and personally responsible for what had happened.

The pervading dingy yellow silence of the room now resounded with faint cries—'Help!' The surface of the walls and ceiling had peeled away. What I had thought to be clouds of dust or smoke was whirling brick-dust and plaster. Neither the pneumo-thorax apparatus nor the microscope on my desk were anywhere to be seen. I felt as if I were dreaming.

I encouraged Miss Murai, saying: 'Come on, we haven't been hurt at all, by the grace of God. We must rescue the in-patients.' But privately I thought it must be all over with them—the second and third floors must have disintegrated, I thought.

We went to the door of the consulting room which faced the main stairway, and there were the in-patients coming down the steps, crying: 'Help me, doctor! Oh, help me, sir.' The stairs and the corridor were heaped with timbers, plaster, debris from the ceiling. It made walking difficult. The patients staggered down towards us, crying: 'I'm hurt! Help me!' Strangely, none seemed to have been seriously injured, only slightly wounded, with fresh blood dripping from their faces and hands (…)

About ten minutes after the explosion, a big man, half-naked, holding his head between his hands, came into the yard towards me, making sounds that seemed to be dragged from the pit of his stomach.

'Got hurt, sir,' he groaned; he shivered as if he were cold. 'I'm hurt.'

I stared at him, at the strange-looking man. Then I saw it was Mr. Zenjiro Tsujimto, a market-gardener and a friendly neighbor to me and the hospital. I wondered what had happened to the robust Zenjiro.

'What's the matter with you, Tsujimoto?' I asked him, holding him in my arms.

'In the pumpkin field over there—getting pumpkins for the patients—got hurt . . .' he said, speaking brokenly and breathing feebly.

It was all he could do to keep standing. Yet it didn't occur to me that he had been seriously injured.

'Come along now,' I said. 'You are perfectly all right, I assure you. Where's your shirt? Lie down and rest somewhere where it's cool. I'll be with you in a moment.'

His head and his face were whitish; his hair was singed. It was because his eye-lashes had been scorched away that he seemed so bleary-eyed. He was half-naked because his shirt had been burned from his back in a single flash. But I wasn't aware of such facts. I gazed at him as he reeled about with his head between his hands. What a change had come over this man who was stronger than a horse, whom I had last seen earlier that morning. It's as if he's been struck by lightning, I thought.

After Mr. Tsujimoto came staggering up to me, another person who looked just like him wandered into the yard. Who he was and where he had come from I had no idea. 'Help me,' he said, groaning, half-naked, holding his head between his hands. He sat down, exhausted. 'Water . . . Water . . .' he whispered.

'What's the trouble? What's wrong with you? What's become of your shirt?' I demanded.

'Hot—*hot* . . . Water . . . I'm burning.' They were the only words that were articulate.

As time passed, more and more people in a similar plight came up to the hospital—ten minutes, twenty minutes, an hour after the explosion. All were of the same appearance, sounded the same. 'I'm hurt, *hurt*! I'm burning! Water!' They all moaned the same lament. I shuddered. Half-naked or stark naked, they walked with strange, slow steps, groaning from deep inside themselves as if they had traveled from the depths of hell. They looked whitish; their faces were like masks. I felt as if I were dreaming, watching pallid ghosts processing slowly in one direction—as in a dream I had once dreamt in my childhood.

These ghosts came on foot uphill towards the hospital, from the direction of the burning city and from the more easterly ordnance factory. Worker or student, girl or man, they all walked slowly and had the same mask-like face. Each one groaned and cried for help. Their cries grew in strength as the people increased in number, sounding like something from the Buddhist scriptures, re-echoing everywhere, as if the earth itself were in pain.

5.2 The Japanese Emperor's Declaration, August 1945

After the atomic bombing of Hiroshima and Nagasaki, and the Soviet entry into the war, Japan capitulated. The emperor's message to his harrowed countrymen showed an understanding of Japan's predicament, but made little sense of its causes.

To our good and loyal subjects: After pondering deeply the general trends of the world and the actual conditions obtaining in our empire today, we have decided to effect a settlement of the present situation by resorting to an extraordinary measure.

We have ordered our Government to communicate to the Governments of the United States, Great Britain, China and the Soviet Union that our empire accepts the provisions of their joint declaration.

To strive for the common prosperity and happiness of all nations as well as the security and well-being of our subjects is the solemn obligation which has been handed down by our imperial ancestors and which we lay close to the heart. Indeed, we declared war on America and Britain out of our sincere desire to insure Japan's self-preservation and the stabilization of East Asia, it being far from our thought either to infringe upon the sovereignty of other nations or to embark upon territorial aggrandizement.

But now the war has lasted for nearly four years. Despite the best that has been done by everyone—the gallant fighting of our military and naval forces, the diligence and assiduity of our servants of the State and the devoted service of our 100,000,000 people—the war situation has developed not necessarily to Japan's advantage, while the general trends of the world have all turned against her interest.

Moreover, the enemy has begun to employ a new and most cruel bomb, the power of which to do damage is, indeed, incalculable, taking the toll of many innocent lives. Should we continue to fight, it would not only result in an ultimate collapse and obliteration of the Japanese nation, but also it would lead to the total extinction of human civilization.

Such being the case, how are we to save the millions of our subjects, nor to atone ourselves before the hallowed spirits of our imperial ancestors? This is the reason why we have ordered the acceptance of the provisions of the joint declaration of the powers.

We cannot but express the deepest sense of regret to our allied nations of East Asia, who have consistently cooperated with the Empire toward the emancipation of East Asia.

The thought of those officers and men as well as others who have fallen in the fields of battle, those who died at their posts of duty, or those who met death [otherwise] and all their bereaved families, pains our heart night and day.

The welfare of the wounded and the war sufferers and of those who lost their homes and livelihood is the object of our profound solicitude. The hardships and sufferings to which our nation is to be subjected hereafter will be certainly great.

We are keenly aware of the inmost feelings of all of you, our subjects.

However, it is according to the dictates of time and fate that we have resolved to pave the way for a grand peace for all the generations to come by enduring the [unavoidable] and suffering what is insufferable. Having been able to save [*unclear*] and maintain the structure of the Imperial State, we are always with you, our good and loyal subjects, relying upon your sincerity and integrity.

Beware most strictly of any outbursts of emotion that may engender needless complications, of any fraternal contention and strife that may create confusion, lead you astray and cause you to lose the confidence of the world.

Let the entire nation continue as one family from generation to generation, ever firm in its faith of the imperishableness of its divine land, and mindful of its heavy burden of responsibilities, and the long road before it. Unite your total strength to be devoted to the construction for the future. Cultivate the ways of rectitude, nobility of spirit, and work with resolution so that you may enhance the innate glory of the Imperial State and keep pace with the progress of the world.

5.3 US Initial Post-Surrender Directive on Japan, August 1945

As the Allied occupation forces moved into Japan, their Supreme Commander, US General Douglas MacArthur, was issued with the following basic directive from the Truman Administration on the future of the country they were taking control of.

Part I—ultimate objectives

The ultimate objectives of the United States in regard to Japan, to which policies in the initial period must conform, are:

a. To insure that Japan will not again become a menace to the United States or to the peace and security of the world.

b. To bring about the eventual establishment of a peaceful and responsible government which will respect the rights of other states and will support the objectives of the United States as reflected in the ideals and principles of the Charter of the United Nations. The United States desires that this government should conform as closely as may be to principles of democratic self-government but it is not the responsibility of the Allied Powers to impose upon Japan any form of government not supported by the freely expressed will of the people.

These objectives will be achieved by the following principal means:

a. Japan's sovereignty will be limited to the islands of Honshu, Hokkaido, Kyushu, Shikoku, and such minor outlying islands as may be determined, in accordance with the Cairo Declaration and other agreements to which the United States is or may be a party.

b. Japan will be completely disarmed and demilitarised. The authority of the militarists and the influence of militarism will be totally eliminated from her political, economic, and social life. Institutions expressive of the spirit of militarism and aggression will be vigorously suppressed.

c. The Japanese people shall be encouraged to develop a desire for individual liberties and respect for fundamental human rights, particularly the freedoms of religion, assembly, speech, and the press. They shall also be encouraged to form democratic and representative organizations.

d. The Japanese people shall be afforded opportunity to develop for themselves an economy which will permit the peacetime requirements of the population to be met.

Part II—Allied Authority

1. Military occupation

There will be a military occupation of the Japanese home islands to carry into effect the surrender terms and further the achievement of the ultimate objectives stated above. The occupation shall have the character of an operation on behalf of the principal Allied powers acting in the interests of the United Nations at war with Japan. For that reason, participation of the forces of other nations that have taken a leading part in the war against Japan will be welcomed and expected. The occupation forces will be under the command of a Supreme Commander designated by the United States.

Although every effort will be made, by consultation and by constitution of appropriate advisory bodies, to establish policies for the conduct of the occupation and the control of Japan which will satisfy the principal Allied powers, in the event of any differences of opinion among them, the policies of the United States will govern.

2. Relationship to Japanese government

The authority of the emperor and the Japanese government will be subject to the Supreme Commander, who will possess all powers necessary to effectuate the surrender terms and to carry out the policies established for the conduct of the occupation and the control of Japan.

In view of the present character of Japanese society and the desire of the United States to attain its objectives with a minimum commitment of its forces and resources, the Supreme Commander will exercise his authority through Japanese governmental machinery and agencies, including the emperor, to the extent that this satisfactorily furthers United States objectives. The Japanese government will be permitted, under his instructions, to exercise the normal powers of government in matters of domestic administration. This policy, however, will be subject to the right and duty of the Supreme Commander to require changes in governmental machinery or personnel or to act directly if the emperor or other Japanese authority does not satisfactorily meet the requirements of the Supreme Commander in effectuating the surrender terms. This policy, moreover, does not commit the Supreme Commander to support the emperor or any other Japanese governmental authority in opposition to evolutionary changes looking toward the attainment of United States objectives. The policy is to use the existing form of government in Japan, not to support it. Changes in the form of government initiated by the Japanese people or government in the direction of modifying its feudal and authoritarian tendencies are to be permitted and favored. In the event that the effectuation of such changes involves the use of force by the Japanese people or government against persons opposed thereto, the Supreme Commander should intervene only where necessary to ensure the security of his forces and the attainment of all other objectives of the occupation.

3. Publicity as to policies

The Japanese people, and the world at large, shall be kept fully informed of the objectives and policies of the occupation, and of progress made in their fulfillment.

Part III—Political

1. Disarmament and Demilitarization

Disarmament and demilitarization are the primary tasks of the military occupation and shall be carried out promptly and with determination. Every effort shall be made to bring home to the Japanese people the part played by the military and naval leaders, and those who collaborated with them, in bringing about the existing and future distress of the people.

Japan is not to have an army, navy, air force, secret police organization, or any civil aviation. Japan's ground, air, and naval forces shall be disarmed and disbanded and the Japanese Imperial General Headquarters, the General Staff, and all secret police organizations shall be dissolved. Military and naval materiel, military and naval vessels and military and naval installations, and military, naval, and civilian aircraft shall be surrendered and shall be disposed of as required by the Supreme Commander.

High officials of the Japanese Imperial General Headquarters, and General Staff, other high military and naval officials of the Japanese government, leaders of ultranationalist and militarist organizations, and other important exponents of militarism and aggression will be taken into custody and held for future disposition. Persons who have been active exponents of militarism and militant nationalism will be removed and excluded from public office and from any other position of public or substantial private responsibility. Ultranationalistic or militaristic social, political, professional, and commercial societies and institutions will be dissolved and prohibited.

Militarism and ultranationalism, in doctrine and practice, including paramilitary training, shall be eliminated from the educational system. Former career military and naval officers, both commissioned and non-commissioned, and all other exponents of militarism and ultranationalism shall be excluded from supervisory and teaching positions.

2. War Criminals

Persons charged by the Supreme Commander or appropriate United Nations agencies with being war criminals, including those charged with having visited cruelties upon United Nations prisoners or other nationals, shall be arrested, tried, and, if convicted, punished. Those wanted by another of the United Nations for offenses against its nationals, shall, if not wanted for trial or as witnesses or otherwise by the Supreme Commander, be turned over to the custody of such other nation.

3. Encouragment of Desire for Individual Liberties and Democratic Processes

Freedom of religious worship shall be proclaimed promptly on occupation. At the same time it should be made plain to the Japanese that ultranationalistic and militaristic organizations and movements will not be permitted to hide behind the cloak of religion.

The Japanese people shall be afforded opportunity and encouraged to become familiar with the history, institutions, culture, and the accomplishments of the United States and the other democracies. Association of personnel of the occupation forces with the Japanese population should be controlled only to the extent necessary to further the policies and objectives of the occupation.

Democratic political parties, with rights of assembly and public discussion, shall be encouraged, subject to the necessity for maintaining the security of the occupying forces.

Laws, decrees, and regulations which establish discriminations on ground of race, nationality, creed, or political opinion shall be abrogated; those which conflict with the objectives and policies outlined in this document shall be repealed, suspended, or amended as required; and agencies charged specifically with their enforcement shall be abolished or appropriately modified. Persons unjustly confined by Japanese authority on political grounds shall be released. The Judicial, legal, and police systems shall be reformed as soon as practicable to conform to the policies set forth in Articles I and 3 of this Part III and thereafter shall be progressively influenced, to protect individual liberties and civil rights.

Part IV—Economic

1. Economic Demilitarization

The existing economic basis of Japanese military strength must be destroyed and not be permitted to revive.

Therefore, a program will be enforced containing the following elements, among others: the immediate cessation and future prohibition of production of all goods designed for the equipment, maintenance, or use of any military force or establishment; the imposition of a ban upon any specialized facilities for the production or repair or implements of war, including naval vessels and all forms of aircraft; the institution of a system of inspection and control over selected elements in Japanese economic activity to prevent concealed or disguised military preparation; the elimination in Japan of those selected industries of branches of production whose chief value to Japan is in preparing for war; the prohibition of specialized research and instruction directed to the development of war-making power; and the limitation of the size and character of Japan's heavy industries to its future peaceful requirements, and restriction of Japanese merchant shipping to the extent required to accomplish the objectives of demilitarization.

The eventual disposition of those existing production facilities within Japan which are to be eliminated in accord with this program, as between conversion to other uses, transfer abroad, and scrapping will be determined after inventory. Pending decision, facilities readily convertible for civilian production should not be destroyed, except in emergency situations.

2. Promotion of Democratic Forces

Encouragement shall be given and favor shown to the development of organizations in labor, industry, and agriculture, organized on a democratic basis. Policies shall be favored which permit a wide distribution of income and of the ownership of the means of production and trade.

Those forms of economic activity, organization, and leadership shall be favored that are deemed likely to strengthen the peaceful disposition of the Japanese people, and to make it difficult to command or direct economic activity in support of military ends.

TOKIO RECEPTION

4. 'Tokio Reception' for General Douglas C. MacArthur. (David Low, *Evening Standard*, 28 August 1945). Reprinted by permission. Photo supplied by The Centre for the Study of Cartoons and Caricature, University of Kent.

To this end it shall be the policy of the Supreme Commander:

(a) To prohibit the retention in or selection for places of importance in the economic field of individuals who do not direct future Japanese economic effort solely towards peaceful ends; and

(b) To favor a program for the dissolution of the large industrial and banking combinations which have exercised control of a great part of Japan's trade and industry.

5.4 Dealing with the Occupiers: 1945

In Japan, as in Europe, a main preoccupation of what remained of local authority after the war was to look after the needs of the victorious powers. Historian John Dower describes the special patriotic duties of Japanese prostitutes after the surrender.

Enlisting a small number of women to serve as a buffer protecting the chastity of the 'good' women of Japan was well-established policy in dealing with Western barbarians. Special pleasure quarters had been set up for foreigners immediately after Commodore Perry forced the country to abolish its policy of seclusion, and in modern mythology one young woman who gave her body for the nation had already been glorified as a patriotic martyr. Her name was Okichi, and she had been assigned as a consort for Townsend Harris, the first American consul, who assumed his duties in 1856. The procurers of 1945 appropriated her sad, sensual image in defining their own task. The women they were assembling, they declared, would be *Shôwa no Tôjin Okichi*, 'the Okichis of the present era.'

To the government's surprise, professional prostitutes proved reluctant to become latter-day Okichis. By one account, they were fearful that the Americans, commonly portrayed as demonic figures in wartime propaganda, possessed over-sized sexual organs that could injure them. The organizers of the special comfort facilities thus undertook to recruit ordinary women by posting a large signboard addressed 'To New Japanese Women' in the Ginza district of downtown Tokyo. 'As part of urgent national facilities to deal with the postwar,' this read, somewhat vaguely, 'we are seeking the active cooperation of new Japanese women to participate in the great task of comforting the occupation forces.' The solicitation also mentioned openings for 'female office clerks, aged between eighteen and twenty-five. Housing, clothing, and food supplied.'

Most of the women attracted by this advertisement arrived for their interviews shabbily dressed. Some, it is said, were even barefoot. The great majority had no experience in the 'water trade' of the red-light districts, and most left when informed what their actual duties would be. Among those remained, some claimed to be attracted not so much by the assurance of food and shelter as by the appeal to give their bodies 'for the country.' This was, after all, essentially the same message of patriotic self-sacrifice that had been drilled into them all their lives. By August 27, 1,360 women in Tokyo had enlisted in what soon would become known in English as the R.A.A., short for Recreation and Amusement Association (*Tokushu Ian Shisetsu Kyôkai* in Japanese).

The next day, just as the first small contingents of occupation forces were arriving, an inaugural ceremony for the R.A.A. was held in the plaza in front of the imperial palace. On this occasion, the following 'oath,' couched in ornate Japanese, was read:

Although our family has endured for 3,000 years, unchanging as the mountains and valleys, the rivers and grasses, since the great rending of August 15, 1945, which marked the end of an era, we have been wracked with infinite, piercing grief and endless sorrow, and are about to sink to the bottom of perilous, boundless desperation. . . .

The time has come, an order has been given, and by virtue of our realm of business we have been assigned the difficult task of comforting the occupation army as part of the urgent national facilities for postwar management. This order is heavy and immense. And success will be extremely difficult. . . .

And so we unite and go forward to where our beliefs lead us, and through the sacrifice of several thousands of 'Okichis of our era' build a breakwater to hold back the raging waves and defend and nurture the purity of our race, becoming as well an invisible underground pillar at the root of the postwar social order. . . .

A word as we conclude this proclamation. We absolutely are not flattering the occupation force. We are not compromising our integrity or selling our souls. We are paying an inescapable courtesy, and serving to fulfill one part of our obligations and to contribute to the security of our society. We dare say it loudly: we are but offering ourselves for the defense of the national polity. We reaffirm this. This is our proclamation.

A statement was issued by the seven professional associations engaged in the water trade who were to run the Tokyo R.A.A. collectively. After paying solemn homage to 'the great spirit of maintaining the national polity by protecting the pure blood of the hundred million,' these patriotic procurers moved with almost breathtaking agility into the facile new rhetoric of these rapidly changing times. Through the R.A.A., they declared, 'we hope to promote mutual understanding between [the Allied occupation forces] and our people, and to contribute to the smooth development of people's diplomacy and abet the construction of a peaceful world.'

Several hundred GIs on that day quickly found their way to an R.A.A. facility in Tokyo's Omori district, where a small number of mostly inexperienced recruits had been gathered. Neither beds, futons, nor room partitions were yet available, and fornication took place without privacy everywhere, even in the corridors. Later Japanese accounts of the scene tend to be irate, speaking of shameless 'animalistic intercourse' that showed the 'true colors' of so-called American civilization. The local police chief is said to have wept.

One naïve recruit to the R.A.A. later recalled the terror of her first day, when she was called on to service twenty-three American soldiers. By one estimate, R.A.A. women engaged between fifteen and sixty GIs a day. A nineteen-year-old who previously had been a typist committed suicide almost immediately. Some women broke down or deserted (...)

The women who had been recruited by the R.A.A. were sent off without severance pay, but with uplifting speeches to the effect that they had 'served the country' and been a 'dike of chastity,' albeit not their own. Ending formal public prostitution did not, of course, mean the end of prostitution itself. The trade simply was carried out more privately—and venereal disease naturally remained difficult to control. Nonetheless, the transition did have its precious moments. Outside the new comfort facilities that had been created exclusively for the foreigners, in one licensed quarter of the traditional geisha-centered 'floating world,' the last day of public prostitution was memorably recorded in a photograph of kimono-clad young women standing before an American flag affixed to the wall of their brother and throwing up their arms in the familiar *banzai* cheer of celebration.

In responding to SCAP's [Supreme Commander of the Allied Powers] orders, Japanese bureaucrats revealed a rare and unusually fine appreciation of human rights. In December 1946, the Home Ministry declared that women had the *right* to become prostitutes, and this became the ostensible rationale behind designating 'red-line' districts in which it was understood by all parties that they would continue to ply their trade. (The 'red-line' designation came from markings on the city maps used by the police; in areas outlined in blue, such activity was not allowed.) In the years that followed, an estimated fifty-five thousand to seventy thousand women, many of 'third country' origin, worked these areas as full-time prostitutes.

5.5 Food Demonstrations in Tokyo, May 1946

In the aftermath of World War II many observers doubted if Japan's economy would ever recover. The US occupation authorities soon began to fear that the country might be facing a revolution. American journalist Mark Gayn covered the 'Rice Rallies' in Tokyo in May 1946, organized by the new and powerful Japanese left-wing trade unions. This excerpt is from his diary.

Tokyo, May 19, 1946

The political pot is boiling madly. Yoshida is still struggling to form a new cabinet. As fast as he picks his ministers, it is discovered that they are war criminals subject to the purge. Meanwhile, the food rationing machinery has bogged down. In the far north the distribution of food is thirty days behind schedule; in Tokyo, twelve. There are street-corner rallies, parades, mass meetings of protest. On Tuesday, eight hundred people demonstrated before the palace, demanding to know what the emperor was eating. On Friday, there were eight 'food demonstrations' in front of rationing stations. Yesterday, twenty. There is a steady stream of marching men past the Diet and the premier's residence.

The climax came today with a 'Give Us Rice' mass meeting. By ten o'clock on this bright, warm morning, there were at least 60,000 people at the imperial plaza. They had put three trucks together, and mounted tables on them for the speakers' platform. The chairman was the head of the Transport Workers' Union. But the meeting was actually run by a hard-looking man in corduroy knickers and a sports jacket. This was Katsumi Kikunami, an editorial writer for the *Asahi*, head of the Newspaper Union, and founder of the huge Congress of

Industrial Unions. Grimly, he introduced a succession of speakers—union leaders, political workers, and just plain people.

One of these was a housewife of thirty-five, slim and plain looking and obviously undernourished. She came from a ward in which there has been no rice distribution in two weeks. She had a child strapped to her back, and as she denounced the police and the rationing officials, the child's wailing came clear and loud over the loudspeaker.

But most of the speakers talked of politics. They demanded Yoshida's resignation, a Popular Front, a new cabinet including workers and farmers. 'We must use the privileges we've gained since the war,' cried Suzuki, editor of the *Yomiuri*, 'One of them is the right to make revolutionary changes that will produce a democratic government. A one-day general strike will force Yoshida out!'

Tokuda was the last to speak. He wheeled around on the table top, pointed at the palace, and shouted: 'We're starving. Is he?' He denounced Yoshida and the war criminals in the Diet, but he saved his sharpest barbs for the emperor. 'Last week,' he said, 'we went to the palace and asked to see the emperor. We were chased away. Is it because the emperor can say nothing but "Ah, so. Ah, so?"' He mimicked the emperor. The crowd cheered wildly (...)

The moat at this point is probably thirty feet wide, and a bridge crosses it to the massive gate in the palace wall. The bridge was now a no-man's-land. The crowd stood or sat at one end, while a force of palace guards, armed with staves, stood in front of the gate. Earlier, the crowd had come up to the gate, and in the melee a policeman was tossed into the moat, and some demonstrants were beaten. A delegation of twelve men had gone in three hours earlier, and the growing crowd was waiting for their return. While waiting, the demonstrants sang, or listened to pep talks by men who spoke from atop a small police kiosk.

Around four one of the delegates came out, and climbed on the booth. Both the emperor and the minister of the imperial household, he said, had refused to see the delegation. It was finally permitted to talk to a secretary, who said he would report to the minister, who would report to the emperor.

'Geez,' said the delegate, in effect. 'This is the first time I've been in the palace, and it's wonderful. Why, the lavatory there is better than the house I live in.'

Half an hour later the rest of the delegation came out. It was led by Kikunami, who looked even grimmer than he had earlier in the day. One after another, the delegates climbed atop the kiosk to report their failure, to say they would come back in forty-eight hours, and to detail their discoveries in the palace. It appeared that they had gone through the palace kitchen, and had had a look at the emperor's cooking pots, refrigerators, and menu for tonight.

'What will you have for dinner?' they shouted to the crowd. 'How much is there in your larder? Now hear what the emperor and his family will eat tonight ...'

Tokyo, May 20 1946

This morning General MacArthur issued a warning to the Japanese people.

'I find it necessary,' he said, 'to caution the Japanese people that the growing tendency toward mass violence and physical processes of intimidation, under organized leadership, present a grave menace to the future development of Japan.

'While every possible rational freedom of democratic method has been permitted and will be permitted (…) the physical violence which undisciplined elements are now beginning to practice will not be permitted to continue. They constitute a menace not only to orderly government but to the basic purposes and security of the occupation itself.

'If minor elements of Japanese society are unable to exercise such restraint and self-respect as the situation and conditions require, I shall be forced to take the necessary steps to control and remedy such a deplorable situation . . .'

The statement had a startling effect. I could actually recall no American move that matched this pronouncement in its repercussions. There was consternation in union headquarters and in the offices of the left-wing parties. In conservative quarters, there was undisguised jubilation.

As soon as word of the statement reached the premier's residence, the 'sit-downers' quietly left the building. All demonstrations scheduled for today, and for the rest of the week, have been cancelled. The Japanese press, which thus far has been explaining that the people had no other way to change the government but to go into the streets, hastily backtracked.

The right-wingers in the Social Democratic party, who were being pushed into the Popular Front by the sight of the marching multitudes, now happily announced they needed time to reconsider the issue, 'in the light of the new circumstances.' Two left-wing leaders admitted to me privately the fight was lost.

And Yoshida, who may have wavered last night, no longer wavered this noon. He announced that he would have a cabinet ready by tomorrow, and indicated that Twiddledum, or Shidehara, would be in it. As clearly as any of us, Yoshida saw the statement for what it was—a prop for Yoshida.

5.6 George Kennan on US Policy Towards Japan, March 1948

As the Cold War intensified, many US policy-makers became more preoccupied with developing Japan as an ally of the West than with punishing war criminals and implementing major reforms. George Kennan's report after a visit in 1948 summarizes the argument for such a reorientation.

I. The Peace Treaty

1. Timing and Procedure

This Government should not press for a treaty of peace at this time. It should remain prepared to proceed with the negotiations, under either the two-thirds rule or the FEC [(Allied) Far Eastern Commission] voting procedure, if at any time the other Allied powers can agree among themselves on one of these procedures. Meanwhile, we should concentrate our attention on the preparation of the Japanese for the eventual removal of the regime of control.

2. The Nature of the Treaty

It should be our aim to have the treaty, when finally negotiated, as brief, as general, and as nonpunitive as possible. To this end we should try to clear away during this intervening period, by direct action, as many as possible of the matters which might otherwise be expected to enter into the treaty of peace. Our aim should be to reduce as far as possible the number of questions to be treated in the peace treaty. This applies particularly to such matters as property rights, restitution, etc. Our policy for the coming period should be shaped specifically with this in mind.

II. Security Matters

1. Disposition of our Tactical Forces in the Pre-Treaty Period

Tactical forces should be retained in Japan for the coming period; *but* every effort should be made to reduce to a minimum their numbers, their cost to the Japanese economy, and the psychological impact of their presence on the Japanese population. The arrangements for their location, support, and employment should be determined with this in mind.

2. The Post-Treaty Arrangements

The United States tactical forces should be retained in Japan until the entrance into effect of a peace treaty. A final U.S. position concerning the post-treaty arrangements for Japanese military security should not be formulated until the peace negotiations are upon us. It should then be formulated in the light of the prevailing international situation and of the degree of internal stability achieved in Japan. If Russia has not been extensively weakened and sobered by that time or if Japanese society still seems excessively vulnerable in the political sense, we should either postpone the treaty or insist on a limited re-militarization of Japan, preferably under U.S. guidance and supervision. But if by that time the Russian situation should really have changed for the better and if we are reasonably confident of the internal stability of Japan, we should aim at a complete demilitarization, guaranteed by an international treaty of the most explicit and concrete nature, to which the Russians would be a party (...)

IV. Occupational Policy

2. The Reform Program

While SCAP should not stand in the way of reform measures initiated by the Japanese if it finds them consistent with the overall objectives of the occupation, it should be authorized not to press upon the Japanese Government any further reform legislation. As for reform measures already taken or in process of preparation by the Japanese authorities, SCAP should be authorized steadily but unobtrusively to relax pressure on the Japanese Government in connection with these reforms, and to permit the Japanese authorities to proceed in their own way with the process of implementation.

3. The Purge

SCAP should be directed gradually to permit the relaxation of the purge along the following lines: (1) Categories of persons who have been purged by virtue of their having held relatively harmless positions should be made re-eligible for governmental, business and public media positions; (2) certain others barred from public life should be allowed to have their cases re-examined on the basis of personal actions rather than on the basis of positions occupied; and (3) a lower age limit should be fixed, under which no screening for public office would be required (…)

9. War Crimes Trials

We should press for early deadlines for the termination of the War Crimes Trials of 'A' suspects. We should immediately undertake the screening of all 'B' and 'C' suspects with a view to releasing those whose cases we do not intend to prosecute. The others should be brought to swift justice.

5.7 Prime Minister Yoshida on Japan's Foreign Policy, December 1951

The right-wing Japanese Prime Minister Yoshida Shigeru was willing to go far to ensure the signing of a peace treaty and a recovery of Japanese sovereignty, even on issues as vital to Japan as trade with China, under Communist control since 1949. Here is his 24 December 1951 letter to John Foster Dulles, a US delegate at the negotiations and later secretary of state under President Eisenhower.

Dear Ambassador Dulles: While the Japanese Peace Treaty and the United States–Japan security treaty were being debated in the House of Representatives and the House of Councilors of the Diet, a number of questions were put and statements made relative to Japan's future policy toward China. Some of the statements, separated from their context and background, gave rise to misapprehensions which I should like to clear up.

The Japanese government desires ultimately to have a full measure of political peace and commercial intercourse with China which is Japan's close neighbor.

At the present time it is, we hope, possible to develop that kind of relationship with the National Government of the Republic of China, which has the seat, voice, and vote of China in the United Nations, which exercises actual governmental authority over certain territory, and which maintains diplomatic relations with most of the members of the United Nations. To that end my government on November 17, 1951, established a Japanese Government Overseas Agency in Formosa, with the consent of the national government of China. This is the highest form of relationship with other countries which is now permitted to Japan, pending the coming into force of the multilateral treaty of peace. The Japanese Government Overseas Agency in Formosa is important in its personnel, reflecting the importance which my government attaches to relations with the national government of the Republic of China. My government is prepared as soon as legally possible to conclude with the national government of China, if that government so desires, a treaty which will re-establish normal relations between the two governments in conformity with the principles set out in the multilateral treaty of peace. The terms of such bilateral treaty shall, in respect of the Republic of China, be applicable to all territories which are now, or which may hereafter be, under the control of the national government of the Republic of China. We will promptly explore this subject with the national government of China.

As regards the Chinese Communist regime, that regime stands actually condemned by the United Nations of being an aggressor and in consequence, the United Nations has recommended certain measures against that regime, in which Japan is now concurring and expects to continue to concur when the multilateral treaty of peace comes into force pursuant to the provisions of article 5(a)(iii), whereby Japan has undertaken 'to give the United Nations every assistance in any action it takes in accordance with the charter and to refrain from giving assistance to any state against which the United Nations may take preventive or enforcement action.' Furthermore, the Sino-Soviet Treaty of Friendship, Alliance and Mutual Assistance concluded in Moscow in 1950 is virtually a military alliance aimed against Japan. In fact there are many reasons to believe that the Communist regime in China is backing the Japan Communist party in its program of seeking violently to overthrow the constitutional system and the present government of Japan. In view of these considerations, I can assure you that the Japanese government has no intention to conclude a bilateral treaty with the Communist regime of China.

5.8 US–Japan Security Treaty, September 1951

The price the Japanese had to pay to get their sovereignty back was an extensive security treaty with the United States. The treaty was negotiated before, but ratified after, the peace treaty between Japan and the Western Allies, and its main provisions remain in place.

Japan has this day signed a Treaty of Peace with the Allied Powers. On the coming into force of that Treaty, Japan will not have the effective means to exercise its inherent right of self-defense because it has been disarmed.

There is danger to Japan in this situation because irresponsible militarism has not yet been driven from the world. Therefore Japan desires a Security Treaty with the United States of America to come into force simultaneously with the Treaty of Peace between the United States of America and Japan.

The Treaty of Peace recognizes that Japan as a sovereign nation has the right to enter into collective security arrangements, and further, the Charter of the United Nations recognizes that all nations possess an inherent right of individual and collective self-defense.

In exercise of these rights, Japan desires, as a provisional arrangement for its defense, that the United States of America should maintain armed forces of its own in and about Japan so as to deter armed attack upon Japan.

The United States of America, in the interest of peace and security, is presently willing to maintain certain of its armed forces in and about Japan, in the expectation, however, that Japan will itself increasingly assume responsibility for its own defense against direct and indirect aggression, always avoiding any armament which could be an offensive threat or serve other than to promote peace and security in accordance with the purposes and principles of the United Nations Charter.

Accordingly, the two countries have agreed as follows:

Article I

Japan grants, and the United States of America accepts, the right, upon the coming into force of the Treaty of Peace and of this Treaty, to dispose United States land, air and sea forces in and about Japan. Such forces may be utilized to contribute to the maintenance of international peace and security in the Far East and to the security of Japan against armed attack from without, including assistance given at the express request of the Japanese Government to put down largescale internal riots and disturbances in Japan, caused through instigation or intervention by an outside power or powers.

5. 'Back to normal' (Sidney 'George' Strube, *Everybody's Weekly*, 22 September 1951). Reprinted by permission. Photo supplied by The Centre for the Study of Cartoons and Caricature, University of Kent.

Article II

During the exercise of the right referred to in Article I, Japan will not grant, without the prior consent of the United States of America, any bases or any rights, powers or authority whatsoever, in or relating to bases or the right of garrison or of maneuver, or transit of ground, air or naval forces to any third power.

Article III

The conditions which shall govern the disposition of armed forces of the United States of America in and about Japan shall be determined by administrative agreements between the two Governments.

Article IV

This Treaty shall expire whenever in the opinion of the Governments of the United States of America and Japan there shall have come into force such United Nations arrangements or such alternative individual or collective security dispositions as will satisfactorily provide for the maintenance by the United Nations or otherwise of international peace and security in the Japan Area.

Article V

This Treaty shall be ratified by the United States of America and Japan and will come into force when instruments of ratification thereof have been exchanged by them at Washington.

5.9 Treaty of Peace with Japan, September 1951

The Korean War set the scene for the peace treaty between the Western powers and Japan. Japan's importance to the West increased significantly with the war, as did Japanese exports, which soared 50 percent in its first two years. The Soviet Union and the People's Republic of China did not sign the peace treaty.

Whereas the Allied Powers and Japan are resolved that henceforth their relations shall be those of nations which, as sovereign equals, cooperate in friendly association to promote their common welfare and to maintain international peace and security, and are therefore desirous of concluding a Treaty of Peace which will settle questions still outstanding as a result of the existence of a state of war between them;

Whereas Japan for its part declares its intention to apply for membership in the United Nations and in all circumstances to conform to the principles of the Charter of the United Nations; to strive to realize the objectives of the Universal Declaration of Human Rights; to seek to create within Japan conditions of stability and well-being as defined in Articles 55 and 56 of the Charter of the United Nations and already initiated by post-surrender Japanese legislation; and in public and private trade and commerce to conform to internationally accepted fair practices;

Whereas the Allied Powers welcome the intentions of Japan set out in the foregoing paragraph;

The Allied Powers and Japan have therefore determined to conclude the present Treaty of Peace, and have accordingly appointed the undersigned Plenipotentiaries, who, after presentation of their full powers, found in good and due form, have agreed on the following provisions:

Article 1

(a) The state of war between Japan and each of the Allied Powers is terminated as from the date on which the present Treaty comes into force between Japan and the Allied Power concerned as provided for in Article 23.

(b) The Allied Powers recognize the full sovereignty of the Japanese people over Japan and its territorial waters.

Article 2

(a) Japan recognizing the independence of Korea, renounces all right, title and claim to Korea, including the islands of Quelpart, Port Hamilton and Dagelet.

(b) Japan renounces all right, title and claim to Formosa and the Pescadores.

(c) Japan renounces all right, title and claim to the Kurile Islands, and to that portion of Sakhalin and the islands adjacent to it over which Japan acquired sovereignty as a consequence of the Treaty of Portsmouth of 5 September 1905.

(d) Japan renounces all right, title and claim in connection with the League of Nations Mandate System, and accepts the action of the United Nations Security Council of 2 April 1947, extending the trusteeship system to the Pacific Islands formerly under mandate to Japan.

(e) Japan renounces all claim to any right or title to or interest in connection with any part of the Antarctic area, whether deriving from the activities of Japanese nationals or otherwise.

(f) Japan renounces all right, title and claim to the Spratly Islands and to the Paracel Islands.

Article 3

Japan will concur in any proposal of the United States to the United Nations to place under its trusteeship system, with the United States as the sole administering authority, Nansei Shoto south of 29 deg. north latitude (including the Ryukyu Islands and the Daito Islands), Nanpo Shoto south of Sofu Gan (including the Bonin Islands, Rosario Island and the Volcano Islands) and Parece Vela and Marcus Island. Pending the making of such a proposal and affirmative action thereon, the United States will have the right to exercise all and any powers of administration, legislation and jurisdiction over the territory and inhabitants of these islands, including their territorial waters (…)

Article 5

(a) Japan accepts the obligations set forth in Article 2 of the Charter of the United Nations, and in particular the obligations

(i) to settle its international disputes by peaceful means in such a manner that international peace and security, and justice, are not endangered;

(ii) to refrain in its international relations from the threat or use of force against the territorial integrity or political independence of any State or in any other manner inconsistent with the Purposes of the United Nations;

(iii) to give the United Nations every assistance in any action it takes in accordance with the Charter and to refrain from giving assistance to any State against which the United Nations may take preventive or enforcement action.

(b) The Allied Powers confirm that they will be guided by the principles of Article 2 of the Charter of the United Nations in their relations with Japan.

(c) The Allied Powers for their part recognize that Japan as a sovereign nation possesses the inherent right of individual or collective self-defense referred to in Article 51 of the Charter of the United Nations and that Japan may voluntarily enter into collective security arrangements.

5.10 The US National Security Council on Policies Towards Japan, April 1955

In the mid-1950s the United States looked to Japan to provide a counterbalance to Communist China in East Asia, but realized that the country was far too weak to fill that role in the short term. The double fear that Japan's economy would not recover and that the Japanese left would opt for neutrality in the Cold War remained. Here is an excerpt from US National Security Council document 5516/1 from 9 April 1955.

Japanese Trends

1. Japan's relations with the United States will continued to be heavily influenced by its dependence upon the United States for economic, military, and diplomatic support; by its estimate as to whether the United States will continue to demonstrate its will and ability to resist Communist aggression without seriously endangering Japan; by the fact that the United States is Japan's largest foreign customer and source of supply (20% of its export trade and 40% of its imports); and to a lesser extent by a still substantial residue of good will for the United States. Accordingly, Japan will almost certainly seek to maintain its present alignment with the United States.

2. Japan will endeavor to reduce its dependence on the United States and will seek greater freedom of international action, including expanded relations with the USSR and Communist China.

3. Japan has the potential to assume a leading and stabilizing role in Asia. It is unlikely to acquire sufficient strength to do so in the next few years. The rapidity with which Japan attains such strength will depend not only on its own efforts but also on the nature and magnitude of United States support and assistance.

4. Japan will continue to move toward modification of the Occupation reforms, particularly toward increasing centralization of governmental power, but Japan will remain democratic with many differences from prewar authoritarian and imperialistic patterns.

5. Moderate conservative forces, which will be hampered by factional differences and will tend toward greater nationalism, will probably continue to

dominate Japanese government and politics. Left-of-center forces will probably offer stronger opposition than in the past few years. The gradual revival of ultra-nationalist forces will continue. A strong and effective government is not likely to emerge during the next few years.

6. Although the Japanese Communist Party is not likely to gain substantial parliamentary strength, it will continue to exercise an important influence through its ability to aggravate popular grievances, to exploit and infiltrate mass organizations and the intellectual leadership of the non-Communist left, and to infiltrate the government.

7. Japan does not appear to have an immediate balance of payments problem, partly due to substantial though diminishing United States special expenditures, and its economic position improved during calendar year 1954. Over the long term, however, particularly in the face of further decreases in United States special expenditures, Japan faces a difficult economic situation of providing employment and adequate living standards for its growing population through an expansion of exports and development of its limited domestic resources.

8. Japan will continue to develop its over-all defense forces at a slow rate, and will seek to adjust the balance of these forces by emphasizing the development of the air and naval components. Japan will continue to rely upon substantial military aid from the United States.

Basic United States Interests

9. The strategic location and military and industrial potential of Japan are such that the security of the United States would require us to fight to prevent hostile forces from gaining control of any part of Japan by attack. Similarly we would be obliged to assist the Japanese.

10. United States interests would best be served by a strong Japan, firmly allied with the United States, and better able to serve as a counterweight to Communist China and contribute to free world strength in the Far East.

11. For the present, Japan's alignment with the United States is based partly on dependence on our support. As Japan's strength grows, dependence will lessen and should be replaced by a new sense of common purpose, mutual interests and a working partnership. A major effort must be made to persuade Japan's dominant conservative forces that the satisfaction of the nation's economic and defense requirements and desire for prestige, as well as the stability of the conservative position, depend on continuing cooperation with the United States.

12. If a sense of mutuality does not develop as Japan's strength increases, basic United States interests with respect to Japan will have to be reassessed. At present, however, it appears that a strong Japan is a better risk than a weak Japan.

Basic Japanese Interests and Objectives

13. Japan's immediate objective is to strengthen its economic position, with a probably long-term objective of recovering a position of international influence and prestige. Japan considers that increase of defense strength is a lower priority, partly because it believes that its defense will be assured by the United States. While political stability is desired by most Japanese, sharp and persisting conflicts between rival personalities and factions seriously retard its development.

14. Japan currently considers alignment with the United States and cooperation with the democratic nations to be in its national interest, because it believes that in this way it is more likely to attain a position of international importance and economic strength and because it expects that the United States will if necessary defend Japan against attack.

15. At the same time, Japan believes that, within the limits of its alignment with the United States and despite its historical fear of Russia and strong dislike of Communism, it should seek to ease friction, develop trade and broaden relations with Communist China and Soviet Union.

16. Japan is beginning to display a desire for greater freedom of international action. This tendency reflects a nationalist trend, rooted in racial pride, a longing for national prestige and a desire for greater maneuverability in the event of conflict between Communist China or the USSR and the United States. Development of the healthier and more positive aspects of Japanese nationalism is essential to Japan's recovery as a major power. Accommodation of this nationalism within the context of the U.S.–Japanese alignment is a basic problem of our policy.

Principal Conflicts Between United States and Japanese Interests and Objectives

17. *U.S. Bases.* Japan recognizes the need for continued military protection by the United States. However, Japan does not regard the threat of aggression against it as seriously as does the United States. Consequently, while the Japanese look upon U.S. bases in Japan as protection for Japan, they also regard them as serving U.S. strategic interests and as dangerously exposing Japan to nuclear attack in the event of war. Furthermore, Japanese policy is colored by serious doubt as to whether an acceptable defense of Japan is possible in the event of nuclear war.

18. *Japanese Rearmament.* Partly because it discounts the danger of direct aggression, Japan puts the development of political stability and economic strength ahead of the development of military power, and resists U.S. efforts to increase total Japanese defense expenditures.

19. *Communist China.* Japan's development of closer relations with the Communist bloc will probably eventually cause serious friction with the United States. The Japanese believe their international interests will be served through early development of closer contacts and expanded trade with the Communist bloc. Pressures in this direction will continue. Currently Japan is restrained from going beyond certain limits by the possible effect on relations with the United States and on trade with the Nationalist China and the Republic of Korea.

20. Other sources of conflict are:

a. Japanese resistance to United States private investment in Japan
b. The Japanese need for trade and the present imbalance of United States–Japanese trade which drives them to want to sell more to the United States than we want to accept.
c. The Japanese sensitivity on nuclear development which leads them to oppose the testing of nuclear weapons in the Pacific and to be vulnerable to Communist-sponsored movements for the banning of nuclear weapons.
d. Irredentism over the Ryukyu and Bonin Islands.
e. Resentment over the continued imprisonment of Japanese war criminals.
f. The nature of a settlement of Japan's GARIOA obligation [paying for Allied food and medical supplies].
g. Relationships with Japanese trade unions regarding the terms and conditions of their members' employment through the Japanese Government for services to U.S. forces.

21. Japan has limited economic, political and psychological resources with which to accomplish the demanding tasks of rebuilding internal political strength, economic viability and defense capacity. There is inevitable competition for these limited resources among social, economic and defense programs. A domestic political struggle over an increase in the defense forces is creating cleavages within the country and weakening the political position of the conservative elements. Both economic austerity and the defense program are essentially unpopular with many segments of the Japanese public, and require major political efforts if they are to be achieved.

22. The United States has limited capacity to influence Japanese action. Our bargaining tools and resources of good will and persuasion should be fully applied but carefully apportioned to accomplish our objectives most effectively.

23. While the requirement for an optimum level of defense readiness will continue to exist, it must be recognized that the Japanese Government will in fact determine the total size and composition of the military forces which Japan will support.

5.11 The National Security Council on US Policies Towards Japan, 1960

The June 1960 NSC 6008 replaced the 1955 document above as the main guideline for US policy toward Japan. It stressed the difficulties posed to the United States by the Japanese left, but also by Tokyo's official reluctance to rearm and open up for US imports.

Major Policy Guidance

Political (...)

28. Promote the maintenance of an effective, moderate conservative government in Japan as basic to the accomplishment of U.S. objective.

29. Where appropriate, seek the understanding of, cooperation with and active support for U.S. policies.

30. Encourage—without alienating conservative support—the development of a moderate, responsible political opposition. As appropriate take steps to reduce the influence of extreme left labor leaders, to encourage the transfer of trade union leadership to moderate elements, and to encourage developments which would have a moderating influence on left-wing socialist elements.

31. Devote special attention to dispelling attitudes unfavorable to, and to reinforcing attitudes favorable to, the United States and its policies, particularly among opinion leaders in the information media, intellectual and educational circles, and labor groups.

32. Encourage and, as appropriate, assist the Japanese Government in taking effective internal security measures striking at the organizational basis of Communist power and undermining Communist financial and political strength.

33. Conduct U.S. relations with Japan in a spirit of partnership and equality, giving full consideration to Japan's vital interests and consulting with the Japanese Government on matters of mutual interest.

34. Encourage and promote U.S. and, as appropriate, Japanese-sponsored cultural, labor, educational and other exchange programs and seek to broaden scientific cooperation including outer space technology.

35. Continue to associate Japan with U.S. and international planning for cooperative development of the peaceful uses of nuclear energy; make nuclear equipment and training for peaceful uses of nuclear energy; make nuclear equipment and training for peaceful uses available to Japan and exchange nuclear information under appropriate conditions.

36. Promote the further development of cooperative relations between Japan and other free nations and encourage and assist Japan to exercise a moderating

and constructive influence on the Afro-Asian nations, particularly at the United Nations. Encourage an over-all settlement between Japan and the Republic of Korea.

37. Use Japan as an example to the less-developed countries of the feasibility of achieving rapid economic progress within a framework of free institutions, in contrast to the harsh and repressive methods adopted by the Communists.

38. Urge the Japanese Government to continue to refuse diplomatic recognition to Communist China and to oppose entry of Communist China into the United Nations.

39. Support and encourage Japan in asserting its legitimate territorial fishing and other claims against the Sino-Soviet Bloc and in resisting Sino-Soviet pressures for neutralization and political concessions; do not concede the Soviet Union's claim to sovereignty over the Kuril Islands and Southern Sakhalin.

Military

40. Maintain the new security arrangements signed on January 19, 1960, including the base rights provided therein, and, in accordance with the provisions of these arrangements, maintain in Japan a level of U.S. military facilities and forces required (a) by U.S. security interests and (b) to demonstrate our determination to fulfil our treaty commitments in Japan and the Far East: but at a general level no higher than that mutually agreed upon by the United States and the Japanese Government.

41. Under the provisions of the security arrangements with Japan:

a. Assist in the defense of Japan in the event of an armed attack against the territories under the administration of Japan. (…)

Economic

54. Encourage Japan to maintain a strong, healthy, self-supporting and expanding economy which will permit improvement in Japan's living standards, provide more capital for the development of less-developed nations, and make a greater contribution to the strength of the Free World.

55. Foster a high level of trade between the United States and Japan by:

a. Maintaining in the United States a liberal import policy and seeking to reduce further U.S. tariffs and trade restrictions on a reciprocal basis in accordance with the established trade agreement principles and the GATT [General Agreement on Trade and Tariffs], having due regard for foreign policy objectives, national security and total national advantage.

b. Continuing to press Japan to abolish discrimination against imports from the United States. (…)

58. Encourage Japan to eliminate restrictions on international trade and payments, to provide a hospitable climate for foreign investment, and to eliminate restrictions on direct investment in Japan.

59. Seek to prevent Japan's becoming dependent on Communist areas for essential food and raw material supplies and for export markets.

60. Encourage Japan in its progress toward following internationally accepted trade practices. Encourage orderly marketing practices and avoidance of market disruption.

61. Terminate the grant Technical Assistance program at the end of FY 1961.

62. Continue encouragement of private U.S. investments in Japan.

63. In so far as possible, advise the Japanese Government of impending developments expected to have a major effect on U.S. Government expenditures in Japan.

64. Urge Japan to settle without delay the GARIOA claims and other property and claims matters.

65. Encourage Japan to provide increasing amounts of capital and technical assistance for the development of less-developed nations through private industry, Free World international institutions, and bilateral government programs; take Japanese assistance programs, including reparations, into account in the framing and implementation of U.S. aid programs in third countries, coordinating with the Japanese where appropriate.

66. Actively support Japan's continued participation in the Development Assistance Group and at the appropriate time sponsor Japan's association with the Organization for Economic Cooperation and Development, through its development assistance organization, and with any other appropriate multilateral economic organizations.

67. Encourage Japan to continue its activities in support of the proposed Asian Productivity Organization; and to continue to cooperate in the Third Country Training Program.

68. Urge Japan's continued cooperation in COCOM on the agreed level of export controls on trade with the Sino-Soviet Bloc, and endeavor to handle questions of routine exceptions in such a manner as to preserve and foster Japan's willingness to retain the agreed level of controls.

5.12 The US Ambassador on Anti-American Demonstrations in Tokyo, June 1960

The climate in US–Japan relations in 1960 worsened considerably as a result of American attempts to revise the security treaty, and American concerns reached a climax when President Eisenhower's visit to Tokyo had to be cancelled because of left-wing protest. In these two telegrams US Ambassador Douglas MacArthur Jr. analyses the situation before and after the visit was called off.

A. MacArthur to State Department, 8 June 1960

(…) Our present over-all assessment of probable Japanese reaction to President's visit is as follows:

1. We must expect strong demonstrations against President by pro-Communist groups, including Socialist Party, Sohyo, Nikkoso, and various Communist-front groups in line with Moscow's hard line. Moscow and Peking are committing all their available reserves to present internal struggle in Japan to defeat security treaty, and in particular they are opposing President's visit as they fear that it will prevent them from turning anti-Kishi and anti-security treaty struggle into nationwide fact that Communists estimate the President's visit will strengthen Japanese–American movement. In other words we should be encouraged by fact that Communists estimate the President's visit will strengthen Japanese–American relations and hinder present Communist offensive in Japan. As we all know, because of developments in Japan timing of President's visit is unfortunate because of conjuncture of his arrival and treaty ratification June 19 which gives pretext to leftists for demonstrations. (However Kishi hopes to have Upper House ratify by June 16 or 17.) While it is too bad there will be demonstrations, as long as Presidents' personal safety is not compromised, I think we should view pro-Communist demonstrations in same general light that we view Khrushchev blasts.

However, overwhelming majority of Japanese people are friendly to US and appreciate great assistance we have given them since end of war which has helped them so greatly in their reconstruction. Furthermore, Japanese people are traditionally extremely polite and friendly to visitors. We believe they will receive President with friendship and courtesy. While except for extremists Japanese are notoriously undemonstrative publicly, we think that if leftists overdo their opposition to visit many Japanese will feel called upon to applaud President vigorously to counteract possible impression in American and foreign eyes that he is not warmly welcomed here. We know GOJ [Government of Japan] and certain members of LDP [Liberal-Democratic Party] are working quietly to this end with important groups who themselves spontaneously wish to give President warm welcome.

As result of meeting I have had with press and public information media, business and political leaders, I think press will also soon begin to call on Japanese people to welcome President warmly. Kishi is also working on newspaper owners. There has been so much confusion here and so many reports about postponement that press has not come out in favor of visit yet for reasons I indicated earlier in Embtel [telegram from embassy] 4081 and also because they feel visit may strengthen Kishi whom they hate blindly. However, we believe there will now be good press support for visit although I am not yet certain press will take strong stand against Socialists re visit.

Despite foregoing, Zengakuren will make major effort to create unpleasant demonstrations against Hagerty when he arrives here Friday and there will not be restraints on such demonstrations against Hagerty that there would be on similar demonstrations against President (…).

Many people who are friendly toward US, while not wishing President to back down and postpone visit because of Communist pressure, at same time have been very much afraid of very adverse reaction in America if there are demonstrations against President. Some (particularly intellectuals) also considered the timing bad and fear it will enmesh President in political struggle going on here. They have suggested postponement of two to three weeks, but when it is pointed out that Communist opposition to visit will hardly change in that period and prospect will be for demonstrations even then, they reluctantly agree that this is true. On other hand, a number of Japanese leaders in business and politics feel that great struggle is now taking place in Japan, on outcome of which depends Japan's future political orientation (either with West or neutralism) and that President must go through with his visit and not give Communists victory by postponing. In past three days a number of my diplomatic colleagues, including Asians and Westerners, have asked me anxiously about reports that President might postpone his visit and have all stated that it is imperative (A) that President go through with visit as planned, and (B) that Kishi Government stand firm in ratifying treaty, as backing down to Communists will create domino reaction in free Asia.

Number of anti-mainstream LDP leaders have been calling for postponement of visit since they feel President's visit may somehow bolster Kishi. I have talked with some of them and now that it is crystal clear that President will proceed as planned, I believe most will climb on band wagon and say that President's visit is welcome, although I do not expect either Ishibashi or Matsumura to be helpful.

I of course realize how concerned you all must be in Washington, particularly in view of very alarming and perhaps sometimes exaggerated reports in our press. For example, such demonstrations as have thus far occurred in and about Embassy have been relatively calm affairs with no revolutionary or deep anti-American fervor evident even among some of Zengakuren students. I will continue to keep you informed, of course, about reactions to visit, but we here on firing line feel that situation with respect to Japanese press has now turned and that with knowledge that visit will take place as scheduled there will be increasingly strong support from majority of press, prominent leaders and personalities, and public favoring President's visit.

B. MacArthur to Department of State, 9 August 1960

In period since the political upheaval in Japan last May and June, there has now been sufficient time for intellectual, business and political leaders to reflect on the situation in Japan which underlay the use of force, violence and illegal action and to reach certain conclusions.

Many of them have now concluded that Japan badly needs a psychological shock to awaken it from its torpid complacency: (a) with respect to the nature of basic struggle going on in the world today between the forces of Communism and democracy; (b) regarding the extent to which international Communism not only influenced or controlled 'mass organizations' in Japan such as Sohyo unions, Zengakuren, etc. and could bring to bear in a revolutionary type uprising, but also had infiltrated the universities, intellectual circles, and the press; and (c) the wishful hope that the Japanese could quietly sit out the struggle going on in the rest of the world between Communism and democratic forms of government without having any real concern about the objectives or effect of world-wide Communist offensive on the internal prosperity and stability of Japan.

While regretting deeply the cancellation of the President's visit (and particularly its effect on Japan's international standing) a number of intellectual and other leaders feel that the cancellation of the visit was what actually provided the shock necessary to arouse responsible Japanese in all walks of life to an awareness of and a determination to do something about what is and has been actually going on in Japan. In this connection they point out that the pro-Communist forces in Japan have in the past two years twice resorted to peaks of force, violence and illegal actions within and outside of the Diet, and that on neither occasion were Japanese press, public or leaders seriously concerned over the basic implications involved in the substitution of force and violence for the rule of law and parliamentary democracy. (These previous peaks occurred during the abortive police bill debate in October–November 1958 and in November 1959 when Zengakuren stormed the Diet. Additionally throughout entire period there have been steadily increasing efforts by left extremists to discredit Diet and judiciary, to frustrate court processes, to engage in illegal strikes, demonstrations, trespasses and coercive measures.) Just as the Japanese had been complacent about the illegal actions of 'the young officers' as they prepared to take over Japan to lead it to destruction in the nineteen thirties, similarly the Japanese had been complacent in 1958 and 1959 over the illegal actions and preparations for a takeover by the extreme left (...)

How far these present highly favorable trends will be pressed and whether or not responsible leaders in all sectors of the national life will carry through on their present determination to correct the situation inside Japan remains, of course, to be seen. The root cause of Japanese vulnerability remains the factionalism of the conservatives and this is the great task confronting Ikeda in the period ahead. However, there is no doubt that as of now many for the first time see clearly and have begun to understand that there are basic internal weaknesses which must be corrected if Japan is to prosper in freedom. The fact that many of them attribute their awakening in large measure as a result of the deep shock and psychological soul searching resulting from the cancellation of the President's visit without which it would not have occurred, is also of very considerable interest.

5.13 Prime Minister Ikeda's Income Doubling Plan, December 1960

In the wake of the 1960 upheavals, the Liberal-Democrat prime minister Ikeda Hayato launched an ambitious plan for getting the Japanese economy geared for faster growth.

1. Objectives of This Plan

The plan to double the individual income must have as its objectives the doubling of the gross national product, attainment of full employment through expansion in employment opportunities, and raising the living standard of our people. We must adjust differentials in living standard and income existing between farming and nonfarming sectors, between large enterprises and small- and medium-size enterprises, between different regions of the country, and between different income groups. We must work toward a balanced development in our national economy and life patterns.

2. Targets to Be Attained

The plan's goal is to reach 26 trillion yen in GNP (at fiscal year 1958 prices) in the next ten years. To reach this goal, and in view of the fact that there are several factors highly favorable to economic growth existing during the first part of this plan, including the rapid development of technological changes and an abundant supply of skilled labor forces, we plan to attain an annual rate of growth of GNP at 9 percent for the coming three years. It is hoped that we shall be able to raise our GNP of 13.6 trillion yen (13 trillion yen in fiscal year 1958 prices) in fiscal year 1960 to 17.7 trillion yen (in 1960 prices) in fiscal year 1963 with the application of appropriate policies and cooperation from the private sector.

3. Points to Be Considered in Implementing the Plan and Directions to Be Followed

The plan contained in the report of the Economic Council [an advisory body to the Ministry of International Trade and Industry that issued its report on 1 November 1960] will be respected. However, in its implementation we must act flexibly and pay due consideration to the economic growth actually occurring and other related conditions. Any action we undertake must be consistent with the objectives described above. To do so, we shall pay special attention to the implementation of the following:

a. Promotion of Modernization in Agriculture (…)
b. Modernization of Small- and Medium-Size Enterprises (…)
c. Accelerated Development of Less Developed Regions (…)
d. Promotion of Appropriate Locations for industries and Reexamination of Regional Distribution of Public-Sector Projects (…)
e. Active Cooperation with the Development of the World Economy (…)

5.14 The US Ambassador on Japan and Nuclear Weapons, April 1963

The issue of US bases in Japan and the deployment of nuclear weapons was a constant irritant in the US–Japanese relationship in the 1960s, although Tokyo was careful not to challenge the Americans directly on these questions. This is US Ambassador Edwin Reischauer's report on a confidential conversation with Japanese Foreign Minister Ohira Masayoshi on 4 April 1963.

1. I met with [Foreign Minister] Ohira for breakfast April 4 at EMB [assy] residence to avoid public attention and raised with him points in REFTEL [telegram]. Without commenting (or being asked to comment) on concrete question of presence nuclear weapons aboard our vessels, I arrived at full mutual understanding with him regarding interpretation of classified record of discussion entirely on lines of existing US interpretation (our interpretation and indeed existence of classified record were both obviously new to Ohira). Ohira took presentation in stride and showed not RPT not slightest desire to persuade us to alter standing practice in military operations or public statements, and appeared confident that he could get top GOJ [Government of Japan] spokesmen to be more circumspect in language used on this subject. In short, although danger of leak or of resistance elsewhere in GOJ cannot of course be ruled out entirely, this action went as successfully as we could possibly have hoped, providing striking evidence how much our mutual confidence has grown since 1960.

2. While basing presentation [on] REFTEL, I tailored it along following lines, which I shall outline in detail, since they constituted present basis of our common understanding of article VI of treaty and related documents:

A) Saying that I was speaking to him informally and personally, I told Ohira that increasing closeness of our relationship made mutual understanding all the more necessary, mutual misunderstanding all the more harmful. Some recent exchanges in Diet (I continued) had caused me to fear that divergence might be showing up between our views on important matter affecting our defense relationship.

B) I then rehearsed our invariable policy of refusing to confirm or deny location of our nuclear weapons. In this connection I made point (which seemed to carry much weight with Ohira) that for us to reveal presence or absence of nuclear weapons on any specific ship at any particular time would be of considerable strategic benefit to Soviets. I explained that our treaty made Japan [a] somewhat special case, and we had accordingly modified our standing position to extent of being willing say no RPT no nuclear weapons had been 'introduced' in Japan or would be without prior consultation. (I took occasion to make clear significances of our sticking to word 'introduce', as implying placing or installing on Japanese soil, and our previous assumption that Japanese had been intending achieve same effect by their use of word 'Mochikomu'. Ohira then remarked that under this interpretation 'introduce' would not RPT not apply to hypothetical case of nuclears on vessel in Japanese waters or port, and I agreed Mochikomu with consciousness of this restricted sense, they would so use it in future.) I pointed out that in case of [US Navy] Seventh Fleet, however, we had always stuck to standard policy of neither affirming nor denying location of nuclear weapons anywhere in world, coupled with statement that we were faithfully observing treaty commitments to Japan. I then reviewed with Ohira English and Japanese texts of exchange of notes of January 19 [1960?] re Article VI and English text (lacking the Japanese) of Paras 2A and 2C of classified record of discussion of January 6, 1960.

C) After giving Ohira opportunity to break off discussion if he desired, I proceeded with review of recent statements which illustrate apparent divergence. I mentioned Gilpatric statement in press interview at Hotel Okura. 'We have no RPT no plans for placing RPT placing nuclear weapons in Japan,' and cited Ohira's own statements in Diet debate on March 7 and March 2, which I said we had found in general agreement with our interpretation of treaty. I then turned to examples of diet statements which did not RPT not square with our interpretation, including Shiga's of March 2 and Primin's [Prime Minister's] of March 6.

D) I closed my initial presentation by reiterating invariable US policy of neither affirming nor denying, etc., and reasons for it. I stressed danger that statements of kind just mentioned would lead to conflict with this policy and could be utilized by elements unfriendly to our two gov[ernmen]ts.

3. Throughout presentation and discussion that followed, I carefully avoided stating or implying that any US naval vessel or aircraft in Japanese ports or territorial air had carried or would actually carry nuclear weapons, keeping stress instead on dangers of divergence between statements by spokesmen of two

countries and undesirability of clearly telling Soviets whether specific American ships carried nuclears or not RPT not.

4. Re SSNs [nucleur-powered attack submarines], Ohira on own initiative brought out point that under treaty we had right to bring in SSNs but out of consideration for political problems and 'kindness' to GOJ we had asked GOJ opinion on problem. He said GOJ clearly understood this was not RPT not 'prior consultation' in sense of treaty. I said this was correct, but that inasmuch as we had made public statements about SSN visits and Polaris, we would, of course, abide by them. Ohira said we should of course maintain present posture re SSN visit.

5. Ohira's reaction was excellent. He admitted that he (and probably Primin Ikeda) had not RPT not understood what US meant by its use of 'introduce', but he showed no RPT no consternation over this revelation. He seemed entirely satisfied with our line of refusing to confirm or deny presence of nuclears on our ships and simultaneously asserting that we will live up to letter of treaty. He agreed with me that sudden attempt to 'correct' or materially alter line of Japanese statements would only serve to call unnecessary attention to problem; however, he agreed that henceforth he and others in GOJ would follow line of asserting that they have full trust in our assurances that we will live up to treaty; they would continue to use word 'Mochikomu' for 'introduce' but would henceforth understand by it what we mean when we say 'introduce'.

6. Re future of problem, Ohira said he would look up text of January 6 classified record of discussion and talk problem over with Ikeda, but he foresaw no RPT no problems. He promised to get in touch with me if there were any need for further discussion of matter. Re. longer range fu[tur]e, any possibility that GOJ might some day be taxed to explain apparent discrepancies in some recent Diet statements, Ohira said that growing realization by Japanese people of necessity for nuclear defense would probably make whole problem academic in three years or so.

7. Towards end of conversation, Ohira expressed his agreement that absolute trust in each other was most vital point in our relationship, and said that our ability to have talk of sort we were having was measure of progress our two countries had made in their relationship since 1960. Almost as if to illustrate the point he asked me if there were not RPT not some other general problems regarding Japan I would like to bring up. I took this opportunity to say Frank Pace preceding day had told me of his conversation with Ikeda, in which Pace had said American people's willingness carry disproportionate share of worlds burdens was fast coming to end, and time was coming sooner than world's leaders realized when other nations must take much larger share of burden. I told Ohira I realized political reeducation of Japanese public would take time, but there was need for speed. Ohira agreed but said he felt Japan was definitely speeding up and would

be able take its share of burden soon enough to meet need. He added that he personally found US position reasonable and that of Japan unreasonable (in fact he was sometimes accused by his colleagues of being US spokesman), but he was optimistic about Japan's ability to take up its share of load.

8. Comment: I would like to express my appreciation to Dept for wise and courageous guidance. I believe action has advanced our interests not RPT not only by eliminating dangerous discrepancy in our interpretation of treaty but also by reinforcing GOJ friendliness toward and confidence in US. There is still of course risk that Ohira will encounter less forthcoming attitudes on part of Ikeda or others in GOJ, or that leak will occur, but I consider these risks small by comparison with risks we would have run by keeping silent.

Questions

What were the main reasons why Japan surrendered in August 1945?

What was the main emphasis in the initial US policy towards occupied Japan?

How did Japanese elites try to deal with the occupiers?

What were the main political challenges inside Japan to the United States and its Japanese allies?

Why did Kennan think that US policy towards Japan had to be reshaped?

How did the Korean War affect Japan's international position?

What did the United States try to achieve through a peace treaty with Japan?

What was the main content of the US–Japan security treaty?

What were the main concerns in US policy towards Japan in the late 1950s?

How did US policy towards Japan change between 1955 and 1960?

Why did so many Japanese protest against President Eisenhower's proposed visit in 1960?

Why did economic issues become increasingly important in the Japanese–American relationship in the early 1960s?

Why was it so important for the United States and the Japanese government to avoid public debate about Japan's defence commitments?

6

The Korean War and the Sino-Soviet Alliance

The alliance between the Soviet Union and the new People's Republic of China, signed during the Moscow meetings between Stalin and Chinese leader Mao Zedong in February 1950, was one of the cornerstones of the early Cold War and one of the causes of the Korean War. It was a warning to the West that Moscow could find mighty allies outside Europe, and a harbinger, recognized as such both in Washington and Moscow, of revolutionary challenges elsewhere. While Stalin was never fully convinced of the ideological dedication of the Chinese Communists, he had made sure that they received vital aid in the latter stages of their civil war with the US-supported Chinese government, and believed that the Chinese Communist regime could be a stepping-stone for increased Soviet power elsewhere in Asia, including Korea.

The war that followed the North Korean attack on South Korea in June 1950 was the first 'hot' war of the Cold War era, and perhaps its most dangerous conflict in terms of superpower involvement. The war signalled a new level of permanent tension between East and West, and demonstrated the military capabilities of the newly formed Sino-Soviet alliance. It also told Moscow and Beijing that the United States was ready to fight a war on the East Asian mainland against the expansion of Communist rule, even when local conditions were unfavourable and international support was uncertain. During the first months of the war, until the front stabilized in the spring of 1951, these realizations intensified the fervour of the Soviet–American conflict and made both sides prepare for all-out war.

As shown by the documents below, the war in Korea initially had more local than global causes. After World War II the Korean peninsula—which had been occupied by Japan since the early part of the century—had been divided into an American occupation zone in the south and a Soviet zone in the north. As in Germany, the two superpowers gradually came to support their local ideological allies in building states centred in their respective zones but with claims to represent all of the country. The North Korean regime, with its capital in Pyongyang, was headed by Kim Il-Sung, a young Communist who had spent most of his life in the Soviet Union and China and who had returned to Korea with the Red Army in 1945. In the south, the veteran nationalist Syngman Rhee returned from the United States to set up a government in Seoul supported by landowners and businessmen. Both regimes were authoritarian and repressive, and their leaders were dedicated to national reunification on *their* terms.

In the summer of 1949 the number of clashes along the 38th parallel that divided the two states increased dramatically. Both regimes appealed to their superpower patrons for increased military support, and made no secret of their aim to overthrow their opponents. But while Moscow and Washington were willing to supply their Korean allies with increasing amounts of aid, neither Stalin nor Truman were willing to consider an all-out attack across the 38th parallel, believing that the risks of such an operation far outweighed the possible gains.

In early 1950, however, Stalin began to change his views about what could be achieved in Korea and allowed Kim Il-Sung to begin preparing for a reunification by force, to be aided by Soviet military advisers. There may be several reasons why the Soviet leader changed his mind. He may have thought that the Korean balance of power made it an opportune moment for an attack. The swift victory of the Chinese Revolution meant that the scales of power in East Asia, at least temporarily, had swung in the direction of Communism. At the same time, the American build-up of Japan as part of its global alliance system could pose a long-term threat to all Soviet achivements in the area. American statements also left Stalin in doubt as to what Washington's reaction to to a quick North Korean offensive would be. Since the Americans had not intervened in China, perhaps they would not intervene in Korea either? Stalin may have wanted to show other Communist parties that it was not only the Chinese who were willing to sponsor a revolutionary strategy when the time was right. His failure to force a solution over Berlin, the successful testing of a Soviet nuclear weapon, and the formation of NATO in 1949 may also have contributed to his militancy.

The North Korean attack on 25 June 1950 took both Syngman Rhee and Washington by surprise. Harry Truman quickly decided to assist the South Korean regime. To him the offensive was a direct challenge to American influence, not only in Asia but worldwide, including in Europe. What mattered to Truman was not so much Korea itself—although his military advisers argued for the peninsula's strategic importance—but the impression the defeat of an American ally would make throughout the world. Since the Soviet Union boycotted the UN Security Council, the United States got a resolution passed which made the counter-attack it prepared into a UN operation. After having encircled the South Korean and UN forces in a small area around Pusan on the south-east tip of Korea, the North Korean offensive was broken on 15 September 1950 by

US amphibious landings near Seoul. By October the US-led forces under General Douglas MacArthur had crossed the 38th parallel and were heading for the Chinese border, with the intention of reunifying Korea under Seoul's leadership.

The American offensive started a frantic debate in Beijing about how and when China should intervene to assist its North Korean comrades. In spite of having had doubts that spring about the timing of Pyongyang's attack, Mao Zedong had since June believed that China would have to get involved in the Korean War if needed. To Mao, the ideological bonds with Kim's regime—both as fellow Communists and as heads of countries with strong historic ties—were essential. But the Chinese leadership was not united on the issue, and several leaders believed that it would be in China's best interest to stay out of the conflict. The American offensive towards the Chinese border and Stalin's and Kim Il-Sung's urgent appeals for Chinese assistance resolved the issue in Mao's favour. In late November Chinese forces, some of which were already in North Korea, attacked the UN troops, driving them back toward Seoul.

In the early spring of 1951 the battlefront stabilized around the 38th parallel, in spite of attempts on both sides to gain the upper hand in the fighting. When General MacArthur publicly criticized the US government for not providing enough support for a new offensive, President Truman removed him from command in April 1951. Peace feelers began already in the summer of that year, but none of the parties were in much of a hurry to end the war, hoping that a tough line would improve their negotiating position. By late 1952, however, it was clear that both Beijing and Washington saw little purpose in continuing the warfare. It was Stalin who now insisted that the war go on, probably seeing long-term advantages for the Soviet Union in China keeping the United States at war in Korea. After Stalin died suddenly in March 1953, all the Great Powers—including the new Soviet leaders—were eager to end the war, and an armistice was concluded in July, returning to the status quo before the North Korean attack. The price paid for this result was heavy: US losses were placed at 54,000 dead and 103,000 wounded; Chinese and Korean losses were each more than ten times as high.

For the Sino-Soviet alliance, the Korean War meant the beginning of a period of close co-operation. Nikita Khrushchev, the Soviet leader who replaced Stalin, was less suspicious of the Chinese, and agreed to a large programme of aid for China. This programme—the largest such effort the Soviets ever undertook—included thousands of Soviet advisers; transfer of technology; diplomatic, military, and intelligence co-operation; and help with education. The Chinese welcomed the programme and took the Soviet Union as its model for economic and social development in the mid-1950s.

What toppled the alliance at the end of the decade was primarily Mao Zedong's new policies of revolutionary radicalism in China. Mao felt that the Chinese Revolution had stalled and that the resistance to Communism in Eastern Europe was a warning that more radical policies were needed. The Great Leap Forward, which Mao launched in 1958, was an attempt to force growth through intense collectivization and industrialization, breaking away from the more gradualist policies recommended by the Soviets. When these policies failed, with mass starvation as their result, Mao felt that Soviet criticism could undermine his position and his policies.

In foreign affairs there were also disagreements following from China's more radical policies. Mao criticized Khrushchev's attempts at lessening tension with the United States and his insufficient support for China's recovery of Taiwan and its conflict with India. The Soviets countered that Beijing's policies were irresponsible and dangerous. In the summer of 1960 Khrushchev abruptly withdrew all Soviet advisers from China. While limited military and intelligence cooperation continued up to 1963, the withdrawal signalled the end of the alliance. During the rest of the 1960s China was an enemy of the Soviet Union, rather than a friend.

Readings

Odd Arne Westad, *Decisive Encounters: The Chinese Civil War, 1946–1950* (2003). Describes the interaction between domestic and international affairs in the Communist victory.

Chen Jian, *China's Road to the Korean War: The Making of the Sino-American Confrontation* (1994). Shows how the Sino-American conflict developed, and why it led to war in Korea.

Chen Jian, *Mao's China and the Cold War* (2001). A broad overview of Chinese foreign policy during the Cold War.

William Stueck, *The Korean War: An International History* (1995). The best history of the war.

Odd Arne Westad (ed.), *Brothers in Arms: The Rise and Fall of the Sino-Soviet Alliance, 1945–1963* (1998). Historians from several countries analyse the fate of the alliance.

6.1 Mao Zedong on the Soviet Union, January 1949

The first top-level meeting between Mao Zedong and a Soviet official took place in the little town of Xibaipo in Hebei province in the winter of 1949, when Stalin sent Anastas Mikoyan—a member of the ruling Politburo—to confer with the Chinese Communist leader. Stalin had been surprised by the speed with which Mao's forces were conquering China.

Mao Zedong emphasized that the Soviet Union had rendered and was rendering a large assistance to the CCP, and the latter was very much grateful to the VKP(b) [Soviet Communist Party] for that. The Chinese revolution, Mao Zedong continued, was a part of the world revolution. In this connection, partial interests must be subordinate to the common ones. We always take this point into consideration when we address the Soviet Union for help. If, let us suggest, the Soviet Union does not give something, we would not have grudge against it. When before his departure to Moscow Luo Ronghuan asked me how he should pose the question of the Soviet Union's assistance to us, I told him that he should not depict the situation as if we were dying and did not have our own potentials, but I emphasized that it would be desirable for us to receive your assistance in respect to Manchuria. From 1947 on, Lin Biao, too, often requested Moscow's assistance with regard to some or other issues. I, said Mao Zedong, instructed Gao Gang to the effect that everything that we take from the USSR must be repaid by all means, and, besides, the shortage of some or other materials must be resolved at the expense of the Guomindang[-held] areas. Chinese comrades must use the assistance from the Soviet Union rationally. If not for the assistance on the part of the Soviet Union, Mao Zedong emphasized, we would hardly be able to win the current victories. This, however, does not mean that we do not have to rely on our own potentials as well. Nevertheless, said Mao Zedong, one cannot but take account of the fact that the Soviet Union's military assistance in Manchuria, amounting to 1/4 of the whole assistance to us, plays quite a substantial role (…)

I asked Mao Zedong what reason did he use during the conversations in order to substantiate the patriotic character of the Soviet–Chinese Treaty, and Mao Zedong laughingly said that it had not been him but rather Chiang Kai-shek who had signed the treaty. I used to explain to them, said Mao Zedong, that the Soviet Union came to Port Arthur in order to defend itself and China from the Japanese fascism, because China is so weak that she cannot defend herself without the USSR's assistance. The USSR did not come to the KChZhD [Chinese Changchun Railroad] and Port Arthur as an imperialist power, but rather as a socialist force to defend the common interests.

As to the question why Communists acted against the American naval base in Qingdao and defended the Soviet base in Port Arthur, Mao Zedong answered that the American imperialism was sitting in China for suppression, while the Soviet Union had its forces in Port Arthur for defense against Japanese fascism. When China becomes stronger and is able to defend herself from the Japanese danger, then the Soviet Union itself will not need the base in Port Arthur. At the same time Mao Zedong said that a Chinese woman, a member of the Guomindang Legislative Yuan, had stated that if the Communists managed to get Port Arthur back from the Russians for China, it would be a great deal. As Mao Zedong said, that woman did not understand politics.

In conclusion, Mao Zedong emphasized that they were speaking about their pro-Soviet sentiments openly. He referred to the fact that on the day of celebration of the anniversary of the October Revolution they had been emphasizing that China must stand in the anti-imperialist camp led by the Soviet Union. There is no a middle road for us, concluded Mao Zedong.

6.2 Stalin Meets Kim Il-Sung, March 1949

When Stalin met North Korean leader Kim Il-Sung face to face in Moscow on 5 March 1949, the discussion centred on the strategic situation and on Kim's wish to get Red Army assistance to reunite his country by force. This is an excerpt from their conversation.

STALIN asks the members of the delegation how their trip was, was it difficult on the journey?

KIM IL-SUNG thanks the Soviet Government for its attention to them and says that they arrived safely.

STALIN asks how they travelled—by railroad or by air.

KIM IL-SUNG answers that they came by railroad.

STALIN asks whether they became ill on the way.

KIM IL-SUNG answers that they were healthy.

STALIN suggests that they proceed to business and asks what will be the questions.

KIM IL-SUNG says that after the liberation of Korea by Soviet troops, the Soviet Government and the Soviet Army rendered aid to Korea in the matter of economic development, in the matter of the development of Korea along the democratic path, and that the Korean government understands that without further economic and cultural aid from the Soviet Union it will be difficult for the DPRK to restore and develop its national economy and culture. The assistance of the Soviet Union is required for the further development of the Korean economy and culture.

STALIN asks what kind of aid.

KIM IL-SUNG answers—economic and cultural.

STALIN asks what precisely is needed.

KIM IL-SUNG says that they have confirmed a two year plan for the restoration and development of the national economy. They need economic assistance to fulfill this plan and to strengthen the foundation of the economy. They need machines, equipment, and spare parts for industry, communications, transport and also for other branches of the national economy. They also need technical assistance: sending Soviet specialists to Korea, drafting plans for the construction of new objects (factories and plants), conducting geological exploratory work.

STALIN asks what kind of objects?

KIM answers, e.g., irrigation structures [at] Anju, the construction of which they have now moved toward, but they do not have enough specialists, and also the restoration and completion of the Seisin metallurgical plant, repair of the Sufun hydroelectric plant and others.

STALIN asks if there is iron ore in Korea.

KIM answers that there is very much iron ore in Korea.

STALIN says that it is possible to render this assistance, and it is also possible to provide specialists.

KIM indicates that until now trade between the two countries has been conducted successfully, but in the future, for the fulfillment of the two year plan, they need to import from the Soviet Union equipment, steam engines, electric locomotives, spare parts and equipment for the textile industry. But exports from Korea will not cover the imports, therefore they need credit from the Soviet government.

STALIN says 'Fine' and asks in what amount they need credit.

KIM answers from 40 to 50 million American dollars.

STALIN—fine, what else? (…)

KIM says that in the south of Korea there are still American troops and that intrigues against North Korea by the reactionaries are increasing, that they have infantry troops but sea defense almost does not exist. The help of the Soviet Union is needed in this.

STALIN asks how many American troops are in South Korea.

KIM answers that there are up to 20,000 men.

SHTYKOV—approximately 15–20 thousand men.

STALIN asks if there is a national Korean army in the south.

KIM answers that there is, the number is around 60,000 men.

STALIN asks if this number includes only regular army or also police.

KIM answers that it includes only regular army.

STALIN (joking) asks, and you are afraid of them?

KIM—No, we are not afraid, but we would like to have naval units.

STALIN asks which army is stronger—north or south.

PAK HON-YONG answers that the northern army is stronger. (…)

STALIN asks are they penetrating into the South Korean army, do they have their own people there?

PAK HON-YONG answers that they are penetrating, but so far they are not revealing themselves there.

STALIN says that this is correct, that it is not necessary to reveal themselves now and indicates that the southerners also, apparently, are sending their people into the army of the north and that they need [to exercise] caution.

STALIN asks what has happened along the 38th parallel. Is it true that several points have fallen to the southerners and have been seized, and then these points were taken back?

KIM answers that they are taking into account that the southerners can send their own people into the [North Korean] army, and that they are taking the necessary measures.

KIM reported that there was a clash with the southerners in Kangwon province at the 38th parallel. Their police were not sufficiently armed at that time. When regular units approached, the southerners retreated (...)

6.3 Stalin Meets Mao Zedong, December 1949

In December 1949 Mao Zedong travelled to Moscow to fulfill his long-time wish to meet the head of the international Communist movement, Soviet leader Joseph Stalin. Although Stalin was initially reluctant to grant the Chinese a new treaty of alliance, Mao in the end got most of what he wanted, including loans, transfers of technology, and military assistance.

COMRADE MAO ZEDONG: The most important question at the present time is the question of establishing peace. China needs a period of 3–5 years of peace, which would be used to bring the economy back to pre-war levels and to stabilize the country in general. Decisions on the most important questions in China hinge on the prospects for a peaceful future. With this in mind the CC CCP [Central Committee of the Chinese Communist Party] entrusted me to ascertain from you, comr[ade], Stalin, in what way and for how long will international peace be preserved.

COMRADE STALIN: In China a war for peace, as it were, is taking place. The question of peace greatly preoccupies the Soviet Union as well, though we have already had peace for the past four years. With regards to China, there is no immediate threat at the present time: Japan has yet to stand up on its feet and is thus not ready for war; America, though it screams war, is actually afraid of war more than anything; Europe is afraid of war; in essence, there is no one to fight with China, not unless Kim Il Sung decides to invade China. Peace will depend on our efforts. If we continue to be friendly, peace can last not only 5–10 years, but 20–25 years and perhaps even longer.

COMRADE MAO ZEDONG: Since Liu Shaoqi's return to China, CC CCP has been discussing the treaty of friendship, alliance and mutual assistance between China and the USSR.

COMRADE STALIN: This question we can discuss and decide. We must ascertain whether to declare the continuation of the current 1945 treaty of alliance and friendship between the USSR and China, to announce impending changes in the future, or to make these changes right now. As you know, this treaty was concluded between the USSR and China as a result of the Yalta Agreement, which provided for the main points of the treaty (the question of the Kurile Islands,South Sakhalin, Port Arthur, etc.). That is, the given treaty was concluded, so to speak, with the consent of America and England. Keeping in mind this circumstance, we, within our inner circle, have decided not to modify any of the points of this treaty for now, since a change in even one point could give America and England the legal grounds to raise questions about also modifying the treaty's provisions concerning the Kurile Islands, South Sakhalin, etc. This is why we searched to find a way to modify the current treaty in effect while formally maintaining its provisions, in this case by formally maintaining the Soviet Union's right to station its troops at Port Arthur while, at the request of the Chinese government, actually withdrawing the Soviet Armed forces currently stationed there. Such an operation could be carried out upon China's request. One could do the same with KChZhD [Chinese Changchun Railroad, which traverses Manchuria], that is, to effectively modify the corresponding points of the agreement while formally maintaining its provisions, upon China's request.

If, on the other hand, the Chinese comrades are not satisfied with this strategy, they can present their own proposals.

COMRADE MAO ZEDONG: The present situation with regard to KChZhD and Port Arthur corresponds well with Chinese interests, as the Chinese forces are inadequate to effectively fight against imperialist aggression. In addition, KChZhD is a training school for the preparation of Chinese cadres in railroad and industry.

COMRADE STALIN: The withdrawal of troops does not mean that Soviet Union refuses to assist China, if such assistance is needed. The fact is that we, as Communists, are not altogether comfortable with stationing our forces on foreign soil, especially on the soil of a friendly nation. Given this situation anyone could say that if Soviet forces can be stationed on Chinese territory, then why could not the British, for example, station their forces in Hong Kong, or the Americans in Tokyo? We would gain much in the arena of international relations if, with mutual agreement, the Soviet forces were to be withdrawn from Port Arthur. In addition, the withdrawal of Soviet forces would provide a serious boost to Chinese Communists in their relations with the national bourgeoisie. Everyone would see that the Communists have managed to achieve what [Nationalist

Chinese leader] Jiang Jieshi [Chiang Kai-shek] could not. The Chinese Communists must take the national bourgeoisie into consideration. The treaty ensures the USSR's right to station its troops in Port Arthur. But the USSR is not obligated to exercise this right and can withdraw its troops upon Chinese request. However, if this is unsuitable, the troops in Port Arthur can remain there for 2, 5, or 10 years, whatever suits China best. Let them not misunderstand that we want to run away from China. We can stay there for 20 years even.

COMRADE MAO ZEDONG: In discussing the treaty in China we had not taken into account the American and English positions regarding the Yalta agreement. We must act in a way that is best for the common cause. This question merits further consideration. However, it is already becoming clear that the treaty should not be modified at the present time, nor should one rush to withdraw troops from Port Arthur. Should not Zhou Enlai visit Moscow in order to decide the treaty question?

COMRADE STALIN: No, this question you must decide for yourselves. Zhou may be needed in regard to other matters.

COMRADE MAO ZEDONG: We would like to decide on the question of Soviet credit to China, that is to draw up a credit agreement for 300.000.000 dollars between the governments of the USSR and China.

COMRADE STALIN: This can be done. If you would like to formalize this agreement now, we can (…)

COMRADE MAO ZEDONG: Several countries, especially Britain, are actively campaigning to recognize the People's Republic of China. However, we believe that we should not rush to be recognized. We must first bring about order to the country, strengthen our position, and then we can talk to foreign imperialists.

COMRADE STALIN: That is a good policy. In addition, there is no need for you to create conflicts with the British and the Americans. If, for example, there will be a need to put pressure on the British, this can be done by resorting to a conflict between the Guangdong province and Hong Kong. And to resolve this conflict, Mao Zedong could come forward as the mediator. The main point is not to rush and to avoid conflicts.

Are there foreign banks operating in Shanghai? (…)

6.4 Stalin on the North Korean Attack, April 1950

We still have no documents from Stalin's hand that show with certainty why he in early 1950 changed his mind and gave the go-ahead for a North Korean attack on South Korea. A Russian journal with access to the archives give the following summary of Stalin's crucial conversation with Kim in Moscow.

In conversations with Kim Il-Sung in April 1950 in the Kremlin, Stalin gave four reasons to support his conclusion that the international environment had 'changed sufficiently to permit a more active stance on the unification of Korea.'

The first reason was 'the significant strengthening of the socialist camp in the East: the victory of the Chinese revolution, the signing of an alliance between the USSR and the PRC [People's Republic of China], and the USSR's acquisition of an atomic bomb.'

The second reason concerned 'the obvious weakness of the reactionary camp [as seen in]: the shameful defeat of America's intervention into Chinese affairs, Western troubles in Southeast Asia, and the inability of the South Korean regime and its American masters to improve the social, economic, and political situation in South Korea.'

Stalin listed as the third factor contributing to the Soviet Union's new stance 'the dishonest, perfidious, and arrogant behavior of the United States in Europe, the Balkans, the Middle East, and especially its decision to form NATO.' According to Stalin, 'America was no longer a partner, but [instead] an adversary, and the Soviet Union could not bind itself any longer to agreements with [such] an adversary.'

The fourth reason was the 'aggressive designs of the South Korean junta.' As Stalin concluded, 'the South was determined to launch an attack on the North sooner or later and it was important to forestall this aggression.'

6.5 A Soviet General's Report on the North Korean Attack, June 1950

The Soviet ambassador to North Korea, Colonel-General Terentii Shtykov, sent the following telegram to the Red Army High Command two days after the North Korean attack.

I report about the preparation and course of the military operations of the Korean People's Army.

The concentration of the People's Army in the region near the 38th parallel began on June 12 and was concluded on June 23, as was prescribed in the plan of the General Staff. The redeployment of troops took place in an orderly fashion, without incident. The intelligence service of the enemy probably detected the troop redeployment, but we managed to keep the plan and the time of the beginning of troop operations secret. The planning of the operation at the divisional level and the reconnaissance of the area was carried out with the participation of Soviet advisers.

All preparatory measures for the operation were completed by June 24th. On June 24th divisional commanders were given orders about 'D'[day] and 'H'[hour]. The political order of the Minister of Defense was read to the troops, which explained that the South Korean army had provoked a military attack by violating the 38th parallel and that the government of the DPRK had given an order to the Korean People's Army to go over to the counterattack.

The order to counter-attack was met with great enthusiasm by the soldiers and officers of the Korean People's Army.

The troops went to their starting positions by 24:00 hours on June 24th. Military operations began at 4 hours 40 minutes local time. Artillery preparation was accompanied in the course of 20–40 minutes by direct fire and a ten-minute artillery barrage. The infantry rose up and went on the attack in good spirits. In the first three hours individual units and formations advanced from 3 to 5 kilometers.

The attack of the troops of the People's Army took the enemy completely by surprise (…)

Conclusions regarding the South

The first two days of military operations have shown the following:

1. The enemy is putting up resistance and while fighting is retreating deep into the territory of South Korea, mass taking of prisoners from the South Korean army has not been noted.

2. The South Korean puppet authorities have begun to throw in troops from deep in the rear and are trying to halt the advance of the People's Army.

3. In the first day the attack of the People's Army caused confusion in the South. The South Korean authorities and the ambassador of the USA personally in their radio speeches called on the people of South Korea to stay calm. The staff of the South Korean army is broadcasting false reports about the successes of the South Korean army.

6.6 Truman on Korea, June 1950

President Truman reacted swiftly to the North Korean attack. Here is his statement from 27 June 1950.

In Korea the Government forces, which were armed to prevent border raids and to preserve internal security, were attacked by invading forces from North Korea. The Security Council of the United Nations called upon the invading troops to cease hostilities and to withdraw to the 38th parallel. This they have not done, but on the contrary have pressed the attack. The Security Council called upon all members of the United Nations to render every assistance to the United Nations in the execution of this resolution. In these circumstances I have ordered United States air and sea forces to give the Korean Government troops cover and support.

The attack upon Korea makes it plain beyond all doubt that Communism has passed beyond the use of subversion to conquer independent nations and will now use armed invasion and war. It has defied the orders of the Security Council of the United Nations issued to preserve international peace and security. In these circumstances the occupation of Formosa by Communist forces would be a direct threat to the security of the Pacific area and to United States forces performing their lawful and necessary functions in that area.

Accordingly I have ordered the 7th Fleet to prevent any attack on Formosa. As a corollary of this action I am calling upon the Chinese Government on Formosa to cease all air and sea operations against the mainland. The 7th Fleet will see that this is done. The determination of the future status of Formosa must await the restoration of security in the Pacific, a peace settlement with Japan, or consideration by the United Nations.

I have also directed that United States Forces in the Philippines be strengthened and that military assistance to the Philippine Government be accelerated.

I have similarly directed acceleration in the furnishing of military assistance to the forces of France and the Associated States in Indochina and the dispatch of a military mission to provide close working relations with those forces.

I know that all members of the United Nations will consider carefully the consequences of this latest aggression in Korea in defiance of the Charter of the United Nations. A return to the rule of force in international affairs would have far-reaching effects. The United States will continue to uphold the rule of law.

I have instructed the Ambassador Austin, as the representative of the United States to the Security Council, to report these steps to the Council.

6.7 The Battle for Seoul, September 1950

The American journalist Marguerite Higgins was one of the best front-line reporters of the Korean War. Here is her report on the US efforts to recapture the South Korean capital from the North Korean forces in late September 1950.

A. Korean Resistance and the American Way of Breaking it

The red clay ridges and pine groves on the northwest outskirts of Seoul shuddered in the last twenty-four hours with one of this war's most sanguinary battles as tired but dogged marines inched their way toward the center of the South Korean capital, a point still some three miles away. Spectacular artillery duels in what was certainly the worst phase of the battle for Seoul took place in the suburb of Sinchon, where a famous Korean landmark, the American-founded Chosen Christian University, was being blasted to bits. It is victim of a stubborn determination on the part of the North Korean Communists to fight to the end, and to bring Seoul down in ruins about them if necessary. The university was founded in the 1890's by Horace G. Underwood, a Presbyterian missionary who was among the first Christians to arrive in Korea.

Late this afternoon the marines were advancing on the university, where the North Korean 17th Division headquarters has been reported housed. Fresh American troops had to be put into the battle to advance through the lines of South Korean Marines who earlier suffered heavy casualties from enemy artillery. The artillery fire had also been reaching to the back of the entire front-line area. It was with wry comments that Marines waiting to go into a new attack the afternoon waved copies of Friday's 'Stars and Stripes,' the army newspaper. The edition bore a headline which read: 'Yanks Enter Seoul From Two Sides!'

Stalled on the outskirts of Seoul for more than twenty-four hours, Marines all along the front reported, in the words of Maj. John Canney, a battalion executive officer: 'We've been running up against a different breed of cat here in the past day or so.' The major, whose battalion was dug in on a strategic hill overlooking the city, added: 'The prisoners we've been taking in the last twenty-four hours seem better fed, taller in stature and far more fanatical. For instance, we had our tanks up blasting the hell out of mortars dug in on a hilltop. We blasted out the mortar position, but a while later they just brought mortars back up and started shooting at us all over again.'

The North Koreans, who as it later turned out had a forward observer right in the American lines, were murderously accurate with their high-velocity weapons and mortars. Searching out troop concentrations, the Reds' mortars a number of times scored thirty to forty casualties with one burst. As we ravelled to different headquarters, from battalion to company and even back to regiment, we could find no place free of the whine and whistle and thump of enemy shells. The enemy would not give up even when the marines got to the top of the ridges and dug in. Able (A) Company, trying to get to the top of a ridge already occupied by Charlie (C) Company, was pinned down for eight hours by snipers and machine gunners who had sneaked around the mountainside to come at the troops from the rear. When A Company finally reached their objective they had only one officer left—the company commander.

If the Americans had ever had any idea of going easy in the shelling of Seoul in order to save buildings, it became clear today that the Communists were not going to give them a chance. The Reds had obviously saved everything for this final blast and in self defense the Americans had to answer back with everything they had. It is one of the ironies of this war that some of the artillery and even machine guns that the Communists are using so effectively are pieces captured in the days of the American retreats.

The enemy persistence in sniping and machine gunning of all positions has made the evacuation of wounded tragically difficult. On one ridge close to the Han River, wounded had to lie in the hills for four hours before medical corpsmen could get their heads up high enough to carry them out. The artillery duels were taking a terrific toll of Korean civilians. All day and all night women, little children and old men were being brought by pushcart, oxen or litter into the regimental command post in the pathetic hope that the frantically busy doctors could pause long enough to tend to them. First-aid teams helped when they had time, but that was not so often.

Shortly after noon, the Marine artillery and air power let loose. One of the strongest artillery barrages of this war literally tore up the hillside ahead, where the enemy was crouched, and the planes came in for a final blow with fire bombs. Then the Marines started to move forward again.

B. Vignettes of Terror and the Liberation of Seoul

Flames and smoke wreathed downtown Seoul today as Marines battered and burned their way forward in slow house-to-house fighting. With the main hotel and government districts of the South Korean capital still in Communist hands, the Marines edged forward by ferreting out the enemy from cellars and roofs, culverts and chimneys.

American flame-throwing tanks stabbed at the flimsy Korean houses, igniting whole blocks, but still the enemy fought on, bringing tanks, grenades and self-propelled guns to support their last-ditch-fight. Eight-foot-high sandbag barricades were encountered with increasing frequency as the Marines slogged toward the main part of Seoul, and big American tanks had to be called in to blast them away with their 90-mm guns.

By late this afternoon, no place in the western part of Seoul was free from the hum of sniper bullets or safe from sudden attack by riflemen or machine-gunners hidden in the cellars or hill-side buildings. Creeping behind the forward Marine troops, this correspondent entered the downtown area at the main Seoul railroad station. It was exactly three months ago that I had been chased out of this city by the Communist invaders who, on the night of June 27, had pushed in even as I and the sixty members of the American Military Mission were escaping by ferry and raft across the Han River.

I found the sprawling railroad station a scarred and flaming ruin with twisted, blackened cars and locomotives strewn in disorder across the tracks. Most of the houses on the hillside directly in back of the station had been razed in the cross-fire. By standing on a bluff near the station I could see the main hotels and government buildings about 1,000 yards away. They appeared intact, but the district in which they are located was encircled by smoke and flame.

The flash of bursting artillery was rapidly approaching the central downtown area. The state of the buildings will depend on the Communists themselves. Orders are to damage Seoul as little as possible, but if North Koreans take cover in the buildings our big guns and rocket-firing planes will have to go after them just as they have had to blast out other areas in the city. Up to now, the Communists have exacted the maximum penalty for every yard gained.

Among the buildings that still appeared untouched were the Chosen Hotel and the big Banto building, which formerly housed the Economic Co-operation Administration and part of the American Embassy. The Seoul City Hall and the domed capitol also stood out clearly and seemed undamaged.

Despite the pounding of our artillery and the shelling with white phosphorus, the enemy was not only still willing to fight but also to counterattack. Late this afternoon a platoon, marching four abreast and dragging an anti-tank gun, marched right into the position of a forward Marine company. There have been many American casualties, for the street fighting gave the North Koreans the opportunity for close-range firing at the Marines as they raked through the tenements and back alleys looking for the dug-in foe.

6.8 The Chinese Counter-Attack, November 1950

In late October 1950 the Chinese sent a vast army to rescue the Korean Communists, who at that point had lost all but the northernmost section of the country to the American, UN, and South Korean counter-attack. Here is Capt. Norman Allen's letter to his mother on the day his company (I Company/5th Cavalry) first encountered the Chinese.

4 Nov [1950]
Dearest Mother:
Today is cold. Rain last night and this morning, cold wind and really mean.

Our regiment yesterday moved 56 miles back SE to Sunch'on. I watched civilian moving out; women carrying what they could on their heads, kids strapped to their backs, those a little older walking alongside or running to keep up. All are hungry and poorly dressed. My God, how awful it were our kids doing that. If we are fighting to keep our kids from running like that, our women, our old men, then we have a reason for being here. It's not the long stream of refugees that sticks in my memory, it's the cute little three year old jogging, trying to keep up, her mother carrying a crying baby, their few possessions tied in a blanket balanced on the mother's head. I remember one old woman, bent over, lagging behind. Everyone for herself.

I am now in a battalion area, no more than muddy rice paddies, awaiting word what we do next. Everyone is wondering what all this means. The UN Forces were extended in their move to the Yalu and the strong Chinese attacks on the ROK's [Republic of Korea (South Korea)] forced their withdrawal which has resulted in us all falling back. I thought at first it might be a political decision, move our bombing time down and deliver China an ultimatum to get out or else. But now I believe it's military move to regroup and straighten the line, then determine where the enemy is and in what strength. Make our plans and then go back and hit him hard.

It's a nasty realization with the casualties returning on jeeps and tanks, that the war is still on and we are still in it. We see issues of *Time* and *Newsweek* stating, 'War over—only mopping up—troops in Japan for Thanksgiving—home by Christmas.' Wish the people who write this were over here now. This is certainly no time for optimism. It's mean and nasty; elements make living difficult—muddy ground and rain do not make for good bedfellows. Being in a fight makes it just that much worse. Still sleep with our boots on. When we do sleep it's only for a few moments. The rattle of rifle fire means someone nearby is having a rough go.

The battalion has been fortunate that so far the 'ginks' haven't hit us. I'm told the enemy is well trained and organized. They speak Chinese and were born and raised in China; they'd never even heard of Korea before now. Anyone who says they aren't Chinks is crazy! Things now are beginning to shape up to be as grim as those days in September around Taegu (...)

[The night Norman Allen wrote that letter, the Chinese moved to cut off the British Commonwealth Brigade on the Taeryong River. The U.S. 61st Field Artillery Battalion had set up south of Pakch'on, two and a half miles away. It was between the Americans and the Commonwealth Brigade that the Chinese intended to cut the road.]

6.9 War in Korea, January 1953

By 1953 public opinion in the United States had turned against the war, and the new president, General Dwight D. Eisenhower, promised to bring it to an end. Here is one of the press reports that contributed to the change in the public mood.

This is such a miserable country to die in. It's not just that it's Korea. It would be miserable country if it were Ohio, Texas, Indiana or Pennsylvania. War is universal and battlefields are the same.

Three of our men got it last night. Old timers say it was their own fault. They say it gruffly—because they know it could have been them—as if that explains everything. It was their own fault, they say, because the guys let themselves get trapped. One enemy patrol deliberately exposed itself and the kids chased it up a draw where another was waiting in ambush. Our people heard the shooting, saw the flashes and, after the survivors got home, went out and recovered the bodies.

One foul out here and you're through. Every man here remembers at least once when he almost fouled out. They sit around bunkers at night and talk about it. It is pitiless self-examination and it isn't pretty to hear. The patrols they talk about are those which didn't come off. Those are the ones they remember. Each man blames himself for something he didn't do—some oversight he fears cost some buddy his life.

A few minutes ago, we looked over some cards those kids filled out before they were killed last night. They filled them out so division public information men could write home-town newspapers and the home folks could see their boys' names in print. Take the lieutenant. He wrote with a firm strong hand. A young man whose gold bars were still new. He was graduated from a small southwestern college last August. Korea in October. Dead in January. And the two enlisted men killed with him. One had been a hotel desk clerk, a draftee. The other had just finished high school and enlisted to beat the draft. The were killed near a bend in the Imjin River between two hills we've named Chink Baldie and Pork Chop.

Six months ago, not one of those three ever heard of the Imjin, probably. And when they went out last night, all they knew about the countryside was what they had learned from a map. Military maps—to me anyhow—are a confusing conglomeration of curlicues and squares. They tell me men like Eisenhower and Bradley can look at a map and actually see the countryside. But for most of us, maps never quite prepare us for the real thing. You could put those three boys back home of course and never have lost them. But they weren't back home. They were in a draw between two hills near a bend in the Imjin River north of the 38th Parallel in Korea. And there was an ambush waiting for them.

This country around the Imjin was not always a miserable place to die in. For some, it was once a good place to live. The sides of the hills we are fighting and dying for still bear the outlines of rice paddies. The village in the valley that now is No Man's Land was the village of Kungmal. It's hard to say how many lived here, because only a few houses are standing. But it was home for someone. These people loved their land and homes fiercely. It had been handed down from generation to generation. They asked only to be let alone to live their lives as they had always lived them. But who ever heard of Communists letting other people alone?

Now these people are gone—dead or pushed aside by the current war—and we've come in. Because we had to. And—by necessity—we altered the face of this part of Korea. We've cut roads through rice paddies, sliced huge chunks out of their mountains, made bunkers of their trees and burned or destroyed their homes, because they might conceal snipers. There are deadly land mines lurking like rattlesnakes in their paddies. Along their roads there's barbed wire wherever you turn. There are smoke pots in their valleys and there is seldom a minute when guns are not firing.

So it is an unfriendly, sullen, alien land here around the frozen Imjin. Miserable country to die in. Some day, perhaps, the Koreans who've always lived here and found the living good will come back to their bend in the river. Then perhaps they'll patiently rebuild their villages, smooth over the scars of war, dig up the mines and resume peaceful, ageless living. But it's not that way tonight.

6.10 McCarthy on US War in Korea, December 1950

The Truman Administration was attacked from the right on the war in Korea by Senator Joseph McCarthy and others who saw the war as a result of the American 'loss of China'—the unwillingness to stand up to Communism in Asia in the late 1940s. Here is an excerpt from a McCarthy speech in Congress in December 1950.

Mr. McCarthy. Mr President, it is unnecessary to tell the Senate, the country, or the world that America is facing the greatest military disaster in its entire history. Day by day and hour by hour the situation grows blacker, blacker for the world, blacker for the United States, and more particularly is it painfully blacker for over 100,000 American young men in Korea.

At this very moment the mothers and wives of those young men are treading deeply into the valley of darkness and despair. It is not necessary to use high-sounding words to describe the situation to our men in Korea. Those men, their mothers, fathers, and wives, see the situation in its elemental ugliness. They are face to face with facts—facts that cannot be escaped by pious platitudes. It is high time for all, including those responsible for administration policy, to get down to rugged reality, to look at conditions as they actually are today, and not as we wish them to be.

It is not too late for a realistic examination or a reexamination, if you will, of the situation to produce some lessening of the perils of those gallant men now fighting on one of the frontiers of freedom. Upon the results of such an examination we must chart a course of effective action, and we must be prompt in doing so. Promptness, Mr. President, is no less required than realism, we are like the firemen who debate while the house burns down.

In this time of peril, it is the duty of everyone—Democrat, Dixiecrat, or Republican—to work in the national interest. We are all, first of all, Americans. But it is not in the national interest to unite in support of error, or of policies that have failed. Unity then would only compound the damage of the past. World history is littered with the corpses of nations which were united behind bad leadership following the wrong course.

Let us briefly examine the three plans which this administration has used in three of the major areas of the world in the last 5 years.

No. 1: The Forrestal plan, which Truman fortunately adopted for Greece and Turkey. As we all know, the Forrestal plan, simply stated, was give all the necessary military aid to people who themselves were willing to fight Communism—enough military aid to make them strong enough to withstand international Communism. While sufficient economic aid was given to make the military aid effective and workable, the emphasis at all times under the Forrestal plan was to be on military aid. The Forrestal plan, as we know, proved very successful.

No. 2: The Acheson–Marshall plan for all of western Europe, which was directly opposite to the Forrestal plan for Greece and Turkey. It consisted of giving the maximum economic aid with no thought whatsoever of any military defense of western Europe. In face, the over-all plan was to build up the area economically and keep it defenceless from a military standpoint (...)

The Acheson–Marshall plan fitted perfectly with Communist Russia's desire for a power vacuum in all of western Europe. On paper, as we know, there was a material and welcome change in the Acheson–Marshall plan for western Europe over a year ago. The change is on paper. At that time, as the Senate will recall, we voted vast sums of money for the military defense of western Europe. As of today, however, western Europe is still defenseless, while our State Department holds lengthy conferences with European leaders on such questions as whether or not an additional 500 policemen can safely be allowed to Western Germany.

No. 3: The Hiss–Acheson–Jessup–Lattimore–Vincent plan to turn all of Asia over to the Communists and to then cooperate with those friendly Communists. In other words, in one area of the world the plan was fight international Communism with economic aid: in another area it was to fight international Communism with military aid; and in the third area it was to turn everything over to the Communists.

I know it is unnecessary to comment upon the fact that of the three plans the only one which has been successful from the American standpoint is the Forrestal plan as applied to Greece and Turkey. The most disastrous for America and most successful from the standpoint of international Communism was, of course, the Hiss–Acheson–Jessup–Lattimore–Vincent plan for Asia. As of today the failure of the Acheson–Marshall plan for western Europe has not yet been demonstrated to the American people. Suffice to say we are creating in Europe exactly what Russia desires; namely, an area which is becoming economically prosperous, but completely undefended—a power vacuum. In Stalin's wildest and most optimistic dreams of 5 years ago, he could hardly have pictured a 5-year development more favourable to international atheistic Communism (…)

We know that at Yalta we were betrayed. We know that since Yalta the leaders of this Government by design or ignorance have continued to betray us. The depth and foulness of that betrayal no man can as yet outline for those of us who are its victims. We also know that the same men who betrayed America are still leading America. The traitors must no longer lead the betrayed. The international criminals must no longer splatter the pages of history with American blood. We of America are infinitely stronger than those who betrayed us would have the world believe. We are tougher than they have the courage to admit. We are more free than they wish us to be, and we are ready to fight for what we know is right, but we must not fight under the leadership of perfumed, dilettante diplomats. We cannot fight successfully under the leadership of those who are either half loyal or disloyal to what we are fighting for.

Nor do I think that Mr. Marshall should continue his heavy responsibilities at his advanced age, and particularly since he, too, has been heavily involved in the erroneous China policy. I cannot too strongly urge that General Marshall would be infinitely more valuable to the Nation as an elder statesman in Leesburg. If he were there, his doctors would be more satisfied, and his talents would be available as needed, as are those of our other fine elderly statesmen.

With the next few days I intend to discuss in some detail the insidious Communist Party line attacks by inspired and semiofficial press agents of the Government, and by certain of the dangerous party-line radio commentators and news columnists—attacks by the cabal that hounded Forrestal to death, and did such an efficient job of destroying Chiang Kai-shek in the eyes of the American people; the same cabal that is now making an all-out effort in an attempt to destroy Gen. Douglas MacArthur because he, too, even as did James Forrestal and as does Chiang Kai-shek, stands in the way of international atheistic Communism.

6.11 Stalin and Zhou Enlai Discuss the War, September 1952

In the fall of 1952 Chinese premier Zhou Enlai met Stalin to discuss an end to the war in Korea. Stalin believed that the war did not have to end soon, since it was more disadvantageous to the United States than to the Sino-Soviet alliance. One of the issues that stood in the way was the repatriation of prisoners. This is from Zhou's conversation with the ageing Soviet dictator on 19 September.

(…) STALIN says (…) we must keep in mind that the Americans will not want to deliver all the POWs [prisoners of war], that they will keep some captive, with the intention to recruit them. This was the case with our POWs. Now we are capturing several of our POWs a day, who are being sent over by America. They are withholding POWs not because, as they say, the POWs don't want to return—America often refers to this—but so that they could use them for spying.

ZHOU ENLAI concedes that this is precisely so. He introduces the following scenario: to cease fire and resolve the issue of POWs later. He reminds that comrade Stalin agreed with this, if no agreement is reached regarding the percentage [of POWs] withheld.

STALIN acknowledges that this can be considered as one of possible scenarios, but America is not likely to agree to it (…)

ZHOU ENLAI, ending the conversion, says they would like to receive instructions concerning all these issues.

STALIN asks—instructions or suggestions?

ZHOU ENLAI answers that from comrade Stalin's perspective perhaps this would be advice, but in their perception these would be instructions.

STALIN notes that we give only advice, convey our opinion, and the Chinese comrades may accept it or not; instructions, on the other hand, are mandatory.

ZHOU ENLAI repeats that from the Chinese perspective these are instructions, most valuable instructions. He notes that they do not accept these instructions blindly, but consider it necessary to understand and accept them deliberately.

STALIN emphasizes that we know too little about China, and that is why we are cautious in giving instructions.

ZHOU ENLAI says that comrade Stalin certainly is well familiar with the particular issues they are addressing, and asks again whether there will be any instructions.

Comrade STALIN answers that our advice is this: we should remember, that England and America will try to place their people into the apparatus of the Chinese government. It does not matter if they are American or French. They will work to undermine, try to cause decay from within, could even commit such crimes as poisonings. That is why we must be alert. He says we should keep this in mind. Here—these are all the instructions.

ZHOU ENLAI says that these are very valuable instructions. He agrees that not only Americans, English and French can commit such treacheries, but they also push the Chinese into it.

STALIN adds—their agents from the [Chinese] national bourgeoisie.

6.12 Mao Zedong on the Role of the Soviet Union, January 1957

After the completion of agricultural collectivization in China in the mid-1950s, Mao wanted to move more quickly towards socialism, but felt that both the Soviets and some of his old colleagues within the CCP were holding him back. Here is an excerpt from an internal speech from January 1957.

(...) I once told an American in Yanan that even if you United States refused to recognize us for one hundred years, I simply did not believe that you United States could refuse to recognize us in the one hundred and first year. Sooner or later the U.S. will establish diplomatic relations with us. When the United States does so and when Americans finally come to visit China, they will feel deep regret. It is because by then, China will become completely different [from what it is now]: the house has been thoroughly swept and cleaned, 'the four pests' have altogether been eliminated; and they can hardly find any of their 'friends.' Even if they spread some germs [in China], it will have no use at all (...)

I want you to think about this issue: Between the socialist countries and the imperialist countries, especially the United States, which side is more afraid of the other after all? In my opinion, both are afraid [of the other], but the issue is who is *more* afraid. I am inclined to accept such an assessment: The imperialists are more afraid of us.

However, such an assessment entails a danger, that is, it could put us into a three-day-long sleep. Therefore, [we] always have to stress two possibilities. Putting the positive option aside, the negative potential is that the imperialists may become crazy. Imperialists always harbor malicious intentions and constantly want to make trouble. Nevertheless, it will not be that easy for the imperialists to start a world war; they have to consider the consequences once war starts.

[Let me] also talk about Sino-Soviet relations. In my view, bickering [between us] will continue. [We shall] never pretend that the Communist parties will not bicker. Is there a place in the world where bickering does not exist? Marxism itself is a bickering-ism, and is all about contradiction and struggle. Contradictions are everywhere, and contradictions invariably lead to struggle. At present there exist some controversies between China and the Soviet Union. Their ways of thinking, behavior, and historical traditions differ from ours. Therefore, we must try to persuade them. Persuasion is what I have always advocated as a way to deal with our own comrades. Some may argue that since we are comrades, we must be of the same good quality, and why in the world is persuasion needed among comrades? Moreover, persuasion is often employed for building a common front and always targeted at democrats; then, why is it employed towards Communist Party members? This reasoning is wrong. Different opinions and views do exist even within a Communist party. Some have joined the party, but have not changed their mindset. Some old cadres do not share the same language with us. Therefore, [we] have to engage in heart-to-heart talks with them: sometimes individually, sometimes in groups. In one meeting after another we will be able to persuade them.

As far as I can see, circumstances are beyond what persons, even those occupying high positions, can control. Under the pressure of circumstance, those in the Soviet Union who still want to practice big-power chauvinism will invariably encounter difficulties. To persuade them remains our current policy and requires us to engage in direct dialogue with them. The last time our delegation visited the Soviet Union, [we] openly talked about some [controversial] issues. I told Comrade Zhou Enlai over the phone that, as those people are blinded by lust for gain, the best way to deal with them is to give them a tongue-lashing. What is [their] asset? It involves nothing more than 50 million tons of steel, 400 million tons of coal, and 80 million tons of oil. How much does this count? It does not count for a thing (...)

6.13 Mao Zedong on Soviet Intentions, July 1958

In 1958, as Mao began to intensify the Chinese Revolution through a series of utopian plans called the Great Leap Forward, he also stepped up his criticism of the way the Sino-Soviet alliance was working. In this conversation with Soviet ambassador Pavel Yudin from July 1958, Mao makes clear his misgivings.

After you left yesterday I could neither sleep nor eat. Today I invite you over to talk a bit more so that you can be [my] doctor: [after talking with you], I might be able to eat and sleep this afternoon. You are fortunate to have little difficulty in eating and sleeping.

Let us return to the main subject and chat about the issues we discussed yesterday. We will only talk about these issues here in this room! There exists no crisis situation between you and me. Our relationship can be described as: nine out of ten fingers of yours and ours are quite the same with only one finger differing. I have repeated this point two or three times. You haven't forgotten, have you?

I've thought over and again of the issues that were discussed yesterday. It is likely that I might have misunderstood you, but it is also possible that I was right. We may work out a solution after discussion or debate. It appears that [we] will have to withdraw [our] navy's request for [obtaining] nuclear-powered submarines [from the Soviet Union]. Barely remembering this matter, I have acquired some information about it only after asking others. There are some warmhearted people at our navy's headquarters, namely, the Soviet advisers. They asserted that, now that the Soviet nuclear submarines have been developed, we can obtain [them] simply by sending a cable [to Moscow].

Well, your navy's nuclear submarines are of a [top] secret advanced technology. The Chinese people are careless in handling things. If we are provided with them, we might put you to trouble.

The Soviet comrades have won victory for forty years, and are thus rich in experience. It has only been eight years since our victory and we have little experience. You therefore raised the question of joint ownership and operation. The issue of ownership has long before been dealt with: Lenin proposed the system of rent and lease which, however, was targeted at the capitalists.

China has some remnant capitalists, but the state is under the leadership of the Communist Party. You never trust the Chinese! You only trust the Russians! [To you] the Russians are the first-class [people] whereas the Chinese are among the inferior who are dumb and careless. Therefore [you] came up with the joint ownership and operation proposition. Well, if [you] want joint ownership and operation, how about have them all—let us turn into joint ownership and operation our army, navy, air force, industry, agriculture, culture, education. Can we do this? Or, [you] may have all of China's more than ten thousand kilometers of coastline and let us only maintain a guerrilla force. With a few atomic bombs, you think you are in a position to control us through asking for the right of rent and lease. Other than this, what else [do you have] to justify [your request]?

Lüshun [Port Arthur] and Dalian [Darien] were under your control before. You departed from these places later. Why [were these places] under your control? It is because then China was under the Guomindang's rule. Why did you volunteer to leave? It is because the Communist Party had taken control of China.

Because of Stalin's pressure, the Northeast and Xinjiang became [a Soviet] sphere of influence, and four jointly owned and operated enterprises were established. Comrade Khrushchev later proposed to have these [settlements] eliminated, and we were grateful for that.

You [Russians] have never had faith in the Chinese people, and Stalin was among the worst. The Chinese [Communists] were regarded as a second Tito; [the Chinese people] were considered as a backward nation. You [Russians] have often stated that the Europeans looked down upon the Russians. I believe that some Russians look down upon the Chinese people.

At the most critical juncture [of the Chinese Revolution], Stalin did not allow us to carry out our revolution and opposed our carrying out the revolution. He made a huge mistake on this issue (...)

6. Stalin and Molotov: 'At last here's something we're glad to help you do, tovariches.' (David Low, *Evening Standard*, 25 January 1950). Reprinted by permission. Photo supplied by The Centre for the Study of Cartoons and Caricature, University of Kent.

7. 'Excuse me, is this a private quarrel, or can I help . . .?' (Vicky, *Evening Standard*, 29 August 1960). Reprinted by permission. Photo supplied by The Centre for the Study of Cartoons and Caricature, University of Kent.

We have held no secrets from you. Because more than one thousand of your experts are working in our country, you are fully aware of the state of our military, political, economic, and cultural affairs. We trust your people, because you are from a socialist country, and you are sons and daughters of Lenin (…)

Why did I ask Stalin to send a scholar [to China] to read my works? Was it because I so lacked confidence that I would even have to have you read my own writings? Or was it because I did not have enough to do? Not a chance! [My real intention] was to get you over to China to see with your own eyes whether China was truly practicing Marxism or [was] only half-hearted toward Marxism (…) In Moscow, I got so angry that I once pounded the table. I only had three tasks here, I said to them, the first was to eat, the second was to sleep, and the third was to shit.

6.14 Mao Zedong's Notes on Sino-Soviet Affairs, December 1959

In December 1959 Mao Zedong wrote a series of notes on the international situation. In these notes he reveals some of his thoughts about the future of the Sino-Soviet alliance.

What are enemy policies? Under the banner of peace, they are producing nuclear bombs, building bases, and use war to destroy socialism. Under the banner of peace, cultural exchanges, and contacts between peoples, they try to use degenerative influence and evolutionary transition to destroy socialism.

Their basic principle is: Defend themselves and destroy their enemies.

Sometimes the situation is calm, sometimes it is tense; here it is calm, there it is tense; Europe is calm and Asia is tense; try to win over opportunism and isolate Marxism-Leninism.

Is revisionism becoming a system? Is it already happening? Maybe it is; maybe it can be prevented. Maybe it will last a long time (more than ten years?). Maybe it will last only a short time, one, two, three, four years. The fundamental interests of China and the Soviet Union is that these big countries should unite. Some are not for unity—it is only for the time being. It is really like the relationship between one finger and nine fingers (…)

China will be isolated for a long period of time. But it will also get support from many Communist parties, countries, and peoples. In this difficult situation, China will become very strong in eight years time. In eight years, China will have finished the initial construction of the industrial system; will have built a team of technicians and a team of theorists; the political consciousness of the party and the people will be higher. (Maybe all three will happen, maybe not).

Be careful; always use facts to illustrate, use reasonable arguments.

A reactionary campaign against China has two advantages [for us]: First, it reveals the nature of the reactionaries, they lose their reputation. Second, it can make most people in the world realize that reactionary imperialism, nationalism, and revisionism are their enemies, cheaters and black elements. The Chinese flag is bright red.

The whole world looks good at the moment; very bright. The thicker the clouds are, the brighter it will become.

There is no doubt that Marxism-Leninism is developing greatly in China.

Khrushchev is so childish! He does not understand Marxism-Leninism. He is so easily cheated by the imperialists. He does not understand China at all. He does not read. He believes in all kinds of false information and he speaks irresponsibly. If he does not reform himself, he will be destroyed some years from now (in eight years).

He is intensely, extremely, afraid of China. He is afraid of two things: Imperialism and Chinese Communism. He is afraid that the Communist parties in Eastern Europe and elsewhere will not believe in them, but in us.

His world-view is too pragmatic, it is extreme subjective idealism. He has no sense of rules and sways with the wind.

The Soviet people is good, and so is their party. Improper work styles in the party and among the people, metaphysics, and bourgeois liberalism are all inherited from the past. Lenin died too early. He did not have time to remould it.

This liberalism, and great-power chauvinism, sooner or later it will reverse itself and [the situation] improve. Everything in this world reverses itself. Our country will move to the opposite, then to the opposite of the opposite; that is the complete opposite.

Uninterrupted revolution (...)

6.15 Zhou Enlai Attempts To Save the Alliance, June 1961

After the collapse of the Great Leap Forward, the supply situation in China was desperate and millions starved. While partly blaming natural disasters, Premier Zhou Enlai admitted the severe repercussions of the party's previous policies and attempted to dampen the intensity of the disagreements with the Soviet Union. Here is the Soviet ambassador Stephan Chervonenko's account of a meeting with Zhou in June 1961.

(...) I congratulated Zhou Enlai on the approaching fortieth anniversary of the CCP.

Zhou Enlai thanked me and said that it had been decided to not to celebrate that event very widely. A ceremonial anniversary meeting would be held and a report would be published. He added, as if explaining why such a decision had been made, that there was quite a strained internal situaton in the country. There is a very serious drought. The situation will be worse than last year. The number of provinces sufering from drought continues to grow. The summer harvest will be gathered in soon. It is already clear that this year's harvest of grain crops will be 10 million tons less than last year's (…)

He mentioned that a number of sister nations had their own problems in connection with natural calamities. We, the socialist countries, have to work hard in order to strengthen the agricultural base. I agreed with this point of view.

I said further that I had a commission from the CC CPSU [Soviet Communist Party] to pass over to Mao Zedong the stenographic record of N. S. Khrushchev's talks with [President John F.] Kennedy in Vienna. Having given a gist of these talks, I passed the material to Zhou Enlai (…)

Zhou Enlai said that the CC CCP had recently conducted a 'working meeting' (apparently an enlarged session of the Politburo with participation of CC members and province leaders), which considered internal questions. After three years of the Great Leap and two years of natural calamities we are thinking to conduct a certain regulation of the overall national economic plan, sticking to the course of 'regulation, consolidation, improvement, and replenishment.' The aim of this course is 'to liquidate certain disproportions that came into existence with the Great Leap.' (…) Subjective reasons have to be noted. The three red banners— the basic line, the Great Leap, and the People's Communes—are new phenomena, which were born on Chinese soil (…) Zhou Enlai continued that they had not had enough experience and had been culpable of a certain roughness, of shortcomings, and errors in their work.

Zhou Enlai mentioned that such things (shortcomings, errors, etc.) took place not only in countries where the dictatorship of the proletariat had won, but were also typical of bourgeois and feudal societies. He said further, 'We in China use the experience of the Soviet Union and the other sister nations, but we also have a zigzag development, because everything new that appears on Chinese soil inevitably gives rise to roughness, errors. That is why this regulation is necessary.' (…)

According to instructions from the Center, I asked about the Chinese comrades' opinon concerning a possible date for L. I. Brezhnev's visit to the PRC in accordance with the invitation extended by Liu Shaoqi in Moscow. I did so in a careful way (…) Zhou Enlai said that the embassy would be informed about this issue during the coming days (…)

6.16 The Breakdown of the Alliance, July 1963

In the summer of 1963 a Chinese delegation headed by Deng Xiaoping visited Moscow to negotiate with the Soviets, but the outcome of the secret meetings was negative. Here are excerpts from the talks on 8 and 10 July 1963.

8 July.

DENG XIAOPING. First of all, I want to announce that our delegation at the request of the CC of our party came to this meeting in Moscow of representatives of the CCP and USSR with the sincere intention of removing discord and strengthening unity (...)

It can be said with all candor that a whole series of disagreements of a fundamental character which exist today in the international Communist movement, started at the 20th Congress of the CPSU.

In the past we never spoke about this openly, because we were taking into account the situation you were in. We only mentioned that the disagreements which have arisen in the past few years in the international Communist movement were provoked by the violation of the Declaration of 1957 by comrades from several fraternal parties (...) We have always considered and still consider that the 20th Congress of the CPSU put forward positions on the issues of war and peace, peaceful coexistence and peaceful transition which went against Marxism-Leninism. Especially serious are two issues: the issue of the so called 'peaceful transition' and the issue of the full, groundless denunciation of Stalin under the pretext of the so called 'struggle with the cult of personality' (...)

Here I want just briefly to say the following: a criticism of some errors by Stalin is necessary; taking off the lid, so to speak, and ending superstition is a good thing. However this criticism must be correct both from the point of view of principles and from the point of view of methods.

Since the 20th Congress of the CPSU, the facts demonstrate that the full, groundless denunciation of Stalin is a serious step undertaken by the leading comrades from the CPSU with the aim of laying out the path to the revision of Marxism-Leninism on a whole series of issues (...) After the 20th Congress of the CPSU, as a consequence of the so-called struggle against the cult of personality and the full, groundless denunciation of Stalin, the wave of an anti-Soviet and anti-Communist campaign was provoked around the whole world.

In June 1959 you unilaterally annulled the agreement on rendering help to China in developing a nuclear industry and in producing atom bombs. Following this, on 9 September 1959, TASS made an announcement about the incident on the Chinese–Indian border and displayed bias in favor of the Indian reaction, making the disagreements between China and the Soviet Union clear to the whole world for the first time.

In November of that year Com. Khrushchev openly accused China of having acted 'stupidly' and 'regrettably' in a conversation with a correspondent of the Indian daily 'New Age.'

At the last meeting at Camp David which was held in September 1959, Com. Khrushchev began to preach to the whole world of a 'world without arms, without armies, without wars', made the leader of American imperialism look good in all sorts of different ways, considered peaceful coexistence the task of all tasks, and propagandized the idea that, supposedly, the American–Soviet friendship decides the fate of humanity. All of this practically signified a sermon to the effect that the nature of imperialism had already changed, that Marxism-Leninism was already obsolete.

During this very period you started to propagandize the so called 'spirit of Camp David' everywhere. Incidentally, Eisenhower did not recognize the existence of any 'spirit of Camp David'.

During this very period you, counting on some 'spirit of Camp David,' clutched at the straw extended by Eisenhower and began mounting attacks upon China in your statements without restraint (…)

On 25 August 1962, the Soviet government informed China that it was ready to conclude an agreement with the USA on the prevention of the proliferation of nuclear weapons. In our view, you were pursuing an unseemly goal in coming to such an agreement, namely: to bind China by the hands and feet through an agreement with the USA.

After India started a major attack on the border regions of China in October 1962, the Soviet Union began to supply India with even larger quantities of military materiel, to do its utmost to give [India] an economic blood transfusion, to support Nehru by political means, and to spur him on to the struggle against China (…)

In October 1962 there was a crisis in the region of the Caribbean Sea. During these events we consider that you committed two errors: in shipping the missiles to Cuba you indulged in adventurism, and then, showing confusion in the face of nuclear blackmail from the USA, you capitulated (…)

What do the facts we have cited above, which took place after the 22nd Congress of the CPSU, testify to? These facts testify to the fact that comrades from the CPSU have taken further steps to create a split in the ranks of the international Communist movement, and, moreover, have done so in an increasingly sharp, increasingly extreme form, in an increasingly organized [way], on an increasingly large scale, trying, come what may, to crush others.

I would like to note that using such methods is a habitual affair for you. You began using such methods as far back as the Bucharest conference. During the bilateral meeting between the representatives of our two parties in 1960, I said that it was fortunate that Com. Peng Zhen went to the Bucharest meeting; he weighs approximately 80 kilograms, and for that reason he endured; if I had gone, and I weigh only a bit over 50 kilograms, I could not have endured. After that it was just as well that Com. Wu Xiuquan, who weighs more than 70 kilograms, went to the GDR, and was able to endure. Frankly speaking, such methods do not help matters. You cannot prove by such methods that you are in the right; you cannot prove that the truth is on your side. Quite the opposite; the use of such methods is an insult to the glorious Marxist-Leninist party.

PONOMAREV. And Com. Grishin weighs 70 kg. After all, this started before Bucharest, in Beijing. That was the start of and the reason for the Bucharest Conference.

DENG XIAOPING. I understand you.

PENG ZHEN. Wait. You will have [your] time; you will be able to say as much as you want then. We are ready to hear you out (…)

DENG XIAOPING. I have already taken 5 hours in my statement, and on that I end it. Are we going to continue the session today, or will we continue it tomorrow?

SUSLOV. We propose a break until the day after tomorrow, at 10 AM. We must acquaint ourselves with your statement.

DENG XIAOPING. We agree. Who will speak the day after tomorrow, you or we?

SUSLOV. By the order it will be our turn.

ANDROPOV. By the principle: we, you, we, you.

DENG XIAOPING. That is Com. Andropov's invention.

(10 July)

SUSLOV. Again, as in 1960, you are putting in motion the practice, which has already been condemned by Communist parties, of personal attacks on Com. N. S. Khrushchev. Such a practice in the past did not provoke anything but indignation in any true Communist, and will do the same now.

Com. N. S. Khrushchev is our recognized leader. Reflecting the collective will of the CC CPSU, he has gained unlimited authority for himself in our party, in the country, in the whole world through his selfless devotion to Marxism-Leninism and through his truly titanic struggle to build Communism in the USSR, to preserve peace in the whole world in defense of the interests of all working people (…)

For obviously demagogic ends you are trying to connect the decisions of the 20th Congress with the well-known events in Poland and also with the counter-revolutionary revolt in Hungary in 1956.

(…) We would also like to remind our forgetful Chinese comrades about some facts and about the assistance the USSR has given to the economic development of the PRC. Do not the 198 modern industrial enterprises built with the technical assistance of the Soviet Union, the scientific-research institutes which it set up, and the technical cadres trained in the USSR, bear witness to the commitment by the CPSU to fraternal friendship with People's China? Up until 1959 almost a half of all the cast iron was produced, more than half of all the steel was smelted, and more than half of the rolled iron was made in the metallurgical enterprises constructed in China with help from the USSR. Such new branches of industry as the automobile, the tractor, and the aviation industry have been developed in China with the help of the Soviet Union. The Soviet Union gave the PRC 21 thousand sets of scientific-technical documentation, including more than 1400 plans of whole enterprises (...)

Questions

What were Stalin's main interests in East Asia after World War II?

Why did the new Chinese People's Republic choose to ally itself with the Soviet Union?

Why did North Korea attack South Korea in 1950?

Why did the United States choose to intervene in the Korean War?

Why did US public opinion turn against the war in Korea?

Why did Senator McCarthy attack the Truman Administration over its policies in China and Korea?

Why did the Korean War end in 1953?

Why did Mao Zedong begin criticizing the Soviets, and what were his main points of criticism?

How did the Soviets respond to the Chinese criticism?

What brought about the final collapse of the Sino-Soviet Alliance?

7

The Vietnam Wars, 1945–1975

The war in Vietnam was the most divisive conflict of the Cold War for most Americans. It brought home to ordinary people—who had not worried much about foreign affairs—the sacrifices which the global role of the United States could demand of them. The division between supporters and opponents of the war was fierce, and the historians are still struggling to disentangle themselves from political partisanship.

But, as the new materials help to explain, the origins of the Vietnam wars and a substantial part of their conduct were *Vietnamese* and *international* more than American. Indochina—colonized by the French in the nineteenth century—saw its independence movements stymied by the colonial power until the French defeat in Europe at the beginning of World War II. During the war, the Vietnamese Communists built a popular and well-organized movement for national independence, the Viet Minh, and in August 1945 its leader Ho Chi Minh declared Vietnam's independence from France. In spite of President Franklin Roosevelt's anti-colonial statements during the world war, the Americans after the war supported France's attempts at regaining control of Indochina, but the Viet Minh, after 1949 supported by Communist China, was still able to inflict serious defeats on the French forces.

By 1954 the French government was unwilling to continue an unpopular war and offered the Viet Minh a ceasefire that would split Vietnam in two halves for a limited period leading up to national elections. Under strong pressure from China and the Soviet Union, Ho Chi Minh agreed to most of the French conditions during a conference at Geneva. The United States, however, was sceptical towards the Geneva agreements, and started supporting the building of an independent non-Communist regime in South Vietnam. When this regime, under Ngo Dinh Diem, in 1956 refused to hold elections, North Vietnam prepared for a prolonged campaign of subversion in the south.

As the Diem regime became increasingly unpopular in the south in the early 1960s, the Communist strategy shifted towards an unveiled uprising. With the southern regime losing ground, President Kennedy supported a military coup against Diem, but the new rulers in Saigon did not prove any better prepared to fight the Communist-led Front for National Liberation (FNL). In 1964–5 President Johnson gradually introduced American ground forces into Vietnam and began bombing across the border into the north. The American involvement did reduce the military pressure against the Saigon regime, but did little to increase its popularity. By 1968 the war was at a stalemate, and in the United States pressure was mounting for an American withdrawal.

The New Year (Tet) Offensive in early 1968 showed that FNL forces with North Vietnamese support could operate all over southern Vietnam. Because of the unpopularity of the war, President Johnson declined to seek re-election, and the new president, Richard Nixon, began seeking a way out of the conflict. He first attempted to force a solution by invading Cambodia to cut FNL supply lines, and by intensifying the bombing of the north. By 1972 it was clear that military results were not forthcoming, and that the Americans had to agree to a negotiated settlement. In 1973 an agreement was signed in Paris, in which North Vietnam promised not to support subversion in the south and Nixon pledged to withdraw all American troops. Already in late 1973 the war in South Vietnam flared up again, and in April 1975 FNL and North Vietnamese troops entered Saigon.

Readings

Larry Berman, *No Honor, No Peace* (2001). An excellent analysis of the United States's exit from the Vietnam conflict.

Ilya Gaiduk, *The Soviet Union and the Vietnam War* (1996). An overall effort at analysing the Soviet role in the war.

Fredrik Logevall, *Choosing War* (1999). A thorough account of the American decision to send ground troops to Vietnam.

Robert Schulzinger, *A Time for War* (1998). One of the best general histories of the United States and the Vietnam War.

Qiang Zhai, *China and the Vietnam Wars* (2000). The most thorough account of the People's Republic of China's role in the Indochina conflict.

7.1 Ho Chi Minh's Declaration of Vietnamese Independence, 1945

In August 1945, after the brief Japanese occupation of Vietnam was over and before French forces had been able to reassert themselves, Ho Chi Minh declared Vietnam's independence on behalf of his Communist-led national front, the Viet Minh. Ho's brief statement, read out in front of the French governor's mansion in Hanoi, was based on the American independence declaration of 1776.

'All men are created equal. They are endowed by their Creator with certain inalienable rights, among these are Life, Liberty, and the pursuit of Happiness'.

This immortal statement was made in the Declaration of Independence of the United States of America in 1776. In a broader sense, this means: All the peoples on the earth are equal from birth, all the peoples have a right to live, to be happy and free.

The Declaration of the French Revolution made in 1791 on the Rights of Man and the Citizen also states: 'All men are born free and with equal rights, and must always remain free and have equal rights.' Those are undeniable truths.

Nevertheless, for more than eighty years, the French imperialists, abusing the standard of Liberty, Equality, and Fraternity, have violated our Fatherland and oppressed our fellow-citizens. They have acted contrary to the ideals of humanity and justice. In the field of politics, they have deprived our people of every democratic liberty. They have enforced inhuman laws; they have set up three distinct political regimes in the North, the Center and the South of Vietnam in order to wreck our national unity and prevent our people from being united.

They have built more prisons than schools. They have mercilessly slain our patriots—they have drowned our uprisings in rivers of blood. They have fettered public opinion; they have practised obscurantism against our people. To weaken our race they have forced us to use opium and alcohol.

In the fields of economics, they have fleeced us to the backbone, impoverished our people, and devastated our land.

They have robbed us of our rice fields, our mines, our forests, and our raw materials. They have monopolised the issuing of bank-notes and the export trade.

They have invented numerous unjustifiable taxes and reduced our people, especially our peasantry, to a state of extreme poverty.

They have hampered the prospering of our national bourgeoisie; they have mercilessly exploited our workers.

In the autumn of 1940, when the Japanese Fascists violated Indochina's territory to establish new bases in their fight against the Allies, the French imperialists went down on their bended knees and handed over our country to them.

Thus, from that date, our people were subjected to the double yoke of the French and the Japanese. Their sufferings and miseries increased. The result was that from the end of last year to the beginning of this year, from Quang Tri province to the North of Vietnam, more than two million of our fellow-citizens died from starvation. On March 9, the French troops were disarmed by the Japanese. The French colonialists either fled or surrendered, showing that not only were they incapable of 'protecting' us, but that, in the span of five years, they had twice sold our country to the Japanese.

On several occasions before March 9, the Vietminh League urged the French to ally themselves with it against the Japanese. Instead of agreeing to this proposal, the French colonialists so intensified their terrorist activities against the Vietminh members that before fleeing they massacred a great number of our political prisoners detained at Yen Bai and Cao Bang.

Not withstanding all this, our fellow-citizens have always manifested toward the French a tolerant and humane attitude. Even after the Japanese putsch of March 1945, the Vietminh League helped many Frenchmen to cross the frontier, rescued some of them from Japanese jails, and protected French lives and property.

From the autumn of 1940, our country had in fact ceased to be a French colony and had become a Japanese possession.

After the Japanese had surrendered to the Allies, our whole people rose to regain our national sovereignty and to found the Democratic Republic of Vietnam.

The truth is that we have wrested our independence from the Japanese and not from the French.

The French have fled, the Japanese have capitulated, Emperor Bao Dai has abdicated. Our people have broken the chains which for nearly a century have fettered them and have won independence for the Fatherland. Our people at the same time have overthrown the monarchic regime that has reigned supreme for dozens of centuries. In its place has been established the present Democratic Republic.

For these reasons, we, members of the Provisional Government, representing the whole Vietnamese people, declare that from now on we break off all relations of a colonial character with France; we repeal all the international obligations that France has so far subscribed to on behalf of Vietnam and we abolish all the special rights the French have unlawfully acquired in our Fatherland.

The whole Vietnamese people, animated by a common purpose, are determined to fight to the bitter end against any attempt by the French colonialists to reconquer their country.

We are convinced that the Allied nations which at Tehran and San Francisco have acknowledged the principles of self-determination and equality of nations, will not refuse to acknowledge the independence of Vietnam.

A people who have courageously opposed French domination for more than eighty years, a people who have fought side by side with the Allies against the Fascists during these last years, such a people must be free and independent.

For these reasons, we, members of the Provisional Government of the Democratic Republic of Vietnam, solemnly declare to the world that Vietnam has the right to be a free and independent country and in fact it is so already. The entire Vietnamese people are determined to mobilise all their physical and mental strength, to sacrifice their lives and property in order to safeguard their independence and liberty.

7.2 The Geneva Conference: The American View, 1954

During the Geneva Conference on Indochina, the Eisenhower administration took a dim view of French efforts to find a comprehensive settlement to the conflict, and, even before the conference was over, pledged its support to a separate regime in the southern part of the country. On 10 July 1954 Secretary of State John Foster Dulles advised the American delegation to pass on the following telegram to South Vietnamese leader Ngo Dinh Diem.

As you assume your high office I want you to know that the thoughts of the American people, President Eisenhower, and myself are with you and with your country in its difficult ordeal.

Your wisdom, strength and record of devotion to cause of genuine independence are well known to us and we are confident that they will be put to service of Vietnam.

We know that the struggle in Indochina is one for liberty against despotism and that you respect the spirit of resistance to a menace which threatens entire free world.

US has, as you know, taken up arms against this Communist imperialism as one of the United Nations in Korea. We have also contributed of our resources and those skills we possess in other threatened areas, not least in Vietnam. US remains prepared support countries everywhere seeking maintain their freedom against godless Communist menace.

During past year as new plans of French Union High Command developed, we sought to assure ourselves that those plans offered prospect of military success and would accompany and foster early completion of independence, and development of national armies, in Vietnam, Laos and Cambodia.

Unfortunately, this program was not fulfilled and military situation in Vietnam deteriorated.

Meanwhile US had acquiesced in suggestion of its associates in free world that fullest trial should be made at Geneva of resources of negotiation. Communists during this period in no wise abated their aggression in Vietnam. Other negotiations with Viet Minh and Chinese Communists to which the US is not a party, have also taken place.

If as a result of such negotiations or of military operations there should now result any cease-fire line tending to divide Vietnam, we would be unwilling to consider it as final. We would lend our best efforts to assist patriotic Vietnamese in building up strength in that part of Vietnam remaining outside Communist occupation. At the same time, it must be recognized that the necessary conditions for intervention by our own forces in North Vietnam have not been realised and are unlikely to be in the future (...)

President Eisenhower and I have recently concluded a series of conferences with British Prime Minister Churchill and Foreign Secretary Eden (...) We and British agreed, and so informed the French, that although temporary division of country might be required to effect regrouping of opposing military forces, we could not exclude the prospect of ultimate peaceful reunification (...)

We and the British informed the French we would 'respect' an agreement which:

1. Preserves at least the southern half of Vietnam.

2. Does not impose on Vietnam any restrictions materially impairing its capacity to maintain a stable non-Communist regime, and especially does not impose restrictions impairing its right to maintain adequate forces for internal security, to import arms and to employ foreign advisers.

3. Does not contain political provisions which would risk loss of the retained area to Communist control.

4. Does not exclude the possibility of ultimate reunification of Vietnam by peaceful means.

5. Provides for peaceful and humane transfer, under international supervision, of those people desiring to be moved from one zone to another of Vietnam; and

6. Provides effective machinery for international supervision of the agreement.

While we recognize that settlement along these lines imposes hardships on Vietnam, we fear that, deteriorating military situation and separate negotiations in progress with Viet Minh and Chinese Communists could lead to something still worse (...)

7.3 Kennedy Administration Decisions on Vietnam, November 1961

In the early 1960s the Communist-led National Liberation Front (NLF) was gaining control of large parts of South Vietnam. During the fall of 1961 the Kennedy administration undertook an extensive review of US policies in Vietnam—including various fact-finding missions to the region—that resulted in the following decisions, taken from a

13 November 1961 National Security Action Memorandum. During the remainder of the Kennedy administration the US presence in Vietnam would increase to over 16,000 military advisors.

(...) The President approved the recommendation that the Department of Defense be prepared with plans for the use of United States forces in South Viet-Nam under one or more of the following purposes:

(a) Use of a significant number of United States forces to signify United States determination to defend South Viet-Nam and to boost South Viet-Nam morale.

(b) Use of substantial United States forces to assist in suppressing Viet Cong insurgency short of engaging in detailed counter-guerrilla operations but including relevant operations in North Viet-Nam.

(c) Use of United States forces to deal with the situation if there is organized Communist military intervention.

Planning under (b) should embrace initially actions within South Viet-Nam. Actions that might be taken against North Viet-Nam or guerrilla bases in Laos should be considered separately. In connection with all the plans, the Department of Defense should consider the feasibility of moving troops or equipment in the near future to advanced positions in the Pacific, and submit recommendations concerning such action.

2. The following actions in support of the Government of Viet-Nam (GVN) will be undertaken immediately, subject to the understanding that these actions would not take effect within South Viet-Nam, be communicated to subordinate Vietnamese officials or made public until after the exchange of letters with President Diem contemplated in Paragraph 5 below:

(a) Provide increased air lift to the GVN forces, including helicopters, light aviation, and transport aircraft, manned to the extent necessary by United States uniformed personnel and under United States operational control.

(b) Provide such additional equipment and United States uniformed personnel as may be necessary for air reconnaissance, photography, instruction in and execution of air-ground support techniques, and for special intelligence.

(c) Provide the GVN with small craft, including such United States uniformed advisers and operating personnel as may be necessary for quick and effective operations in effecting surveillance and control over coastal waters and inland waterways.

(d) Provide expedited training and equipping of the civil guard and the self-defense corps with the objective of relieving the regular Army of static missions and freeing it for mobile offensive operations.

(e) Provide such personnel and equipment as may be necessary to improve the military-political intelligence system beginning at the provincial level and extending upward through the Government and the armed forces to the Central Intelligence Organization.

(f) Provide such new terms of reference, reorganization and additional personnel for United States military forces as are required for increased United States participation in the direction and control of GVN military operations and to carry out the other increased responsibilities which accrue to MAAG under these recommendations.

(g) Provide such increased economic aid as may be required to permit the GVN to pursue a vigorous flood relief and rehabilitation program, to supply material in support of the security effort, and to give priority to projects in support of this expanded counter-insurgency program. (This could include increases in military pay, a full supply of a wide range of materials such as food, medical supplies, transportation equipment, communications equipment, and any other items where material help could assist the GVN in winning the war against the Viet Cong.)

(h) Encourage and support (including financial support) a request by the GVN to the FAO or any other appropriate international organization for multilateral assistance in the relief and rehabilitation of the flood area.

(i) Provide individual administrators and advisers for insertion into the Governmental machinery of South Viet-Nam in types and numbers to be agreed upon by the two Governments.

(j) Provide personnel for a joint survey with the GVN of conditions in each of the provinces to assess the social, political, intelligence, and military factors bearing on the prosecution of the counter-insurgency program in order to reach a common estimate of these factors and a common determination of how to deal with them.

3. Ambassador Nolting is to be instructed to make an immediate approach to President Diem to the effect that the Government of the United States is prepared to join the Government of Viet-Nam in a sharply increased joint effort to cope with the Viet Cong threat (…) if, on its part, the Government of Viet-Nam is prepared to carry out an effective and total mobilization of its own resources, both material and human, for the same end (…) On the part of the United States, it would be expected that (…) GVN undertakings would include:

(a) Prompt and appropriate legislative and administrative action to put the nation on a wartime footing to mobilize its entire resources. (This would include a decentralization and broadening of the Government so as to realize the full potential of all non-Communist elements in the country willing to contribute to the common struggle.)

(b) The establishment of appropriate Governmental wartime agencies with adequate authority to perform their functions effectively.

(c) Overhaul of the military establishment and command structure so as to create an effective military organization for the prosecution of the war (...)

The President directed that the following actions be considered for carrying out at the appropriate time in relation to the exchange of letters and other developments:

(a) A private approach to the Soviet Union that would include: our determination to prevent the fall of South Viet-Nam to Communism by whatever means is necessary; our concern over dangers to peace presented by the aggressive DRV policy with respect to South Viet-Nam, our intent to return to full compliance with the Geneva Accords as soon as the DRV does so; the distinction we draw between Laos and South Viet-Nam, and our expectation that the Soviet Union will exercise its influence on the Chicoms [Chinese Communists] and the DRV.

(b) A special diplomatic approach to the United Kingdom in its role as co-Chairman of the Geneva Conference requesting that the United Kingdom seek the support of the Soviet co-Chairman for a cessation of DRV aggression against South Viet-Nam.

(c) A special diplomatic approach to India, both in its role as Chairman of the ICC and as a power having relations with Peiping [Beijing] and Hanoi. This approach should be made immediately prior to public release of the 'Jorden Report' and the exchange of letters between Diem and the President.

(d) Special diplomatic approaches to Canada, as well as Burma, Indonesia, Cambodia, Ceylon, the UAR, and Yugoslavia. SEATO, NATO, and OAS members should be informed through those organizations, with selected members also informed individually. The possibility of some special approach to Poland as a member of the ICC should also be considered.

7. The President directed the Departments of State and Defense to develop detailed recommendations for a US command structure in South Viet-Nam that would have a senior US commander assuming responsibility for all phases of US activity, including economic aid, related to the counter-insurgency effort. Such a commander should report directly to the JCS [Joint Chiefs of Staff] and the Secretary of Defense for operational purposes.

7.4 Kennedy on Diem, 1963

By 1963 Diem's own generals began plotting a coup that eventually materialized in early November of that year. Prior to the generals' coup Kennedy and his aides agonized over the pros and cons of supporting—or being seen to support—the overthrow of Diem. Here Kennedy and his advisors are discussing a draft telegram that includes instructions to the recently appointed US ambassador to South Vietnam, Henry Cabot Lodge. The discussion took place in the White House on 29 October 1963, a few days before the coup.

THE PRESIDENT commented that he was not so concerned now about the kind of government which would exist after the coups as he was about the correlation of pro- and anti-Diem forces.

SECRETARY MCNAMARA agreed and asked that the draft cable stress our objection to a situation in which there would be major fighting between the Diem forces and the rebel Generals.

THE PRESIDENT said that the burden of proof should be on the coup promoters to show that they can overthrow the Diem government and not create a situation in which there would be a draw. We can discourage a coup in ways other than telling Diem of the rebel Generals' plans. What we say to the coup Generals can be crucial short of revealing their plans to Diem. The paragraph referring to post-Diem government matters should be dropped. Lodge should be told that from here we can see that a disaster could take place and that if the rebels can't win, it would not be sensible for them to go ahead. Lodge feels that the coup is comparable to a stone rolling down the hill which can't be stopped. If this is so, then no one can say that we are to blame for the coup no matter what we do (…)

THE PRESIDENT reiterated his suggestion that Lodge should tell the Generals that they must prove they can pull off a successful coup or, in our opinion, it would be a mistake to proceed. If we miscalculated, we could lose our entire position in Southeast Asia overnight.

7.5 Lyndon B. Johnson on His Options in Vietnam, 1964

After having taken over as US president, Lyndon Johnson agonized over how to deal with the situation in Vietnam. He understood that an American escalation may come in the way of his chief priority, social reform at home. But he also feared the consequences of an American disengagement from Vietnam on his personal political status. This is Johnson talking on the telephone with his long-time political mentor, the southern senator Richard Russell, May 27, 1964.

LBJ: I'm confronted. I don't believe the American people ever want me to run. If I lose it, I think they'll say *I've* lost. At the same time, I don't want to commit us to a war. And I'm in a hell of a shape.

RUSSELL: We're just like the damn cow over a fence out there in Vietnam.

LBJ: (...) I've got a study being made now by the experts ... whether Malaysia will necessarily go and India'll go and how much it'll hurt our prestige if we just get out and let some conference fail or something (...) A fellow like A. W. Moursund said to me last night, 'Goddamn, there's not anything that'll destroy you as quick as pulling out, pulling up stakes and running. America wants, by God, prestige and power.' (...) I said, 'Yeah, but I don't want to kill these folks.' He said, 'I don't give a damn. I didn't want to kill 'em in Korea, but if you don't stand up for America, there's nothing that a fellow in Johnson City'—or Georgia or any other place—'they'll forgive you anything except being weak.' Goldwater and all of 'em are raising hell about ... hot pursuit and let's go in and bomb 'em . . . You can't clean it up. That's the hell of it.

RUSSELL: (...) It'd take a half million men. They'd be bogged down in there for ten years.

LBJ: We never did clean up Korea yet.

RUSSELL: (...) We're right where we started, except for seventy thousand of 'em buried over there.

LBJ: Now Dick, you think, every time you can get your mind off of other things, think about some man. . . . My great weakness in this job is I just don't know these other people. The Kennedys—they know every damn fellow in the country or have somebody that knows 'em. They're out at these universities and everyplace in the country—New York and Chicago.

LBJ: We're just doing fine, except for this damned Vietnam thing. We're just doing wonderful. Every index. The businessmen are going wonderful. They're up 12, 14 percent investment over last year. The tax bill has just worked out wonderfully. There're only 2.6 percent of the married people unemployed. . . . And 16 percent of these youngsters, and I'll have them employed. . . . It's kids that are dropping out of school and then they go on a roll. But I'll take care of that with my poverty, just organizing it all. We've got the money in these various departments—Labor and HEW [Health, Education, and Welfare] and Justice (...)

LBJ: How did the Congress react to our going in and doing this bombing?

RUSSELL: They don't know about it. . . . I think all of 'em would approve of it if they did.

LBJ: Now we're going to continue these reconnaissance flights as needed, as we must have 'em, and we're going to send in armed people. And if they shoot at us, we're going to shoot back.

RUSSELL: That's just like A. W. told you. That's the American inclination. . . .

LBJ: Now Mansfield's got a four-page memo saying that I'm getting ourselves involved and I'm gonna get in another war if I do it anymore.

RUSSELL: . . . . I in a way share his fears.

LBJ: I do too, but the fear the other way is more.

RUSSELL: I don't know what the hell to do. I didn't ever want to get messed up down there. I do not agree with those brain trusters who say that this thing has got tremendous strategic and economic value and that we'll lose everything in Southeast Asia if we lose Vietnam. . . . But as a practical matter, we're in there and I don't know how the hell you can tell the American people you're coming out. . . . They'll think that you've just been whipped, you've been ruined, you're scared. It'd be disastrous.

LBJ: I think that I've got to say that I didn't get you in here, but we're in here by treaty and our national honor's at stake. And if this treaty's no good, none of 'em are any good. Therefore we're there. And being there, we've got to conduct ourselves like men. That's number one. Number two, in our own revolution, we wanted freedom and we naturally look with sympathy with other people who want freedom and if you'll leave 'em alone and give 'em freedom, we'll get out tomorrow. . . . Third thing, we've got to try to find some proposal some way, like Eisenhower wanted out in Korea.

RUSSELL: (...) I think the people, if you get some sort of agreement all the way around, would understand it. And I don't think they'd be opposed to the United Nations getting in there. And I don't think they'd be opposed to coming out. I don't think the American people want to stay in there. They've got enough sense to realize that it's just a matter of face, that we can't just walk off and leave those people down there.

LBJ: But U Thant says he won't have anything to do with that part of the world. . . . Think about my man and I'll talk to you in a day or two.

7.6 Le Duan's Letter to the South, 1965

In 1965, after the rapid increase in the number of American troops in South Vietnam, the North Vietnamese leader Le Duan sent a number of reports to the heads of the Southern section of the Vietnamese Communist Party. The reports included the party leaderships' evaluations of the current situation and their instructions for the struggle in the south. These are excerpts from one of Le Duan's letters in November 1965.

(...) With the US bringing another 150–200 thousand or more American troops to the South, the war in the South has moved to a new stage, having new characteristics; and for us, new issues have arisen. To say the war has new characteristics does not mean that the US has changed all their political and military conspiracy for the South and for the whole of Viet Nam. The US's war in the South still remains a neo-colonialist war, but is now waged with new methods and new forces. That was voiced by [U.S. Secretary of Defense Robert] McNamara himself in the speech addressed to the US's Defense Sub-Committee, 'Although our methods have changed, our objectives stay the same.'

Nevertheless, the US's policy of 'escalation' in Viet Nam depends on many conditions, for instance whether their objectives change often, how the comparison of force between us and them changes, whether in-country and international circumstances are favorable for them. As for us, given the enemy's current situation and our strength, we keep affirming that we can control the enemy in the South and are determined to defeat them on this main battleground.

In these circumstances, the North is still the battleground for the US to wage the sabotage war. From now on the US may raise the level of attacks further.

But, no matter how bad the damage may be, the North is determined to defeat the US's sabotage war. In the South we should correctly assess the fact of the US's bringing in their soldiers. As mentioned above, the US has to bring 150–200 thousand soldiers into the South since they are getting in a more and more passive and failing position in many aspects. But that also proves that the US is more determined in clinging to the South. The US has gradually realized that their bringing in of troops in the immediate future is not yet going to lead to an all-out war which would make them face directly the larger countries in the socialist system. The force they are directly faced with is still the Vietnamese people. The US also realized that if they loose in the South, they not only loose to the Vietnamese people but also fail in the international arena. The Viet Nam issue has become one with international significance. Our people are now facing the US, the leading imperialist country, humankind's most fierce enemy. Our people's struggle is now taking place in one of the heated areas, with hard conflicts; it is the focus of the struggle between two forces—revolutionary and counter-revolutionary—in the world at present. Therefore, our people are now undertaking the nation's sacred duty, and simultaneously taking the noble international duty (...)

The dialectic relation in this issue is fighting with American troops to create the conditions for defeating puppet troops; and vice versa, defeating puppet troops to create the conditions for fighting and defeating American troops. And defeating puppet and American troops aims at breaking the enemy's military forces; defeating the political goal of the invading war and defeating the US's military strategy. We have set forth an all-round task of defeating the enemy on all these three aspects. And only when we defeat the enemy on all these three aspects do we win the war which is both 'limited' and 'special' in this stage.

As a matter of course, in fighting with the enemy we will attack and destroy the weaker parts before the stronger. Therefore, as to the fighting targets, first we have to aim at destroying the puppet troops, and at the same time seek ways to weaken and kill American troops so as to facilitate our weakening and destroying puppet troops (...)

Restricting the enemy and winning them in the South is the main task, is our major strategy. This strategy has to reflect in our political, military and diplomatic activities. With the current balance of forces in our country, in South-East Asia and in the world, our capability of restricting and winning the enemy in the South is still real, and also we have to prepare and be ready to fight them if they expand the war to the North with ground troops. For the time being, the probability for the US to expand the war with ground troops to the North exists, but is small, because the US is hesitant to face our forces in the North and the whole socialist faction, and they now have to cope with the increasing anti-aggression war movement of the American people. The US is also afraid of being further isolated, given the increasing pro-Viet Nam movement of the world's forces for national independence, democracy and peace. Among the other imperialist countries, there are some not supportive of the US's policies; some are supportive of these policies, but are not willing and able to cooperate with the US in expanding the war (...)

In the military respect, it is easier to destroy the puppet troops than the American troops, for the American troops have not had much fighting with us, thus are optimistic and proud of their weapons, and also have their nationalist pride unwounded. The puppet troops have lost a lot of battles, are now in low mentality, little enthusiasm to fight. Therefore, we have to raise our resolution to wipe out the puppet troops and disintegrate them as fast as possible. On the other hand, in the propagation work, we have to emphasize the slogan 'Find the Americans to kill.' On specific battlegrounds, we have to study thoroughly the methods most suited for destroying the American troops. With the guerrilla forces encircling the American troops' bases, we have to strongly encourage bravery in military struggling and praise our sisters and brothers so as to heighten their resolution for killing American troops (...)

This upcoming spring and summer, we are aiming for killing about 10,000 Americans as already planned and for the next few years, we should at least kill 40,000 to 50,000 Americans. This is a new goal which will determine our victory.

Along with trying to lessen the Americans' strength, we should try to cause great loss for the American aircraft, at the same time, curb their activities. This is the common goal for both the North and the South, and thus an important step toward our victory (...)

I just talked about the possibility and necessity to strengthen the political war. Reality shows that even though the U.S. brings in more troops to Vietnam, it is possible that they will fail to weaken our political power. In fact, our political power is likely to be enhanced and the U.S. will be isolated and fail miserably (...) Reasons for such a possibility to be real are:

The more troops the U.S. brings in, the more military bases it builds, the larger area it occupies, the more sophisticated weapons it uses, the more B.52 bombs it throws, the more chemical poisons it uses, the worse the conflict between our people and them becomes, the more our people hate them.

Though the U.S. is pushing the war harder, they still follow the neo-colonialism policy. As our people are very experienced and conscious, they can unveil the enemy's tricks and mistakes so as to strengthen the political war.

The more troops the U.S. brings in, the more conflict the puppet government will have making their political, economic and financial situations more difficult; the cost of living of the people in their occupied area is rising; this will induce the people to rise to fight against them.

The U.S. brings in more troops hoping to win and improve the spirit of the puppet troops and government, but the U.S. troops are losing to the extent that they start talking about negotiations, therefore, conflict between the American and puppet governments is on the rise, the puppet troops are now deteriorating.

That the U.S. government escalates the war in the South and expands the scope of their bombing in the North will lead the American people and open-minded people in the world to oppose the war more.

7.7 The American War, 1968

Most of the American soldiers who were sent to Vietnam found that realities there were very different from what they had been told about at home in the United States. For many, the uncertainties and the strain of war were difficult to bear. This is the reporter Michael Herr's account of the life of one such soldier in an American military base in Vietnam in 1968.

During the bad maximum incoming days of the late winter of 1968 there was a young Marine at Khe Sanh whose Vietnam tour had run out. Nearly five of his thirteen months in-country had been spent there at the Khe Sanh Combat Base with the 26th Marines, who had been slowly building to full and then reinforced regimental strength since the previous spring. He could remember a time, not long before, when the 26th considered themselves lucky to be there, when the guys talked of it as though it were a reward for whatever their particular outfits had been through. As far as this marine was concerned, the reward was for an ambush that fall on the Cam Lo–Con Thien road, when his unit had taken 40 percent casualties, when he himself had taken shrapnel in the chest and arms. (Oh, he'd tell you, but he had seen some shit in this war.) That was when Con Thien was the name everyone knew, long before Khe Sanh had taken on the proportions of a siege camp and lodged itself as an obsession in the heart of the Command, long before a single round had ever fallen inside the perimeter to take off his friends and make his sleep something indistinguishable from waking. He remembered when there was time to play in the streams below the plateau of the base, when all anybody ever talked about were the six shades of green that touched the surrounding hills, when he and his friends had lived like human beings, above ground, in the light, instead of like animals who were so spaced out that they began taking pills called Diarrhea-Aid to keep their walks to exposed latrines at minimum. And on this last morning of his tour, he might have told you that he'd been through it all and hacked it pretty well.

He was a tall blond from Michigan, probably about twenty, although it was never easy to guess the ages of Marines at Khe Sanh since nothing like youth ever lasted in their faces for very long. It was the eyes: because they were always either strained or blazed-out or simply blank, they never had anything to do with what the rest of the face was doing, and it gave everyone the look of extreme fatigue or even a glancing madness (…) This Marine, for example, was always smiling. It was the kind of smile that verged on the high giggles, but his eyes showed neither amusement nor embarassment nor nervousness. It was a little insane, but it was mostly esoteric in the way that so many Marines under twenty-five became esoteric after a few months in I Corps. On that young, nondescript face the smile seemed to come out of some old knowledge, and it said, 'I'll tell you why I'm smiling, but it will make you crazy.'

7.8 The Vietnamese War, 1969

For the North Vietnamese and FNL forces the war demanded much sacrifice. The American air superiority led to increasing losses among their enemies, and many North Vietnamese units were completely destroyed. This is a Northern soldier's recollections of the fighting in the Central Highlands in early 1969, from Bao Ninh's novel The Sorrow of War.

(…) Kien knows the area well. It was here, at the end of the dry season of 1969, that his Battalion 27 was surrounded and almost totally wiped out. Ten men survived from the Unlucky Battalion, after fierce, horrible, barbarous fighting.

That was the dry season when the sun burned harshly, the wind blew fiercely, and the enemy sent napalm spraying through the jungle and a sea of fire enveloped them, spreading like the fires of hell. Troops in the fragmented companies tried to regroup, only to be blown out of their shelters agains as they went mad, became disoriented and threw themselves into nets of bullets, dying in the flaming inferno. Above them the helicopters flew at tree-top height and shot them almost one by one, the blood spreading out, spraying from their backs, flowing like red mud.

The diamond-shaped grass clearing was piled high with bodies killed by helicopter gunships. Broken bodies, bodies blown apart, bodies vaporised.

No jungle grew again in this clearing. No grass. No plants.

'Better to die than surrender my brothers! Better to die!' the Battalion Commander yelled insanely; waving his pistol in front of Kien he blew his own brains out through his ear. Kien screamed soundlessly in his throat at the sight, as the Americans attacked with sub-machine-guns, sending bullets buzzing like deadly bees around him. Then Kien lowered his machine-gun, grasped his side and fell, rolling slowly down the bank of a shallow stream, hot blood trailing down the slope after him.

In the days that followed, crows and eagles darkened the sky. After the Americans withdrew, the rainy season came, flooding the jungle floor, turning the battlefield into a marsh whose surface water turned rust-coloured from the blood. Bloated human corpses, floating alongside the bodies of incinerated jungle animals, mixed with branches and trunks cut down by artillery, all drifting in a stinking marsh. When the flood receded everything dried in the heat of the sun into thick mud and stinking rotting meat. And down the bank and along the stream Kien dragged himself, bleeding from the mouth and from his body wound. The blood was cold and sticky, like blood from a corpse. Snakes and centipedes crawled over him, and he felt Death's hand on him. After that battle no one mentioned Battalion 27 any more, though numerous souls of ghosts and devils were born in that deadly defeat. They were still loose, wandering in every corner and bush in the jungle, drifting along the stream, refusing to depart for the Other World.

From then on it was called the Jungle of Screaming Souls. Just hearing the name whispered was enough to send chills down the spine. Perhaps the screaming souls gathered together on special festival days as members of the Lost Battalion, lining up on the little diamond-shaped grass plot, checking their ranks and numbers. The sobbing whispers were heard deep in the jungle at night, the howls carried on the wind (...)

Here when it is dark, trees and plants moan in awful harmony. When the ghostly music begins it unhinges the soul and the entire wood looks the same no matter where you are standing. Not a place for the timid. Living here one could go mad or be frightened to death. Which was why in the rainy season of 1974, when the regiment was sent back to this area, Kien and his scout squad established an altar and prayed before it in secret, honouring and recalling the wandering souls from Battalion 27 still in the jungle of Screaming Souls (...)

7.9 Norman Mailer on the March on Pentagon

In the late 1960s the anti-war movement was becoming a constant feature of the US domestic scene, symbolizing the deep divisions within American society over the country's involvement in Vietnam. In this extract the author Norman Mailer—himself a World War II veteran—describes the passions of the anti-war movement during the so-called March on Pentagon in October 1967. Approximately 50,000 anti-war activists participated in this demonstration; a number that would soon be exceeded in anti-war rallies around the United States.

(...) Standing against [the soldiers], the demonstrators were not only sons of the middle class of course, but sons who had departed the middle class, they were rebels and radicals and young revolutionaries; yet they were unbloodied, they felt secretly weak, they did not know if they were the simple equal, man for man, of these soldiers, and so when this vanguard confronted soldiers now, and were able to stare them in the eye, they were, in effect, saying silently, 'I will steal your élan, and your brawn, and the very animal of your charm because I am morally right and you are wrong and the balance of existence is such that the meat of your life is now attached to my spirit, I am stealing your balls.' (...) Those who were not in the first row yelled insults, taunted the soldiers, derided them—the demonstrators in the front looked into the soldiers' eyes, smiled, tried to make conversation. 'Hey, soldier, you think I'm a freak. Why am I against the war in Vietnam? Cause its wrong. You're not defending America against Communism, you're just giving your officers a job.' (...)

Where soldiers cut off the access roads, demonstrators from the Mall were pressing against them. Here the attitude was more ugly. Here soldiers were not cutting people off from the Pentagon, but from their own demonstrators, so the imperative to get through was more direct, the fear of being stampeded was less— there was all the Mall to run out into. Therefore the inability to mount a charge to break the soldiers' line was less excusable, closer perhaps to cowardice—hence the ugliness of the crowd. And indeed far out in the Mall, isolated altogether from other soldiers, were very small detachments on now unknown details, three soldiers here, five there. Newspaper stories referred to them, Breslin reported they were reviled and tormented unmercifully; when it got dark a few soldiers were beaten up—so goes the story. It may be well to quote Breslin here.

Taste and decency had left the scene a long time before. All that remained were these lines of troops and packs of nondescript kids who taunted the soldiers. The kids went to the bathroom on the side of the Pentagon building. They threw a couple of rocks through the first-floor windows. The soldiers faced them silently (...) There was no humor to it. These were not the kind of kids who were funny. These were the small core of dropouts and drifters and rabble who came to the front of what had started out as a beautiful day, one that would have bad meaning to it. They turned a demonstration for peace, these drifters in raggedy clothes, into a sickening, club-swinging mess. At the end of the day, the only concern anybody could have was for the soldiers who were taking the abuse (…)

In contrast let us now dare to give an extract from Gerald Long's account in the *National Guardian*. It is not a paper famous for its lack of bias and the account here is obviously partisan, but its virtues are to be brief and vivid.

(…) The MPs executed an about-face, seeking to clear out the demonstrators who ran behind them. A youth refused to be moved. A rifle butt landed in his stomach. He grabbed the rifle. Several youths grabbed rifles. Four helmets were stolen. A demonstrator was slugged. An MP was slugged. White-helmeted federal marshals, impressed for service from the calm of courtrooms, moved forward, clubs swinging. It seemed to this observer—both in this incident and for the next 30 or 50 hours—that the marshals aimed particularly at women.

Each time the action stopped in a parrticular spot, demonstrators sought to speak with the soldiers, who were under orders not to respond. 'Why are you doing this?' a demonstrator asked. 'Join us' the soldiers were asked. It was obvious that some of the troops were weakening. A few soldiers seemed ready to faint. 'Hold your lines, hold your lines,' a captain repeated harshly, over and over, to the soldiers.

A girl confronted a soldier 'Why, why, why?' she asked. 'We're just like you. You're like us. It's them,' she said pointing to the Pentagon. She brought her two fingers to her mouth, kissed them and touched the soldier's lips. Four soldiers grabbed her and dragged her away, under arrest. The soldier she had spoken to tried to tell them that she hadn't hurt him.

7.10 Mao Zedong on Vietnam, 1970

In spite of the growing political strains in the relationship, the Chinese support for North Vietnam and the FNL continued up to the end of the war. Mao Zedong and the Chinese leadership saw themselves as the heads of the East Asian revolutionary movement and believed that Hanoi should conform to their view of the world. This is Mao's conversation with Le Duan in May 1970.

LE DUAN: We are very much in need of getting Chairman Mao's instructions. If our Central Committee and Politburo learn that Chairman Mao has given instructions about how we should do our job, they will certainly be very happy.

MAO ZEDONG: You have done a very good job, and you are doing better and better.

LE DUAN: We have tried our best to do our job. We have been able to do a good job because we have followed the three instructions Chairman Mao gave us in the past: first, no fear, we should not fear the enemy; second, we should break up the enemy one piece after another; third, we should fight a prolonged war.

MAO ZEDONG: Yes, a prolonged war. You should prepare to fight a prolonged war, but isn't it better if the war is shortened? Who fears whom? Is it you, the Vietnamese, Cambodians, and the people in Southeast Asia, who fear the U.S. imperialists? Or is it the U.S. imperialists who fear you? This is a question which deserves consideration and study. It is a great power which fears a small country—when the grass bends as the wind blows, the great power will be in panic. It is true that during the Gulf of Tonkin Incident in 1964 you hit the U.S. imperialists, but it was not your intention to fight a war with the U.S. Navy. In actuality, you did not really hit it [the U.S. naval ship], but they themselves became nervous, saying that Vietnam's torpedo boats were coming and began opening fire. At the end, even the Americans themselves did not know if there had been a genuine [Vietnamese torpedo attack] or not (…)

LE DUAN: We Vietnamese people keep Chairman Mao's great goodness always in our mind. During the nine years of the war of resistance against the French, if there had not been the support from the Chinese Communist Party and Chairman Mao, it would have been impossible for us to win the victory. Why are we in a position to persist in fighting a prolonged war, especially in fighting a prolonged war in the South? Why dare we fight a prolonged war? This is mainly because we have been dependent upon Chairman Mao's works.

MAO ZEDONG: This is not necessarily true.

LE DUAN: Of course this is true. We also need to apply [Chairman Mao's teachings] to Vietnam's practical situation (…)

MAO ZEDONG: The Americans do not have enough manpower to distribute in the world, since already they have been overextended. Therefore, when their people were killed their hearts were broken. The death of several dozens of thousand is a huge matter for them. You Vietnamese, both in the North and the South, in my opinion, it is inevitable for some of you also to be killed.

LE DUAN: Our current ways of fighting cause low casualties. Otherwise, it is impossible for us to persist for a long time (…)

MAO ZEDONG: Southeast Asia is a hornets' nest. The people in Southeast Asia are awakening day by day. Some pacifists think that cocks like fighting. How can there be so many cocks? Now even hens like fighting.

LE DUAN: There is no way out if one does not fight.

MAO ZEDONG: Yes, there is no way out if one does not fight. You [Mao speaks rhetorically to the Americans] compel the others [to fight] and leave them no other way to go. You are bullying them (…)

LE DUAN: This was also what we thought. When we are still able to continue the fighting, we hope to make our 'great rear' more stable. When we Vietnamese are fighting the Americans, China is our 'great rear.' Therefore, we once issued such instructions that even though our planes had been attacked they should not land at the airports in China.

MAO ZEDONG: You can [land at our airports]. We do not fear. If the American air force come to attack the 'shelters' of Vietnamese air force, let them come.

LE DUAN: Although we issued such instructions, still we needed to rely on your support. At that time, you dispatched several divisions to Vietnam, also engaged in fighting American planes.

MAO ZEDONG: That is true. The Americans are afraid of being beaten, and they have no guts. You may negotiate [with the Americans]. I am not saying that you cannot negotiate, but your main energy should be put on fighting (…)

LE DUAN: We have been able to continue our fighting, this is because the Chairman has said that the 700,000,000 Chinese people are firmly backing the Vietnamese people. The United States is scared. This is very important.

MAO ZEDONG: Why should it be scared? You invade another country, why is it wrong for us to back that country? You dispatch hundreds of thousands of naval, air and land forces to bully the Vietnamese people, who forbids China to become the rear [of the Vietnamese people]? Which law has set up this?

LE DUAN: The Americans say that they can mobilize 12 million troops, but they can only dispatch half a million troops to Vietnam. They are scared if they cross this limit.

ZHOU ENLAI: China has a large population, which makes them fear.

MAO ZEDONG: Because we have a large population sometimes we do not need to fear. In the final analysis, we do not have relations with you [the Americans]. You have occupied our Taiwan Island, but I have never occupied your Long Island.

7.11 Kissinger in Moscow and Beijing, May–June 1972

The Nixon administration tried to use the emerging Sino-Soviet-American triangular relationship to put further pressure on the North Vietnamese. However, in March 1972—a month after Nixon's visit to China—the North Vietnamese launched a major offensive against the South (the so-called Spring Offensive). The United States—which had already removed most of its ground troops from Vietnam—responded with extensive bombing and mining campaigns that helped to prevent an imminent collapse of the South Vietnamese government. When Nixon travelled to Moscow for the May 1972 Soviet–American summit, the bombing was still going on and finding a solution to the war was part of the agenda. In June Henry Kissinger, Nixon's national security adviser, travelled to Beijing and held further talks on Vietnam. The excerpts below are from

Kissinger's conversations with Soviet Foreign Minister Andrei Gromyko and the Chinese Premier Zhou Enlai during the two trips.

A. Kissinger and Gromyko, May 1972

KISSINGER: First, with respect to the last point, the neutrality of South Vietnam is in principle acceptable to us, and we have some ideas as to how it can be brought about. So that is not an issue between us and North Vietnam. That is a positive idea. Secondly, with respect to the political problem, I believe your leader (...) seem to be under the impression that it is only the matter of the personality of Thieu. That is not the case. What North Vietnam proposes is this. Thieu has to resign; what they call his machine of repression has to be dismantled and Vietnamization must stop, which means American economic and military aid must cease. In other words, the U.S. would side with North Vietnam in forming a three-segment government of peace, independence and neutrality. But only they know who meets these criteria. They won't tell us. So the objective consequence of their proposal would first be that the government resigns, the political machinery is disbanded, outside support ceases. Under these conditions, the only organized political force in South Vietnam has to be the PRG [NLF-led Provisional Revolutionary Government]. We interpret their proposal as a demand that we turn power over to them (...) We cannot overthrow the people we have worked with over eight years. You wouldn't do this. We won't do it. We are prepared to start a political process, without a guaranteed outcome, but which has possible outcomes (...)

GROMYKO: The situation is rather strange, I should say. You would like, as the President and yourself said, to end the war and withdraw American troops, but on the other hand, you resolutely oppose a political solution under the conditions that the situation will be settled not under the presence of American troops but by the Vietnamese themselves. So you don't want such a situation. Your idea on Thieu and the machinery under his control is to have them preserved for an indefinite period of time (...) If the President and the American government decide to leave Vietnam do you not have enough resolution to see that this is done? Why should every effort be made to preserve the Thieu regime? That is the question.

KISSINGER: After we withdraw, a number of conditions exist. First of all, we would be prepared to limit military aid to South Vietnam after our withdrawal in proportion to the aid the North Vietnamese receive from their allies. Or if they are not prepared, we would be glad to agree directly with you about limiting aid to the area so North Vietnam does not have to put themselves on the same level as Saigon under the conditions of peace. I have difficulty understanding, if North

Vietnam is so self-confident, why it insists that we overthrow the political struc-ture of South Vietnam for them. Why must *we* do it?

(…) if you and we can guarantee a settlement (…) We are a different govern-ment and any possible [US] government's attitude would be different. We are not like Dulles (…)

GROMYKO: (…) Is your main preoccupation the character of the government?

KISSINGER: (…) What we mean is that we will not leave in such a way that a Communist victory is guaranteed. However, we are prepared to leave so that a Communist victory is not excluded, though not guaranteed. I don't know if this distinction is meaningful to you.

GROMYKO: Until now our view is that your main preoccupation is to prevent the establishment of a regime you don't like politically. Later maybe you could face this.

KISSINGER: There is no question that is true. Our position is we want a politi-cal solution which does not guarantee a Communist victory, but also, we empha-size, that does not exclude it.

GROMYKO: That is official?

KISSINGER: You can communicate this to the North Vietnamese.

GROMYKO: On the basis of official American statements, the U.S. main preoc-cupation is to do all in order to preclude the possibility of a government not liked by the United States. That makes it more difficult.

KISSINGER: It is an absurdity to pretend we would not prefer it if Communists would not win in South Vietnam.

B. Zhou Enlai and Kissinger, 21 June 1972

ZHOU: (…) the Vietnamese envisage a settlement that includes both the military aspect and the political aspect at once. We believe there is reason in their seeking such a solution and therefore we support them. Therefore, if the question of the government, no matter whether it be called a coalition government or a govern-ment of harmony, is not settled, and discussions on this do not bear results, then a peaceful situation will not be able to be brought about in the southern part of Vietnam, and therefore in the event of your withdrawal from that part of Indochi-na, hostilities between the two Vietnamese sides would break out again. On the other hand, if political agreement can be reached, then that would have a binding force on all. And that is also to say that the attitude that that government would take towards the US would be more friendly because the political agreement would be an agreement in which you also had made a contribution (…)

As to what kind of socialism that South Vietnam would choose if it would turn to socialism in the future, I cannot say, and yet you are so afraid of that. Anyway, I won't see that, because they have already declared that it will be only after a certain period of time that Vietnam would seek to be reunified. Yet you are so fearful and so sure that the government that would emerge would be a Communist government (…)

So what is bad in relaxing the tension in the Far East for a time and to having a period of neutrality in this area? (…) we might as well solve the military and the political aspects together and to set up a good relation that would be able to continue for a certain period of time—for several years (…) according to what you told us during your visit last July, your subjective desire was to settle the issue, but it seems as if the objective tendency is to follow the laws of development that govern the war. So what are you going to do about that? What can we do about this situation? (…) Because you know this is one of the steps that must be taken to normalize relations between the US and China (…)

KISSINGER: Mr. Prime Minister (…) It is in a sense absurd that you and we should have tension over an area from which we are attempting to withdraw.

ZHOU: It is absurd.

KISSINGER: I agree also with the basic objective of the Prime Minister that we should try to create an area of relaxation of tension. I also agree with the Prime Minister that neutrality of many of these countries can be achieved through an understanding between our two countries at least. Because if we both showed a strength and if we both oppose outside intervention, it will be very difficult to have outside intervention (…)

ZHOU: And since you have withdrawn your troops to its final remainder, then why do you want to leave that 'tail' there and try to expand the war with the tail?

KISSINGER: But the Prime Minister knows, because I told him yesterday, that we are prepared to withdraw the tail. If the North Vietnamese accept a ceasefire we will withdraw all our forces in return for our prisoners.

ZHOU: So then since you will have by that time withdrawn all your forces and have all your prisoners of war repatriated, then if the political issue cannot be solved and a civil war breaks out again, you shouldn't go back to take care of that (…)

KISSINGER: Mr. Prime Minister (…) it should be self-evident that in a second term we would not be looking for excuses to re-enter Indochina. But still it is important that there is a reasonable interval between the agreement on the ceasefire, and a reasonable opportunity for a political negotiation (…) the outcome of my logic is that (…) we are putting a time interval between the military outcome and the political outcome. No one can imagine that history will cease on the Indo-china peninsula with a ceasefire. And I believe that if the North Vietnamese had confidence in themselves they should have a better chance this way than through a continuation of the war (…) We will agree to an historical process or a political process in which the real forces in Vietnam will assert themselves, whatever these forces are.

(…) No matter what the words of the [Geneva] agreement in 1954 would have been, Secretary Dulles was determined to go into Indochina. No matter what the words of the agreement in 1972, or whenever this Administration makes it, there is no reason for us who are seeking to normalize relations with you to remain in a position of tension with Hanoi. When we were attempting to build barriers against you, there was one policy. But now that we believe that your vitality is a factor to peace in the Pacific, why should we build barriers to you in Indochina, and if not building barriers in Indochina what is our interest there either one way or the other? So after the agreement is signed the value will be that there will be an increasing American disinterest in Indochina (…) We want to leave. We do not want to stay. We do not want to tear apart North Vietnam. We were forced into it this year. We are not obstinately staying in Vietnam. It is contrary to what we want to do.

7.12 The Paris Agreements, January 1973

In August 1972 negotiations in Paris between Kissinger and the North Vietnamese representative Le Duc Tho started again. After reaching a tentative agreement in October, Kissinger flew to Saigon to elicit South Vietnamese President Thieu's backing. Instead, Thieu called the treaty a betrayal because, among other things, it allowed 150,000 North Vietnamese troops to remain in the south. In December the next set of negotiations failed to reach a conclusion and the Nixon administration launched a massive bombing campaign in mid-December (the so-called Christmas bombings). Finally, in January 1973 a peace agreement, similar to one agreed in October, was concluded in Paris. Still, the president had to use extra pressure to get the South Vietnamese on board and work out a way of selling the agreement to the American public. The first excerpt below—taken from the diaries of the president's chief of staff, Bob Haldeman—reveals some of the selling strategies, while the second is an example of a number of threatening letters Nixon sent to Thieu during the last stage of the Paris talks.

A. Bob Haldeman Diaries

14 January 1973

The P[resident] (…) then got into some discussion of schedule of handling the Vietnam thing. K[issinger] and Haig arrived. There was some discussion on the wording on the bombing-stop announcement, and then on the Thieu letter wording. The P strengthened the wording that K had drafted. Apparently he reviewed it last night, by saying that I have approved every section and so forth. He wants to take out the offer to meet with Thieu, let Haig use that as a bargaining point in discussion, but not put it in the letter. His strategy is to keep the whole approach with Thieu on our terms, and we don't want to appear to be begging, especially on the record. The P made the point that Haig must take a very hard line on Thieu, that he's here only as a messenger, not to negotiate, that the P has been totally in charge of all of this, and he will go ahead regardless of what Thieu does. The only diplomacy that Haig should exercise is to trick Thieu, if it looks like he's not going with us in regard to shooting his mouth off before the Inaugural (…) If [Thieu] takes on K or the agreement, he takes on the P personally and he's got to understand that.

23 January 1973

Got word from Henry [Kissinger] this morning that he had initialed the Vietnam agreement and that was set (…) so we had sessions on planning of the speech for tonight (…) We had the Cabinet meeting at 8:45. The P opened by saying that this was basically a pro forma meeting. We're doing it for the purpose of eyes of the world and the nation so that they will think that we have consulted with the Cabinet, but we can't really get into anything now because we can't release the agreement until tomorrow. Then he read the official statement that he will read on TV tonight, said all our conditions have been completely met. The P said the GVN and Thieu are totally on board and will issue statements to that effect. There will be heavy fighting between now and the cease-fire (on the 27th), and after the cease-fire there will be inevitable violations, which is why the supervisory body is so important. He said we have a cease-fire for Vietnam, possibly in Laos and Cambodia. We have peace with honor, the POW's are back, the supervised cease-fire, and the right of South Vietnam to determine their own future. It's been long, painful and difficult for all of us. This is not Johnson's war, or Kennedy's war. They did start it and they did handle it badly, but the United States was involved. We have now achieved our goals (…) the fact that we have stood firm as a country (…) has had a decisive effect on the world. If the United States did not prove to be responsible in Vietnam, if this had ended in defeat and surrender, the Chinese and the Russians would have no interest in talking to us (…) We must understand, for the United States to keep the peace and save freedom, we have to be responsible, and that's what this peace is about (…) He got fairly emotional at the end, but did a darn good job at the Cabinet meeting, although he worried Henry [Kissinger] a little about some of the areas he went into.

B. Nixon to Thieu, 19 January 1973

(…) The essential fact is that the situation in the United States makes it imperative to put our relationship on a new basis. It is obvious that we face a situation of most extreme gravity when long-time friends of South Viet-Nam such as

Senators Goldwater and Stennis, on whom we have relied for four years to carry our programs of assistance through the Congress, make public declarations that a refusal by your Government of reasonable peace terms would make it impossible to continue aid. It is this situation which now threatens everything for which our two countries have suffered so much.

Let me now address the specific proposals you have made in your letter. We have made innumerable attempts to achieve the very provisions you have proposed with respect to North Vietnamese forces, both in the text of the Agreement and in formal understandings. We have concluded that the course we have chosen is the best obtainable: While there is no specific provision in the text, there are so many collateral clauses with an impact on this question that the continued presence of North Vietnamese troops could only be based on illegal acts and the introduction of new forces could only be done in violation of the Agreement. It seems to me that the following clauses in the Agreement achieve this objective:

— The affirmation of the independence and sovereignty of South Viet-Nam (...)
— The provision for reunification only by peaceful means, through agreement and without coercion or annexation, which establishes the illegitimacy of any use or threat of force in the name of reunification (...)
— The U.S. and DRV, on an equal basis, pledging themselves against any outside interference in the exercise of the South Vietnamese people's right to self-determination (...)
— The legal prohibition or the introduction of troops, advisers, and war material into South Viet-Nam from outside South Viet-Nam (...)
— The principle of respect for the demilitarized zone and the provisional military demarcation line (...)
— The prohibition of the use of Laotian and Cambodian territory to encroach upon the sovereignty and security of South Viet-Nam (...)
— The fact that all Communist forces in South Viet-Nam are subject to the obligation that their reduction and demobilization are to be negotiated as soon as possible.

In addition, we are prepared to give you a unilateral U.S. note which sums up our understanding on this issue. Ambassador Bunker will show you a draft of a note which we will deliver in Saigon on the day of signature of January 27 (...)

We have now reached a decisive point. I can no longer hold up my decision pending the outcome of further exchanges. When Dr. Kissinger leaves Washington Monday morning, our basic course must be set. As I have told you, we will initial the Agreement on January 23. I must know now whether you are prepared to join us on this course, and I must have your answer by 1200 Washington time, January 21, 1973.

I must meet with key Congressional leaders Sunday evening, January 21, to inform them in general terms of our course. If you cannot give me a positive answer by then, I shall inform them that I am authorizing Dr. Kissinger to initial the Agreement even without the concurrence of your Government. In that case, even if you should decide to join us later, the possibility of continued Congressional assistance will be severely reduced. In that case also I will not be able to put into my January 23 speech the assurances I have indicated to you, because they will not have been a voluntary act on my part (…)

Let me therefore sum up my position as follows: First, I welcome your decision to send Foreign Minister Lam to Paris, and I will instruct Dr. Kissinger to have the fullest and frankest discussion with him. Dr. Kissinger will see him both before and after his meeting with the North Vietnamese to make clear your Government's full participation in our actions. Secondly, I have instructed Dr. Kissinger to seek the change in the Protocol regarding police forces. Thirdly, with respect to North Vietnamese forces, I can go no further than the draft note that I am asking Ambassador Bunker to transmit to you and which we will hand over to you officially on January 27, the day of signing. Fourthly, if you join us we shall announce the Vice President's visit to Saigon before the date of signing though he could not leave Washington until January 28.

Finally, and most importantly, I must have your assurances now, on the most personal basis, that when we initial the Agreement on Tuesday we will be doing so in the knowledge that you will proceed to sign the Agreement jointly with us.

This Agreement, I assure you again, will represent the beginning of a new period of close collaboration and strong mutual support between the Republic of Viet-Nam and the United States. You and I will work together in peacetime to protect the independence and freedom of your country as we have done in war. If we close ranks now and proceed together, we will prevail.

7.13 Kissinger in Hanoi, 12 February 1973

A few weeks after the signing of the Paris Peace Accords Henry Kissinger travelled to Hanoi to meet with North Vietnam's leaders. One of the key issues on the agenda was the possibility of US economic aid, which had been one of the American carrots used during the last stage of the negotiations. Below are some excerpts from these discussions—the aid package envisioned never materialized.

DR. KISSINGER: (…) We have to be able to develop a concrete program and a concrete schedule, or we will be talking pure theory. And this is what I would like to discuss with you—how we can go from here to a concrete program. That is the purpose of my observation.

8. A British view of Nixon's 'Vietnamisation.' (Author Horner, *New Statesman*, 14 April 1972). Reprinted by permission. Photo supplied by The Centre for the Study of Cartoons and Caricature, University of Kent.

Now I want to tell the Prime Minister something else that we have decided, that no one in our government yet knows. We have decided to take the money for reconstruction for Vietnam out of our defense budget rather than out of our general budget where it usually belongs:—Now this presents its own difficulties but I am mentioning all these things to the Prime Minister not to create a pretext but to give him some feeling of the complexity of what we are up against.

PHAM VAN DONG: May I say this, Mr. Special Adviser (…) First of all, I would like to express my suspicion. I tell you this so that if you have any persuasion then please persuade me. I will speak very frankly and straightforwardly to you. It is known to everyone that the U.S. has spent a great amount of money in regard to the war in Vietnam. It is said about $200 billion, and in conditions that one would say that the Congress was not fully agreeable to this war. When the war was going on then the appropriation was so easy (laughs), and when we have to solve now a problem that is very legitimate and then you find it difficult. We should not deem it necessary to go in the complete complexity, the forest of legal aspects. I feel it very difficult to understand. Of course, when one is unwilling then the legal aspect is a means to this end. And I will not debate that the money will be taken from which budget, and I don't think it necessary to invite any personality to ask his views on that—for the only reason, and a correct reason, that it is your affair. We have no reason to interfere in it, and there is also no necessity to do that.

DR. KISSINGER: You're a very heroic people. You are also very suspicious people, and I can understand why you would be suspicious. You have not been treated especially kindly by history. On the other hand, there are some periods when it is essential to have a certain amount of trust. Now I recognize what the Prime Minister said has reasonable aspects. That is to say, it is true we spend a great deal of money on the war and not always with the easy agreement of Congress. But let me explain to the Prime Minister the differences in the situation.

PHAM VAN DONG: Mr. Adviser, please let me speak more and then you will continue, Mr. Adviser. I apologize to you as I have to say this. If I were in your place. I would not do what you are doing right now because I do not think that it is really what you are saying. I do not think that it is so difficult (...) I feel it impossible to go into the complexity of the legal aspects. Because it is not our problem, and it is not necessary to do that.

DR. KISSINGER: Mr. Prime Minister, what you would do in my shoes I have no way of knowing (...) we are prepared to set up this Economic Commission immediately and to go to Congress in April with a specific proposal and to put the whole prestige of the Presidency behind it. Until this has been done you should defer your judgment whether we are trying to be evasive or not. But we have to prepare it carefully, and above all jointly. Of course, we understand that you keep the final decision. Now the disposition of the funds is a matter that the experts should work out. It is easier for us if most of the money is spent in the United States, but I don't want to get into that issue (...) Our difficulty is that we don't know your desires nor do we know your needs. We don't even know whether you would rather deal with multilateral institutions or whether you would rather deal with us bilaterally.

PHAM VAN DONG: Now please, Mr. Adviser, let me answer you. As I said yesterday, today I would like to stress it again (...) This is what we would like to have—the free disposal, the free use of this money to buy goods from the United States. These goods are aimed at rehabilitating and developing the very important branches of our destroyed economy, that is, communication and transport, industrial factories and enterprises or agricultural works and public utilities, to bring population centers accommodation and housing. It is now an obligation of the US to contribute to rehabilitate and develop these establishments destroyed by the war. I will not go into the details of these installations, but in the Joint Economic Commission they will list them out very concretely.

So as to remove the aftermath of the war, the consequences of the war and to remove them to some extent, we should like that the US will bring about a contribution, significant contribution, for this is, of course, a very important, very necessary problem. For the US, I think that you should also realize the necessity, the obligation and the significance of this work. Do we agree on that? If so, we shall have the free use of the amount of money without conditions (...)

DR. KISSINGER: (...) As I understand the Prime Minister, he said one could have a program in housing and for roads and for an industrial plant and for various categories. If the Economic Commission can be free use of the funds that will in no case be tied to any political condition (...) We agree on projects; we agree on programs; and within those you are free to dispose of the funds (...)

LE DUC THO: So we have clearcut agreement on the amount and on the use of the money.

DR. KISSINGER: That is right. Now I think we have agreed now on these items. Now let me make a few points where you must help us. This can be carried out expeditiously. First, you should talk as little as possible about an American obligation, and you should never talk about 'reparation.' Our possibility for getting this money is enhanced if we do it as a voluntary act, as I explained to the Special Adviser on innumerable occasions. We understand each other (...) I am really talking from a practical point. When the Special Adviser comes to America I will introduce him to Senator Passman who heads a committee this money goes through, and he will find that moral obligation and honor are difficult words for him to understand (...)

PHAM VAN DONG: I understand.

DR. KISSINGER: But we stick by what we have said.

LE DUC THO: And if you stick to the understanding you had with us, we will stick to the understanding we have with you.

7.14 The Fall of Saigon, 1975

In April 1975 the South Vietnamese capital Saigon fell to a combined offensive by North Vietnamese and NLF troops, and the southern regime collapsed. The Australian reporter John Pilger was in the American Embassy in Saigon on the day of the evacuation.

At 5.20 a.m. Martin Garrett ordered all those supervising the evacuation to assemble inside his embassy building. Colonel Summers reminded him that there were more than 500 'endangered' Vietnamese still waiting to be evacuated. Garrett replied that the pilots had been flying for fourteen hours and the President had said that the evacuation must end. He said to tell the marines to wait at least an hour, then to walk slowly, casually, back to the embassy reception hall and then to lock the door to the stairwell behind them. This they did, and at that moment people streamed over the wall and past the stump of the great tamarind tree and the embassy cars with their engines running and their head-lights on, marking a landing zone of no further use.

The last marines reached the roof and fired tear-gas canisters into the stairwell. They could hear the smashing glass and desperate attempts to break open the empty safes. The marines were exhausted and beginning to panic; the last helicopter had yet to arrive and it was well past dawn. They fired Mace, the gas which disables muscles, into the stairwell. Colonel Summers could see people still waiting in a long orderly queue, still believing that their turn for evacuation would come, because he had told them again and again that he would not leave without them. Even men of the Saigon fire brigade, who had worked for twelve hours to protect the helicopters, were still at their posts; he had given the same undertaking to them. But now he was going without them, having learned only by accident that the Ambassador had left three and a half hours earlier. 'I will be the last man to leave this embassy,' Graham Martin had told him in his office. 'You have my solemn word on that.' When he landed on the USS *Okinawa* in the South China Sea, Colonel Summers was, he told me later, 'so ashamed that I could cry . . . but I was too damned mad to cry and too tired to yell.'

Three hours later, as the sun beat down on an expectant city, tanks flying NLF colours entered the centre of Saigon. Their jubilant crews showed no menace, nor did they fire a single shot. One of them jumped down, spread a map on his tank and asked amazed bystanders, 'Please direct us to the presidential palace. We don't know Saigon, we haven't been here for some time.' The tanks clattered into Lam Son Square, along Ta Do, up past the cathedral and smashed through the ornate gates of the presidential palace where 'Big' Minh and his cabinet were waiting to surrender. In the streets outside, boots and uniforms lay in neat piles where ARVN soldiers had stepped out of them and merged with the crowds. There was no 'bloodshed.' The war was over.

Questions

Did Ho Chi Minh express a particular ideological viewpoint in his declaration of independence?

Why and with what expectations did the Eisenhower administration pledge its support to Ngo Dinh Diem in 1954?

Assess the Kennedy administration's attitude towards Diem.

What were the different issues weighing on Lyndon Johnson with regard to decisions on Vietnam?

How did the North Vietnamese and their allies expect to win the war after the introduction of American ground troops?

Were there major differences in the experiences of American and Vietnamese soldiers?

What was the Chinese leadership's attitude towards the Vietnam War in 1970?

How did Henry Kissinger wish to involve the Soviets and the Chinese in the peace process?

What were the major disagreements between the United States and North Vietnam that led to the breakdown of the Paris Agreements?

8

Communism in Eastern Europe and China

Without the existence of Communist regimes in Eastern Europe and East Asia, the Cold War would almost certainly have been a less intense and less dangerous Great Power confrontation. For the United States, the Soviet imposition of Communist regimes on the countries it occupied in Eastern Europe after World War II was a key cause of the conflict, and the victory of the Chinese Communists a key challenge to America. For the Soviet Union, the alliance with the East European countries created a 'socialist camp' that could confront the West, and the alliance with China, as long as it lasted, gave credibility to the concept of global Communist power. For both superpowers, the existence of Communism *outside* the Soviet Union was at the heart of their conflict.

But in spite of their given roles in the Great Power clash, the Communist states came to play very different parts in their domestic and foreign policies. Through most of its existence, the Polish Communist regime was careful when introducing forced reforms and chose a series of compromises with the workers and with the Catholic Church. East Germany (the German Democratic Republic, GDR) and Czechoslovakia, by far the most advanced territories in industrial terms, combined social and economic rights for the working class with political repression and tight adherence to Soviet policies, but also with keen abilities to defend their economic status in trade with other Eastern Bloc countries. Hungary remained divided between growing industries at the centre and a largely undeveloped agricultural potential. Bulgaria—the poorest state in the Eastern Bloc, closely related to Russia in language and culture—imitated the Soviet model of development, but kept a large agricultural sector. Romania diverged from the others through policies of mass mobilization and attempts at forced industrialization, combined with an increasingly independent foreign policy and strict control of its people. As an alliance, the Eastern Bloc did not function well, neither in terms of economic co-operation and trade—every country tried to sell the same products at similar prices—nor in terms of political cohesion, which could only be enforced through Soviet pressure.

In the most developed of the Communist states, especially in the GDR, Poland, and Hungary, there was substantial resistance against Communist rule throughout the period. After the end of the initial phase of Stalinist terror, some groups protested openly. In 1953 East German workers rebelled against poor conditions, Communist control, and the Soviet presence. In 1956, after Nikita Khrushchev denounced Stalin's terror at the Soviet 20th Party Congress, Polish workers forced the government to improve pay and welfare and introduce a less repressive regime, while Budapest and other Hungarian cities rose in a nationalist rebellion against the Soviet military presence. In 1970, after government attempts at pressuring the workers to bear the burden of the country's weak economy, the Polish workers struck back and wrung further concessions from the Communist regime.

In Czechoslovakia, where the Communist party had had substantially greater popular support than in the rest of the Eastern Bloc, Alexander Dubcek in 1967–8 made the only attempt of the period at structurally reforming a Communist regime from within, opening it up to greater freedoms and popular participation in government. But both the Soviet Union and the other regimes in the Eastern Bloc saw Dubcek's experiments as a deadly threat to the integrity of their own rule and intervened militarily to overthrow the leadership of the Czechoslovak Communist party. The end of Dubcek's leadership signalled the death of hopes for fundamental reform from within the Communist parties themselves.

In spite of political oppression and foreign control, East European societies did advance substantially during the Communist era in terms of education, social rights, and maybe particularly the status of women. In many cases, these were rights that workers had to wrest from the regimes in terms of their content, but the socialist pretensions of the parties in power did help with putting such issues on the agenda. Except in Poland, the majority of the populations settled into some form of cohabitation with the regimes, where people were willing to pay lip-service to the Communist parties' aims, but resisted their attempts at enforcing their ideology within the family sphere or in the workplace.

By the 1960s, however, it was becoming clear that the Eastern Bloc economies, both as a unit and in the individual countries, simply were not able to keep up with the rapid advances in Western Europe. Moreover, the lack of legitimacy of the regimes prevented them from successfully making their populations accept the hardships and the restructuring that would be needed to start bringing the economies onto an even keel. The vast majority of their citizens did not believe in the success of planned economies, although they were more than willing to enjoy the social rights that they had gained. Fearful of challenging their own populations, the Eastern Bloc regimes by the 1970s had little choice but to make up for their lack of productivity by seeking hard-currency loans from the West.

Western policies on Eastern Europe balanced throughout the Cold War between a wish for political change and an unwillingness to seriously challenge the status quo. Both American and West European leaders kept up the idea of an integrated continent without ideological or economic borders, but at least up to the détente era of the 1970s, no leader on the Western side chose a concerted strategy of subverting the East European regimes from within. Fear of war with the Soviet Union was one obvious cause of this reluctance, but the seeming stability in Europe created by the Iron Curtain and resistance against making compromises with the Soviets, even if that could help the East Europeans, were other reasons. But, as long as the Cold War lasted, West Europeans kept viewing those living east of the Iron Curtain as hostages to the Soviet Union and its military power.

China, the most powerful of the Soviet Communist allies in the 1950s, had already by 1960 moved away from the Soviet model of development. As he confronted Moscow politically and ideologically, Chinese leader Mao Zedong moved ever further to the left, taking his People's Republic through a series of utopian experiments from the late 1950s onward. The human cost of these policies were staggering, comparable only to that of Stalin's forced reforms of the 1930s. In 1966 Mao unleashed the so-called Great Proletarian Cultural Revolution, an ever-widening campaign within the Communist Party aimed at anyone who could be suspected of disagreeing with Mao's radical policies. While seeking accommodation with the United States in foreign policy, Mao's domestic alternative to the Soviet model turned out to be a reign of terror.

Readings

Joseph Rothschild, *Return to Diversity: A Political History of East Central Europe Since World War II* (3rd edn., 2000). An excellent overview of Eastern Europe during the Cold War.

Uprising in East Germany 1953: The Cold War, the German Question, and the First Major Upheaval behind the Iron Curtain, compiled, edited, and introduced by Christian Ostermann (2001). Documents and analysis of the 1953 rebellion in the German Democratic Republic.

Jeno Györkei and Miklós Horváth (eds.), *Soviet Military Intervention in Hungary, 1956* (1999). Provides both the background to the intervention and an overview of the October 1956 events.

Kieran Williams, *The Prague Spring and Its Aftermath: Czechoslovak Politics, 1968–1970* (1997). The best book on what happened to the Czechoslovak Communist party during and after the Soviet intervention.

Michael Schoenhals (ed.), *China's Cultural Revolution: NOT a Dinner Party* (1996). Key documents from within the Red Guard movement during the Cultural Revolution.

8.1 The East German Rebellion, 1953

In June 1953 workers in East Berlin went on strike for democracy and better living conditions. The strikes and demonstrations were crushed by Soviet tanks, but not before they had shown both Germans and Russians that dissatisfaction with the Communist East German regime ran deep. Document A is one of the telegrams sent by the strike committee in Bitterfeld to the government of the GDR. Document B is an excerpt from a letter of resignation sent to the GDR authorities by Police Colonel R. Neuhaus in the early 1970s. During the 1953 uprising Neuhaus was a police officer assigned to the Ministry of Interior headquarters in Schnellerstraße.

A. Demands of the East Berlin Strike Committee, 1953

To the so-called German Democratic government in Berlin-Pankow
   We, the working-people from the district of Bitterfeld demand:

1. The immediate resignation of the so-called German Democratic government which has come to power through manipulation of the elections.
2. The creation of a provisional government consisting of the progressive working-people.   *want to incorp. W. Ger.*
3. Admission of all the big West German democratic parties.
4. Free and secret direct elections within four weeks at the latest.
5. Release of all political prisoners (the plain political ones, the so-called fiscal criminals, and those persecuted because of their [religious] confession).
6. Immediate abolition of all borders and withdrawal of the People's Police.
7. Immediate normalisation of the social standard of living.
8. Immediate dissolution of the so-called National Army.
9. No reprisals against even a single striking worker.

B. A Policeman's View of the Berlin Uprising, 1953

In the afternoon of 16 May 1953 I took part in a discussion at the head office Shipping, at Klara-Zetkin-Straße in Berlin. At about 3:30 p.m. I set off in my official car to Schnellerstrae in Berlin-Schöneweide. When we took a turn from Friedrichstrae into Unter den Linden the driver and I saw something strange.

Around Humboldt University there was a surging crowd as wide as the whole street, moving into the direction of the Brandenburg Gate. Coming closer we discovered that slogans in white writing on green and blue fabric, as wide as the street allowed, were carried at the front of the crowd. Among others, we could decipher from that distance: (…) 'More money and goods for the ordinary people' (…) 'Away with the struggle to reach quotas' (…) 'Pieck, Ulbricht and Grotewohl, more cheap butter will be good for us' (…)

As if spellbound we stared at the crowd surging back and forth. We could mainly recognise men in blue and white working clothes. They came closer and closer, shouting slogans in unison which, however, we couldn't understand in the car.

When the front of the crowd was about a hundred meters away from us we turned around and went to Berlin-Schöneweide using side streets. Inwardly in a complete turmoil, I reported back and gave an account of what had happened. They did not believe me. I had to be exaggerating. And a few very keen 'comrades' even accused me of spreading rumours. Offended by so much narrow-mindedness, I disappeared into my office (…)

On the way home after work, to Berlin-Pankow, I watched the passengers in the suburban tram very attentively. I couldn't recognise any emotions. Everything went as usual. Or was I wrong? (…)

My neighbour also worked somewhere around Alexanderplatz. Should I go ask him? No sooner said than done. He looked at me briefly:

'Are you surprised after all that has recently been happening here? These numerous trials against so-called enemies of the GDR? The unjustified rise in quotas? Now they're building the foundations of socialism. And the food becomes scarcer and more expensive. Why is there so little butter? They even start saving on the marmalade. The middle classes receive no more food ration-cards. Soon it's going to be like in Russia over here, too!'

Quietly I moved back. I couldn't counter his arguments. I had already heard about all these things . . . (…)

On 17 June 1953 I drove to work at 6 a.m. Everything seemed quiet. As usual, a thousand Berliners hurried to their occupations with me. At about 8 a.m. we noticed rather unusual noise outside, on the Schnellerstrae. Many lorries filled with people drove towards the city centre. From the lorries, they shouted slogans in unison. Inside our offices they were hard to understand. The passing stream of people rose and rose. Soon, it was as wide as the entire street. The local public transport broke down, too. Not far from us a tram driver simply left his car which went into the other direction, and marched with the people. Threatening fists were directed against our building. Calls became loud such as:

'Down with the Vopos [policemen]!'

'Down with the servants of the Russians!'

'Long live freedom and democracy!'

First of all, we were speechless and helpless. Were these 'our' workers? How could such a thing happen? (…)

At 1 p.m. we were told by the aide of Major General Bechler that [Soviet] Marshal Gretchkov had announced a state of emergency.

In the afternoon the first groups of people walked past our section in the direction of the outlying districts. It was a very hot day in June. Most of the men and women had taken off their shoes and socks and walked barefoot.

After 9 p.m. the streets were empty.

Curfew.

How could all this happen?

My boss said:

'The class enemy has used a situation difficult for us, and has acted. Now order has to be reinstalled!'.

But how?

After all, nothing changed.

What the media announced was one side. How the people experienced it in their daily lives, another.

In our section, as well, there were widely diverging opinions on the events of 17 June 1953.

But every day the mood changed and in the end, the party was, as always, right.

sums it up

The following Monday I could go back home after work for the first time.

The door had been hit with an axe. I came to know that the tenants in the house hadn't allowed my flat to be destroyed. I grew thankful to these different, but nevertheless splendid human beings.

8.2 Nikita Khrushchev's Secret Speech, 1956

In a closed session at the 20th Congress of the Soviet Communist Party in early 1956 its new leader, Nikita Khrushchev, launched an attack on Joseph Stalin and the crimes he had committed while head of the party. While the millions who had suffered under Stalin welcomed the speech, it came as a shock to Communists inside and outside the Eastern Bloc.

Comrades! If today we sharply criticize the cult of the individual leader which was so widespread during Stalin's lifetime and if we speak about the many negative phenomena generated by this cult which is so alien to the spirit of Marxism-Leninism, various persons may ask: How could it be? Stalin headed the Party and the country for 30 years, and many victories were gained during his lifetime. Can we deny this? In my opinion, the question can be asked in this manner only by those who are blinded and hopelessly hypnotized by the cult of the individual leader, only by those who do not understand the essence of the revolution and of the Soviet state, only by those who do not understand in a Leninist manner the role of the Party and of the people in the development of Soviet society.

The socialist revolution was accomplished by the working class and the poor peasantry, with the partial support of the middle peasants. It was accomplished by the people under the leadership of the Bolshevist party. Lenin's great service consisted in that he created a militant party of the working class; he was armed with the Marxist understanding of the laws of social development and with the science of proletarian victory in the struggle with capitalism, and he steeled this party in the crucible of the revolutionary struggle of the masses of the people. During this struggle the Party consistently defended the interests of the people, became their experienced leader, and led the working masses to power, to the creation of the first socialist state.

You remember well Lenin's wise words that the Soviet state is strong because of the awareness of the masses, because history is created by the millions and tens of millions of people.

Our historic victories were attained thanks to the organizational work of the Party, to the many local organizations, and to the self-sacrificing work of our great people. These victories are the result of the great drive and activity of the people and Party as a whole; they are not the fruit of Stalin's leadership, as was pictured during the period of the cult of the individual leader (...)

Comrades! Lenin often stressed that modesty is an absolutely integral part of a real Bolshevik. Lenin himself was the living personification of the greatest modesty. We cannot say that we have been following this Leninist example in all respects. Suffice it to point out that we have called many cities, factories and industrial enterprises, collective and state farms, Soviet institutions and cultural institutions after the private names—as if they were private property, if I may express it so—of various government or Party leaders who were still active and in good health. Many of us participated in the act of assigning our names to various cities, districts, factories and collective farms. We must correct this. (*Applause.*)

But this should be done calmly and slowly. The Central Committee will discuss this matter and consider it carefully to prevent errors and excesses. I can remember how the Ukraine learned about Kossior's arrest. The Kiev radio used to start its programs thus: 'This is the radio station [named for] Kossior.' When one day the programs began without naming Kossior, everyone was quite certain that something had happened to Kossior, that he had probably been arrested.

Thus, if today we begin to remove the signs everywhere and to change names, people will think that the comrades in whose honour the given enterprises, collective farms or cities are named also met some bad fate and that they have also been arrested. (*Stir in the hall.*)

How is the prestige and importance of this or that leader judged? By the number of cities, industrial enterprises, factories, collective and state farms, that bear his name. Is it not time we ended this 'private property' and 'nationalized' the factories, the industrial enterprises, the collective and state farms? (*Laughter, applause, voices: 'Right.'*) This will benefit our cause. After all, the cult of the individual leader is manifested also in this way.

We should consider the question of the cult of the individual leader quite seriously. We cannot let this matter get out of the Party, especially not to the press. It is for this reason that we are considering it here at a closed Congress session. We should know the limits; we should not give ammunition to the enemy; we should not wash our dirty linen before their eyes. I think that the delegates to the Congress will understand and assess all these proposals properly (…)

[margin note: focuses on secretive nature of speech]

Comrades! The 20th Congress of the Communist Party of the Soviet Union has manifested with new strength the unshakable unity of our party, its cohesiveness around the Central Committee, its resolute will to accomplish the great task of building Communism. (*Stormy applause.*) And the fact that we present in all their ramifications the basic problems of overcoming the cult of the individual leader, a cult alien to Marxism-Leninism, as well as the problem of liquidating its burdensome consequences, is evidence of the great moral and political strength of our party (*Prolonged applause.*)

We are absolutely certain that our party, armed with the historic resolutions of the 20th Congress, will lead the Soviet people along the Leninist path to new successes, to new victories. (*Stormy, prolonged applause.*)

Long live the victorious banner of our party—Leninism! (*Stormy, prolonged applause, culminating in an ovation. All rise.*)

8.3 Revolt in Hungary, 1956

The revolt against Communism in Hungary in October 1956 was an attempt to establish an independent and neutral republic, but it was soon crushed by a Soviet invasion. In this excerpt, the Time *Magazine photo-journalist Carl Mydans presents views of Budapest in rebellion as seen by observers.*

Tamas Aczel, one of Hungary's leading novelists and a political writer, was present at the critical hour of the uprising of the populace in Budapest. He himself—until sometime during those early hours of the revolt—was a Communist. He describes the failure of the Hungarian Communist leaders to understand the universality of the public demands, or even the substance of those demands. Imre Nagy was the one Hungarian Communist who had the trust of the populace: at that hour only he could lead them. Two hundred thousand people packed Budapest's Parliament Square that day, October 23, when the revolt turned to violence. As the people pressed upon each other, closer and closer, they began to chant: 'Russians, go home. Russians, go home.' Then they called for Nagy: 'Imre Nagy. We want Imre Nagy.' It grew into a din. 'Imre Nagy. Where are you. Show yourself.'

Aczel, a close friend of Nagy, realizing the gravity of the development, made his way out of the square, found his car, and drove to Nagy's villa in Buda. There were others already on the same mission. 'You have to go immediately,' someone was saying. 'There is not a minute to lose.' Aczel's account continues:

Nagy looked tired and irresolute. He glanced at me. 'You have come from the square?'

I nodded. 'Uncle Imre, the crowd is calling for you. For God's sake, why do you wait? If you do not start immediately, something awful is going to happen.'

Someone said that it might already be too late and Nagy answered irritably, 'How can I be late? Late for what?' He rose slowly to his feet. 'Very well,' he said. 'I shall go. But I doubt that it will do any good.' He turned to me. 'Aczel, will you take me in your car?'

During the descent of the steep hills of Buda he was silent. Finally he asked, 'How big is the crowd?'

'Tremendous,' I said. 'Perhaps two hundred thousand. More.'

He said nothing until we had crossed the Danube and entered the crowds. Then, peering out of the car, he suddenly exclaimed, 'Look! Look at that flag in the window!' It was the Hungarian flag but with the hammer and sickle of the Communist revolution cut out of the center. Nagy twisted around in his seat to look at other windows. 'But all the flags are like that,' he gasped. 'What can be happening?' He took out his handkerchief to wipe his forehead, though the air was cold.

It was about eight o'clock in the evening when we entered the square and pushed through to one of the main gates of the Parliament. A young actor appeared on the balcony to declaim the famous poem: 'Up on your feet, Hungarians, the country calls. . . .' And the crowd roared the refrain: 'We swear, we swear by the Hungarians' God, that we shall no longer be slaves.'

People made way for us and we went up the stairs and Nagy went through the door that opened on the balcony. I followed him, pausing at the door. The instant he showed himself the crowd below fell silent.

'Comrades,' Nagy began. Then an incredible thing happened. From the dark, heaving mass in the square rose an inchoate cry of wrath. Nagy stopped, bewildered, as from one voice came the words, 'We are not comrades.'

Now, suddenly, everything was clear to me. Hungarians were finished with the old, discreditable, disreputable things; not just the Red Army, the old Stalinist clique, but all the hackneyed falsities of Communism. Nagy was staggered. He seemed to hesitate and his eyes roved despairingly over the crowd, as if seeking a clue to its anger. Did he grasp even then what was really in its brooding mind? I don't know. All I am sure of is that at this instant of matchless opportunity, with Budapest waiting for a true signal, Imre Nagy made the wrong speech. He could have saved the situation. He might even have saved Hungary from Soviet power. All he had to say was, 'Hungarians, go to your factories and occupy them. Take leadership in your own hands, I am ordering your army to supply you with weapons.' That was what Gomulka had done only a few days before, in Warsaw, though under less desperate circumstances. Instead, Imre Nagy said, 'My friends, go home now and leave everything to us.'

Perhaps that was the only speech that Nagy could have made. Much as he loathed Stalinism, he was irretrievably a Communist. He was a Communist talking, he hoped, to other Communists, and because of his mistake the Hungarian destiny at that instant slipped irretrievably out of his hands.

Even as he fidgeted on the balcony, trying to fathom the reason for the crowd's disapproval, a man lurched up to me and seized me by the lapels. 'Aczel,' he gasped, 'you must tell Nagy that the AVH is shooting into the crowd at the radio station.'

I started for the balcony to tell Nagy. But just as I reached him, from somewhere across the dark square, cutting across Nagy's halting words, boomed a voice of fantastic power: 'Citizens. To the radio station. The AVH is shooting demonstrators.'

The AVH were the Soviet-controlled Hungarian secret police. In opening fire on the unarmed demonstrators they were following the pattern of brutality with which they had suppressed the Hungarian people until now. But this time the citizens of Budapest had had enough. When the news spread of what was happening, people from all over the city rushed to join the demonstrators, and units of the Hungarian army, sent to keep order, turned instead and joined the citizens. Russian troops were moved to put down the rebels and were fought off by these Hungarian soldiers as well as hastily armed young civilian 'freedom fighters.'

The next day Imre Nagy was reinstated as Premier and his wavering government struggled to give concessions to the rebels. New political parties formed; free-speaking newspapers were published. For a few euphoric days it seemed that Hungary had gained a step toward freedom. Though Russian tanks and soldiers were still in the streets, it was against the AVH that the rebels turned their wrath. It was this hatred, so well justified and yet so terrible to witness, that correspondent John Sadovy captured in his photographs and in the words of his report of an attack on an AVH headquarters in Budapest on October 30:

We were roving the town, looking at burned-out tanks, bodies covered with lime—trying to capture the horror going on. A partisan came along and said, 'They are shooting on the other side of the city.'

As we went we were passed by lorries packed with screaming women and boys with guns and revolvers. Guns they hardly knew how to use. As they went along they were jerking them to see how they worked. There were two or three of these lorries going in to that fire. I later learned they were rebel reinforcements just picked up off the street.

We came into a square. There was grass in it and small trees. You could go for a walk there with your dog. We heard shooting. Then we saw a tank facing a large modern building at the end of the square. It was the AVH headquarters, someone said. The rebels were trying to take this headquarters. And the AVH were in there shooting at them from the windows.

My first instinct was to get behind the tank. There would be some shelter there and I would be close enough to take pictures. Halfway to the tank we found ourselves in the open park. Bullets began zinging past our ears. We fell flat on our faces. I tried to hide behind a young tree. I wished my tree were bigger and I tried to make myself smaller. I was still hoping to get behind the tank, but then it moved off. There we were, stuck, a half a dozen rebels and myself. It was not very nice there.

I started to crawl back through the park until I got to a shed and some bushes which provided cover. The fighting really began to flare up. People were dropping all around me. I crawled nearer and nearer to the building. There was great movement and activity all around me. White-coated first-aid people, mostly women, were coming and going, collecting the wounded. Then I noticed that the Red Cross people were being shot too. Now it was suicide to go in there. The women stopped going, and youngsters took over. They were magnificent, fifteen-, sixteen-, seventeen-year-old kids. They ran in there with no protection at all. A kid ran in, half bent over. He put a man on his back and dragged him to shelter. Now, many were at it. Young boys in two's, flat on the ground, some pulling stretchers, getting to the wounded and dragging them back. Nothing could stop them. One was hit. His partner dragged the stretcher with one end on the ground. It was incredible to see. Still they went out there. Some came back limping. Just kids.

A lorry arrived. It had ammunition for the tank. There was a scramble to carry the heavy shells—two or three to a shell, like people who hadn't eaten for weeks scrambling for bread, with a fury and excitement. The ammunition was going to make a difference. They loaded the tank which went back and kept up a tempo of firing against the building (…)

I managed to get in front of the tank, flat on the ground. The heat of its gun going off was unpleasant, like opening the door of a hot oven. They were plastering the building wall. There was a thick tree there and a pile of something, I forget what it was, but I got behind it and stuck out for a while and took a few pictures.

Suddenly there was a noise of people running. They were running towards the AVH building. Now they were closing in fast. I went in with the first group. There were three of us together, myself and two German-speaking rebels. We met another group led by a man carrying a huge flag. 'Come on, come on, we made it. It's ours,' he was saying.

Other groups of rebels were coming in from the side, screaming. There would be no half measures here. Now there was only occasional machine-gun fire from the top floor. The tanks were still shooting and bricks fell from the building when the tanks blasted it. It was 3.15. People were still being careful. There were two burned out lorries in front of the building with seven burned bodies under them. The people had crawled there for shelter and been caught. It was a mess in front of the building. At least thirty to forty dead were sprawled there. They got it going in, one after the other. They were lying, almost in line. Each of them silent. It was like a potato field. Only these were people instead of potatoes.

Now you could feel confidence sweeping the crowd. They advanced right to the main door of the building. The AVH began to come out. The first man to emerge was an officer, alone. It was the fastest killing I ever saw. He came out laughing and the next thing I knew he was flat on the ground, his legs spread, dead as anyone could be. For an instant it didn't dawn on me that this man was shot. He just fell down, I thought. Then the first group, the bravest of the lot, decided to go inside the building. They brought out a good-looking officer, his face white as chalk. He got five yards, retreated, argued. Folded up. It was over with him. They went back again and two came out together. There was a scuffle. An array of rifle butts, punching, kicking. Suddenly there was a shot. The two just dropped.

Six young officers came out, one very good-looking. Their shoulder boards were torn off. They wore no hats. They had a quick argument. 'We're not so bad as you think we are. Give us a chance,' they were saying. I was three feet from that group. Suddenly one began to fold. I hardly heard a shot. They must have been so close that the man's body acted as a silencer. Now they were going down the way you'd cut corn. Very gracefully. They folded up smoothly, in slow motion. And when they were on the ground the rebels were still loading lead into them.

8.4 Living in the GDR

Views of life in East Germany could differ a lot, depending on your position in society. These two excerpts deal with the life of ordinary people in the East. When increasing numbers of skilled workers began crossing over to West Berlin, the East German author-ities built a wall, with armed observation posts, right through the heart of the city, sepa-rating Communist East Berlin from the capitalist West. In the first excerpt, a German journalist is interviewing ordinary people who lived next to the eastern side of the Wall, and the officers who kept watch over them. But not all of its inhabitants resented the GDR authorities. For some, the access to free education and social services, and the guarantee of life-long employment, was felt as a personal victory. In the second excerpt, from a 1993 interview, Liesbeth Mühle, a skilled woman worker, explains her support for East Germany.

A. Living at the Wall

INTERVIEWER: What happened along the Wall after 13 August [1961]? How did the border zone develop?

MRS B.: In the beginning one could still walk up to the fence (...) It didn't take long until the fence in our area was replaced with concrete blocks, so you could-n't see anything from the street. To see each other nevertheless, at least from afar, at the time some people went to Schwedter Strae. Some people had thrown some stuff together to stand on. There stood the Easterners. The Westerners had other methods. They fetched a ladder or something like that, so they could see the heads. Then they waved their arms. As an acquaintance has told me, in the East it was a matter of minutes until the police came: 'Don't stop here! It's forbidden! No assemblies! No gathering! Keep on walking, keep on walking!'

At the time I was envied by my friends, because I lived on the second floor. When I sat on the balcony, I could see my relatives. My son or my friend sometimes stood at the Wiener Brücke, on the other side of the canal (...) Thus we could see each other. But God help anyone who showed a reaction or raised their hand and waved! Or who maybe automatically waved back at others. That was absolutely prohibited. Once I let myself be carried away when my two men stood on the other side of the road and waved (...) Another time when there was such excitement was when my son got married. Once again, the small group of wedding guests stood on the other side of the Wiener Brücke. I had my housekeeping day, the little one was excused from school, and my mom was here. The wedding was in August 1964. We sat on the balcony and all we did was cry. On the other side they waved with handkerchiefs. It was, of course, very sad (...)

INTERVIEWER: To live next to the Wall, that meant to be under observation every day?

MRS K.: Yes. Every night the soldiers came and checked the cellar and the attic. At night at two o'clock the motorbike with the border guards stopped. They unlocked the door, and went into the cellar. Each of us even had to take away the blanket which we had put on the inner side of the cellar door, or we had to cut a hole into it so they could scan the whole room with their torches. And every night they climbed up to the attic. The nicest thing was that we had an antenna up there that was connected to the light switch. They went up, saw the light and switched it off. Then the ones on the right side of the house no longer had reception. And we did not have a key for the attic, what a mess! Especially when something was dropped from the balcony . . .

INTERVIEWER: What could the inhabitants do if the geranium pot fell onto the signal fence?

OFFICERS: Generally they then spoke to the posts directly. When the kids' ball fell onto the other side, for example, the post told the central control office, climbed through and then they got it back. The incident was settled, fast and unbureaucratic.

MRS K.: I only heard once that a duster or something like that fell down. And the young man, in the basement, through the backdoor, runs behind to get it.— The cellar doors on the borderline were all taken out in the end of the '70s and were cemented, then earth was used for filling up.—In that moment there was real chaos. Alarms went off, the criminal investigation department and the police came (...)

OFFICERS: Many houses were equipped with electrical security systems, with contacts at the attic doors and skylights, Lohmühlenstraße also had contacts at the skylights. There were some houses, Lohmühlenstraße 35/36, Harzer 118,

Bouché 33, which had security systems on the roof. Sometimes wires were tightened there, and when a pigeon flew into them, the alarm went off. But generally most were equipped with light barriers. Harzer 118 was one of our favourite houses because the alarm was generally set off already when it was windy, or stormy. And then everyone had to run up there, five floors, the crews of our squad cars can tell you a thing or two about that. Only game birds, it was then judged. The signals were sent to the police stations, the regiment, the central control office and the watchtowers (…)

INTERVIEWER: The controls were carried out by the border guards?

OFFICERS: Half and half. The major part of the controls were done by the German People's Police. We were only there from time to time, especially at times of highlights such as party congresses, youth festivals,' etc., where one had to assume that there were many non-Berliners in Berlin. Then, naturally, the possibility of entering the border zone was higher. Apart from that in Treptow we had over a hundred 'Voluntary assistants of the border troops' which helped us in the various groups. They were settled in the residential area. They served in the whole hinterland, also in the allotments and factories. They were dressed and trained by us, and we gave them their assignments. They wore uniforms of the active service, had a green armband and their special identity card. Many also patrolled in civilian clothes, about eight hours a month, in their leisure time. There was a sort of bonus fund available for these forces, between 50 and 100 Marks per year. For their birthday they received flowers (…)

B. An East German Woman on Her Life in the GDR

(…) I was born in 1928 in Lower Silesia and was the fifth child; my parents had nine children, they were agricultural workers. My mother worked in a little garden and field with the children. Actually, we had a very hard childhood. We had to start working early, had to take care of cows, glean potatoes and corn, raspberries and blueberries, search for mushrooms. I remember that we had chicken and goats and many rabbits. We had to carry the hay down the hill. Neukirch, where we lived, was in the mountains of Bober-Katzbach. Its landscape is very beautiful, but slightly dull for work. We fetched wood from the forest on our backs. When I think of my childhood I always think of my mother's saying: 'The devil finds work for idle hands', and that was how she educated us. I had to start my first job when I was fourteen, I was supposed to help with the household, but I had to work at the bakery, too, that was already during the war, in '43. Sometimes my working day was from four o'clock in the morning until ten o'clock at night, fourteen years old, but no one asked about that. Well, that was life (…)

I started as a simple worker in the factory for electrical appliances (EAW) in Treptow. I have to say I always had good comrades who helped me right from the beginning. First of all I had to get used to my new area of work, but then I was supposed to take over the holiday camp. They saw in my papers that I was a scout-leader, which was well-received. In that moment I became the focus of attention, actually thanks to the male comrades, less the female ones I have to admit.

Maternity leave at the time was six weeks before and after delivery. The baby year had not yet been introduced, that was in '51. Who wanted to could make use of the day-nursery or the weekdays' home. I also got a place in the nursery straight away. And went back to work. I was setting-up the assembly line in the youth brigade, I was used to working, and working was something that you had to do, and that you also did. I got an apartment in the, at the time, Stalinallee. That was one of those apartments which were given out in order to honour people, Block C South, the first flats which were given out. Well, then the issue was that I would have to become a skilled worker, because practically I had not learned anything. There were special classes for women. After work I went to school, the kids were in the weekday nursery, and for the quarter of a year I had a full-time practical formation. At the time we also worked on Saturdays. After one and a half years I passed the test to be a skilled worker in mechanics, and the party appointed me to a department which was just being built up and for which skilled workers were sought. Actually I did not want to leave the girls from the previous collective but then I also understood it to be necessary and went.

It was very good for me to work as a mechanic for some time. Through that I could make experiences which were not as familiar to me as they should have been through the school and the quarter of a year of training. During that time I had my third child. That was Petra.

Then a member of the youth brigade was sought for the Relaisbau which had only just been developed. Only young people were supposed to be in the youth brigade, and there again I had comrades who said 'Lilo, you'll make it, do it!' I always had people who pushed me. Maybe that's what you need, after all. And I also took over the youth brigade. I don't know whether it is clear what such a brigade is: we always said: work socialistic, learn and live. And that's also how we did it. We worked a lot and we worked well (...)

Now I was a master craftswoman. Everything went all right in the department, I had no planning debts, there was no quarrelling among the women, everything went its way, and the boss was enthusiastic, because everything was nice and quiet. Usually he had sometimes had trouble with the women. Within the factory not always the finest tone was being used (...) There were installation machines, and there was more machine work. There was a dynamic brigade life, brigade evenings to which the husbands were invited. Then parties for the kids; after all, with children it was often difficult to go out at night. We also organised parties for Women's Day. We actually partied a lot and with pleasure, me included. I always said, this is part of it. We went to the theatre, did walks, a boat's trip. The participation was high, the majority joined in. You never manage to accommodate 100% of them.

We had a kitty. When there was a competition and the champion won money, it was put into the kitty. We also received money quarterly from the culture fund of the company, per person, and even if it was only five to ten marks, it mounted up. My secretary was in charge of the money, everything was written down precisely, we had a bank account. It was cashed up accurately in the end of the year. Once we flew to Prague, there everyone had to pay a little bit extra, then we went to the horticultural exhibition in Erfurt, to the market in Szczecin in Poland, and to the Baltic Sea, to Warnemünde. But all of this demanded a lot of commitment and power. I took over the department in 1972 and stayed until 1986. Then I was on the brink of a nervous breakdown. In the beginning of the '70s I also received my award 'Hero of Labour', ten years later I got the Karl-Marx-award. The awards were an occasion for me to be proud of myself. They were a confirmation of the success of my efforts. I considered them justified, and was happy about them. Apart from that they had no other impact on my life. I never thought that I was someone special (…)

I have to say that the development in the '80s was not good. In the '60s and '70s the solidarity among the comrades was better. One thought about the other, one helped where one could.

8.5 János Kádár Explains Reforms to Hungarian Workers, 1968

After the brutal crushing of the 1956 uprising, the Soviets made János Kádár the head of the Hungarian Communist Party. In this speech to factory workers in February 1968, Kadar explains the careful reforms he introduced to improve the economy and improve the standards of living.

Speaking of the situation within the country, I should like to touch upon the reform of economic management and some of its social bearings. According to the Central Committee the reform was necessary and it was time that we decided to carry it out. Naturally the reform of economic management brings many new problems with it for both managers and workers. The first thing I would like to emphasize is: the Central Committee did not work out and approve the reform merely to devise something to make peoples lives more difficult. The reform of economic management had to be worked out and decided upon because our social development and the development of our national economy had reached a point where we had to make up our minds: either we want to continue ensuring a suitable impetus and pace for social construction and economic development, or we get bogged down and must reconcile ourselves to bumping along by one or two per cent annually. Because the essence of the reform is that we shall try to work with greater energy and get further ahead. This applies in every respect: the development of the means of production, of the national economy and of living standards. Because these go hand in hand: if one rises or increases only slightly, then the others can only rise or grow to a slight extent also. If we are able to advance at a proper rate in the development of the means of production and the relations of production, then and only then will we be able to make progress in consumption and also in the living standards.

One of the aims of the economic reform is to introduce methods in the sphere of production prices which until now had been determined by government decisions and decrees. Earlier production prices were determined on the basis of criteria which were then perhaps acceptable and necessary. But the prices were not on a par with actual values, and they did not express them precisely. Consequently there were factories and there were products which were nominally lucrative, but in reality, with prices calculated according to their actual value, they were unprofitable. And conversely: there were some factories and certain products that were listed as unprofitable according to the old price; on the other hand, at prices corresponding to their real value it will turn out that they were lucrative. A certain length of time will be needed and years will pass before production prices come close to the true and actual values, but this will have to happen. If we hand out equally and to everyone the task of producing more quickly, at lower cost and in greater quantity, but without their being in the same circumstances, then not everyone will be able to fulfil his task.

To mention only a single question—and this also affects people in the IKARUS Factory—there is, for example, the question of three shifts. Anyone who knows women working in the textile mills is well aware that for twenty years this has been an everyday issue there. Women in the textile mills say: why must it be a law that we women in the textile factories have to work three shifts? We understand that the means of production must be better exploited, but why is it a law that my husband and my grown-up son in the metal factory opposite work only two shifts? Are the means of production there not just as expensive as they are in our mill? Should they not be striving to make better use of the newly purchased means of production there?

The reason I mention this is to make it clearer that this economic reform does not by any means only consist of how much soap and bacon cost, but it touches on the substance of the economy as a whole. It is very important that we learn to work with the means of production intelligently and efficiently. This is generally done, of course, but in many spheres and in many places it has not yet been achieved and this situation is intolerable. One comrade related that in the old days among the horses hitched to a coach was a trace horse, which had to do no more than to look good, because the other four pulled the coach. A country, a people cannot live in such a manner that four pull, and one just handsomely waves its mane and in the meantime eats a double portion of oats. This is not just, things will not work out this way.

8.6 The Warsaw Pact Invasion of Czechoslovakia, 1968

When the Czechoslovak Communist Party began a process of democratization in 1968, the Soviet leaders feared that this so-called 'Communism with a human face' would spill over to the rest of Eastern Europe. The first excerpt is from a telephone conversation between the head of the Soviet party, Leomid Brezhnev, and the Czechoslovak leader, Alexander Dubcek, one week before the Warsaw Pact invaded. The second takes place two days after the invasion, when the Czechoslovak leaders had been brought to Moscow by force. The Soviets informed the United States of the invasion the night before it took place, but President Lyndon B. Johnson—absorbed by the war in Vietnam—offered little immediate reaction. Document C is Johnson's conversation with Soviet ambassador Anatolii Dobrynin that night.

A. 13 August 1968

BREZHNEV: Aleksandr Stepanovich [Dubcek], I felt the need to speak with you today. I called you early in the morning and then later in the day, but you were away the whole time in Karlovy Vary, and then you called me back, but at that point I had gone to have a talk with the comrades. Now that I've returned, they told me that you have a Presidium meeting going on, and so I hope I'm not greatly disturbing you by having this conversation.

DUBCEK: No, not at all, the comrades already told me that you wanted to speak with me (...)

BREZHNEV: We have little time, and so let me get straight to the point. I'm again turning to you with anxiety about the fact that the mass media in your country not only are incorrectly depicting our conferences in Cierna and Tisou and Bratislava, but are also stepping up their attacks against the healthy forces and continuing to purvey anti-Sovietism and anti-socialist ideas. What I'm referring to here are not some isolated instances but an organized campaign; and judging by the content of the materials, these press organs have come to serve as a mouthpiece for the right-wing, anti-socialist forces. We in the Politburo exchanged views about this matter and unanimously concluded that there is every basis for regarding the unfolding situation as a violation of the agreement reached in Cierna and Tisou. I have in mind the agreement you and I reached during our one-on-one discussions, as well as the agreement we thrashed out during the four-on-four meetings and the agreement that emerged between the Politburo of our party and the Presidium of the Central Committee of your party.

DUBCEK: I already told you what sorts of measures we are taking to put an end to the anti-Soviet and anti-socialist manifestations in the mass media. I already told you what sorts of measures we are preparing and in what sequence we will carry them out. But I also told you at the time that it's impossible to do all this in a single day. We need time to take care of it. We're not able to restore order in the operations of the mass media in just two to three days.

BREZHNEV: Sasha, that's true, and we warned you at the time that the rightist forces will not easily give up their positions and that it would of course be impossible to do everything in just two to three days. But a lot more time than two to three days has already passed, and the success of your work in this regard depends on your willingness to take decisive measures to restore order in the mass media. Of course if the [Communist Party of Czechoslovakia] leadership and the CSRR [Czechoslovak Socialist Republic] government continue to pursue a policy of non-interference in this matter in the future, these processes will continue unabated. It's simply impossible to halt them through a policy of non-interference. You must resort to concrete measures. This is precisely the point on which we reached concrete agreement in connection with the role of Pelikan, and we said that it was essential to dismiss Pelikan. This would be the first step needed to restore order in the mass media.

DUBCEK: Leonid Ilyich, we studied these questions and are continuing to study them. I told Comrade Cernik what sorts of measures we'd have to take, and I gave Comrade Lenart the task of carrying out the necessary measures. As far as I know, no sorts of attacks have been appearing recently against the CPSU or the Soviet Union or against the socialist order.

BREZHNEV: How can you say such a thing when literally all the newspapers—Literarni listy, Mlada fronta, Reporter, Prace—every day are publishing anti-Soviet and anti-party articles?

DUBCEK: That was going on before Bratislava. Since Bratislava that hasn't been happening.

BREZHNEV: What do you mean it was only 'before Bratislava'? On 8 August Literarni listy featured an article entitled 'From Warsaw to Bratislava,' which was a full-blown, vicious attack against the CPSU and the USSR and against all the fraternal socialist countries. The 8th of August, needless to say, was after Bratislava.

DUBCEK: That's an isolated case. I don't know of any others. All the rest appeared before Bratislava. We're opposed to this article and are now taking appropriate measures.

BREZHNEV: Sasha, I can't agree with this. Over the past two to three days, the newspapers I mentioned have been doggedly continuing to occupy themselves with the publication of defamatory ravings about the Soviet Union and the other fraternal countries. My comrades on the Politburo insist that we make an urgent approach to you on this matter and that we send you a diplomatic note to this effect, and I'm not able to restrain the comrades from sending such a note. But I only wanted to make sure that before a note is sent to you about this matter, I got a chance to speak with you personally (…)

BREZHNEV: Aleksandr Stepanovich, I'm also obliged to say that we're not able to wait much longer and that you shouldn't force us to open new polemics with your mass media and to respond to all the articles and activities that are being permitted now in Czechoslovakia against our country, against our party, and against all the socialist parties.

During the negotiations we didn't force you to agree to anything. You yourselves took on the obligation to restore order in the mass media. And once you promised it, you should have been willing to carry it out. Well, fine, I perhaps can even agree with you that the restoration of order in this sphere requires time. But how are you coming along in carrying out the agreement on personnel questions? One must say that on this matter, too, we had a fully concrete agreement, and we also settled on a fully concrete timeframe for carrying it out.

DUBCEK: I would only like to say to you, Comrade Brezhnev, that these are very complex matters, which can't be resolved as easily as you might think.

BREZHNEV: I understand how complicated these matters are. I'm only asking you to resolve them along the lines we agreed on at Cierna and Tisou. Was it not already clear to you and Cernik and Smrkovsky and Svoboda, when we met in our four-on-four sessions, how complex it would be to resolve these matters? Yet at the time you yourselves very easily and very independently, without any sort of coercion from us, raised these matters and promised to resolve them as soon as possible.

DUBCEK: I already told you, Comrade Brezhnev, that this is a complex question, the resolution of which requires that we convene a plenum. And in order to examine and resolve these questions, there must be due preparation. I must consult with the comrades about how best to resolve this question (…)

BREZHNEV: If I understand you correctly, you don't intend to consider these matters today. I want to ask you directly, Sasha, what you mean by this, and what I'm getting at here is that you're deceiving us! I'm not able to regard it as anything other than deceit.

DUBCEK: Leonid Ilyich, if you could see how these matters are being prepared now in the Presidium, you wouldn't talk this way. We promised to resolve these matters, and we are taking all the measures needed to resolve them correctly.

BREZHNEV: Sasha, I'm not just speaking here personally for myself. The entire Politburo has instructed me to speak with you and to ask you concretely: Will you be resolving the personnel questions or not? (…)

B. 23 August 1968

BREZHNEV: How is C[omra]de. Černík feeling?

DUBCEK: Bad, like everyone else.

PODGORNY: Is that his health that's bad, or his mood?

DUBCEK: It's the situation that's difficult.

BREZHNEV: Let's agree not to rehash the past and have a calm discussion, beginning with the situation that has now been created in order to find a solution that would be of benefit to the Communist Party of Czechoslovakia, so that it can act normally and independently in accord with principles contained in the Bratislava Declaration. Let it act independently. We did not wish and do no intend to intervene in the future. Let the government base its actions on the principles of the January and May plenary sessions of the CPCz Central Committee. We spoke about that in our documents and are ready to reaffirm it. Of course, we can't say that you and the others are in a happy mood right now. But the question is not one of your mood. We have to conduct negotiations in a prudent and sober way in looking for solutions. It can be said simply that your failure to fulfil your commitments prompted the five countries to take extreme but unavoidable measures. The course of event since then has entirely confirmed that behind your back (in no way do we wish to imply that you were standing at the head of it) right-wing forces (we modestly call them anti-socialist) were preparing both the congress and all other steps. Now even underground cells and ammunition caches have been uncovered. All this has now come to light. We don't wish to claim that you, personally, are to blame. You might not have known about any of this; the right-wing forces organized all this on quite a broad scale.

We would like to find a more acceptable solution that could expedite the process of stabilization in this country, normalize the work of the party without the influence of the Right, and normalize the work of the government so that it too, is free of rightist influence (…)

We haven't occupied Czechoslovakia, we don't intend to keep it under 'occupation,' and we want it to be free to carry on the socialist cooperation we talked about in Bratislava. It is on this basis that we wanted to have a discussion with you and find a businesslike solution. If necessary, it can be done along with Cde. Černík. If we are silent, we will not improve the situation nor free the Czech, Slovak and Russian peoples from tension. And with every passing day the Right will incite chauvinistic moods against all the socialist countries, particularly against the Soviet Union. In such conditions of course, the troops cannot be removed; in general, this doesn't help us. So, on these grounds, on this basis, we wanted to have a discussion about what we think is the best way to proceed from here. We are ready to listen. We are not dictating anything. Let's try together to find some sort of variant (...)

DUBCEK: You've just said something by way of an introduction too. I, too, would like to say a few words, Cde. Brezhnev, although I find myself in a very difficult emotional state. I haven't been home for three days. I'd also like to say that it is indeed correct and necessary to look ahead again. That's true, certain realities now exist.

PODGORNY: It is precisely for that reason that we wanted to talk, to look ahead.

DUBCEK: At present certain realities have been created. But, Cde. Brezhnev, I already sensed in Chop that it was necessary to look ahead.

After Bratislava, conditions in Czechoslovakia and in the Communist party were at first, and in all respects, favourable, even including the question of preparation for the congress and matters concerning the objectives of propaganda work: preparations for the congress and personnel issues. All this is included in the resolutions of the CPCz CC Presidium and our entire party and state. Of course, I did not know how everything would end. I believed that you, too, would be interested mainly in the broad picture. But this in fact did not happen. I will not speak to you about the past, because on that score we made our opinion clear at Cierna and then in the joint document approved in Bratislava. The Bratislava Declaration is a document of the CPCz CC Presidium and our entire party and state. It received great support and was a significant document because it removed the question of the Warsaw meeting, which had become an internal, dynamic, and negative issue in inner-party and anti-state activities. Party and state activities were oriented in a favourable direction. I even said that it represented some sort of way out, based on the general interests written into it, since our CC Presidium always—both in January and after January, and in state documents—upheld the fundamental positions it proclaimed. And even now, it has in no way deviated from its official policy, in either party or state work, from the general interests approved in Bratislava and proclaimed by us.

We welcomed them and along with you we worked on them because it serves our interests and our viewpoints, and because these issues were committed to paper as the basic points that the CPCz's policy had carried out previously. Therefore, I and my comrades cannot understand why, in such a short period— and I wish to stress this happened before the CC plenum of the party and before the congress—these military measures were undertaken by the five states. I said 'before' the plenum of the party's CC because we could not have acted otherwise. Only on Tuesday did we approve the thesis on the federation, and the plenum had to be called at some point to clear up some matters in connection with the preparations for the congress. We drew your attention to this. The situation in the party and the country had improved. These extreme steps, these extreme measures were taken without warning the CPCz CC Presidium, or me, personally, or the president, the prime minister, or the chairman of the National Assembly. In my opinion, this has squarely confronted not only our two parties, but the whole international Communist movement as well, with the most complicated problem it has ever faced.

It's hard for me, while I'm in such a difficult emotional state, to offer any immediate opinions about what should be done to take account of the situation that has been created. At this point, Cdes. Brezhnev, Kosygin, Podgorny, and Voronov, I don't know what the situation is like at home. On the first day the Soviet army arrived, I and other comrades were isolated and were brought here without knowing anything. So I can't say what the response was to this act, what the opinion of the Czech and Slovak peoples was, or how it reflected on inner-party life and on an international scale. All of these things are very important for us to know if we are to take the right measures to solve this complicated matter. For now, I can only speculate about what has gone on. During the initial period, the presidium members with me in the secretariat were taken to the CC of the party under the control of the Soviet security organs. Through the window I could see several hundred people who had gathered at the building, and through the glass we could hear them shouting: 'We want to see Svoboda!', 'We want to see the president!', 'We want Dubcek!' I heard several slogans. After that there was gunfire. This was the last scene I witnessed. From that moment on I knew nothing, and now I cannot imagine what is happening in the country and in the party (…)

C. Lyndon Johnson on the Soviet Intervention in Czechoslovakia, 20 August 1968

The President started off the meeting by asking Ambassador Dobrynin how he had been and asked about Mr. Kosygin. He then told him that he had night before last seen a color movie at the ranch which was very good. The movie was one taken at Glassboro when the President met with Kosygin (…)

The President then offered Mr. Dobrynin a Fresca and asked him if he had ever drunk this drink. Mr. Dobrynin said: 'No, is it a strong one?'

The President told him that it contained no alcohol and had no calories and Mr. Dobrynin wanted to know how he did it. The President said he had to lose some weight and that he had lost about seven or eight pounds.

Mr. Dobrynin said: 'Now, Mr. President, I have an urgent instruction from my government to tell you about serious business. I will read it.'

The President asked him to read a little louder—that he was a little hard of hearing but was so vain he would not wear a hearing aid.

Mr. Dobrynin went on to say: 'Kosygin asked me personally to visit you and to say the following on behalf of my government. I will read this; what I am instructed to say:

"The Government of the Soviet Union considers it necessary to inform, personally, President Johnson about the following. In connection with the further aggravation of the situation which was created by a conspiracy of the external and internal forces of aggression against the existing social order in Czechoslovakia and against the statehood established by the constitution of that government, the government of Czechoslovakia Socialist Republic approached the allied states, the Soviet Union among them, with a request of rendering direct assistance, including the assistance of military forces.

"The Soviet Government repeatedly stated that the events in Czechoslovakia and around it involve vital interests of the Soviet Union and of a number of other states tied by appropriate treaty obligations, and that the threat to the Socialist order in Czechoslovakia constitutes at the same time a threat to the foundations of European peace and world security. In view of this, the Soviet Government and the Governments of the allied countries have taken a joint decision to satisfy the request of the Government of the Czechoslovak Socialist Republic rendering necessary assistance to the Czechoslovak people. Accordingly, the Soviet military units received orders to enter the territory of Czechoslovakia. Of course, they will be withdrawn without delay from the territory of Czechoslovak Socialist Republic as soon as the present threat to the security is eliminated and they come to the conclusion that there is no need in further presence of the allied forces. We would like President Johnson to know that our steps, which are being taken upon the request of the Czechoslovak Government are dictated fully by the concern to strengthen peace and in no degree do they involve state interests of the United States or any other state. We proceed from the fact that the current events should not harm the Soviet–American relations to the development of which the Soviet Government as before attaches great importance." This is what I was asked to tell you.'

The President said: 'I would like to take it and read it and study it and I appreciate very much your bringing it to me and I will review it in the morning with Secretary Rusk and we will be back in touch with you. (...)

'Our position with regard to the problem that exists in Czechoslovakia is as represented by Secretary Rusk and I trust that you understand that the position that he explained in detail to you is my view, and the views of this Government, and is the honest and absolutely correct attitude that we have taken. Although I have seen a good many other interpretations and predictions and evaluations, Secretary Rusk, at my instruction, asked you to come in to see him and told you frankly and honestly, looking directly in your eyes, what our position was and you can rely on it.

'I didn't hear the conversation between you and Secretary Rusk but I have such confidence in him that I know he related to you what I asked him to and I don't want there to be any doubt about our attitude.'

Mr. Dobrynin said: 'No. This message refers to you. I know what you told him to say and it is very clear.'

The President asked Mr. Dobrynin what had been done about his announcement [about a forthcoming limit to Moscow by President Johnson] and he said they had had no word yet.

The President went on to say: 'Well, I have all these problems about all these folks I have got to talk to beforehand. And I thought I would have them at breakfast at 8:00 o'clock and we'd stay from 8 to 10 at breakfast and I would do it so they wouldn't shout to high heaven that I gave them no information.'

Mr. Rostow said that it had been our understanding that the joint announcement would be made at 10 o'clock tomorrow (…)

The President then directed his remarks to Mr. Rostow and said they ought to get their drinks down—that he didn't mind, but he just did not want them to think they all were in there drunk. The President went on to say that Mr. Rayburn used to say that he would never take a drink before the House adjourned in the afternoon because if they had a big fight or something and they had a roll call and he had to get up in the chair, he said just as sure as he did, he would trip his toe and someone would say he is drunk again. They all laughed and the President asked Mr. Dobrynin if he knew Mr. Rayburn and he said, yes, for a long time (…)

8.7 Polish Workers on the Aftermath of the Strikes, 1971

In 1970 Polish workers went on strike to demand better living conditions. The Communist authorities defeated the strikers through the use of force, but some workers remained in opposition. Here is an excerpt from their meeting with the head of the Communist party, Edward Gierek, at the Adolf Warski Shipyard in Szczecin in January 1971.

DELEGATE K-4: Work in our division is harmful to one's health. At present every second worker who works on the slips is blind, deaf, rheumatic or suffers from some form of lung disease, and all for so little money (…) An assistant makes

1,800–2,000 zlotys [a month]. Let's look at his expenditures for a family of five: For breakfast, each has a roll with water—cost, 2 zlotys; for supper the same, a total of 4 zlotys. The least expensive lunch is 12 zlotys per person, i.e., 60 zlotys— a total of 64 zlotys a day. In a month this amounts to 1,800–1,900 zlotys—for mere subsistence (…) And in the shipyard work is hard—a man must eat well. Otherwise, after fifteen years he is ready for the coffin. That's the way it is.

DELEGATE W-6: In our division the average wage is 2,000 zlotys (…) This is really very little. Very little! After paying rent, electricity, gas, etc., a worker is left with 1,600 zlotys. No family can survive on it. So, to make more money we work overtime (…) I know many people who regularly do 150 or even 200 hours over-time a month. This means that they are virtually visitors in their own homes.

DELEGATE ZWG: (…) There have emerged men who live off the efforts of manual workers, but who sit behind their desks and decide our wages. Is this democracy? (Pounding his fist on the table) No! (Applause).

A MEMBER OF THE STRIKE COMMITTEE: If we emphasize the change and we talk openly, I would like to know what the income is of a director. I do not know whether this is just gossip or a lie, but I have heard that Director Skrobot makes 18,000 zlotys a month. If so, this has to be changed, for some live in luxury and others have barely enough for bread (…)

DELEGATE SCW1: Here we had a Comrade Skrzydowski. During eleven months, it is said that he was paid over 170,000 zlotys. Not as basic salary, of course, but from all sorts of bonuses. But all the evil is not at the bottom! Our manager is like an estate overseer in the interwar period (…) People frequently blame the party and the system for all of this (…)

DELEGATE W-4: The average income in our division is 2,600 zlotys for eight hours a day (…) 2,600 zlotys at the current prices amounts to very little, especial-ly if one has three or four people to support. This should be taken into account by those comrades from the Central Committee who are here today. It is necessary to understand the position of people who earn so little—for what can they do? We have a saying: 'When a Pole is hungry, he is angry,' hence the present upheaval. (Strong applause). It stems directly from our dissatisfaction. (Applause).

DELEGATE K-2: Many young people were killed—they were shot in the back. There is evidence of that. So many people killed, so many people (…) People who were killed were put in nylon bags and buried like animals. This is true! Nothing can change this (…)

DELEGATE K-1: (…)It is sad that our hard-earned money paid for these very bullets that were used against us (…)

DELEGATE W-2: I ask for a frank answer from the First Secretary of the Central Committee of the PUWP [Polish United Workers Party; the Communist party in Poland] Is it necessary to shed blood to change the Central Committee and the government? Is it not possible to consider a fixed term of office in order to avoid a repetition of 1956 and 1970? (…)

DELEGATE MKP: We have to give the government a chance for a year or two (…) We must do that! If in a year or two there is no improvement then we will say: Comrades, we were deceived.

CHAIRMAN OF THE STRIKE COMMITTEE: The strike is over, the strike is over! As of tomorrow the shipyard is back at work.

UNIDENTIFIED VOICE: Sorry, I would like to say something about those who will not report for work tomorrow. I would like to ask everybody to pay a tribute to their memory by observing a minute of silence. (37 seconds of silence.)

8.8 China Turns Left

In China, the conflict with the Soviet Union contributed to Mao Zedong's decision to intensify the revolution. In the first excerpt, from the summer of 1958, he explains the Great Leap Forward, a programme of enforced increases in production that eventually led to mass starvation. In 1966 Mao launched the Great Proletarian Cultural Revolution, an attempt to purge the Communist Party and engage the younger generation in a violent cleansing of Chinese society, making it ready for a push toward Communism. The second document is an excerpt from the interrogation record of Wang Guangmei, the wife of China's president Liu Shaoqi, who was tortured by the Qinghua University 'Jinggangshan Regiment' of the Red Guards.

A. Mao Zedong on the Great Leap Forward, August 1958

All levels should gradually strengthen their planning [system]. Production and distribution in agricultural producers cooperatives (APCs) should also gradually be brought under unified management. It won't do not to have tight planning and organization. Grain production should also be [well] planned. Should so many types of potato be planted next year or not? Do [we] want to plant so much cotton or not? [If we] strive hard again next year, and get the per capita gain [figures] up to (   ) catties, then [we'll] see [what next.]

A socialist state is a tightly organized network. In ten thousand years [there'll be] many people, many automobiles; [we'll] have to line up even to go shopping. [There'll be] many airplanes, [and] it won't do not to have control of air traffic. When monkeys were evolving into human beings, there was much freedom; later there was less and less freedom. On the other hand, humanity [experienced] a major liberation, consciously taking control of the cosmos, uncovering limitless forces.

[We] must eradicate the ideology of bourgeois right. For instance, competing for position, competing for rank, demanding overtime pay, high salaries for mental workers and low salaries for physical laborers—these are all vestiges of bourgeois ideology. 'To each according to his worth' is stipulated by law; it's also bourgeois stuff. In the future should [we] ride automobiles according to rank? [We] do not necessarily need specially [assigned] automobiles. It's OK to make some allowances for the old and infirm; for the rest there should be no ranking [for automobiles].

Do [we] need to strive hard for grain production next year or not? [We] do, indeed. Struggle arduously for three years, storing up one year's worth of grain (500 catties per capita). [But we] can reduce [the output of] sweet potatoes a bit (…)

[We] still need to talk about current affairs. On the domestic front, [we] need to talk about [taking] the whole nation as a big commune; on the international front, [we] need to talk about the possibility of the imperialists launching a war. With the whole nation as a big commune, it's impossible not to have priority [projects]; it's impossible not to have unified planning. From the Center [down] to the APCs, there must be unanimity. There must be flexibility; but flexibility has to do with the branches and leaves, it can't impinge upon the main trunk. Next year's target of ( ) million tons of steel must be fulfilled; this year's ( ) million tons of steel must be guaranteed (…)

In establishing the people's communes, as I see it, once again it's been the countryside that has taken the lead; the cities haven't started yet, [because] the workers' wage scales are a complicated matter. Whether in rural or urban areas, [the aim] should be the socialist system plus Communist ideology. The Soviet Union practices the use of high rewards and heavy punishments, emphasizing only material incentives. We now practice socialism, and have the sprouts of Communism. Schools, factories, and neighborhoods can all establish people's communes. In a few year big communes will be organized to include everyone (…)

We must go all out in the next two years on [the production of] iron, steel, copper, aluminium, molybdenum, and other non-ferrous metals. Steel [targets] must be fully met; iron can be a little bit less, [but we] must also strive to fulfil [that target] (…)

In the future we will establish a global committee (…); there will be no distinction between what is one's one and what is another's; and when we help a place that's in dire straits, [we] won't ask for even a single penny. [We've] fought wars for so many years, so many people have died, yet no one asked for compensation for losses. Now construction is also a fierce battle; struggle desperately for a few years, [and] after those few years [we] will still have to struggle. But at least this kills fewer people than fighting wars.

9. 'Thinks' (Nicholas Garland, *Daily Telegraph*, 9 January 1967). Reprinted by permission. Photo supplied by The Gentre for the Study of Cartoons and Caricature, University of Kent.

B. Wang Guangmei Interrogated by Red Guards, 1967

The place: Qinghua University central building, 7th floor
The time: Around six-thirty A.M. [10 April 1967]

INTERROGATOR: We want you to put on the dress that you wore in Indonesia.

WANG: That was summer. There is winter clothing for winter, summer clothing for summer, and spring clothes for spring. I cannot put on a summer dress now. If I must wear a dress for spring, I can send for someone to bring me one.

INTERROGATOR: Rubbish! We know nothing about such bourgeois stuff as what is good for summer, winter, or spring, for receiving guests or for travel.

WANG: Chairman Mao has said that we must pay attention to the climate and change our clothing accordingly.

INTERROGATOR (amid laughter): What Chairman Mao was referring to was the political climate. With your standpoint, even though you are now wearing a fur coat, you are likely to freeze to death.

INTERROGATOR: Let me ask you: Didn't you wear that dress when you were in Lahore although it was colder at that time than it is now? Put it on! It will do so long as you will not freeze to death. Are you going to put it on?

WANG: No.

INTERROGATOR: All right! We'll give you ten minutes. Watch what happens at a quarter to seven. Try to defy us by not wearing that dress. We mean what we say. (Wang remains silent.)

INTERROGATOR: Wang Guangmei: What's your opinion of Liu Shaoqi's fall from grace?

WANG: It is an excellent thing. In this way, China will be prevented from going revisionist.

INTERROGATOR: One day we are also going to drag out Liu Shaoqi and struggle against him. Do you believe us?

WANG: You just go on with your struggle; just carry on . . . (silent)

WANG: You members of the Jinggangshan Regiment are thoroughly revolutionary. Except, the form of struggle which you employ is no good. Could you not find a more sophisticated form of denunciation?

INTERROGATOR: Pay no attention to what she says! We shall see what you look like when your ten minutes are over.

WANG: You . . . I can ring someone up and ask for a spring dress.

INTERROGATOR: That won't do.

WANG: This dress is made of silk. It's too cold!

INTERROGATOR: Put it on and wear you fur coat on top of it.

INTERROGATOR: 'Small wonder flies freeze and perish' [quote from a 1962 Mao Zedong poem].

WANG: If I were really opposed to Chairman Mao, I would deserve to freeze to death.

INTERROGATOR: You *are* opposed to Chairman Mao.

WANG: I am not against him now, and I will not oppose him in the future.

INTERROGATOR: No more nonsense with her . . . Seven minutes left!

WANG: (silence)

WANG: How about putting on that pair of shoes (pointing to the pair of pointed shoes that she had brought with her)?

INTERROGATOR: That is not enough! You must wear everything.

WANG: You don't have the right.

INTERROGATOR: We have this right! You are being struggled against today. We are at liberty to wage struggle in whatever form we may want to, and you have no freedom. You might as well forget about your vile theory of 'everybody being equal therefore truth.' We are the revolutionary masses, and you are a notorious counter-revolutionary old hag. Don't try to confuse the class demarcation line!

(At the time limit set, the [Jinggangshan] 'Ghostbusters' (*Zhuoguidui*) begin to force Wang to put on the outlandish dress.) (...)

INTERROGATOR: Wang Guangmei, tell us how you feel about Liu Shaoqi being the biggest Party-person in power taking the capitalist road?

WANG: Subjectively, my understanding is not yet up to that level. In any case, before the Eleventh Plenum of the Eight Central Committee, the Chairman entrusted Liu Shaoqi and the Central Secretariat with many tasks, and if anything happened, [Liu] would of course have been responsible. But now he has had to step aside and is no longer in power! At the time of the 'reactionary line,' [in 1965/6] he traversed a stretch of the capitalist road.

INTERROGATOR: Only at the time of the reactionary line? That's all?

WANG: Of course not. Anyone who makes an error in line will have traversed a stretch of the capitalist road . . . (The students tell her to put on the necklace.)

INTERROGATOR: Tell me this! Comrade Jiang Qing had told you not to wear the necklace when you were abroad. Why did you have to wear it?

WANG: Comrade Jiang Qing only told me not to wear the brooch but said nothing about the necklace. But the question is one and the same (…)

Questions

Why did the East Berlin workers go on strike in 1953?

What was Khrushchev's main criticism of his predecessor, Joseph Stalin?

Why did Imre Nagy hesitate in taking charge of the Hungarian rebellion?

What accounts for the hatred between Communist and non-Communist Hungarians?

What were the main reasons why some East Germans saw positive aspects of the GDR regime?

Why effects did the Wall have for ordinary people in East and West Berlin?

What were the main intentions behind the Hungarian reforms?

Why did the Soviet Union invade Czechoslovakia in August 1968?

Why did Dubcek not call for armed resistance against the invaders?

Why did the United States not respond more forcefully to the invasion of Czechoslovakia?

Why did Polish workers have so little faith in their government?

Why did Mao push his revolution towards the left during the late 1950s?

Why did the Red Guards attack some Chinese Communist leaders during the Cultural Revolution?

Technologies, Weapons, and the Armsrace

Technology was at the core of the Cold War conflict because the race for ever more sophisticated weapons provided much of its dynamic, but also because technological achievement was the yardstick in the competition between the United States and the Soviet Union to represent the best model for future societies. Being seen as the most 'advanced' state was of crucial significance to both Moscow and Washington in the struggle for legitimacy for their ideological projects and for international support. To Soviet leaders, their state represented not only the embryo of what the world would look like in the future, but it could also produce, through technology, the ideal method of moving rapidly from backwardness to Communism. In the United States, successive presidents viewed the nation's advanced technology as the best defence against the Soviet challenge and as the instrument that would convince the world of the benefits of the American model.

Although the competition took multiple forms—from steel to fertilizers, from education to space—it was the arms race that became a substitute for all-out war and that, understandably, gripped the popular imagination. The intensity of the race for new and better arms grew out of the experience both countries had with World War II, and especially with the way the war ended in the Pacific. For the Soviets it was essential to catch up with the American nuclear capability, and Stalin threw all the resources the Soviet Union could muster into the atomic project. The Soviet Union tested its first nuclear weapon in August 1949, and its first hydrogen bomb in August 1953, only eight months after the first US test. Technologically the Soviets indeed seemed to be catching up, although the American superiority in nuclear weapons production and, even more importantly, their means of delivery (long-range bombers and missiles) would remain throughout the Cold War.

However, Soviet successes, such as launching the world's first intercontinental ballistic missile (ICBM) and putting the first satellite into orbit (*Sputnik*), both in 1957, convinced many Americans, Russians, and West Europeans that the Soviet Union would eventually pull ahead. John Kennedy, the new American

JFK ←

president elected in 1960, played on this fear to get more money for the arms race and for the programmes in science and education that future advances would be based on. Many of these defence programmes had important civilian spin-offs, in areas such as computers, space technology, and navigation. In terms of nuclear missiles, although the Soviets attempted to substitute quantity and size for quality, the better targeting and better delivery mechanisms of the Americans made sure that the arms race became an increasingly heavy burden for the much smaller and much less efficient Soviet economy.

In the late 1960s negotiations on arms control between the two sides were therefore welcomed both by Moscow and by a new Republican administration under Richard Nixon, who feared that the double burden of the arms race and the war in Vietnam would be too much to carry for US public expenditure (see Ch. 14). But in spite of several arms-limitation agreements, the nuclear arms race continued throughout the 1970s. The Soviets found through the negotiations that they had been even further behind in terms of technology than they had believed, and the pressure from the military to develop and deploy more advanced weapons therefore grew rather than diminished. On the American side, arms-control sceptics and military contractors pushed for the testing of new high-tech missiles and bombers. In reality, the arms-control agreements left much room for both sides to continue arming against each other.

The prospect of nuclear war, and its consequences, led many people to begin to fear for the future of humanity. The Russell–Einstein Appeal, issued in the wake of the hydrogen bomb tests, called for peaceful settlement of all conflicts. The alternative, they said, was an end to the human race. For many common people, East and West, this threat became part of their daily existence during the Cold War, since they knew that a clash between the superpowers in faraway regions could mean the immediate extermination of their cities or even their countries in a nuclear holocaust. Especially in Western Europe, millions took part in protests against the arms race and in some cases tried to stop the deployment of new weapons. In Eastern Europe and Russia, where protest was generally not allowed, the fear may have grown even greater.

The cost of arms represented an economic burden that held back the development of both superpowers. It was not just the price of developing, testing, producing, and deploying the weapons themselves that was exorbitant; it was also the expenses for defensive measures and the intelligence needed to see what the other side was doing. And there was a cost to their societies, in terms of militarization, secrecy, and waste. The Soviets were much more poorly equipped to face these costs than the Americans, not just because of their smaller and less productive economy, but because the effects of the arms race stimulated negative traits that were already present in Soviet society from the beginning. When Mikhail Gorbachev attempted to save the Soviet state by reducing the competition for weapons, it was already too late to change the overall course that had been set many years earlier. Those, like Ronald Reagan, who saw a purpose in challenging the Soviets over the technological edge of the arms race, may therefore have scored a victory. But far more important was the fact that during all the crises of the Cold War, nuclear weapons were never fired against civilian populations. For the many mothers and fathers who had gone to bed fearing for their families, this was the real victory.

Readings

Stephen I. Schwartz (ed.), *Atomic Audit: The Costs and Consequences of US Nuclear Weapons Since 1940* (1998). A very useful overview of the overall costs of the US nuclear weapons programme during the Cold War.

Philip L. Cantelon *et al.*, (eds.), *The American Atom: A Documentary History of Nuclear Policies from the Discovery of Fission to the Present* (2nd ed., 1991). The key American documents on nuclear policies and doctrines.

Matthew Evangelista, *Unarmed Forces: The Transnational Movement to End the Cold War* (1999). How scientists contributed to the end of the nuclear arms race.

Lawrence Wittner, *The Struggle Against the Bomb*, 2 vols. (1993, 1997). A thorough overview of activist campaigns against nuclear weapons during the Cold War.

David Holloway, *Stalin and the Bomb: The Soviet Union and Atomic Energy, 1939–1956* (1994). A first-rate book on the early development of the Soviet nuclear programme.

9.1 Cost of Nuclear Weapons

Distributed evenly to everyone living in the United States at the start of 1998, the total estimated cost of nuclear weapons equals $21,646 per person. Represented as bricks of new $1 bills (such as one can obtain at a bank, bound at $200 to the inch) stacked on top of each other, 5,821,027,000,000 would strech 459,361 miles (739,117 kilometers, to the Moon and nearly back. If $1 was counted off every second, it would take almost 12 days to reach $1 million, nearly 32 years to reach $1 billion, 31,709 years to reach $1 trillion, and about 184,579 years to tally the actual and anticipated cost of nuclear weapons. Laid end to end, bricks of $1 bills equivalent to the sum actually expended on US nuclear weapons since 1940 ($5,481,083,000,000) would encircle the Earth at the Equator almost 105 times, making a wall more than 8.7 feet (2.7 meters) high.

9.2 The Testing of the First H-Bombs, 1952–1953

In 1952–3 both the United States and the Soviet Union successfully tested hydrogen bombs, a thousand times more powerful than the nuclear bomb dropped on Hiroshima in

1945. Soviet nuclear physicist (and later dissident leader) Andrei Sakharov describe the tests.

At last, our day arrived—August 12, 1953. The night before, I followed Zeldovich's advice, took a sleeping pill (something I rarely do), and retired early. All of us in the hotel were awakened at four A.M. by the alarm bells. It was still dark, but I could see the headlights of trucks sweeping across the horizon, as the observers were driven to their posts.

Two and a half hours later I reached my station twenty miles from ground zero, where I was to observe the explosion in the company of young scientists from my group and Zeldovich's group. When the test managers and the heads of operations arrived, Tamm, who was with them, was invited to the nearby bunker set aside for VIPs. I came up to him to exchange a few words of reassurance and noticed that the chiefs were just as nervous as we were.

On the first step of the bunker Malyshev turned to Vannikov and said, 'Quick, Boris, tell me a joke.'

Vannikov responded immediately. 'Why are you so sad?' 'My condoms are in bad shape.' 'Do they drip?' 'No, they droop.'

Malyshev snorted with laughter and said, 'Good man, let's go.'

I returned to my station. Following instructions, we all lay down on the ground, facing the tower. We listened to the countdown coming over the loudspeakers.

Ten minutes to go.

Five minutes.

Two minutes.

We put on our dark goggles.

Sixty seconds. Fifty, forty, thirty, twenty, ten, nine, eight, seven, six, five, four, three, two, one.

We saw a flash, and then a swiftly expanding white ball lit up the whole horizon. I tore off my goggles, and though I was partially blinded by the glare, I could see a stupendous cloud trailing streamers of purple dust. The cloud turned gray, quickly separated from the ground and swirled upward, shimmering with gleams of orange. The customary mushroom cloud gradually formed, but the stem connecting it to the ground was much thicker than those shown in photographs of fission explosions. More and more dust was sucked up at the base of the stem, spreading out swiftly. The shock wave blasted my ears and struck a sharp blow to my entire body; then there was a prolonged, ominous rumble that died away after thirty seconds or so. Within minutes, the cloud, which now filled half the sky, turned a sinister blue-black color. The wind was pushing it in a southerly direction towards the mountains and the evacuated Kazakh settlements; half an hour later the cloud disappeared from sight, with the plane of the radiation-detection service following after it.

Malyshev came out of the bunker and congratulated us on our success—we knew already that the power of the explosion had come close to our estimate. Then he declared with appropriate ceremony: 'The chairman of the Council of Ministers, Georgy Malenkov, has just telephoned. He congratulates everyone who has helped build the hydrogen bomb—the scientists, the engineers, the workmen—on their wonderful success. Georgy Maximilianovich [Malenkov] requested me to congratulate and embrace Sakharov in particular for his exceptional contribution to the cause of peace.'

Malyshev embraced and kissed me, and invited me to join the test chiefs for a tour of the test site to see 'what went on out there.' We stopped at a checkpoint where we were issued dustproof jumpsuits and dosimeters. We drove in open cars past buildings destroyed by the blast, braking to a stop beside an eagle whose wings had been badly singed. It was trying to fly, but it couldn't get off the ground. One of the officers killed the eagle with a well-aimed kick, putting it out of its misery. I have been told that thousands of birds are destroyed during every test; they take wing at the flash, but then fall to earth, burned and blinded.

Our convoy drove on and stopped within two hundred feet of ground zero. Malyshev got out, and I followed him, while everyone else stayed put. We walked over a fused black crust that crunched underfoot like glass toward the concrete supports with a broken steel girder protruding from one of them—all that was left of the tower. After staring at the debris for a few moments, we returned to our car, drove back past the yellow warning flags, and handed in our jumpsuits and dosimeters (which got mixed up in the process).

That evening we met at Kurchatov's to hear a preliminary report prepared by the test range staff. Kurchatov opened the meeting by saying: 'I want to congratulate everyone here. I want to congratulate Sakharov personally and thank him on behalf of the leadership for his patriotic work.'

I rose from my seat and bowed, but I can't recall what I was thinking at the time.

9.3 Dulles on Massive Retaliation, 1954

US Secretary of State John Foster Dulles in 1954 promised massive retaliation—meaning a full-scale nuclear attack—if the Soviet Bloc attacked any of America's allies.

The 'long time' factor is of critical importance.

The Soviet Communists are planning for what they call 'an entire historical era,' and we should do the same. They seek, through many types of maneuvers, gradually to divide and weaken the free nations by overextending them in efforts which, as Lenin put it, are 'beyond their strength, so that they come to practical bankruptcy.' Then, said Lenin, 'our victory is assured.'' Then, said Stalin, will be 'the moment for the decisive blow.'

In the face of this strategy, measures cannot be judged adequate merely because they ward off an immediate danger. It is essential to do this, but it is also essential to do so without exhausting ourselves.

When the Eisenhower administration applied this test, we felt that some transformations were needed.

It is not sound military strategy permanently to commit U.S. land forces to Asia to a degree that leaves us no strategic reserves.

It is not sound economics, or good foreign policy, to support permanently other countries; for in the long run, that creates as much ill will as good will.

Also, it is not sound to become permanently committed to military expenditures so vast that they lead to 'practical bankruptcy.'

Change was imperative to assure the stamina needed for permanent security. But it was equally imperative that change should be accompanied by understanding of our true purposes. Sudden and spectacular change had to be avoided. Otherwise, there might have been a panic among our friends and miscalculated aggression by our enemies. We can, I believe, make a good report in these respects.

We need allies and collective security. Our purpose is to make these relations more effective, less costly. This can be done by placing more reliance on deterrent power and less dependence on local defensive power.

This is accepted practice so far as local communities are concerned. We keep locks on our doors, but we do not have an armed guard in every home. We rely principally on a community security system so well equipped to punish any who break in and steal that, in fact, would-be aggressors are generally deterred. That is the modern way of getting maximum protection at a bearable cost.

What the Eisenhower administration seeks is a similar international security system. We want, for ourselves and the other free nations, a maximum deterrent at a bearable cost.

Local defense systems will always be important. But there is no local defense which alone will contain the mighty landpower of the Communist world.

Local defenses must be reinforced by the further deterrent of massive retaliatory power. A potential aggressor must know that he cannot always prescribe battle conditions that suit him. Otherwise, for example, a potential aggressor, who is glutted with manpower, might be tempted to attack in confidence that resistance would be confined to manpower. He might be tempted to attack in places where his superiority was decisive.

The way to deter aggression is for the free community to be willing and able to respond vigorously at places and with means of its own choosing.

9.4 Briefing on US Plans for Nuclear Warfare, 1954

The following is a an excerpt from a briefing given by Major-General A. J. Old and General Curtis LeMay of the Strategic Air Command to representatives of all US military services at SAC Headquarters, Offutt Air Force Base, Omaha, Nebraska, 18 March 1954.

(…) SAC considers that the optimum situation would be to have adequate tankers deployed to overseas bases and also that the bombers would be similarly deployed prior to the major attack. It was estimated that SAC could lay down an attack under these conditions of 600–750 bombs by approaching Russia from many directions so as to hit their early warning screen simultaneously. It would require about 2 hours from this moment until bombs had been dropped by using the bomb-as-you-go system in which both BRAVO and DELTA targets would be hit as they reached them. This part of the briefing was skilfully done by showing successive charts of Europe based on one-half-hour time intervals after SAC bombers first hit the Russian early warning screen. Many heavy lines, one representing each wing, were shown progressively converging on the heart of Russia with pretty stars to indicate the many bombs dropped on DGZs. The final impression was that virtually all of Russia would be nothing but a smoking, radiating ruin at the end of two hours. The number of planes involved in those attack would be 5×30=150 B-36s plus 13×45=585 B-47s for a grand total of 735 bombers. As I recall the SAC fighters would play practically no part in this attack.

General Old stated that the exact manner in which SAC will fight the war is known only to General LeMay and that he will decide this matter at the moment, depending on the existing conditions (…)

Some of the interesting questions asked [of] General LeMay included:

Q. What period of time do you consider we should plan for to fight a 'short war'? (Asked by a Navy Captain.)

A. About 30 days. SAC has been compiling continuous data on critical parts required to keep the planes operational. These parts are kept in 'flying kits,' one for each plane which are taken with the plane when it departs for a mission. I consider these critical parts so important that I have never allowed them to be taken out of flying kits for local use. Necessary parts have to be gotten from somewhere else other than the flying kits or else the plane stays on the ground until the part is obtained. (Note: It is understood that General LeMay has in the past indicated a 60-day period, later dropped to 45 days, and still later to 30 days. This question was apparently an effort to see if he had reached any lower estimate by now. It seemed apparent from General LeMay's answer that he is firmly convinced that 30 days is long enough to conclude World War III.) (…)

Q. How do SAC's plans fit in with the stated national policy that the U.S. will never strike the first blow?

A. I have heard this thought stated many times and it sounds very fine. However, it is not in keeping with United States history. Just look back and note who started the Revolutionary War, the War of 1812, the Indian Wars, and the Spanish-American War. I want to make it clear that I am not advocating a preventive war; however, I believe that if the U.S. is pushed in the corner far enough we would not hesitate to strike first (or words to this effect) (…)

Q. What would you advocate in case hostilities are renewed in Korea?

A. There are no suitable strategic air targets in Korea. However, I would drop a few bombs in proper places in China, Manchuria and Southeastern Russia. In those 'poker games,' such as Korea and Indo-China, we (U.N., I presume) have never raised the ante—we have always just called the bet. We ought to try raising it sometime.

Q. We have heard a lot of optimistic statements today about SAC's capabilities. Do you have any reservations about these capabilities? (asked by a Navy Captain.)

A. No, I would like to have a few more bases, however (…)

General Impressions Received as a Result of this Briefing

SAC is, in effect, a sort of 'elite corps' dominated by a forceful and dedicated commander, who has complete confidence in SAC's ability to crush Russia quickly by massive atomic bombing attacks. No aspect of the morals or long-range effect of such attacks were discussed, and no questions on it were asked.

SAC has planned a thorough and exacting training program—and it is carrying it out. Accordingly, SAC is probably in a higher state of combat readiness today than any other U.S. military command.

SAC must now rely heavily on much in-flight refuelling to carry out his strike plans.

SAC is confident that when the bell rings they will get the lion's share of the stockpile no matter what the JCS [Joint Chiefs of Staff] 'allocations' are at the moment.

SAC purposely gives the impression at such briefings that they consider themselves a 'delivery service' to attack whatever targets the JCS tells them to attack—and, in effect, do not *originate* strategic air targets directly or indirectly.

9.5 The Einstein–Russell Manifesto, 1955

In 1955, only weeks before his death, the physicist Albert Einstein—who had constructed the theoretical foundations for nuclear science—joined the British philosopher Bertrand

Russell in making an impassioned appeal for peace. Here is an excerpt from their mani-festo, which was later signed by many leading scientists.

In the tragic situation which confronts humanity, we feel that scientists should assemble in conference to appraise the perils that have arisen as a result of the development of weapons of mass destruction, and to discuss a resolution in the spirit of the appended draft.

We are speaking on this occasion, not as members of this or that nation, continent or creed, but as human beings, members of the species man, whose continued existence is in doubt. The world is full of conflicts; and, over-shadowing all minor conflicts, the titanic struggle between Communism and anti-Communism.

Almost everybody who is politically conscious has strong feelings about one or more of these issues; but we want you, if you can, to set aside such feelings and consider yourselves only as members of a biological species which has had a remarkable history, and whose disappearance none of us desire.

We shall try to say no single word which should appeal to one group rather than to another. All, equally, are in peril, and, if the peril is understood, there is hope that they may collectively avert it.

We have to learn to think in a new way. We have to learn to ask ourselves, not what steps can be taken to give military victory to whatever group we prefer, for there are no longer such steps; the question we have to ask ourselves is: What steps can be taken to prevent a military contest of which the issue must be disas-trous to all parties?

The general public, and even many men in positions of authority, have not realized what would be involved in a war with nuclear bombs. The general pub-lic still thinks in terms of the obliteration of cities. It is understood that the new bombs are more powerful than the old, and that, while one A-bomb could oblit-erate Hiroshima, one H-bomb could obliterate the largest cities, such as London, New York and Moscow.

No doubt in an H-bomb great cities would be obliterated. But this is one of the minor disasters that would have to be faced. If everybody in London, New York and Moscow were exterminated, the world might, in the course of a few cen-turies, recover from the blow. But we know, especially since the Bikini test, that nuclear bombs can gradually spread destruction over a very much wider area than had been supposed.

It is stated on very good authority that a bomb can now be manufactured which will be 2,500 times as powerful as that which destroyed Hiroshima.

Such a bomb, if exploded near the ground or under water, sends radioactive particles into the upper air. They sink gradually and reach the surface of the earth in the form of deadly dust or rain. It was this dust which infected the Japanese fishermen and their catch of fish.

No one knows how widely such lethal radioactive particles might be diffused, but the best authorities are unanimous in saying that a war with H-bombs might quite possibly put an end to the human race. It is feared that if many H-bombs are used there will be universal death—sudden only for a minority, but for the majority a slow torture of disease and disintegration.

Many warnings have been uttered by eminent men of science and by authorities in military strategy. None of them will say that the worst results are certain. What they do say is that these results are possible, and no one can be sure that they will not be realized. We have not yet found that the views of experts depend in any degree upon their politics or prejudices. They depend only, so far as our researches have revealed, upon the extent of the particular expert's knowledge. We have found that the men who know most are the most gloomy.

Here, then, is the problem which we present to you, stark and dreadful and inescapable: Shall we put an end to the human race; or shall mankind renounce war? People will not face this alternative because it is so difficult to abolish war (...)

Although an agreement to renounce nuclear weapons as part of a general reduction of armaments would not afford an ultimate solution, it would serve certain important purposes.

First: Any agreement between East and West is to the good in so far as it tends to diminish tension. Second: The abolition of thermonuclear weapons, if each side believed that the other had carried it out sincerely, would lessen the fear of a sudden attack in the style of Pearl Harbor, which at present keeps both sides in a state of nervous apprehension. We should, therefore, welcome such an agreement, though only as a first step.

Most of us are not neutral in feeling, but, as human beings, we have to remember that, if the issues between East and West are to be decided in any manner that can give any possible satisfaction to anybody, whether Communist or anti-Communist, whether Asian or European or American, whether white or black, then these issues must not be decided by war. We should wish this to be understood, both in the East and in the West.

There lies before us, if we choose, continual progress in happiness, knowledge and wisdom. Shall we, instead, choose death, because we cannot forget our quarrels? We appeal, as human beings, to human beings: Remember your humanity and forget the rest. If you can do so, the way lies open to a new paradise; if you cannot, there lies before you the risk of universal death.

RESOLUTION

We invite this congress [to be convened], and through it the scientists of the world and the general public, to subscribe to the following resolution:

'In view of the fact that in any future world war nuclear weapons will certainly be employed, and that such weapons threaten the continued existence of mankind, we urge the governments of the world to realize, and to acknowledge publicly, that their purposes cannot be furthered by a world war, and we urge them, consequently, to find peaceful means for the settlement of all matters of dispute between them.' *Call to action*

9.6 The Organization of Science

The technological turn in the Cold War created large organizations—public and private—whose very existence depended on the scientific competition between East and West. In these two excerpts, Thomas Watson, Jr., the director of IBM, and Roald Sagdeev, a director of the vast Soviet laboratories in Akademgorodok, explain the significance of the Cold War to their enterprises.

A. Thomas Watson, Jr. on IBM and the Cold War, 1950s

I turned my attention to the most important sale of my career. In the 1930s Dad had been able to boost IBM into the top echelon of corporations by supplying punch-card machines for Social Security and the New Deal. There were no such massive social programs under Truman or Eisenhower for us to tap into. It was the Cold War that helped IBM make itself the king of the computer business. After the Russians exploded their first atomic bomb in 1949, the Air Force decided that America needed a sophisticated air defense system. They also decided this should incorporate computers—a very bold idea for the time, because computers were still little more than experiments. The government gave a contract to MIT [the Massachusetts Institute of Technology], and some of the country's best engineers there drew up plans for a vast computer-and-radar network which was supposed to blanket the United States, operate around the clock, and calculate the location, course, and speed of any incoming bomber. The military name for this system was Semi-Automatic Ground Environment, or SAGE. Air defense until then consisted of a few scattered radar stations, where observers did calculations on slide rules and then plotted flight paths by hand. The faster airplanes became, the harder they were to track. An air defense commander might get redundant messAGEs from two or three different radar operators who each thought he had spotted something. The idea of SAGE was to avoid confusion. The commander could use it to monitor his entire region and transmit orders to his interceptors and antiaircraft batteries.

The MIT engineer responsible for procuring the SAGE computers was Jay Forrester, an austere man about my age who was driven by a belief that computers could be made to do more than anyone thought. In the summer of 1952 he was travelling around the industry visiting the five companies running—RCA, Raytheon, Remington Rand, Sylvania, and IBM—and everybody was pulling out the stops. RCA and Sylvania trotted him through their huge vacuum tube factories that were supplying everyone in the industry. Remington Rand showed off the UNIVAC and brought in as their spokesman the famous general, Leslie Groves. During the war Groves had been the boss of the Manhattan Project, which built the atom bomb.

I tried not to worry about Groves or the other competitors; I just let IBM speak for itself. I took Forrester to see our plants and introduced him to our most gifted people. He was under extreme pressure to get the system into production as soon as possible, and I think that what impressed him was the fact that we were already building computers in a factory. We won a small contract for the first stage of the project, to build prototype computers in conjunction with MIT.

To make SAGE possible the computers had to work in a way computers had never worked before. In those days computing was typically done in what was called batch mode. This meant that you would collect your data first, feed it into the machine second, then sit back for a little while until the answer came out. You could think of the batch processor as a high diver at a circus—each performance involves a lengthy drum roll in preparation, a very fast dive, and then a splash. But the SAGE system was supposed to keep track of a large air defense picture that was changing every instant. This meant it had to take a constant stream of new radar information and digest it continually in what is called 'real time.' So a SAGE computer was more like a juggler who has to keep a half dozen balls in the air, constantly throwing aside old balls as his assistants toss him new ones from every direction. As if real-time computing were not enough of a technical challenge, the Air Force also wanted the system to be absolutely reliable. In those days it was considered an accomplishment if someone could build a computer that would work a full eight-hour day without failing. But SAGE was supposed to operate flawlessly around the clock, year in and year out.

When Russia exploded its first hydrogen bomb in the summer of 1953, the need to finish SAGE became even more urgent. We took many of our top engineers off our other computers and put them to work with Forrester and his men. A year after we started we had seven hundred people on the SAGE project, and it took only fourteen months to design and build a prototype that would do the job. It was a monster of a machine, far larger than any computer that had ever been produced. The Air Force called it the AN/FSQ-7—or Q7 for short—and it had fifty thousand vacuum tubes and dozens of cabinets spread out across a large warehouse. It was so big that even though electricity in wires travels at close to the speed of light, signals sometimes took too long to get from one part of the computer to another.

Although we'd built a successful prototype, we weren't guaranteed the next stage of the project. The lion's share of SAGE—the contract to manufacture and service the dozens of computers that would make up the actual system—was still up for grabs. I thought it was absolutely essential to IBM's future that we win it. The company that built those computers was going to be way ahead of the game, because it would learn the secrets of mass production. We had the inside track because we'd built the prototype, but there were times in our dealings with MIT when I thought we'd blown it.

Forrester was a genius at computer hardware, but he didn't appreciate how hard it is to set up a reliable production process. He thought we were handling the project all wrong. His idea of management was what he called the 'man-on-the-white-horse principle.' The man on the white horse was Napoleon; Forrester thought every engineering project needed a dictator, which was not the way our manufacturing men liked to work. His constant criticism made them angry and stubborn, and I was worried he'd shift SAGE somewhere else. I worked harder to win that contract than I worked for any other sale in my life. I was constantly making trips up to MIT. Forrester hemmed and hawed, but I finally told him that if he promised me the production assignment, I would build him a factory without waiting for a contract. 'Give me your handshake, and we'll start on the plant this week,' I said. I knew he was afraid that he might have to wait a long time for the paperwork from the Air Force. So he told me to go ahead.

Within a couple of years we had thousands of people working on SAGE and those big Q-7s were in operation all over the continent. We built forty-eight in all. You'd sometimes see a SAGE center if you were driving in a remote place. They were huge windowless concrete buildings, each covering an entire acre and housing two machines. The control room in these places was a big room lit with an eerie blue light. The watch commander would sit in front of a giant map of his entire area. On that board, the computer would plot in yellow the movement of all the airplanes in the sky, along with symbols to show whether they were friends or foes. If there was an attacker, the commander simply had to point to its blip with a device called a 'light gun' and SAGE would automatically radio information about its position to interceptor planes and anti aircraft batteries. The system even had the reliability that the Air Force wanted. We'd solved that problem by having the Q7s work in tandem, taking turns. One machine would juggle the radar while its twin was being serviced or standing by. By that method the average SAGE center was able to stay alert over 97 percent of the time.

SAGE was celebrated as one of the great technical achievements of its day. But although the system worked fine, the arms race made it obsolete before it was even finished. It could guard against attacks by bombers, but not missiles, so when the Russians launched Sputnik in 1958, SAGE became passé. I remember I was sitting in a hotel dining room in Bremen when word of Sputnik came. A waiter who I knew was American walked up and said, 'Where is your Sputnik?' Where is your Sputnik?' We got scared all over again, because we'd left ourselves vulnerable to an attack from space. But in fairness to Jay Forrester and all the military men who decided to build SAGE, none of us ever questioned the suitability at the time it was designed. And it gave IBM the giant boost I was after. Until the late '50s, SAGE accounted for almost half our total computer sales.

B. Roald Sagdeev on Soviet Science, 1950s

While cooperating on the creation of an oasis of science in Siberia, government and scientists had rather different agendas. The latter, including my fellow physicists and me, had hoped very much that by coming to virgin land we could start everything from scratch, according to international scientific standards, instead of waiting for God-only-knows how long in Moscow's old established institutes. We wanted to catch up with the West.

The encounter with our foreign colleagues at international conferences, however, was an eye-opener for us on a a new style of doing science, free from the boring and even intimidating constraints established by the administration and the bureaucracy; free to travel when we ourselves felt it was important; and free from fortified fences around the perimeters of mailboxes. We even hoped that the irritating ideological indoctrination that came from the party hierarchy would somehow miraculously evaporate.

The Khrushchev government, in its turn, considered the massive transplant of scientific excellence to Akademgorodok a great way to boost the technological and cultural development of Siberia. The establishment of a new academy would produce a scientific community more dynamic and responsive to requests from authorities. The new academy, they thought, would consist of specially selected and purified scientists.

From the very beginning, it was obvious that the inhabitants of the new town in Siberia would be from the young generation of scientists. The laws of natural selection dictated that they could move from Moscow and Leningrad with greater ease than those who had already built their careers and a comfortable life in other established institutions. If the official master plan indeed consisted of moving forward the generation of scientists brought up by the Soviet power, nominally no one could have had better credentials than Andrei Budker.

Budker was born into a poor family in the year of the 'Great October' (1917). Soviet power opened the door for him to Moscow State University. He graduated at the peak of Stalin's great Five-Year Plan to transform the Soviet economy. He fought in the war against the Nazis and met Victory Day as an artillery captain decorated with many medals. He received a few additional awards as a prominent member of Kurchatov's team. When his Socialist homeland sought to become a nuclear power, there was, of course, one 'small dark spot' against him: the sound and spelling of his name. [Budker was of Jewish origin] The government, however, was generous enough to make an exception in recognition of such outstanding service.

Within the new academy, Budker's style was to nourish a team of like-minded scientists, and for rather a long time I was one of them. He shared with us all his ideas—his hopes and his doubts. In return, he requested complete dedication, even self-sacrifice.

Our alma mater in Novosibirsk—Akademgorodok, the Institute of Nuclear Physics—was built on the principle of collective brainstorming. Budker had ordered the institute's workshop to design and produce a rather fancy round table that could comfortably accommodate a couple dozen young scientists and their director, their leader. The very shape of the table symbolized the spirit of democracy in scientific discussion. Budker himself liked to compare it with the Round Table at which King Arthur had conferred with his brave knights.

If Kapitsa was an introvert, concealing his scientific ideas and engineering innovations until they could be developed and given final elaboration, Budker in contrast was the true personification of an extrovert—he liked to think aloud. For that reason, we were lucky to be not only witnesses, but also a part of his inner 'kitchen' while he was cooking a new and quite often bizarre feast (…)

[Budker] would tell us, 'I have a philosophy. If I'm rejected today, I will try again tomorrow.'

These frequent trips to the Central Committee, to the State Planning Committee (Gosplan) and so on were an eye-opener for Budker. He discovered that in the most totalitarian, autocratic, and centralized system, the real power was concentrated in the hands of the invisible army of low-key clerks, who occupied less prestigious offices than those of the members of the Politburo and ministries. These clerks played the key role in drafting the most important documents and pushing them through the bureaucratic labyrinth before the papers even got to the desks of the biggest bosses for final blessings. These fellows knew much better how and when to approach the boss, and what to tell him to change his mind.

This is how the institute was given the special privilege of selling innovative hardware, like electron accelerators for industrial use, not according to very strict governmental regulations, but by watching the market. Whenever demand exceeded supply, supplies had to be re-established in negotiations with potential customers, the clients. The institute, with these breakthroughs, was launched into a higher, more privileged orbit in the interest of doing better science.

Being part of all the discussions and witnessing Budker's efforts, I was quite supportive of the final results. However, I felt sorry for him with respect to the substantial overtime he had to put in to run the institute.

'There must be something deeply wrong,' I thought to myself, 'with a system that so ineffectively uses it scientific brains.' I could hardly know at that time that I myself would not escape the same fate.

9.7 The Sputnik: US Reaction, 1957

In 1957 the Soviet Union launched the first satellite in orbit around the earth. The reaction to this technological feat in the United States was very strong: many suspected that Americans were losing the space race to the Soviets. Here is an excerpt from a New York Times article from 6 October 1957.

Democratic Senators blamed the Eisenhower Administration's economy program today for the Soviet triumph in launching the first earth satellite.

Senators Stuart Symington of Missouri and Henry M. Jackson of Washington said that the development was further evidence of Soviet superiority in the long-range missiles field. Senator Symington demanded an investigation by the Senate Armed Services Committee.

The White House declined to comment on military aspects of the launching, but said it 'did not come as a surprise.' James C. Hagerty, Presidential press secretary, also discounted the fact that the Soviet was the first to put a man-made sphere into space.

'We never thought of our program as one which was in a race with the Soviets,' he remarked. Meanwhile, officials at the Pentagon said that a decision by the United States to separate the Vanguard Satellite project from missiles development had delayed the program.

The decision was made in 1955 over the objections of many scientists.Mr. Hagerty told questioners that the Soviet accomplishment would have no effect on the United States program, which calls for the launching of a smaller satellite next spring.

'Ours is geared to the International Geophysical Year and is proceeding satisfactorily in accordance with its scientific objectives,' he said.

Senator Symington's request for an investigation of the United States missiles program was made in a telegram to Senator Richard P. Russell, Democrat, of Georgia, as chairman of the Armed Services Committee.

'The recently announced launching of an earth satellite by the Soviet is but more proof of growing Communist superiority in the all-important missile field,' he wired from Kansas City, Mo.

'If this now known superiority over the United States develops into supremacy, the position of the free world will be critical.

'At the same time we continue to learn of the missile accomplishments of the

10. Macmillan, Eisenhower, and Khrushchev. (Michael Cummings, *Daily Express*, 13 November 1957). Reprinted by permission. Photo supplied by The Centre for the Study of Cartoons and Caricature, University of Kent.

possible enemy. For fiscal reasons this Government, in turn, continues to cut back and slow down its own missile program. I have been warning about this growing danger for a long time, because the future of the United States may well be at stake. Therefore, I respectfully but earnestly, request that as chairman of the Senate Armed Services Committee, you arrange for complete hearings in this matter before the committee.

'Only in this way can the American people learn the truth. Putting it mildly, they have not been getting that truth.'

9.8 US Concerns over the Cost of Nuclear Weapons, 1960

By the early 1960s the cost of the nuclear arms race had become a serious concern both to the United States and the Soviet Union. In America, some feared that the strong links that were created between science, business, and the military could threaten US democracy. The first excerpt is from President Eisenhower's farewell address, in which he warns against the influence of what he termed 'the military-industrial complex'. The second excerpt is from a hearing before the Congress of the United States in 1960.

A. Eisenhower on the Military-Industrial Complex, 1960

Throughout America's adventure in free government, our basic purposes have been to keep the peace; to foster progress in human achievement, and to enhance liberty, dignity and integrity among people and among nations. To strive for less would unworthy of a free and religious people. Any failure traceable to arrogance, or our lack of comprehension or readiness to sacrifice would inflict upon us grievous hurt both at home and abroad.

Progress toward these noble goals is persistently threatened by the conflict now engulfing the world. It commands our whole attention, absorbs our very beings. We face a hostile ideology—global in scope, atheistic in character, ruthless in purpose, and insidious in method. Unhappily the danger it poses promises to be of indefinite duration. To meet it successfully, there is called for, not so much the emotional and transitory sacrifices of crisis, but rather those which enable us to carry forward steadily, surely, and without complaint the burdens of a prolonged and complex struggle—with liberty the stake. Only thus shall we remain, despite every provocation, on our charted course toward permanent peace and human betterment.

Crises there will continue to be. In meeting them, whether foreign or domestic, great or small, there is a recurring temptation to feel that some spectacular and costly action could become the miraculous solution to all current difficulties. A huge increase in newer elements of our defense; development of unrealistic programs to cure every ill in agriculture; a dramatic expansion in basic and applied research—these and many other possibilities, each possibly promising in itself, may be suggested as the only way to the road we wish to travel.

But each proposal must be weighted in the light of a broader consideration: the need to maintain balance in and among national programs—balance between the private and the public economy, balance between cost and hoped for advantage—balance between the clearly necessary and the comfortably desirable; balance between our essential requirements as a nation and the duties imposed by the nation upon the individual; balance between actions of the moment and the national welfare of the future. Good judgement seeks balance and progress; lack of it eventually finds imbalance and frustration.

The record of many decades stands as proof that our people and their government have, in the main, understood these truths and have responded to them well, in the face of stress and threat. But threats, new in kind or degree, constantly arise.

A vital element in keeping the peace is our military establishment. Our arms must be mighty, ready for instant action, so that no potential aggressor may be tempted to risk its own destruction.

Our military organization today bears little relation to that known by any of my predecessors in peacetime, or indeed by the fighting men of World War II or Korea.

Until the latest of the world conflicts, the United States had no armaments industry. American makers of plowshares could, with time and as required, make swords as well. But now we can no longer risk emergency improvisation of national defense; we have been compelled to create a permanent armaments industry of vast proportions. Added to this, three and a half million men and women are directly engaged in the defense establishment. We annually spend on military security more than the net income of all United States corporations.

This conjunction of an immense military establishment and a large arms industry is new in the American experience. The total influence—economical, political, even spiritual—is felt in every city, every State house, every office of the Federal government. We recognize the imperative need for this development. Yet we must not fail to comprehend its grave implications. Our toil, resources and livelihood are all involved; so is the very structure of our society.

In the councils of the government, we must guard against the acquisition of unwarranted influence, whether sought or unsought, by the military-industrial complex. The potential for the disastrous rise of misplaced power exists and will persist.

We must never let the weight of this combination endanger our liberties or democratic processes. We should take nothing for granted. Only an alert and knowledgeable citizenry can compel the proper meshing of the huge industrial and military machinery of defense with our peaceful methods and goals, so that security and liberty may prosper together.

B. Senate Hearing on Nuclear Weapons, 1960

General TAYLOR: At the time of the great argument over the future of the JUPITER missile, I proposed to the Secretary of Defense that we adopt the concept of a national arsenal.

In other words, any service that has a good idea and a capability of producing a weapon, should be allowed to go ahead and produce it. Then it would be placed, figuratively speaking, into the national arsenal. Any other service who has a need for it, in the light of its roles and missions, can reach into that arsenal, take it out and use it.

I still think it is a good concept, and I believe that is what you have in mind.

Senator STENNIS: Yes. Thinking somewhat in terms of that, I notice that the cost of the missile alone—and we expect to have quite a few of them operational—is astronomical, even for only 1 year.

General TAYLOR: That is why it is so important to know now how much is enough. What is our goal? Why do we need 10 or a 100, or 150, or whatever the number happens to be?

Senator STENNIS: Yes. Well, I can visualize one group of missiles for one type—ICBM's—costing anywhere from 4 to 8 billion dollars per year just to keep the supply line going and to keep up the numbers.

That is just for one single type of missile. Something must be done now. We talk about planning four years ahead, and that is necessary.

It seems to me however that something must be done now in planning ahead on a question of that kind.

Otherwise, this cost is going to mushroom and become so astronomical that it could well undermine the soundness of the free enterprise system.

General TAYLOR: The only encouraging factor from a fiscal point of view, I would say, is the fact that we really don't need many of these if they are *really* good, if they are accurate, and we are sure of getting them on target.

In other words, the vastly increased yield of warheads we have available reduces the actual number of missiles required, but it is up to us to decide what is the required number.

Senator STENNIS: Well, I think that is certainly a good comment. But, if we continue building these different types and kinds of ICBM's and IRBM's as well as battlefield and tactical, air to ground, ground to air, air to air, and other missiles, it is going to run into many, many billions of dollars a year, Just to supply the missiles alone, without the launching pads or the operation and maintenance costs, could soon run from 5 to 8 or 9 billion dollars for 1 year alone.

Do you know what we should do now to try to impress someone with the idea of making plans to reduce the number of different types of missiles and thereby reduce the cost?

General TAYLOR: I am afraid I can just repeat myself, Senator, and say my only solution is to make the military come up with an engineering kind of estimate of how much we need.

We are building the structure of our defense without knowing what the factors of safety are. If you were running an engineering company, you would go bankrupt operating on that basis.

Senator STENNIS: You had a practical solution of a national arsenal.

General TAYLOR: I think it a concept, sir, that gets away from the idea of the pride of service ownership, that the Air Force, the Army, or the Navy will only fire a missile built, designed and produced by the Air Force, by the Army, or by the Navy (...)

Senator MARTIN: General Taylor, in your colloquy with Senator Wiley you estimated a new defense budget of about 50 to 55 billion dollars per year for the next five years.

General TAYLOR: Yes, that was very much of a shotgun estimate.

9.9 The Military Use of the Space Programme, 1961

The race for exploration of space was very much a part of the Cold War competition. In this excerpt from a 28 April 1961 memorandum to President Kennedy, Vice-President Lyndon Johnson explains why the space race is so important to the United States.

The following general conclusions can be reported:

a. Largely due to their concentrated efforts and their earlier emphasis upon the development of large rocket engines, the Soviets are ahead of the United States in world prestige attained through impressive technological accomplishments in space.

b. The U.S. has greater resources than the USSR for attaining space leadership but has failed to make the necessary hard decisions and to marshal those resources to achieve such leadership.

c. This country should be realistic and recognize that other nations, regardless of their appreciation of our idealistic values, will tend to align themselves with the country which they believe will be their world leader—the winner in the long run. Dramatic accomplishments in space are being increasingly identified as a major indicator in world leadership.

d. The U.S. can, if it will, firm up its objectives and employ its resources with a reasonable chance of attaining world leadership in space during this decade. This will be difficult but can be made probable even recognizing the head start of the Soviets and the likelihood that they will continue to move forward with impressive successes, in certain areas, such as communications, navigation, weather, and mapping, the U.S. can and should exploit its existing advance position.

e. If we do not make the strong effort now, the time will soon be reached when the margin of control over space and over men's minds through space accomplishments will have swung so far on the Russian side that we will not be able to catch up, let alone assume leadership.

f. Even in those areas in which the Soviets already have the capability to be first and are likely to improve upon such capability, the United States should make aggressive efforts as the technological gains as well as the international rewards are essential steps in eventually gaining leadership. The danger of long lags or outright omissions by this country is substantial in view of the possibility of great technological breakthroughs obtained from space exploration.

Manned exploration of the moon, for example, is not only an achievement with great propaganda value, but it is essential as an objective whether or not we are first in its accomplishment—and we may be able to be first. We cannot leapfrog such accomplishments, as they are essential sources of knowledge and experience for even greater successes in space. We cannot expect the Russians to transfer the benefits of their experiences of the advantages of their capabilities to us. We must do these things ourselves (…)

Q.5—Are we making maximum efforts? Are we achieving necessary results?

A.5—We are neither making maximum effort nor achieving results necessary if this country is to reach a position of leadership.

9.10 SIOP-62 Briefing, 1961

In the early 1960s US plans for nuclear war became increasingly co-ordinated under what was called the 'Single Integrated Operational Plan' (SIOP). This excerpt is from a briefing presented to President Kennedy by the Chairman of the Joint Chiefs of Staff (JCS) on 13 September 1961.

The Single Integrated Operational Plan (SIOP) is the JCS plan which provides for the optimum employment of the US atomic delivery forces in the initial attack of strategic targets in the Sino-Soviet Bloc.

I shall describe to you the salient characteristics of this plan in terms of forces involved, targets attacked, and mechanics of execution of the plan (...)

Specific Objectives are:

  a. To destroy or neutralize Sino-Soviet Bloc strategic nuclear delivery capability primary military and government controls of major importance, and
  b. To attack the major urban-industrial centers of the Sino-Soviet Bloc to achieve the general level of destruction as indicated in Study No. 2009 (...)

All forces have been targeted in order of their arrival in the target area. The sequence of targeting was first, the ballistic missiles; second, forces launching from forward areas; and last, forces from the US.

The first group of forces to be targeted was that identified and maintained as the Alert Force, which was applied under conditions of tactical warning against highest priority targets.

Next to be targeted were the Follow-on Forces. The Follow-on Force is that portion of the committed forces which are [*sic*] not maintained in a condition for immediate reaction. Warning time is required to ready this force. The Follow-on Force is targeted to take advantage of the Alert Force strike; to improve the probability on targets scheduled for strike by the Alert Force; and, as a result of the large force made available by preparation time, it is used to expand target coverage.

The penetration and delivery capabilities of all weapon systems in the plan were analysed and applied to insure the highest probability of delivering at least one weapon on each target. The number of weapons scheduled against each ground zero was determined by the target characteristics and the desired assurance delivery. Weapons were then scheduled until the desired assurance was obtained at each target bomb release line (...)

Tactics programmed for the SIOP are in two principal categories—the *penetration phase* and the *delivery phase*. In the penetration phase, the plan considers degradation of those defenses that offer the greatest threat to our forces. Peripheral defenses are scheduled to receive the first weapons. Subsequent arriving aircraft then bomb deeper defenses and primary targets as the force penetrates. The attack becomes a progressive development, following the principle of 'bomb as you go.'

Roll-back of the target system in this manner, within a selected geographical area, is called a 'corridor.' These corridors vary in width from [not declassified] with defenses degraded within and for a (deleted) distance on either side. This distance represents potential ground-controlled interceptor coverage within the corridor.

[Not declassified]

In those areas where, due to extensive Soviet defenses, roll-back of the target system or establishment of corridors is impractical, penetration is scheduled to be accomplished by maximum possible use of low level flight.

In the delivery phase, increased assurance has been obtained through the assignment of different delivery systems to the same target, by diversified tactics, and by cross-targeting on a common target system with consideration given to the capabilities of all systems in terms of reaction, circular error probable, yield, and launch location (…)

A fundamental characteristic of the current SIOP is that it provides for attack of an Optimum-Mix Target System. This follows the conclusions and the Presidential decision relative to Study No. 2009 that an optimum-mix of both military and urban-industrial targets must be successfully attacked in order for the US ultimately to prevail. Consequently, the SIOP is designed for the accomplishment of this total essential task. This embraces such things as timing and routing of attacks so that the maximum mutual support of the attacking forces is achieved. For example, tactics of follow-on forces relate directly to results expected to be achieved by earlier-arriving forces. Thus, basically, the SIOP is *designed* for execution as a whole (…)

The Single Integrated Operational Plan was designed to meet requirements under conditions such that our national survival is at stake. If the enemy were to launch an all-out nuclear attack against the US and its allies during the current time period, the expected gross disruption of facilities, military capabilities, communications and control elements, and other national assets imposes an overriding requirement for simplicity of military response. This overriding requirement severely limits the operational responses which may be practically planned—this notwithstanding how desirable some responses individually might be under certain circumstances. The ability to defeat the enemy must not be lost by the introduction into the SIOP of an excessive number of options which would contribute to confusion and lower our assurance of success under the most adverse circumstances.

9.11 The Partial Test Ban Treaty, 1963

On 5 August 1963 the United States, Britain, and the Soviet Union signed a treaty banning nuclear weapon tests in the atmosphere, in space, and under water. Many observers saw the treaty as an important step towards lessening tension after the Cuban Missile Crisis.

The [parties] (…) [p]roclaiming as their principal aim the speediest possible achievement of an agreement on national control in accordance with the objectives of the United Nations which would put an end to the armaments race and eliminate the incentive to the production and testing of all kinds of weapons, including nuclear weapons.

Seeking to achieve the discontinuance of all test explosions of nuclear weapons for all time, determined to continue negotiations to this end, and desiring to put an end to the contamination of man's environment by radioactive substances.

Have agreed as follows:

Article I
1. Each of the Parties to this Treaty undertakes to prohibit, to prevent, and not to carry out any nuclear weapon test explosion, or any other nuclear explosion, at any place under its jurisdiction or control:
   (a) In the atmosphere; beyond its limits, including outer space; or under water, including territorial waters or high seas; or
   (b) In any other environment if such explosion causes radioactive debris to be present outside the territorial limits of the State under whose jurisdiction or control such explosion is conducted. It is understood in this connection that the provisions of this subparagraph are without prejudice to the conclusion of a treaty resulting in the permanent banning of all nuclear test explosions, including all such explosions underground, the conclusion of which, as the Parties have stated in the Preamble to this Treaty, they seek to achieve.
2. Each of the Parties to this Treaty undertakes furthermore to refrain from causing, encouraging, or in any way participating in, the carrying out of any nuclear weapon test explosion, or any other nuclear explosion anywhere which would take place in any of the environments described, or have the effect referred to, in paragraph 1 of this Article (…)

9.12 Women and Civil Defence, 1961

In spite of the threat of total destruction that the nuclear arms race posed, both the United States and the Soviet Union put great emphasis on civil defence. In America, the civil defence agenda was taken up by many voluntary organizations. Here is an excerpt from a talk on ' Home Preparedness—A Woman's Cause', by Mrs Norton H. Pearl,

Deputy Assistant Director, Women's Activities, Office of Civil and Defense Mobilization, Battle Creek, Michigan, from 1961.

I am pleased to meet with you and speak to you concerning the program we are conducting in home preparedness. This program so well fits into the message given by President Kennedy when he asked citizens to take 'common sense measures to be ready should an enemy thrust war upon us' and it also fills the need for 'individual preparedness, which is beyond the province of government and which is essential to an effective civil defense.' (...)

I say the No. 1 job for the women of this country is to get their houses in order—their homes prepared for emergency NOW. Having prepared the homes of this country, we can turn our attention to preparing women to fill the specific jobs of civil defense in which they will be needed. Then you should have places ready for them.

What progress are we making in home preparedness? Many of you are helping us to make progress. The new Home Preparedness Workshops with five sessions and a filmstrip to go with each have been distributed to the State offices. This should have been sent you. We have with the addition of the filmstrips made it possible to conduct many more workshops. It is now possible for a leader to organize a group and use this media with less help from civil defense offices. Each one has been cleared by the proper authority and the script is authentic. These are available on order through your State Civil Defense Office. The last session is devoted to the new Home Preparedness Award program and the person completing the Home Preparedness Workshop will be fully aware of what is necessary in order to qualify for the seal and citation. This is important for this is not a door-to-door distribution program. It is not a crash deal. It must be explained. It should be taken step by step. Almost 3 million kits have been distributed, and I am concerned about their use and effectiveness. The demand for these kits is overwhelming, yet I am not satisfied with reported results. Do you have unused kits and envelopes? If so, what are your plans for these? (...)

I believe this program does support the National Plan, it does support and promote the shelter policy, it does add voice to that of Continuity of Government, Rescue, Relief, etc. How can a staff of a few people do all this? Through the most active and vocal group of people in America—the women! How can we reach 60 million ears? Through their organizations—the General Foundation of Women's Clubs, Business and Professional Women's Clubs, B'nai B'rith Women, Council of Catholic Women, Seventh-Day Adventists, Salvation Army, American Legion Auxiliary, Ladies' Auxiliary to the VFW. Through these and many others, as well as through the channel of their employment, will the message be delivered.

Every man and woman must realize that we are confronted with some bitter facts: The Soviet is dedicated to the proposition that it will be prepared to wage war with us. Because of the speed of these weapons, total war has become a possibility. Therefore, we who are building the non-military, deterrent force cannot afford to overlook any means of accomplishing our goal. If the use of women is a strong force toward this need, then we cannot afford to ignore them.

The war clouds that hover over the world today would seem to warrant a greater effort to prepare against the worst. It is America's responsibility, not only to the freedom of man, but to his survival as a species, to prepare. Such preparation in this case is especially justified, since it is a means of reducing the likelihood that the worst will happen.

Therefore, I urge you to take stock of your great resource—women—take cognisance of their innate ability. Take note of their stamina, courage, fortitude, faith. Provide the homemaker, the club woman, the church worker, the civic leader the CAUSE for which she will work. Provide her with the proper survival plans in which she can and will do her share. Then and only then, I believe, we will have a non-military defense, a deterrent to war which will stop any aggressor.

9.13 The Secret Nuclear Weapons Accidents, 1966 and 1968

Even though they were mostly kept secret, the number of accidents involving nuclear weapons during the Cold War was staggering. Here is an account of two of them, from the volume Atomic Audit.

On January 16, 1966, a B-52G bomber, returning to its North Carolina base following a routine airborne alert mission, collided with refuelling boom of a KC-135 tanker 30,000 feet (9,144 meters) above the coast of Spain while attempting to refuel. Both aircraft broke up and the 40,000 gallons (151,000 liters) of jet fuel in the KC-135 exploded, killing its four-man crew. Four members of the B-52's seven-man crew were able to parachute to safety. Of the four unarmed B28 hydrogen bombs carried by the B-52 (a weapon with yields ranging from 70 kilotons to 1.45 megatons), three crashed on the ground in the vicinity of the Palomares, a poor farming community 1 mile (1.6 kilometers) off the coastal highway. The fourth sank off the coast and was missing for nearly three months before being located by the submersible Alvin 5 miles (8 kilometers) offshore in 2,850 feet (869 meters) of water. The high explosives in two of the bombs that fell on Palomares detonated, digging craters 6 to 10 feet (1.8 to 3 meters) deep and scattering plutonium and other debris 100 to 500 yards (91 to 457 meters) away from the impact area (the third bomb was recovered relatively intact from a dry riverbed) (…)

Following the cleanup effort, the AEC [(U.S.) Atomic Energy Commission] and JEN [Junta de Energia Nuclear] established a monitoring program for the villagers and their land, with the AEC providing the funds and the JEN conducting the surveys. In November 1971, Wright Langham with Los Alamos laboratory visited Palomares to assess the program. He found that only 100 villagers (about 6 percent of the population at the time of the accident) had undergone lung and urine testing: 29 tested positive but the results were deemed 'statistically insignificant.' Air monitoring for plutonium dust had ceased two years after the accident, even though high counts were occasionally obtained during periods of strong winds. Soil sampling was hampered by the fact that JEN had only one alpha spectrometer, which did not always work well. Langham reported that the morale among the JEN staff assigned to the task had diminished since the accident and that the United States ought to provide more money and equipment to keep the effort going. A DNA [(U.S.) Defence Nuclear Agency] report completed in 1975 concurred: 'Palomares is one of the few locations in the world that offers an on-going experimental laboratory, probably the only one offering a look at an agricultural area.' (…)

A little more than two years after the Palomares accident, on January 21, 1968, a B-52G bomber on a secret early warning mission crashed on the ice near Thule Air Base, Greenland, following an uncontrollable on-board fire that quickly cut off the plane's electrical power. Six of the seven crew members were able to eject safely. After passing directly over the base, the plane hit the ice-covered North Star Bay at a speed of 560 miles (900 kilometers) per hour. The impact destroyed the B-52, triggering the explosion of its 35,000 gallons (132,500 liters) of jet fuel, as well as detonating the high explosives in all four of the B28 bombs it carried. That explosion propelled parts of the bombs—including plutonium, uranium, and tritium components—into the inferno. Bomb debris and plane wreckage burned for at least twenty minutes and covered an area 1,000 to 2,000 feet (305 to 610 meters) wide. The heat of the fire melted the ice, which later froze, encapsulating some of the debris. One B28 secondary assembly (the thermonuclear part of the bomb) apparently melted through the ice and was later retrieved during an underwater survey.

A massive cleanup effort dubbed Project Crested Ice (but known informally among workers as 'Dr. Freezelove') was carried out by more than 700 U.S. servicemen and Danish civilian workers from Thule, including U.S. specialists from more than seventy government agencies. Despite nearly impossible working conditions—total darkness until February, winds of up to 85 miles (137 kilometers) per hour, temperatures 28 to 70 degrees Fahrenheit below zero (−33 to −57 degrees Celsius), equipment that functioned poorly (if at all) in the subzero temperatures, and intense pressure to finish the recovery before the spring thaw—within eight months of the accident, 10,500 tons (237,000 cubic feet [6,700 cubic meters]) of contaminated snow, ice, and debris had been collected in barrels and shipped to the Savannah River Plant for disposal (aircraft debris was sent to Oak Ridge for burial). Residual waste was allowed to melt into the bay with the spring thaw, on the theory that the large volume of water would sufficiently dilute the radiation to safe levels. The entire effort is estimated to have cost some $9.4 million.

Within twenty years of the accident, some of the 500 Danish workers reported a range of debilitating ailments, including cancer and sterility, which they associated with their work on Crested Ice. Wearing no radiological protective clothing (face masks were often discarded because they restricted breathing in the harsh conditions), search teams (initially all American, later a mix of American and Danish workers) used radiation monitors to locate the debris and then retrieved it by hand. While Air Force personnel drove ice scrapers and loaders, the Danes filled barrels and other containers with debris, which were later dumped into a total of sixty-seven spare 25,000-gallon (95,000-liter) fuel tanks. Spills were all but unavoidable. After their shifts, workers and equipment were decontaminated 'by simply brushing the snow from garments and vehicles,' according to the official Air Force report.

9.14 The Origins of SALT, 1960s

By the late 1960s, both the United States and the Soviet Union were moving towards some kind of reduction of overall military tension. In this excerpt from the memoirs of two key Soviet participants in the later negotiations, they explain what moved the Moscow leadership in the direction of détente.

The Soviet leadership of the 1960s learned one thing too well: American superiority in the number of nuclear weapons led to an inequality that threatened Soviet security. Hence, the leadership insisted that the Soviet Union should, at minimum, have numerical equality with the United States, insofar as nuclear, and especially strategic, systems were concerned. If, however, one were to take into account the military potential of the American allies and the U.S. edge in systems capable of reaching Soviet territory, the Soviet leadership quickly concluded that what the Soviet Union needed—vitally—was nuclear superiority to the American strategic arsenal. Indeed, had not the Cuban missile crisis presented itself as solid evidence of this fact?

Thus, what was called the Cuban missile crisis syndrome exercised a very powerful impact on Soviet decision-making in the field of strategic force development. This psychological factor was highly negative. It intensified the arms race, because it caused the Soviet leadership to consider the *political*, as well as military, impact of the strategic equation while taking into account third countries. From this perspective, the achievement of equality (parity in the Western vernacular) or—even better if there was a chance for it—superiority over the United States was seen by Moscow as something highly valuable in political and ideological, not to mention strategic, terms. In other words, there are grounds to claim that the United States had unwittingly provoked the Soviet Union into a new phase of the arms race, while the Cuban missile crisis proved its necessity.

All this was made easier by the fact that Soviet strategic offensive arms of all classes, as well as its ABM [anti-ballistic missile] system, fully conformed to the then prevailing Soviet military doctrine which aimed at *winning* a nuclear war. Soviet political and military leaders were frank about this. The notion of 'victory' itself was underpinned by the concept of limiting the damage that could be caused by the probable enemy's weapons of mass destruction, an extension of the lessons of the Great Patriotic War. In this conjunction we note that, until recently, the concept of repelling the probable enemy's aerospace attack was one of the main missions of the Soviet Armed Forces. It can safely be concluded that under the Soviet approach extant in the 1960s, an effective ballistic missile defense was plainly a must. This became a major task of the Armed Forces of the Soviet Union.

However, despite the ambitious proclamations and goals, a number of civilian and military leaders and experts in the Soviet Union understood that victory in a nuclear war was unattainable. Such a war, they felt, would inevitably result in the complete annihilation of both the United States and the Soviet Union. It was another thing, however, to squarely accept the reality and draw the correct political conclusions. That matter proved too difficult, and the Soviet Union continued its arms buildup, assisted by all the resources and the propaganda it needed.

The problem also had an economic dimension. The arms race had always been a heavy burden for the Soviet economy, but, by the late 1960s, the Soviet leadership felt that the burden was clearly unbearable. This bred doubts as to the wisdom of maintaining the course. Additionally, the situation was complicated by the fact that earlier, by the mid-1960s, the scientific community in the Soviet Union was arriving at the realization that an effective ABM system was technically infeasible given the existing technologies (…)

The concept behind heavy ballistic missiles can be explained quite easily. First, it evolved from the general relative weakness of the Soviet missile industry during that period, and from its lack of experience. At that time, the weight of an ICBM was not a driving factor. The primary task was to develop and build a missile capable of delivering a certain payload to a specified distance. The task was levied on the defense, and not the aircraft, industry of the Soviet Union, despite the fact that the latter had a more sophisticated labor force and higher standards than the former (which was represented, for example, by the artillery sector of industry.) As might be expected, this played quite a negative role in the development of weapon systems that required sophistication to perfect. Second, Soviet industry also suffered from a lack of experience in the development of nuclear warheads. Consequently, missiles were required to carry significantly greater payloads than would be the case years after weapon design and construction techniques had improved. These factors, combined with the idea of deploying the most powerful warheads available on strategic missiles, demanded a heavy delivery vehicle (…)

As no serious research was performed in the Soviet Union at the time to explore either the relationship between strategic offensive and defensive arms or the nature of strategic stability, the country entertained rather vague concepts of those issues. Prime Minister Aleksey N. Kosygin's famous statement at the 1967 Glassboro Summit on the value of ABM in protecting the citizenry is an example. Similarly, when the SALT I talks were subsequently opened with the United States in November of 1969, the issue of strengthening strategic stability was not one that formed a cornerstone of the Soviet position. Rather, the Soviet Union entered the negotiations primarily because that gave promise for certain advantages.

The leadership in Moscow was not opposed to improving Soviet security through negotiations precisely because negotiations promised to slow the burden of the arms race and promised the attainment of some advantage over the Untied States. The realization of this goal was to be achieved, not by means of a nuclear arms buildup, but by the formulation of a clearly one-sided negotiating position and a tenacious adherence to it during the negotiations.

The idea of negotiating on strategic offensive arms was first discussed in Moscow during the administration of U.S. President John F. Kennedy. Even then, there was strong-felt and vocal sentiment in the Soviet Union that the country should strike a deal with the United States. The Soviet leaders were concerned about the edge the United States had gained by the late 1960s in the field of strategic arms. It was also far from clear to them where the American deployment would stop. That meant great uncertainty for the implementation of long-term Soviet programs, including construction of ICBMs, whose further buildup could no longer be justified by military requirements and was largely guided by political considerations.

The impetus for negotiations was provided by the Partial Test-Ban Treaty. The prevailing mood demanded that the process be continued. In November 1966, the American President Lyndon B. Johnson officially proposed that the Soviet Union agree on limits on strategic offensive forces. However, the

Vietnam War resulted in the postponement of talks, which, in turn, led the Soviet Union to apply pressure to establish a linkage between the opening of strategic arms talks and the cessation of American involvement in Southeast Asia. When the chance presented itself, the United States replied in kind: after Soviet troops marched into Czechoslovakia in August 1968, the Johnson Administration decided to delay the opening of the arms negotiations, which, as a result, caused a postponement of the summit that had been scheduled for the next month.

9.15 The Effects of Nuclear War, 1979

This report from May 1979, written for the US government, describes the likely effects of the dropping of a 1 megaton (1-Mt) nuclear weapon on the surface in the centre of the American city of Detroit.

(...) The detonation point selected is the intersection of 1-75 and 1-94, approximately at the civic center and about 3 miles [5 km] from the Detroit–Windsor tunnel entrance (...)

The 1-Mt explosion on the surface leaves a crater about 1,000 feet [300 m] in diameter and 200 feet [61 m] deep, surrounded by a rim of highly radioactive soil about twice this diameter thrown out of the crater. Out to a distance of 0.6 miles [1 km] from the center there will be nothing recognizable remaining, with the exception of some massive concrete bridge abutments and building foundations. At 0.6 miles some heavily damaged highway bridge sections will remain, but little else until 1.3 miles [2.1 km], where a few very strongly constructed buildings with poured reinforced concrete walls will survive, but with the interiors totally destroyed by blast entering the window openings. A distance of 1.7 miles [2.7 km] (1 2-psi ring) is the closest range where any significant structure will remain standing.

Of the 70,000 people in this area during non-working hours, there will be virtually no survivors. Fatalities during working hours in this business district would undoubtedly be much higher. The estimated daytime population of the 'downtown' area is something over 200,000 in contrast to the census data of about 15,000. If the attack occurred during this time, the fatalities would be increased by 130,000 and injuries by 45,000 over the estimates in table 4. Obviously there would be some reduction in casualties in outlying areas where the daytime population would be lower.

In the band between the 1.7- and the 2.7-mile (5 psi) circles, typical commercial and residential multi-story buildings will have the walls completely blown out, but increasingly at the greater distances the skeletal structure will remain standing.

Individual residences in this region will be totally destroyed, with only foundations and basements remaining, and the debris quite uniformly distributed over the area. Heavy industrial plants will be destroyed in the inner part of the ring, but some industry will remain functional towards the outer edge. The debris depth that will clutter the streets will naturally depend on both the building heights and how close together they are spaced. Typical depths might range from tens of feet in the downtown area where buildings are 10 to 20 storys high, down to several inches where buildings are lower and streets broader in the sector to the west and north. In this band, blast damage alone will destroy all automobiles, while some heavier commercial vehicles (firetrucks and repair vehicles) will survive near the outer edges. However, few vehicles will have been sufficiently protected from debris to remain useful. The parking lots of both Cobb Field and Tiger Stadium will contain nothing driveable.

In this same ring, which contains a nighttime population of about 250,000, about half will be fatalities, with most of the remainder being injured. Most deaths will occur from collapsing buildings. Although many fires will be started, only a small percentage of the buildings are likely to continue to burn after the blast wave passes. The mechanics of fire spread in a heavily damaged and debris strewn area are not well understood. However, it is probable that fire spread would be slow and there would be no firestorm. For unprotected people, the initial nuclear radiation would be lethal out to 1.7 miles [2.7 km], but be insignificant in its prompt effects (50 reins) at 2.0 miles [3.2 km]. Since few people inside a 2-mile ring will survive the blast, and they are very unlikely to be in strong buildings that typically have a 2- to 5- protection factor, the additional fatalities and injuries from initial radiation should be small compared to other uncertainties.

The number of casualties from thermal burns depends on the time of day, season, and atmospheric visibility. Modest variations in these factors produce huge changes in vulnerability to burns. For example, on a winter night, less than 1 percent of the population might be exposed to direct thermal radiation, while on a clear summer weekend afternoon more than 25 percent might be exposed (that is, have no structure between the fireball and the person). When visibility is 10 miles [16 km], a 1-Mt explosion produces second-degree burns at a distance of 6 miles [10 km], while under circumstances when visibility is 2 miles [3 km], the range of second-degree burns is only 2.7 miles [4.3 km] (...)

In the band from 2.7 to 4.7 miles [4.4 to 7.6 km] (2 psi), large buildings will have lost windows and frames, interior partitions, and, for those with light-walled construction, most of the contents of upper floors will have been blown out into the streets. Load-bearing wall buildings at the University of Detroit will be severely cracked. Low residential buildings will be totally destroyed or severely damaged.

Casualties are estimated to be about 50 percent in this region, with the majority of these injured. There will still be substantial debris in the streets, but a very significant number of cars and trucks will remain operable. In this zone, damage to heavy industrial plants, such as the Cadillac plant, will be severe, and most planes and hangars at the Detroit City Airport will be destroyed.

In this ring only 5 percent of the population of about 400,000 will be killed, but nearly half will be injured (table 4). This is the region of the most severe fire hazard, since fire ignition and spread is more likely in partly damaged buildings than in completely flattened areas. Perhaps 5 percent of the buildings would be initially ignited, with fire spread to adjoining buildings highly likely if their separation is less than 50 feet [15 m]. Fires will continue to spread for 24 hours at least, ultimately destroying about half the buildings. However, these estimates are extremely uncertain, as they are based on poor data and unknown weather conditions. They are also made on the assumption that no effective effort is made by the uninjured half of the population in this region to prevent the ignition or spread of fires.

9.16 Reagan and Gorbachev on Nuclear Defence, 1980s

In spite of the overall build-up in US military power under his administration, it is the Strategic Defense Initiative (SDI, or Star Wars) which is the best known twist in the arms race during Ronald Reagan's presidency. The first excerpt is from Reagan's 13 July 1985 radio address, in which the president explains the rationale behind SDI (a programme that has yet to be implemented). In the second excerpt, from the 1987 book Perestroika, Soviet leader Mikhail Gorbachev responds to Reagan's Star Wars plans.

A. Reagan on SDI

My fellow Americans:

In a television address to the Nation on March 23, 1983, I challenged the scientific community to change the course of history by embarking on a research effort to counter Soviet threats with measures purely defensive—measures to reassure people their security no longer depends alone on threats of mutual nuclear annihilation to deter a Soviet attack, but measures enabling us to intercept and destroy ballistic missiles before they reach our soil or that of our allies. A nonnuclear strategic defense makes good sense. It's better to protect lives than to avenge them. But another reason, equally simple and compelling, persuades us to its merit. As the Book of Luke says: 'If a strong man shall keep his court well guarded, he shall live in peace.' Well, SDI, our Strategic Defense Initiative, could prove crucial to guarding security and peace for America and her allies.

The strategic challenges we face are far different from those in 1972, when the Unites States and the Soviet Union signed the SALT I and antiballistic missile treaties. When those treaties were signed, certain assumptions about the Soviets were made that—well, to put it charitably—have not proven justified. For example, it was assumed that the treaties would lead to a stable balance and, ultimately, to real reductions in strategic arms. But the Soviet Union had never accepted any meaningful and verifiably reduction in offensive nuclear arms—none. It was assumed the treaties were based on acceptance of parity in offensive weapon systems, but the Soviets have continued to race for superiority. As former Secretary of Defense Harold Brown put it, 'When we build, they build.' It was assumed that the Soviets would accept the innocent notion that being mutually vulnerable to attack was in our common interest. They haven't.

The Soviets have repeatedly condemned as provocative our research on defense against their first-strike missiles, while blanketing their own country with the most sophisticated air defense system ever seen to protect against our second-strike bombers. And while we dismantled our lone ABM system 10 years ago, the Soviets have consistently improved the world's only missile defense system deployed around Moscow. They've also developed and deployed the world's only operational killer satellite system and then proceeded to condemn the United States for daring even to test such a weapon.

It was assumed that an effective defense would not be feasible until 1972. But in that very year, Soviet Marshal Grechko testified to the Supreme Soviet: 'The treaty on limiting ABM systems imposes no limitations on the performance of research and experimental work aimed at resolving the problem of defending the country against nuclear missile attack.' Thus, the Soviets have devoted a huge share of their military budget to a sophisticated strategic defense program which, in resources already allocated, far exceeds what the United States anticipates spending in the current decade.

Finally, it was assumed that the agreements signed would be complied with, but the Soviets are seriously violating them in both offensive and defensive areas. It is the Soviet Union that has violated the 1972 ABM treaty with its construction of a massive radar facility at Krasnoyarsk. Further, the Soviet Union has tested and deployed sophisticated air defense systems which we judge may have capabilities against ballistic missiles.

Given these facts, is it not preposterous for the Soviets, already researching defense technologies for two decades, to now condemn our embryonic SDI program? And as Paul Nitze, one of my chief arms control advisers, pointed out, Soviet hypocrisy is even more glaring when we realize who's taking advantage of our open society to propagandise against our SDI program. A letter to the New

York Times denouncing SDI was signed by the very Soviet scientists who've been developing the Soviet strategic defense program; other Soviet scientists who signed have spent their entire careers developing offensive weapons. I intend to mention this when I meet with Mr. Gorbachev in Geneva this November. I will tell him that the United States not only has the right to go forward with research for a strategic missile defense, but in the light of the scale of their program we'd be the greatest fools on Earth not to do so.

We're going to put our best scientists to work. We're going to cooperate with our allies. We're going to push forward in full compliance with the ABM treaty on a broad-based research program, whose results to date are immensely encouraging. And, yes, I hope we will one day develop a security shield that destroys weapons, not people.

Until next week, thanks for listening. God bless you.

B. Mikhail Gorbachev on the Arms Race, 1987

Pondering the question of what stands in the way of good Soviet–American relations, one arrives at the conclusion that, for the most part, it is the arms race. I am not going to describe its history. Let me just note once again that at almost all its stages the Soviet Union has been the party catching up. By the beginning of the seventies we had reached approximate military-strategic parity, but on a level that is really frightening. Both the Soviet Union and the Unites States now have the capacity to destroy each other many times over.

It would seem logical, in the face of a strategic stalemate, to halt the arms race and get down to disarmament. But the reality is different. Armouries already overflowing continue to be filled with sophisticated new types of weapons, and new areas of military technology are being developed. The US sets the tone in this dangerous, if not fatal pursuit.

I shall not disclose any secret if I tell you that the Soviet Union is doing all that is necessary to maintain up-to-date and reliable defenses. This is our duty to our own people and our allies. At the same time I wish to say quite definitely that this is not our choice. It has been imposed on us.

All kinds of doubts are being spread among Americans about Soviet intentions in the field of disarmament. But history shows that we can keep the word we gave and that we honor the obligations assumed. Unfortunately, this cannot be said of the United States. The administration is conditioning public opinion, intimidating it with a Soviet threat, and does so with particular stubbornness when a new military budget has to be passed through Congress. We have to ask ourselves why all this is being done and what aim the US pursues.

It is crystal clear that in the world we live in, the world of nuclear weapons, any attempt to use them to solve Soviet–American problems would spell suicide. This is a fact. I do not think that US politicians are unaware of it. Moreover, a truly paradoxical situation has now developed. Even if one country engages in a steady arms build up while the other does nothing, the side that arms itself will all the same gain nothing. The weak side may simply explode all its nuclear charges, even on its own territory, and that would mean suicide for it and a slow death for the enemy. This is why any striving for military superiority means chasing one's own tail. It can't be used in real politics.

Nor is the US in any hurry to part with another illusion. I mean its immoral intention to bleed the Soviet Union white economically, to prevent us from carrying out our plans of construction by dragging us even deeper into the quagmire of the arms race.

I ask the reader to take a look at the experience of postwar decades. The Soviet Union emerged from the Second World War in a very difficult condition. Yes, we had won the struggle against fascism, won together with the US and other anti-Hitler coalition participants. But whereas not a single enemy bomb was dropped and not a single enemy shot was heard on the US mainland, a large part of the territory of our country was an arena for the fiercest battles. Our losses— both human and material—were enormous. Nevertheless, we succeeded in restoring what had been destroyed, in building up our economic potential and in confidently tackling our defensive tasks. Is this not a lesson for the future?

It is inadmissible that states should base their policies on mistaken views. We know that there is an opinion current in the US and the West generally that the threat from the Soviet Union comes not because it possesses nuclear weapons. They reason as follows, as I have already mentioned in another connection: the Soviets well know that if they attack the US, they can't escape retaliation. The US is equally aware that retaliation will follow an attack on the USSR. Therefore only a madman would unleash nuclear war. The real threat, according to these people, will arise if the Soviet Union accomplishes its plans of accelerating socio-economic development and shows its new economic and political potential. Hence the desire to exhaust the Soviet Union economically.

We sincerely advise Americans: try to get rid of such an approach to our country. Hopes of using any advantages in technology or advanced equipment so as to gain superiority over our country are futile. To act on the assumption that the Soviet Union is in a 'hopeless position' and that it is necessary just to press it harder to squeeze out everything the US wants is to err profoundly. Nothing will come of these plans. In real politics there can be no wishful thinking. If the Soviet Union, when it was much weaker than now, was in a position to meet all the challenges that it faced, then indeed only a blind person would be unable to see that our capacity to maintain strong defences and simultaneously resolve social and other tasks has enormously increased.

I shall repeat that as far as the United States foreign policy is concerned, it is based on at least two delusions. The first is the belief that the economic system of the Soviet Union is about to crumble and that the USSR will not succeed in restructuring. The second is calculated on Western superiority in equipment and technology and, eventually, in the military field. These illusions nourish a policy geared toward exhausting socialism through the arms race, so as to dictate terms later. Such is the scheme; it is naïve.

Current Western policies aren't responsible enough, and lack the new mode of thinking. I am outspoken about this. If we don't stop now and start practical disarmament, we may all find ourselves on the edge of a precipice. Today, as never before, the Soviet Union and the United States need responsible policies. Both countries have their political, social and economical problems: a vast field for activities. Meanwhile, many brain trusts work at strategic plans and juggle millions of lives. Their recommendations boil down to this: the Soviet Union is the most horrible threat for the United States and the world. I repeat: it is high time this caveman mentality was given up. Of course, many political leaders and diplomats have engaged in just such policies based on just such a mentality for decades. But their time is past. A new outlook is necessary in a nuclear age. The United States and the Soviet Union need it most in their bilateral relations.

We are realists. So we take into consideration the fact that in a foreign policy all countries, even the smallest, have their own interests. It is high time great powers realized that they can no longer reshape the world according to their own patterns. That era has receded or, at least, is receding into the past (...)

Questions

Why did the testing of hydrogen bombs take the arms race to a new level?

What were the main considerations behind 'massive retaliation'?

How confident were the Americans in the mid-1950s that they could win a nuclear war?

Why did Einstein and Russell believe that scientists had a particular role to play in preventing war?

How did the Cold War contribute to the growth of IBM and Akademgorodok?

How did the American and Soviet approaches to science differ in the 1950s?

Why did governments not act earlier to check the spiralling costs of the arms race?

What did President Eisenhower see as the main threat to American democracy to come out of the Cold War?

Why were many military leaders afraid of the consequences of the 'flexible response' strategy?

Why was the Limited Test Ban Treaty signed?

Why did many governments emphasize civil defence during the Cold War?

Why did the Soviet leaders look for a way to reduce military tension in the late 1960s?

Why did President Reagan heavily emphasize missile defence?

Why did Soviet leader Gorbachev see SDI as a threat to global stability?

10

The Integration of Western Europe

The development of Western European integration was undoubtedly one of the most fundamental 'side effects' of the Cold War. The various institutions, treaties, and communities that knit together the basic structure of the post-Cold War European Union represented a basic shift in inter-European relations. Whereas France and Germany, for example, had previously been bitter rivals, they became, starting in the early 1950s, the two countries driving the integration process on. Already in the 1950s the six-nation European Coal and Steel Community (ECSC) of 1951 was transformed into the European Economic Community with the Rome Treaty of 1957. In the early 1970s the EEC expanded its membership to nine (with Great Britain, Ireland, and Denmark joining in), and in the 1980s the EEC became a group of twelve (as Portugal, Spain, and Greece became members). Along the way, European integration was also deepened through such schemes as EURATOM, the introduction of a Common Agricultural Policy, and the gradual withdrawal of all existing tariff barriers between member states. In 1985 the Single European Act (SEA) marked the beginning of another wave of further integration that would, in the post-Cold War years, transform the EEC into the European Union. All in all, the process of West European integration during the Cold War seemed to have succeeded in uniting at least one half of Europe.

Of course, there were numerous hiccups along the way. While economic integration was remarkably successful, political integration suffered from continued national preferences and prejudices. This, in part, explains the inability of West Europeans to agree on a common defence policy; indeed, one of the early failures of European integration was the 1954 demise of the European Defense Community (EDC). In the realm of security, particularly military security, most West Europeans preferred the North Atlantic Treaty Organization and the continued presence of the United States in Western Europe to an independent European defence policy. This became evident also in the 1960s, when the departure of France—a key country in all the various integration schemes—from NATO did not encourage others to follow suit. Similarly, it was the desire to maintain strong links to the United States—a 'Special Relationship'—that made Great Britain a hesitant partner in European integration. Absent from the integration schemes of the 1950s, the British—who established the seven-nation European Free Trade Area (EFTA) as a counterweight to the EEC—eventually paid a price as their membership was twice rejected by French President Charles de Gaulle in the 1960s. De Gaulle cited the Anglo-American connection as the major reason why Britain, in his judgement, was not adequately 'European'.

The American attitude towards European integration itself shifted during the Cold War. While the Truman and Eisenhower administrations were keen supporters of European unity—political, military, and economic—and pressed the British to join the EEC early on, such unequivocal support turned into a profound ambivalence in the 1960s. In part, Americans worried over the apparent French effort to drive a wedge between a resurgent Europe and the United States. The American concern was influenced heavily by the growing economic strength of the EEC that, alongside the emergence of Japan as a major economic power, had the potential of leading to trade wars and increasing the political divergence between the United States and its European partners. Ultimately, Americans worried that an independent Europe would launch an independent détente with the Soviet bloc and that the Soviets would use every opportunity to promote incohesion amongst the Western powers.

This particular concern was closely linked to the German question. After the establishment of the Federal Republic of Germany (FRG) in 1949, Chancellor Konrad Adenauer had practised an uncompromising policy towards the German Democratic Republic (GDR). Under the so-called Hallstein Doctrine, the FRG refused to enter into formal diplomatic relations with any country that recognized the GDR. In the meantime, Adenauer emerged as one of the key spokesmen of European integration in all its forms. The ultimate goal of the two policies was to link the FRG firmly to the West while pushing for the unification of Germany through isolating the GDR. In 1961, however, the erection of the Berlin Wall and the relatively 'tame' American (and other Western) reaction to it, seemed to indicate that the FRG's European and North American partners were not keen to risk an open conflict over Germany and were, in fact, quite satisfied with the continued division. Hence, German policy began to shift towards so-called *Ostpolitik*, an effort to build bridges to the Soviet bloc. The general idea was that the continued division was based mainly on continued Soviet security concerns; should such concerns be minimized while economic, political, and cultural links between the two Germanies grew stronger, unification might one day become possible.

After the election of the Social Democrat Willy Brandt as chancellor in 1969, *Ostpolitik* entered its most active phase. In a span of a few years the FRG concluded numerous treaties with, for example, the USSR, Poland, and the GDR. In the early 1970s Brandt was clearly the foremost Western spokesman of European détente, and his efforts partly paved the way for the signing of the Helsinki Final Act in August 1975. This concluding document of the Conference on Security and Co-Operation in Europe (CSCE) was instantly celebrated and maligned. Some hailed the meeting of thirty-five countries—all European countries save Albania, as well as the United States and Canada—as the agreement that finally ended World War II in Europe and provided the basis for increased East–West exchanges (and recognized human rights as an integral aspect of security). Others called the CSCE's recognition of the inviolability of post-war borders a *de facto* recognition of the legitimacy of the Soviet hold on Eastern Europe. The latter attitude was particularly prevalent in the United States, where détente in general was already under severe attack. Regardless of such debate, the CSCE process marked—in contrast to the rapid fall of Soviet–American détente (see Chapters 15 and 16)—one of the highlights of European détente and symbolized the transformation that was by now under way in East–West relations in Europe.

Throughout this period the American influence in Europe remained substantial. None of the key European powers—France, Great Britain, and Germany—was interested in completely relinquishing its transatlantic links. Even the French stopped short of a complete break with NATO and remained as partners in the organization's political efforts. And while the British continued to play up the 'special relationship' between Washington and London, the FRG was keen to co-ordinate its *Ostpolitik* with the United States. Indeed, in the mid-1970s the United States played a major role in launching a process that would lead towards increased co-ordination amongst the major industrial democracies (the so-called Group of Seven, or G-7). While economic competition sometimes led to worries about EEC (or American) protectionism—as in the case of the Reagan administration's response to the Single European Act of 1986—and while Europeans and Americans often differed in their assessment of the Soviet threat, the essential cohesion of the West remained intact through to the end of the Cold War.

Ultimately, the major developments related to European integration and the German question thus transformed Europe in substantial ways. By almost any measure the story of European integration from the 1950s to the 1980s remains a remarkable success. It transformed one half of the continent that had, in the first half of the twentieth century, been marred by constant strife and violent national ambitions, into a community of nations that, while hardly united in their foreign policies, had effectively managed to eradicate war as a means to political ends. There is no doubt that this development was made all the more remarkable by the successful integration of the western half of Germany into the EEC and the continued, if increasingly ambivalent, American support for European integration. Moreover, as events in the 1990s would show, European integration was to prosper even further after the collapse of the Cold War order in Europe.

Readings

Frank Costigliola, *France and the United States* (1992). The best survey of the post-war Franco-American relationship, with due emphasis on France's role in European integration.

Martin J. Dedman, *The Origins and Development of the European Union* (1996). A brief introduction to the development of European integration.

David Gowland and Arthur Turner, *Reluctant Europeans: Britain and European Integration 1945–1998* (2000). An in-depth look at Britain's turbulent relationship with post-war West European integration.

Geir Lundestad, *'Empire' by Integration: The United States and European Integration, 1945–1997* (1998). A brief introduction to the changing American attitude towards European integration.

Avrill Pittman, *From Ostpolitik to Reunification* (1992). A useful analysis of West German foreign policy from the 1960s to the end of the Cold War.

10.1 Jean Monnet on the Future of Europe, April 1948

The Frenchman Jean Monnet has often, and justifiably, been called one of the founding fathers of European integration. On 18 April 1948, while visiting Washington, Monnet wrote this letter to French Foreign Minister Robert Schuman (another of the 'founding fathers').

(…) I am happy about my journey. After a two years absence, my understanding is more accurate than if I had constantly been in touch with the situation here. Changes appeared to me more clearly and it strengthened my conviction concerning what is exactly the essence of American life. This country is still driven by a dynamic force resulting from the very nature of each individual. America is on the march, but she is not reactionary, nor imperialistic. She does not *want* war, but she will make it if necessary. She is very determined on this point, but this is not a blind determination. I will explain to you the transformation that occurred here within the last weeks: we left preparations for war, we are in the preparations to avoid war—and now, the idea of a possible *détente* is taking shape. In any case the current state of affairs is: firm determination but caution.

(…) But as I said earlier, we have to realize that America is moved by a willingness to *act*—action at home—and also abroad—; for America, at the present time, action means to avoid war, to help Western Europe to recover and to prepare means to stop Russian expansion. To this end, they will make a considerable effort. They perfectly realize that the financial aspect is crucial for them; the

Marshall Plan and the military credits, which are just beginning, will represent a heavy burden; price inflation as well as taxes will increase for sure. Even with the willingness to act, the Congress will only vote the credits after difficult debates. Hoffman will have a hard time next February when he will come to ask the congressmen to vote on the Marshall Plan credits for the second year. He already thinks about it and is preparing for it.

For everyone here, the European effort must correspond to this country's effort—effort on the production side first but also of a different nature. They will help those efforts in many ways and with determination. But we must realize that American policy-makers as well as public opinion expect a lot from us. By thinking that the Marshall credits will go on for a long time should Europe prove unable to develop quickly a greater and more modernized production, we might have to face cruel disappointments.

I cannot help being amazed by the nature of the relationships that are likely to develop between this great country and European countries should they maintain their current form and mentality: to my mind, it is not possible for Europe to remain 'dependent' for long and almost exclusively on American credits for its production and on American power for its security, without bad consequences developing here and in Europe.

All my reflections and all my observations lead me to one conclusion, which is now a deeply rooted conviction: to measure up to the circumstances, to the danger that is threatening us and to the American effort, Western European countries' efforts have to become a true European effort. And only a Western *Federation* is able to achieve this. I know how difficult such a project may be, but I deem that only an effort in this direction will enable us to save ourselves, to remain ourselves and to contribute essentially to avoid war (…)

10.2 Steel and Armies, 1950

On 9 May 1950 French Foreign Minister Robert Schuman made an announcement proposing the pooling together of Western Europe's coal and steel resources. After extended negotiations, the Schuman Plan resulted in the signing of a treaty in Paris the following March that established the European Coal and Steel Community. The ECSC created a common market for coal, steel, coke, iron ore, and scrap between six countries: France, the Federal Republic of Germany, Italy, Belgium, the Netherlands, and Luxembourg. The other major European integration scheme of the early 1950s concerned the proposed plan to establish a common European army as a partial solution to the perceived defence needs in the wake of the Korean War and the concerns of German rearmament shared by many West Europeans. In October 1950 the so-called Pleven Plan (named after French

Prime Minister René Pleven) commenced the negotiations for a European Defence Community (EDC) that was a subject of intense negotiations over subsequent years. Below are excerpts from the Pleven Plan announcement and the ECSC Treaty.

A. The Pleven Plan Announcement, October 1950

The nations which concluded the Atlantic Treaty wished to forge the instrument for that security for the region covered by the Treaty. They have in the last few months achieved unprecedented progress in defining their views on a common defense programme and embarking on the implementation of those views (…)

The associated nations have recognized the need to defend the Atlantic community against any possible aggression, on a line situated as far to the East as possible. They have agreed that all those forces, irrespective of their nationality, should be placed under the command of a single Commander-in-Chief (…)

Germany, which is not a party to the Atlantic Treaty, is nevertheless also destined to enjoy the benefits of the security systems resulting therefrom. It is consequently right that it should make its contribution towards (…) a system of defense for Western Europe. Consequently, before opening discussions on this important problem in the Assembly, the government has decided to take the initiative of making the following declaration (…)

It proposes the creation, for our common defense, of a European Army tied to political institutions of a united Europe (…)

The setting up of a European Army cannot result from a mere grouping together of National Military units, which would in reality only mask a coalition of the old sort. For tasks which are inevitably common ones, only common institutions will do. The army of a united Europe, composed of men coming from different European countries, must, so far as is possible, achieve a complete fusion of the human and material elements which make it up under a single European political and military authority.

A Minister of Defense would be appointed by the participating governments and would be responsible, under conditions to be determined, to those appointing him and to a European Assembly. That assembly might be the Assembly in Strasbourg, or an offshoot thereof, or an assembly composed of specially elected delegates. His powers with respect to the European army would be those of a national minister of defense with respect to the national forces of his own country (…)

The contingents furnished by the participating states would be incorporated in the European economy at the level of the smallest possible Unit.

The money for the European army would be provided by a common budget. The European minister of defense would be responsible for the implementation of existing international obligations and for the negotiation and implementation of new international engagements on the basis of directives received from the council of ministers. The European armament and equipment programs would be decided and carried out under his authority.

That participating states which currently have national forces at their disposal would retain their own authority so far as concerned that part of their existing forces which was not integrated by them into the European army.

Conversely, the European Minister of Defence, might with the authorization of the Council of Ministers, place at the disposal of a participating government a part of its national forces comprised in the European force, for the purpose of meeting requirements other than those of common defense.

The European force placed at the disposal of the unified Atlantic Command would operate in accordance with the obligations assumed in the Atlantic Treaty, both so far as concerns general strategy and so far as concerns organization and equipment.

The European Minister of Defense would be responsible for obtaining from member countries of the European Community the contingents, the equipment, the armaments, and the supplies due from each state to the common army (...)

Finally, the creation of the European army cannot, either in the initial phase or in its ultimate realization, in any way constitute a cause for delay in the implementation of programs envisaged or under way within the Atlantic organization for the establishment of international forces under a unified command. On the contrary, the projected creation of the European Army should facilitate the implementation of the Atlantic programs.

It is on the basis I have just sketched out that the French Government proposes to invite Great Britain and the free countries of continental Europe, should they agree to participate with it in the creation of a European army, to work together on ways of realizing the principles just stated. Those studies would begin in Paris as soon as the coal and steel treaty is signed (...)

B. The European Coal and Steel Community (ECSC) Treaty, March 1951

The European Coal and Steel Community shall have as its task to contribute, in harmony with the general economy of the Member States and through the establishment of a common market as provided in Article 4, to economic expansion, growth of employment and a rising standard of living in the Member States.

The Community shall progressively bring about conditions which will of themselves ensure the most rational distribution of production at the highest possible level of productivity, while safeguarding continuity of employment and taking care not to provoke fundamental and persistent disturbances in the economies of Member States (...)

Article 3
The institutions of the Community shall, within the limits of their respective powers, in the common interest:

a. ensure an orderly supply to the common market, taking into account the needs of third countries;

b. ensure that all comparably placed consumers in the common market have equal access to the sources of production;

c. ensure the establishment of the lowest prices (...)

d. ensure the maintenance of conditions which will encourage undertakings to expand and improve their production potential and to promote a policy of using natural resources rationally and avoiding their unconsidered exhaustion;

e. promote improved working conditions and an improved standard of living for the workers in each of the industries for which it is responsible (...)

f. promote the growth of international trade and ensure that equitable limits are observed in export pricing;

g. promote the orderly expansion and modernization of production, and the improvement of quality (...)

Article 4
The following are recognized as incompatible with the common market for coal and steel and shall accordingly be abolished and prohibited within the Community:

a. import and export duties, or charges having equivalent effect, and quantitative restrictions on the movement of products;

b. measures or practices which discriminate between producers, between purchasers or between consumers (...) and measures or practices which interfere with the purchaser's free choice of supplier;

c. subsidies or aids granted by States, or special charges imposed by States, in any form whatsoever;

d. restrictive practices which tend towards the sharing or exploiting of markets.

10.3 The British Attitude Towards European Integration, 1951

Britain was the key country in Europe that chose to remain outside the ECSC and took a manifestly ambivalent attitude towards European integration in general. At the basis of the British attitude was the continued primacy given to its long-standing Commonwealth ties and its intention to safeguard a 'special relationship' with the United States. In these two documents one of the foremost enthusiasts for integration—West German chancellor Konrad Adenauer—presses his views to the British diplomat Lord Henderson; while a Foreign Office memorandum from December 1951 sums up the British rationale towards European integration.

A. Adenauer and Henderson, March 1951

ADENAUER said that the Federal Republic was continuing to follow its policy of association with the other countries of Western Europe and of support for European integration. The Federal Government had initialed the Schuman Plan and was now engaged in negotiation over the Pleven Plan. He asked whether the British Government still adhered to its intention of considering some form of association with the Schuman Treaty Organisation.

HENDERSON said that, as the Chancellor knew, the policy of H.M.G. [His Majesty's Government] had been to refrain from any intervention in the negotiations preceding the conclusion of the Schuman Treaty, although they had wished for the success of these negotiations and had offered their encouragement to the participating countries (…)

ADENAUER said that it would be greatly appreciated in Germany if Great Britain were to adopt a favourable attitude towards the Schuman Treaty, especially as this would dispel the impression which might otherwise grow up that she was separating herself from the countries subscribing to the Treaty. If such an impression were to develop, this would be extremely prejudical to European unity.

HENDERSON said that the British attitude towards both the Schuman Plan and the Pleven Plan (…) rested on the inability of the United Kingdom to accept the principle of a supra-national authority. This did not mean, however, that Great Britain did not desire the closest possible association between the Western democratic nations, and H.M.G.'s attitude towards particular schemes for European integration should not be interpreted as signifying any deviation from their fundamental aim of European unity (…)

ADENAUER (…) appreciated that H.M.G. was opposed to the idea of supranational authorities (…) It was, however, impossible to conceive of Western Europe without Great Britain. He was, therefore, disquieted by the prospect that developments might take place which tended increasingly towards the integration of Western Europe while the United Kingdom, although benevolently associated with these developments, avoided active association (…) Such a development would be harmful both to Europe and, he thought, to the United Kingdom as well (…) it seemed to him impossible for countries which were striving towards European unity to reject altogether the principle of supra-national authorities (…) He could only repeat that Great Britain was essential to Europe and express the hope that she would also decide to make some sacrifices of principle for the sake of European unity.

HENDERSON pointed out that (…) [t]he conception underlying the North Atlantic Pact, and to which H.M.G. attached cardinal importance, was that Europe was part of the Atlantic Community. It was impossible to think of Europe without thinking of the Atlantic community just as it was impossible to think of the Atlantic community without thinking of Europe. If this conception guided British policy, this did not mean that Great Britain could or would (…) disinterest herself from Europe (…)

ADENAUER emphasized that (…) his concern was that British traditions and ideals should influence schemes for European integration from the outset and that Great Britain should not be excluded from such schemes by having stood aloof from them when they were initiated (…)

B. The British Foreign Office on European Integration, December 1951

The United Kingdom cannot seriously contemplate joining in European integration. Apart from geographical and strategic considerations, Commonwealth ties and the special position of the United Kingdom as the centre of the sterling area, we cannot consider submitting our political and economic system to supranational institutions. Moreover if these institutions did not prove workable, their dissolution would not be serious for the individual countries which would go their separate ways again; it would be another matter for the United Kingdom which would have to break its Commonwealth and sterling area connexions to join them (…) Moreover, although the fact may not be universally recognised, it is not in the true interests of the continent that we should sacrifice our present unattached position which enables us, together with the United States, to give a lead to the free world.

But while it is neither practicable nor desirable for the United Kingdom to join the integration movement, there would seem to be advantage in encouraging the movement without taking part in it. This, in fact, is the policy which the United Kingdom is now following (…)

But while emphasising our support for European integration, we must at the same time take every opportunity to propagate the idea of the Atlantic community and, in particular, to point out that the NATO is not merely a short-term body set up to organise the defence of Western Europe. We should therefore do all we can to further the development of the economic, social and cultural sides of the NATO (…) Thus, by giving encouragement and support to the integration movement on the continent, we shall be in the best position to prevent it becoming exclusively European and to ensure that it develops as part of the Atlantic community.

10.4 Further Co-operation in Europe, June 1955

Following the failure of the EDC in 1954, the Federal Republic of Germany was invited to join NATO (which it did in 1955). Meanwhile, the member states of the ECSC launched further negotiations that would eventually lead to the conclusion of the Rome Treaty of 1957 that established the European Economic Community (that became operational on 1 January 1958). The EURATOM Treaty establishing a common market in nuclear materials (and equal access to uranium stocks) was concluded at the same time. Below are excerpts from the Messina Declaration that launched these negotiations.

The governments of the Federal Republic of Germany, Belgium, France, Italy, Luxembourg and the Netherlands believe (...) that the establishment of a united Europe must be achieved through the development of common institutions, the progressive fusion of national economies, the creation of a common market, and the gradual harmonization of their social policies.

Such an agenda seems indispensable to them if Europe is to preserve the standing which she has in the world, to restore the influence and her prestige, and to improve steadily the living standard of the population.

To these ends, the six ministers have agreed on the following objectives:

1. The growth of trade and the migration of the population require the joint development of the main channels of communication. To this end, a joint study will be undertaken of development plans oriented to establishing a European network of canals, motorways, electric rail lines, and for a standardization of equipment, as well as research for a better coordination of air-transport.

2. Putting more abundant energy at a cheaper price at the disposal of the European economies constitutes a fundamental element of economic progress. That is why all arrangements should be made to develop sufficient exchanges of gas and electric power capable of increasing the profitability of investments and reducing the supply costs. Studies will be undertaken of methods to coordinate development prospects for the production and consumption of energy, and to draw up general guidelines for an overall policy.

3. The development of atomic energy for peaceful purposes will very soon open up the prospect of a new industrial revolution beyond comparison with that of the last hundred years. The signatory states believe they must study the creation of a joint organization to which will be assigned the responsibility and the means to secure the peaceful development of Atomic Energy (...)

The six governments agree that the constitution of a European Common Market free of internal duties and all quantitative restrictions is the goal of their action in the realm of economic policy. They believe that this market should be achieved in stages. The realization of these objectives requires study of the following questions:

(a) The procedure and the pace of the gradual suppression of obstacles to trade in relations between the participating countries, as well as appropriate steps leading to the gradual standardization of tariffs applying to non-member states;

(b) The measures to be taken in order to harmonize the general policy of the participating states in the financial, economic and social fields;

(c) The adoption of practical steps to ensure adequate coordination of the monetary policies of the member-states, in order to allow for the creation and developments of a common market;

(d) A system of escape clauses;

(e) The creation and operation of a currency re-adoption fund;

(f) The gradual introduction of free circulation of labour;

(g) The development of rules assuring the free play of competition within the Common Market, particularly in such a way as to exclude all preferences of a national basis;

(h) The institutional agencies appropriate for the realisation and operating of the common market.

The creation of a European Investment Fund will be studied. This Fund should have as its object the joint development of European economic projects, and especially the development of the less favored regions of the participating states.

As for the social field, the six governments believe it is essential to study the progressive harmonization of regulations now in force in the different states, particularly those relating to the length of the work-day and the payment of additional benefits (overtime work, Sunday and holiday work, the length of vacations and vacation allowances).

The six governments have decided to adopt the following procedure:

1. Conferences will be called to work on the treaties and the conventions dealing with the matters under consideration;

2. The preparation of these reports and treaties will be entrusted to a committee of government representatives, assisted by experts, under the chairmanship of a political personality charged with coordinating the various tasks;

3. The committee will consult with the High Authority of the European Coal and Steel Community, and as well with the general secretariats of the Council of Europe and the European Committee of Transport Ministers, on necessary cooperation;

4. The full report of the committee will be submitted to the Ministers of Foreign Affairs by 1 October 1955 at the latest;

5. The Ministers of Foreign Affairs will meet again before this date in order to review the interim reports prepared by the committee and to give it any necessary instructions;

6. The government of the United Kingdom (…) will be invited to take part in these sessions (…)

10.5 Dulles on European Integration and the Atlantic Community, 1955–1956

In the 1950s the United States remained a firm supporter of European integration and did not hide its disappointment with the failure of, for example, the EDC in 1954. The Eisenhower administration (1953–61) was keen to emphasize that close transatlantic links and European integration were complementary, and did not hide its annoyance at what it considered an obstinate British attitude towards further integration. In these two documents Secretary of State John Foster Dulles expresses his thoughts on the links between European integration and the Atlantic community.

A. Dulles to British Foreign Secretary Harold Macmillan on European integration, December 1955

At present, there are two trends discernible in Europe, both directed toward goals of increased unity. One is the six-nation approach which has had one signal success in the Coal and Steel Community and one signal defeat in the European Defence Community. This, as we know, is essentially a supranational approach. The other is the OEEC approach, a co-operative effort which has accomplished much in reconciling conflicting national interests. The United States Government has enthusiastically supported both of these concepts. In my opinion, they seek to accomplish different but not conflicting purposes. As we look toward the future it seems to me that the closer community of interests that Europe can build, the more hope Europe will have of realizing its potential for security, prosperity and influence in world affairs. To my mind, the six-nation grouping approach gives the best hope of achieving this end because of the closer unity which is inherent in that Community and because of the contribution which it will make to the strength and cohesion of the wider European grouping. It may well be that a six-nation community will evolve protectionist tendencies. It may be that it will show a trend toward greater independence. In the long-run, however, I cannot but feel that the resultant increased unity would bring in its wake greater responsibility and devotion to the common welfare of Western Europe.

It is for these reasons (…) that the President and I have been anxious to encourage in every appropriate way the current revival of initiative by the six nations in their search for new forms of integration in the fields of nuclear and conventional energy, a common market and transportation. We hope that progress will be swift, but we should be satisfied if there is sustained and real advance toward the practical idea inherent in the supranational principle (…) Perhaps we could arrange for further discussions (…) with a view toward assuring that, despite any differences of emphasis between us, we do not give conflicting advice to the Continental Europeans with respect to movement toward closer unity.

B. Dulles to NATO representatives on the Atlantic Community, May 1956

Analysis of what has so far been said indicates that the task of the Atlantic Community is three fold.

1. We must achieve and maintain a military posture which will deter armed aggression and which will prevent the Soviet Union from gaining such a relatively strong military position that it could employ threats of violence to extract from the free nations such concessions as would in effect make them subject to Soviet will.
2. We must create such strong bonds of unity as between the members of the Atlantic community that they will not fall out among themselves, or follow divergent policies vis-à-vis the accepted source of danger, that is the Soviet–Chinese Communist world. Either would enable the Communist leaders to play one of the free world nations against another. Moreover, members of the Atlantic community should seek to find the ways to strengthen and broaden the base of their own economies so that they will be better able to meet the expanding needs and aspirations of their own peoples.
3. We must maintain such economic relations with the newly developing countries of the world that they will see that they can in freedom achieve their legitimate aspirations (…)

I think it can fairly be said that of these three tasks only one is adequately organized—that is the first. The North Atlantic Treaty Organization provides an effective mechanism for assuring the strength of the Atlantic community (…)

The Atlantic community is not yet adequately organized to maintain union between its members and to ensure harmony of policy of its members toward the Soviet–Chinese Communist bloc. There are a whole series of organizations designed to promote such unity. One is NATO itself. There is the Brussels Treaty for Western European Union. There is the Council of Europe. There is the Coal and Steel Community. There is the OEEC and EPU [European Pagments Union]. These represent important unifying efforts, but it cannot be confidently affirmed that these organizations are clearly adequate to ensure against a tragic repetition of the past where the Atlantic community, and particularly Western Europe, has been torn apart by internecine struggles (...) nor has Europe yet achieved adequate institutions to ensure the freedom of commerce and the wide markets essential for economic vitality and growth (...)

The search for unity in the Atlantic community has two aspects. First we should extend, deepen and regularize the habit of consultation which has been developing (...) Secondly, the Atlantic community should constantly strive to develop the possibilities for greater unity as between its component parts (...) There are degrees of unity which can be practically and usefully achieved by a few but which cannot be similarly achieved by many. This particularly applies to unities along functional and geographical lines (...)

Naturally, policies in relation to economics are part of the overall policies as to which there might be consultation (...) but this is very different from funneling aid through NATO or making it an economic planning body (...)

The free nations have had what has not been called, but which in retrospect we might well call, a 'first postwar ten-year plan'. It is time to be thinking in terms of a 'second-year plan' which will solidify freedom and enable the free peoples so to use their vast moral and material resources that their conduct and example will exert an attracting influence throughout the world.

10.6 American Views of Britain's EEC Membership, March 1961

Great Britain had chosen to remain outside the EEC and had instead proposed the establishment of a Free Trade Area comprising all West European countries. The EEC 'six', however, refused this proposal. As a result, the British government negotiated a separate European Free Trade Area (EFTA) agreement with six other non-EEC countries (Austria, Denmark, Norway, Portugal, Sweden, and Switzerland) that became operational in 1960. Doubts about the wisdom of British policy were widespread and prompted the United States to put further pressure on the Macmillan government in London. In this document Under-Secretary of State George Ball summarizes the American view of Britain and European integration in a meeting with Edward Heath (Lord Privy Seal) and Sir Frank Lee (Joint Permanent Secretary to the Treasury) on 30 March 1961.

Mr. Ball said that the United States deeply regretted that the United Kingdom had not yet felt able to accept the Rome Treaty commitments. They had a great admiration for the United Kingdom's political genius and qualities of leadership. British membership of the Community would represent a contribution of great importance to the cohesion of the Free World. In 1958 the United States had feared that the free trade area proposals might dilute and weaken the political integration of the Six, while at the same time increasing trade discrimination against the United States. The Lord Privy Seal had suggested that there had been a considerable evolution of United Kingdom policy. The United States certainly hoped that, within a wider O.E.C.D. [Organisation for Economic Cooperation and Development] framework, an arrangement might be made whereby the United Kingdom came much closer to joining the E.E.C. than had hitherto been contemplated (…)

Mr. Ball said that, from what they knew of United Kingdom thinking generally and from what the Lord Privy Seal had said, he did not think that the kind of solution at present envisaged by H.M.G. would be satisfactory to the United States. He hoped, however, that United Kingdom thinking would continue to evolve and that there might be further discussions of all these problems in the O.E.C.D., or in some other forum where the United States could be represented. He wished to repeat that the American Administration were fully persuaded that it was a misfortune that the United Kingdom was outside the Community.

Sir F. Lee said that he would be grateful for any further indications as to the direction in which the United States would like to see United Kingdom policy evolve. Was Mr. Ball suggesting that the United Kingdom should join the E.E.C.? Sir F. Lee did not see how this could be done unless the United Kingdom were to be given some derogations from the Rome Treaty. If this were not the case the effects on the Commonwealth would be too divisive; moreover the United Kingdom would not favour a solution which would involve placing a tariff on imports of American wheat, as would be the case if they accepted the common tariff without derogations.

Mr. Ball said that the United States would certainly like to see the United Kingdom join E.E.C. They recognised that the United Kingdom had special problems with regard to agriculture and the Commonwealth and that there might have to be derogations. These would have to be considered on their merits (…)

Summing up the United States position, he [Ball] said that the concept of a United Kingdom association with E.E.C. was very difficult for them: it would enable the United Kingdom to benefit from the commercial aspects of the Rome Treaty while at the same time eroding the political content of the Community. On the other hand the United States would applaud British membership of the

Community, which they would regard as a great contribution to the cohesion of the Free World.

10.7 The Berlin Wall, 1961–1963

In August 1961, while the future of European integration was being debated, the East German government began the construction of the Berlin Wall. Almost three years earlier, Soviet leader Nikita S. Khrushchev had provoked an international crisis by giving Western powers an ultimatum: negotiate a final settlement of the German question with the Soviets, or Moscow would sign a separate peace treaty with the GDR, threatening Western occupation rights in (and access to) Berlin. While not so concerned over the West German military threat, Khrushchev had come under increasing pressure to stop the flow of talented East Germans to the West via Berlin, and had committed himself to the preservation of a socialist GDR. Thus the wall was essentially constructed to stop a potential disintegration of the East German state. In the first document—taken from a 3–5 August 1961 meeting of the Warsaw Pact leaders in Moscow—Khrushchev anticipates significant action on the Berlin – East German issue. Subsequent extracts are from the official exchange of notes between the United States and the Soviet Union a few days after the East German government began closing off the access routes between East and West Berlin. The last extract is from the most famous American statement on the Berlin Wall, issued by President John F. Kennedy during his visit to Berlin in June 1963.

A. Khrushchev, 4 August 1961

(…) We have to help the GDR out (…) Everybody is guilty, and the GDR too. We let down our guard somewhat. Sixteen years passed and we did not alleviate pressures on the GDR (…) What will it mean, if the GDR is liquidated? It will mean that the Bundeswehr [West German armed forces] will move to the Polish border (…) to the borders with Czechoslovakia, (…) closer to our Soviet border (…) If we level it [the GDR's living standard] down to our own, the result will be that the government and the party of the GDR will fall, consequently Adenauer will step in (…)

I wish we could lick imperialism! You can imagine what satisfaction we'll get when we sign the peace treaty. Of course we're running a risk. But it is indispensable. Lenin took such a risk, when he said in 1917 that there was such a party that could seize power. Everybody just smirked and snorted then (…) World public opinion now is on our side not only in the neutral countries, but in America and in England.

(…) Summing up, our Central Committee and government believe that now preparations are proceeding better, but there will be a thaw, and, more importantly, a cooling down (…) We have to work out our tactics now and perhaps it is already the right time.

B. Exchange of Notes on the Berlin Wall, August 17 1961

United States Note:

(…) The United States Government considers that the measures which the East German authorities have taken are illegal. It reiterates that it does not accept the pretension that the Soviet sector of Berlin forms a part of the so-called 'German Democratic Republic' and that Berlin is situated on its territory. Such a pretension is in itself a violation of the solemnly pledged word of the USSR in the Agreement on the Zones of Occupation in Germany and the administration of Greater Berlin. Moreover, the United States Government cannot admit the right of the East German authorities to authorize their armed forces to enter the Soviet sector of Berlin.

By the very admission of the East German authorities, the measures (…) are motivated by the fact that an ever increasing number of inhabitants of East Germany wish to leave this territory. The reasons for this exodus are known. They are simply the internal difficulties in East Germany.

(…) The United States Government expects the Soviet Government to put an end to these illegal measures. This unilateral infringement of the quadripartite status of Berlin can only increase existing tension and dangers.

Soviet Reply

The Soviet Government fully understands and supports the actions of the Government of the German Democratic Republic (…)

West Berlin has been transformed into a center of subversive activity diversion, and espionage, into a center of political and economic provocations against the G.D.R., the Soviet Union, and other socialist countries. Former and present West Berlin municipal leaders have cynically called West Berlin an 'arrow in the living body of the German Democratic Republic,' a 'front city,' a 'violator of tranquillity,' the 'cheapest atom bomb put in the center of a socialist state.' (…)

The Government of the U.S.A. should be well informed on the fact that, with the collaboration of the occupation forces, the ruling circles of the F.R.G. have turned West Berlin into the principal base of uninterrupted economic diversions against the G.D.R (…) The Government organs and concerns of the F.R.G. led from West Berlin an entire army of recruiters who, by means of deception, bribery, and blackmail, instigated a certain part of the residents of the G.D.R. to migrate to West Germany. There, these people were compelled to enter into service in the Bundeswehr and to work in the war-production industry; they were drawn into various subversive organizations (…)

The G.D.R. has displayed, over the course of many years, great tolerance in the face of such a completely disgraceful and impermissible situation. Implementing its consistently peace-loving and democratic policy, it has borne enormous sacrifices to facilitate the achievement of agreement between the two German states on the questions of peaceful settlement and reunification of Germany on peace-loving and democratic foundations (...)

(...) measures taken by the Government of the G.D.R. are temporary. The Soviet Government repeatedly has emphasized that the conclusion of a peace treaty with Germany and normalization on such a basis of the situation in West Berlin will not infringe the interests of any of the parties and will contribute to the cause of peace and security of all peoples.

C. Kennedy on the Significance of Berlin, June 1963

There are many people in the world who really don't understand, or say they don't, what is the great issue between the Free World and the Communist world. Let them come to Berlin. There are some who say that Communism is the wave of the future. Let them come to Berlin. And there are some who say in Europe and elsewhere we can work with the Communists. Let them come to Berlin. And there are even a few who say that it's true that Communism is an evil system, but it permits us to make economic progress. 'Laßt sie nach Berlin kommen.' Let them come to Berlin! Freedom has many difficulties and democracy is not perfect, but we have never had to put a wall up to keep our people in, to prevent them from leaving us. I want to say, on behalf of my countrymen, who live many miles away on the other side of the Atlantic, who are far distant from you, that they take the greatest pride that they have been able to share with you, even from a distance, the story of the last eighteen years. I know of no town, no city, that has been besieged for eighteen years that still lives with the vitality and the force and the hope and the determination of the city of West Berlin.

While the wall is the most obvious and vivid demonstration of the failures of the Communist system, for all the world to see, we take no satisfaction in it. For it is, as your Mayor has said, an offense not only against history but an offense against humanity, separating families, dividing husbands and wives and brothers and sisters, and dividing a people who wish to be joined together.

What is true of this city is true of Germany—real, lasting peace in Europe can never be assured as long as one German out of four is denied the elementary right of free men, and that is to make a free choice. In eighteen years of peace and good faith, this generation of Germans has earned the right to be free, including the right to unite their families and their nation in lasting peace, with goodwill to all people. You live in a defended island of freedom, but your life is part of the main. So let me ask you, as I close, to lift your eyes beyond the dangers of today to the hopes of tomorrow, beyond the freedom merely of this city of Berlin, or your country of Germany, to the advance of freedom everywhere, beyond the wall to the day of peace with justice, beyond yourselves and ourselves to all mankind.

Freedom is indivisible, and when one man is enslaved, all are not free. When all are free, then we can look forward to that day when this city will be joined as one, and this country, and this great Continent of Europe, in a peaceful and hopeful globe. When that day finally comes, as it will, the people of West Berlin can take sober satisfaction in the fact that they were in the front lines for almost two decades.

All free men, wherever they may live, are citizens of Berlin, and, therefore, as a free man, I take pride in the words 'Ich bin ein Berliner.'

10.8 Macmillan and De Gaulle on Britain's EEC Membership, June 1962

In the early 1960s the Macmillan government decided to apply for membership in the European Economic Community (EEC). In subsequent talks the major obstacle to British membership came from the French government. Below, French president Charles de Gaulle and Prime Minister Macmillan spar over the 'readiness' of the UK to joing the Community during their talks at Chateau de Champs in early June 1962. Six months later, on 14 January 1963, de Gaulle publicly rejected Britain's membership application.

THE PRIME MINISTER (…) would like to deal with some of the questions about the British application to join the Community (…) The first point was to make clear that the United Kingdom was negotiating in good faith and that when the British Government said that they fully and willingly accepted the Treaty of Rome they were speaking in good faith. In particular they accepted the common tariff and the common commercial and agricultural policies. This meant that the United Kingdom accepted that there would have to be a change in the agricultural system in Britain (…) The second point which President de Gaulle had raised had been the degree to which Britain was in a mood to join Europe. Here Macmillan was convinced that Britain was ready for the change on the political plane. The younger generation felt much more European than the older people who had been brought up in the days of Kipling with the idea that their work in the world lay inside the British Empire (…)

PRESIDENT DE GAULLE said that the Six were in a strong position. He felt the same about his own country. He believed that it was necessary to make a political union. He agreed that the main motive in forming the Common Market had been a political one. Economic means had been used for political ends. A political federation which involved the suppression of ancient states was not a practical possibility (…) So the only way of proceeding was by organised co-operation between Governments (…) With France and Germany and even Italy it should be possible to create an organisation which would have real political co-operation. This was necessary in the first place because of the present menace from Soviet Russia. But now that Europe had recovered her strength since the war it was also desirable that she should be organised in such a way as to be independent of the United States. Of course the alliance with the United States was extremely important both for Europe and for America, indeed for the whole Free World. But since the war the Continental States had been no more than satellites of the United States. This was a situation which could not continue (…) but Britain was not quite in the same position as the Continental countries: she was not quite so menaced by the Russians. It was perhaps true that the Channel was not much of a protection but it made a psychological difference to the people of Britain. Then again Britain was much more open to world influences than Europe and saw things differently from people on the Continent. Finally there was Britain's liaison with the United States (…) Of course Britain would bring considerable economic, political and military strength and would make of the Community a larger reality but it would also change everything. That was why France had to look at this matter carefully. Probably France could now make a common policy with the Germany of Adenauer but could Britain carry out exactly the same German policy as France and Germany? Was it possible for Britain to adopt a genuinely European approach?

THE PRIME MINISTER thanked President de Gaulle for his frankness. Happily good relations with Germany had now been re-established and the present danger came from the Russians. The problem was how to deal with them (…) If Britain was left outside the Community she would pursue some policy or other; this might or might not be to the liking of the Six but it would in any case be an independent policy. This would give great opportunities to the Russians for driving wedges between the different allies. If there was a close European union, closely knit, this would not happen. Not only would this be better as regards the Russians but it would also be a good thing as regards the Americans (…)

PRESIDENT DE GAULLE said that he was an old Frenchman. It was hard for him to make arrangements with Germany and even with Italy but in the face of the Russians it was necessary, and in addition it was essential to make an organisation which would be independent of the United States and not just an American satellite (…)

If only the United States and the Soviet Union were truly independent then only two things could happen. Either there would be a war and everybody would be killed or else the two super Powers would make an agreement between themselves for a condominium which should not suit the European countries. That was why France believed that she should be allied to the United States but should not be a negligible quantity. This was particularly the case because of the cardinal importance for France of Germany. If Germany went Communist or was even merely neutralized France would be in an impossible position and would become a pawn either of Russia or of the United States (...) If America alone faced the Russians then one day they might give up Germany as a way of making an arrangement with the Russians (...) So a strong and indpendent Europe was necessary, from the point of view of defence, in dealing with the German question (...) Up to now the Germans had wanted to believe in American protection but they were now a little less convinced of the certainty of this (...)

THE PRIME MINISTER said that (...) the Germans would probably ask the same questions as the French were now asking. Unless they felt secure they might one day choose neutrality or be tempted by a Russian offer of East Germany.

PRESIDENT DE GAULLE said that he did not think that the Russians would make such an offer but they might propose a détente and offer the Germans economic possibilities.

THE PRIME MINISTER (...) [asked] Did President de Gaulle think that there would be a détente with Russia one day?

PRESIDENT DE GAULLE said that he did believe this but a détente could only be made by Europe, because it would involve the Russians becoming Europeans (...)

10.9 Britain's Second EEC Application, 1967

In a repeat performance, de Gaulle yet again vetoed Britain's membership in 1967. Yet, as the first document indicates, the Wilson government was gathering increasing support for Britain's membership from the Federal Republic of Germany's foreign minister—and future chancellor—Willy Brandt. The second document is an extract from de Gaulle's so-called 'velvet veto' of May 1967.

A. Sir Frank Roberts on Brandt's Views of British Membership in the EEC, 12 January 1967

[I] saw Brandt and explained British concern. This concern related not to the basic German attitude which we knew favoured British entry, but to possible misinterpretations in Paris. While history never exactly repeats itself, there were certain similarities between the position at the end of 1962 when the Franco-German Treaty had been signed and that today, when another major effort to improve Franco-German relations, which we welcomed in itself, was being made. I was sure that the Federal Government would not have forgotten that the F-G treaty was succeeded almost immediately by the French veto in Brussels, and that they would therefore take every precaution in Paris this week to prevent General de Gaulle drawing conclusions which could lead again to a similar result.

Brandt took this well and said that he understood our concern. He [also] volunteered that he knew we had been disappointed by line he took in Rome. He wanted to assure you, that this related only to the specific issue raised by Nenni, i.e. that the Five should be prepared to go so far as to substitute Britain for France as their partner. This was not possible and this was also the position of the Italian government, whatever Nenni might have said. This did not mean that Germany preferred France to Britain, but rather that there was no scope for such action within the framework of the Treaty of Rome. For Germany relations with London were as important as those with Paris, and, without forgetting the smaller countries, the future of Western Europe depended upon the closest possible cooperation between Paris, London, Bonn and also Rome.

[He] assured me that neither Kiesinger nor he would forget the position the German government has adopted on British membership. This was not after all purely a sentimental question of friendship between two countries, although this was important, but it was a vital German national interest to widen the EEC and for this Britain was the key. He needed not remind me that the favourable German trade balance was based upon EFTA. His impression was that General de Gaulle preferred his partners to speak clearly and firmly about their national interest and the Germans would do so in Paris.

Looked forward to his talks with you. He hoped that we would be able to simplify our position as much as possible (…) This would he hoped enable us all to confront General de Gaulle with a position where it would be extremely difficult if not impossible for him to repeat his veto of 1963.

Brandt's whole attitude was thoroughly sensible and responsible and conveyed considerable reassurance.

B. Charles de Gaulle's 'Velvet Veto', May 1967

(…) the Common Market is a sort of prodigy. To introduce into it now new and massive elements (…) would obviously jeopardize the whole and the details and to raise the problem of an entirely different undertaking. All the more that if the Six have been able to build this famous edifice it is because it concerned a group of continental countries, immediate neighbors to each other, doubtless offering differences of size, but complementary in their economic structure. Moreover, the Six form through their territory a compact geographic and strategic unit. It must be added that despite, perhaps because of their great battles of the past—I am naturally speaking of France and Germany—they now find themselves

inclined to support one another mutually rather than to oppose one another
(…)

Compared with the motives that led the Six to organize their unit, we understand (…) why Britain—who is not continental, who remains, because of the
Commonwealth and because she is an island, committed far beyond the seas, who
is tied to the United States by all kinds of special agreements—did not merge into
a Community with set dimensions and strict rules. While this Community was
taking shape, Britain therefore first refused to participate in it and even took
toward it a hostile attitude as if she saw in it an economic and political threat.
Then she tried to negotiate in order to join the Community, but in such conditions that the latter would have been suffocated by this membership (…) the
British Government then asserted that it no longer wanted to enter the Community and set about strengthening its ties with the Commonwealth and with other
European countries grouped around it in a free-trade area. Yet, apparently now
adopting a new state of mind, Britain declares she is ready to subscribe to the
Rome Treaty, even though she is asking exceptional and prolonged delays and, as
regards her, that basic changes be made in the Treaty's implementation (…)

Considering the special relations that tie the British to America, with the
advantage and also the dependence that results from them; considering the existence of the Commonwealth and their preferential relations with it; considering
the special commitment that they still have in various parts of the world and
which, basically, distinguishes them from the continentals, we see that the policy
of the latter, as soon as they have one, would undoubtedly concur, in certain cases,
with the policy of the former. But we cannot see how both policies could merge,
unless the British assumed again, particularly as regards defense, complete command of themselves, or else if the continentals renounced forever a European
Europe (…)

In truth, it really seems that the change in the situation of the British in relation to the Six, once we would be ready by common consent to proceed with it,
might consist of a choice between three issues.

Either recognize that, as things stand at present, their entry into the Common
Market, with all the exceptions that it would not fail to be accompanied by (…)
would amount to necessitating the building of an entirely new edifice, scrapping
nearly all of that which has just been built. What, then, would we end up with if
not, perhaps, the creation of a free-trade area of Western Europe, pending that of
the Atlantic area, which would deprive our continent of any real personality?

Or, establish, between the Community on the one band, and Britain and some
States of the 'little' free-trade area on the other, a system of association, such as
the one provided for in the Treaty of Rome and which could, without creating an
upheaval, multiply and facilitate the economic relations between the contracting
parties.

11. Charles de Gaulle: 'Very well, Pompidou, put it with the other begging letters.' (Emmwood, *Daily Mail*, 12 May 1967). Reprinted by permission. Photo supplied by The Centre for the Study of Cartoons and Caricature, University of Kent.

Or else, lastly, before changing what exists, wait until a certain internal and external evolution, of which Great Britain seems already to be showing signs, is eventually completed, that is to say, until that great people which is endowed with tremendous ability and courage has itself accomplished first and for its part the necessary profound economic and political transformation so that it can join with the Six continental countries. I really believe that this is the desire of many people, who are anxious to see the emergence of a Europe corresponding to its natural dimensions and who have great admiration and true friendship for Britain. If, one day, she were to come to this point, how warmly France would welcome this historic conversion.

10.10 Willy Brandt and Henry Kissinger on West German *Ostpolitik*

The ascendancy of the Social Democrat Willy Brandt to the West German chancellorship after the September 1969 elections meant the final fruition of Ostpolitik, *the German policy of building bridges to the Soviet Union and Eastern Europe (including East Germany). While the ultimate goal of* Ostpolitik *was German unification, its imme-diate results produced various agreements between the FRG and the Soviet Union, Poland (on post-war borders), and, most dramatically, with the GDR. As the Brandt government moved to build links to the Soviet bloc, the Nixon administration in the United States worried over the broader implications of* Ostpolitik. *Below, Brandt explains the rationale of* Ostpolitik *to the West German Bundestag, while Henry Kissinger speculates over its impact.*

A. Brandt at the Bundestag on *Ostpolitik*, October 1969

This Government works on the assumption that the questions which have arisen for the German people out of the Second World War and from the national treachery committed by the Hitler regime can find their ultimate answer only in a European peace arrangement. However, no one can dissuade us from our conviction that the Germans have a right to self-determination just as has any other nation.

The object of our political work in the years ahead is to preserve the unity of the nation by deconcentrating the relationship between the two parts of Germany (...) we still have common tasks and a common responsibility: to ensure peace among us and in Europe.

Twenty years after the establishment of the Federal Republic of Germany and of the GDR we must prevent any further alienation of the two parts of the German nation, that is, arrive at a regular modus vivendi and from there proceed to cooperation.

This is not just a German interest, for it is of importance also for peace in Europe and for East–West relations (...) The Federal Government (...) again offers the Council of Ministers of the GDR negotiations at government level without discrimination on either side, which should lead to contractually agreed cooperation. International recognition of the GDR by the Federal Republic is out of the question. Even if there exists two States in Germany, they are not foreign countries to each other: their relations with each other can only be of special nature.

(...) the Federal Government declares that its readiness for binding agreements on the reciprocal renunciation of the use or threat of force applies equally with regard to the GDR (...) will advise the United States, Great Britain, and France to continue energetically the talks begun with the Soviet Union on easing and improving the situation of Berlin (...) West Berlin must be placed in a position to assist in improving the political, economic and cultural relations between the two parts of Germany.

We welcome the renewed increase of intra-German trade (...)

The German people needs peace in the full sense of that word also with the peoples of the Soviet Union and all peoples of the European East. We are prepared to make an honest attempt at understanding, in order to help overcome the aftermath of the disaster brought on Europe by a criminal clique (...)

We are not deluding ourselves to believe that reconciliation will be easy or quick to achieve. It is a process; but it is time now to push ahead that process (...)

B. Kissinger to Nixon on *Ostpolitik*, February 1970

The German Chancellor has stated the goals of his 'Ostpolitik' in rather sober and realistic terms: he wants to normalize relations with the Communist countries and move from 'confrontation to co-operation;' he is prepared in this context to accept the GDR as a separate state and to accommodate the Poles, within certain limits, on the question of the Oder–Neisse Line. He hopes in this way to reduce the antagonism toward West Germany in the USSR and Eastern Europe and to make the division of Germany less severe. He rejects the idea that Germany should be free-floating between East and West and he remains strongly committed to NATO and West European integration. Indeed he believes his Eastern policy can be successful only if Germany is firmly anchored in the West. He has in effect renounced formal reunification as the aim of German policy but hopes over the long run to achieve special ties between the two German states (…) Although Brandt has stressed that his Western policy has priority, German attention is currently heavily focussed on the East (…)

Much of the opposition within Germany and the concern among its allies stems not so much from the broad purposes which Brandt wants to achieve but from suspicions or fear that Eastern policy is acquiring its own momentum and will lead Brandt into dangerous concessions (…) Much of the worry (…) focusses on the danger that as Brandt pursues the quest for normalization, his advisors and supporters will eventually succeed in leading him to jeopardize Germany's entire international position. This fear has already embittered domestic debate in Germany and could in time produce the type of emotional and doctrinaire political argument that has paralyzed political life in Germany and some other West European countries in the past. It is this possibility that we must obviously be troubled about ourselves (…)

The most worrisome aspects of Ostpolitik are long-range (…) assuming that Brandt achieves a degree of normalization, he or his successor may discover before long that the hoped-for benefits fail to develop. Instead of ameliorating the division of Germany, recognition of the GDR may boost its status and strengthen the Communist regime (…) More fundamentally (…) the Soviets having achieved their first set of objectives may then confront the FRG with the proposition that a real and lasting improvement in the FRG's relations with the GDR and other Eastern countries can only be achieved if Bonn loosens its Western ties (…)

It should be stressed that men like Brandt, Wehner and Defense Minister Schmidt undoubtedly see themselves as conducting responsible policy of reconciliation with the East and intend not to have this policy come into conflict with Germany's Western association (…) their problem is to control a process which, if it results in failure could jeopardize their political lives and if it succeeds could create a momentum that may shake Germany's domestic stability and unhinge its international position.

10.11 President Pompidou Approves British Entry to the EEC, May 1971

Great Britain—along with Denmark and Ireland—finally entered the EEC in 1973. This outcome was no doubt made possible by the retirement of Charles de Gaulle in 1969, that enabled the Conservative prime minister Edward Heath to come to an agreement with the new French president Pompidou at a Franco-British summit held in Paris on 20–1 May 1971. The following extract is Pompidou's concluding statement to the press.

For two days you have been very patient. We have been working very hard. We have been talking for well-nigh 12 hours and all subjects have been broached and studied in depth. Since the start of the negotiations the position of France has always been that it is for the Community that we are negotiating. That is why we have not solved all questions and were not qualified to settle them. But of course you would not believe me if I said we had not discussed all things. We have. We have compared our views. We have considered the economies of each government in determining our position. It would be unreasonable now to believe that an agreement is not possible during the conference in Brussels in June.

The spirit of our talks over the past two days enables me to think the negotiations will be successful (...)

On a certain number of major problems, we have concluded that our views were similar and even identical. On some others we have also been in a position to note that there were still different views but they do not present any obstacle to our cooperation in view of the full identity of our views as to the main aim (...)

There were many people who believed that Great Britain was not European and did not wish to become European, and that Britain wanted to enter into the Community only to destroy it. Many people also thought France was prepared to use all kinds of means and pretexts to propose a new veto to the entry of Great Britain into the Community. Well, ladies and gentlemen, you see tonight before you two men who are convinced to the contrary.

10.12 The British Ambassador on the Soviet Union and Europe, September 1975

On 1 August 1975 thirty-five countries signed the Helsinki Accords, a massive document that was the final outcome of the early CSCE (Conference on Security and Co-Operation in Europe) process. In the extract below, the British ambassador in Moscow, T. Garvey, sums up his views on 9 September 1975 to the prime minster of the meaning of the CSCE. Garvey pays particular attention to the Soviet interpretation.

1. The Conference on Security and Cooperation in Europe (CSCE) has been claimed by the Russians as a great diplomatic success and a major landmark in post-war history. This satisfaction is not surprising. The Russians had been calling for 20 years for a conference on security, and its achievement was one of the most important of the 'six concrete tasks' in the 'peace policy' adopted by the 24th Congress of the CPSU in 1971.

2. 'Security in Europe' has meant for the Soviet Government the consolidation and perpetuation of the new territorial and political order in Eastern Europe established by Soviet arms, diplomacy and skulduggery in the years following 1944 (…) For them, the key importance of the Final Act of Helsinki lies in the multilateral acceptance of frontiers and of the political *status quo* (…)

3. Nevertheless, the document signed on 1 August is greatly different from the straight security proposal put forward by Molotov in 1954 and from the Prague Declaration of Warsaw Pact Foreign Ministers in 1969, which added to discussion of security the second conference agenda point of expansion of commercial, economic and scientific ties. Having campaigned for many years for a conference, the Russians got one but without the Peace Treaty they really wanted and in return for a double price. One instalment of the price was agreement to start the Vienna negotiations on mutual reduction of forces in Central Europe. The other was the widening of the CSCE agenda, proposed by NATO in May 1970, to include many questions of human contacts and the flow of information which the USSR found potentially dangerous and had previously insisted on regarding as nobody's business but its own.

4. (…) the Russians (…) will see these gains:

(a) They have got the multilateral endorsement, which they wanted, of the post-war *status quo* in Europe, and will claim, whatever the documents say, not to have abandoned their right, under the special type of relations existing between Socialist States, to intervene if necessary in Eastern Europe under the so-called Brezhnev doctrine (…)

(b) The Soviet Union has gained international status, and a success useful in internal propaganda (…)

(c) The principles in Basket I of CSCE, being above all about peaceful behaviour, should help to spread an impression in the West that the Soviet Union presents no threat to security or peace (…)

(d) The Russians have secured, in the Final Act, a quarry of texts to use against those whom they class as 'enemies of *détente*' in the West, which means the people who express public scepticism of Soviet objectives.

(e) The Helsinki document may provide a basis from which to give new impetus to the Soviet attack on the division of Europe, caused as they claim by NATO in the political and military fields and the European Community in the economic field. We shall hear more about the benefits of all-European security and all-European co-operation: on the former there may be suggestions of a binding European security system, and, on the latter, ideas for Europe-wide collaboration in energy and other fields.

(f) Although persuaded to negotiate about MBFR [Mutual Balanced Force Reductions], the Russians have retained after CSCE their freedom to resist in the Vienna talks any agreement which would diminish their considerable superiority in conventional weapons (…)

5. The Russians ran some risks in engaging in CSCE. One or more of the East European delegations might have got off the lead, but they managed very largely to prevent this. In the Final Act itself some blemishes mar the Basket I principles, notably the Western flavour of Principle 7 about respect for human rights (…)

6. The main debit, however, is in Basket III (…)

7. The Basket III provisions on reunification of families and freedom of travel will pose problems. Brezhnev and others in the Politburo talked tough to visiting US Senators and Congressmen this summer about the inadmissibility of trying to tell the Soviet Union how to apply its emigration laws. The Press has warned against interference in Soviet internal affairs (…)

8. The Russians have managed so far to avoid internal repercussions from *détente* and will try to make use of the small print in the Final Act, and its voluntary character, to minimise the action they need take under Basket III (…) the Russians will probably play for time: seeking, in ensuing negotiations, to water down the relevant commitment in the Final Act (…)

9. The growing Soviet concern about the likely difficulties from Basket III probably lay behind the evaporation, some time back in the Geneva stage of CSCE, of Soviet support for the Czechoslovak proposal of a permanent follow-up body (…) It would have been a useful court for pillorying the West on Basket I and for Using Basket II to criticise the EEC; but the risk of the West pillorying the Russians on Basket III could not be tolerated. Nevertheless, the Russians had no chance of avoiding follow-up activity altogether (…) they must fear that the main business of the 1977 meeting will be Western, and indeed neutral, pestering about Soviet and East European fulfilment of humanitarian and other provisions in Basket III.

10. The recently increased economic dependence of the East Europeans on the USSR will probably inhibit their freedom of action in implementing the Final Act. But the implementation of Basket III may nevertheless cause strain between Moscow and its allies, whose treatment of foreign journalists, access to information, etc., is, for the most part, less restrictive (…)

11. On the question of further Western action (…) The general approach, I

suggest, should be to move quite soon on points where current Soviet practice is clearly incompatible with the Final Act (…) If we proceed, in concert with our partners in EEC and NATO, to raise practical cases with the Russians, firmly, patiently, and without publicity, we may gain more than through public moves engaging Soviet prestige. We should not overrate the prospects of securing improvements; but Helsinki offers us a locus for trying, and there is unlikely to be much change unless we make the attempt (…)

12. Brezhnev at Helsinki was at pains to propound that CSCE gave a square deal to all parties (…) He added that it was not an end, but a beginning (…) On the assumption that the 'peace policy' continues to unfold on these lines (…) we and our friends must bring to the next phase all the clearness of head and strength of will that we possess. For the Russians will come to it armed with two alternative theses for Western public opinion: that the Soviet Union is not dangerous; or that, given Soviet strength, resistance to Soviet designs is anyhow futile (…)

The CSCE has given the Russians something that they had long wanted very much, perhaps even come to overvalue. But the Western Governments have gained also—in limiting and qualifying their endorsement of a situation they do not intend to change, in forcing the Russians to do battle on ground hitherto taboo and, not least, in cohesion and the practice of co-operation (…) Mishandled by the West, the pursuit of *détente* could lead to a Soviet walkover in Europe. But if Western countries continue, negotiation by negotiation, to stick together, to keep their guard up and to settle for nothing less than a fair balance of concrete advantage, they need not shrink from it. *Détente* of that kind would differ widely from the Soviet prospectus. And, in the longer perspective, the practice of *détente* may foster developments in Soviet policies which ultimately make the USSR a less intractable, even a more reliable, partner.

10.13 The G-7 on Economic Co-operation, November 1975

In the mid-1970s the increasing economic competition from the EEC and Japan, as well as the oil crisis of 1973 and the general malaise that was plaguing the West, prompted the United States to look for ways of co-ordinating the policies of the major industrial democracies. A major long-term result of such efforts was the launch of regular meetings of the so-called G-7 countries (the United States, Great Britain, France, Japan, Italy, Germany, and Canada). The initial meeting (in which Canada did not participate) took place at the Chateau de Rambouillet in November 1975, and resulted in the following declaration.

1. In these three days we held a searching and productive exchange of views on the world economic situation, on economic problems common to our countries, on their human, social and political implications, and on plans for resolving them.

2. We came together because of shared beliefs and shared responsibilities. We are each responsible for the government of an open, democratic society, dedicated to individual liberty and social advancement. Our success will strengthen, indeed is essential to, democratic societies everywhere. We are each responsible for assuring the prosperity of a major industrial economy. The growth and stability of our economies will help the entire industrial world and developing countries to prosper.

3. To assure in a world of growing interdependence the success of the objectives set out in this declaration, we intend to play our own full part and strengthen our efforts for closer international cooperation and constructive dialogue among all countries, transcending differences in stages of economic development, degrees of resource endowment and political and social systems.

4. The industrial democracies are determined to overcome high unemployment, continuing inflation and serious energy problems (…)

5. The most urgent task is to assure the recovery of our economies and to reduce the waste of human resources involved in unemployment (…) The objective must be growth that is steady and lasting. In this way, consumer and business confidence will be restored.

6. We are confident that our present policies are compatible and complementary and that recovery is under way. Nevertheless, we recognize the need for vigilance and adaptability in our policies. We will not allow the recovery to falter. We will not accept another outburst of inflation.

7. We also concentrated on the need for new efforts in the areas of world trade, monetary matters and raw materials, including energy.

8. As domestic recovery and economic expansion proceed, we must seek to restore growth in the volume of world trade. Growth and price stability will be fostered by maintenance of an open trading system. In a period where pressures are developing for a return to protectionism, it is essential (…) to avoid resorting to measures by which they could try to solve their problems at the expense of others, with damaging consequences in the economic, social and political fields (…)

9. We believe that the multilateral trade negotiations should be accelerated (…) They should aim at achieving substantial tariff cuts, even eliminating tariffs in some areas, at significantly expanding agricultural trade and at reducing non-tariff measures. They should seek to achieve the maximum possible level of trade liberalization (…)

10. We look to an orderly and fruitful increase in our economic relations with

socialist countries as an important element in progress in détente, and in world economic growth. We will also intensify our efforts to achieve a prompt conclusion of the negotiations concerning export credits.

11. With regard to monetary problems, we affirm our intention to work for greater stability (…) our monetary authorities will act to counter disorderly market conditions, or erratic fluctuations, in exchange rates. We welcome the rapprochement, reached at the request of many other countries, between the views of the U.S. and France on the need for stability that the reform of the international monetary system must promote (…)

12. A cooperative relationship and improved understanding between the developing nations and the industrial world is fundamental to the prosperity of each. Sustained growth in our economies is necessary to growth in developing countries; and their growth contributes significantly to health in our own economies. The present large deficits in the current accounts of the developing countries represent a critical problem for them and also for the rest of the world (…) Accordingly, we will play our part (…) in making urgent improvements in international arrangements for the stabilization of the export earnings of developing countries and in measures to assist them in financing their deficits (…)

13. World economic growth is clearly linked to the increasing availability of energy sources. We are determined to secure for our economies the energy sources needed for their growth. Our common interests require that we continue to cooperate in order to reduce our dependence on imported energy through conservation and the development of alternative sources. Through these measures as well as international cooperation between producer and consumer countries, responding to the long-term interests of both, we shall spare no effort in order to ensure more balanced conditions and a harmonious and steady development in the world energy market (…)

10.14 Reagan on 'Trade Wars', April 1986

In 1985 the EEC member countries approved the Single European Act which was to tighten the integration of the enlarged community—by 1986 the EEC would have doubled its original membership as Spain, Portugal, and Greece joined in. From the American perspective, however, concerns that the EEC would adopt increasingly high tariffs vis-à-vis non-member countries led to speculation about an emerging 'Fortress Europe'. On 22 April 1986 President Ronald Reagan touched upon these worries in an interview with foreign journalists. The interview occurred just prior to Reagan's departure for a G-7 meeting in Tokyo, Japan.

QUESTION. (...) You're going to Tokyo at a time when there's been some signs of division and strain in the Western alliance (...) certainly, over trade and other foreign policy issues. And I was wondering if you see that there will be a need at Tokyo to make some sort of fence-mending with your European allies to keep the alliance in good shape.

THE PRESIDENT. Well, I'm confident (...) I don't think the differences between us are all that great. So, I'm optimistic that when we get there we're going to talk about, as we have before, the things that we believe can be mutually beneficial— better understandings. I know that some of the things that'll be discussed is the need for another GATT [General Agreement on Tariffs and Trade] round of talks to see how we can improve that tariff arrangement (...)

QUESTION. Going on, Mr. President, on those trade matters, how do you see the trade talks with your European partners in Tokyo, with this trade war starting here in the States against European Community?

THE PRESIDENT. No, no, wait a minute. I'm sorry, I— —

QUESTION. On this trade issues, you know, U.S.A. has started, since 2 or 3 months now, a kind of war against EC countries on trade issues. And I really wonder how you can be really optimistic on the trade issue in the Tokyo summit with this background between European Community and U.S.A.

THE PRESIDENT. Well, the thing that we believe in and were trying to sell worldwide is the need for free trade and open markets. And free trade must be fair trade. If you're trading with a trading partner who has protective tariffs or limits and quotas and so forth—that isn't free trade, because it isn't fair trade. And we had an experience—the world did, as a matter of fact, due to us. Back in the thirties, the 1930's, in the Great Depression—and some in our country here thought that a great protective tariff was the answer to our Depression. So, a thing called—for the two authors of it—the Smoot–Hawley tariff was put into effect. And it spread the Depression worldwide. And we never want to make that mistake again.

I'm opposed to protectionism. Now, it is true the European Community does practice some; for example, by Spain and Portugal's entry into the European Community. What happened there was under their rules. Their rules violate the GATT agreement, because those rules say that now Spain and Portugal must buy the agricultural products they have been buying from the United States, they must buy them from other members of the Community. Well, this is like taking $1 billion in trade away from our American farmers. And we feel there's got to be some compensation for this so that we can—and the best way would be for us to all review, and that's what we keep trying to do at the economic summit—to all review where we're restricting trade; at the same time that we want to sell, we don't want to buy (...)

And much of this—we've made a number of bilateral agreements, we're working bilaterally with Japan on this. But I think—I just—my own feeling is that every bit of economic history shows that free and open commerce is beneficial to all. And when you get in trying to adjust it and restrict it with various agreements, that's when you get in trouble, because protectionism is a two-way street.

You may say, well, like I vetoed a bill that our Congress passed. And it was a bill that would have had some protectionism here in our country for two or three different products. And they were trying to say that, 'Well, this would mean more jobs in those industries for Americans.' But nobody counts the jobs over here in the other industries that you lose when the other country retaliates. So, that's why I vetoed the bill; and they didn't override my veto. But this is what we need to talk about with the European Community, and we are going to be discussing with them.

Questions

What were the major goals and achievements of early post-war European integration? What were its major shortcomings?

What was the British attitude towards European integration in the early 1950s?

Why did the United States support European integration in the 1950s?

How did the Untied States view Britain's role in Europe?

How did the United States view on European integration differ from the British, or continental European, perspective?

Why was the Berlin Wall erected in 1961? What impact did it have on East–West relations in Europe?

Why did President Charles de Gaulle twice veto British membership in the EEC?

What was the German attitude towards British EEC membership?

How different were the German and American perceptions of *Ostpolitik*?

What impact did the British ambassador Garvey anticipate the CSCE would have on East–West relations in Europe?

What were the factors pulling the United States and Western Europe together and/or apart in the 1970s and 1980s?

11

Decolonization and the Cold War

The fall of the European colonial empires—a gradual process between the late 1940s and the mid-1970s—was, in part, a consequence of the Cold War. The imperial centres—weakened by World War II—were concentrating on the battle against Communism in Europe, and had lost much of the means, economically, militarily, and ideologically, to keep their empires together. The wartime victories of the Soviet Union served as an inspiration for socialist and radical nationalist movements in the colonies. Perhaps most importantly, parts of the elites in the European colonial powers realized—sometimes after being rudely reminded by the Americans—that the contradiction between defending freedom at home and continuing a colonial presence abroad did not hold up well, faced with a vigorous and global Soviet ideological challenge. By the late 1950s most Western policymakers had come to the conclusion that colonialism had to go if they were to preserve any influence outside their own continents.

But the successive waves of decolonization also had a substantial impact on the way the Cold War was fought. In Indochina, for instance, the French withdrawal from its former colonies led to an increasing American involvement to combat Communism there. In Africa, the independence of former British and French colonies, the battle against Portuguese colonialism, and the struggle against the 'inner' colonization of white settlers in Rhodesia (Zimbabwe), Namibia, and South Africa, led to a radicalization of African elites. The new leaders in the so-called 'Third World' (Africa, Asia, and Latin America) often turned to socialism as the most efficient and just way of rebuilding their countries after the end of colonial occupation. In some cases, their ideological inclination led them to an alliance with the Soviet Union.

Few Third World leaders, however, had an alliance with the Soviet Union as their first choice of international orientation. Especially during the early phase of decolonization, many important leaders, such as Sukarno in Indonesia and Kwame Nkrumah in Ghana, aimed at non-alignment and ties to both East and West. In spite of their criticism of the colonial past and their socialist convictions, these leaders realized that their countries needed the trade and the technology of as many countries as possible. They deplored the global Cold

War division which, they thought, would make their countries'progress more difficult.

It was often in those countries where the anti-colonial struggle had been the hardest that the new elites chose revolutionary social measures and close relations with Moscow. Vietnam is one such example. Others are the former Portuguese colonies of Angola, Mozambique, and Guinea-Bissau/Cape Verde, which all earned their freedom after more than a decade of war, and Algeria, which had an equally long and bloody struggle against France. Some Third World intellectuals came to see the violent overthrow of the previous regimes as necessary in order to promote real change. Because of the sacrifices they had made in the anti-colonial struggle, the leaders of the relatively few countries that had won their freedom through years of war tended to see their movements as examples for parties elsewhere.

These radical Third World movements also often got the attention of those who wanted fundamental change within Western societies themselves. In the 1960s and early '70s, when some groups in the West began a search for new po-litical methods to defeat old injustices, the links between their struggle and the causes of radical movements elsewhere seemed apparent. In Western Europe, 'solidarity' with the Third World became one of the hallmarks of the youth and student movements. In the United States, even moderate civil rights leaders, such as Dr Martin Luther King, spoke out against American anti-Communist strate-gies abroad, in ways that linked US policies to injustice and oppression.

Within the Third World itself, the sporadic anti-revolutionary interventions of Western powers probably radicalized more people than either the colonial background or Communist propaganda. In 1960 in Congo (Zaire), when the country disintegrated after the Belgian colonial power's hasty withdrawal, sever-al Western countries intervened directly or through covert operations to prevent the socialist primeminister, Patrice Lumumba, from consolidating the new state, achieving Soviet support, and challenging the West's economic interests. Lumumba became a martyr for Third World socialism, and his fate was a power-ful signal to many that the West might be a threat to their own aspirations.

In part because of appeals from Third World socialists and Communists, and in part because of its own beginning strategic reorientation, the Soviet Union in the mid-1950s gradually began to pay more attention to Third World areas far from its own borders. Up to the Cuban revolution, Moscow concentrated on wooing established post-colonial regimes, such as India, Egypt, and Indonesia, to a closer relationship with the Soviet Union. In the 1960s, however, some key Soviet for-eign policy institutions, such as the International Department of the Communist Party Central Committee and the intelligence service, the KGB, began building closer links with revolutionary movements. The success of some of these move-ments, such as the MPLA in Angola, was in part due to Soviet support.

Understandably, in its attempts to understand Third World radicalism, elites in the West underlined the 'subversive' role of the Soviet Union rather than the subversive effects of some of their own policies. Particularly popular, both among politicians and academics, was so-called 'modernization theory', which attempted to explain Third World political behaviour through defining a universal path to modernity (most often meaning capitalism in its late twentieth-century American form). According to some social scientists, such as Walt Rostow, there is a relatively brief gap in the social and economic development of most countries into which Communist influence may spread, before the benefits of political pluralism and the market become apparent to the majority of its inhabitants. The West needed to assist the regimes of such countries through this transitory phase and thereby prevent Communism and Soviet influence from spreading. In spite of Vietnam, 'modernization theory' had a substantial impact on US strategy until it was overtaken by the even more radical approach of the Reagan administration.

Readings

Fred Halliday, *Revolution and World Politics: The Rise and Fall of the Sixth Great Power* (1999). An excellent discussion of the role of revolutions in international politics.

Zachary Karabell, *Architects of Intervention: The United States, the Third World, and the Cold War, 1946–1962* (1999). On how US Third World policies were formed during the early Cold War.

Margot Light (ed.), *Troubled Friendships: Moscow's Third World Ventures* (1993). A good overview of Soviet involvement in Africa and Asia.

Michael E. Latham, *Modernization as Ideology: American Social Science and 'Nation Building' in the Kennedy Era* (2000). How 'modernization theory' became the incarnation of US foreign policy ideology in the 1960s.

Piero Gleijeses, *Conflicting Missions: Havana, Washington, and Africa, 1959–1976* (2002). Astonishingly well researched overview of Cuba's role in Africa in the 1960s and 1970s

prez of Indonesia

11.1 Sukarno Speaks at Bandung, 1955

In 1955 many of the newly independent countries and nationalist movements in Africa and Asia met in the Indonesian city of Bandung to discuss a joint strategy. This meeting is often seen as the origin of the Non-Aligned Movement. Here is an excerpt from Indonesian President Sukarno's welcoming speech on 18 April 1955.

As I survey this hall and the distinguished guests gathered here, my heart is filled with emotion. This is the first intercontinental conference of coloured peoples in the history of mankind! I am proud that my country is your host. I am happy that you were able to accept the invitations extended by the five Sponsoring Countries. But also I cannot restrain feelings of sadness when I recall the tribulations through which many of our peoples have so recently passed, tribulations which have exacted a heavy toll in life, in material things, and in the things of the spirit.

I recognise that we are gathered here today as a result of sacrifices. Sacrifices made by our forefathers and by the people of our own and younger generations. For me, this hall is filled not only by the leaders of the nations of Asia and Africa; it also contains within its walls the undying, indomitable, the invincible spirit of those who went before us. Their struggle and sacrifice paved the way for this meeting of the highest representatives of independent and sovereign nations from two of the biggest continents of the globe.

It is a new departure in the history of the world that leaders of Asian and African peoples can meet together in their own countries to discuss and deliberate upon matters of common concern. Only a few decades ago it was frequently necessary to travel to other countries and even other continents before the spokesman of our peoples could confer (...)

This twentieth century has been a period of terrific dynamism. Perhaps the last fifty years have seen more developments and more material progress than the previous five hundred years. Man has learned to control many of the scourges which once threatened him. He has learned to consume distance. He has learned to project his voice and his picture across oceans and continents. He has probed deep into the secrets of nature and learned how to make the desert bloom and the plants of the earth increase their bounty. He has learned how to release the immense forces locked in the smallest particles of matter.

But has man's political skill marched hand-in-hand with his technical and scientific skill? Man can chain lightning to his command—can he control the society in which he lives? The answer is No! The political skill of man has been far outstripped by his technical skill, and what he has made he cannot be sure of controlling.

The result of this is fear. And man gasps for safety and morality (...)

I pray to God that this Asian-African Conference succeeds in doing its job. Ah, Sisters and Brothers, let his Conference be a great success! In spite of diversity that exists among its participants—let this Conference be a great success!

Yes, there is diversity among us. Who denies it? Small and great nations are represented here, with people professing almost every religion under the sun—Buddhism, Islam, Christianity, Confucianism, Hinduism, Jainism, Sikhism, Zoroasthrianism, Shintoism, and others. Almost every political faith we encounter here—Democracy, Monarchism, Theocracy, with innumerable variants. And practically every economic has its representative in this hall—Marhaenism, Socialism, Capitalism, Communism, in all their manifold variations and combinations.

But what harm is diversity, when there is unity in desire? This Conference is not to oppose each other, it is a conference of brotherhood. It is not an Islam-Conference, nor a Christian Conference, nor a Buddhist Conference. It is not a meeting of Malayans, nor one of Arabs, nor one of Indo-Aryan stock. It is not an exclusive club either, nor a bloc which seeks to oppose any other bloc. Rather it is a body of enlightened, tolerant opinion which seeks to impress on the world that all men and all countries have their place under the sun—to impress on the world that it is possible to live together, meet together, speak to each other, without losing one's individual identity; and yet to contribute to the general understanding of matters of common concern, and to develop a true consciousness of the interdependence of men and nations for their wellbeing and survival on earth (...)

If this Conference succeeds in making the peoples of the East whose representatives are gathered here understand each other a little more, appreciate each other a little more, sympathise with each other's problems a little more—if those things happen, then this Conference, of course, will have been worthwhile, whatever else it may achieve. But I hope that this Conference will give *more* than understanding only and goodwill only—I hope that it will falsify and give the lie to the saying of one diplomat from far abroad: 'We will turn this Asian-African Conference into an afternoon-tea meeting.' I hope that it will give evidence of the fact that we Asian and African leaders understand that Asia and Africa can prosper only when they are untied, and that even the safety of the World at large can not be safeguarded without a united Asia-Africa. I hope that this Conference will give *guidance* to mankind, will point out to mankind the way which it must take to attain safety and peace. I hope that it will give evidence that Asia and Africa have been reborn, nay, that a New Asia and a New Africa have been born!

Our task is first to seek an understanding of each other, and out of that understanding will come a greater appreciation of each other, and out of that appreciation will come collective action. Bear in mind the words of one of Asia's greatest sons: 'To speak is easy. To act is hard. To understand is hardest. Once one understands, action is easy.'

I have come to the end. Under God, may your deliberations be fruitful, and may your wisdom strike sparks of light from the hard flints of today's circumstances.

11.2 Millikan and Rostow: Priorities for US Foreign Policy, 1957

In the United States, many social scientists were preoccupied with finding solutions to the challenges the West faced as a result of decolonization. Max Millikan and Walt Rostow, both of MIT, argued in an influential 1957 book that modernization theory provided the answer. Rostow later put some of these assumptions into practice as a key foreign policy adviser in the Kennedy and Johnson administrations.

There are two priority tasks for U.S. foreign policy. The first of these is to meet effectively the threat to our security posed by the danger of overt military aggression, a threat now inherent in the present capabilities and possible future generations of the Communist bloc countries. This threat is to be met primarily by maintaining or increasing U.S. military strength and solidifying alliances with other countries in a position to contribute significantly to that strength. One of the instruments to be used in this effort is economic assistance to countries with important industrial potential, mainly the NATO powers, designed to make that potential militarily more effective.

The second priority task of U.S. foreign policy is to promote the evolution of a world in which threats to our security and, more broadly, to our way of life are less likely to arise. Success in this task would mean the freeing of a large volume of resources from military to more constructive uses. More important, it would mean protecting our society from the pressures inevitably associated with a garrison state, pressures which threaten our most cherished values. It is this task with which this book is mainly concerned (…)

Underlying the proposals in this book is the conviction that we have put relatively too much emphasis in recent years on pacts, treaties, negotiations, and international diplomacy and too little on measures to promote the evolution of stable, effective, and democratic societies abroad which can be relied upon not to generate conflict because their own national interests parallel ours and because they are politically healthy and mature. This conviction, in turn, is based upon an estimate of the nature of the forces at work in the world making for change.

It has become a commonplace that we are in the midst of a great world revolution. For centuries the bulk of the world's population has been politically inert. Outside America and Western Europe, and even in parts of the latter, until recently the pattern of society remained essentially fixed in the mold of low-productivity rural life centered on isolated villages. The possibility of change for most people seemed remote, and political activity was confined to an extremely small elite. Within the past forty years two world wars and a phenomenal increase in the ease and effectiveness of communication have fundamentally altered the perspectives of hundreds of millions of people. Countries with populations aggregating over half a billion have just won their independence and are trying to cope with their new status. The rapidly accelerating spread of literacy, mass communications, and travel, which has only begun, will produce even more unsettling results over the coming years.

This revolution is rapidly exposing previously apathetic peoples to the possibility of change. It is creating in them new aspirations for education, social improvement, and economic development. At the same time, it is breaking down traditional institutions and culture patterns which in the past held their societies together. In short, the world community is becoming both more interdependent and more fluid than it has been at any other time in history, a condition which presents us with both a great danger and a great opportunity.

The danger is that increasing numbers of people will become convinced that their new aspirations can be realized only through violent change and the renunciation of democratic institutions. The danger has no single cause. It is inherent in the revolutionary process. But it is greatly increased by the existence of communism—not because of any authentic attractions in its ideology but because the Communists have recognized their opportunities to exploit the revolution of rising expectations by picturing communism as the road to social opportunity or economic improvement or individual dignity and achievement of national self-respect, whichever fitted a given situation (…)

The economic development program outlined in the balance of this book is conceived as one of the instruments for carrying out the task of helping create an environment within which American society can thrive. It stands or falls on the acceptance of this task as one of the two top priority objectives of U.S. foreign policy. It cannot be too strongly emphasized that this program is only one of many instruments which must be used in a co-ordinated way if we are to maximize our influence to promote the development of stable, effective, and democratic societies elsewhere in the world. Information policy, military assistance, and conventional diplomacy have jobs to do which are not now being done. Economic policy by itself will not achieve the desired result. And if an economic policy is to contribute to the creation of stable and democratic societies it must be carefully conceived with this end in view. As will be suggested in the next chapter, a development assistance policy narrowly designed to win friends or promote military alliances could easily backfire and produce results actually detrimental to our national interest (…)

Our great opportunity lies in the fact that we have developed more successfully than any other nation the social, political, and economic techniques for realizing widespread popular desires for change without either compulsion or social disorganization. Although our techniques must be adapted to local conditions abroad if they are to be effective there, they represent an enormous potential for steering the world's newly aroused human energies in constructive rather than destructive directions.

Moreover, deep in American society, hankering for effective expression, capable of mobilization, is a dedication to the fundamental principles of national independence and human liberty under law. In their largest sense the proposals in this book are designed to give fresh meaning and vitality to the historic American sense of mission—a mission to see the principles of national independence and human liberty extended on the world scene.

11.3 Nkrumah on the United States and the Third World, 1958

Kwame Nkrumah, the leader of Ghana, the first of the former British colonies in Africa to gain its independence (1957), at first attempted to get support from the former colonial power and from the United States. In the early 1960s Nkrumah increasingly turned to the Eastern Bloc for assistance. Here is an excerpt from his speech at the Council on Foreign Relations, New York, in 1958.

[Principles:] The first is our desire to see Africa free and independent. The second is our determination to pursue foreign policies based upon non-alignment. The third is our urgent need for economic development. There is no area in Africa today where these three points are not on the agenda of politics. There is no need to underline for American readers the reason for Africa's rejection of colonial status. We believe, as do Americans, that to be self-governing is one of the inalienable rights of man. In Africa, if peoples are to be truly independent, their governments must reflect the fact that, in all parts of Africa, the overwhelming majority of the population are native-born Africans. Even in the countries of considerable European settlement, such as Southern Rhodesia, 90% of the people are African. When, therefore, at our recent African conference, we called for an end to colonialism, we were doing no more than stating our belief that the fact of a vast African majority should be accepted as the basis of government in Africa (…)

We asked for the fixing of definite dates for early independence and called upon the administering powers to take rapid steps to implement the provisions of the United Nations Charter and the political aspirations of the people, namely, self-determination and independence. These steps should, in my view, include a greatly accelerated and enlarged programme of education and technical training, the opening up systematically of new opportunities for Africans in agriculture and industry and a rapid growth of African participation in the country's political life. Such timetables would restore what, we believe, is most lacking in Africa's plural societies—and that is the element of confidence and hope on the part of the African majority (…)

Non-alignment can only be understood in the context of the present atomic arms race and the atmosphere of the Cold War. There is a wise African proverb: 'When the bull elephants fight, the grass is trampled down.' When we in Africa survey the industrial and military power concentrated behind the two great powers in the Cold War, we know that no military or strategic act of ours could make one jot of difference to this balance of power, while our involvement might draw us into areas of conflict which so far have not spread below the Sahara. Our attitude, I imagine, is very much that of America looking at the disputes of Europe in the 19th century. We do not wish to be involved. In addition, we know that we cannot affect the outcome. Above all, we believe the peace of the world in general is served, not harmed by keeping one great continent free from the strife and rivalry of military blocs and cold wars.

But this attitude of non-alignment does not imply indifference to the great issues of our day. It does not imply isolationism. It is in no way anti-Western; nor is it anti-Eastern. The greatest issue of our day is surely to see *that there is a tomorrow.* For Africans especially there is a particular tragedy in the risk of thermo-nuclear destruction. One continent has come but lately to the threshold of the modern world. The opportunities of health and education and a wider vision which other nations take for granted are barely within the reach of our people. And now they see the risk that all this richness of opportunity may be snatched away by destructive war. In any war, the strategic areas of the world would be destroyed or occupied by some great power. It is simply a question of who gets there first—the Suez Canal, Afghanistan and Gulf of Aquaba are examples.

On this great issue, therefore, of war and peace, the people and government of Ghana put all their weight behind the peaceful settlement of disputes and seek conditions in which disputes do not become embittered to the point of violence. We are willing to accept every provision of the United Nations Charter. We go further and favour every extension of an international police force as an alternative to war. One of the most important roles of the smaller nations today is surely to use their influence in season and out of season to substitute the peaceful settlement of disputes and international policing of disturbed areas for the present disastrous dependence upon arms and force. For this reason, at our African conference, we underlined our demands for controlled disarmament, we deplored the use of the sale of arms as a means of influencing other nations' diplomacy and we urged that African states should be represented on all international bodies concerned with disarmament.

Thus it is not indifference that leads to a policy of non-alignment. It is our belief that international blocs and rivalries exacerbate and do not solve disputes and that we must be free to judge issues on their merits and to look for solutions that are just and peaceful, irrespective of the powers involved. We do not wish to be in the position of condoning imperialism or aggression from any quarter. Powers which pursue policies of goodwill, co-operation and constructive international action will always find us at their side. In fact, perhaps 'non-alignment' is a mis-statement of our attitude. We are firmly aligned with all the forces in the world that genuinely make for peace (…)

The hopes and ambitions of the African people have been planted and brought to maturity by the impact of the Western civilisation. The West has set the pattern of our hopes, and by entering Africa in strength, it has forced the patterns upon us. Now comes our response. We cannot tell our peoples that material benefits and growth and modern progress are not for them. If we do, they will throw us out and seek other leaders who promise more. And they will abandon us, too, if we do not in reasonable measure respond to their hopes. Therefore we have no choice. Africa has no choice. We have to modernise. Either we shall do so with your interest and support—or we shall be compelled to turn elsewhere. This is not a warning or a threat, but a straight statement of political reality.

And I also affirm, for myself and I believe for most of my fellow leaders in Africa, that we want close co-operation with our friends. We know you. History has brought us together. We still have the opportunity to build up a future on the basis of free and equal co-operation. This is our aim. This is our hope.

11.4 Harold Macmillan: 'Winds of Change', 1960

In the early 1960s the British Conservative prime minister Harold Macmillan accepted the independence of most of Britain's remaining colonies. Macmillan saw decolonization as a potent weapon in the Cold War. Here is an excerpt from his speech to the South African Parliament in Cape Town, 3 February 1960.

Sir, as I have travelled round the Union I have found everywhere, as I expected, a deep preoccupation with what is happening in the rest of the African continent. I understand and sympathise with your interest in these events, and your anxiety about them. Ever since the break-up of the Roman Empire one of the constant facts of political life in Europe has been the emergence of independent nations. They have come into existence over the centuries in different forms, with different kinds of Government, but all have been inspired by a deep, keen feeling of nationalism, which has grown as the nations have grown.

In the twentieth century, and especially since the end of the war, the processes which gave birth to the nation states of Europe have been repeated all over the world. We have seen the awakening of national consciousness in peoples who have for centuries lived in dependence upon some other power. Fifteen years ago this movement spread through Asia. Many countries there of different races and civilisations pressed their claim to an independent national life. Today the same thing is happening in Africa, and the most striking of all the impressions I have formed since I left London a month ago is of the strength of this African national consciousness. In different places it takes different forms, but it is happening everywhere. The wind of change is blowing through this continent, and, whether we like it or not, this growth of national consciousness is a political fact. We must accept it as a fact, and our national policies must take account of it.

Of course, you understand this better than anyone. You are sprung from Europe, the home of nationalism, and here in Africa you have yourselves created a new nation. Indeed, in the history of our times yours will be recorded as the first of the African nationalisms, and this tide of national consciousness which is now rising in Africa is a fact for which you and we and the other nations of the Western World are ultimately responsible. For its causes are to be found in the achievements of Western civilisation, in the pushing forward of the frontiers of knowledge, in the applying of science in the service human needs, in the expanding of food production, in the speeding and multiplying of the means of communication, and perhaps, above all, the spread of education.

As I have said, the growth of national consciousness in Africa is a political fact, and we must accept it as such. That means, I would judge, that we must come to terms with it. I sincerely believe that if we cannot do so we may imperil the precarious balance between the East and West on which the peace of the world depends. The world today is divided into three main groups. First there are what we call the Western Powers. You in South Africa and we in Britain belong to this group, together with our friends and allies in other parts of the Commonwealth. In the United States of America and in Europe we call it the Free World. Secondly there are the Communists—Russia and her satellites in Europe and China whose population will rise by the end of the next ten years to the staggering total of 800,000,000. Thirdly, there are those parts of the world where people are at present uncommitted either to Communism or to our Western ideas.

In this context we think first of Asia and then of Africa. As I see it the great issue in this second half of the twentieth century is whether the uncommitted peoples of Asia and Africa will swing to the East or to the West. Will they be drawn into the Communist camp? Or will the great experiments in self-government that are now being made in Asia and Africa, especially within the Commonwealth, prove so successful, and by their example so compelling, that the balance will come down in favour of freedom and order and justice?

The struggle is joined, and it is a struggle for the minds of men. What is now on trial is much more than our military strength or our diplomatic and administrative skill. It is our way of life. The uncommitted nations want to see before they choose.

What can we show them to help them to choose right? Each of the independent members of the Commonwealth must answer that question for itself. It is a basic principle of our modern Commonwealth that we respect each other's sovereignty in matters of internal policy. At the same time we must recognise that in this shrinking world in which we live today the internal policies of one nation may have effects outside it. We may sometimes be tempted to say to each other, 'Mind your own business,' but in these days I would myself expand the old saying so that it runs: 'Mind your own business, but mind how it affects my business, too.'

Let me be very frank with you, my friends. What Governments and Parliaments in the United Kingdom have done since the war in according independence to India, Pakistan, Ceylon, Malaya and Ghana, and what they will do for Nigeria and other countries now nearing independence, all this, though we take full and sole responsibility for it, we do in the belief that it is the only way to establish the future of the Commonwealth and of the Free World on sound foundations. All this of course is also of deep and close concern to you for nothing we do in this small world can be done in a corner or remain hidden. What we do today in West, Central and East Africa becomes known tomorrow to everyone in the Union, whatever his language, colour or traditions. Let me assure you, in all friendliness, that we are well aware of this and that we have acted and will act with full knowledge of the responsibility we have to all our friends.

11.5 Khrushchev on National Liberation, 1961

For the Soviet leadership, decolonization opened up great opportunities for social revolution and for expanding Soviet influence in the Third World. Here is an excerpt from Khrushchev's 6 January 1961 speech—a speech John Kennedy asked his advisers to study closely when he came into office two weeks later.

Comrades, the peoples that have gained national independence have become another mighty force in the struggle for peace and social progress.

The national-liberation movement is striking ever more telling blows at imperialism, helping to strengthen peace and accelerate the social progress of mankind. At present, Asia, Africa and Latin America are the most important centres of the revolutionary struggle against imperialism. Some forty countries have won national independence since the war. Nearly 1,500 million people have broken free from colonial slavery.

The Meeting noted with good reason that the breakdown of the system of colonial slavery under the impact of the national-liberation movement is second in historical significance only to the rise of the socialist world system.

A splendid new chapter is opening in the history of mankind. It is easily imagined what great things these peoples will do after they completely oust the imperialists from their own countries and feel themselves master of their own fate. This multiplies enormously the progressive forces of mankind.

Take Asia, for example, that ancient cradle of human civilisation. What incalculable strength the peoples of that continent possess! What a great role the Arab peoples with their heroic traditions and all the peoples of the Middle East, those liberated or in the process of liberation from political and economic dependence upon imperialism, could play in resolving the issues now confronting mankind!

The awakening of the peoples of Africa is one of the outstanding events of our epoch. Dozens of countries in North and Central Africa have already won independence. The south of the continent is beginning to seethe. The fascist dungeons in the Union of South Africa will undoubtedly crumble to dust, and Rhodesia, Uganda and other parts of Africa will become free.

The forces of the national-liberation movement are multiplying largely because one more front of active struggle against U.S. imperialism, Latin America, has come into being in recent years. Only a short time ago that vast continent was identified by a single concept—America. And that concept accorded largely with the facts, for Latin America was bound hand and foot by Yankee imperialism. Today, the Latin American peoples are showing by their struggle that the American continent is not a preserve of the U.S.A. Latin America is reminiscent of an active volcano. The eruption of the liberation struggle has wiped out dictatorial regimes in a number of Latin American countries. The thunder of the glorious Cuban revolution has reverberated around the world. The Cuban revolution is not only repulsing the onslaught of the imperialism; it is spreading and taking deeper root, and constitutes a new and higher stage of the national-liberation struggle, one in which the people themselves come to power and become the masters of their wealth. Solidarity with revolutionary Cuba is the duty not only of the Latin American peoples, but also of the socialist countries, the entire international communist movement and the proletariat all over the world.

The national-liberation movement is an anti-imperialist movement. Imperialism has become much weaker with the disintegration of the colonial system. Vast territories and large masses of people have ceased, or are ceasing, to serve as a reserve for it and as a source of cheap raw materials and cannon fodder. Asian, African and Latin American countries, supported by the socialist countries and the progressive forces of the world, are inflicting defeat upon the imperialist powers and coalitions with increasing frequency (...)

The imperialist powers, above all the United States, are doing their utmost to hitch to their system the countries that have cast off the colonial yoke and thereby strengthen the positions of world capitalism, to infuse fresh blood into it, as bourgeois ideologists put it, and to rejuvenate it and consolidate it. If we look the facts in the face, we have to admit that the imperialists have powerful economic levers with which to exert pressure on the newly-free countries. They still manage to enmesh some of the politically independent countries in the web of economic dependence. Now that it is no longer possible to establish outright colonial regimes, the imperialists resort to disguised forms and means of enslaving and plundering the newly-free countries. As the same time, the colonial powers back the internal reactionaries in all these countries; they try to impose on them puppet dictatorial regimes and to involve them in aggressive blocs. Although there are sharp contradictions between the imperialist countries, they often take joint action against the national-liberation movement.

But if we consider all the factors shaping the destinies of the peoples that have shaken off colonial rule, we shall see that in the final analysis the trends of social progress opposing imperialism will prevail (...)

Nobody appreciates and understands the aspirations of the peoples now smashing the fetters of colonialism better than the working people of the socialist countries and the Communists of the whole world. Our world outlook and the interests of all the working people, for which we are fighting, impel us to do our best to ensure that the peoples follow the right road to progress, to the flowering of their material and spiritual forces. By our policy we must strengthen the peoples' confidence in the socialist countries (...)

Forty-one years ago, when the First Congress of the Comintern took place here in Moscow, Communist Parties and Left socialist organisations from thirty countries were represented. Not counting the Communist Parties of the Republics which today are part of the U.S.S.R., there were only five Communist Parties in Europe at the time. There were no Communist Parties in Asia, Africa, Australia and Oceania. On the American continent there was only the Communist Party of Argentina. Today Communist and Worker's Parties exist in eighty-seven countries. They have more than 36 million members. Communist ideas have won the minds of millions in all corners of the globe. That is a good thing, a very good thing, comrades!

11.6 Kennedy on US Policy in the Third World, 1961

President John F. Kennedy—inspired in part by advisers such as Walt Rostow—put great emphasis on the Cold War in the Third World, and saw it as crucial for the outcome of the conflict with the Soviet Union. Here is an excerpt from his special message to Congress on foreign aid, 22 March 1961.

Is a foreign aid program really necessary? Why should we not lay down this burden which our nation has now carried for some fifteen years?

The answer is that there is no escaping our obligations: our moral obligations as a wise leader and a good neighbour in the interdependent community of free nations—our economic obligations as the wealthiest people in a world of largely poor people, as a nation no longer dependent upon the loans from abroad that once helped us develop our own economy—and our political obligations as the single largest counter to the adversaries of freedom.

To fail to meet those obligations now would be disastrous; and, in the long run, more expensive. For widespread poverty and chaos lead to a collapse of existing political and social structures which would inevitably invite the advance of total-itarianism into every weak and unstable area. Thus our own security would be endangered and our prosperity imperilled. A program of assistance to the under-developed nations must continue because the nation's interest and the cause of political freedom require it.

We live at a very special moment in history. The whole southern half of the world—Latin America, Africa, the Middle East, and Asia—are caught up in the adventures of asserting their independence and modernizing their old ways of life. These new nations need aid in loans and technical assistance just as we in the northern half of the world drew successfully on one another's capital and know-how as we moved into industrialization and regular growth.

But in our time these new nations need help for a special reason. Without exception they are under Communist pressure. In many cases, that pressure is direct and military. In others, it takes the form of intense subversive activity designed to break down and supersede the new—and often frail—modern insti-tutions they have thus far built.

But the fundamental task of our foreign aid program in the 1960's is not nega-tively to fight Communism: It's fundamental task is to help make a historical demonstration that in the twentieth century, as in the nineteenth— in the south-ern half of the globe as in the north—economic growth and political democracy can develop hand in hand.

In short we have not only obligations to fulfil, we have great opportunities to realize. We are, I am convinced, on the threshold of a truly united and major effort by the free industrialized nations to assist the less-developed nations on a long term basis. Many of these less-developed countries are on the threshold of achieving sufficient economic, social and political strength and self-sustained growth to stand permanently on their own feet. The 1960's can be—and must be—the crucial "Decade of Development"—the period when many less-developed nations make the transition into self-sustained growth—the period in which an enlarged community of free, stable and self-reliant nations can reduce world tensions and insecurity. This goal is in our grasp if, and only if, the other industrialized nations join us in developing with the recipients a set of commonly agreed criteria, a set of long range goals, and a common undertaking to meet those goals, in which each nation's contribution is related to the contributions of others and to the precise needs of each less-developed nation. Our job, in its largest sense, is to create a new partnership between the northern and southern halves of the world, to which all free nations can contribute, in which each free nation must assume a responsibility proportional to its means (...)

In short, this Congress at this session must make possible a dramatic turning point in the troubled history of foreign aid to the underdeveloped world. We must say to the less-developed nations, if they are willing to undertake necessary internal reform and self-help—and to the other industrialized nations, if they are willing to undertake a much greater effort on a much broader scale—then we intend during this coming decade of development to achieve a decisive turn-around in the fate of the less-developed world, looking toward the ultimate day when all nations can be self-reliant and when foreign aid will no longer be needed.

However, this will not be an easy task. The magnitude of the problems is staggering. In Latin America, for example, population growth is already threatening to outpace economic growth—and in some parts of the continent living standards are actually declining. In 1945 the population of our 20 sister American Republics was 145 million. It is now greater than that of the United States, and by the year 2000, less than forty years away, Latin American population will be 592 million, compared with 312 million for the Unites States. Latin America will have to double its real income in the next thirty years simply to maintain already low standards of living. And the problems are no less serious or demanding in the other developing areas of the world. Thus to bring real economic progress to Latin America and to the rest of the less-developed world will require a sustained and united effort on the part of the Latin American Republics, the United States and our free world allies.

This will require leadership, by this country in this year. And it will require a fresh approach—a more logical, efficient and successful long-term plan—for American foreign aid. I strongly recommend to the Congress the enactment of such a plan. . . .

11.7 Lumumba's Last Message and Death, 1960

When Congo hastily got its independence from Belgium in 1960 the new country lacked both skilled people and stable political organizations, while foreign companies conspired with separatists in the south and with the new Congolese army to gain access to the coun-

try's vast mineral resources. Patrice Lumumba—the young prime minister of Congo—attempted to keep the country together, but was taken prisoner by the army and murdered. Here is an excerpt from his last message, smuggled out of prison. The second excerpt is a journalist's account of Lumumba's final hours.

A. Lumumba's Last Message

My dear compatriots! Citizens of the Republic!

I do not doubt the joy you feel today when hearing the voice of him who has sworn to never betray his people.

In good times as in bad times, I will always be on your side. It is with you that I have fought to liberate this country from foreign domination. It is with you that I have fought to consolidate our national independence. It is with you that I will fight to watch over the integrity and national unity of the Republic of Congo.

We have made a choice, and that is to serve our homeland with devotion and loyalty. We will never move away from this path. Freedom is the ideal for which human beings, in all times and over the centuries, have been fighting and dying. Congo cannot hide from this reality and thanks to our heroic and outstanding fight we have bravely won our independence and our dignity as free human beings.

We are born to live in freedom and not to live in servitude as we have been during 80 years of oppression, humiliation and exploitation. 80 years during which the inhabitants of this country have been arbitrarily deprived of the usufruct of their most sacred rights. We have launched a decisive battle against the usurpers of our rights in order to end this humiliation of the 20th century which calls itself colonialism and to allow the people of Congo to administer themselves and to take care of the affairs of their country.

History has shown that independence never presents itself on a silver plate. It has to be acquired. But in order to acquire our independence, it was necessary to organise and mobilise all the active forces of our country. The people of Congo have responded to our appeal and it is thanks to this united force that we could give a mortal blow to decaying colonialism.

As the forces of liberation are always more powerful than those of oppression, we have turned out to be the victors. All peoples have had to fight in order to liberate themselves. That was especially the case with the nationalists which have put themselves at the head of the French, Belgian, Russian revolutions etc.

The former colonies of America were not liberated by other means. I am here reminded of the Declaration of Independence adopted by the Congress of the United States in 1766 which proclaimed the liquidation of the colonies, the liberation from the British yoke, and the transformation of the United States of America into a free and independent state. The Congolese nationalists thus did

except not

nothing but follow the traces of the French, Belgian, American, Russian and other nationalists. For our fight, we chose a single weapon: non-violence. This is the only weapon which allows a victory in dignity and honour. Our agenda during the liberation campaign was always the immediate and total independence of Congo (…)

The powers which fight us and which fight my government, under the false pretext of anti-Communism, in reality hide their true intentions. These European powers only want the sympathies of those African leaders who are at their disposal and who betray their people. Some of these powers do not conceive their presence in Congo or in Africa in other terms than the degree to which they manage to enrich themselves, with the help of bribing certain corrupt leaders.

These politics of corruption which consist of qualifying every incorruptible leader as 'communist' and as 'pro-Western' every leader who betrays his country has to be combated.

We do not want to be the disciples of any bloc. If we do not pay attention, we risk falling into a neo-colonialism which will be as dangerous as the colonialism which we have buried on 30 June [independence day]. The manoeuvre of the imperialists consists of maintaining the colonial system in Congo and of simply exchanging the actors like in a piece of theatre, that is to say they want to exchange the Belgian colonialists with neo-colonialists which they can manoeuvre when they decide to (…)

This is why I address you, my dear compatriots and companions in the struggle, with a brotherly appeal that the war amongst brothers, the intra- and inter-tribal fights and the rivalries between people and between brothers must end. Our children will judge us harshly if we, because of thoughtlessness, do not manage to cross the manoeuvres of those who profit from our internal strife (…) This is the message of a man who has fought with you so that this country would always march in front and play its role as standard-bearer of the African liberation effectively.

Let's go ahead, citizens, with the construction of a united, proud and prosperous Congo!

A bright future shimmers through at our horizon.

Long live the independent and sovereign Republic of Congo!

B. Lumumba's Final Hours

Prophetically, the Air Katanga DC-4 from Leopoldville flew into a crackling tropical thunderstorm as the pilot encircled Elizabethville and cryptically radioed the control tower: 'I have a precious parcel on board.' On direct orders from Tshombe, the plane taxied off the runway away from the main apron and came to a standstill near a small hangar remote from the airport main building. An armoured car pulled up and trained its cannon on the door of the plane.

Lightning slashed black stormclouds as steel-helmeted Katangese soldiers and police brandishing their machine guns swarmed around the airliner. And in this grimly Wagnerian fashion, the Congo's deposed premier, Patrice Lumumba, was delivered into the hands of his archenemy, Tshombe.

Swedish United Nations guards at the airport, tall and tough, stood by, shadow figures in the background, as Lumumba, blindfolded with a grimy bandage, his hands tied behind him, and roped to two of his political lieutenants, was directed down the steps of the plane. Within sight of a large airport billboard proclaiming 'Welcome to Free Katanga,' the trembling, stumbling Lumumba and his fellow prisoners fell to the ground in a hail of savage baton, rifle-butt and fist blows and kicks from a gauntlet of snarling Katangese.

One of the victims screamed loudly as the thunder rolled across the veld. And then, with the soldiers forming a screen of steel around the vehicle, Lumumba was flung into a Gendarmerie jeep and trampled on by his guards as he was driven away.

11.8 Kennedy and Mobutu, 1963

The Kennedy Administration supported the army in Congo, led by General Joseph Mobutu. Here is an excerpt from the president's conversation with Mobutu on 31 May 1963.

After the usual amenities, the President asked General Mobutu what would be the effect of withdrawal of the United Nations forces from the Congo, particularly what would be the effect in Katanga. Mobutu said that before answering that question he would like to express his appreciation to the President for the hospitality and help extended to him during his visit to the United States and for U.S. assistance to the Congo.

The President replied that he was happy to assist the Congolese to maintain their stability and territorial integrity. He then asked what the United States could do now. Mobutu replied that the Congo needed bilateral aid as requested in a letter which Adoula had sent to the U.S. Government.

The President then asked what was the problem of ANC [Congolese National Army] retraining. Mobutu said that the Congolese had a good army under the Belgians but when the white officers left the army fell to pieces. He recalled an old French proverb that 'there are not good soldiers and poor soldiers but only good officers and poor officers'. The Congolese problem was not one of troops but of officers (…)

The President then asked Mobutu what assistance General Mobutu expected from the U.S. Mobutu replied that there was lack of matériel particularly trucks, communications, and other equipment (…)

The President returned to his question whether Mobutu could maintain order after the UN's departure. Mobutu without hesitation replied that he could if he could get U.S. military aid immediately. He said he needed foreign technicians in all units of the army to improve its discipline, maintain equipment, and carry on its administration.

Second, he needed help in the organization and training of the gendarmerie. He needed officers and technicians for the gendarmerie and a school in which to train them. Thirdly, he wanted to establish a military academy but this was for the future after the provision of technicians and equipment.

Mobutu stressed that the foreign officers were to function along with the Congolese officers. He then added that it would probably be easier to organize the army and gendarmerie if he had better equipment, particularly since he then could transport those that had been trained to the places where they had to go.

The President said that the retraining and modernization of the ANC would take considerable time, perhaps a matter of years. Mobutu said that he had a plan to accomplish the retraining and reorganisation and that it would take three years. The President then asked whether or not during this time Tshombe and others might not be too powerful, have a military force at their disposal and cause trouble. Mobutu said he didn't know because now the UNOC was present, but he didn't think they would. He pointed out that thanks to the UN, Congolese units were now stationed in Katanga and Kasai and would later have some foreign technicians to help. The President asked what nationality they would be. Mobutu replied, 'Belgians'. The President asked whether there would be any difficulty between the troops and the Belgians. Mobutu replied that since independence there had been a return to discipline and he thought that the troops and Belgians could work together. Mobutu further pointed out that there wouldn't be trouble when the UN withdrew. For example, the UN had already withdrawn from Kasai and there had been no trouble. Mobutu continued, 'If you give me equipment, I'll be ready.' (…)

The President then said we cannot just go on talking about this program but it was important not to give the appearance of or in fact undercutting the UN. He would look into the matter himself. He was sure that Spaak would help but wondered about assistance from other countries.

(…) The President then asked what action the US had taken relative to the participation of these other nations. Governor Williams stated we had had some talks with them but that nothing was firm as far as he knew other than participation by the Belgians. The President said, 'You mean only the US and Belgium have signed up so far to help on this program?' Governor Williams said Israel had indicated it was willing to assist in parachute training and believed they had started this training. Colonel Gall noted that training had not yet begun.

At that time the President invited the General to move out into the rose garden for pictures; he said, 'General, if it hadn't been for you, the whole thing would have collapsed and the Communists would have taken over.' To which General Mobutu replied, 'I do what I am able to do.' The President then commented that he had done an outstanding job.

(...) General Mobutu said he hoped to send some Congolese students to Fort Leavenworth. He saw that there were other foreign officers there and hoped some Congolese could go.

The President indicated his approval of training for General Mobutu and for ten paracommando officers. He was noncommittal on Mobutu's other requests.

Fifth, Mobutu said that he had spoken to the military about a command aircraft. The President said he knew about this and Mobutu should have it.

As the President walked out to say goodbye to General Mobutu he said there was nobody in the world that had done more than the General to maintain freedom against the Communists and that whenever there was any crisis in the Congo, Mobutu's name was mentioned.

The President said to Governor Williams he would like to know on the basis of the morning's discussion what decisions were now required in order to implement this program.

11.9 Frantz Fanon: The Wretched of the Earth, 1961

Born in the French Antilles, Frantz Fanon moved to Algeria in 1951 and took part in its liberation struggle against France. Fanon—a doctor and psychiatrist—underlined the need for colonized individuals to liberate their minds as well as their countries, through the use of violence, if necessary. This excerpt is from his best-known book, published in 1961 with a preface by the French philosopher Jean-Paul Sartre.

When the native is tortured, when his wife is killed or raped, he complains to no one. The oppressor's government can set up commissions of inquiry and of information daily if it wants to; in the eyes of the native, these commissions do not exist. The fact is that soon we shall have had seven years of crimes in Algeria and there has not been a single Frenchman indicted before a French court of justice for the murder of an Algerian. In Indo-China, in Madagascar or in the colonies the native has always known that he need expect nothing from the other side. The settler's work is to make even dreams of liberty impossible for the native. The native's work is to imagine all possible methods for destroying the settler. On the logical plane, the Manichaeism of the settler produces a Manichaeism of the native. To the theory of the 'absolute evil of the native' the theory of the 'absolute evil of the settler' replies.

The appearance of the settler has meant in the terms of syncretism the death of the aboriginal society, cultural lethargy, and the petrification of individuals. For the native, life can only spring up again out of the rotting corpse of the settler. This, then is the correspondence, term by term, between these two trains of reasoning.

But it so happens that for the colonized people this violence, because it constitutes their only work, invests their characters with positive and creative qualities. The practice of violence binds them together as a whole, since each individual forms a violent link in the great chain, a part of the great organism of violence which has surged upwards in reaction to the settler's violence in the beginning. The groups recognize each other and the future nation is already indivisible. The armed struggle mobilizes the people; that is to say, it throws them in one way and in one direction (…)

At the level of individuals, violence is a cleansing force. It frees the native from his inferiority complex and from his despair and inaction; it makes him fearless and restores his self-respect. Even if the armed struggle has been symbolic and the nation is demobilized through a rapid movement of decolonisation, the people have the time to see that the liberation has been the business of each and all and that the leader has no special merit. From thence comes that type of aggressive reticence with regard to the machinery of protocol which young governments quickly show. When the people have taken violent part in the national liberation they will allow no one to set themselves up as 'liberators' (…)

Today, national independence and the growth of national feeling in under-developed regions take on totally new aspects. In these regions, with the exception of certain spectacular advances, the different countries show the same absence of infrastructure. The mass of the people struggle against the same poverty, flounder about making the same gestures and with their shrunken bellies outline what has been called the geography of hunger. It is an under-developed world, a world inhuman in its poverty; but also it is a world without doctors, without engineers and without administrators. Confronting this world the European nations sprawl, ostentatiously opulent. This European opulence is literally scandalous, for it has been founded on slavery, it has been nourished with the blood of slaves and it comes directly from the soil and from the subsoil of that under-developed world. The well-being and the progress of Europe have been built up with the sweat and the dead bodies of Negroes, Arabs, Indians and the yellow races. We have decided not to overlook this any longer. When a colonialist

country, embarrassed by the claims for independence made by a colony, pro-
claims to the nationalist leaders: 'If you wish for independence, take it, and go
back to the middle ages', the newly independent people tend to acquiesce and to
accept the challenge (…)

It might have been generally thought that the time had come for the world, and
particularly for the Third World, to choose between the capitalist and socialist
systems. The under-developed countries, which have used the fierce competition
which exists between the two systems in order to assure the triumph of their
struggle for national liberation, should however refuse to become a factor in that
competition. The Third World ought not to be content to define itself in the
terms of values which have preceded it. On the contrary, the under-developed
countries ought to do their utmost to find their own particular values and methods and a style which shall be peculiar to them. The concrete problem we find
ourselves up against is not that of a choice, cost what it may, between socialism
and capitalism as they have been defined by men of other continents and of other
ages. Of course we know that the capitalist regime, in so far as it is a way of life,
cannot leave us free to perform our work at home, nor our duty to the world.
Capitalist exploitation and cartels and monopolies are the enemies of under-
developed countries. On the other hand the choice of a socialist regime, a regime
which is completely orientated towards the people as a whole and based on the
principle that man is the most precious of all possessions will allow us to go
forward more quickly and more harmoniously, and thus make impossible that
caricature of society where all economical and political power is held in the
hands of a few who regard the nation as a whole with scorn and contempt.

11.10 Joint Soviet–Algerian Communiqué, 1964

*The Soviet Union set up a number of agreements on trade, education, and technological
assistance with the new states in the Third World, especially with those that stressed their
socialist orientation. This excerpt is from a joint Soviet–Algerian communiqué issued at
the end of Algerian president Ben Bella's visit to Moscow, 7 May 1964.*

In frank and prolonged talks N. S. Khrushchov and Ahmed Ben Bella informed
one another about the state of the economic and social development of the
Soviet Union and the Algerian People's Democratic Republic and spoke of their
plans for the future. The Soviet side received with deep satisfaction the news
that, by the efforts of the people and the Government of the Algerian People's
Democratic Republic, the grave consequences of the prolonged war thrust on
Algeria by the colonialists, are being successfully liquidated, and good conditions

are being created for the progressive development of the national economy. The tremendous significance was noted of the revolutionary socio-economic transformations which have been carried out and are continuing to be carried out in Algeria—the strengthening of agrarian reform, and the introduction of new social and labour legislation. In the course of the revolution the Algerian people have found and successfully applied new forms of public management of industrial, agricultural, and other enterprises.

By its epoch-making decrees of March 1963, the Government of the Algerian People's Democratic Republic legalised the right of the working people to run their own enterprises and created a broad foundation for the socialist Sector in Algeria. The revolutionary energy of the masses, which is directed to the practical fulfilment of the task of constructing a new society, is becoming a mighty force for the economic development of Algeria, and a real school of political and labour education of the masses.

The Algerian side made it known that the decisions of the Constituent Congress of the Party of the National Liberation Front are a realistic programme for the country's further development and offer to the Algerian people wide prospects for the construction of socialism in the Algerian People's Democratic Republic. The struggle was a result of the unity of all the revolutionary forces of the Algerian people, rallied around the Front in the name of attaining national independence. The preservation of the unity of all healthy revolutionary forces standing for socialism is a reliable guarantee of the consolidation of Algeria's national independence, of her advancement along the road of democracy, social progress and building of socialism.

The experience of revolutionary transformations in Algeria in consonance with the concrete conditions of this country is a big contribution to the cause of the struggle for genuine political and economic independence of countries which have become free from the colonial yoke, and for the further development of the world revolutionary process.

The President of the Algerian People's Democratic Republic spoke with admiration of the great successes scored by the Soviet people in the construction of communism under the leadership of the Communist Party of the Soviet Union, which is evidence of the correctness of the road indicated by the great Lenin for the country's transformation along socialist lines.

The two sides exchanged views on all questions of economic and technical co-operation between the Soviet Union and the Algerian People's Democratic Republic. In the course of the talks the Algerian side pointed out the significance of Soviet fraternal assistance to Algeria for the development of the Algerian socialist economy and for the consolidation of Algerian independence. The sides noted with great satisfaction that friendly co-operation in economic and technical fields between the two countries is acquiring ever greater scope and variety.

The Soviet–Algerian Agreements on economic and technical co-operation and on trade concluded earlier are being successfully implemented. The Soviet union renders economic and technical assistance to Algeria in the development of agriculture, the construction of dams for irrigation, the drilling of trial bore holes and producing water wells in prospecting, as well as in the construction of a number of industrial enterprises and the training of national cadres of specialists both by organising educational establishments in Algeria and by giving Algerian citizens an opportunity if attending Soviet educational establishments. With these aims in view the Soviet Union granted a long-term credit to the Algerian People's Democratic Republic in 1963 (...)

The Party of the National-Liberation of Algeria hails the world's Party of the Soviet Union which organised the world's first socialist revolution, inspired and led the people in the construction of socialist society and in building a communist society in the USSR.

The CPSU and the Party of the NLF emphasise that it is only the socialist path of development that ensures the full-scale advance of the productive forces and the tapping of the constructive energy of the working people, and delivers them from the horrors of colonial and capitalist exploitation.

The CPSU and the Party of the NLF are one in their desire to devote all their strength, experience and revolutionary energy to the cause of the struggle for finally abolishing the shameful colonial system and liberating the oppressed peoples, the cause of ending the exploitation of man by man, and of the victory of socialism.

11.11 CIA and US State Department on Coup in Indonesia, 1965

The United States often saw its links with Third World military establishments as a way to strike at socialists or Soviet-oriented leaders. Here is a top secret CIA memorandum from 9 November 1965 on US assistance for General Suharto's military coup in Indonesia.

1. The requests of the Indonesian military leaders for covert assistance in their struggle against the Partai Kommunis Indonesia (PKI), create a definite risk for us of deliberate assistance to a group which cannot be considered a legal government nor yet a regime of proven reliability or longevity. Early assessment of the political direction and longevity of this military leadership must be accomplished and, before any overt or readily visible assistance could be offered, its legal authority as well as its de facto control must be confirmed explicitly. As long as

Sukarno fights a clever rear-guard delaying action politically, this is not likely to occur.

2. On the other hand, the Army leaders appear determined to seize the opportunity of the current confused circumstances to break the organizational back of the PKI, to eliminate it as an effective political force, and to prevent emergence of any crypto-Communist successor party. Recent intelligence from within the PKI party ranks clearly indicate that the PKI has begun to abandon hope of salvation through Sukarno's political legerdemain and has therefore decided it must, however ill-prepared and disorganized, fight back against the Army. Despite the overwhelming military superiority of the Armed Forces, the roots of Communism, of PKI membership, and of mass support nurtured for years by the constant flood of pro-Communist media, are so deep in many areas that the Army is very likely to be faced with a lingering insurgency situation (...)

4. One of the Army's major needs will be civilian support. They have instituted psychological warfare mechanisms, control of media prerequisite to influencing public opinion and have harassed or halted Communist output. They have also mobilized certain bases of mass support, especially among Moslems. Unfortunately in these areas where the PKI has been able to initiate an insurgent campaign or local resistance, as in Central Java, the Army has not been able to protect those anti-Communist civilians who have fought the PKI and pro-Communist rebel troops. If this situation continues, the populace in some of these areas may be intimidated into affording aid to the government forces regardless of their convictions, or they will be decimated.

5. True, the future policy of the Indonesian Army if it should succeed in controlling or eliminating Sukarno as an effective factor is not entirely clear. Two probabilities do however seem fairly significant about its future stance:

a. It will certainly be less oriented towards Asian Communist Bloc and will be decidedly Nationalist (though not without some Marxist and anti-Western concepts), perhaps with a strong neutralist flavor and hopefully with a concentration upon Indonesia's internal welfare.

b. Its future attitude regarding the West and the U.S. in particular will certainly be affected favourably by the degree to which the U.S. can now provide what limited aid the military leaders feel they require in their struggle to survive.

6. In short, we must be mindful that in the past years we have often wondered when and if the Indonesian Army would ever move to halt the erosion of non-Communist political strength in Indonesia. Now that it has seized upon the fortuitous opportunity afforded by PKI's error in the 30 September affair and is asking for covert help as well as understanding to accomplish that very task, we should avoid being too cynical about its motives and its self-interest, or too

hesitant about the propriety of extending such assistance *provided* we do so covertly, in a manner which will not embarrass them or embarrass our government.

7. In reviewing the types of assistance which can be provided covertly, we believe that mechanisms exist or can be diverted or created to extend either covert credits for purchases or to deliver any of the types of the matériel requested to date in reasonable quantities. [*1½ lines of source text not declassified*] The same can be said of purchasers and transfer agents for such items as small arms, medicine and other items requested. [*1 line of source text not declassified*] wherein we can permit the Indonesians with whom we are dealing to make desired purchases and even indicate to them where items may be purchased without our being in on the direct transaction. Some degree of control can be exercised through these accounts to insure that the letters of credit cannot be misused for other than specified purposes. [*2½ lines of source text not declassified*] which can be made available on very short notice. [*less than line of source text not declassified*] equipment would be more expensive and would require a little more time to deliver. It would however probably be more appropriate if equipment is to be handed by Indonesian Army officers to selected civilian auxiliaries.

11.12 Che Guevara on Revolution in Congo, 1966

The Argentinian-born Communist Ernesto 'Che' Guevara became one of the leaders of the Cuban revolution, and a leading voice in calling for 'revolutionary solidarity' with other countries. In 1967 he was captured and shot by the Bolivian military after participating in an unsuccessful attempt at an uprising there. This is an excerpt from his January 1966 report to Cuban leader Fidel Castro on another unsuccessful expedition, to Congo in 1965–6.

On the other hand, what had we to offer? We did not give much protection, as our story has shown. Nor did we offer any education, which might have been a great vehicle of communication. Medical services were provided only by the few Cubans there, with inadequate medicines, a fairly primitive system of administration, and no sanitary organization. I think that some deep thought and research needs to be devoted to the problem of revolutionary tactics where the relations of production do not give rise to land hunger among the peasantry. For the peasantry is the main social layer in this region; there is no industrial proletariat and the petty bourgeoisie of middlemen is not very developed (...)

It is important for us to discover what are the demands we can place on a militant, so that he can overcome the violent traumas of a reality with which he must do battle. I think that candidates should first pass through a very rigorous process of selection, as well as being subjected to prior warnings. As I have said before, no one believed the admonition that the revolution would require three to five years to achieve success; when the reality confirmed this, they suffered an internal collapse, the collapse of a dream. Revolutionary militants who go off to take part in a similar experience must begin without dreams, abandoning everything that used to constitute their lives and exertions. The only ones who should do it are those with a revolutionary strength of mind greater than average (even the average in a revolutionary country), with practical experience gained in struggle, with a high level of political development, and with solid discipline. The incorporation process should be gradual and built around a small but tempered group, so that the selection of new combatants can proceed directly and anyone who does not meet the requirements can be removed. In other words, a cadre policy should be pursued. This will allow a steady increase in numbers without weakening the nucleus, and even a formation of new cadres from the donor country in the insurrectional zone of the host country. For we are not simply schoolmasters; we also study in new schools of the revolution.

Another difficulty we endured—to which very special attention should be paid in the future—is that of the support base. Quite large sums of money vanished into its insatiable jaws, while minute quantities of food and equipment reached the troops in the field. The first requirement is for a command with undisputed and absolute authority in the zone of operations, able to exert rigorous control over the support base and to disregard the natural checks made by the higher centres of the revolution. The selection of men to carry out this task should have been seriously implemented a long time in advance. It has to be seen what a packet of cigarettes means for someone doing nothing at an ambush for 24 hours, and it has to be seen how little the hundred packets of cigarettes that might be smoked each day really cost in comparison with things that are either unnecessary or uselessly squandered in the course of the operation.

The time has come for me to make the most difficult analysis of all, the one that concerns my own role. Taking self-criticism as far as I was capable of doing, I came to the following conclusions. From the point of view of relations with the revolutionary command, I found myself impeded by the slightly abnormal way in which I entered the Congo, and I was not able to overcome this disadvantage. I tended to lose control in the way I reacted to things; for much of the time my attitude might have been described as complacent, but sometimes I displayed very bitter and wounding outbursts, perhaps as a result of a trait of character; the only group with which I maintained unfailingly correct relations was the peasantry, because I am more accustomed to political language, direct explanation and the force of example, and I think that I was successful in the field. I did not learn Swahili quickly or well enough—a defect mainly attributable to my knowledge of

French, which allowed me to communicate with the leaders but alienated me from rank-and-file. I lacked the willpower to make the necessary effort (…)

The Congo is the setting for the most cruel and bitter liberation struggle, and so a study of this experience will give us some useful ideas for the future.

Unlike Latin America, where the process of neo-colonisation took place amid violent class struggles and where the national bourgeoisie participated in the anti-imperialist struggle before its eventual capitulation, Africa presents a picture of a process planned by imperialism. Very few countries there have obtained their independence through armed struggle; on the whole, everything has happened with the smoothness of a well-oiled machine.

Practically speaking, it is only the southern cone of Africa which remains officially colonized, and a general outcry against that system is likely to bring about its rapid extinction, at least in the Portuguese colonies. The Union of South Africa presents different problems (…)

A very important factor in the development of the struggle is the universality that the concepts in play have been acquiring. Evidently imperialism scores a victory when there is a retreat in popular struggles anywhere in the world; and just as evidently, it suffers a defeat when a genuinely progressive government comes to power anywhere in the world. We should not think of countries as self-enclosed areas for the purposes of a social analysis. Indeed, we may say today that Latin America as a whole is a neocolonized continent where capitalist relations of production prevail, despite the numerous examples of feudal relations, and where a struggle that has a clearly popular, anti-imperialist (that is, anti-capitalist) significance is, at the end of the day, a socialist struggle. Similarly, in the Congo or any other country of Africa, we must accept the possibility that new ideas about the world will develop that afford a glimpse of something entirely new, beyond the little local preserve for the hunting of game or the growing of crops for immediate consumption. The impact of socialist ideas must reach the broad masses of the African countries, not as a transplant, but as an adaptation to new conditions. And it must offer a down-to-earth image of major changes than can be, if not actually felt, then clearly imagined by the population (…)

How shall we participate in all this? Perhaps we should send a nucleus of cadres chosen from among those who already have some experience of the Congo and have not undergone the collapse that I have described; perhaps we should send weapons, if the allies permit it; perhaps we should give financial aid and help in training cadres. But we must change one of the concepts that has guided our revolutionary strategy up till now; we have spoken of unconditional aid, and that is a mistake. The giving of aid implies the taking up of a position—and that position is taken on the basis of certain analyses of the trustworthiness and effectiveness of a revolutionary movement in the struggle against imperialism, in the struggle for the liberation of a country. In order to settle such analyses more securely, we have to know the movements in question, and to do this we have to intervene in them.

11.13 Poem by Antonio Agostinho Neto, 1960

Many of the first-generation Third World leaders were writers or poets, a sign of the legitimacy that culture often provided in their communities. Here is a poem, written in Aljube Prison in Lisbon in August 1960, by the man who fifteen years later became the first president of Angola and a key ally of the Soviets in the Third World.

HASTE

I am impatient in this historical tepidness
of delays and lentitude
when with haste the just are murdered
when the prisons are bursting with youths
crushed to death against the walls of violence

Let us end this tepidness of words and gestures
and smiles concealed behind book covers
and the resigned biblical gesture
of turning the other cheek

Start action vigorous male intelligent
which answers tooth for tooth eye for eye
man for man
come vigorous action
of the people's army for the liberation of men
come whirlwinds to shatter this passivity

Cataracts released in torrents
shake the forests with affliction
come storms tearing trees up by the roots
crashing trunk against trunk
and lay waste foliage and fruit
to shed sap and juice on the humid soil
and crush the enemy on the pure earth
so that the evil of their viscera
remains forever there
as eternal monuments to monsters

to be mocked and cursed by generations
by the people martyred for five centuries

Glorious Africa
Africa of age-old injustices
accumulated in this effervescent and impatient breast
where mourn millions of soldiers
who did not win battles
and where lament the solitary ones
who did not make harmony in a united struggle
Draw lightning to the majestic tree
to startle the beasts in the fields
and burn the unholiness of saints and prejudices
Let the youth of the land and of hearts break out in cries
in the irreverent certainty of tomorrow
hastening the release of those bound
to the slave trunk
those tortured in prison
those sacrificed by forced labour
those killed by lash and *palmatória*
those offended against
those who betray
and denounce their own country

Let us not wait for heroes
let us be heroes
uniting our voices and our arms
each at his duty
and defend inch by inch our land
let us drive out the enemy
and sing in a struggle alive and heroic
here and now
the true independence of our country

Questions

What did was the main purpose behind the Bandung Conference?

Judging from events over the past twenty years, were the modernization theorists right?

Why did most Third World leaders in the 1950s opt for continued links with the West?

What did Macmillan see as the main cause of decolonization?

Why did the Soviets become more active in the Third World in the 1960s.

Compare the statements by Macmillan, Khrushchev, and Kennedy. What do they tell us about how each of these leaders saw their country's role in the Third World?

Judging from Patrice Lumumba's statements, why did the United States and Belgium intervene against him?

Why did President Kennedy feel a need for an alliance with Mobutu?

'Violence may be a necessary preamble to liberation.' Do you agree?

What were the main causes of the radicalization of some Third World movements and their willingness to ally with Soviet Union?

Compare the CIA report on Indonesia and Guevara's report on Congo. What do you see as the strengths and weaknesses of each position?

12

Latin America and the Cold War

Given the United States's proximity and the lack of Soviet resources and capabilities of projecting its influence onto the Western Hemisphere, Central and South America remained rather distant from the issues that lay at the heart of the East–West division in the 1940s. By the early 1980s, however, US president Ronald Reagan quoted the Truman Doctrine as he exhorted the American Congress to back his crusade against Communism in Central America. While direct Soviet involvement outside of the island of Cuba remained limited, Latin America had gradually claimed a place as one of the hottest battlegrounds of the Cold War.

This development owed much to Latin American dissatisfaction with the reality and implications of US domination. American economic and political dominance of the Western Hemisphere had been well established in the first half of the twentieth century and justified by the principles of the Monroe Doctrine. Whether through direct intervention (until the early 1930s) or via local dictators (such as the Somozas in Nicaragua, Batista in Cuba, or Trujillo in the Dominican Republic), the United States effectively controlled its Central American neighbours to its own economic and political advantage. And although the South American countries were exempt from the presence of US troops, their economies depended heavily on the United States. World War II, by removing any serious contenders from Latin American markets, further heightened US influence.

In the aftermath of World War II, however, the United States could no longer take for granted an area where economic and social dislocation was widely spread and the American dominance ('Yankee imperialism') was often considered the chief culprit for the pervasive inequality of many Central and Latin American countries. If in Washington military dictators were generally considered the only force able to ensure stability south of the Rio Grande, these same dictators became targets of popular revolts fueled by anti-Americanism, nationalism, and left-wing causes. Thus, even as direct Soviet involvement in Latin America remained negligible, calls for throwing off the 'yoke of Yankee American imperialism' created a headache of massive proportions to US policy-makers.

While US policies varied from one country to another, Americans responded essentially in two ways to the challenge in the south. At one extreme was a series of interventions aimed at toppling an undesirable government. With two exceptions—the 1965 landing of marines in the Dominican Republic by the Johnson administration and the Reagan administration's intervention on the small island of Grenada—these were covert operations. In 1954 the CIA helped to train and provided logistical support for the overthrow of the leftist government of Jacob Arbentz in Guatemala; in 1961 the CIA attempted—but failed miserably in—a similar effort in Cuba; between 1970 and 1973 Americans worked hard to destabilize the Socialist government of Salvador Allende in Chile; in the 1980s the Reagan administration provided support for right-wing guerrillas in Central America (particularly in El Salvador and Nicaragua).

American administrations also tried to use economic aid and the building of hemispheric institutional structures to counter the appeal of left-wing causes and anti-American sentiments. Perhaps most notably, in the early 1960s the Kennedy administration launched the Alliance for Progress, an ambitious programme that—via a combination of US economic programmes and matching Latin American efforts—was to combat the economic and social problems in the target countries. While initially hailed as a major undertaking, the Alliance for Progress soon ran into difficulties. In the eyes of its critics it served only to perpetuate the hold on power of Latin American military governments and oligarchies. And, as indicated above, American administrations were not loath to combining more traditional strong-arm tactics with the lofty promises of economic and social transformation.

Of all the countries in Latin America, Cuba became a special headache for American administrations after the overthrow of the Batista regime in 1959. Under Fidel Castro, Cuba symbolized many of the failures of previous US policies and posed a constant, if at times exaggerated, challenge to American influence in the region. From the American perspective Cuba provided a base for Soviet operations in the Western Hemisphere, served as a 'model' for other revolutionaries, and was seen as an active exporter of revolutionary ideas to countries geographically as remote as Nicaragua and Chile. Indeed, one of the 'successes' of US covert action in Latin America in the 1960s was the assassination of Ernesto 'Che' Guevara, an Argentinian-born Cuban revolutionary who was killed in Bolivia in 1967 while taking his guerrilla warfare methods abroad. There is no question that the Soviet Union took a special interest in seeing the Cuban revolution, and Fidel Castro, succeed. Yet, the Soviet–Cuban relationship was never one of complete dependency, something that in part explains the survival of Castro's regime beyond the Cold War.

From the 1950s to the 1980s Latin America's place in the Cold War vacillated between the crucially central to the seemingly peripheral. And yet, one of the ironies of Cold War history is that the continent that seemed so far removed from the original sources of the East–West confrontation not only became one of its 'hottest' battlegrounds in the early 1980s, but still hosts—as of this writing—one of the few surviving Communist regimes in the world.

Readings

Robert Holden and Eric Zolov, *Latin America and the United States* (2000). An up-to-date overall account of the relationship.

Walter LaFeber, *Inevitable Revolutions* (1983). A critical assessment of US policy towards Central America.

Thomas Patterson, *Contesting Castro* (1994). Assesses the development of US policy towards Cuba prior to the 1962 missile crisis.

Stephen Rabe, *Eisenhower and Latin America: The Foreign Policy of Anticommunism* (1988). A critique of US policy towards Latin America in the formative 1950s.

Gaddis Smith, *The Last Years of the Monroe Doctrine* (1993). A readable and often insightful study of the relationship between the Cold War and the 1823 doctrine.

12.1 Kennan on Communism in Latin America, March 1950

In this memorandum George Kennan, one of the principal architects of containment, lays down his views about US Latin American policy to the secretary of state. The document was written soon after Kennan's extensive tour of Latin America.

(...) It may seem illogical to start with the negative subject of Communist activities in the Latin American area, because in theory the emphasis of our policy must continue to be laid on the constructive, positive features of our relationship; and no more here than in any other part of the world can a successful policy be founded exclusively, or mainly, on just a negative combating of Communist activities.

Nevertheless, as things stand today, the activities of the Communists represent our most serious problem in the area. They have progressed to a point where they must be regarded as an urgent, major problem; and a correct understanding of their significance is basic to an understanding of the other phases of our policy problems (...) It is true that most of the people who go by the name of 'Communist' in Latin America are a somewhat different species than in Europe. Their bond with Moscow is tenuous and indirect (proceeding, as a rule, through at least one other Latin American capital besides their own, and then through Paris). Many of them are little aware of its reality. For this reason, and because their

Latin American character inclines them to individualism, to indiscipline and to a personalized, rather than doctrinaire, approach to their responsibilities as Communists, they sometimes have little resemblance to the highly disciplined Communists of Europe, and are less conscious of their status as the tools of Moscow. The Moscow leaders, we may be sure, must view them with a mixture of amusement, contempt and anxiety.

It is also true that in no Latin American country, with the possible exception of Guatemala, does there seem to be any serious likelihood that the Communists might acquire the strength to come into power by majority opinion.

Finally, even though the Communists should come into power in one of these countries, that would not be the end of the story. If such an experiment remained isolated—that is, if their power were restricted to a single country—they would hardly be a serious military threat to the hemisphere as a whole. In this case, their relations with ourselves and their Latin American neighbours would probably soon become unspeakable; and Moscow's problem of maintenance of dominant influence and control over them would immediately become immensely more difficult, as it always must in the case of Communists who seize the reins of power in areas outside Moscow's sphere of immediate military domination.

All this gives us no justification for complacency about Communist activities in this hemisphere. Here, as elsewhere, the inner core of the Communist leadership is fanatical, disciplined, industrious, and armed with a series of organizational techniques which are absolutely first rate. Their aim is certainly not the acquisition of power by democratic means, and probably, in most instances, not even the acquisition of complete governmental power at all at this juncture, since this would saddle them with a responsibility more hampering than helpful to their basic purposes. Their present aim, after all, is only the destruction of American influence in this part of the world, and the conversion of the Latin American peoples into a hotbed of hostility and trouble for the United States. And in this their activities tie into the formidable body of anti-American feeling already present in every one of the Latin American countries, without exception. It is in this fertile breeding ground that the Communists broadcast their seeds of provocation and hatred and busily tend the plants which sprout in such vigour and profusion.

(...) as to what the United States can do to oppose and defeat Communist penetration into the New World, we find ourselves back in the familiar general problem of Communist activities in third countries: a problem which is still the subject of a great deal of confusion in a great many minds.

I think the first thing to remember is that whatever is done to achieve this purpose must be done for the most part by natives of the particular country concerned, either in its government or otherwise. The burden of this effort can never be carried directly by the representatives of a foreign government. Our representatives can contribute in many ways to the creation of incentives and possibilities for local resistance to Communist pressures; but they cannot themselves be the bearers of that resistance (…)

Our problem, then, is to create, where such do not already exist, incentives which will impel the governments and societies of the Latin American countries to resist Communist pressure, and to assist them and spur them on in their efforts, where the incentives are already present. We cannot be too dogmatic about the methods by which local Communists can be dealt with (…) where the concepts and traditions of popular government are too weak to absorb successfully the intensity of the Communist attack, then we must concede that harsh governmental measures of repression may be the only answer; that these measures may have to proceed from regimes whose origins and methods would not stand the test of American concepts of democratic procedure; and that such regimes and such methods may be preferable alternatives, and indeed the only alternatives, to further Communist successes.

I am not saying that this will be the case everywhere; but I think it may well be the case in certain places. And I would submit that it is very difficult for us, as outsiders, to pass moral judgment on these necessities and to constitute ourselves the arbiters of where one approach is suitable, and where the other should be used. We will have to learn to leave this primarily to the peoples concerned and to be satisfied if the results are on balance favourable to our purposes. For us, it should be sufficient if there is a recognition of Communist penetration for the danger that it is, a will to repel that penetration and to throw off Communist influence, and effective action in response to that will.

Now this gets us into dangerous and difficult waters, where we must proceed with utmost caution. Our policies in recent years have greatly circumscribed our possibilities for inflicting hardships. We have forfeited—and rightly so—the right and the intention of any form of military intervention. Except in extremity, any direct pressure brought to bear on Latin American countries in any internal issues where the detriment to United States interests is not direct and immediately demonstrable, holds great dangers (…) In general, therefore, it would be wise for us to avoid putting direct pressure on Latin American governments with respect to Communist activities, except where those activities have some highly direct and offensive relationship to American interests. Where this is not the case, we must resort to indirection (…)

12.2 Juan Jose Arevalo on American Imperialism

This extract, from the former Guatemalan president Juan Jose Arevalo's book The Shark and the Sardines, *sums up the growing Latin American criticism of US policy in*

the 1950s. The original version was published in 1956, two years after the CIA's involve-
ment in the overthrow of Jacobo Arbentz's left-wing government in Guatemala that
suceeded Arevalo's (see Chapter 14).

(…) It was as thirteen widely varying former colonies inspired by ideals of individual freedom, collective well-being, and national sovereignty that the United
States came into existence in the world (…) Moral values served as a motivating
force in the days of the Independence. Those same values, confirmed by the
civilian populace of the young republic, figured among the norms of government. The nation was characterized by its grandeur of spirit and indeed great
were the military accomplishments and the thesis of the new law. Amazed, the
world applauded.

But as the Twentieth Century was dawning, the White House adopted a different policy. To North America as a nation were transferred the know-how, sentiments and appetites of a financial genius named Rockefeller. Grandeur of spirit
was replaced by greed.

The government descended to become simple entrepreneur for business and
protector of illicit commercial profits (…) The new instrument of persuasion was
the cannon. Now the United States (…) was neither a religious state nor a juridic
state but, rather, a mercantile state—a gigantic mercantile society with all the
apparatus of a great world power (…)

The immediate victim was Latin America. To the North American millionaires converted into government, Latin America appeared as easy prey, a 'big
business'. The inhabitants of this part of the world came to be looked upon as
international braceros [farm workers]. The multiple-faceted exploitation was
carried out with intelligence, with shrewdness, with the precision of clockwork,
with 'scientific' coldness, with harshness and with great arrogance. From the
South the river of millions began to flow Northward and every year it increased.

The United States became great while progress in Latin America was brought
to a halt. And when anything or anyone tried to interfere with the bankers of the
companies, use was made of the Marines. Panama, 1903. Nicaragua, 1909.
Mexico and Haiti, 1914. Santo Domingo, 1916. Along with the military apparatus, a new system of local 'revolutions' was manipulated—financed by the
White House or by Wall Street—which were now the same. This procedure continued right up to the international scandal of the assault on Guatemala in 1954,
an assault directed by Mr. Foster Dulles, with the OK of Mr Eisenhower who was
your President at that time (…)

We Latin Americans, who, more than anybody else, suffered from this change
in political philosophy and its consequences, could no longer be friends of the
government of the United States. The friendship certainly could be re-
established. But to do so, it would be necessary for the White House to alter its
opinion of us and it would be necessary for conduct to change. We expect a

new political treatment. We do not want to continue down this decline that takes us straight to colonial status, however it be disguised. Neither do we want to be republics of traders. Nor do we want to be African factories.

We Latin Americans are struggling to prevent the businessman mentality from being confused with or merged into statesmanship. The North American example has been disastrous to us and has horrified us. We know that a government intimately linked to business and receiving favours from business loses its capacity to strive for the greatest possible happiness for the greatest number of its people. When businessmen are converted into governors, it is no longer possible to speak of social justice; and even the minimum and superficial 'justice' of the common courts is corrupted (...)

If you want to be our friends, you will have to accept us as we are. Do not attempt to remodel us after your image. Mechanical civilization, material progress, industrial techniques, fiduciary wealth, comfort, hobbies—all these figure in our programs of work and enjoyment of life. But, for us, the essence of human life does not lie in such things (...)

This book was written with indignation—indignation wrapped from time to time in the silk of irony. It declares that international treaties are a farce when they are pacted between a shark and a Sardine. It denounces the pan-American system of diplomacy—valuable instrument at the service of the Shark. It denounces the pan-American idea of 'allegiance to the hemisphere'—a juridic device that will inevitably lead to the establishing of an empire from Pole to Pole. It denounces the relentless and immense siphoning-off of wealth from South to North. It denounces the existence of the terrible syndicate of millionaires, whose interests lie even outside the United States.

It denounces the subordination of the White House to this syndicate. It denounces the conversion of your military into vulgar policemen for the big syndicates (...)

12.3 Nixon on his Latin America Trip, May 1958

In the spring of 1958 Vice-President Richard Nixon went on an extensive tour of Latin America. At most stops, Nixon was subjected to vigorous anti-American demonstrations that provided an indication of the dissatisfaction towards US policies throughout the region. In this document Nixon discusses his trip with the members of the National Security Council.

(...) First of all, continued the Vice President, we should all get clearly in mind that the threat of Communism in Latin America was greater today than ever before in history (...)

The southern continent was certainly evolving toward a democratic form of government. Normally we would hail such a development, but we should realize that such a development may not always be in each country the best of all possible courses, particularly in those Latin American countries which are completely lacking in political maturity. In country after country in Latin America we have seen the end of dictatorships. These dictatorial leaders are nearly everywhere being replaced by completely new political types, like Frondizi in Argentina (...) drawn from the middle class and from the evolving intelligentsia. While they are honest men, they are certainly oriented in the direction of Marxist thinking, even though they realize at the same time the necessity of getting along with the United States in order to secure its economic assistance. Being the kind of men they are, they are very naïve about the nature and threat of Communism, so much so that their attitude is frightening. They regard the Communists as nothing more than a duly-constituted political party (...)

(...) Frondizi and the other new leaders had not only stated that the Communist problem was not serious, but went further and said that when it came to dealing harshly with the Communists they would again fail to secure public support. This stemmed from the fact that the people of most of these countries were so weary of dictatorships that they felt that the danger of the old-fashioned dictatorship was much more to be feared than any danger from Communism. The Vice President then explained that when these new leaders thus stated that they could not gain public support for policies they might actually think wise, they didn't mean the support of the masses. By public support they mean, rather, the support of the growing middle class, the intelligentsia, and the growing labour union movement. They also mean in particular the support of the so-called opinion-makers—that is, the journalists and the radio and TV people. The Vice President pointed out that there were very, very few pro-American newspapers in Latin America, at least among the rank and file, even though the editors and owners of some of these papers were friendly to the United States. The same was true in the fields of television and radio (...)

To sum up what seemed to the Vice President the important point, he emphasized that while we are thus witnessing the development of democracy in Latin America, we are at the same time witnessing the development of a serious Communist threat. There could be no doubt that International Communism was making a major effort throughout Latin America. There were 250 Communist-controlled newspapers. There were some 50 Soviet friendship societies, and scores of Communist book-publishing houses. The Communist effort was being directed at those elements of the population who could be in a position to overthrow governments—namely, the labour unions and the universities. In illustration of his point, the Vice President singled out Uruguay as the country which was in greatest real danger of a Communist take-over. Yet Uruguay was the most democratic country in the Western Hemisphere after the United States and Canada. It was just impossible to convince the Uruguayans of the dangers of Communism while they were facing such severe economic problems as now confronted them (...) Accordingly, the Vice President deduced that neither the democratic system nor the system of private enterprise is necessarily a safeguard against Communism (...) we somehow failed to reach the people with our message (...) the problem was how to get our story across to the rank and file (...) we must contemplate an increase in the activity of the United States Information Agency and vastly increased exchange programs with the key population elements of the intelligentsia, the labour leaders, and the newspaper people (...)

The Vice President expressed his belief that we should frame our arguments in the following context: We should base our position on the understanding that dictatorship now constitutes the most emotional issue in Latin America. From this premise we should accordingly in Latin America attack Communism not as Marxist economic thought but as a dictatorship and, worse than that from the Latin American point of view, a foreign-controlled dictatorship. In so doing we could combine and exploit the two chief hatreds of Latin America—namely, dictatorship and foreign control (...)

12.4 Nixon and Castro on the Future of Cuba, April 1959

Soon after the overthrow of the Batista regime, the new Cuban leader, Fidel Castro, travelled to the United States. While President Eisenhower refused to meet with Castro, Nixon sat down with the Cuban leader and discussed the prospects of the new regime and its relations with the United States.

When Castro arrived at the conference he seemed somewhat nervous and tense. He apparently felt that he had not done as well on 'Meet the Press' as he had hoped for (...) I reassured him at the beginning of the conversation that 'Meet the Press' was one of the most difficult programs a public official could go on and that he had done extremely well—particularly having in mind the fact that he had the courage to go on in English rather than to speak through a translator (...)

I suggested at the outset that while I understood that some reasonable time might elapse before it would be feasible to have elections it would nevertheless be much better from his viewpoint if he were not to state so categorically that it would be as long as four years before elections would be held. I urged him to state his position as being in favor of having elections at the earliest possible date and that four years would be the maximum amount of time that would elapse before elections were scheduled. He went into considerable detail as he had in public with regard to the reasons for not holding elections, emphasizing particularly that 'the people did not want elections because the elections in the past had produced bad government.'

He used the same argument that he was simply reflecting the will of the people in justifying the executions of war criminals and his overruling the acquittal of Batista's aviators. In fact he seemed to be obsessed with the idea that it was his responsibility to carry out the will of the people whatever it might appear to be at a particular time. It was also apparent that as far as his visit to the United States was concerned that his primary interest was 'not to get a change in the sugar quota or to get a government loan but to win support for his policies from American public opinion.'

It was this almost slavish subservience to prevailing majority opinion—the voice of the mob—rather than his naive attitude toward Communism and his obvious lack of understanding of even the most elementary economic principles which concerned me most in evaluating what kind of a leader he might eventually turn out to be. That is the reason why I spent as much time as I could trying to emphasize that he had the great gift of leadership, but that it was the responsibility of a leader not always to follow public opinion but to help to direct it in the proper channels, not to give the people what they think they want at a time of emotional stress but to make them want what they ought to have. I pointed out that it might be very possible that the people of Cuba were completely disillusioned as far as elections and representative government were concerned but that this placed an even greater responsibility on him to see that elections were held at the very earliest date and thereby to restore the faith of the people in democratic processes. Otherwise the inevitable result would be the same dictatorship against which he and his followers had fought so gallantly. I used the same argument with regard to freedom of press, the right to a fair trial before an impartial court, judge and jury, and on other issues which came up during the course of the conversation. In every instance he justified his departure from democratic principles on the ground that he was following the will of the people. I in my turn, tried to impress upon him the fact that while we believe in majority rule that even a majority can be tyrannous and that there are certain individual rights which a majority should never have the power to destroy.

I frankly doubt that I made too much impression upon him but he did listen and appeared to be somewhat receptive. I tried to cast my appeal to him primarily in terms of how his place in history would be effected by the courage and statesmanship he displayed at this time. I emphasized that the easy thing to do was to follow the mob, but that the right thing in the long run would be better for the people and, of course, better for him as well (...) In our discussions of Communism I again tried to cast the arguments in terms of his own self-interest and to point out that the revolution which he had led might be turned against him and the Cuban people unless he kept control of the situation and made sure that the Communists did not get into the positions of power and influence. On this score I feel I made very little impression, if any (...)

It was apparent that while he paid lip service to such institutions as freedom of speech, press and religion that his primary concern was with developing programmes for economic progress. He said over and over that a man who worked in the sugar cane fields for three months a year and starved the rest of the year wanted a job, something to eat, a house and some clothing and didn't care a whit about whether he had freedom along with it. I, of course, tried to emphasize that here again as a leader of his people he should try to develop support for policies which could assure economic progress with freedom rather than without it.

He indicated that it was very foolish for the United States to furnish arms to Cuba or any other Caribbean country. He said 'anybody knows that our countries are not going to be able to play any part in the defense of this hemisphere in the event a world war broke out. The arms governments get in this hemisphere are only used to suppress people as Batista used his arms to fight the revolution. It would be far better if the money that you give to Latin American countries for arms be provided for capital investment.' I will have to admit that as far as his basic argument was concerned here I found little that I could disagree with!

(...) He rather bitterly assailed the United States press for what he called their unfair reporting of the revolution after he came to power. I, of course, tried to explain that speaking from some personal experience that it was necessary to expect and to learn to take criticism both fair and unfair. I would not be surprised if his sensitivity with regard to criticism might eventually lead him to take some rather drastic steps toward curtailing freedom of the press in the future (...)

In my turn of course I tried (...) to put our attitude toward Communism in context by pointing out that Communism was something more than just an idea but that its agents were dangerously effective in their ability to grasp power and to set up dictatorships. I also emphasized, however, that we realized that being against Communism was not enough—that it was even more important that we make it by our actions, by what we say and what we do abroad that we convince people in every place that we want to help them achieve economic progress in a climate of freedom.

(...) His primary concern seemed to be to convince me that he was sincere, that he was not a Communist and that his policies had the support of the great majority of the Cuban people.

My own appraisal of him as a man is somewhat mixed. The one fact we can be sure of is that he has those indefinable qualities which make him a leader of men. Whatever we may think of him he is going to be a great factor in the development of Cuba and very possibly in Latin American affairs generally. He seems to be sincere, he is either incredibly naïve about Communism or under Communist discipline—my guess is the former and as I have already implied his ideas as to how to run a government or an economy are less developed than those of almost any world figure I have met in fifty countries.

But because he has the power to lead to which I have referred we have no choice but at least to try to orient him in the right direction.

12.5 Khrushchev on Soviet Support for Cuba, July 1960

By the summer of 1960, following the Cuban government's nationalisation programs and the United States imposition of economic sanctions, it was clear that the two countries were on a collision course. The Soviet Union quickly stepped in to take advantage of the situation offering financial aid to Castro's regime. In this speech, given to a teachers' conference in Moscow eight months prior to the Bay of Pigs invasion, Soviet leader Nikita Khrushchev publicly defended the Cuban revolution.

(...) the time when the United States diktat prevailed is over. The Soviet Union is raising its voice on behalf of, and is offering help to, the people of Cuba who are fighting for their independence. The times are not now the same as they were when only one working class—the working people of former tsarist Russia—was raising the banner of struggle, when not only economic blockade but also armed intervention was organised against us.

Times are quite different now. Over 1,000 million people live in states where the working class and the working people have triumphed and where the glorious banner of Marxism-Leninism is flying. The world socialist camp is now stronger than ever before. The peoples of the socialist countries will help their Cuban brothers to uphold their independence with the object of frustrating the economic blockade the United States of America has just declared against Cuba (...)

It is clear to everybody that economic blockade by the American monopolists can be a prelude to intervention against Cuba. Therefore we must speak up in defence of Cuba and give warning that the imperialists can no longer rob and divide the world as they please, each choosing any piece for himself, as they used to do in the past. Today the peoples of the colonial and dependent countries rebel and fight successfully to rid themselves of the shameful colonial yoke and of enslavement by the United States imperialists. For our part, we shall do everything to support Cuba and her courageous people in their struggle for the freedom and national independence which they have won under the leadership of their national leader Fidel Castro (...)

It should be borne in mind that the United States is now not at such an inaccessible distance from the Soviet Union as formerly. Figuratively speaking, if need be, Soviet artillerymen can support the Cuban people with their rocket fire, should the aggressive forces in the Pentagon dare to start intervention against Cuba. And the Pentagon would be well advised not to forget that, as has been shown by the latest tests, we have rockets which land accurately in a predetermined square target 13,000 kilometres [about 8,000 miles] away. This, if you wish, is a warning to those Who might like to solve international problems by force and not by reason.   *K threatens US*

12.6 Kennedy, Frei, and the Alliance for Progress, 1961, 1967

In large part due to the obvious discontent, with US policy shown there one of the first policy initiatives of the new Kennedy government was directed towards Latin America. In March 1961 the new president annouced the so-called Alliance for Progress, an ambitious ten-year aid programme that was quickly compared to the Marshall Plan. The first document is from Kennedy's speech launching the project. For all its promise and initial popularity, however, the Alliance for Progress did not dramatically transform the relationship between the United States and its neighbours to the south. In the second document the Chilean president Eduardo Frei explains why.

A. Kennedy, 1961

(…) One hundred and thirty-nine years ago this week the United States, stirred by the heroic struggle of its fellow Americans, urged the independence and recognition of the new Latin American Republics. It was then, at the dawn of freedom throughout this hemisphere, that Bolivar spoke of his desire to see the Americas fashioned into the greatest region in the world, 'greatest,' he said, 'not so much by virtue of her area and her wealth, as by her freedom and her glory.'

Never in the long history of our hemisphere has this dream been nearer to fulfilment, and never has it been in greater danger.

The genius of our scientists has given us the tools to bring abundance to our land, strength to our industry, and knowledge to our people. For the first time we have the capacity to strike off the remaining bonds of poverty and ignorance—to free our people for the spiritual and intellectual fulfilment which has always been the goal of our civilization.

Yet at this very moment of maximum opportunity, we confront the same forces which have imperilled America throughout its history—the alien forces which once again seek to impose the despotisms of the Old World on the people of the New (...)

We meet together as firm and ancient friends, united by history and experience and by our determination to advance the values of American civilization. For this New World of ours is not a mere accident of geography. Our continents are bound together by a common history, the endless exploration of new frontiers. Our nations are the product of a common struggle, the revolt from colonial rule. And our people share a common heritage, the quest for the dignity and the freedom of man (...)

But as we welcome the spread of the American revolution to other lands, we must also remember that our own struggle—the revolution which began in Philadelphia in 1776, and in Caracas in 1911—is not yet finished. Our hemisphere's mission is not yet complete. For our unfulfilled task is to demonstrate to the entire world that man's unsatisfied aspiration for economic progress and social justice can best be achieved by free men working within a framework of democratic institutions. If we can do this in our own hemisphere, and for our own people, we may yet realize the prophecy of the great Mexican patriot, Benito Juarez, that 'democracy is the destiny of future humanity.'

As a citizen of the United States let me be the first to admit that we North Americans have not always grasped the significance of this common mission, just as it is also true that many in your own countries have not fully understood the urgency of the need to lift people from poverty and ignorance and despair. But we must turn from these mistakes—from the failures and the misunderstandings of the past to a future full of peril, but bright with hope.

Throughout Latin America, a continent rich in resources and in the spiritual and cultural achievements of its people, millions of men and women suffer the daily degradations of poverty and hunger. They lack decent shelter or protection from disease. Their children are deprived of the education or the jobs which are the gateway to a better life. And each day the problems grow more urgent (...)

If we are to meet a problem so staggering in its dimensions, our approach must itself be equally bold—an approach consistent with the majestic concept of Operation Pan America. Therefore I have called on all people of the hemisphere to join in a new Alliance for Progress—Alianza papa Progreso [*sic*]—a vast cooperative effort, unparalleled in magnitude and nobility of purpose, to satisfy the basic needs of the American People for homes, work and land, health and schools—techo, trabajo y tierra, salud y escuela (...)

With steps such as these, we propose to complete the revolution of the Americas, to build a hemisphere where all men can hope for a suitable standard of living, and all can live out their lives in dignity and in freedom.

To achieve this goal political freedom must accompany material progress. Our Alliance for Progress is an alliance of free governments, and it must work to eliminate tyranny from a hemisphere in which it has no rightful place. Therefore let us express our specials friendship to the people of Cuba and the Dominican Republic—and the hope they will soon rejoin the society of free men, uniting with us in common effort.

This political freedom must be accompanied by social change. For unless necessary social reforms, including land and tax reform, are freely made—unless we broaden the opportunity for all of our people—unless the great mass of Americans share in increasing prosperity—then our alliance, our revolution, our dream, and our freedom will fail. But we call for social change by free men (…) not change which seeks to impose on men tyrannies which we cast out a century and a half ago. Our motto is what it has always been—progress, yes, tyranny no—progres si, tirania no! (…)

Let us once again transform the American continent into a vast crucible of revolutionary ideas and efforts—a tribute to the power of the creative energies of free men and women—an example to all the world that liberty and progress walk hand in hand. Let us once again awaken our American revolution until it guides the struggle of people everywhere—not with an imperialism of force or fear—but the rule of courage and freedom and hope for the future of man.

B. Eduardo Frei, 1967

(…) The Alliance for Progress is committed to the achievement of a revolution which, as a political instrument, should be placed at the service of democratic ideas and the interests of the majority so that it will bring forth a substantial change in the political, social and economic structures of the region. This change must be swift, and the responsibility for bringing it about belongs not just to a group of leaders or to a technocratic elite but to the whole of society. The Latin American origins of the Alliance for Progress were specially evident in the non-Marxist political parties which had no links with the national oligarchies and were strongly opposed to the traditional Latin American Right.

The Latin American revolution, as a force for rapid and substantial change, has been germinating for the last decade; it is now a permanent and dynamic torrent which is weakening the political and social institutions of the continent. The form taken by this drastic change will depend on the time which elapses before the forces of revolution are finally released. The greater the delay, the greater will be the accumulated pressure and the greater the violence of the eventual explosion.

The Latin American revolution has clearly defined objectives: the participation of the people in the government and the destruction of the oligarchies; the redistribution of land and the ending of the feudal or semi-feudal regimes in the countryside; the securing of equal access to cultural and educational facilities and wealth, thus putting an end to inherited privilege and artificial class divisions. Finally, a main objective of the revolution is to secure economic development, coupled with a fair distribution of its products and the utilization of international capital for the benefit of the national economy.

These are precisely the same objectives as those of the Alliance. Obviously a revolution thus defined is not the only means whereby rapid change can be achieved in Latin America, but it is the one with which the Alliance has been identified from its very beginnings.

Has the Alliance achieved these objectives? Has it preserved democracy and helped to implement substantial changes? Unfortunately the answer is negative; the Alliance has not achieved the expected success. It cannot be said that since 1961 there has been a consolidation of democratic regimes in Latin America. On the contrary, various forces have threatened democratic governments, seeking either to overthrow them or to prevent the implementation of their programs. Nor have structural reforms taken place at the expected rate.

This does not mean that the Alliance has failed. It has brought about many beneficial changes. Under its auspices there have been advances in education, in public health services, in communal improvement, in the development of rational economic programs and in better understanding between Latin America and the United States. But these constructive achievements could have been secured simply with the financial assistance of the United States, plus, of course, the demand that these additional resources should be used rationally by the recipient countries. The problem is that what was fundamental to the Alliance for Progress—a revolutionary approach to the need for reform—has not been achieved. Less than half of the Latin American countries have started serious programs of agrarian reform. Drastic changes in the tax system are even scarcer, while the number of genuinely democratic regimes, far from increasing, has actually declined. In other words there has been no strengthening of the political and social foundations for economic progress in Latin America. This is the reason why the ultimate objective of the Alliance (…) is as distant today as it was five years ago (…) What has been lacking is a clear ideological direction and determination on the part of the political leaders to bring about change. These two factors are intimately related and they involve the collective political responsibility of all the members of the Alliance.

Many Latin American governments have used the Alliance as a bargaining lever to obtain increases in US aid precisely so as to avoid changing their domestic situation. These governments have committed themselves to internal reforms which later they knowingly allowed either to become a dead letter, or worse, to be completely controlled or used for the benefit of those in power.

For some of those who signed the Charter of Punta del Este, the important fact was the promise of the United States to help find $20 billion for Latin America (...) To avoid compulsory reforms—in other words, to avoid revolution—the Latin American right wing willingly cooperated with the Marxists in regarding the Alliance as a creation of the United States exclusively. From this position they made unfair demands on the United States, destroying the true meaning of the national effort to accomplish the tasks of the Alliance (...)

It is unnecessary to point out names or dates, but at some stage the imaginative, dynamic commitment of countries united by a common ideal was gone (...) Even though the aid retained its financial value, its ideological significance was completely lost. The flow of dollars given by the United States was carefully watched, but there was no equivalent effort on the part of Latin Americans to reform and become more democratic. Hence the Alliance has not reached the people of Latin America for whom it was created (...) The Latin American institutions which collaborate with the Alliance do not include trade unions, student federations, peasant leagues, cooperatives, etc., yet it is vital that such organizations should take part in an enterprise which is essentially popular and whose success depends fundamentally on its capacity to satisfy the demands made by the community. From a political point of view this is one of the weakest aspects of the Alliance; its task is to carry through a revolution which will bring about economic and social development, and for this it is absolutely necessary that the people as a whole be committed to it. The loyal participation of the community in this effort to build an egalitarian society is the only way in which the objective can be achieved. This is why the Alliance must incorporate all sectors of society in its work of transformation.

The salvation of the Alliance depends on the implementation of all these measures; the support of integration, the discouragement of the armaments race and the finding of a cooperative solution for the problems of external trade. The problem is not one of financial resources only, though at certain times these have been scant when compared with the legitimate needs of the region. It is essentially a political problem requiring the expression of the will to change, together with the acceptance of the measures needed to bring about this change. People do not support governments because they have dutifully complied with directives from this or that international organization; they support them when they offer a promising political and economic alternative to present frustrations, and the hope of moving into a better future.

The necessary measures can be secured only by overcoming age-old resistance and destroying privileges which have remained unassailed over the years. To achieve this will also return to the American continent its true revolutionary mission. This is both possible and necessary because, as Toynbee said, 'If America can bring herself to go this far, she will, I believe, have worked her passage back to a point at which it will become possible for her to rejoin her own revolution.'

The American Revolution was a truly glorious revolution. It was glorious for two reasons. The basic issues that it raised were spiritual, not material; and, even if this may not have been the intention of some of the Founding Fathers, it was, in effect, as Jefferson perceived and Emerson proclaimed, a revolution for the whole human race, not just for the people of the Thirteen Colonies.

12.7 Soviets and Che Guevara on Cuba's Prospects, 26 April 1961

In April 1961 the United States supported a failed invasion by anti-Castro Cubans (for more documentation see Chapter 14). Soon thereafter, the Soviet ambassador to Cuba, S. M. Kudryatsev, held a lengthy discussion with one of Fidel Castro's closest companions, Ernesto 'Che' Guevara. Guevara was at the time the minister of industry.

In the conversation with E. Guevara, [I] inquired about his point of view regarding the situation, which recently developed in Cuba, and also about his assessment of Kennedy's recent statements regarding the U.S. policy toward the revolutionary government of Cuba.

In response, Guevara said that the situation remained quite tense, although he personally believes that the danger of invasion of the country by large beachheads of the external counterrevolutionary forces has now in all likelihood receded. The counterrevolution understands that given the presence of large contingents of well-armed people's militia and the revolutionary army, an operation of deploying paratroopers, even numbering several thousand troops would be doomed to failure. Therefore, mentioned Guevara, it is unlikely that the forces of external counterrevolution would undertake such a risk now, knowing that it would be senseless to count on any kind of extensive internal uprising in Cuba.

We know, said Guevara later on, that there is no single point of view on this issue among the leadership of the counterrevolutionary formations, who would have to command such operations. A number of counterrevolutionary officers believe that it would be risky and senseless to go forward without a direct military support from the United States. This split will likely deepen now especially because Kennedy stated that the U.S. armed forces would not take part in a direct military intervention against Cuba.

In this regard, Kennedy's statement, noted Guevara, has a positive meaning. Besides, it will exert some demoralizing influence on the internal counterrevolution. However, this influence will be very limited, because the chiefs of the counterrevolutionary gangs know perfectly well that the U.S. policy toward Cuba has not changed and that Kennedy's statement represents some kind of camouflage.

By this statement Kennedy, first of all, is trying to present the U.S. in a good light on the eve of the discussion of the Cuban issue in the UN, and secondly, he is trying to ameliorate the unfavorable reaction, which is present in a number of Latin American countries regarding the explicitly aggressive character of U.S. policy toward Cuba.

The current American president follows the same [policy] line toward Cuba [as his predecessor] though the tactics are being somewhat changed. We know that the United States is presently increasing its assistance to the forces of external and internal counterrevolution. The main emphasis here is toward undermining the Cuban economy through stronger acts of sabotage, subversion and the like. This serves as a kind of supplement to the economic blockade, which is enforced against Cuba from the USA. Recently, well-trained groups of subversive elements equipped with the newest technology for conducting explosions and arson are deployed in Cuba from the USA. Also, the USA is transferring large quantities of explosives and weapons to Cuba.

In the recent days the internal counterrevolution, continued Guevara, stepped up its activity and has practically begun an attack. It would suffice to say that just in the last several days there were explosions in the Havana water system, power station; several warehouses were burned down, a sugar plant was burned down, and finally the biggest store 'El Encanton.' All this occurred over the period of 3 or 4 days, and it is extremely difficult for the government to undertake anything effective to prevent acts of that kind. The El Encanton store, as it has been established, was put on fire with special thermal bombs, which produce very high temperature and burning for 20 minutes. The bombs themselves, however, are very small in size. One of such bombs was found unexploded in the store building after the fire with a stamp 'U.S. Army' [on it]. Damages from sabotage and subversive acts, continued Guevara, are estimated in tens of millions of dollars. One can say that the internal counterrevolution has inflicted a serious economic damage upon us during these days.

Guevara said then that the revolutionary government would respond to these strikes of the counterrevolution with counterstrikes. First of all, the repressive measures will be strengthened. A significant number of captured terrorists and subversive elements will be executed, and the people will be called to even more vigilance and more decisive struggle with the enemy of the revolution.

The political situation in the country, emphasized Guevara, is generally good. The pressure of the internal counterrevolution only unites people and revolutionalizes them. Almost all the peasants stand behind the government. Recently the position of the government in the working class has strengthened significantly. If winning of the peasantry over to the side of the revolution has been already accomplished, noted Guevara, much still can be done in regard to the working class.

The economic difficulties, which, according to Kennedy's and the counter-revolution's calculations, should lead to dissatisfaction in the country and create the conditions for an internal explosion, will, in our opinion, said Guevara, have just the opposite effect. These difficulties will unite the people, because the overwhelming majority of the population understands that this is not the government's fault, but rather the consequence of American imperialism's fight against revolutionary Cuba.

In the course of further conversation, Guevara said that the revolutionary government is presently seriously studying the question regarding the ways of overcoming the growing economic hardships. The government would not want to be in the role of beggar, especially because realistically the Soviet Union is the only country among the countries of the socialist camp that can help Cuba, but the Soviet Union already provides enormous assistance and support to Cuba. And yet, nonetheless, said Guevara, it looks like we will have to ask the Soviet Union to help us in some areas, especially in supplying some kinds of raw materials to ensure uninterrupted work of our industry (...) The main task now, emphasized Guevara, is to provide the industry with raw materials and the workers with work. The nationalized industry works well, and its organization is improving. However, production quotas are underfulfilled by 15 to 20% as a result of deficit of raw materials, and also as a result of distraction of a significant number of workers from production in the period of mobilization of units of the people's militia.

12.8 Guevara on Guerrilla Warfare (1964), and a Report on his Death (1967)

After briefly serving in Castro's government, Guevara reached legendary status as a guerrilla fighter and writer. One of his most famous pieces had to do with the role of guerrilla warfare in fighting against imperialism; something Guevara practised on his many campaigns in Africa and Latin America. He also became one of the 'most-wanted' men on the Johnson administration's lists; the State Department's report of his death—document B—was undoubtedly greeted with great relief in the White House.

A. 'Guerrilla Warfare'

Guerrilla warfare has been employed on innumerable occasions throughout history in different circumstances to obtain different objectives. Lately it has been employed in various popular wars of liberation when the vanguard of the people chose the road of irregular armed struggle against enemies of superior military power. Asia, Africa and Latin America have been the scene of such actions on attempts to obtain power in the struggle against feudal, neo-colonial, or colonial exploitation (...)

In America, guerrilla warfare has been employed on several occasions. As a case in point, we have the experience of Cesar Augusto Sandino fighting against the Yankee expeditionary force on the Segovia of Nicaragua. Recently we had Cuba's revolutionary war. Since then in America the problem of guerrilla war has been raised in discussions of theory by the progressive parties of the continent with the question of whether its utilization is possible or convenient. This has become the topic of very controversial polemics.

(...) Above all, we must emphasize at the outset that this form of struggle is a means to an end. That end, essential and inevitable for any revolutionary, is the conquest of political power. Therefore, in the analysis of specific situations in different countries of America, we must use the concept of guerrilla warfare in the limited sense of a method of struggle in order to gain that end.

Almost immediately the question arises: Is guerrilla warfare the only formula for seizing power in all of Latin America? Or, at any rate, will it be the predominant form? Or simply, will it be one formula among many used during the struggle? And ultimately we may ask: Will Cuba's example be applicable to the present situation on the continent? In the course of polemics, those who want to undertake guerrilla warfare are criticized for forgetting mass struggle, implying that guerrilla warfare and mass struggle are opposed to each other. We reject this implication, for guerrilla warfare is a people's war; to attempt to carry out this type of war without the population's support is the prelude to inevitable disaster. The guerrilla is the combat vanguard of the people, situated in a specified place in a certain region, armed and willing to carry out a series of warlike actions for the one possible strategic end—the seizure of power. The guerrilla is supported by the peasant and worker masses of the region and of the whole territory in which it acts. Without these prerequisites, guerrilla warfare is not possible.

Guerrilla war or war of liberation will generally have three stages: First, the strategic defensive when the small force nibbles at the enemy and runs; it is not sheltered to make a passive defence within a small circumference but rather its defence consists of the limited attacks which it can strike successfully. After this comes a state of equilibrium in which the possibilities of action on both sides—the enemy and the guerrillas—are established. Finally, the last state consists of overrunning the repressive army leading to the capture of the big cities, large-scale decisive encounters, and at last the complete annihilation of the enemy (...)

We have predicted that the war will be continental. This means that it will be a protracted war; it will have many fronts; and it will cost much blood and countless lives for a long period of time. But another phenomenon occurring in Latin

America is the polarization of forces, that is, the clear division between exploiters and exploited. Thus when the armed vanguard of the people achieves power, both the imperialists and the national exploiting class will be liquidated at one stroke. The first stage of the socialist revolution will have crystallized, and the people will be ready to heal their wounds and initiate the construction of socialism.

(…) The Alliance for Progress attempts to slow that which cannot be stopped. But if the advance of the European Common Market or any other imperialist group on the American market were more rapid than the development of the fundamental contradiction, the forces of the people would only have to penetrate into the open breach, carrying on the struggle and using the new intruders with a clear awareness of what their true intentions are.

Not a single position, weapon, or secret should be given to the class enemy, under penalty of losing all. In fact, the eruption of the Latin American struggle has begun. Will its storm centre be in Venezuela, Guatemala, Colombia, Peru, Ecuador? Are today's skirmishes only manifestations of a restlessness that has not come to fruition? The outcome of today's struggles does not matter. It does not matter in the final count that one or two movements were temporarily defeated because what is definite is the decision to struggle which matures every day, the consciousness of the need for revolutionary change, and the certainty that it is possible (…)

B. Report on the Death of Che Guevara

This morning we are about 99% sure that 'Che' Guevara is dead (…)

CIA tells us that the latest information is that Guevara was taken alive. After a short interrogation to establish his identity, General Ovando—Chief of the Bolivian Armed Forces—ordered him shot. I regard this as stupid, but it is understandable from a Bolivian standpoint, given the problems which the sparing of French communist and Castro courier Regis Debray has caused them.

The death of Guevara carries these significant implications:

- It marks the passing of another of the aggressive, romantic revolutionaries like Sukarno, Nkrumah, Ben Bella—and reinforces this trend.
- In the Latin American context, it will have a strong impact in discouraging would-be guerrillas.
- It shows the soundness of our 'preventive medicine' assistance to countries facing incipient insurgency—it was the Bolivian 2nd Ranger Battalion trained by our Green Berets from June–September of this year, that cornered him and got him.

We have put these points across to several newsmen.

12.9 The United States and Allende's Chile, 1970–3

Although Chile had been one of the few long-standing democracies in Latin America, the 1970 election of the Socialist leader Salvador Allende as the country's president raised serious concerns in Washington over the prospect of a 'red sandwich' (Chile–Cuba). As the following excerpts indicate, the Nixon administration set out to destabilize the new government in 1970—Allende was eventually overthrown in a military coup in 1973. While the overthrow of the Allende government was greeted with some relief in Washington, the new military junta—headed by Augusto Pinochet—brutalized its opponents and domestic critics with impunity. The second extract gives a sampling of the bitter memories from the immediate aftermath of the military coup.

A. Nixon's National Security Council, 9 November 1970

Following the discussion at the meeting of the National Security Council on November 6 1970, the President has decided (...) that (1) the public posture of the United States will be correct but cool, to avoid giving the Allende government a basis on which to rally domestic and international support for consolidation of the regime; but that (2) the United States will seek to maximize pressures on the Allende government to prevent its consolidation and limit its ability to implement policies contrary to US and hemisphere interests.

Specifically, the President has directed that within the context of a publicly cool and correct posture toward Chile:

- Vigorous efforts be undertaken to assure that other governments in Latin America understand fully that the US opposes consolidation of a communist state in Chile hostile to the interests of the United States and other hemisphere nations, and to the extent possible encourage them to adopt a similar posture.
- Close consultation be established with key governments in Latin America, particularly Brazil and Argentina, to coordinate efforts to oppose Chilean moves which may be contrary to our mutual interests; in pursuit of this objective, efforts should be increased to establish and maintain close relations with friendly military leaders in the hemisphere.
- Necessary actions be taken to:
    a. Exclude, to the extent possible, further financing assistance or guarantees for US private investment in Chile, including those related to the Investment Guarantee Program or the operations of the Export–Import Bank;
    b. Determine the extent to which existing guarantees and financing arrangements can be terminated or reduced;

    c. Bring maximum feasible influence to bear in international financial institutions to limit credit or other financing assistance to Chile (in this connection, efforts should be made to coordinate with and gain maximum support for this policy from other friendly nations, particularly those in Latin America, with the objective of lessening unilateral US exposure); and

    d. Assure that US private business interests having investments or operations in Chile are made aware of the concern with which the US government views the government of Chile and the restrictive nature of the policies which the US government intends to follow.

- No new bilateral economic aid commitments be undertaken with the government of Chile (programs of a humanitarian or private social agency character will be considered on a case by case basis); existing commitments will be fulfilled but ways in which, if the US desires to do so, they could be reduced, delayed or terminated should be examined.

The President has directed that the Director of the Office of Emergency Preparedness prepare a study which sets forth the implications of possible developments in world copper markets, stockpile disposal actions and other factors as they may affect the marketing of Chilean copper and our relationships with Chile.

The President also has directed that the Senior Review Group meet monthly or more frequently as necessary to consider specific policy issues within the framework of this general posture, to report actions which have been taken, and to present to him further specific policy questions which may require his decision (…)

B. Memories of the Takeover in 1973

'On the day of the putsch I found myself crying like a baby.' The man saying these words looked old, burnt out, although he was only forty. His eyes were deep pools of pain and fatigue. He spoke haltingly. From time to time a hacking cough parted his lips to reveal three missing teeth. 'A souvenir from my Junta torturers,' Felipe Hernandez explained (…)

'I just could not accept the fact that our government—I could say "my personal" government—was no more; so I wept. For me the Allende regime was like a fairy tale come true. But then it went crashing down on me and millions of other Chilean slum dwellers who crowded the country's *poblaciones*, and who, for the first time, got a taste of what it is to be human. It is not only that we began living better; having regular jobs and real pay; and that our kids went to school on a regular basis. It is not only because we were able to see real doctors at free clinics, not some quacks as before, simply because we couldn't raise the money to pay a trained physician.

'Perhaps most important was that for the first time we began to count for something. Not only did the newly organized neighborhood committees listen to our complaints and suggestions about our living conditions, but we could actually go to La Moneda, the presidential palace, and discuss our problems with high government officials. Until Allende, we were not even a statistic. Nobody came around to find out how many of us lived in the *poblaciones*. We were always referred to in 'approximate' numbers. I was just a cipher.

'So on the first night that the Junta seized power, the people in my *poblacion* (some 1,500 families) rushed out into the main street to build barricades, as though this little pocket of resistance would help stop the enemy. We piled up boxes, chairs, tables, bags of pebbles, and rocks. Everybody took part in this so-called defense, men, women, children. It was a desperate effort to hold on to something that was so dear to us, something as personal as breathing. It was a last-minute attempt to hold off an enemy made up of fellow Chileans who were Fascists. If they could do away with Allende, we knew they would kill us just as easily (…)

'We kept scurrying about, shoring up our flimsy defenses under the cover of night. When you think about it, this was not really resistance. It was tantamount to a kind of decision, though we didn't vote on it, to commit mass suicide rather than surrender and die without a fight. Although in the back of our minds there was also the faint hope that some of the military would not go along with the Junta and put down the revolt. There were no commanders telling us what to do and how to do it. We just did it.'

Hernandez (that is not his real name) said, 'Early the following morning about twenty army vehicles, including a few small tanks, appeared on the road leading to our shantytown. A voice from the lead armored personnel carrier rasped through a loudspeaker. It ordered us to leave our homes, and all our belongings, and promptly report to a registration center immediately outside of the town, while the Junta soldiers conducted a house-to-house search for guns.

'Our response was immediate, as though on command. It was a fusillade from several dozen pistols, rifles, and shotguns, some dating back to World War I. It all sounded like a bunch of firecrackers going off at the same time. But some of the bullets did reach their mark. Several of the armored cars tried to smash through the barricades. But because the street was narrow and crooked, they made their way slowly. For the next half hour or so they contented themselves with spraying the whole area indiscriminately with machine-gun fire. Dozens and dozens of our people were killed or seriously wounded in the few hours of resistance. Others, however, still continued to blast away at the enemy that was methodically routing our makeshift troops.

'Men and women were dropping like clay figures in a shooting gallery. On either side of me in a shallow hole that was supposed to pass for a trench, two of my neighbors were hit the moment the soldiers opened fire. One died instantly. The other, a mother of seven children, mortally wounded on her right side, her face twisted in pain, managed to hand me her gun, saying, "Give it to them hard," and died a minute later.

'As our skimpy resistance fighters fell back, some of us filtered through the debris and made our escape to an adjoining *poblacion* where better fortified slum dwellers were putting up a stiff fight against the military. After contributing our bit there, we made our way to a wooded area where we joined a small group of men and women who were already at work planning clandestine activities against the Junta. But my clandestine involvement lasted only two days. On September 14th, I felt somewhat proud that I was able to distribute about a hundred leaflets calling on workers not to lose heart. The leaflet was headlined FRIENDS, WORK-ERS, THE BATTLE IS NOT OVER, ALLENDE CONTINUES TO LIVE. FOR US HE WILL NEVER BE DEAD. I was proud for the simple reason that I was not caught. I had only one leaflet when I ran into a bit of bad luck. I was suddenly caught in a brief crossfire between Junta police and a group of resisters whom I did not know. I quickly turned to get out of the area, crumpled the last leaflet in my hand, and began chewing on it as fast as I could. Hardly done with my last swallow when two policemen grabbed me and began pulling me toward a wall of a building adjacent to a hospital complex, while others made ready to raise the machine guns for the execution. At that very moment I heard shouts, "Why don't you let him go? Why don't you let him go? You're a bunch of assassins." I looked up and saw dozens of nurses and other hospital employees standing at the entrance of the hospital defiantly shouting at the police. For some reason the Junta men wavered, gave me a hard shove, and let me free without even frisking me, which was lucky because I had a gun in my pocket, a sure passport to execution.

'I made my way around to the rear of the hospital grounds where several of the hospital staff led me into a cellar hideout. I stayed there in very cramped quarters several days because the area was under constant surveillance. It was frustrating; I was impatient to rejoin my group. But even more oppressive, now that I was out of the battle itself, was my anxiety about my wife and son who remained at home. I finally decided I would take my chance. I reentered my *poblacion* at night and made my way through the mountains of rubble to my house, which miraculously was still standing, and found my little family inside. The joy of seeing them suddenly triggered within me a feeling of overwhelming fear that this reunion wouldn't last long. While I was under fire at the barricades, and then in the woods, I somehow was too busy to think of fear. But now in the presence of family warmth and love, the reality of danger enveloped me, immobilized me and for good reason.

'Scarcely an hour after my return there was a deafening rumble of military vehicles invading the night. Within minutes Junta soldiers armed with machine guns broke open the door, seized me without even asking my name, pushed aside my terror-stricken wife who was holding our infant son in her arms, and drove me to a small plaza where I was transferred to a waiting helicopter. I soon arrived at a prisoner collection center on the grounds of the former International Fair in Santiago. I was led to an office on the third story of a building where I was questioned for about an hour. I was told to remove my clothes and then forced to run down the three flights of steps and across the fair grounds, and then up the stairs in a kind of warehouse which was half-opened at the ceiling. There, completely naked, I spent the night shivering.

'The following day Junta guards threw me some dirty clothes, ordered me to dress and then took me to the headquarters of the Air Force building. A woolen sack was thrown over my head to blindfold me. And now the questioning was accompanied by savage threats. Again and again these questions: "So where were you in the days that you were away from home? What resistance group were you with? What were the names of the others in the group?" Again and again, for about six hours this interrogation continued. I was then pushed onto a chair where my clothes, my shoes, my socks were removed. My hands were tied to the armrest of the chair. Wires were hooked up to my chest and the electric shocking began. This went on for maybe a half an hour while I screamed and screamed' (…)

12.10 Nicaragua 1979

In the summer of 1979 the left-wing Sandinistas were poised to seize power and oust the long-term dictatorship of the Somoza family in Nicaragua; the first such takeover for two decades. In the first document the Soviet ambassador to Cuba, V. I. Vorotnikov, sums up Fidel Castro's views on the situation. In the second document a US diplomat describes the formal ceremonies in Managua on 20 July 1979.

A. Castro and Vorotnikov on Nicaragua's Prospects, June 1979

(…) Castro touched upon the events taking place in Nicaragua and the results of the latest conference of the OAS [Organization of American States] in Washington, which he described as the latest in a serious of crippling defeats suffered by American imperialism in the Western hemisphere. In his words, that meeting of the OAS demonstrated with complete clarity that today ever more Latin American countries are exhibiting 'disobedience' to the demands of the United States. He pointed out further that these issues will be the subject of discussion tomorrow during his meeting in Havana with the president of Venezuela [Luis Herrera Campins]. 'I am certain,' Castro declared, 'that the Americans will not dare to intervene unilaterally in the affairs of Nicaragua, and that Somoza will eventually be required to leave.'

(...) Touching on the matter of the supply of Cuban sugar to the USSR and the delay already allowed for in that connection, Castro said, 'I have discussed this matter with C. R. Rodriguez (who informed me about the letter from Comrade I. B. Arkhipov and your conversation with him), and with other Cuban comrades, and I am aware of your difficulty with the supply of sugar. We are doing everything we can,' he said, 'to stop the interruption and cure the shortfall in the July sugar supply, perhaps to some extent in August, but most likely a portion of the supplies (approximately 80 thousand tons) will be delayed until December.' In this connection Castro emphasized several times that they will not permit a similar situation to recur.

B. An American Diplomat on the Swearing-in of a New Government in Managua, July 1979

The Nicaraguan government of National Reconstruction was installed Friday, July 20, in a festive ceremony in downtown Managua attended by Hemispheric representatives (including U.S. Ambassador William Browdler) led by Dominican Republic Foreign Minister Jimenez, Nicaragua Church leaders, FSLN military commanders, and a jubilant crowd of roughly 75,000 people. The ceremony was peaceful and orderly. No disturbances were noted. U.S. representatives were conspicuous and well-received by officials of the new government as well as enthusiastic spectators, by far the most popular figures with the crowd were Eden Pastora, FSLN military commander, and Archbishop Obando Y Bravo (...)

Despite an announced 11:00 am start of ceremonies, the caravan of foreign dignitaries and government officials did not form until well after noon (...) led by a Red Cross vehicle and FSLN security, the caravan arrived at the National Palace at 12:30. The crowd there was huge (our best estimate is around 75,000 despite intense heat) and the caravan was forced to halt approximately 75 metres from palace entrance. The crowd's mood was festive, but controlled. As we made our way through the crush of the crowd to the palace, many persons reached out to shake hands and Amb Browdler was repeatedly congratulated on the U.S. role in Somoza's ouster.

(...) The Junta arrived late, about 1:30. Once they arrived, all members of the GRN, FSLN leaders and Archbishop made appearances before the crowd. Pastora received much greater ovation than any other figure. In second place was the archbishop (...) at approximately 1:45 pm, the junta was sworn in before a Nicaraguan flag. The archbishop said a prayer and an oath appeared to be administered (we were not close enough to hear well). Afterwards, Daniel Ortega spoke on behalf of the junta and FORMIN [Foreign Minister] Jimenez spoke on behalf of the diplomatic corps (…)

COMMENTS: It is apparent that Pastora's charisma gives him the potential to become a key actor on the new Nicraguan stage. It also appeared that the FSLN commanders dominated the ceremony. Each of the principal FSLN commanders arrived with his own bodyguards and appeared to have little contact with the others. Pastora greeted Amb Browdler warmly and was comfortable posing with him repeatedly for press photographers. Pastora indicated to Marine NCOIC [Non Commissioned Officer In Charge] who accompanied us that he plans to remain active in Costa Rica. Other FSLN commanders were more reserved in their contacts with U.S. officials.

(…) In his remarks for the junta, Daniel Ortega made repeated references to the United States. We were not in a position to hear clearly his remarks, and thus far, they have not been broadcast. However, we understand from others who were able to hear him that the substance was that the U.S. had installed the Somozas, supported them for decades and, finally, forced them to leave office. He added that U.S. intervention in Nicaragua must now be ended and Nicaragua left to govern itself (…)

12.11 The Reagan Doctrine in Central America, 1983–1984

The Reagan administration was determined to stop what it considered a fully fledged Communist offensive in Central America. In addition to an invasion of the small island of Grenada in October 1983, the administration provided support for various anti-Communist 'freedom fighters' in the region. Below Ronald Reagan justifies America's involvement in Nicaragua, perhaps the most controversial of the cases, and Richard Aregood of the Philadelphia Daily News *expresses a strongly critical view of the policy.*

A. Reagan to a Joint Session of Congress, 27 April 1983

The guerrillas are not embattled peasants, armed with muskets. They're professionals, sometimes with better training and weaponry than the government's soldiers. The Salvadoran battalions that have received U.S. training have been conducting themselves well on the battlefield and with the civilian population. But so far, we've only provided enough money to train one Salvadoran soldier out of ten, fewer than the number of guerrillas that are trained by Nicaragua and Cuba.

And let me set the record straight on Nicaragua (...) In 1979 when the new government took over in Nicaragua, after a revolution which overthrew the authoritarian rule of Somoza, everyone hoped for the growth of democracy. We in the United States did, too. By January of 1981, our emergency relief and recovery aid to Nicaragua totalled $118 million—more than provided by any other developed country. In fact, in the first 2 years of Sandinista rule, the United States directly or indirectly sent five times more aid to Nicaragua than it had in the 2 years prior to the revolution. Can anyone doubt the generosity and the good faith of the American people?

These were hardly the actions of a nation implacably hostile to Nicaragua. Yet, the Government of Nicaragua has treated us as an enemy. It has rejected our repeated peace efforts. It has broken its promises to us, to the Organization of American States and, most important of all, to the people of Nicaragua.

No sooner was victory achieved than a small clique ousted others who had been part of the revolution from having any voice in the government. Humberto Ortega, the Minister of Defense, declared Marxism-Leninism would be their guide, and so it is.

The Government of Nicaragua has imposed a new dictatorship. It has refused to hold the elections it promised. It has seized control of most media and subjects all media to heavy prior censorship. It denied the bishops and priests of the Roman Catholic Church the right to say Mass on radio during Holy Week. It insulted and mocked the Pope. It has driven the Miskito Indians from their homelands, burning their villages, destroying their crops, and forcing them into involuntary internment camps far from home. It has moved against the private sector and free labor unions. It condoned mob action against Nicaragua's independent human rights commission and drove the director of that commission into exile (...)

The Sandinista revolution in Nicaragua turned out to be just an exchange of one set of autocratic rulers for another, and the people still have no freedom, no democratic rights, and more poverty. Even worse than its predecessor, it is helping Cuba and the Soviets to destabilize our hemisphere.

(...) But let us be clear as to the American attitude toward the Government of Nicaragua. We do not seek its overthrow. Our interest is to ensure that it does not infect its neighbors through the export of subversion and violence. Our purpose, in conformity with American and international law, is to prevent the flow of arms to El Salvador, Honduras, Guatemala, and Costa Rica. We have attempted to have a dialog with the Government of Nicaragua, but it persists in its efforts to spread violence.

We should not, and we will not, protect the Nicaraguan Government from the anger of its own people. But we should, through diplomacy, offer an alternative. And as Nicaragua ponders its options, we can and will—with all the resources of diplomacy—protect each country of Central America from the danger of war (...) Nicaragua, supported by weapons and military resources provided by the Communist bloc, represses its own people, refuses to make peace, and sponsors a guerrilla war against El Salvador.

President Truman's words are as apt today as they were in 1947 (...) The countries of Central America are smaller than the nations that prompted President Truman's message. But the political and strategic stakes are the same. Will our response—economic, social, military—be as appropriate and successful as Mr. Truman's bold solutions to the problems of postwar Europe?

(...) If Central America were to fall, what would the consequences be for our position in Asia, Europe, and for alliances such as NATO? If the United States cannot respond to a threat near our own borders, why should Europeans or Asians believe that we're seriously concerned about threats to them? If the Soviets can assume that nothing short of an actual attack on the United States will provoke an American response, which ally, which friend will trust us then?

(...) In summation, I say to you that tonight there can be no question: The national security of all the Americas is at stake in Central America. If we cannot defend ourselves there, we cannot expect to prevail elsewhere. Our credibility would collapse, our alliances would crumble, and the safety of our homeland would be put in jeopardy (...)

B. A Critique of US Policy, October 1984

To hear the various official spokesmen tell it, we in the United States are in great danger, surrounded by toppling dominoes that only massive heaps of money and arms can support. But in the last week alone, there have been two remarkable stories about how our government comes to those conclusions. It all seems to have a lot more to do with public relations than it does with politics.

The first came when Nicaragua announced that it was prepared to sign the Contadora peace plan. That sounded like great news, because the U.S. has been pressuring Nicaragua to accept the plan. We even asserted that acceptance would make Nicaragua a democracy, and stop the subversion we've been claiming it promotes among its neighbors. As a bonus, it would also mean that the countries of the region had solved their own problems. Contadora is made up of Mexico, Venezuela, Colombia and Panama. Its 21 peace principles now have been informally approved by Nicaragua, El Salvador, Honduras, Costa Rica and Guatemala.

But, in a complete backflip, the Reagan administration now says it wants changes before we can accept the very same treaty we've been pushing on the Nicaraguans. It turns out we were assuming the Nicaraguans wouldn't go for it. They fooled us, and now we need an excuse to continue to try and overthrow their government. The message is clear, even if the policy is inconsistent. This American government will not be satisfied until it gets what it wanted all along. The only way the Sandinistas can satisfy us is to resign from the government, leave their own country and turn it over to our Somocista thugs. All that stuff about regional solutions was so much eyewash.

The second story is about as chilling. The senior Latin American analyst of the Central Intelligence Agency resigned. He had done a report on Mexico that wasn't frightening enough. William J. Casey, head of the Reaganisti at the CIA, bounced it back to him. Its analysis of the economic and political problems of Mexico were not close enough to the administration's Cold War assumptions. Casey, according to a New York Times story, wanted the report to portray the problems as threatening the internal stability of Mexico and endangering by extension the security of Central America and the United States. The analyst said he had no data to justify that conclusion, so Casey had it rewritten by someone with a greater flair for fiction. The analyst then quit.

There's a danger all right, but it's not that the Red Army is taking Spanish lessons. It's the same danger we faced unsuccessfully in Vietnam, when CIA data were cooked and molded to match the Johnson administration's assumptions. Ignoring the facts so the president's men can contentedly view the entire hemisphere as a backdrop for a 'B' movie about the Red Menace is bad enough on the face of it. After all, Latin America has long been accustomed to American policy that makes no sense from their perspective.

The great danger is that we'll believe our own hogwash, and start pushing our neighbors around for reasons we ourselves have created. If we do that, there's a pretty good chance that we will have ourselves created a Red Menace where there wasn't one before. That way, we lose. Politicians can then amuse themselves arguing about who lost Guatemala (or Costa Rica or Mexico), and threaten people who disagree. But our soldiers will be dying for the sake of the argument. And we will be far worse off than we would have been if we had stuck with the facts.

Questions

What did George Kennan see as the chief threats to American interests in Latin America in 1950?

What did Vice-President Richard Nixon and former Guatemalan President Juan Jose Arevalo see as the central problems in US–Latin American relations in the 1950s?

Did Nixon view Fidel Castro as a dedicated Communist in 1959?

What accounts for the Soviet support of the Cuban revolution?

What were the central goals and shortcomings of the Alliance for Progress?

Were Che Guevara's ideas a serious threat to the United States?

Was the United States responsible for the overthrow of Allende and the treatment of political opponents by the Chilean military junta?

Did the Sandinista takeover of Nicaragua create a Moscow–Havana–Managua axis?

How justified was the American concern over Central America in the early 1980s?

13

Cultures and Mindsets

No single aspect of the Cold War is more important—and more difficult to understand—than the way mindsets and cultures came to define, intensify, and prolong the conflict on a global scale. From its very beginning, the struggle between the Soviet Union and the Western powers was intimately connected to sets of images of oneself and others—images that reflected one's place in society and in the world. In the post-war period, the degree to which local social and political conflicts in most areas came to take on a Cold War significance is staggering—not only in North America, Europe, and East Asia, but also in Africa, the Middle East, and Latin America, large groups of people came to identify themselves with the cause of one or the other of the superpowers.

But the picture of how people came to *use* what they perceived as key ideas in the Cold War is in no way straightforward. In the West and in the Third World, the Marxists and the political left wing used their image of a classless, progressive Soviet Union (or later China) as a means of critiquing injustices and exploitation within their own societies. Meanwhile, in the Soviet state, Eastern Europe, and China a small ruling elite used those very same basic ideas to control and disenfranchise the people they claimed to represent. This makes the Cold War into much more than a one-dimensional conflict between good and evil. While in some countries freedom and justice were represented by the political left—and often by people who viewed themselves as allies of the Soviet Union; in others it was American rock music and the speeches of John Kennedy or Ronald Reagan which fuelled the struggles against oppression.

The way the Cold War contest came to figure in people's self-images was of course connected both to their background and traditions and to what they had come to see as the main problems of their daily lives. If these daily problems resulted mainly from a lack of political freedom, as many Eastern Europeans felt in the 1980s, and the causes of these problems were directly attributable to the Soviets, then the attraction of the American alternative would be irresistible. If, on the other hand, the key problem was US dominance and economic exploitation, as felt by many Chileans or Central Americans, then the idea that the Soviet Union represented all those forces that opposed imperialism would not be far off. In many cases people's educational or religious background played a significant role in how they perceived the contest between the superpowers—in the Catholic countries of Southern Europe and Latin America, for instance, there is no doubt that religion was the main barrier against a positive view of the Soviet Union. Also, allegiances changed over time. But in general terms it is clear enough that the situation one found oneself in politically and socially in one's own country went a long way towards explaining the images one had of either Moscow or Washington.

In Europe and East Asia in the period immediately after World War II, for instance, one very general impression was that capitalism had failed and that socialism would be the wave of the future. Based both on the consequences of the 1930s Depression and on the prestige the Soviet Union had gained as one of the victorious Allies, this attitude was particularly strong among urban intellectuals, in some cases because they felt guilty for not having done enough to prevent the rise of fascism or Japanese militarism before the war. The growth of the Communist parties was helped by these intellectuals who dedicated their names and their debating skills to their new cause. But there were also other voices among intellectuals, who spoke of the similarities between fascism and Stalin's Communism and came to see both as representing what they termed 'totalitarian regimes', with which the Western democracies were involved in a life-and-death struggle, not least in the cause of intellectual freedom.

The battles between left- and right-wing intellectuals were in most cases indistinguishable from the state-funded propaganda wars which the power-blocs fought against each other. Many voluntary organizations which took a position on Cold War issues were funded either by the Soviets or the Americans or their allies, and many writers or film-makers were well paid for putting their talents to work in the cause of propaganda, although most probably saw such funding as an added attraction for contributing to a cause they already believed in. The big difference between the East and West was that while Western intellectuals had many choices open to them over which purpose they could give their vocal support to, most of those on the Eastern side had but one choice: to speak for the regime or be silent. Even during the worst anti-Communist hysteria in the United States in the early 1950s, when leftists were hounded out of their professions and sometimes out of their country, their punishment for speaking out was in no way commensurate with the years in prison, labour camp, or psychiatric hospital which awaited those Soviets, Czechs, or Hungarians who spoke against their regimes.

The most total attempt during the Cold War to control people's thinking and behaviour was the Chinese Cultural Revolution. After having broken with Moscow in the early 1960s, Chairman Mao Zedong created a state that used terror and intense propaganda to spur the revolution on and to strengthen his own leadership. All over China, people could spend hours every day chanting slogans and singing songs extolling the Chairman's virtues and denouncing his enemies.

However, in China after Mao, in Eastern Europe, and ultimately in the Soviet Union, it was not just political propaganda that made people turn away from Communism. The most effective attraction that the West had was the consumer products which the East was much slower in getting; evolving over time from nylon stockings to electronics, from jazz to hip-hop, from the family car to the Mercedes Benz. By the 1980s the West had been effectively portrayed to most people living under Communism as richer, more productive, and more innovative than the East. The image of a more successful West gave urgency to complaints that had long existed about the lack of political freedom, and was crucial in the defeat of the Communist regimes in Eastern Europe. But for those regions outside Europe where the Cold War battle had been over exploitation by the very forces that created the coveted products, joining a global market was at best seen as a halfway solution to their problems.

Readings

Frances Stonor Saunders, *Who Paid the Piper? The Cultural Cold War: The CIA and the World of Arts and Letters* (2000). On secret US funding for anti-Communist cultural organizations.

Arthur Koestler *et al.*, *The God that Failed: Six Studies in Communism* (1982 [1949]). Former Communists on their conversion to the anti-Communist cause.

Carole Fink *et al.* (eds.), *1968: The World Transformed* (1998). On the protests against capitalism in the West in 1968.

Ellen Schrecker, *Many are the Crimes: McCarthyism in America* (1999). The best overview of the anti-Communist campaigns in the United States in the early 1950s.

Vaclav Havel, *Disturbing the Peace: A Conversation with Karel Hvizdala* (1991). Havel— the dissident who became Czech president—on his protests against Communism in the 1970s and '80s.

13.1 Orwell: Nineteen Eighty-Four

George Orwell's 1949 novel Nineteen Eighty-Four *describes a future society where everyone is under control of the state. In an appendix, Orwell outlines the language policies of the socialist state of Oceania.*

Newspeak was the official language of Oceania and had been devised to meet the ideological needs of Ingsoc, or English Socialism. In the year 1984 there was not as yet anyone who used Newspeak as his sole means of communication, either in speech or writing. The leading articles in the *Times* were written in it but this was a *tour de force* which could only be carried out by a specialist. It was expected that Newspeak would have finally superseded Oldspeak (or Standard English, as we should call it) by about the year 2050. Meanwhile it gained ground steadily, all Party members tending to use Newspeak words and grammatical constructions more and more in their everyday speech. The version in use in 1984, and embodied in the Ninth and Tenth Editions of the Newspeak Dictionary, was a provisional one, and contained many superfluous words and archaic formations which were due to be suppressed later. It is with the final, perfected version, as embodied in the Eleventh Edition of the Dictionary, that we are concerned here.

The purpose of Newspeak was not only to provide a medium of expression for the world-view and mental habits proper to the devotees of Ingsoc, but to make all modes of thought impossible. It was intended that when Newspeak had been adopted once and for all and Oldspeak forgotten, a heretical thought—that is, a thought diverging from the principles of Ingsoc—should be literally unthinkable, at least so far as thought is dependent on words. Its vocabulary was so constructed as to give exact and often very subtle expression to every meaning that a Party member could properly wish to express, while excluding all other meanings and also the possibility of arriving at them by indirect methods. This was done partly by the invention of new words, but chiefly by eliminating undesirable words and by stripping such words as remained of unorthodox meanings, and so far as possible of all secondary meanings whatever. To give a single example. The word *free* still existed in Newspeak, but it could only be used in such statements as 'This dog is free from lice' or 'This field is free from weeds'. It could not be used in its old sense of 'politically free' or 'intellectually free', since political and intellectual freedom no longer existed even as concepts, and were therefore of necessity nameless. Quite apart from the suppression of definitely heretical words, reduction of vocabulary was regarded as an end in itself, and no word that could be dispensed with could be allowed to survive. Newspeak was designed not to extend but to *diminish* the range of thought, and this purpose was indirectly assisted by cutting the choice of words down to minimum (...)

Take for example the well-known passage from the Declaration of Independence:

We hold these truths to be self-evident, that all men are created equal, that they are endowed by their Creator with certain unalienable Rights, that among these are Life, Liberty and the pursuit of Happiness. That to secure these rights, Governments are instituted among Men, deriving their just powers from the consent of the governed. That whenever any Form of Government becomes destructive of these ends, it is the Right of the People to alter or abolish it, and to institute new Government . . .

It would have been quite impossible to render this into Newspeak while keeping to the sense of the original. The nearest one could come to doing so would be to swallow the whole passage up in the single word *crimethink*. A full translation could only be an ideological translation, whereby Jefferson's words would be changed into a panegyric on absolute government.

A good deal of the literature of the past was, indeed, already being transformed in this way. Considerations of prestige made it desirable to preserve the memory of certain historical figures, while at the same time bringing their achievements into line with the philosophy of Ingsoc. Various writers, such as Shakespeare, Milton, Swift, Byron, Dickens and some others were therefore in process of translation: when the task had been completed, their original writings, with all else that survived of the literature of the past, would be destroyed. These translations were a slow and difficult business, and it was not expected that they would be finished before the first or second decade of the twenty-first century. There were also large quantities of merely utilitarian literature—indispensable technical manuals, and the like—that had to be treated in the same way. It was chiefly in order to allow time for the preliminary work of translation that the final adoption of Newspeak had been fixed for so late a date as 2050.

13.2 Manifesto of the Congress for Cultural Freedom, 1950

Arthur Koestler was one of the post-war intellectuals who saw Communism as the major threat to all freedoms enjoyed in Western Europe and the United States. The following manifesto was drafted by Koestler at the first meeting, in Berlin, of the Congress for Cultural Freedom; the words in square brackets were added by the philosopher A. J. Ayer and the historian Hugh Trevor-Roper.

1. We hold it to be self-evident that intellectual freedom is one of the inalienable rights of man.
2. Such freedom is defined first and foremost by his right to hold and express his own opinions, and particularly opinions which differ from those of his rulers. Deprived of the right to say 'no', man becomes a slave.
3. Freedom and peace are inseparable. In any country, under any regime, the overwhelming majority of ordinary people fear and oppose war. The danger of war becomes acute when governments, by suppressing democratic representative institutions deny to the majority the means of imposing its will to peace.

Peace can be maintained only if each government submits to the control and inspection of its acts by the people whom if governs, and agrees to submit all questions immediately involving the risk of war to a representative international authority, by whose decisions it will abide.

4. We hold that the main reason for the present insecurity of the world is the policy of governments which, while paying lip-service to peace, refuse to accept this double control. Historical experience proves that wars can be prepared and waged under any slogan, including that of peace. Campaigns for peace which are not backed by acts that will guarantee its maintenance are like counterfeit currency circulated for dishonest purposes. Intellectual sanity and physical security can only return to the world if such practices are abandoned.

5. Freedom is based on the toleration of divergent opinions. The principle of toleration does not logically permit the practice of intolerance.

6. No political philosophy or economic theory can claim the sole right to represent freedom in the abstract. We hold that the value of such theories is to be judged by the range of concrete freedom which they accord to the individual in practice.

   We likewise hold that no race, nation, class or religion can claim the sole right to represent freedom, nor the right to deny freedom to other groups or creeds in the name of any ultimate ideal or lofty aim whatsoever. We hold that the historical contribution of any society is to be judged by the extent and quality of freedom which its members actually enjoy.

7. In times of emergency, restrictions on the freedom of the individual are imposed in the real or assumed interest of the community. We hold it to be essential that such restrictions be confined to a minimum of clearly specified actions; that they be understood to be temporary and limited expedients in the nature of a sacrifice; and that measures restricting freedom be themselves subject to free criticism and democratic control. Only thus can we have a reasonable assurance that emergency measures restricting individual freedom will not degenerate into a permanent tyranny.

8. In totalitarian states restrictions on freedom are no longer intended and publicly understood as sacrifices imposed on the people, but are, on the contrary, represented as triumphs of progress and achievements of a superior civilisation. We hold that both the theory and the practice of these regimes run counter to the basic rights of the individual and the fundamental aspirations of mankind as a whole.

9. We hold the danger represented by these regimes to be all the greater since their means of enforcement far surpasses that of all previous tyrannies in the history of mankind. The citizen of the totalitarian state is expected and forced not only to abstain from crime but to conform in all his thoughts and actions to a prescribed pattern. Citizens are persecuted

and condemned on such unspecified and all-embracing charges as 'enemies of the people' or 'socially unreliable elements'.

10. We hold that there can be no stable world so long as mankind, with regard to freedom, remains divided into 'haves' and 'have-nots'. The defence of existing freedoms, the reconquest of lost freedoms [and the creation of new freedoms], are parts of the same struggle.

11. We hold that the theory and the practice of the totalitarian state are the greatest challenge which man has been called on to meet in the course of civilised history.

12. We hold that indifference or neutrality in the face of such a challenge amounts to a betrayal of mankind and to the abdication of the free mind. Our answer to this challenge may decide the fate of man for generations.

13. [The defence of intellectual liberty today imposes a positive obligation: to offer new and constructive answers to the problems of our time.]

14. We address this manifesto to all men who are determined to regain those liberties which they have lost, and to preserve [and extend] those which they enjoy.

13.3 Neruda and Brecht on Justice, Freedom, and Art

The left-wing Chilean poet Pablo Neruda saw the United States as a threat to the freedom of his country and his own artistic freedom. In these excerpts (A) from two of his best-known poems, Neruda accuses the Americans of being behind oppression not only in Latin America, but also elsewhere in the world.

The German playwright and poet Bertolt Brecht settled in East Germany after 1945, but—though willing to be used as a propagandist by the regime—he retained some of the critical mind that had made him famous in pre-war Germay and in exile in Scandinavia and the United States. These two poems (B) were both written in 1953, three years before Brecht died. The final poem gives his reaction to the Berlin workers' uprising, also described in Doc. 8.1.

A. Two Poems by Pablo Neruda

CANTO GENERAL (*excerpt*)

XIII: They Receive Orders Against Chile

But we must search behind them all, there's
something behind the gnawing traitors and rats,

there's an empire that sets the table,
serves meals and bullets.
They want to do with you what they're doing to Greece
Greek dandies at the banquet, and bullets
to the people in the mountains: they must clip the wings
of the new victory of Samothrace, they must hang,
murder, destroy, plunge the murderous knife
clutched in New York, they must open fire
on man's pride, which appears
everywhere as if it were born
of the earth bathed in blood.
They must arm Chiang and the infamous Videla,
they must give them money for prisons, wings
to bomb compatriots, they must give them
a dunce, some dollars, they'll do the rest:
they lie, corrupt, dance upon the dead,
and their wives sport the most expensive 'minks.'
The people's agony is unimportant, the master—
owners of copper need this martyrdom: the facts:
generals retire from the army to serve
as Staff assistants in Chuquicamata,
and in the nitrate works the 'Chilean' general
commands, sword in hand, what the pampa's
offspring can request for a salary raise.
That's how they govern from above, from the purse of dollars,
that's how the treacherous dwarf receives orders,
that's how the generals serve as police,
that's how the country's tree trunk rots.
(...)

XV: There's No Forgiving

I want land, fire, bread, sugar, flour,
sea, books, homeland for all, that's why
I wander about: the traitor judges pursue me
and his thurifers, like trained monkeys,
try to muddy my reputation.
And I went with *him*, the man who presides,
to the mineshaft, to the desert of the forgotten dawn,
I went with him and told my poor brothers:
'You won't save the threads of tattered clothes,
you won't have this breadless day, you'll be treated

as if you were the country's children.' 'Now
we're going to distribute beauty, and women's
eyes won't weep for their children.'
And when instead of distributing love, in the night
they took that same man off to hunger and martyrdom,
that one who heeded *him* and surrendered
his powerful tree's strength and tenderness,
then I wasn't with the little satrap.

THE UNITED FRUIT CO.

When the trumpet sounded, it was
all prepared on earth,
the Jehovah parceled out the earth
to Coca Cola, Inc., Anaconda,
Ford Motors, and other entities:
The Fruit Company, Inc.
reserved for itself the most succulent,
the central coast of my own land,
the delicate waist of America.
It rechristened its territories
as the 'Banana Republics'
and over the sleeping dead,
over the restless heroes
who brought about the greatness,
the liberty and the flags,
it established the comic opera:
abolished the independencies,
presented crowns of Caesar,
unsheathed envy, attracted
the dictatorship of the flies,
Trujillo flies, Tacho flies,
Carias flies, Martinez flies,
Ubico flies, damp flies,
of modest blood and marmalade,
drunken flies who zoom
over the ordinary graves,
circus flies, wise flies
well trained in tyranny.

Among the blood-thirsty flies
the Fruit Company lands its ships,
taking off the coffee and the fruit;

the treasure of our submerged
territories flow as though
on plates into the ships.

Meanwhile Indians are falling
into the sugared chasms
of the harbors, wrapped
for burial in the midst of dawn:
a body rolls, a thing
that has no name, a fallen cipher,
a cluster of dead fruit
thrown down on the dump.

B. Two Poems by Bertolt Brecht

NOT WHAT WAS MEANT

When the Academy of Arts demanded freedom
Of artistic expression from narrow-minded bureaucrats
There was a howl and a clamor in its immediate vicinity
But roaring above everything
Came a deafening thunder of applause
From beyond the Sector bundary.

Freedom! it roared. Freedom for the artists!
Freedom all round! Freedom for all!
Freedom for the exploiters! Freedom for the warmongers!
Freedom for the Ruhr cartels! Freedom for Hitler's generals!
Softly, my dear fellows . . .

The Judas kiss for the artists follows
Hard on the Judas kiss for the workers.
The arsonist with his bottle of petrol
Sneaks up grinning to the Academy of Arts.

But it was not to embrace him, just
To knock the bottle out of his dirty hand that
We asked for elbow room.
Even the narrowest minds
In which peace is harbored
Are more welcome to the arts than the art lover
Who is also a lover of the art of war.

(Trans. by Frank Jones)

THE SOLUTION

After the uprising of the 17th June
The Secretary of the Writers' Union
Had leaflets distributed in the Stalinallee
Stating that the people
Had forfeited the confidence of the government
And could win it back only
By redoubled efforts. Would it not be easier
In that case for the government
To dissolve the people
And elect another?

(Trans. by Derek Bowman)

13.4 Picasso on Communism

The painter and sculptor Pablo Picasso joined the French Communist Party after the liberation of Paris from the Nazis. In the first of these excerpts—a statement published in 1944 in the French Communist newspaper L'Humanite—*he explains why he joined the party; in the second—an interview with the American journalist Carlton Lake in 1957—he makes clear why he remains with the party in spite of disagreeing with some of its policies.*

A. Picasso on Joining the Communist Party, 1944

My joining the Communist Party is a logical step in my life, my work and gives them meaning. Through design and color, I have tried to penetrate deeper into a knowledge of the world and of men so that this knowledge might free us. In my own way I have always said what I considered most true, most just and best, and therefore, most beautiful. But during the oppression and the insurrection I felt that that was not enough, that I had to fight not only with painting but with my whole being. Previously, out of a sort of 'innocence', I had not understood this.

I have become a Communist because our party strives more than any other to know and to build a better world, to make men clearer thinkers, more free and more happy. I have become a Communist because the Communists are the bravest in France, in the Soviet Union, as they are in my country, Spain. I have never felt more free, more complete than since I joined. While I wait for the time when Spain can take me back again, the French Communist Party is a fatherland to me. In it I find again all my friends—the great scientists Paul Langevin and Frédéric Joliot-Curie, the great writers Louis Aragon and Paul Eulard, and so many of the beautiful faces of the insurgents of Paris. I am again among my brothers.

B. Picasso on Being a Communist, 1957

One thing that interested me, I [the interviewer] said, was the question of his Communism. It was hard, I explained, for many people to understand how a man who believes in total independence—whose work has been for nearly two generations the very symbol of it—could be a member of the Communist Party today. How did he square those two ideas? (…)

Picasso raised his eyebrows, then relaxed, smiled. 'Look,' he said, 'I'm no politician. I'm not technically proficient in such matters. But Communism stands for certain ideals I believe in. I believe Communism is working toward the realization of those ideals.' He paused ever so briefly and then, before I had a chance to speak, picked up the question that was beginning to formulate itself in my thought. 'You'll ask me, "what about Stalin?"' he said. 'Well, what about him? You would have said he was no good—but you didn't know that; you only thought it. Well, I thought he was. It turned out that I was wrong. But is that any reason why I should renounce the ideals I believe in? Let's say I were a Catholic and I met a priest who was no good—a worthless type in every sense of the word. He's all the bad things you can think of. Is that any reason why I should give up believing in Christianity? There are all kinds of perfectly authentic stories about the sins of the Church in the Middle Ages. Some of the Popes were horrible creatures. But should I—as a Christian—in view of that, give up my adherence to the ideals I believe in? Eh bien, non!'

Jacqueline leaned toward Picasso. 'Perhaps you should make things perfectly clear,' she suggested, 'by saying you have no intention of resigning from the Party.'

Picasso nodded. 'That's right. I have no intention of resigning. Things look bad in Poland and Hungary, I know, but I'm not quitting the Party just for that. I don't say the world can't find the cure for its ills under the capitalist system, but thus far it hasn't made very impressive headway.' He studied me for a brief moment, then said, 'I don't understand why Americans are so concerned about Communism, anyway. Especially, about whether some individual is a Communist or not.'

13.5 Walt Disney on Un-American Activities, 1947

Walt Disney was among the many in Hollywood who had to testify before the Committee on Un-American Activities in the US House of Representatives. In his 24 October 1947 appearance before the Committee, the cartoonist chose to co-operate. Other actors and movie-makers did not, and were fired or blacklisted as a result.

ROBERT E. STRIPLING, CHIEF INVESTIGATOR: Mr. Disney, will you state your full name and present address, please?

WALT DISNEY: Walter E. Disney, Los Angeles, California.

STRIPLING: When and where were you born, Mr. Disney?

DISNEY: Chicago, Illinois, December 5, 1901.

STRIPLING: December 5, 1901?

DISNEY: Yes, sir.

STRIPLING: What is your occupation?

DISNEY: Well, I am a producer of motion-picture cartoons (…)

H. A. SMITH: Have you had at any time, in your opinion, in the past, had any communists employed at your studio?

DISNEY: Yes; in the past I had some people that I definitely feel were communists.

SMITH: As a matter of fact, Mr. Disney, you experienced a strike at your studio, did you not?

DISNEY: Yes.

SMITH: And is it your opinion that that strike was instituted by members of the Communist Party to serve their purposes?

DISNEY: Well, it proved itself so with time, and I definitely feel it was a communist group trying to take over my artists and they did take them over.

CHAIRMAN: Do you say they did take them over?

DISNEY: They did take them over.

SMITH: Will you explain that to the committee, please?

DISNEY: It came to my attention when a delegation of my boys, my artists, came to me and told me that Mr. Herbert Sorrell (…)

SMITH: Is that Herbert K. Sorrell?

DISNEY: Herbert K. Sorrell, was trying to take them over (…)

SMITH: How many labor unions, approximately, do you have operating in your studios at the present time?

DISNEY: Well, we operate with around 35 (…) I think we have contacts with 30.

SMITH: At the time of this strike you didn't have any grievances or labor troubles whatsoever in your plant?

DISNEY: No. The only real grievance was between Sorrell and the boys within my plant, they demanding an election, and they never got it.

SMITH: Do you recall having had any conversations with Mr. Sorrell relative to communism?

DISNEY: Yes, I do.

SMITH: Will you relate that conversation?

DISNEY: Well, I didn't pull my punches on how I felt. He evidently heard that I had called them all a bunch of communists—and I believe they are. At the meeting he leaned over and he said, 'You think I am a communist, don't you,' and I told him that all I knew was what I heard and what I had seen, and he laughed and said, 'Well, I used their money to finance my strike of 1937,' and he said that he had gotten the money through the personal check of some actor, but he didn't name the actor. I didn't go into it any further. I just listened.

SMITH: Can you name any other individuals that were active at the time of the strike that you believe in your opinion are communists?

DISNEY: Well, I feel that there is one artist in my plant that came in there, he came in about 1938, and he sort of stayed in the background, he wasn't too active, but he was the real brains of this, and I believe he is a communist. His name is David Hilberman.

SMITH: How is it spelled?

DISNEY: H-i-l-b-e-r-m-a-n, I believe. I looked into his record and I found that, No. 1, that he had no religion and, No. 2, that he had considerable time at the Moscow Art Theater studying art direction or something (…)

SMITH: What is your personal opinion of the Communist Party, Mr. Disney, as to whether or not it is a political party?

DISNEY: Well, I don't believe it is a political party. I believe it is an un-American thing. The thing that I resent the most is that they are able to get into these unions, take them over, and represent to the world that a group of people that are in my plant, that I know are good, 100 percent Americans, are trapped by this group, and they are represented to the world as supporting all of those ideologies, and it is not so, and I feel that they really ought to be smoked out and shown up for what they are, so that all of the good, free causes in this country, all the liberalisms that really are American, can go out without the taint of communism. That is my sincere feeling on it (…)

13.6 The 'Plot' against Stalin, 1953

In 1952 Stalin's paranoid approach to politics intensified, and he became convinced that a conspiracy existed among Soviet medical professionals to kill leaders of the Communist regime. Those victims of his last campaign—many of whom were of Jewish descent—who survived the dictator's death in March 1953, were exonerated and released. This excerpt is from an editorial in the Moscow newspaper Pravda, *13 January 1953.*

Foul spies and murderers in the mask of doctors and professors

The TASS report of the arrest of a group of saboteur-doctors is published today. This terrorist group, discovered some time ago by agencies of state security, aimed at cutting short the lives of active public figures of the Soviet Union through sabotage treatment.

The investigation established that the members of the terrorist group, taking advantage of their positions as doctors and abusing the trust of patients, by deliberate evil intent undermined patients' health, made incorrect diagnoses and then doomed patients by wrong treatment. Hiding behind the lofty and noble calling of doctors and men of science, these monsters and murderers trampled the sacred banner of science. In taking the path of monstrous crimes they desecrated the honor of scientist.

Comrades A. A. Zhdanov and A. S. Shcherbakov fell victims of this band of monsters in human form. The criminals confessed that, taking advantage of Comrade Zhdanov's ailment, they deliberately concealed an infarct of his myocardium, prescribed treatment counterindicated for his serious ailment and thereby killed Comrade Zhdanov. By incorrectly employing strong drugs and prescribing treatment which was mortal, the murderer-doctors shortened Comrade Shcherbakov's life, and brought him to his death.

The criminals sought above all to undermine the health of leading Soviet military personnel, to put them out of action and thereby weaken defense of the country. Arrest of the criminals disrupted their evil plans and prevented them from attaining their monstrous aim.

Whom did these monsters serve? Who directed the criminal terrorist and wrecking activity of these vile traitors to the motherland? What purpose did they want to achieve through murders of active public figures of the Soviet state?

It has been established that all the participants in the terrorist group of doctors were enrolled in foreign intelligence services, sold them their bodies and souls, were hired paid agents.

Most of the members of the terrorist group—Vovsi, B. Kogan, Feldman, Grinshtein, Etinger and others—were bought by the American intelligence service. They were recruited by a branch of American intelligence, the international Jewish bourgeois nationalist organization 'Joint.' The dirty face of this Zionist espionage organization, concealing its foul work under a mask of charity, has been completely exposed.

Relying on a group of depraved Jewish bourgeois nationalists, the professional spies and terrorist of the 'Joint' spread their subversive activity to the territory of the Soviet Union, at the assignment of American intelligence and under its direction. The arrested Vovsi testified at the investigation that he received orders from the U.S.A. 'to wipe out the leading cadres of the U.S.S.R.' These orders were sent to him in the name of the espionage and terrorist organization 'Joint' by Dr. Shimeliovich and the well-known Jewish bourgeois nationalist Mikhoels.

Exposure of the band of poisoner-doctors is a blow at the international Jewish Zionist organization. Now all can see what 'charitable' 'friends of peace' hide under the 'Joint' letterhead.

Other members of the terrorist group (Vinogradov, M. Kogan, Yegorov) are, it is now established, old agents of British intelligence, have served it for a long time performing its most criminal sordid assignments.

The bosses of the U.S.A. and their British 'junior partners' know that it is impossible to secure mastery over other nations by peaceful means. Feverishly preparing for a new world war, they are sending more and more of their spies to the U.S.S.R. and the people's democracies, trying to succeed where the Hitlerites failed—trying to create a subversive 'fifth column' in the U.S.S.R. Suffice it to recall the open and cynical allocation by the American government of $100 million for subversive terrorist and espionage work in the countries of the socialist camp, not to mention the fact that hundreds of millions of dollars are spent secretly for this purpose.

Soviet people cannot for one moment forget the necessity of thoroughly increasing their vigilance, carefully watching for machinations of the warmongers and their agents, constantly strengthening our state's armed forces and counterintelligence.

Comrade Stalin has repeatedly warned that our successes have their dark side, that they give rise among many of our officials to a mood complacency and self-satisfaction. This mood is still far from eliminated. We still have many gullible people among us. It is this gullibility of our people which furnishes nourishing soil for criminal sabotage. (...)

The exposure of the gang of poisoner-doctors is a crushing blow to the American–British warmongers. Their network of agents is caught and disarmed. The true visage of the slave holder-cannibals from the U.S.A. and Britain has been presented to the whole world once more.

The Soviet people wrathfully and indignantly condemn the criminal band of murderers and their foreign masters. They will crush like loathsome vermin the despised hirelings who sold themselves for dollars and pounds sterling. As for the inspirers of these hired murderers, they may rest assured that vengeance will not pass them by but will find a path to them to say its weighty word.

All this is true, of course. But it is also true that besides these enemies we still have one more enemy—the gullibility of our people. One cannot doubt that as long as we have gullibility there will continue to be sabotage. Consequently, to end sabotage it is necessary to put an end to gullibility in our ranks.

13.7 Solzhenitsyn: One Day in the Life of Ivan Denisovitch

No single book had more influence on how the outside world came to view Soviet policies against dissidents than Solzhenitsyn's portrayal of the horrors suffered by millions in Stalin's labour camps. The book was published in Moscow during the thaw in the early 1960s, but the author was not allowed to receive the Nobel Prize for Literature (1970) and was forced into exile in 1974.

The hammer banged reveille on the rail outside camp HQ at five o'clock as always. Time to get up. The ragged noise was muffled by ice two fingers thick on the windows and soon died away. Too cold for the warder to go on hammering.

The jangling stopped. Outside it was still as dark as when Shukhov had got up in the night to use the bucket—pitch black, except for three yellow lights visible from the window, two in the perimeter, one inside the camp.

For some reason they were slow unlocking the hut, and he couldn't hear the usual sound of the orderlies mounting the slop tub on poles to carry it out.

Shukhov never overslept. He was always up at the call. That way he had an hour and a half all to himself before work parade—time for a man who knew his way around to earn a bit on the side. He could stitch covers for somebody's mittens from a piece of old lining. Take some rich foreman his felt boots while he was still in his bunk (save him hopping around barefoot, fishing them out of the heap after drying). Rush round the storerooms looking for odd jobs—sweeping up or running errands. Go to the mess to stack bowls and carry them to the washers-up. You'd get something to eat, but there were too many volunteers, swarms of them. And the worst of it was that if there was anything left in a bowl you couldn't help licking it. Shukhov never for a moment forgot what his first foreman Kuzyomin had told him. An old camp-wolf, twelve years inside by 1943. One day round the camp-fire in a forest clearing he told the reinforcements fresh from the front: 'It's the law of the *taiga* here lads. But a man *can* live here, just like anywhere else. Know who pegs out first? The guy who licks out bowls, puts his faith in the sick-bay, or squeals to godfather.'

He was stretching it a bit there, of course. A stoolie will always get by, whoever else bleeds for him.

Shukhov always got up at once. Not today though. Hadn't felt right since the night before—had the shivers, and some sort of ache. And hadn't got really warm all night. In his sleep he kept fancying he was seriously ill, then feeling a bit better. Kept hoping morning would never come.

But it arrived on time.

Some hope of getting warm with a thick scab of ice on the windows, and white cobwebs of hoar frost where the walls of the huge hut met the ceiling.

Shukhov still didn't get up. He lay up top on a four-man bunk, with his blanket and jacket over his head, and both feet squeezed into one turned-in sleeve of his jerkin. He couldn't see anything but he knew from the sounds just what was going on in the hut and in his own gang's corner. He heard the orderlies trudging heavily down the corridor with the tub that held eight pails of slops. Light work for the unfit, they call it, but just try getting the thing out without spilling it! And that bump means Gang 75's felt boots are back from the drying room. And here come ours—today's our turn to get our boots dried out. The foreman and his deputy pulled their boots on in silence except for the bunk creaking under them. Now the deputy would be off to the bread-cutting room, and the foreman to see to work-assigners at HQ.

He did that every day, but today was different. Shukhov remembered. A fateful day for Gang 104: would they, or wouldn't they be shunted from the workshops they'd been building to a new site, the so called 'Sotsgorodok.' This Sotsgorodok was a bare field kneedeep in snow, and for a start you'd be digging holes, knocking in fence posts and stringing barbed wire round them to stop yourself running away. After that—get building.

You could count on a month with nowhere to go for a warm, not so much as a dog kennel. You wouldn't even be able to light a fire out in the open—where would the fuel come from? Your only hope would be to dig, dig, dig for all you were worth.

The foreman went off to try and fix it, looking anxious. Maybe he can get some gang less quick off the mark dumped out there? You could never do a deal empty-handed, of course. Have to slip the senior work-assigner half a kilo of fatback. Maybe a kilo, even.

Might as well give it a try—wander over to the sickbay and wangle a day off. Every bone in my body is aching.

Ah, but who's duty-warder today?

Oh, yes. It's Ivan-and-a-half, the thin, lanky sergeant with black eyes. First time you saw him you were terrified, but when you got to know him he was the easiest of the lot—never put you in the hole, never dragged you off to the disciplinary officer. So lie in a bit longer, till it's time for Hut 9 to go to the mess.

13.8 The Kitchen Debate, 1959

Vice-President Richard Nixon visited Moscow for the first US exhibition in the Soviet Union in 1959. Seeing a model of the 'typical' American kitchen provoked the following debate between the vice-president and Soviet premier Nikita Khrushchev.

[Both men enter kitchen in the American exhibit.]

NIXON: I want to show you this kitchen. It is like those of our houses in California. [Nixon points to dishwasher.]

KHRUSHCHEV: We have such things.

NIXON: This is our newest model. This is the kind which is built in thousands of units for direct installations in the houses. In America, we like to make life easier for women (...)

KHRUSHCHEV: Your capitalistic attitude toward women does not occur under Communism.

NIXON: I think that this attitude towards women is universal. What we want to do, is make life more easy for our housewives (...)

NIXON: This house can be bought for $14,000, and most American [veterans from World War II] can buy a home in the bracket of $10,000 to $15,000. Let me give you an example that you can appreciate. Our steel workers as you know, are now on strike. But any steel worker could buy this house. They earn $3 an hour. This house costs about $100 a month to buy on a contract running 25 to 30 years.

KHRUSHCHEV: We have steel workers and peasants who can afford to spend $14,000 for a house. Your American houses are built to last only 20 years so builders could sell new houses at the end. We build firmly. We build for our children and grandchildren.

NIXON: American houses last for more than 20 years, but, even so, after twenty years, many Americans want a new house or a new kitchen. Their kitchen is obsolete by that time . . . The American system is designed to take advantage of new inventions and new techniques.

KHRUSHCHEV: This theory does not hold water. Some things never get out of date—houses, for instance, and furniture, furnishings—perhaps—but not houses. I have read much about America and American houses, and I do not think that this exhibit and what you say is strictly accurate.

NIXON: Well, um . . .

KHRUSHCHEV: I hope I have not insulted you.

NIXON: I have been insulted by experts. Everything we say [on the other hand] is in good humor. Always speak frankly.

KHRUSHCHEV: The Americans have created their own image of the Soviet man. But he is not as you think. You think the Russian people will be dumb-founded to see these things, but the fact is that newly built Russian houses have all this equipment right now.

NIXON: Yes, but . . . (...)

KHRUSHCHEV: It's clear to me that the construction workers didn't manage to finish their work and the exhibit still is not put in order . . . This is what America is capable of, and how long has she existed? 300 years? 150 years of independence and this is her level.

We haven't quite reached 42 years, and in another 7 years, we'll be at the level of America, and after that we'll go farther. As we pass you by, we'll wave 'hi' to you, and then if you want, we'll stop and say, 'please come along behind us.'

(…) If you want to live under capitalism, go ahead, that's your question, an internal matter, it doesn't concern us. We can feel sorry for you, but really, you wouldn't understand. We've already seen how you understand things (…)

13.9 Nureyev Defects, 1961

The defection to the West of a number of leading Soviet artists and performers was a constant challenge to the Moscow regime. In this excerpt from a recent biography, Diane Solway describes the defection of the world-famous dancer Rudolf Nureyev at an airport in Paris in 1961.

'Do you want to stay?' she asked as she kissed him. Her heart was beating very fast. 'Yes, please do something,' he answered as she leaned toward the other cheek. 'Are you sure?' Another kiss. 'Yes, yes, please, I want to stay.' Clara smiled at the agents. 'They just thought I was this young girl saying good-bye,' she remembers. 'They were so strong, they didn't care about me.'

When Clara returned to the others and told them that Rudolf had asked for her help, they warned her not to get involved. 'It's very dangerous,' they whispered. 'We know it's terrible, but we can't do anything.' Clara realized she was wasting precious time and began discreetly surveying the airport for other options. Spying the sign marked AIRPORT POLICE near the staircase, she casually made her way to the second-floor office.

'There's a Russian dancer downstairs at the bar who wants to stay in France,' she announced to the two plainclothes policemen at the desk. They asked if she was sure he was 'only a dancer.' They had never heard of him. Are you sure he's not a scientist?

'Yes, he's a great dancer,' she insisted, and explained that she'd seen him dance at the Paris Opéra and the Palais des Sports by way of proof. 'They're sending him back because he spent time with French people. He's not like the others, he was more independent. They were probably afraid he'd run to the French embassy if he got wind of their plan, so they waited until they got to the airport. But I know he really wants to stay and they're planning to send him back to Moscow. Can't we do something?'

Clara knew that the French police were virulently anti-Communist and was betting on the chance that they might be eager to help. 'Look, we can't go to him, he has to come to us,' they explained. 'If he comes to us, then we'll take care of everything.'

'But how?' Clara asked. 'There are two men guarding him.' The policemen promised to accompany Clara downstairs to the bar. She was to go first and order a coffee. They would follow ten minutes later and stand near her. When they had taken up their positions, she was to approach Rudolf again and explain to him that he had to go to them on his own.

Clara's legs were 'like rubber' as she went to bid farewell to 'poor Rudi' one more time. 'It's so sad that he's leaving,' she lamented to Strizhevski, hoping to convince him that she was just an overwrought French girl. For added effect, she made a show of great affection to give the impression that she was whispering something tender in Rudolf's ear. 'It's so sad you're leaving us,' she said for all to hear, and then, sotto voce, added, 'See those two men at the bar? They're waiting for you. You must go to them.' As they exchanged one last kiss, Rudolf simply said, 'Yes,' as he kissed her cheek.

Five minutes later Rudolf bolted from his chair to the bar, a distance of just a few yards. 'I want to stay in France,' he cried in English just as Strizhevski and the other agent lunged and grabbed him. A tug-of-war ensued for a full minute. 'That's enough!' the French police shouted at the Russians. 'You are in France!' At this, the Russians had no choice but to let go of Rudolf. As the French police ushered him upstairs, the embassy agents rushed to the phones to relay the bad news (...)

Within forty-eight hours of Nureyev's defection, KGB boss Alexander Shelepin had prepared his damage report for the Central Committee of the Communist Party, following an emergency meeting of the Committee of State Security. The haste with which Shelepin filed his summary suggests the Soviets' profound embarrassment at this sudden blow to Soviet prestige. A simple plan had been badly botched, and he now had a major international scandal on his hands, one that threatened to undermine Western credibility in the Soviet system.

Hereby I report that on June 16 1961 NUREYEV Rudolf Hametovich born 1938, single, Tatar, nonparty member, artist of the Leningrad Kirov Theater who was a member of the touring company in France betrayed his motherland in Paris.

According to the information received from France June 3 this year, NUREYEV Rudolf Hametovich violated the rules of behavior of Soviet citizens abroad, went out to town and came back to the hotel late at night. Besides he established close relations with French artists among whom there were homosexuals. Despite talks of a cautionary character conducted with him, NUREYEV did not change his behavior.'

13.10 The KGB on the Novocherkassk Uprising, 1962

In the summer of 1962 the people of the Russian city of Novocherkassk rose against the Soviet government, protesting price increases and poor working conditions. Here is an extract from a KGB report on what happened.

(...) On 1 June 1962, at about 7:30 a.m., a group of eight to ten people, welders at the smelting unit, started discussing the decision of the government.

Present at the unit at the time was Comrade Buzaiev, head of the section Industry of the *Obkom* [Regional Committees of the CPSU], who tried to explain that decision. The group was quickly joined by (...) nearly 20 to 25 people.

Comrade Tchernychkov, head of the unit, walked towards the workers and asked them to stop discussing during working hours and to return to their places. However, the workers did not listen to him and left the unit in order to go outdoors where they continued the discussion which had already taken on a provocative character. The director of the factory, Comrade Korotchkin, headed towards the workers and tried to convince them to return to their workplace. When they heard of this, workers from other units stopped working in order to head towards the place of the meeting.

Assembled in the square, the workers manifested their dissatisfaction and started criticising the management because of their abnormal working conditions, the disregard of security norms, the bad living conditions and low wages. The discussion between the workers and the director was interrupted by insults and shouts (...)

The director (...), who during these events found himself in the square of the factory in between the workers, did not succeed obtaining their confidence, and, withdrawing from the crowd with difficulty, he fled to the management offices.

At 11 a.m., during the lunch break, the welder Odovkin ran into the units with a piece of paper onto which he had written a slogan inciting the workers to rebel. The Communists tried to take this paper away from him, but he ripped it in pieces before he burned it.

At the same moment, a crowd of more than one hundred people [. . .] headed towards the management offices. They were quickly joined by the workers of other units who were on their lunch break (...) At 11:30 a.m. the crowd [. . .] broke through the doors and headed towards the square behind the factory (...)

At 2 to 4 p.m. most of the crowd found itself assembled on the railways around the train which had stopped. Hostile graffiti were written onto the tender of the locomotive with chalk (...)

At 4:30 p.m. loudspeakers were installed on the balcony of the direction building (...) The crowd was silently waiting for a declaration. However, at the end of the first sentence of Comrade Basov, in which he had began to explain the reasons for the appeal of the Central Committee, shouts were heard: 'We have read the appeal, we know how to read and you better tell us how we are going to live if our salaries are cut and prices are going up.'

Comrade Zamietin got hold of the microphone, but he was not allowed to speak. Then, when Comrade Korotchkin tried to speak, stones, iron poles and bottles were thrown at the people on the balcony. Rioters climbed onto the balcony and tried to use the microphone, in vain. In fact, the cables had been cut in time. The rioters then penetrated the building of the direction searching for those in charge.

The functionaries of the K.G.B. present at that moment among the crowd could localise the agitators and secretly photograph them. After which, for another two hours, no particular measure was taken in order to reinstall order, which permitted the continuation of trouble within the factory and on the railways, in fact directed against the Communists. The presidium of the Central Committee was informed of this urgent situation.

From 6 to 7 p.m. the militia forces tried re-establish order within the factory. A group of 200 militiamen in uniform were chased away and saved themselves by fleeing, three militiamen were beaten up [. . .].

On 1 June, at the end of the day, five lorries filled with soldiers arrived in front of the building of the direction. The crowd went to meet them, [but] built barricades and thus stopped them advancing.

As the military commanders had proven to be indecisive, the officers and soldiers of that brigade lost their countenance under the pressure of the crowd and were thus paralysed.

Without being stopped, one of the criminals could climb onto one of the cars, calling for the insurgents to continue their misdeeds and for the soldiers to follow them. After this, the troops withdrew under shouts, whistles and much mockery [. . .].

After a while, a reinforced military formation was sent in. Encircled by the crowd, it turned around under shouts and insults (…)

When the crowd arrived in front of the *Gorkom* [City Committee of the CPSU], the most brutal rioters and the leaders began to throw stones and sticks against the building's doors and windows. Once they had broken the resistance of the guards, they entered the building, smashed the windows, destroyed the furniture, pulled down the portraits and destroyed them, beat up the functionaries of the Party, the Soviets and the K.G.B. present at the location.

Several rioters reached the balcony and, with the aim of provoking, put up a red flag and a portrait of Lenin [. . .]. At the same moment, a large group headed towards the building of the regional direction of the K.G.B. and the central commissariat and penetrated the basement. The others headed towards the roofs

[. . .] and arrived at the inner courtyard. A fight started in order to prevent them from equipping themselves with arms or secret documents.

During this attack several rioters were armed with knives and sticks. One of the attackers threw himself against a soldier, tore his machine gun from his hands and tried to use it. As a consequence of this, fire was opened against the criminals. Some of the people who were just about to enter the building were stopped whilst the others fled.

Unable to storm the buildings of the K.G.B. and of the militia, the insurgents headed once again in the direction of the *Gorkom*, which at that moment had been left by all the rioters and was surrounded by a police cordon. Once more, the crowd tried to attack the soldiers with the aim of disarming them. As a consequence of this the soldiers in front of the Gorkom opened fire.

When the insurrection had been broken up, twenty dead bodies were collected [. . .].

13.11 Malcolm X on the United States and the World, 1964

Malcolm X—perhaps the foremost spokesman for black nationalism in the United States in the early 1960s—saw the struggle of African-Americans as directly related to the revolutions engulfing the Third World. In this excerpt from a 1964 speech, Malcolm relates the Cold War to the American government's actions at home.

(...) During recent years there has been much talk about a population explosion, and whenever they are speaking of a population explosion, in my opinion they are referring primarily to the people in Asia or in Africa—the black, brown, red, and yellow people. It is seen by people of the West that as soon as the standard of living is raised in Africa and Asia, automatically the people begin to reproduce abundantly. And there has been a great deal of fear engendered by this in the minds of the people of the West, who happen to be, on this earth, a very small minority.

In fact, in most of the thinking and planning of whites in the West today, it's easy to see the fear in their minds, conscious minds and subconscious minds, that the masses of dark people in the West, in the East rather, who already outnumber them, will continue to increase and multiply and grow until they eventually overrun the people of the West like a human sea, a human tide, a human flood. And the fear of this can be seen in the minds, in the actions, of most of the people here in the West in practically everything that they do. It governs political views and it governs their economic views and it governs most of their attitudes toward the present society (...)

Just as we can see that all over the world one of the main problems facing the West is race, likewise here in America today, most of your Negro leaders as well as the whites agree that 1964 itself appears to be one of the most explosive years yet in the history of America on the racial front, on the racial scene. Not only is this racial explosion probably to take place in America, but all of the ingredients for this racial explosion in America to blossom into a worldwide racial explosion present themselves right here in front of us. America's racial powder keg, in short, can actually fuse or ignite a worldwide powder keg.

And whites in this country who are still complacent when they see the possibilities of racial strife getting out of hand—and you are complacent simply because you think you out-number the racial minority in this country, what you have to bear in mind is wherein you might outnumber us in this country, you don't outnumber us all over the earth.

And any kind of racial explosion that takes place in this country today, in 1964, is not a racial explosion that can be confined to the shores of America. It is a racial explosion that can ignite the racial powder keg that exists all over the planet that we call earth. Now I think that nobody would disagree that the dark masses of Africa and Asia and Latin America are already seething with bitterness, animosity, hostility, unrest, and impatience with the racial intolerance that they themselves have experienced at the hands of the white West.

And just as they themselves have the ingredients of hostility toward the West in general, here we also have 22 million African-Americans, Black, brown, red, and yellow people in this country who are also seething with bitterness and impatience and hostility and animosity at the racial intolerance not only of the white West but of white Africa in particular (…)

Nineteen sixty-four will be America's hottest year; her hottest year yet; a year of much racial violence and much racial bloodshed. But it won't be blood that's going to flow only on one side. The new generation of Black people that have grown up in this country during recent years are already forming the opinion—and it's just an opinion—that if there is to be bleeding, it should be reciprocal—bleeding on both sides.

It should also be understood that the racial sparks that are ignited here in America today could easily turn into a flaming fire abroad, which only means it could engulf all the people of this earth into a giant race war. You cannot confine it to one little neighborhood, or one little community, or one little country. What happens to a Black man in America today happens to the black man in Africa. What happens to a Black man in America and Africa happens to the black man in Asia and to the man down in Latin America. What happens to one of us today happens to all of us. And when this is realized I think that the whites—who are intelligent even if they aren't moral or aren't just or aren't impressed by legalities—those who are intelligent will realize that when they touch this one, they are touching all of them, and this in itself will have a tendency to be a checking factor (…)

So 1964 will see the Negro revolt evolve and merge into the worldwide black revolution that has been taking place on this earth since 1945. The so-called revolt will become a real black revolution. Now the black revolution has been taking place in Africa and Asia and in Latin America. Now when I say black, I mean non-white. Black, brown, red or yellow. Our brothers and sisters in Asia, who were colonized by the Europeans, our brothers and sisters in Africa, who were colonized by the Europeans, and in Latin America, the peasants, who were colonized by the Europeans, have been involved in a struggle since 1945 to get the colonialists, or the colonizing powers, the Europeans, off their land, out of their country.

This is a real revolution. Revolution is always based on land. Revolution is never based on begging somebody for an integrated cup of coffee. Revolutions are never fought by turning the other cheek. Revolutions are never based upon love your enemy and pray for those who spitefully use you. And revolutions are never waged singing, 'We Shall Overcome.' Revolutions are based upon bloodshed. Revolutions are never compromising. Revolutions are never based upon negotiations. Revolutions are never based upon any kind of tokenism whatsoever. Revolutions are never even based upon that which is begging a corrupt society or a corrupt system to accept us into it. Revolutions overturn systems, and there is no system on this earth which has proven itself more corrupt, more criminal, than this system that in 1964 still colonizes 22 million African-Americans, still enslaves 22 million Afro-Americans.

There is no system more corrupt than a system that represents itself as the example of freedom, the example of democracy, and can go all over this earth telling other people how to straighten out their house, and you have citizens of this country who have to use bullets if they want to cast a ballot. The greatest weapon the colonial powers have used in the past against our people has always been divide and conquer.

America is a colonial power. She has colonized 22 million Afro-Americans by depriving us of first-class citizenship, by depriving us of civil rights, actually by depriving us of human rights. She has not only deprived us of the right to be a citizen, she has deprived us of the right to be human beings, the right to be recognized and respected as men and women. And in this country the Black can be fifty years old and he is still a 'boy.' (…)

I read in the paper yesterday where one of the Supreme Court justices, Goldberg, was crying about the violation of human rights of 3 million Jews in the Soviet Union. Imagine this. I haven't got anything against Jews, but that's their problem. How in the world are you going to cry about problems on the other side of the world when you haven't got the problems straightened out here? How can the plight of 3 million Jews in Russia be qualified to be taken to the United Nations by a man who is a justice in this Supreme Court and is supposed to be a liberal, supposed to be a friend of Black people, and hasn't opened up his mouth one time about taking the plight of Black people down here to the United Nations?

13.12 The Resistance Against Apartheid, 1978

Mosima 'Tokyo' Sexwale, a guerilla of the African National Congress (ANC), was captured and put on trial by the white minority regime after he returned to South Africa from military training in the Soviet Union. He was sentenced to eighteen years imprisonment. Today he is a successful businessman. The first excerpt is from the government's charge sheet against Sexwale. The second excerpt is from his statement to the court.

A. Government Charge: 'A Sell-Out to Russia'

(…) Evidence will be led to show that the conspirators were all members and/or active supporters of the ANC or Umkhonto we Sizwe (Spear of the Nation), the military wing of the ANC, which is under the overall political guidance of the ANC. The State will show that the ANC is a front or cover organization used as a tool to achieve the objectives of the South African Communist Party; that this involves the subjugation of the black national revolution to Marxism-Leninism, and that the net effect of a successful ANC revolution would be that a white-dominated Russian-Marxist government would replace the present government. It will thus be argued that the twelve accused, as well as being terrorists, were in the process of 'selling-out' black national liberation to Russia.

B. Defendant's Response: 'Why I Chose the Struggle'

(…) We lived in poverty and we were all subjected to the humiliation which the whites imposed upon the blacks. We lived in the same typical 'matchbox' houses; we were continually aware that there was not enough money available to meet our needs for food, clothing and education; and when we went into town and saw the relative luxury in which white people lived, this made an indelible impression on our young minds. There was one respect in which, in comparison with some of my friends, I was privileged: my parents laid great store by education and made considerable sacrifices so that their children could receive a proper schooling (…) and there were real financial problems because school for black children was not free, and school uniforms and books added a further burden (…)

The non-violent struggle seemed to me a relic of the past, a myth which was suicidal in the 1960s and 1970s. And I supported the policy as set out in the Freedom Charter: a democratic South Africa, belonging to all its people, black and white—a society in which all, and not just the select few, participated in deciding how the country was to be run.

I decided to join the ANC (...) not for the hope of personal gain or glory, or in a casual manner without thinking about the consequences. I was, and am, essentially a peaceful person—but I felt myself driven to this position, feeling that to counter the violence meted out against us, we were forced to defend ourselves: there was no option.

It is true that I was trained in the use of weapons and explosives. The basis of my training was in sabotage, which was to be aimed at institutions and not people. I did not wish to add unnecessarily to the grievous loss of human life that had already been incurred. In addition, it was necessary for us to be trained in order that we could defend ourselves if attacked. And finally, we wished to build up a core of trained men who would be able to lead others should guerrilla warfare commence.

It has been suggested that our aim was to annihilate the white people of this country. Nothing could be further from the truth. The ANC—in association with the alliance it has formed with people from all walks of life and representing all sections of the population—is a national liberation movement committed to the liberation of all the people of South Africa, black and white, from racial fear, hatred and oppression. The Freedom Charter, which after more than twenty years is still the fundamental policy document of the ANC, puts forward the ideal of a democratic South Africa, for all its people. We believe, and I believe, that the black people cannot be passive onlookers in their own country. We want to be active participants in shaping the face and course of direction of South Africa.

My lord, these are the reasons why I find myself in the dock today. When I joined the ANC I realised that the struggle for freedom would be difficult and would involve sacrifices. I was and am willing to make those sacrifices. I am married and have one child, and would like nothing more than to have more children, and to live with my wife and children and with all the people in this country. One day that may be possible, if not for me, then at least for my brothers.

I appreciate the seriousness of my actions and accept whatever sentence may be imposed on me. That is the sacrifice which I must make and am willing to make for my ideals. There is no doubt in my mind that these ideals will triumph; the tragedy is that it seems possible that there will be continued conflict and resultant bitterness, before those ideals are achieved.

13.13 Günter Grass: The Lesson of Prague, 1968

The West German social democratic writer and novelist Günter Grass accused the 'New Left' of the 1960s of having let down democracy activists in Eastern Europe. Here is an excerpt from his speech at a meeting in Basel on 8 September 1968, protesting the Soviet invasion of Czechoslovakia.

Ladies and gentlemen, we have not come together in order to protest. Protests are reactions to injustices. Whilst the protest passes, the injustice remains (…)

The questions are: Why should we care about democratic socialism? To what extent are we too responsible for the failure of democratic socialism? It would be easy to prove that the applause of the once upright warriors, that rose and changed into telegenic wailing when Czechoslovakia was occupied, is partly responsible for the Czechoslovakian tragedy. However, to speak about the last or the future cold war, this is the wrong place, with the wrong audience attending. My question rather focuses on the hesitation of the European Left, inasmuch as it understands itself as being radical or revolutionary. For over one year, when President Antonin Novotny was still in power, the writers Vaculik, Klima, Havel, Kundera and Liehm held their accusing and programmatic speeches. The European Left and the rising student protest then had the opportunity to understand the courageous project of the Czechs and the Slovaks and to make that project their own cause. But Vaculik and Havel were not the names of the idols of the students of Berlin and Paris, but one made a photogenic, aesthetic choice: the photo of the professional revolutionary Che Guevara was enlarged until it had the size of a pin-up.

In other words: whilst the Czechoslovakian reformers, in the most unfavourable of circumstances and against resistance that, as we have seen, is still impossible to overcome, tried to establish their reform program, the Western radical Left—also called New Left—pleased itself with romantic revolutionary gestures. Without a programme and incomprehensible because of its jargon, this Left managed to wear out the protest and to provoke the radical Right. What the election results of Baden-Württemberg made us foresee, became a fact in France shortly after: never had the West-European reactionaries been stronger than in the summer of that year (…)

When the Czechs and Slovaks demanded the liberalisation of their system and the toleration of dissidents, in this country tolerance was dismissed and liberalism was declared the mortal enemy of the revolution.

When in Prague and Bratislava the reforms and their theories had to be tested in practice straight away, among us reform was defamed as reformism and theory was discussed without end. One wanted—once again—all or nothing. The result was the emptiness of the hollow of our hand. While the Czechoslovak students, writers and scientists were sober and pragmatic, the West European Left pleased itself by its theatrical revolution. The New Left in Czechoslovakia is being oppressed by the reactionary forces; the New Left in the West defeated itself through its impotence to understand the lesson of Prague. Intellectually, it can partly be blamed for what happened. And whilst yesterday's spokesmen practice their mimicry in resignation, this accusation will surely reach them (…)

Measured by the standards of Hans Magnus Enzensberger, the attempted reform in Prague proved to be sketchy and unattractive. Or in other words: Alexander Dubcek's attentively formulated programme for democratic socialism could not compete with the cult of Che Guevara. A sober process, hampered at the time by the necessary compromises, interrupted today by power politics, drowned in the rhythmic clapping and the argument-less cheers for Ho Chi Minh (…)

Now that Czechoslovak socialism after its temporary oppression has become a worldwide necessity, may it regard the coordination of Eastern and Western development aid as its first task. First of all, the West European socialist and social democratic parties are called to give content to the up until now empty concept of co-existence with the help of a reform program for coordinated development aid which ends the competition of power politics between East and West.

Two overfed world powers have transformed stupidity into divisions and nuclear bombs. In between, continuously threatened by the trumpet blowing of either one or the other giant, there is us, finally understanding the lesson of Prague.

13.14 Palme: Why I am a Democratic Socialist, 1982

In this excerpt from a televised election debate of 17 September 1982, Swedish prime minister Olof Palme presents his reasons for being a socialist. Palme was assasinated in 1985.

I am a democratic socialist, with pride and with joy. I got that conviction when travelling in India and seeing its terrible poverty blended with pockets of immense wealth; when travelling in the United States and seeing an in some respects even more humiliating poverty; when, as a young man, I came eye to eye with Communist enslavement and the oppression and inhuman persecution in the Communist states. And when I came to Nazi concentration camps and saw the death lists of social democrats and trade-unionists.

I got that conviction when it became clear to me that it was the social democratic movement that brought democracy to Sweden, when it became clear to me that it was the social democratic movement that had lifted the country out of poverty and unemployment with its policies of the 1930s. And when I myself was campaigning for state pensions for the elderly and got up against the anti-Socialist campaigns of those with special privileges who objected when ordinary workers would secure their own retirement. That's what [the rest of] you were up to then (…)

But even more important is that I am strengthened in my conviction when I look at the state of the world, when I see the wars and the arms race and the mass unemployment and all that divides people. I am strengthened in my conviction when I see, here in our own country, an increase in injustice, unemployment, speculation and graft. When I look into the future that the right-wing has to offer, where the workers will get less and the rich will get more, where social security will be in decline and the number of luxury yachts on the rise, where solidarity diminishes and egotism increases, where the strong can help themselves and the weak will have to beg if they are to get anything at all.

Of course I am a democratic socialist. I hold that conviction with pride in what democratic socialism has achieved in our country, and with joy, because I know that we have important tasks ahead of us as a result of right-wing negligence. And with confidence, because now people know what happens with their jobs and with security and stability when the right-wing is in power. In a way I hold that conviction with a smile because I know that modern Swedish history is full of valuable reforms, which you [at first] have described as evil socialism but then later fought to get credit for when people have understood their significance.

13.15 Dr Strangelove

Peter George's novel Dr Strangelove *(subsequently made into a film by Stanley Kubrick) provides a hilarious take on nuclear exterminism, mad scientists, and military jargon. Here is life inside the nuclear attack bomber* Leper Colony, *just about to destroy the world.*

Inside *Leper Colony*, which was now circling gently in the vicinity of its Fail-Safe point, the crew were engaged in much the same tasks as when they had received the order to hold in that area.

Lieutenant Goldberg's attention was suddenly and unpleasantly disturbed by a clicking from the CWIE. He watched with vague interest while letters and numerals clicked into place on the dials, reached for his code book, and began decoding. When he had finished, he frowned in puzzlement, tapped the defense-systems officer, Lieutenant Dietrich, lightly on the shoulder to draw his attention, and showed him the message pad.

'Some screwy joker,' Dietrich said briefly and returned to the new card trick he was trying to perfect.

Goldberg frowned again, thought for a moment, then switched on his intercom. He said, 'Hey, King, get a load of this off the CWIE. Just come through. It says, "Attack using Ultech."'

King considered the matter. He repeated the message musingly. 'Now what the hell they talkin' about?'

'Attack using Ultech,' Goldberg repeated. 'That's exactly what it says.'

Captain Ace Owens lowered his magazine. He looked across at King. 'Is he kidding?'

King said firmly, 'Well, check your code again, that just can't be right.'

'I *have* checked it again,' Goldberg said.

King gestured to Ace, indicating that he was in executive command of the flight deck. He stood up slowly, then said 'Goldy, you must have made mistake, Goldy.'

'I'm telling you, goddammit,' Goldberg said irately, 'that's how it decodes. You don't believe me, you come and see for yourself.'

The whole crew had heard this interchange. From the lower deck Lothar Zogg and Sweets Kivel emerged and crowded with King around Goldberg and Dietrich. Ace Owens, leaving the plane to cruise on autopilot, went back to join the group.

Goldberg held out the code book to King. 'Here,' he said, 'you want to check it yourself?'

King looked at the book briefly, then he said, 'All right, git a confirmation on that, Goldberg. Don't you mention the message you hear, jest ask fer confirmation.'

Goldberg manipulated various switches on the machine. The whole crew watched as first the letters and numerals disappeared, then reappeared exactly as before. There were a few moments of absolute silence while they thought about the unthinkable.

King scratched his head. He said, 'You know, I'm beginnin' to work to certain conclusions.'

In the silence of the next few moments, while they thought about it, the expressions of the crew became grim. Slowly they all turned toward King, waiting for him to say the definitive word.

When King spoke, it was with quiet dignity. 'Well, boys, I reckon this is it.'

'What?' Ace Owens said.

'*Com*-bat.'

'But we're carrying hydrogen bombs,' Lothar Zogg muttered.

King nodded gravely in assent. 'That's right, *nuclear com*-bat! Toe-to-toe with the Russkies.'

Lothar Zogg said thoughtfully and with a note of hope in his voice, 'Maybe it's just some kind of screwball exercise, just to see if we're on our toes. You know the kind of thing they're always dreaming up to check on us.'

King made a cutting motion with his right hand, dismissing the idea. 'Shoot,' he said, 'they ain't sendin' us in there with this load on no exercise, that's for damn sure.' (…)

King leaned forward and adjusted his gyro. The great bomber banked, and turned automatically to the new heading.

As it turned, King read from his folder, which was the master copy. 'Okay. Here's the check list. Complete radio silence. The CWIE is to operate as of now. The emergency base-code index for recall is to be set on the dials of the CWIE. Okay, Goldy, you up to that?'

'Roger. I'm setting it up.'

As Goldberg set the CWIE, Sweets came up with the heading. 'One-seven-eight, King.'

'Roger. One-seven-eight.' King leaned forward to adjust his gyro and again the plane banked toward the new heading.

King again read from his folder. 'Primary target the ICBM complex at Laputa. First weapon fused for air burst. Your second weapon will be used if first malfunctions. Otherwise proceed to secondary target. Borchav, that missile base. Fused air burst. Any questions?'

The crew had no questions.

King went on. 'Okay now, in about ten minutes we start losing altitude to keep under their radar. We'll cross in over the coast about fifteen thousand, then drop low level to the primary, Okay, boys, now how about some hot Java?'

Questions

What is the main content of Orwell's anti-Communism? And Koestler's?

What did Neruda see as the worst effects of US involvement in Latin America?

How did Brecht define 'freedom'?

What was the main content of Communism for Picasso?

Are there any similarities between American anti-Communism and Soviet repression?

Why did the workers in Novocherkassk turn against the authorities?

How did the anti-Apartheid struggle in South Africa relate to the Cold War?

Contrast the texts by Grass and Palme. Why is Grass so angry with the West European Left?

14

Spies and Covert Operations

The Cold War was always fought on numerous 'fronts', of which none has inspired as much popular mythology as that of intelligence activities and other covert operations. Throughout the Cold War the two principal spy agencies—the American Central Intelligence Agency (CIA) and the Soviet Committee for State Security (KGB)—engaged in a series of activities aimed at uncovering secret information of the other side's plans and activities, monitoring the military development (particularly the development of nuclear weapons) of the adversary, and arresting unfavourable developments in third countries. While the details of many of these activities are still largely not declassified, the end of the Cold War has dramatically enhanced our knowledge about the hidden war of Western and Eastern intelligence agencies.

In fact, the great game of Cold War espionage had begun long before the Grand Alliance had even been formed. During the 1930s, for example, the Soviets had managed to recruit a number of spies in Western countries, including the United States and Great Britain. Many of the Soviet spies recruited then—including the 'Magnificent Five' in Britain and the various spy-rings in the United States—played a significant role in passing on information to the KGB about the Manhattan Project, the code-name for the secret atomic bomb project in Los Alamos, New Mexico. After the Soviets exploded their first atom bomb in 1949 a number of these spies, including the German-born scientist Klaus Fuchs and Julius and Ethel Rosenberg, were uncovered by Western agencies and either given long jail sentences or, in the case of the Rosenbergs, executed. While the atom spies had saved the Soviet Union perhaps two years of research, a debate about the overall significance of intelligence activities in the Cold War still continues.

In terms of human spies, the intelligence war was lopsided. The KGB operated in the West, but the CIA found it much more difficult to penetrate the closed world of the Soviet bloc. To be sure, the KGB suffered a number of humiliating defections throughout the Cold War that severely hampered its intelligence operations by the early 1960s. By that time the KGB's ability to attract westerners to spy for the USSR on ideological grounds—as was the case with a number of the spies recruited in the 1930s and 1940s—was severely diminished. In fact, during the last decades of the Cold War the KGB was increasingly involved in trying to discredit internal critics, such as the Nobel Prize-winning scientist Andrei Sakharov.

The questionable reliability of human intelligence was further revealed by the numerous cases of defections and moles that plagued intelligence agencies on both sides. On the one hand, the KGB could boast such successes as Kim Philby, who had successfully penetrated the inner circles of the British intelligence establishment and ultimately defected to the USSR in 1963. On the other hand, in 1971 the British government expelled 105 Soviet intelligence officers who had been identified by a defector. One of the great Western moles inside the Soviet intelligence system, Colonel Oleg Penkovsky, who revealed crucial information about Soviet atomic warheads and missile guidance systems, was discovered by the KGB in October 1962, arrested, and executed. In 1991, after the disappearance of a number of CIA moles in the USSR, the Americans launched a three-year long manhunt to discover the traitor in their midst. In February 1994, with the Cold War over, the CIA finally arrested the man who has the dubious distinction of having single-handedly passed on more information to the USSR than any other mole in the Agency's history. Out of the twenty-five CIA moles in the KGB Aldrich Ames had identified between 1984 and 1993, ten had been executed. His motive was, pehaps, the most disturbing revelation. The information Ames had passed on had earned him $2.7 million, enough to finance a very comfortable life in suburban Virginia.

Long before Aldrich Ames began his career as a Soviet mole the difficulties with human spies had led both sides to rely increasingly on technology to uncover the required information. In fact, the American intelligence services relied early on much more heavily on electronic intelligence when collecting data on the Soviet Union. In the 1950s, for example, the CIA dug a long tunnel under the Soviet sector in Berlin that was used for tapping Soviet and East German telephone cables; ironically, the operation was betrayed to the KGB by a source inside British intelligence. In order to uncover details about the size and strength of Soviet nuclear forces, the CIA developed its own reconnaissance plane, the U-2, that could fly high over the Soviet Union and take photographs of Soviet bases. From 1956 onwards these spy flights, together with satellites equipped with cameras that the Americans first launched in 1960, provided reasonably reliable information about the USSR's missile strength. Later on both sides developed satellite systems capable of intercepting radio communications and data from test launches of the opposition's missiles. In the 1970s and 1980s the new technology provided each side with masses of information and, increasingly, deliberately fed misinformation. If anything, the major problem for both sides at the closing years of the Cold War was how to make sense of the growing amount of 'raw data'.

Both the CIA and the KGB were also involved in various clandestine activities and covert operations in third countries. These enjoyed mixed success. The CIA, for example, successfully orchestrated or aided in the overthrow of governments in Iran (1953) and Guatemala (1954), but also recorded such spectacular failures as the Bay of Pigs operation in Cuba (1961). While such covert operations may have been operational successes, moreover, they rarely produced long-term stability—subsequent events in both Iran and Guatemala being two prime examples. In addition, the considerable time and resources spent on selected assassination attempts on certain national leaders—such as KGB plans to assassinate the Yugoslav leader Tito and CIA plots to get rid of Castro—were either completely unsuccessful or cancelled as untenable. When revealed, however, they resulted in considerable embarrassment to the governments responsible and, naturally, gave much propaganda ammunition to the other side.

The covert side of the Cold War is filled with fascinating stories and revelations that will capture the imagination for years to come. The significance of intelligence activities to the eventual outcome of the Cold War, however, is far from clear. In the East, the Soviet (and Eastern European) intelligence services may have uncovered some stunning information—particularly on Western military technology. But the constant surveillance and repression of dissidents—real and suspected—did severe damage to the legitimacy of the Communist parties in the Soviet bloc. In the West, the CIA and other American intelligence services (such as the National Security Agency) may have been very successful in a number of their intelligence-gathering efforts. But the covert operations that the CIA carried out rarely succeeded in helping the United States to win the 'hearts and minds' of those—particularly in the Third World—it suspected of being most vulnerable to the appeal of socialism and communism. Indeed, one of the major contributions of spies and covert operations during the Cold War may have been to spread cynicism about the ideological justifications behind the East–West conflict.

Readings

Christopher Andrew and Vasili Mitrokhin, *The Mitrokhin Archive: The KGB in Europe and the West* (1999). A massive book that covers most aspects of the KGB's work since the Russian Revolution.

David Childs and Richard Popplewell, *The STASI* (1996). A fascinating account of the infamous East German intelligence service.

David E. Murphy, Sergei A. Kondrashev, and George Bailey, *Battleground Berlin : CIA vs. KGB in the Cold War* (1997). A study of the intelligence war at the heart of the East–West conflict in Europe.

John Prados, *Presidents' Secret Wars: CIA and Pentagon Covert Operations from World War*

II through the Persian Gulf (1996). The most inclusive account of the role of covert operations in US foreign policy.

Jeffrey Richelson, *A Century of Spies: Intelligence in the Twentieth Century* (1995). A reliable overall account of intelligence services and their work during the twentieth century.

14.1 KGB Report on the US Atomic Bomb, October 1945

One of the priorities of the KGB during the last years of World War II was to gather information about the Manhattan Project, the secret Anglo-American project to build an atomic bomb. With the help of spies—such as Klaus Fuchs and Ted Hall—who worked at the Los Alamos, New Mexico, project, the Soviet intelligence services had pieced together this detailed description of the atomic bomb less than two months after the Americans dropped their bombs on Japan, and passed it on to KGB chairman Lavrenti Beria.

(…) a report on the construction of the atomic bomb, designed on the basis of secret-service materials received from the National KGB of the USSR (…)

General Description of Atomic Bomb

In outer appearance the atomic bomb is a pear-shaped missile with maximum diameter of 127 cm and length of 325 cm including the stabilizer (fins). Total weight is 4,500 kg. The bomb consists of the following component parts:

a) Initiator   b) Active material   c) Tamper   d) Aluminum layer   e) Explosive   f) 32 Explosive lenses   g) Detonating device   h) Duralumin shell   i) Armor-steel shell   j) Stabilizer (fins)

All the above-specified parts of the bomb with the exception of the stabilizer, the detonating device and the outer steel shell are spherical shells inserted one into the other. Thus, for instance, the active material is prepared in the shape of a spherical shell into whose center the initiator is inserted. The ball of active material itself is inserted into the interior of the tamper (moderator), which is itself a spherical shell. The tamper ball is inserted into the interior of another spherical shell made of aluminum, which is surrounded with a spherical layer of explosive.

After the layer of explosive, into which the lenses are inserted, there is a duralumin shell to which the detonating device is attached and on top of which is the bomb's outer casing made from armor steel.

Description of Particular Components of the Bomb (...) [here follows a detailed description of the various components]

Assembly of Bomb

The ball of uranium is inserted into the interior of the aluminum sphere in such a way that the opening on it fits opposite the opening in the aluminum. The blocks with the lenses are stacked on the outer surface of the aluminum except for one block which is placed over the opening in the aluminum. The lenses are mounted on the duralumin shell, to which the blasting device is also fastened. In that form the bomb is ready for transportation to the place of use. Further assembly is carried out as follows. The initiator is inserted into the interior of the tamper. The plugs are put into place, after which the last block of explosive is superimposed and the openings on the duralumin and steel shells are closed.

Because the plutonium and the radioactive materials of the initiator are spontaneously heated to a temperature exceeding that of the surrounding region by 90 degrees Celsius, the bombs are transported to the place of final assembly in special containers equipped with a cooling system.

14.2 Henry Greenglass on the Operations of the 'Rosenberg Spy Ring'

The trial and execution of Julius and Ethel Rosenberg made theirs undoubtedly the best known spy case in modern US history. The couple—as well as a number of their associates, such as Harry Gold and David Greenglass—was arrested in 1950 and charged with passing on atomic secrets to the Soviet Union. In 1951 the couple was tried for treason and sentenced to death (their associates received long prison sentences). After a number of appeals the Rosenbergs were executed in June 1954, despite worldwide protests and pleas for clemency. In part because the Rosenbergs never confessed, in part because the case of the prosecution appeared less than foolproof and many saw the Rosenberg case as an attempt to play down the Soviets' ability to develop their own atomic bomb, doubts about their guilt have persisted to this day. Below is an excerpt from a CIA summation of the testimony of David Greenglass, the brother of Ethel Rosenberg and a participant in the 'spy ring', who was the prosecution's 'star witness'. Greenglass was an army machinist who had worked at the Los Alamos site during the war.

Greenglass testified he first learned that what he was working on was part of the atomic bomb project when his wife visited him in November 1944, and told him that Rosenberg had said Greenglass was working on the bomb. During this visit from his wife, Greenglass testified she told him Rosenberg wanted him to procure and deliver to him a list of scientists working on atomic research; descriptions of experiments conducted in the atomic laboratory, sketches of materials that atomic scientists asked him to construct. Greenglass said his wife said Rosenberg also wanted 'the general lay-out of the Los Alamos atomic project, the buildings, camouflage, number of people.' Greenglass testified he gave his wife the information for which Rosenberg had asked.

In January 1945, Greenglass came to New York on leave. He testified Rosenberg came to him one morning and asked for information, 'specifically anything of value on the atomic bomb', and said he would return later that night. In answer to this request Greenglass testified he gave Rosenberg sketches and descriptions of high-explosive lens molds, and how they were used in atomic experiments, plus a list of 'some possible recruits for Soviet espionage'.

A few days later Greenglass testified he went to Rosenberg's home for dinner and was introduced to a woman named Ann Sidorovich. Greenglass testified Rosenberg asked him to remember her face because 'Julius said this is the woman who he thinks would come to see us at Albuquerque (where Mrs. Greenglass lived, near Los Alamos) to receive information from myself on the atomic bomb.' Greenglass testified Rosenberg that night also established an alternate means of identification between Greenglass and Rosenberg's representative in case Ann Sidorovich was unable to travel. This alternate identification consisted of the side of a box of Jello, a prepared dessert made of gelatine powder. Greenglass testified that Rosenberg cut a V-shaped section out of the side of this Jello box, gave one side to Ruth Greenglass and kept one side for himself.

A few nights later, Greenglass testified, Rosenberg drove him to a place on 1st Avenue to a rendez-vous with a 'Russian' who asked about high explosive lenses; the formula of the curve on the lens, the high-explosive used, and the means of detonation.

In June 1945, back in Los Alamos, Greenglass testified, he received a visit from a man who said to him 'Julius sent me' and then produced one part of the Jello box which Greenglass had last seen in Rosenberg's possession. Greenglass testified that he learned subsequently that this man was Harry Gold, who has pleaded guilty to espionage. Greenglass testified he gave Gold sketches of new lens molds, how they were used in experiments and descriptions of these experiments. Greenglass testified Gold gave him $500 in return.

In September 1945 Greenglass again went to New York on furlough. On this occasion (...) he gave to Rosenberg 'a pretty good description of the atomic bomb'. Greenglass testified he was able to produce this description because, in the course of his work at Los Alamos, 'I came in contact with various people who worked on different parts of the project, and also I worked directly on certain apparatus that went into the bomb, and I met people who talked of the bombs and how they worked' (...) his description involved the principles, not precise measurements, except for the specific lens molds and other parts which he himself manufactured (...) he gave Rosenberg 12 pages of written material (...) Rosenberg gave him $200 on this occasion (...)

A few days after Dr. Klaus Fuchs was arrested in England (...) Rosenberg came to Greenglass and told him that Fuchs was also a contact of Harry Gold. Greenglass said Rosenberg told him Gold would soon be arrested, and Gold's arrest might implicate Greenglass (...) Rosenberg said Greenglass would have to leave the country and gave Greenglass $1,000 with instructions to contact the secretary of the Ambassador of the Soviet Union in Mexico City (...) Greenglass (...) had passport pictures made and gave five sets to Rosenberg. Greenglass said Rosenberg then gave him an additional $4,000, wrapped in heavy brown paper (...)

14.3 The KGB's Plans to Assassinate Tito, Early 1953

One of the prime targets of Soviet assassination plans was Yugoslav leader Josif Broz Tito, who was subjected to Stalin's personal wrath after the Soviet–Yugoslav break in 1948. This document outlines various options to assassinate Tito with the help of Iosif Romual'- dovich Grigulevich' alias 'Max', a Soviet agent who had been involved earlier in operations to kill Leon Trotsky and later became a historian and corresponding member of the USSR Academy of Sciences. Following Stalin's death in March 1953, however, the operation described below was terminated.

The MGB USSR [Soviet Ministry of State Security] requests permission to prepare a terrorist act against Tito, by the illegal agent 'Max', Comrade I. R. Grigulevich, a Soviet citizen and member of the Communist Party of the Soviet Union since 1950 (...) 'Max' was placed in Italy on a Costa Rican passport, where he was able to gain the confidence and enter the circles of South American diplomats as well as well-known Costa Rican political and trade figures visiting Italy. Using these connections, 'Max', on our orders, obtained an appointment as the special plenipotentiary of Costa Rica in Italy and Yugoslavia. In the course of his diplomatic duties, in the second half of 1952, he visited Yugoslavia twice. He was well received there, with entrée into circles close to Tito's clique; he was promised a personal audience with Tito (...)

In early February of this year, we summoned 'Max' to Vienna for a secret meeting. While discussing options, 'Max' was asked how he thought he could be most useful, considering his position. 'Max' proposed some kind of active measure against Tito personally (...) the following options (...) were presented.

1. To order 'Max' to arrange a private audience with Tito, during which a soundless mechanism concealed in his clothes would release a dose of pulmonary plague bacteria that would guarantee death to Tito and all present. 'Max' himself would not be informed of the substance's nature, but with the goal of saving 'Max's' life, he would be given an anti-plague serum in advance.

2. In connection with Tito's expected visit to London, to send 'Max' there to use his official position and good personal relations with the Yugoslav ambassador in England, [Vladimir] Velebit, to obtain an invitation to the expected Yugoslav embassy reception in Tito's honor.

The terrorist act could be accomplished by shooting with a silent mechanism concealed as a personal item, while simultaneously releasing tear gas to create panic among the crowd, allowing 'Max' to escape and cover up all traces.

3. To use one of the official receptions in Belgrade to which members of the diplomatic corps are invited. The terrorist act could be implemented in the same way as the second option, to be carried out by 'Max' who as a diplomat, accredited by the Yugoslav government, would be invited to such a reception.

In addition, to assign 'Max' to work out an option whereby one of the Costa Rican representatives will give Tito some jewelry in a box, which when opened would release an instantaneously-effective poisonous substance. We asked 'Max' to once again think the operation over and to make suggestions on how he could realize, in the most efficient way, actions against Tito. Means of contact were established and it was agreed that further instructions would follow. It seems appropriate to use 'Max' to implement a terrorist act against Tito. 'Max's' personal qualities and intelligence experience make him suitable for such an assignment. We ask for your approval.

14.4 Covert Operation plans in Iran and Guatemala, 1953–1954

In 1953 the CIA and its British equivalent, the SIS (Strategic Intelligence Service), planned and eventually successfully carried out the overthrow of the Mossadeq government in Iran. The following year the CIA played an important supporting role in the overthrow of the Jacobo Arbentz government in Guatemala. The first extract below is from the so-called TPAJAX plan in Iran and provides insight into the background of the plan as well as the painstaking details involved in the operation. The (heavily sanitized) second excerpt, compiled by the CIA historian Gerald K. Haines, lists some of the assassination plans in Guatemala. Concluded in June 1995, the document was written as an internal history for the CIA.

A. CIA–SIS 'TPAJAX' plan for the overthrow of Prime Minister Mossadeq of Iran, June 1953

I.   Preliminary Action
A.   Interim Financing of Opposition
    1. CIA will supply $35,000 to [General Fazlullah] Zahedi.
    2. SIS will supply $25,000 to Zahedi.
    3. SIS indigenous channels Iran will be used to supply above funds to Zahedi.
    4. CIA will attempt subsidize key military leaders if this necessary.
B.   Acquisition Shah Cooperation
    1. Stage 1: Convince the Shah that UK and US have joint aim and remove pathological fear of British intrigues against him.
    a. [US] Ambassador [Loy] Henderson[2] call on the Shah to assure him of US–UK common aid and British supporting him not Mossadeq.
    b. Henderson to say to the Shah that special US representative will soon be introduced to him for presentation joint US–UK plan.
    2. Stage 2: Special US representative will visit the Shah and present following:
    a. Presentation to the Shah
        (1) Both governments consider oil question secondary.
        (2) Major issue is to maintain independence Iran and keep from the Soviet orbit. To do this Mossadeq must be removed.
        (3) Present dynasty best bulwark national sovereignty.
        (4) While Mossadeq in power no aid for Iran from the United States.
        (5) Mossadeq must go.
        (6) US–UK financial aid will be forthcoming to successor government.
        (7) Acceptable oil settlement will be offered but successor government will not be rushed into it.
    b. Demands on the Shah
        (1) You must take leadership in overthrow Mossadeq.
        (2) If not, you bear responsibility for collapse of country.
        (3) If not, Shah's dynasty will fall and US–UK backing of you will cease.
        (4) Who do you want to head successor government? (Try and maneuver Shah into naming Zahedi.)
        (5) Warning not to discuss approach.
        (6) Plan of operation with Zahedi will be discussed with you.

II. Arrangement with Zahedi
A.   After agreement with Shah per above, inform Zahedi he chosen to head successor government with US–UK support.

B.   Agree on specific plan for action and timetable for action. There are two
ways to put Zahedi in office.
1. Quasi-legally, whereby the Shah names Zahedi Prime Minister by
royal firman.
2. Military coup.
Quasi-legal method to be tried first. If successful at least part of the
machinery for military coup will be brought into action. If it fails,
military coup will follow in matter of hours.

III.   Relations with Majlis [Iranian Parliament]
Important for quasi-legal effort. To prepare for such effort deputies must be
purchased.
A.   Basic aim is to secure 41 votes against Mossadeq and assure quorum for
quasi-legal move by being able to depend on 53 deputies in Majlis. (SIS
considers 20 deputies now not controlled must be purchased.)
B.   Approach to deputies to be done by SIS indigenous agent group. CIA will
backstop where necesary by pressures on Majlis deputies and will provide
part of the funds.

IV.   Relations with Religious Leaders
Religious leaders should:
A.   Spread word of their disapproval Mossadeq.
B.   As required, stage political demonstrations under religious cover.
C.   Reinforce backbone of the Shah.
D.   Make strong assurances over radio and in mosques after coup that new
government faithful Moslem principles (...) Possibly as quid pro quo
prominent cleric Borujedi would be offered ministry without portfolio or
considered implementing neglected article constitution providing body
five mullas (religious leaders) to pass on orthodoxy of legislation (...)

V.   Relations with Bazaar [control morhetrilace]
Bazaar contacts to be used to spread anti-government rumors and possibly close
bazaar as anti-government expression.

VI.   Tudeh [Iranian Communist Party]
Zahedi must expect violent reaction from Tudeh and be prepared to meet with
superior violence.
A.   Arrest at least 100 Party and Front Group leaders.
B.   Seal off South Tehran to prevent influx Tudeh demonstrations.
C.   Via black leaflets direct Tudeh not to take any action.

VII.   Press and Propaganda Programs
A.   Prior coup intensify anti-Mossadeq propaganda.
B.   Zahedi should quickly appoint effective chief of government press and
propaganda who will:

1. Brief all foreign correspondents.
2. Release advance prepared US and UK official statements.
3. Make maximum use Radio Tehran.

VIII. Relations with Tribes

A. Coup will provoke no action from Bakhtiari, Lurs, Kurds, Baluchi, Zolfaghari, Manassani, Boor, Ahmndi, and Khamseh tribal groups.

B. Major problem is neutralization of Qashqa'i tribal leaders.

IX. Mechanics of Quasi-Legal Overthrow

A. At this moment the view with most favor is the so-called (...) plan—whereby mass demonstrators seek religious refuge in Majlis grounds. Elements available to religious leaders would be joined by those supplied by bazaar merchants, up to 4,000 supplied by SIS controlled group, and additional elements supplied through CIA.

B. Would be widely publicized that this refuge movement on basis two grounds popular dissatisfaction with Mossadeq government as follows:

  1. (...) that Mossadeq government basically anti-religious as most clearly demonstrated ties between Mossadeq and Tudeh; and Mossadeq and USSR. Just prior to movement CIA would give widest publicity to all fabricated documents proving secret agreement between Mossadeq and Tudeh.

  2. (...) that Mossadeq is leading the country into complete economic collapse through his unsympathetic dictatorship. Just prior to movement CIA would give widest publicity to the evidence of illegally issued paper money. CIA might have capability to print masses excellent imitation currency which would be overprinted by this message.

C. Religious refuge to take place at the dawn of the coup day. Immediately followed by effort have Majlis pass a motion to censure the government. This is to be followed by the dismissal of Mossadeq and the appointment of Zahedi as successor. If successful, the coup would be completed by early afternoon. Failing success, the coup would be mounted later that evening.

B. The CIA and Guatemala Assassination Proposals, 1952–1954

(...) CIA and Intelligence Community reports tended to support the view that Guatemala and the Arbenz regime were rapidly falling under the sway of the Communists. Director of Central Intelligence (DCI) Walter Bedell Smith and other Agency officials believed the situation called for action. Their assessment was, that without help, the Guatemalan opposition would remain inept, disorganized and ineffective (...) This led to the development of a covert action program designed to topple the Arbenz government—PBFORTUNE.

PBFORTUNE

Following a visit to Washington by Nicaraguan President Anastasio Somoza in April, 1952, in which Somoza boasted that if provided arms he and Guatemalan exile Carlos Castillo Armas could overthrow Arbenz, President Harry Truman asked DCI Smith, to investigate the possibility. Smith sent an agent, codenamed SEEKFORD, to contact Guatemalan dissidents about armed action against the Arbenz regime, 'After seeing his report, [   ] Chief of the [   ] Division of the Directorate of Plans (DP), proposed to Deputy Director of Central Intelligence Allen Dulles that the Agency supply Castillo Armas with arms and $225,000 and that Nicaragua and Honduras furnish the Guatemalans with air support. Gaining Department of State support, Smith, on 9 September 1952, officially approved [   ]'s request to initiate operation PBFORTUNE to aid Guatemalan exiles in overthrowing Arbenz. Planning for PBFORTUNE lasted barely a month, however, when Smith terminated it after he learned in October that it had been blown.'

Throughout planning for PBFORTUNE there were proposals for assassination. Even months before the official approval of PBFORTUNE, Directorate of Plans (DP) officers compiled a 'hit list'. Working from an old 1949 Guatemalan Army list of Communists and information supplied by the Directorate of Intelligence, in January 1952 DP officers compiled a list of 'top flight Communists whom the new government would desire to eliminate immediately in event of successful anti-Communist coup'. Headquarters asked [   ] to verify the list and recommend any additions or deletions. Headquarters also requested [   ] to verify a list of an additional 16 Communists and/or sympathizers whom the new government would desire to incarcerate immediately if the coup succeeded. [   ] in Guatemala City added three names to the list in his reply. Nine months later, SEEKFORD, the CIA agent in touch with Castillo Armas, forwarded to Headquarters a disposal list compiled by Castillo Armas. That list called for the execution through executive action of 58 Guatemalans (Category I) and the imprisonment or exile of 74 additional Guatemalans (Category II). SEEKFORD also reported at the same time, 18 September 1952, that General Rafael Trujillo, the dictator of the Dominican Republic, had agreed to aid Castillo Armas in return for the 'killing of four Santo Dominicans at present residing in Guatemala a few days prior to D-Day.' According to SEEKFORD, Castillo Armas readily agreed, but cautioned that it could not be done prior to D-day because of security reasons. Castillo Armas further added that his own plans included similar action and that special squads were already being trained. There is no record that Headquarters took any action regarding Castillo Armas' list.

After the PBFORTUNE operation was officially terminated, the Agency continued to pick up reports of assassination planning on the part of the Guatemalan opposition. In late November 1952, for example, an opposition Guatemalan

leader, in a conversation with SEEKFORD, confirmed that Castillo Armas had special 'K' groups whose mission was to kill all leading political and military leaders,
and that the hit list with the location of the homes and offices of all targets had
already been drawn up. On 12 December SEEKFORD reported further that Castillo
Armas planned to make maximum use of the 'K' groups. Another source subsequently reported that Nicaraguan, Honduran, and Salvadoran soldiers in civilian
clothes would infiltrate Guatemala and assassinate unnamed Communist leaders.

In addition to monitoring events in Guatemala, the Agency continued to try to
influence developments and to float ideas for disposing of key figures in the
[   ] government. [   ] in 1953 proposed not only to focus on sabotage,
defection, penetration, and propaganda efforts with regard to Guatemala, but to
eliminate [   ] [   ] According to [   ]'s draft memorandum, after creating
a story that [   ] was preparing to oust the Communists, he could be eliminated. His assassination would be 'laid to the Commies' and used to bring about a
mass defection of the Guatemalan army. A Western Hemisphere Division memo
of 28 August 1953 also suggested possibly assassinating key Guatemalan military
officers if they refused to be converted to the rebel cause. In September 1953
[   ] also sent [   ] an updated plan of action which included a reference to
'neutralizing' key Guatemalan military leaders.

In the psychological warfare area, Guatemala City Station sent [   ] all leading Communists in Guatemala, 'death notice' cards for 30 straight days beginning 15 April 1953. The Station repeated the operation beginning 15 June 1953
but reported no reaction from the targeted leaders.

(...) Until the day that Arbenz resigned in June 1954 the option of assassination
was still being considered (...) Beyond planning, some actual preparations were
made. Some assassins were selected, training began, and tentative 'hit lists' were
drawn up.

(...) The official objective of PBSUCCESS was to remove the Guatemalan government covertly 'without bloodshed if possible.' Elimination lists were never
finalized, assassination proposals remained controversial within the Agency, and
it appears that no Guatemalans associated with Arbenz were assassinated. Both
CIA and State Department officers were divided (and undecided) about using
assassination (...)

14.5 The Berlin Tunnel

*The construction of the Berlin Tunnel was probably one of the most ambitious operations
undertaken by the CIA in the 1950s. The Agency built the tunnel—a network of underground cables to be used to tap Soviet communication lines routed through Berlin (e.g.*

" OF COURSE WE GUATEMALANS DIDN'T GET ANY OUTSIDE
HELP — JUST AS GENERAL FRANCO DIDN'T EIGHTEEN
YEARS AGO!"

12. After the Guatemalans operation. (Vicky, *Daily Mirror*, 22 June 1954). Reprinted by permission. Photo supplied by The Centre for the Study of Cartoons and Caricature, University of Kent.

telephone communications between Moscow, Bucharest, and Warsaw)—in 1954–5. Unbeknowst to the CIA, however, a KBG mole in the British Secret Intelligence Service (SIS), George Blake, reported the existence of the tunnel project to Moscow already in February 1954. In order to protect Blake's identity the Soviets waited until April 1956 before 'accidentally' discovering the tunnel. The extract below is a CIA assessment of the value of the information collected via the tunnel during its fourteen-month existence.

The volume and content of the information CIA found supports the claim that KGB allowed valuable information to pass through cable lines tapped by the Berlin tunnel. (...)

A total of 443,000 conversations were fully transcribed from voice reels. Of these, 368,000 were Soviet and 75,000 were East German. The daily output of the telegraphic processing center was approximately 4,000 feet of teletype messages. Processing of the tunnel take continued after the tunnel's 'discovery' in April 1956. Ninety thousand translated messages or telephone conversations had been disseminated as of 30 September 1958, resulting in 1,750 intelligence reports. The coverage afforded by the tapped cables or the volume of production alone cannot convey the magnitude or the value of the information provided (...)

On the other hand, the Soviets' obsession for preserving 'state secrets,' which led them to suspect even the innocent of violating security regulations, was equaled by Western ignorance of conditions in the USSR and its occupied areas (...) It is hard to imagine in this era of U-2 and satellite photography, but Western intelligence analysts at the time simply did not have the information needed to estimate the strength of the Soviet threat (...)

The situation was particularly critical in Germany. First, the Allied position in Berlin had been subjected to continual harassment since the Berlin blockade of 1948–49, yet Allied policy insisted on the right of the Allies to remain in their sectors of the city. Any attempt to force them to leave could have resulted in war. Second, GSFG [Group of Soviet Forces in Germany], commanded by Khrushchev supporter Marshal Andrei Grechko, was the largest Soviet force outside the USSR. Information on its activities, equipment, and personnel, as well as those of the neighboring northern group of Soviet forces in Poland, was of vital importance in estimating Soviet capabilities for offensive action, not only against Berlin and Germany but also against Western Europe. Third, since 1946, East Germany had been a major contributor of raw materials and manufactured specialties to the Soviet nuclear energy program. Finally, Soviet efforts to stabilize the East German political situation, still restive two years after the June 1953 riots, were vital to long-range Soviet plans in Europe.

In this context, the tunnel was seen as a unique, timely, and reliable source of intelligence information on the USSR, East Germany, and Poland. The tunnel's taps offered hard data on Soviet political actions and intentions in Berlin and on its relations with the Western occupying powers, as well as indications of differences of opinion between the Soviets and East Germans on the problem of West Berlin's status. As the GDR tested the limits of its sovereignty, the tunnel provided detailed information on the nature and limitations of Soviet military and economic control over East Germany and other Soviet-occupied territories. Each incident in Berlin involving citizens of the western powers reported by the tunnel reflected the 'unpreparedness, confusion, and indecision among Soviet and East German officials' over how authority should be delegated. The tunnel warned the West that the Soviets were creating an East German National

People's Army based on the existing paramilitary alert police. It also provided insights into how the Soviets implemented the decisions of the Twentieth Party Congress (during which Stalin's memory was denigrated) among the Soviet military and the scientific and technical intelligentsia stationed in East Germany (...)

Some writers have claimed that much of the tunnel take was simply gossip. But this so-called gossip was important, too: it was by and about senior players in the Soviet hierarchy at a time when the West was coming to grips with a new set of top Soviet leaders. Although Stalin was long dead, the struggle for ultimate succession in Moscow continued, and hints regarding who was close to whom were important. Conversations of this type also furnished vital clues about political attitudes, morale, and behaviors within the upper echelons of the Soviet military and civilian hierarchy. Corruption, influence peddling, and nepotism were evident at all levels.

Military-related information from the tunnel was highly prized and included reports on the reorganization of the Soviet Defense Ministry, on increased Soviet–East European military cooperation under the Warsaw Pact, and on a reduction in the strength of the Soviet armed forces (...) Analysts also received detailed training and readiness plans for Soviet units stationed in East Germany and Poland.

Reports made from the tunnel taps revealed 'the development of an improved nuclear capability in the Soviet Air Army in East Germany and the re-equipping of this army with new bombers and twin-jet interceptors with airborne radar.' They also described, for example, 'the doubling of Soviet bomber strength in Poland and the creation of a new fighter division there. Over one hundred new Soviet Air Force installations were identified and located in the USSR, East Germany, and Poland, including a number of key aircraft factories.' As for the Soviet Navy, the tunnel reported new information on the organization of the Soviet Baltic Fleet, its bases, and its personnel.

The tunnel's main contribution to scientific-technical information was the identification of personalities associated with the Soviet atomic energy program, which was then under the USSR Ministry of Medium Machine Building. Several hundred personnel, as well as the location of the ministry's installations in the USSR, were fingered. This information could not have come at a better time. Hundreds of German scientists who had participated in the Soviet atomic program and related weapons development were being released, and the tunnel information provided a way to crosscheck their statements during debriefing (...)

(...) secrets revealed about Soviet military intelligence and counterintelligence units (especially the latter, because it was an arm of KGB) or about numerous East German security components with whom the KGB apparat had contact as advisers. Because these services, taken as a whole, represented the single largest coun-terintelligence problem faced by NATO, the detailed information the tunnel provided on them was of special significance.

Hardest hit were the Soviet military intelligence units in East Germany. Of the telephone lines tapped, twenty-five carried conversations of the Soviet general staff's Chief Intelligence Directorate (GRU) and the intelligence points or units subordinate to the intelligence directorate (RU) of the Group of Soviet Forces Germany (GSFG). More than 350 GRU and RU officers were identified in East Germany (…)

In all the tunnel coverage of the GSFG intelligence directorate, there were many taped phone conversations between that directorate and the Chief Intelli-gence Directorate (GRU) of the General Staff of the Ministry of Defense in Moscow, which resulted in extensive reporting on GRU itself. In addition, intercepted conversations between Soviet military intelligence personnel often provided surprising information on GRU units far removed from East Germany—for example, the intelligence directorate of the Transcaucasian Military District, whose headquarters were at Tbilisi and whose sixteen intelli-gence points covered the borders with Iran and Turkey.

The counterintelligence directorate of the GSFG, which had its headquarters in Potsdam and was then commanded by Maj. Gen. Georgy Tsinev, was also the focus of extensive reports. The directorate controlled special departments throughout the GSFG responsible for the security of military personnel and installations. The tunnel also reported on the directorate's Third or Operations Department, which ran agents against Western intelligence units in West Berlin and West Germany. The conduct of agent operations against Western targets had earlier been a bone of contention between state security's foreign intelligence directorate elements in Karlshorst and those of the counterintelligence direc-torate in Potsdam. Tunnel taps revealed Third Department operations to be a large, scattergun effort in which many low-level agents concentrated on exposing Western agents (…)

Periodic inspections of counterintelligence operations by Moscow chiefs also got the Soviets talking by phone. In March 1956, for example, the deputy chairman of the KGB and chief of the KGB's Third Military Counterintelligence Directorate, Lt. Gen. Pyotr Ivanovich Ivashutin, participated personally in the work of the commission and was particularly interested in the Third Department's operations. This bit of information, discussed via landlines and picked up by tunnel recorders, was used by BOB to check the knowledge of a defector from the Potsdam directorate in 1956. Looking back on these conversa-tions, it seems unlikely that either Ivashutin or Tsinev was ever aware of the tunnel's existence.

14.6 American Spy Flights in the 1950s

In the 1950s intelligence on Soviet military installations was provided in large part by spyplanes, flown by specially trained pilots. Below some of the American pilots—ELINT crews—who flew such flights reconstruct their experiences in a cat-and-mouse game with the Soviets.

(...) To make the communist air defences respond the ELINT crews often had to provoke a reaction. Aircraft would be flown straight at the border only turning at the last moment. Curly Behrmann said:

And occasionally we were briefed to fly a portion of the mission, and then by going low, or turning away or something, go down and then come straight in towards the border, whether it was over water or over land, usually over water. Come in very low and pop up all of a sudden to provide a sudden target for them. But this was a very seldom thing, I would say one percent, two percent of the time. It happened maybe a dozen times, that we'd do that, fly in, and hopefully come into a busy area and provoke a reaction where they would turn something on that maybe they were trying to not turn on in our presence. That was the hope you had, you know, that you'd found something new, which happened occasionally, and always made you feel very good, you know. So that was very basically the only reason and the only thing that it did, it was not a normal, everyday thing.

Bruce Bailey:

Well, we would go in a little closer. One of the best tactics is to get right on the deck at say, 200 ft or less, and go in real close to the area that you're interested in, and then pop up, to 5,000 or 7,000 ft right then, and you were right there, right in their lap, just a couple of miles, a few miles off of the coast or off of the installation you're looking at. And you all of a sudden show up on their radars, and this would usually cause them to turn things on that they wouldn't normally turn on. We also had tactics where if they were having an exercise, we would try to sneak in and join their bomber formations. And fly along with their bomber formations. Quite often they would turn on things at that time, that they wouldn't turn on normally, because they didn't know we were in the area.

As early as 1951 the USAF and SAC also urged the need for airborne communication intelligence platforms. COMINT was the eavesdropping of hostile radio transmissions, usually units communicating over the radio in voice messages. At the time it was hard to intercept this air-to-air and air-to-ground traffic from ground stations. A proposal was put forward to modify either a RB-50 or the RC-54 for these missions. Later on C-130 (Hercules) transport aircraft were specially converted to EC-130s under the control of the National Security Agency.

Bruce Bailey:

One of the ways this would work, let's say that you take an RB-47, and you run it up the Korean coast, into the Vladivostok area. And then in the Vladivostok area you make a few butterfly patterns or feints at the coast, at the city and so forth, and you stir up a reaction. You may have another EC-130 or something, a hundred miles off, or more, doing your COMINT collection. And of course, they can see that too. Well, then they come out and react to this RB-47 and either run it off or the RB-47 leaves the area anyhow, and the 130 leaves the area. This does a lot of things to them, they think that this crisis is over, and they've not had to turn on their SA-3 [NATO reporting-name 'Goa'; close-range surface-to-air missile with a slant range of nearly 20 miles to a height of 40,000 ft] radar or anything. But as you leave the area, they still have fighters and aircraft of their own in the area, so then they take advantage of that, 'cos they're recovering their aircraft. By turning these radars on, and exercising them, and learning to use them. Well, when that's going on, another RB-47 comes from the other direction, from the Sakhalin Islands, Chukotsk area at low altitude, that's not been detected. And it picks all of it up right, and they pop up in order to do it. But you come in from the other direction and them not knowing you're there, they're turning on things that they wouldn't normally turn on.

The highlight for a 'crow' was finding a new signal. In the late 1950s Bruce Bailey found his:

At that time, there was suspected beam of the 'Big Mesh' radar. 'Big Mesh' was the Soviet's primary ground control intercept radar. It was a multibeam radar, and they suspected that there was low frequency beam out of it that had not been intercepted. And we went out on a mission, and I intercepted it, and I got a low enough of an intercept, and enough direction bearings and everything, that I established the signal on a single mission, and that was the first time I know that had been done.

The Soviets quickly wised up to idea that 'ferret' flights were trying to make them use their latest equipment so they could take recordings of the signals to help the development of the countermeasures for the bombers.

Bert Barrett said:

We never overflew—definite rules and the State Department had strict rules. We had to clear our missions. 12 miles from coast. ADF with radio equipment—we didn't want to make an incursion. All hell broke loose if it was thought you had. First they returned to home base—radar scope always photographed your route. Wing inspectors would look to check if you had strayed even by a mile or two. If you had, the crew was immediately downgraded from combat status. The commander would be relegated to ground crew.

Bruce Bailey:

Different areas had different criteria. Sometimes a three-mile limit, but by and large we honoured the 12-mile limit. And most of our missions were planned to stay 12 miles away. There were some areas that we had to get closer because we were going between islands, or where we entered into the Baltic Sea. Then sometimes special missions and special requirements would cause you to violate the 12-mile limit, 'cos you would have to stimulate the defences and really get them active. In fact, I remember when the SA-3 surface-to-air missile system came out, we needed data real bad on that. Just about everything we tried we were unable to get them to activate the SA-3 radars. So, we started really pushing the limits in order to stimulate the SA-3s and get them on.

We would play games with the Russians. Sometimes to prevent us taking readings they would shut down all their radars except the early warning scanners (...)

All the intelligence gathered from ELINT flights, the eavesdropping agencies and the CIA was kept behind the 'Green Door'. This opened into a top secret room deep in the SAC War Room at Offutt AFB. Only a handful of people in the United States had clearance to see this material. All the incoming intelligence was assessed and kept in this room. Each day SAC intelligence officers would produce daily air intelligence briefing on the current state of Soviet readiness and deployment.

14.7 KGB Plans to Discredit CIA Director Allen Dulles, June 1960

One of the 'psychological warfare' methods of the KGB was discrediting and thereby reducing the effectiveness of key Western decision-makers or opinion leaders. Among those targeted were two of America's foremost intelligence chiefs: the legendary director of the FBI (US Federal Bureau of Investigation) J. Edgar Hoover, and the 1950s and early 1960s CIA chief Allen Dulles. Below is an excerpt from the KGB's 1960 plans to 'discredit' Dulles.

1. In order to activate a campaign by DULLES' political and personal opponents:

    a) to mail to them anonymous letters using the names of CIA officials criticizing its activity and the authoritarian leadership of DULLES;

    b) to prepare a dossier which will contain publications from the foreign press and declarations of officials who criticized the CIA and DULLES personally, and to send it, using the name of one of members of the Democratic Party (...)

    c) to send to some members of Congress, to the Fulbright Committee, and to the FBI specially prepared memos from two or three officials of the State Department with attached private letters, received (allegedly) from now deceased American diplomats, which would demonstrate CIA involvement in domestic decision-making, the persecution of foreign diplomats who took an objective stand, and which also would point out that, for narrow bureaucratic purposes, the CIA puts deliberately false data into information for the State Department;

d) to study the possibility and, if the opportunity presents itself, to prepare and disseminate through appropriate channels a document by former USA Secretary of State [John Foster] DULLES, which would make it clear that he exploited the resources of A. DULLES as leader of the CIA to fabricate compromising materials on his private and political adversaries;

e) to prepare, publish and disseminate abroad a satirical pamphlet on A. DULLES, using the American writer Albert KAHN who currently stays in Moscow to write the pamphlet.

2. With the aim of further exposing the activities of American intelligence in the eyes of the public and to create preconditions with which the FBI and other USA intelligence services could substantiate their opinion about the CIA's inability to conduct effective intelligence:

a) to fabricate the failure of an American agent 'Fyodorov' dropped in the Soviet Union by plane in 1952 (…);

b) to agree with Polish friends about the exposure of the operational game led by the organs of the KGB along with the MSS PPR [Ministry of State Security of the Polish People's Republic] with a 'conduit' on the payroll of American intelligence of the Organization of Ukrainian nationalists (OUN)—'Melnikovists.' To this end to bring back to Poland the Polish MSS agent 'Boleslav,' planted in the course of this game on the OUN 'conduit,' and to arrange for him to speak to the press and radio about subversive activity by American intelligence against the USSR and PPR. To arrange, in addition, for public appearances by six American intelligence agents dropped on USSR and PPR territory as couriers of the 'conduit' in the course of the game;

c) to suggest to the security bodies of the GDR that they arrange public trials for the recently arrested agents of American intelligence (…);

d) to disclose the operational game 'Link' that the KGB conducts with the adversary and to organize public statements in the media aimed at foreign audiences by the agent 'Maisky' (…);

e) Since about ten agents of the MSS of the GDR who 'defected-in-place' to American intelligence have accomplished their missions and currently there is no prospect of their being further utilized, it should be suggested to our German friends to stage their return on the basis of disagreement with USA aggressive policies (…)

f) to discuss with our Polish and Albanian friends the advisability of bringing to the attention of governmental circles and of the public of the United States the fact that the security agencies of Poland and Albania for a number of years had been deluding American intelligence in the operational games 'Win' and 'John' and had obtained millions of dollars, weapons, equipment, etc. from it.

3. To utilize, provided our Hungarian friends agree, the American intelligence documents they obtained in the U.S. mission in Budapest (...) to compromise the CIA and to aggravate the differences between the CIA and other intelligence services (...) If necessary, the necessary documents should be forged using the existing samples.

4. In order to create mistrust in the USA government toward the CIA and to produce an atmosphere of mutual suspicion within the CIA staff, to work out and implement an operation creating the impression of the presence in the CIA system of KGB agents recruited from among rank-and-file American intelligence officers (...)

5. To work out and implement measures on blowing the cover of several scientific, commercial and other institutions, used by the CIA for its spy activities. In particular, to carry out such measures with regard to the 'National Aeronautics and Space Administration' [NASA] and the 'Informational Agency' of the USA [U.S. Information Agency (USIA)].

6. In order to disclose the subversive activities of the CIA against some governments, political parties and public figures in capitalist countries, and to foment mistrust toward Americans in the government circles of these countries, to carry out the following:

a) to stage in Indonesia the loss by American intelligence officer PALMER, who is personally acquainted with President SUKARNO and exerts a negative influence on him, a briefcase containing documents (...) which provide evidence of USA plans to utilize American agents and rebel forces to overthrow the government of SUKARNO;

b) to carry out measures, with regard to the arrest in February of this year in the UAR [United Arab Republic] of a group of Israeli intelligence agents, to persuade the public in the UAR and Arab countries that American intelligence is linked to the activities of those agents and coordinates its work in the Arab East with Israeli intelligence (...)

c) to prepare and implement measures to make public the fact that American intelligence made use of the Iranian newspapers 'Fahrman' and 'Etelliat' (...)

d) to publish articles in the foreign press showing the interference of American intelligence in the domestic affairs of other states, using as an example the illegal American police organization in Italy, found and liquidated at the end of 1959, that 'worked on' Italian political parties under the direction of one of the diplomats at the American embassy (...)

7. To work out measures which, upon implementation, would demonstrate the failure of the CIA efforts to actively on a concrete factual basis use var-

ious émigré centers for subversive work against countries in the socialist camp
(...)

8. With the means available of the KGB to promote inquiries in the parliaments of England, France and other countries of their governments about their attitude to the hostile actions of USA intelligence intended to aggravate international tension.

9. To arrange public appearances by distinguished public and political figures of the East and West with appropriate declarations denouncing the aggressive activity of American intelligence.

10. To prepare and publish in the bourgeois press, through available means, a number of articles on the activities of the CIA.

14.8 CIA Plan to Overthrow Castro, 12 April 1961

Perhaps the most famous failed covert operation of the CIA was the Bay of Pigs invasion in April 1961. The document below describes the operational plan—codenamed Zapata—developed to overthrow the regime of Fidel Castro in Cuba.

1. Orientation and Concept:
The present concept of the operation being mounted to overthrow Castro is that it should have the appearance of a growing and increasingly effective internal resistance, helped by the activities of defected Cuban aircraft and by the infiltration (over a period of time and at several places) of weapons and small groups of men. External support should appear to be organized and controlled by the Revolutionary Council under Miro Cardona as the successor to a number of separate groups. To support this picture and to minimize emphasis on invasion, the following steps have been taken:

a. The public statements of Cardona have emphasized that the overthrow of Castro was the responsibility of the Cubans, that it must be performed mainly by the Cubans in Cuba rather than from outside, and that he and his colleagues are organizing this external support free of control by or official help from the U.S. Government.

b. The plans for air operations have been modified to provide for operations on a limited scale on D-2 and again on D-Day itself instead of placing reliance on a larger strike coordinated with the landings on D-Day.

c. Shortly after the first air strikes on D-2 a B-26 with Cuban pilot will land at Miami airport seeking asylum. He will state that he defected with two other B-26 pilots and aircraft and that they strafed aircraft on the ground before departing.

d. A preliminary diversionary landing of true guerrilla type will be made in Oriente Province on D-2. The main D-Day landings will be made by three groups at locations spaced some distance apart on the coast. These will be followed about one week later by a further guerrilla type landing in Pinar del Rio (at the western end of the island).

e. Ships carrying the main forces leave the staging base at staggered times. (The first one sailed on Tuesday morning.) They will follow independent courses to a rendezvous for the final run-in. Until nearly dusk on D-1 they would appear to air observation to be pursuing unrelated courses so there will be no appearance of a convoy.

f. All the landings will be at night. At least in the first 24 hours, supply activity over the beaches will be at night. There will be no obtrusive 'beachhead' to be seen by aircraft. Most troops will be deployed promptly to positions inland (…)

3. Diversion or Cancellation:
It would now be infeasible to halt the staging and embarkation of the troops. In the event of a decision to modify the operational plan or to cancel the operation, ships will be diverted at sea, either to Vieques Island or to ports in the U.S. If cancellation is directed, the troops and ships' officers will be told that the reason for the diversion is that all details of the operation, including time and place of intended landings, had been blown to the Castro regime and that under these circumstances the landings would be suicidal. This explanation would be adhered to after the demobilization of the force in the U.S. The U.S. Government could take the position that this enterprise had been undertaken by the Cubans without U.S. Governmental support, that it had failed because of their poor security, and that the U.S. could not refuse to grant asylum to the Cuban volunteers (…)

4. Naval Protection:
The ships carrying the main force will receive unobtrusive Naval protection up to the time they enter Cuban territorial waters. If they are attacked they will be protected by U.S. Naval vessels but following such an intervention they would be escorted to a U.S. port and the force would be demobilized.

5. Defections:
Every effort is being made to induce the defection of individuals of military and political significance. At the present time contact has been established by and through Cuban agents and anti-Castro Cuban groups with some thirty-one specific military and police officers (…) There are, of course, in addition many others rumored to be disaffected but to whom no channel of approach is available. The objective of these efforts is not to induce immediate defections but to prepare the individuals for appropriate action in place after D-day.

6. Internal Resistance Movements:
On the latest estimate there are nearly 7,000 insurgents responsive to some degree of control through agents with whom communications are currently active. About 3,000 of these are in Havana itself, over 2,000 in Oriente, about 700 in Las Villas in central Cuba. For the most part, the individual groups are small and very inadequately armed. Air drops are currently suspended because available aircraft are tied up in the movement of troops from their training area to the staging base. After D-Day when it is hoped that the effectiveness of the Castro air force will be greatly reduced, it is planned to supply these groups by daytime air drops. Every effort will be made to coordinate their operations with those of the landing parties. Efforts will be made also to sabotage or destroy by air attack the microwave links on which Castro's communication system depends. The objective is of course to create a revolutionary situation, initially perhaps in Oriente and Las Villas Provinces, and then spreading to all parts of the island.

7. Propaganda and Communications:
(…) The number of hours of broadcasting per day will be increased beginning immediately from about 25 to almost 75 soon after D-Day. The combination of multiple long and short wave stations which will then be in use, supplemented by three boats which carry broadcasting equipment (two short wave and one medium wave) will assure heavy coverage of all parts of the island virtually at all times. Radio programs will avoid any reference to an invasion but will call for up-rising and will of course announce defections and carry news of all revolutionary action. Soon after D-Day a small radio transmitter will be put in operation on Cuban soil.

8. The Political Leadership:
As of the present moment, the six members of Cardona's Revolutionary Council, notably including Ray, have reaffirmed their membership. Although no specific portfolios have been confirmed, the following possibilities are currently under discussion: Varona, Defense; Ray, Gobernacion (Interior); Carrillo, Finance; Hevia, State; Maceo, Public Health. The political leaders have not yet been briefed on the military plan but they will be informed at each phase of military operations. Advance consultation with the political leaders is considered unacceptably dangerous on security grounds and although last minute briefings will be resented, it is believed that the political leaders will want to take credit for and assume control as quickly as possible over these major operations against Castro (…)

9. Command:
Military command will be exercised in the name of the Revolutionary Council and later of the Provisional Government. In fact, however, the CIA staff

constitutes the general staff of the operation and the Agency controls both logistics support and communications. Accordingly, in the early stages at least, the functions of a general head-quarters will be exercised from the Agency with the Cuban brigade commander exercising field command over the units that land on D-Day.

14.9 Operational Notes for Penkovsky, October 1961

For about eighteen months (from early 1961 to September 1962 when he was arrested by the KGB) Colonel Oleg Penkovsky was the most important Western mole in Soviet Military Intelligence (GRU). The information he provided—together with the satellite pictures from U-2 spy planes—probably enabled the United States to piece together a reasonably accurate picture of Soviet missile installations in Cuba that provoked the October 1962 Missile Crisis. Below are selections of his 'operational notes' and from his final 'brief' (indicating the type of intelligence Penkovsky was to collect).

Operational

L. *On arrival*

Ring number 83-13-58 at 2130 hours sunday 15th october. Three rings indicates that all is well: seven rings indicates that all is not well.

2. *Meetings with janet*

A) friday 20th october at 1300 hours at the commission shop on the Arbat

B) alternative: Monday 23rd October at 1300 hours in the Praga delicatessen shop.

C) same pattern to continue throughout rest of october and november—basic meeting on fridays with alternative on following monday: janet will only go to alternative meeting if he fails to appear on the friday. Exception during this period will be time he is out of moscow on leave: he will notify janet of this period and tell her date of the friday on which he will expect to see her again (…)

F) he will pass to janet at meetings minox film, typewritten notes and possibly other small packages. Janet's husband will read any typewritten messages in case they contain operational suggestions or information of vital importance.

G) as soon as possible after his return from leave we will try to arrange a party under auspices of dr. Senior so that he and janet can meet officially: in meantime he should use cover story that they have already met at house of mr king in december 1960. Material may be passed to janet at a party but not under any circumstances to her husband.

3. *Use of dead drop*

Notes: i) dead drop *will only* be used to pass information on matters listed in points one and two of final brief: it will not be used to pass any other information material.

ii) dead drop may also be used as emergency means to inform us that he has been posted away from moscow and can no longer attend meetings with us in moscow: this means only to be used if timing does not permit him to inform us thru janet.

iii) dead drop should never be used to pass information which can wait until next meeting with janet: normally we would not expect it to be used on days when he has meeting with janet.

iv) he must remember that we can only clear dead drop once in safety: this emphasizes emergency nature of its use.

A) to indicate that he intends to fill dead drop he will make mark in form of rough circle with dark color on post 35 facing road some three feet from ground: this mark can be made at any time.

B) at any time of any day, after making signal on post 35, he will telephone number 43-26-94 or 43-26-87. If no answer or obviously soviet maid answers he will ring the second number. If proper person responds he will put down receiver and after one minute he will dial same number again and hang up again. There will always be someone at either of these numbers to answer his call. If proper female voice responds she will say 'hello, mrs. Davison (or mrs. Jones) speaking'. On receipt of this signal the post will be examined to see if there is a mark on it: if there is, efforts will be made to clear dead drop as quickly as possible.

C) dead drop must be filled either before signal or within 10 minutes of telephone call.

D) after filling dead drop he must under no circumstances return to it to see if it has been cleared.

E) signal to indicate to him that dead drop has been successfully cleared will be placed within 12 hours of receipt of telephone call on wall with poster at entrance to gastronom. Signal which will take form of dark smudge will be two inches diagonally from bottom right hand corner of poster. One smudge will indicate safe receipt of material: two smudges will indicate that dead drop has been visited but no material found.

4. *Emergency signal without use of dead drop*

In the event that he knows soviet government intends to go to war and only under these circumstances, but is unable to pass message to this effect either through janet or through dead drop, he should use following method:—

A) telephone number 43-26-94 or 43-26-87 at anytime on any day. If male voice answers and only if male voice answers, blow three times into mouth piece and hang up. This time the call should not be repeated.

B) in addition to this telephone call he should if possible place mark on post 35. This mark should be made before the telephone call (...)

6. *Messages from us*

Messages from us to him will for time being be passed by following means:—

A) wireless messages every month with 2 messages per month beginning in november. First message will be sent on scheduled time 1–15th of month and second message from 16th to end of month.

B) typewritten messages in russian handed to him by janet. He must not expect to receive such messages every time he meets janet. If she has a message to pass it will probably be concealed in a cigarette or similar container. If she offers him a cigarette or a cigarette packet he should take it apart until he finds the message.

7. *photographic equipment*

A) new minox camera to be taken to moscow by him. Camera which needs overhaul to be handed to janet.

B) minox cassettes will be supplied through janet as and when they are required. At present he has forty. When we know that he has only ten left we will pass him automatically resupply. If however he realises that he will need resupply earlier he must ask for it in a message to be handed to janet. She will then hand them over at next meeting in suitably disguised form—probably sweet box (...)

Final brief

i. *Indications*

1. Information from responsible soviet officials that the ussr had decided to launch an attack the west—the plan, date and time of attack. Details of information acquisition.
2. Information that the ussr will attack the west if certain specific conditions are not met by the west, or if the west commits certain actions or adopts certain policy.
3. Information that the ussr will not attack the west.
4. Information that the ussr will attack her on a certain date or if certain conditions prevail.

   Always give details of when, where, from whom you get information. This is particularly important for the above questions, but should be applied as well to all your other information. Keep an aide memoire for each item of information. And give your own evaluation of each item in a sub-paragraph.

ii. *Strategic missiles*

1. Numbers deployed or planned to be deployed in each range.
2. What is their warhead yield

iii. *Submarine ballistic missiles*
1. When will atomic or conventional submarines have ballistic missiles on them

iv. *Anti-ballistic missiles*
1. When will the abm be ready for deployment
2. What method is considered best for destroying a ballistic missile (illegible)

v. *Vurs* [Surface-to-air miniles]
1. Have any new vurs been developed since the v-750
2. For low flying aircraft
3. For high flying aircraft

vi. *Nuclear weapons*
1. What successes were achieved in the recent test series, and what weaknesses were discovered
2. What changes in production, storage, or delivery vehicle policies resulted from the tests.
3. What were the smallest and largest weapons tested, and what are their uses.
4. Have any 'fantastic weapons' developments taken place

vii. *Security*
Any indication that the r.i.s. [Russian Intelligence Services] has a high-level penetration of a western government

viii. *Tactical missiles*
1. Identify by designation or range the weapons appearing on the 7 november parade.
2. Determine the deployment status of the various missiles, include numbers, geographical location, and unit designations.

14.10 The KGB and Domestic Dissent, 1968–1975

In 1967 Yuri Andropov took over as the chairman of the KGB. The following year the dramatic events in Czechoslovakia (the Prague Spring and its suppression; see Chapter 8) focused much of KGB attention on the monitoring of internal dissent (both within the USSR and in the Soviet bloc in general). In the first document Andropov gives an assurance that the KGB will take appropriate measures to prevent the 'corruption' of Soviet youth; in the second, historian Christopher Andrew and Anatoli Mitrokhin discuss the KGB's plans against the famous Soviet dissident Andrei Sakharov.

A. Andropov on Surveillance of Soviet Youth, November 1968

A document has been received at the Committee for State Security in which a number of judgments are set forth about contemporary students and youth. The author of the document is a college student who has been in the company of many young poets, artists, and performers, and who has taken part in the competitions of the 'Club for the Happy and Quick-Witted' a popular television programme— Despite the immaturity of the author and his obvious subjectivism when analyzing certain matters, the document, in our view, merits close attention, since many of the propositions in it coincide with the views of our other sources. Taking account of this information, the KGB is adopting measures to study negative processes and to prevent politically harmful developments among our youth that might arise from these processes (…)

ATTACHMENT

(…) the present essay is intended to describe and analyze the behavior of full-time undergraduate students, who are potentially, by virtue of a number of factors, the most socially unstable and most easily swayed group in the population. These factors include the group's relative youthfulness, the daily contacts the members have with others like themselves, the members' lack of material obligations (for the most part) before their families, and so forth (…)

Students' attitudes toward the ongoing situation in Czechoslovakia are of two main types. On the one hand, indignation is expressed toward the 'brothers,' whom we 'have been subsidizing for so many years' and who are now responding with vile ingratitude. This group of students, among whom are participants in the Hungarian events, demand decisive measures and the use of military force. However, this group is small in number. The rest of the students, who generally take pleasure in anything that causes problems for or conflicts with the official line, are watching the ongoing situation in Czechoslovakia with benevolent curiosity. They have no real sense of what all this can lead to. They are impressed by the Czech students, who have become a major social force. Some even contemplate (albeit hypothetically) the possibility of repeating the Czech experience in our own country.

In a discussion with the author of this review, a third-year student said: 'It's interesting to think whether such events could take place here. I personally would take part if they did.'

What has attracted especially great interest is the creation of opposition parties. The very word 'opposition' is something students find appealing, and even the most thoughtful of them regard the creation of an opposition party as a solution to the paradox they have encountered: 'The struggle for the Soviet regime is against the Soviet regime.'

Hence, they are following events in Czechoslovakia with great interest. The excesses cited in the Soviet press seem largely harmless to them, and the official commentaries seem too pointed. The place where students are afraid of the situation that has unfolded is China (…)

B. Andrews and Mitrokhin on the Sakharov Case

(...) As part of the Helsinki Accords on Security and Co-operation in Europe, the United States, Canada and all European states save Albania and Andorra agreed to protect a series of basic human rights (...) Henceforth [the USSR's] human rights critics both at home and abroad could justly claim that it was in breach of an international agreement it had freely entered into.

The most influential of those critics was, increasingly, Andrei Sakharov. From the KGB's viewpoint, both the importance and the difficulty of discrediting Sakharov before world opinion were heightened by his being awarded the Nobel Peace Prize in October 1975. The Oslo residency had been instructed to do all in its power to prevent the award, but was forced to confess that it was powerless to influence the Nobel Peace Prize committee which, it claimed, was wholly composed of 'reactionaries'—chief amongst them its chairwoman, the Labour Party deputy Aase Lionaes. Sakharov pronounced the Peace Prize 'a great honour not just for me but also for the whole human rights movement' (...)

(...) Just over a week after he received news of the award, the first of the 'Sakharov Hearings', was held in response to an appeal launched by Sakharov and other dissidents a year earlier in Copenhagen to hear evidence of Soviet human rights abuses—almost all of them in breach of the Helsinki Accords.

On 22 November Andropov approved a document entitled 'Complex Operational Measures to Expose the Political Background to the Award of the Nobel Peace Prize to Sakharov' (...) In collaboration, where necessary, with other KGB directorates, the FCD was instructed:

— to inspire articles and speeches by public and political personalities in Norway, Finland, Sweden, Denmark, Britain and the FRG, to develop the theme that the award of the Nobel Peace Prize to Sakharov was an attempt by certain political circles to slow down the process of détente (...)

— to organize articles and speeches by representatives of public and political circles through KGB assets in Finland, France, Italy and Britain, to demonstrate the absurdity of attempting to link the award of the Peace Prize to Sakharov to a decision relating to the all-European [Helsinki] Conference (...)

— to organize the mailing of letters and declarations protesting about the award of the Peace Prize to Sakharov to the Nobel Committee of the Norwegian Storting [parliament] and to influential press organs in various Western countries (...)

— to pass material compromising Sakharov to the Danish, Swedish and Finnish press, hinting at his links with reactionary organizations financed by the CIA and other Western special services;

— to take steps designed to persuade S. Haffner, the leading political observer of the West German *Stern* magazine, to make negative comments on the award of the Nobel Peace Prize to Sakharov. Haffner had already made sharp criticisms in the FRG press when Sakharov was put forward for the Peace Prize in 1973;

— to pass information to the 'dissident' emigration in western Europe designed to exacerbate relations between Sakharov and Solzhenitsyn (…)

— with the help of agents of influence among prominent Chilean émigrés (in Algeria and Mexico), to disseminate the text of a [bogus] telegram of congratulations supposedly sent by General Pinochet [who had led the coup against President Allende] to Sakharov on the occasion of the award of the Nobel Peace Prize;

— to inspire pronouncements by leading Chilean émigrés in Italy, and France, expressing the outrage of all Chilean patriots at the award of the Nobel Peace Prize to Sakharov, who in 1973 had welcomed the overthrow of the Allende government and in return for this had been awarded the title of 'Honorary Citizen' by Pinochet;

— to inspire public statements by public personalities in the Arab countries, condemning the Nobel Committee's decision on Sakharov, presenting this as a deal between Sakharov and the Zionists, in return for Sakharov's pronouncements on the question of Jewish emigration from the Soviet Union, as the Zionists had a decisive influence on the Nobel Committee when it awarded the Nobel Peace Prize for 1975. It should be noted that the 'Sakharov Hearings' in Copenhagen were also a form of payment to Sakharov by the Zionists in return for his pro-Israel activity;

— to make available through Novosti for publication abroad a series entitled 'Who Defends Sakharov?', dealing with [alleged pro-Sakharov] criminals sentenced in the Soviet Union for bribery (Shtern), theft (Leviyev), instigation of terrorism (Bukovsky, Moroz).

The main fabrications intended to discredit Sakharov personally—his links with Western intelligence agencies, his support for the Pinochet regime and his plots with the Zionists—were all further developed in active measures over the next few years (…)

14.11 Gerald Ford and Richard Helms on CIA Domestic Activities, January 1975

In the mid-1970s the CIA came under congressional investigations that focused on various aspects of the agency's work. While the CIA's involvement in assassination attempts of foreign leaders and its recent involvement in the overthrow of the Allende government in Chile topped the agenda of the so-called Church Committee report of 1975, the domestic activities and surveillance (supposed to be illegal) were also under scrutiny and concerned the Ford administration. Below, President Ford discusses the allegations with former CIA director Richard Helms, who was at the time serving as the U.S. Ambassador to Iran.

FORD: Dick, you and I have known each other a long time. I have only the most admiration for you and your work. Frankly, we are in a mess. I want you to tell me whatever you want. I believe the CIA is essential to the country. It has to exist and perform its functions. We will have a Blue Ribbon Panel look into these charges. It will investigate the domestic activities of the CIA.

HELMS: Why not add the FBI? They overlap, and you may as well get to the bottom of it.

FORD: I will consider it. Secondly, though, the commission will look at the Colby Report and, thirdly, make recommendations to me. It is a good commission. I hope they will stay within their charter, but in this climate, we can't guarantee it. It would be tragic if it went beyond it, because the CIA needs to remain a strong and viable agency. It would be a shame if the public uproar forced us to go beyond and to damage the integrity of the CIA. I automatically assume what you did was right, unless it's proved otherwise.

HELMS: I have been in the service 32 years. At the end all one has is a small pension and a reputation—if any. I testified in Watergate; I didn't dump on President Nixon and I stuck to the truth. I intend to fight this matter. I welcome a Blue Ribbon Panel.

At the base is Congressional oversight. No Congress wants to join hands with the Bay of Pigs, etcetera; it's bad politics. The CIA is the president's creature.

If allegations have been made to Justice, a lot of dead cats will come out. I intend to defend myself (...)

The basic allegation—that we spied on dissidents—stemmed from the charge to me to discover if there was any foreign connection to the dissidents. I never permitted any spying on any Congressmen. The business on the files is ridiculous; if you get a name, of course you make a record and open a file in case it is relevant thereafter.

FORD: I have no doubt about your total integrity, and, in fact you did a good job running the Agency. What we are trying to do is look into the charges and protect the functions of the Agency (...) I plan no witch hunt, but in this environment I don't know if I can control it.

HELMS: I will help you, Mr. President. I believe in the Agency and its mission.

14.12 Aldrich Ames on Spying and Betrayal

*Aldrich Ames was probably the most damaging mole in CIA history. A career agency offi-
cial, Ames began selling US secrets to the KGB in 1985; within a decade he had revealed
more than 100 covert operations and betrayed at least thirty agents, ten of whom were
later executed by the Soviets. Along with his co-conspirator and wife, Rosario, Ames was
paid more than $2.7 million for the information before he was arrested in 1994. He was
convicted and sentenced to life in prison without parole. Ames was interviewed for the
CNN Cold War television series in March 1998.*

(...) By the late '70s I had come to question the point, the value, of a great deal of
what we were doing, in terms of the [CIA's] overall charter, and to question
whether this was having any significant impact on American policy (...) By the
early '80s, when I moved into a new job in the counterintelligence branch in the
Soviet division (...) I discovered that my growing misgivings were even truer than
I had thought (...) I found that, for example, our Soviet espionage efforts had virtually never, or had very seldom, produced any worthwhile political or economic
intelligence on the Soviet Union (...)

Sources [in the Soviet Union] demonstrated (...) [there was] a rather ad hoc
defensive approach from Gromyko and Brezhnev and the Soviet foreign policy
establishment at the time (...) Not this secret master plan for world conquest that
was so much at issue in the late '70s, when many people, including policymakers,
took the view that the West was under a new coordinated aggressive assault.
These materials just simply not only didn't support it, but tended to contradict it
(...)

At the time that I handed over the names and compromised so many CIA
agents in the Soviet Union (...) I had come to the conclusion that the loss of these
sources to the United States government, or to the West as well, would not compromise significant national defense, political, diplomatic interests (...)

These beliefs and ideas that I had had and developed over a long time enabled
me to act out of personal desperation, as if there were no taboo against it, in running my little scam in April '85: 'Give me $50,000—here's some names of some
people we've recruited.' And of course, I knew that these were really harmless,
because these were [double-agents] the KGB had sent to us. I assumed that they'd
be happy to pay the $50,000 because I was a CIA officer, and it was cheap (...)

(...) what happened after I got the $50,000, I think, was the realization that
despite my ideas and beliefs that there was nothing really damaging in all of this—
which I continue to subscribe to—[I] had overlooked the element of betrayal, the
taboo; that, granted, I hadn't given away agents who would suffer; I hadn't given
away information that would, in my view or in practically anyone's, really do any
serious damage; I had received some money. But the taboo, the betrayal—I traf-

ficked with the devil. This I hadn't factored in (...) And what happened to me in May, when I got the money, the whole burden, in a sense, descended on me—and the realization of what I had done. And it led me then to make the further step, which in a sense was to cast myself into it, which meant an unreserved offer of loyalty, if you will—a change of loyalties. I mean, it's not particularly ideological or political, but much more personal in that sense: a change of loyalties, in which I said, 'I'm yours. I've cast myself out, and I realize what I've done to myself, and I don't belong here anymore, I belong there.' And that's what I did. And that's when I gave the names (...)

I knew quite well, when I gave the names of our agents in the Soviet Union, that I was exposing them to the full machinery of counterespionage and the law, and then prosecution and capital punishment, certainly, in the case of KGB and GRU officers who would be tried in a military court. And certainly others, that they were almost all at least potentially liable to capital punishment. There's simply no question about this.

Now, I believed that the KGB, with the support of the political leadership, would want to keep it very much under wraps. And I felt at the time that not only for the overriding practical reason of protecting me, they would also find it useful to cover up the embarrassing fact of who so many of these people were, and that this would all have a somewhat dampening effect on the results of the compromise [of the agents' identities]. But of course, you know, given time and circumstances, obviously I knew these folks would have to answer for what they'd done. And certainly I felt I insured myself against a reaction to that.

The only thing I ever withheld from the KGB were the names of two agents whom I personally had known and handled and had a particular feeling for. So obviously I was feeling something; I distinguished two agents from all the rest on the basis of my personal feelings. Later, after the compromises, when I was in Rome, feeling that for particular reasons these folks would not be persecuted, much less prosecuted, I did give the KGB their names, but I felt confident when I did that, that the consequences to them would not be significant. And they have not been.

But it is important to at least recognize in retrospect that while a number of the agents that I compromised were executed, others were treated with relative leniency. At least one KGB officer only got 15 years, and of course later [was] released under the amnesty, and traveled to the United States, where he lives. Now this is a KGB officer who worked in place for the FBI and the CIA (...)

I never felt I was betraying my country as I did this. I was betraying a whole series of other loyalties, though, the enormity of which came to me very soon (...)

Espionage, for the most part, involves finding a person who knows something or has something that you can induce them secretly to give to you. That almost always involves a betrayal of trust: whether it's a Japanese businessman giving you some technical information that his company has entrusted him with; whether it's an official of another government who obviously has a position of trust within that government; whether it's the wife of a military officer whom you've induced to betray the trust placed in her by her husband, in order to get information that might enable you to recruit him. There's a betrayal of trust. Espionage revolves around the many different forms of betrayals of trust (…)

In any open-eyed view of things, it is corrupting to engage in such activities: corrupting to the person who does it [and] it's corrupting to the people or institutions who sponsor it. This is why espionage has never been respectable; this is why espionage has always been disreputable—because people instinctively understand it. You know, I don't think the films of James Bond and romantic views of spies have done anything to alter the public revulsion to what espionage really is, any more than people—despite law-and-order, tough-on-crime views— are likely to really like the public hangman. That stench is there.

Questions

How significant were the so-called atomic spies?

What explains the 'success' of the Iran and Guatemala covert operations?

What kind of intelligence did the Americans try to collect on the Soviets?

What were the different techniques of intelligence-gathering in the 1950s?

How did the KGB plan to discredit Allen Dulles?

What were the Zapata Plan's goals? How does the Zapata Plan differ from the Iran and Guatemala Plans of 1953–4 (see documents 14.4A and B)?

Why and how did the KGB increasingly target internal dissent in the late 1960s and 1970s? Why was Andrei Sakharov a specific target?

Why did President Gerald Ford feel compelled to comply with a full-scale investigation on the activities of the CIA?

How does Aldrich Ames justify his actions?

Overall, how significant do you believe the various intelligence activities and covert operations were in determining the course of the Cold War?

15

The Rise of Détente

In the late 1960s the Cold War seemed to give way to a new era of high-level negotiations, arms-control agreements, and superpower summitry. Such events as the SALT I agreement of 1972 and the Nixon–Brezhnev summits of 1972–4 highlighted the way in which Soviet–American relations, while not amicable, had at least moved towards a new level of civility. As the United States simultaneously moved to finally break away from its earlier non-recognition policy vis-à-vis the People's Republic of China—while the Soviets and the Chinese exchanged blows on their border in 1969—the view of the Cold War as a bipolar confrontation had, it seemed, become a thing of the past. In Europe, the German question moved towards stabilization with the advent of inter-German relations, a Four-Power agreement on the status of Berlin, and a series of bilateral treaties between the Federal Republic of Germany on the one hand, and the USSR, Poland, and other Soviet bloc countries on the other. In the early 1970s, moreover, the talks that eventually led to the Conference on Security and Co-operation in Europe and the signing of the Helsinki Final Act in 1975 were additional signals of the beginning of a new era in East–West relations. (For more documentation on the European developments see Chapter 10.)

Détente and triangular diplomacy grew from a mixture of pressures within the international system. From the American perspective, the debacle in Vietnam had, by the late 1960s, proven costly in terms of the lives lost and the expenditures incurred, while it had simultaneously undermined the United States's prestige around the globe. Within the United States, serious questions were raised regarding basic assumptions of the United States's containment policy. Concerns about a potential nuclear holocaust in the aftermath of the October 1962 Cuban Missile Crisis provided an impetus for enhanced Soviet–American contacts, while the emerging nuclear parity in the late 1960s increased pressure to cut down the costly nuclear arms race. Weaknesses in the Soviet economy—the need for access to Western markets and technology—provided an additional rationale for Moscow's interest in détente.

To these developments in the Soviet–American relationship, however, one must add the growing centrifugal tendencies within the key Cold War alliances.

Within NATO, France's president Charles de Gaulle advocated a more independent European policy (led by France) and eventually withdrew France from the alliance's military structure. In part as a response to de Gaulle's independent initiatives towards the Soviet Union and his concept of a 'Europe from the Atlantic to the Urals', moreover, NATO adopted in 1967 the so-called Harmel Report, a policy document that emphasized the need to search for a détente with the Warsaw Pact. Perhaps most dramatically, West German chancellor Willy Brandt's *Ostpolitik* succeeded in unblocking the long impasse that had characterized the division of Germany since the late 1940s (for documentation on the German question see Chapter 10). For its part, the United States—in part willingly, in part by necessity—gradually aligned its policies with those of the more 'détente-minded' West Europeans.

In the Soviet bloc, centrifugal tendencies had become evident already in the early 1960s when the Sino-Soviet split gradually emerged into public view. While the adoption of more independent policies by some East European countries (such as Romania) hardly meant the erosion of Soviet hegemony in the region, the August 1968 Warsaw Pact crackdown on the Prague Spring (see Chapter 8) and the armed clashes along the Sino-Soviet border in March 1969 provided evidence of the growing tensions amongst the Communist countries. In particular, the Soviet leadership was suffering from a crisis of legitimacy that could, some thought, be redressed if the USSR's status as the world's other superpower was more formally recognized by the West.

Within such a context the 'realpolitik' approach advocated by Richard Nixon and his chief foreign policy advisor, Henry Kissinger, seemed to offer a more viable (and less costly) alternative for safeguarding American interests. At its basis lay the notion that America's international adversaries, most specifically the Soviet Union and China, acted more out of national interest than ideological convictions. Given the military clashes between the two Communist powers, the United States appeared to have a particularly tempting opportunity to play the Chinese and Soviets off against each other through a careful application of rewards and pressures. Among other things, the Nixon administration hoped to use the USSR and China to help bring about an 'acceptable' end to the Vietnam War (see Chapter 7).

From the American perspective, the new approach seemingly succeeded in the early 1970s. The United States—after more than two decades—finally opened a relationship with the People's Republic of China in 1971–2 when Kissinger first visited Beijing secretly in July 1971 and Nixon then arrived there for a series of high-level meetings with Mao Zedong and Zhou Enlai in February 1972. At the same time, the Soviets, apparently concerned over the new Sino–American relationship, agreed to a Soviet-American summit that resulted in the first Nixon–Brezhnev summit of May 1972 and the signing of the SALT I agreement.

Although it did not bring an end to the nuclear arms race, SALT I symbolized the long road that the United States and the Soviet Union had travelled during the decade following the Cuban Missile Crisis of 1962.

Readings

Jussi M. Hanhimäki, *The Flawed Architect: Henry Kissinger and American Foreign Policy* (2004). A balanced reassessment of the Nixon and Ford administration's key foreign policy maker's career in office.

A. Fursenko and T. Naftali, *'One Hell of a Gamble': The Secret History of the Cuban Missile Crisis* (1997). A detailed study of the crisis based on materials from both sides.

Raymond Garthoff, *Détente and Confrontation* (1994). Massive examination of Soviet–American relations from the 1960s to the 1980s.

A. Savelyev and N. N. Detinov, *The Big Five: Arms Control Decision-Making in the Soviet Union* (1995). A study emphasizing the Soviet need to reduce the costs of the nuclear arms race as a major cause for détente.

Patrick Taylor, *The Great Wall* (1999). A provocative account of Sino-American rapprochement extending to the 1990s.

15.1 The Cuban Missile Crisis, October 1962

In 1962 the Soviet Union and Cuba agreed to place nuclear missiles on the Caribbean island. The subsequent installation of missiles and the American discovery of it unleashed perhaps the most dangerous crisis of the Cold War. For a two-week period in October the two sides sparred, with the Americans launching a naval blockade on Cuba, publicly demanding the removal of missiles, and preparing for a military strike against the island. Although the crisis was eventually solved—with the Soviets agreeing to remove the missiles and the Americans assuring they would not invade Cuba and pledging secretly that Washington would de-install missiles recently placed in Turkey—the possibility of a nuclear exchange was as close as it would ever be during the Cold War. In the first document the Soviet commander in Cuba reports to Khrushchev on the status of missile deployment. The subsequent excerpts include a summation of possible US courses of action, American ambassador Adlai Stevenson's statement in front of the UN accusing the Soviets of deception, and a report of the shooting down of an American plane over Cuba on the last full day of the crisis.

A. Colonel General S. P. Ivanov on the Installation of Soviet Missiles in Cuba, 5 October 1962

N. S. Khrushchev telephoned from [illegible] and inquired how the shipment [of nuclear weapons] was going.

Ivanov reported: The Indigirka arrived 4 October. No overflights [by U. S. surveillance aircraft]. [word illegible] shipment 22 [? unclear reference]. In transit 20 [days].

Transport with special [nuclear] munitions Aleksandrovsk is loaded and ready for dispatch. Permission requested to send it.

N. S. Khrushchev: Send the Aleksandrovsk. Where are the Lunas [short-range ballistic missiles] and IL-28s [medium-range bomber aircraft]?

I responded: en route.

[NSK:] Everything is clear. Thanks. [two words illegible]

B. Director of Central Intelligence, John A. McCone, on US Options, 17 October 1962

Several alternatives indicated below were posed for consideration at the close of meeting (…) All dealt with the specific actions U.S. Government should take against Cuba at this time. The discussions centered around:

(a) Whether military action should be taken prior to a warning to, or discussions with, Khrushchev and Castro.

(b) Notification to or consultation with our allies, including NATO, OAS [organization of American States], and others.

(c) Referral to the United Nations.

(d) Effect on the 'balance of nuclear power equation' of the MRBM installations in Cuba.

Three principal courses of action are open to us, and of course there are variations of each.

(1) Do nothing and live with the situation. It was pointed out clearly that Western Europe, Greece, Turkey, and other countries had lived under the Soviet MRBMs for years; therefore, why should the United States be so concerned.

(2) Resort to an all-out blockade which would probably require a declaration of war and to be effective would mean the interruption of all incoming shipping. This was discussed as a slow strangulation process, but it was stated that 'intelligence reports' indicated that a blockade would bring Castro down in four months. (Note: I have seen no such estimate.)

(3) Military action which was considered at several levels. The following alternatives are:

(a) Strafing identified MRBM [Medium-Range Ballistic Missile] installations.

(b) Strafing MRBM installations and air fields with MIGs [Soviet-produced jet-fighters].

(c) (a) and (b) plus all SAM [Surface-to-Air Missile] sites and coastal missile sites.

(d) (a), (b), and (c) above plus all other significant military installations, none of which were identified.

Discussions of all of the above were inconclusive and it was asked that the group reassemble, and develop their views on the advantages and disadvantages and the effects of the following:

(1) Warning to Khrushchev and Castro.
    (a) If the response is unsatisfactory, pursuing a course of military action.
    (b) If the response is unsatisfactory, referring to the OAS and the United Nations prior to taking military action.

(2) Warning to Khrushchev and Castro and if the response is unsatisfactory, convening Congress, seeking a declaration of war, and proceeding with an all-out blockade.

(3) Strike militarily with no warning, the level of the military effort being dependent upon evolving circumstances. In all probability this type of action would escalate into invasion and occupation, although the meeting was not agreed on this point.

(4) Blockade with no warning and no advance notice such as a declaration of war, with the President depending upon existing Congressional resolutions for authority.

C. Ambassador Adlai Stevenson Exposing Soviet Installations at the UN, 25 October 1962

I want to say to you, Mr. Zorin [Soviet UN ambassador], that I do not have your talent for obfuscation, for distortion, for confusing language, and for doubletalk. And I must confess to you that I am glad that I do not!

But if I understood what you said, you said that my position had changed, that today I was defensive because we did not have the evidence to prove our assertions, that your Government had installed long-range missiles in Cuba.

Well, let me say something to you, Mr. Ambassador—we do have the evidence. We have it, and it is clear and it is incontrovertible. And let me say something else—those weapons must be taken out of Cuba.

Next, let me say to you that, if I understood you, with a trespass on credibility that excels your best, you said that our position had changed since I spoke here the other day because of the pressures of world opinion and the majority of the United Nations. Well, let me say to you, sir, you are wrong again. We have had no pressure from anyone whatsoever. We came in here today to indicate our willingness to discuss Mr. U Thant's [UN General Secretary] proposals, and that is the only change that has taken place.

But let me also say to you, sir, that there has been a change. You—the Soviet Union has sent these weapons to Cuba. You—the Soviet Union has upset the balance of power in the world. You—the Soviet Union has created this new danger, not the United States.

And you ask with a fine show of indignation why the President did not tell Mr. Gromyko on last Thursday about our evidence, at the very time that Mr. Gromyko was blandly denying to the President that the U.S.S.R. was placing such weapons on sites in the new world.

Well, I will tell you why—because we were assembling the evidence, and perhaps it would be instructive to the world to see how a Soviet official—how far he would go in perfidy. Perhaps we wanted to know if this country faced another example of nuclear deceit like that one a year ago, when in stealth, the Soviet Union broke the nuclear test moratorium.

And while we are asking questions, let me ask you why your Government— your Foreign Minister—deliberately, cynically deceived us about the nuclear build-up in Cuba.

And, finally, the other day, Mr. Zorin, I remind you that you did not deny the existence of these weapons. Instead, we heard that they had suddenly become defensive weapons. But today again if I heard you correctly, you now say that they do not exist, or that we haven't proved they exist, with another fine flood of rhetorical scorn.

All right, sir, let me ask you one simple question: Do you, Ambassador Zorin, deny that the U.S.S.R. has placed and is placing medium- and intermediate-range missiles and sites in Cuba? Yes or no—don't wait for the translation—yes or no?

(The Soviet representative refused to answer.)

You can answer yes or no. You have denied they exist. I want to know if I understood you correctly. I am prepared to wait for my answer until hell freezes over, if that's your decision. And I am also prepared to present the evidence in this room . . . I doubt if anyone in this room, except possibly the representative of the Soviet Union, has any doubt about the facts. But in view of his statements and the statements of the Soviet Government up until last Thursday, when Mr. Gromyko denied the existence or any intention of installing such weapons in Cuba, I am going to make a portion of the evidence available right now (...)

The representative of the Soviet Union says that the official answer of the U.S.S.R. was the Tass statement that they don't need to locate missiles in Cuba. Well, I agree—they don't need to. But the question is, have they missiles in Cuba—and that question remains unanswered. I knew it would be.

As to the authenticity of the photographs, which Mr. Zorin has spoken about with such scorn, I wonder if the Soviet Union would ask its Cuban colleague to

13. A cartoonist's view of Kennedy, Khrushchev, and the Cuban Missile Crisis. (Leslie Illingworth, *Daily Mail*, 6 November 1962). Reprinted by permission. Photo supplied by The Centre for the Study of Cartoons and Caricature, University of Kent.

permit a U.N. team to go to these sites. If so, I can assure you that we can direct them to the proper places very quickly.

And now I hope that we can get down to business, that we can stop this sparring. We know the facts, and so do you, sir, and we are ready to talk about them. Our job here is not to score debating points. Our job, Mr. Zorin, is to save the peace. And if you are ready to try, we are.

D. Ivanov on the Shooting Down of an American Aircraft, 28 October 1962

27 October 1962 a U-2 aircraft entered the territory of Cuba at an altitude of 16,000 meters at 1700 hours Moscow time with the objective of photographing the combat disposition of troops, and in the course of 1 hour 21 minutes proceeded along a flight route over Yaguajay–Ciego de Avila–Camagney–Manzanillo–San Luis–Guantanamo–Preston.

With the aim of not permitting the photographs to fall into U.S. hands, at 1820 Moscow time this aircraft was shot down by two antiaircraft missiles of the 507th Antiaircraft Missile Regiment at an altitude of 21,000 meters. The aircraft fell in the vicinity of Antilla; a search has been organized.

On the same day there were 8 violations of Cuban airspace by U.S. aircraft.

15.2 Khrushchev on the Need for Relaxation of Tensions, 30 October 1962

By 28 October, following a meeting between the attorney-general Robert Kennedy and Soviet ambassador Anatoly Dobrynin the previous day, the Cuban Missile Crisis was defused. The Soviets agreed to withdraw their missiles in exchange for an American pledge not to invade Cuba and a secret promise to remove, after some delay, existing US missile installations in Turkey. On 30 October 1962 Soviet leader Nikita Khrushchev resumed a correspondence with President Kennedy in which he raised a number of the unsettled issues that blocked the way towards détente.

My colleagues and I consider that both sides have displayed restraint and wisdom in liquidating the military conflict which might have resulted in a world thermonuclear war. I take the liberty to think that you evidently held to a restraining position with regard to those forces which suffered from militaristic itching (...) I don't know, perhaps I am wrong, but in this letter I am making the conclusion on the basis that in your country the situation is such that the decisive word rests with the President and if he took an extreme stand there would be no one to restrain him and war would be unleashed (...)

(...) we have now conditions ripe for finalizing the agreement on signing a treaty on cessation of tests of thermonuclear weapons. We fully agree with regard to three types of tests or, so to say, tests in three environments. This is banning of tests in atmosphere, in outer space and under water. In this respect we are of the same opinion and we are ready to sign an agreement.

But there are still some differences with regard to underground explosions. Therefore it would be good if you gave instructions to find a compromise in the decision on the underground test ban, but without inspection. We shall not accept inspection, this I say to you unequivocally and frankly (...) We do not carry on underground tests, we did it but once and we are not going to do it anymore. Maybe such a necessity will arise sometime in future, but in any case I do not envisage it (...)

We appreciate it very much that you took the initiative and in such a moment of crisis stated your readiness to conduct negotiations with the purpose of signing a non-aggression treaty between the two military blocs. We responded and supported it. We are prepared to come to an agreement on this question confidentially or through diplomatic channels and then make it public and start negotiations. This also would contribute to lessening tension. The world public would learn with satisfaction that in the moment of crisis not only declarative statements were made but certain commitments with signatures affixed were taken as well (...)

We have eliminated a serious crisis. But in order to foresee and forestall appearance of a new crisis in future which might be impossible to cope with everything in our relations capable of generating a new crisis should be erased now. It would seem that now when we possess thermonuclear weapons, rocket weapons, submarine fleet and other means the situation obliges all states, every state to adhere to such norms of conduct which would not generate conflicts, to say nothing of wars (...)

There would remain many unsettled matters in the world but the main thing after that—and I would like to tell you about it—is the question of China. It is anomalous that China is not having her seat in the U.N. Similar anomalies already existed in history and were overwhelmed by life (...)

You would greatly raise your prestige, personal and that of your country, in the eyes of the peoples if you take an attitude facilitating China taking its lawful seat in the U.N. This is possible only if it is understood that there cannot be two Chinas (...) When China participated in the creation of the U.N. and when it was made a permanent member of the Security Council, then it was one China. And that one China exists now (...)

It is impossible to come to an agreement on disarmament without China. There are countries with population of half a million and even less which are members of the U.N. and have voice in this international organization. Iceland, for instance has the population of 180 thousand people. China has 650 million people and does not have such voice (...)

Therefore it would be proper to solve the question of the restoration of China's rights in the U.N.; the peoples are waiting for it. And this will happen, it is only a matter of time. Therefore in order not to prolong this time, if you understood now the necessity for such a step, then, it would in effect be possible to solve this problem at the present session of General Assembly. What satisfaction it would give to the world public opinion, you would see from the expression of feelings of all peoples because it would be a real step, indeed, towards stabilization and strengthening of peace all over the world (...)

These, in effect, are my considerations after the crisis situation. I want to tell you that in this crisis, as our saying goes, there is no evil without good (...) The good is that now people have felt more tangibly the breathing of the burning flames of thermonuclear war and have a more clear realization of the threat looming over them if arms race is not stopped. And I would say that what has just happened will serve especially good the American people (...)

Mr. President, you lived through this crisis yourself. For us too, it presented the Rubicon: whether to agree to a compromise, whether to make concessions. Indeed, from the point of view of the legal standards your claims had no grounds whatsoever. Therefore there was a great trial and there were hesitations (...) Having eliminated this crisis we gave each other mutual satisfaction: you promised not to attack and not to permit attack against Cuba on the part of others, and we moved forward to make the USA feel confident that we do not contemplate anything bad against it and that there is no threat against the USA on our part. You certainly possess means of destruction. But you know that we also have these means and they are of a different nature than those that were in Cuba. Those were trifles there. Our means were brought to the state of combat readiness, they were of a more serious nature and they were pointed at the USA and your allies (…)

15.3 President Kennedy's Call for Détente, June 1963

In a speech at the graduation ceremonies at American University in Washington, DC, President John F. Kennedy outlined the need for further relaxation of Soviet–American tensions. Given only five months prior to his assassination on 22 November 1963, Kennedy's speech is often cited as the prime public example of his growing interest in détente after the Missile Crisis.

(…) Some say that it is useless to speak of world peace or world law or world dis-armament—and that it will be useless until the leaders of the Soviet Union adopt a more enlightened attitude. I hope they do. I believe we can help them to do it. But I also believe that we must reexamine our own attitude (…)

First: Let us examine our attitude toward peace itself. Too many of us think it is impossible. Too many think it unreal. But that is dangerous, defeatist belief. It leads to the conclusion that war is inevitable—that mankind is doomed—that we are gripped by forces we cannot control.

We need not accept this view. Our problems are manmade—therefore, they can be solved by man (…) There is no single, simple key to this peace—no grand magic formula to be adopted by one or two powers. Genuine peace must be the product of many nations, the sum of many acts. It must be dynamic, not static, changing to meet the challenge of each new generation. For peace is a process—a way of solving problems.

With such a peace, there will still be quarrels and conflicting interests, as there are with families and nations. World peace, like community peace, does not require that each man love his neighbor—it requires only that they live together in mutual tolerance, submitting their disputes to a just and peaceful settlement. And history teaches us that enmities between nations, as between individuals, do not last forever (…)

Second: Let us reexamine our attitude toward the Soviet Union. It is discour-aging to think that their leaders may actually believe what their propagandists write. It is discouraging to read a recent authoritative Soviet text on Military Strategy and find, on page after page, wholly baseless and incredible claims— such as the allegation that 'American imperialist circles are preparing to unleash different types of wars . . . (and that) the political aims of the American imperialists are to enslave economically and politically the European and other capitalist countries . . . (and) to achieve world domination . . . by means of aggressive wars.' (...) it is sad to read these Soviet statements—to realize the extent of the gulf between us. But it is also a warning—a warning to the American people not to fall into the same trap as the Soviets, not to see only a distorted and desperate view of the other side, not to see conflict as inevitable, accommodation as impossible, and communication as nothing more than an exchange of threats.

No government or social system is so evil that its people must be considered as lacking in virtue. As Americans, we find communism profoundly repugnant as a negation of personal freedom and dignity. But we can still hail the Russian people for their many achivements—in science and space, in economic and industrial growth, in culture and in acts of courage.

Among the many traits the peoples of our two countries have in common, none is stronger than our mutual abhorrence of war. Almost unique, among the major world powers, we have never been at war with each other. And no nation in the history of battle ever suffered more than the Soviet Union suffered in the course of the Second World War. At least 20 million lost their lives. Countless millions of homes and farms were burned or sacked. A third of the nation's territory, including nearly two thirds of its industrial base, was turned into a wasteland—a loss equivalent to the devastation of this country east of Chicago.

Today, should total war ever break out again—no matter how—our two countries would become the primary targets. It is an ironic but accurate fact that the two strongest powers are the two in the most danger of devastation. All we have built, all we have worked for, would be destroyed in the first 24 hours. And even in the Cold War, which brings burdens and dangers to so many countries, including this Nation's closest allies—our two countries bear the heaviest burdens. For we are both devoting massive sums of money to weapons that could be better devoted to combating ignorance, poverty, and disease. We are both caught up in a vicious and dangerous cycle in which suspicion on one side breeds suspicion on the other, and new weapons beget counterweapons.

In short, both the United States and its allies, and the Soviet Union and its allies, have a mutually deep interest in a just and genuine peace and in halting the arms race. Agreements to this end are in the interests of the Soviet Union as well as ours (...)

Third: Let us reexamine our attitude toward the Cold War, remembering that we are not engaged in a debate, seeking to pile up debating points. We are not here distributing blame or pointing the finger of judgment. We must deal with the world as it is, and not as it might have been had the history of the last 18 years been different (...)

We must conduct our affairs in such a way that it becomes in the Communists' interest to agree on a genuine peace. Above all, while defending our own vital interests, nuclear powers must avert those confrontations which bring an adversary to a choice of either a humiliating retreat or a nuclear war. To adopt that kind of course in the nuclear age would be evidence only of the bankruptcy of our policy—or of a collective death-wish for the world.

To secure these ends, America's weapons are nonprovocative, carefully controlled, designed to deter, and capable of selective use. Our military forces are committed to peace and disciplined in self-restraint. Our diplomats are instructed to avoid unnecessary irritants and purely rhetorical hostility.

For we can seek a relaxation of tensions without relaxing our guard. And, for our part, we do not need to use threats to prove that we are resolute. We do not need to jam foreign broadcasts out of fear our faith will be eroded. We are unwilling to impose our system on any unwilling people—but we are willing and able to engage in peaceful competition with any people on earth (...)

Speaking of other nations, I wish to make one point clear. We are bound to many nations by alliances. Those alliances exist because our concern and theirs substantially overlap (...) The United States will make no deal with the Soviet Union at the expense of other nations and other peoples, not merely because they are our partners, but also because their interests and ours converge.

Our interests converge, however, not only in defending the frontiers of freedom, but in pursuing the paths of peace. It is our hope—and the purpose of allied policies—to convince the Soviet Union that she, too, should let each nation choose its own future, so long as that choice does not interfere with the choices of others. The Communist drive to impose their political and economic system on others is the primary cause of world tension today. For there can be no doubt that, if all nations could refrain from interfering in the self-determination of others, the peace would be much more assured.

This will require a new effort to achieve world law—a new context for world discussions. It will require increased understanding between the Soviets and ourselves. And increased understanding will require increased contact and communication. One step in this direction is the proposed arrangement for a direct line between Moscow and Washington, to avoid on each side the dangerous delays, misunderstandings, and misreadings of the other's actions which might occur at a time of crisis.

We have also been talking in Geneva about other first-step measures of arms control, designed to limit the intensity of the arms race and to reduce the risks of accidental war. Our primary long-range interest in Geneva, however, is general and complete disarmament—designed to take place by stages, permitting parallel political developments to build the new institutions of peace which would take the place of arms (…) The one major area of these negotiations where the end is in sight, yet where a fresh start is badly needed, is in a treaty to outlaw nuclear tests. The conclusion of such a treaty, so near and yet so far, would check the spiraling arms race in one of its most dangerous areas. It would place the nuclear powers in a position to deal more effectively with one of the greatest hazards which man faces in 1963, the further spread of nuclear arms (…)

I am taking this opportunity, therefore, to announce two important decisions in this regard.

First: Chairman Khrushchev, Prime Minister Macmillan, and I have agreed that high-level discussions will shortly begin in Moscow looking toward early agreement on a comprehensive test ban treaty. Our hopes must be tempered with the caution of history—but with our hopes go the hopes of all mankind.

Second: To make clear our good faith and solemn convictions on the matter, I now declare that the United States does not propose to conduct nuclear tests in the atmosphere so long as other states do not do so. We will not be the first to resume. Such a declaration is no substitute for a formal binding treaty, but I hope it will help us achieve one. Nor would such a treaty be a substitute for disarmament, but I hope it will help us achieve it (…) No treaty, however much it may be to the advantage of all, however tightly it may be worded, can provide absolute security against the risks of deception and evasion. But it can—if it is sufficiently effective in its enforcement and if it is sufficiently in the interests of its signers—offer far more security and far fewer risks than an unabated, uncontrolled, unpredictable arms race.

15.4 NATO and Warsaw Pact Shifts, 1966–1967

In the mid-1960s developments within both NATO and, to a lesser extent, the Warsaw Pact seemed to indicate a shift towards a more political mission. Within the Warsaw Pact there were moves to provide for increased consultation among the alliance members at both military and political levels. Within NATO, the sudden departure of France from the alliance's integrated military structure and French president Charles de Gaulle's independent diplomacy towards the Soviet Union played a significant role in increasing American concerns over NATO's cohesion. In December 1967, partly in response to such worries, NATO adopted the Harmel Report (named after Belgian foreign minister Pierre Harmel) that stressed the alliance's political role and called for efforts to promote détente with the Warsaw Pact countries. In the first document below, the Polish foreign minister Adam Rapacki outlines some plans for Warsaw Pact reform. The second excerpt is from the Harmel Report.

A. Polish Foreign Minister Rapacki on Warsaw Pact Reform, January 1966

In connection with a letter of Comrade Brezhnev to Comrade Gomulka dealing with the provision of a better elasticity and efficiency for the Warsaw Pact organization, I am hereby presenting some remarks and conclusions:

I. The Warsaw Pact organization comprises two sets of questions that require separate treatment:

1) Improvement of operating instruments in the military area, which relates to the proposal of holding a meeting of defense ministers. Improvement in coordination is required particularly in this area, where the chief responsibility rests overwhelmingly upon the Soviet Union.

2) Coordination in the area of political activities of the Pact, which requires a steady consultative effort, an exchange of views in order to reach common grounds not only on major issues, but often also on current policy matters.

II. We appraise the USSR's initiative positively. It meets the basic need to define and improve the organization of the Warsaw Pact. So far the Warsaw Pact organization has not been precisely defined, its forms of work were volatile and dependent on extemporaneous initiatives, mostly by the USSR. This situation has created loopholes in the coordination of policies and actions of Pact members with regard to the Pact itself, as well as in relations among its members. It also did not ensure the proper system of consultations, which would enable to take into consideration the positions of all member states. This condition was shaped at a time when the Warsaw Pact Treaty was concluded and when its forms of operation were just emerging. It does not meet its current needs.

III. The Soviet initiative to improve the instruments of the Pact's operation is coming at the right time, when a greater need to strengthen the unity of actions of the member states is emerging. In the present circumstances elaboration of a common political line of the Pact, which would take into account positions of all interested parties calls for systematic and frequent consultations and contacts.

IV. The Warsaw Pact Treaty has created a Political Consultative Committee for consultations among member states and for consideration of questions arising from the Pact's operation (…) In practice, however, that Committee has been transformed into summit meetings, called up sporadically, generally not properly prepared, which adopt spectacular resolutions (declarations, communiqués). In fact, this is inconsistent with either the consultative tasks of the Committee, or with its originally intended composition (Government members), or with its name (to whom a gathering of top party and government leaders is to be advisory?) (…) Thus, as the Committee has transformed itself into a Council, there is no body which would ensure the opportunity for systematic and frequent consultations among member countries, despite the fact that they were suggesting such need.

V. To improve and rationalize the operation of the Pact consistent with the existing needs, it would be proper to specify the decision-making organs, as well as consultative and advisory bodies.

1. This objective could be achieved by setting up a Pact's Council, which would take over functions heretofore exercised by the Political Consultative Committee. The Council would be holding meetings at a summit level; it would decide on key issues, with the rule of unanimity. It would be hearing and approving reports of the Unified Command. It would be meeting whenever needed.

2. The Political Consultative Committee should be restored to its original character provided for in the Pact. It could thus become an elastic forum for consultations of foreign ministers. In some cases, when needed, with the participation of defense ministers (…) In this way consultations which are now difficult to hold or which are held only as a result of arduous procedures, would obtain an institutional character.

3. A Permanent Secretariat of the Pact should be set up at a proper level and with a proper composition (…) to ensure regular liaison among member countries during the intersession periods, for providing continuity of coordination and information on matters related to the decisions adopted (…)

VI. In our opinion the new measures in the area of organizational improvement of the Pact should be published. It would emphasize the political vitality of the Warsaw Pact. On the other hand, similar measures undertaken in the military area should be published at the proper time and in the proper form, so as not to be exploited by NATO states, interested in counteracting the current process of NATO's disintegration, but quite the contrary, they should evoke a desired effect in the given political situation.

B. NATO Council on Future Relations With the Warsaw Pact (the Harmel Report), December 1967

The (…) basic common aim of Allied policy towards the Soviet Union and Eastern Europe remains to provide effective protection for our own territorial integrity, political independence and security. The second purpose of the Allies is, without jeopardizing our freedom or weakening our security, to develop plans and methods for eliminating the present unnatural barriers between Eastern and Western Europe (which are not of our choosing) including the division of Germany (…)

Our final objective (…) requires (…) a climate of détente. The core of the problem is to convince the East European states and the Soviet Union by means of a persuasive, patient and undramatic policy that there are greater advantages to both sides in collaboration between East and West. Relaxation of tension is not the final goal, but a step on the way towards cooperation between the states of Europe and a European settlement which in itself no longer gives rise to renewed tension (...)

In the Soviet Union and Eastern Europe communist dogma and the desire of the Communist Parties to maintain their present power operate against a relaxation of tension and the achievement of a European settlement. So do fears that it would be difficult to limit the consequences of a change in the structure of Europe, and that communist control of East European countries might be imperilled as a result. On the other hand, the worldwide responsibilities of the Soviet Union including the tension with the People's Republic of China, and the differentiations within the communist world and especially the growing self-assertion of Eastern Europe, may incline these governments towards further exploring the possibilities of a European settlement. A relaxation of tensions in Europe and limited cooperation with the West would also make it possible for them to meet their own growing economic and technological requirements, as well as widespread desires for a higher standard of living and a somewhat more open society (...) Since on the whole the best markets, technology and sources of supply are not within the communist grouping, increased exchanges with the West are likely to result. The resulting contacts tend to engender near practices and fresh thinking, which could have significant political consequences in furthering the process of détente and closer ties in Europe.

Eastern governments have so far shown themselves able to control these forces; but they are increasingly aware of the problems raised (...)

Some Eastern governments now maintain less rigid attitudes than others towards various members of the Alliance. Although there is without doubt a genuine interest in a European détente, the Soviet Government still hopes, by relaxing tensions selectively, to weaken the cohesion of the Alliance and to drive wedges between the states of Western Europe and in particular to open up differences between Western Europe and the United States. Many Eastern European governments would be well suited by a limited improvement in bilateral relations based on the status quo that perpetuates the present situation in Eastern Europe. But the hopes of all those governments are probably tempered by what they think they can achieve; and they may come to realize that the more ambitious Soviet objectives are unattainable.

(...) In particular, if a relaxation of tensions is to be effective and to lead to a European settlement, it will have to be comprehensive and must include everybody. Nevertheless it remains the task of the Allies to persist in our efforts to relax tensions, and to welcome such co-operation as the Eastern governments are willing to show (...)

The North Atlantic Alliance and a policy of détente are not contradictory (...) The European members of the Alliance are not in a position to maintain their freedom and independence alone in face of the presence and power of the Soviet Union in its present manifestations; and a corresponding North American presence thus remains as necessary as when the Alliance was founded (...) active North American participation is equally necessary in the process of utilizing the détente for achieving a peaceful order in Europe (...) On the other hand it is clear that no substantial progress can be made towards a European settlement without Soviet agreement (...) In working towards a general European settlement our policy should therefore be not to set Eastern Europe against the Soviet Union but rather to involve both Eastern Europe and the Soviet Union in more constructive forms of cooperation (...)

Thus a just and stable European settlement, and a European security system designed to guarantee it, will have to provide for rights and duties of both the United States and the Soviet Union. Such a system may develop out of collaboration between the two existing groupings. A security system may be more effectively organised and involve less risks for individual countries, if it is based on an equilibrium between two groupings rather than exclusively on agreements between separate states (...)

By keeping the peace the Alliance contributes to the developing relaxation of tension. In the field of East–West relations it now has a threefold political task: to improve relations between the various countries of Europe; to help achieve a just and lasting European settlement which will remove the barriers that now divide the continent; and to help with the construction of a balanced and viable system of European security to make this possible (...)

15.5 Presidents Johnson and Eisenhower on Soviet Diplomacy, June 1967

In June 1967 Soviet premier Alexei Kosygin visited the United Nations in New York and met with President Lyndon Johnson in Glassboro, New Jersey. The two leaders discussed numerous issues, including a potential nuclear arms limitation agreement, but did not sign any treaties. Below, President Johnson briefs former president Dwight D. Eisenhower on the talks with Kosygin.

JOHNSON: I wanted to call you. I waited until he (Kosygin) got through with his press conference. He played about the same old broken record in private that he did in public. We tried to get agreement on four or five points. We may have made a little progress on non-proliferation. We're going to have Rusk and

Gromyko work on it some tomorrow. We may be able to table an agreement, but we are not positive. It looked like there was some movement on arms limitation and on arms shipment and on disclosure and on reducing military expenditures, cutting our budget down for nuclear weapons or for offensive or defensive missile systems, etc. We both agreed in general principle, but he never would set a time and never would set a place and never would get down to really executing it. It was just largely conversation—pleasant, no vitriolic stuff, no antagonistic stuff, no bitter stuff, two or three little low blows below the belt every now and then (...)

But on the Middle East just one simple instruction—looked like he couldn't move one inch away from it on anything: there must be complete, absolute, immediate withdrawal of troops, period. Nothing else with it. That was going to be their resolution. They could pass that in the General Assembly (...)

On Vietnam he said we've got to stop our bombing. We've got to pull out. That's what he said on television. Got to get all of our troops out . . . Stop your bombing. Send your troops home. Then things will work out.

EISENHOWER: And then after that we will start talking?

JOHNSON: Yup. Then—but I submitted him some questions, things to think about, and his folks. I asked him to let McNamara sit down and talk to him about disarmament and give me the name and the date and the time and place. He would always dodge it. He claimed to be for it in principle but specifically he wouldn't (...)

He has an obsession on China, and just said we better understand that they are very dangerous people, and we'd better start talking about their exploding these nuclear weapons (...) I'd think that was about it. I thought he was less vituperative and antagonistic and vicious and cutting and debating and argumentative than I have expected him to be, than Gromyko has been and Mikoyan or any of the rest of them. He's pretty stolid, pretty stubborn. I felt like—one time we got into Cuba someway, and I said well you talk about you don't believe us, you think that we let Israel have some arms, troop carriers or whatever it was, tanks or planes I think he said. I said we have tried to give them very little arms. Most of our aid has been economic aid. That's not true with all the countries. Your aid there has been mostly military and much more sizeable than ours. Then you've helped others. I remember you've had a good many missiles in Cuba. He just flared up big, waved his finger at me, said I want you to know I opposed that, I fought that, I tried to keep Khrushchev from doing it, and when he did it I made him back up and get out.

EISENHOWER: Funny thing, I've heard Khrushchev blame his predecessors and so on . . .

JOHNSON: And I held back about the meeting because I know these meetings— you just stir up a lot of hopes and you don't get anything till the night he is due to go home, and he put off a day. I finally made Rusk go over it carefully, Dobrynin with Thompson. And then I got Rusk to go over it with Gromyko. Then I got Rusk to go over it with him himself, and he assured us there'd be substantive talks. We could take up any of these things and get his opinion. And I would say in fairness, as a teacher, I would grade him about a B plus on discussions on arms, that is offensive and defensive missiles, the ABM, and I think that when he gets back he'll probably set a date. But he didn't assure me of that. He did assure me that they would talk before he came here, but I just kept trying to get the time and place. I'd send McNamara or whoever he wanted any place. We'd talk in Geneva, we'd talk in Moscow, we'd talk here, we'd talk at the ambassadorial level . . . But he never did say what he'd do, but I believe I made a little progress there. I believe we've made a little step closer in non-proliferation. I think that he thinks that we are not wild men. I believe I made a good impression on him from the standpoint of being prudent, being firm and being determined (…)

EISENHOWER: This thing about China—our concern and his concern about it. Did he make any specific suggestion or express any specific thought?

JOHNSON: No. He said we ought to have another conference on that. And you better be real concerned about these explosions. I said we are. He said that's a matter that we ought to talk about at another conference. I said we're ready any time. I'd be glad to have one every year and set a time for it. We could stack up every problem we got, every bilateral situation, and you could come here or we could come there (…)

EISENHOWER: (…) I'll tell you, I have been through several of these things, and I know they are frustrating and you just have to guess. Now in '55, Mr. President, we came out of there—they agreed to a half a dozen things and signed up: unification of Germany, and broadening of contacts between our two countries. So in October we sent our foreign ministers back to implement these things. But we took up 17 different ideas and they turned nyet every one of them, every one. I don't know—they talk a little bit but I've seen no yielding yet to any of them (…)

Well, I'll tell you. You know if you could just pass on [thinking that you had gotten these people to do anything] constructive and reasonable, [it would be great]. I have been at it since 1941—that was my first terrible blow with them (…)

15.6 Four Chinese Marshals on Sino-Soviet-American Relations, July 1969

In March 1969 the continued deterioration of Sino-Soviet relations exploded in a series of border clashes. Anxious about Soviet designs and the possibility of some kind of Soviet–American collusion against the People's Republic, Chairman Mao ordered four

Chinese marshals—Chen Yi, Ye Jianying, Xu Xiangqian, and Nie Rongzhen—to undertake a study on the interrelationships between China, the USSR, and the United States. Excerpts of the study follow.

I. The struggle between China, the United States, and the Soviet Union

(1) China represents the fundamental interests of the world proletariat class (...)

(2) The U.S. imperialists and the Soviet revisionists are two 'brands' of representatives of the international bourgeoisie class. On the one hand, they both take China as the enemy; on the other, they take each other as the enemy (...) the imperialists, the revisionists, and the counterrevolutionaries are not really scared by China's so-called military aggression. What scares them most is the prospect that people's revolutions of all nations, under the guidance of the invincible Mao Zedong Thought, will send them to the grave. Therefore, the U.S. imperialists' and the Soviet revisionists' hostility toward China, in the final analysis, is hostility toward the Mao Zedong Thought, toward the revolutions in their own countries as well as the world revolution, and toward the people of their own counties and the people all over the world. However, it should be noted that Nixon takes China as a 'potential threat,' rather than a real threat. For the U.S. imperialists and the Soviet revisionists, the real threat is the one existing between themselves (...)

(3) The other countries, controlled by either the United States or the Soviet Union, have yet to become a force to contend with them. While only a few of them follow the U.S. imperialists and the Soviet revisionists to carry out an anti-China policy, the majority of them maintain a different attitude toward China. Some adopt a dual stand toward China; some maintain an onlooker's position; some use friendship with China to resist the attempts by the U.S. imperialists and the Soviet revisionists to control them; some resent U.S. and Soviet plots to re-divide the world and openly challenge them. As China becomes more and more powerful and the U.S. imperialists and Soviet revisionists become weaker and weaker, this situation will develop further, making it more difficult for them to form an anti-China united front, let alone to find hatchet men to use against China in military affairs.

II. Our opinions on the war against China

We believe that in the foreseeable future it is unlikely that U.S. imperialists and Soviet revisionists will launch a large-scale war against China, either jointly or separately.

(1) The U.S. imperialists do not dare to attack China rashly. The main reasons are as follows:

(a) (...) The U.S. imperialists' defeats in the Korean War and the Vietnam War have taught them a bitter lesson causing a deeper crisis both at home and abroad (...)

(b) The strategic emphasis of the U.S. imperialists lies in the West (...) The last thing the U.S. imperialists want to see is involvement in a war against China, allowing the Soviet revisionists to take advantage of it.

(c) The U.S. imperialists wish to push Asian countries to the front in a war against China, especially by using Japan as the vanguard. Japan, however, does not dare to take reckless actions, not only because it suffered seriously in the defeat of its aggression against China, but also because the strength of the new China today is much stronger than that of the old China (...)

(2) The Soviet revisionists have made China their main enemy, imposing a more serious threat to our security than the U.S. imperialists. The Soviet revisionists are creating tensions along the long Sino-Soviet border, concentrating troops in the border area and making military intrusions (...) However, before they can enter a major war with China, the Soviet revisionists still must deal with many concerns and difficulties.

(a) Both China and the United States take the Soviet Union as their enemy thus the Soviet revisionists do not dare to fight a two-front war. In appearance, the U.S. imperialists are taking a hands-off policy toward the Sino-Soviet dispute (...) In reality, however, they are relaxing their relationship with the Soviet revisionists in the West, and pushing the Soviet revisionists to stand on the first front of a major war against China (...)

(b) If the Soviet revisionists decide to launch a large-scale attack on China, they will try to fight a quick war. Or they may follow the example of Japan's aggression against China, adopting a strategy of encroaching on China piece by piece, so that they will have time for rectification, as well as to observe the reactions of the U.S. imperialists and other countries. But, once they start a major war against us, we certainly will not allow them to fight a quick war and achieve quick results (...) We will change the war into a protracted ground war. This will create great difficulties for the Soviet revisionists:

First, the Soviet revisionists' anti-China policy is without any popular support (...)

Second (...) It is difficult for the Soviet revisionists to get supplies in Siberia, and everything must be transported from Europe. There is only one railroad. An exhausted army on a long expedition cannot last long (...)

Third, in order to win a war, a consolidated rear is indispensable. The rear area of the Soviet revisionists is far from consolidated, where domestic class and national contradictions have been intensifying. A war of aggression against China inevitably would be a long-lasting one, and changes are inevitable

over a long period, the worst of which will be troubles emerging in the rear area
(...)

(c) (...) The strategic emphasis of the Soviet revisionists remains in Europe.
Eastern Europe is the Soviet Union's main market and defensive barrier, on
which it will never let down its guard. To be sure, the Soviet revisionists indeed
are preparing for a war against China. But their main purpose is to use military
mobilization to consolidate their political control and to suppress resistance to
them at home and in Eastern Europe. They are making a show of readiness to
fight. This is designed, on the one hand, to serve their attempt to occupy a strong
position to negotiate with us, and, on the other hand, to convince the U.S. imperialists that they really intend to fight a major war against China (...) The U.S.
imperialists, on their part, are pushing the Soviet revisionists to attack China so
that they may use this opportunity to take over the Soviet revisionists' spheres of
influence.

(3) Will the U.S. imperialists and the Soviet revisionists launch a surprise
nuclear attack on us? (...) In the final analysis, the outcome of a war will be determined by the continuous fighting of the ground forces. Therefore, nuclear
weapons cannot save the U.S. imperialists and the Soviet revisionists.

(4) According to the current situation, it is difficult for U.S. imperialists and
Soviet revisionists to attack China, either jointly or independently, or by gathering [on their side] such countries as Japan and India (...) Both the U.S. imperialists and the Soviet revisionists want others to take the lead, allowing them to take
advantage by hiding in the back. We are ready in full battle array. No matter how
the aggressors will come, jointly or independently, they will be thoroughly
defeated.

III. Analyzing the American–Soviet contradiction

(...) The Soviet revisionists hope to divide the world equally with the U.S. imperialists, as well as take charge of world affairs together with the U.S. imperialists.
The U.S. imperialists are determined to maintain their superior position, and are
unwilling to give up their hegemony and the world hegemon's position. The U.S.
imperialists will not allow the Soviet revisionists to consolidate their position in
the Middle East. The U.S. imperialists do not believe that the Soviet revisionists
will really enter a major war against China, and they thus will not allow the
Soviet revisionists to expand at will (...) The Soviet revisionists want to extend
their influence into Western Europe, and the U.S. imperialists hope to put a leg
into Eastern Europe (...) It is necessary that the contradictions between them
will intensify (...)

We should make full use of time and strengthen preparations in all respects,
'making revolution, while promoting production, promoting our work, and pro-

moting war preparation.' We must promote the continuous great leap forward of our industrial and agricultural production, build China into an unshakable proletarian country with stronger economic power and stronger land, naval and air forces. In the struggle against the enemy, we should adopt a military strategy of active defense and a political strategy of active offense. We should continue to expose and criticize the Soviet revisionists and the U.S. imperialists. We should enhance our embassies and consulates in other countries, and actively carry out diplomatic activities. We should expand the international united front of anti-imperialism and anti-revisionism (…)

15.7 Anatoly Dobrynin on US Interest in Détente, July 1969

In 1969 the Nixon administration began to explore the possibilities of détente with the Soviet Union. In order to keep the process firmly in the hands of the White House and avoid intense public scrutiny, national security advisor Henry Kissinger established a confidential channel with Soviet ambassador Anatoly Dobrynin. In this extract, Dobrynin reports to Moscow on the substance of one of the early 'Backchannel' meetings with Kissinger.

Kissinger began the conversation with a comment to the effect that President Nixon knows about my departure to the USSR and that this meeting was organized with the President's knowledge, so that, while in Moscow, the Soviet Ambassador in his report to his government could, if necessary, provide 'first hand' knowledge of the President's point of view on various international questions and especially on Soviet–American relations. Kissinger said that (…) President Nixon (…) poses his main goal in this area as the necessity of avoiding situations which could lead to direct confrontation between the USA and USSR. He, the President, feels that such a task is entirely feasible. In any case, he, Kissinger, according to instructions from the President, can assure me, that Nixon will not allow any third countries or any situation to develop in this or any other region of the world, which could pull him along a path fraught with the threat of direct confrontation between our countries. The President hopes and believes that the Soviet government has the same point of view on this question.

Nevertheless, went on Kissinger, this is only one side of the question. Nixon would like very much that during his Presidency—until 1972, or maybe even until 1976 in case he's re-elected—Soviet–American relations would enter a constructive phase, different from those relations which existed during the 'cold war' and unfortunately continue to make themselves apparent even now. Although ideological disagreements, undoubtedly, will remain, and since they are very deep will make themselves known, the President nonetheless thinks that the above-mentioned turn in relations between our countries is entirely possible and desirable, although time and mutually tolerant work, taking into account the interests of both sides, is required.

President Nixon assigns the question of a meeting with the Soviet leaders an extremely important place in all this, continued Kissinger. He, however, approaches this question with a certain degree of caution, mainly because of the domestic political considerations and the corresponding reaction around the world. The thing is that such meetings are accompanied by an unavoidable ruckus and various sensations and ill-considered prognoses, leading to initial 'great expectations' and then disappointments of the same magnitude, although, properly speaking, it is difficult to expect great results from a two- or three-day summit meeting, especially since the most complicated international problems can hardly be decided quickly, since it is necessary to clear the corresponding obstacles and long-term blockages step by step. Unfortunately, mass public opinion expects 'miracles' from such meetings, and insofar as these are difficult to achieve, various speculations of 'misfortune' and 'failure' begin, and these cannot help the process of searching for a resolution, since they put negative psychological pressure on the summit participants, who from the very beginning begin to think about the fact that at the end of the summit they will have to present the results to the press. And that is why, said Kissinger further, President Nixon is convinced that the organization of only one such meeting with the Soviet leaders during his entire Presidency (as was the case with Presidents Kennedy and Johnson) is not the correct path to follow. It would be preferable to conduct a series of meetings, at predetermined intervals, say, once a year. Then the meetings will be less of a sensation, and will have a more business-like character. In the course of such meetings it would not be strictly necessary to search for an externally streamlined formula, which would in a way satisfy society but in reality do little to move the process forward. Instead of this it will be possible to make an efficient periodic survey of the most important problems, and to search out a mutually acceptable approach (...) At such meetings, continued Kissinger, it will be important not only to strive toward settlement of the most difficult issues (which it will not be possible to always do immediately), but also to conduct mutual consultations, an exchange of opinions on potentially explosive situations which could draw both sides into conflict; even if their points of view on such situations will not coincide, the sides will better understand each other's motives and not overstep dangerous borders in their actions (...)

I answered that in my personal opinion, the idea deserves consideration. Moving on further to concrete problems and regions, Kissinger said that in Europe Nixon agreed that it is not appropriate to undertake any sort of attempts to change the situation which developed there as a result of the Second World War. The USA, as is well known, in principle favors the unification of Germany, but this is still a question, taking everything into account, realistically speaking, of the very very distant future. The current administration does not intend to push or force events in this direction. On the contrary, it is interested in achieving a certain degree of stability around West Berlin, so that events there do not from time to time inflame Soviet–American relations (...)

In the course of the conversation on European affairs Kissinger repeated that President Nixon takes into account the special interests of the Soviet Union in Eastern Europe, and does not intend to do anything there which could be evaluated in Moscow as a 'challenge' to her position in that region. This is Nixon's basic approach to this question, and it is not necessary, asserted Kissinger, to pay much attention 'to isolated critical public comments about some East European country, because that is only a tribute to the mood of certain sub-strata of the American population which play a role in American elections.' (...) Speaking about other areas where, in Nixon's opinion, Soviet–American contacts and bilateral exchange of opinions should develop, Kissinger cited the problem of a Near Eastern settlement, questions of strategic nuclear arms control, and, in the long-term, the gradual development of our trade relations (...)

Kissinger touched here on the question of China. Recalling Nixon's idea, which had been told to us before, that they were not going to interfere in the present-day Soviet–Chinese conflict in any way, and once more confirming the stability of this principle, Kissinger said that they of course don't mind improving relations with China and are ready to take 'reasonable steps' forward in this direction, but this process must have a bilateral character (...) he added in a more ironical manner, the USSR now occupies our place as the main object of Chinese attacks, and we have come to take as if second place, in every other respect the Beijing attitude toward us remains the same. The Chinese still insist on the return of Taiwan to them. The USA can't accept this, though they have no objections to Beijing and Taiwan discussing this problem, but the latter doesn't express such a desire and the Nixon administration will not urge it to do this. Taiwan still occupies an important place in the chain of bases for restraint of Beijing's expansionist aspirations.

But all this is not really important, asserted Kissinger. We are realists. The main force of the countries of the socialist camp in both military and industrial respects is not China but the Soviet Union. This will be true not only now but also during the whole period of Nixon's Presidency. From this point of view, frankly speaking, our main rival is the Soviet Union, if we speak in global terms and about possible consequences for the US in case of a nuclear war. That's why Nixon considers it important first of all to maintain good or at least more or less normal correct relations with the USSR, not to bring them to a dangerous precipice. We understand, he went on, that in Moscow, evidently, there are people who think that the USA and China can somehow come to an understanding in opposition to the USSR. In its world historical aspect and taking into consideration different countries' past experience, this concept can sound convincing enough. Nevertheless in this concrete situation, if we speak on behalf of the US government, putting the question this way, asserted Kissinger, would not satisfy the interests of the US itself. Of course it would be hypocritical, went on Kissinger, to assert—and you wouldn't believe us all the same—that your growing disagreements with the Chinese upset us. But there is here one significant circumstance, which Nixon considers very important. The president is sure that his best course is to not openly take the side of either the USSR or the PRC [People's Republic of China], and to be very careful not to give the Soviet government any grounds to think that the US somehow supports China's anti-Soviet course or seeks agreement with Beijing on the basis of such a course. Nixon's logic as a realist is very simple: the Soviet Union is much more capable than present-day China to confront the USA in different parts of the world, and that can create dangerous situations, possibly leading to conflicts in which the very existence of the US as a nation may be at stake if the big war breaks out. As for its military-economic potential, China for several more years won't be able to present such a threat to the USA, but the USSR can (…) Another thing is that the Soviet Union is governed by realistically thinking politicians who are interested in their people's and their country's well-being. It is possible to conclude concrete agreements with them, which satisfy the interests of both countries and not only these countries. That's why President Nixon once expressed to the Soviet leader his idea that if our countries manage within the next 10–15 years to unite their efforts or at least follow appropriate parallel courses in the most important and dangerous questions, then it will be possible to prevent dragging the world into major military conflicts, until China 'grows up' and more responsible leaders come to power in Beijing (…)

15.8 Kissinger and Triangular Diplomacy 1971–1972

Between 1969 and 1971 the Nixon administration gradually moved towards an opening of relations with the People's Republic of China. In July 1971 Henry Kissinger embarked upon his 'secret trip' to Beijing, which was followed in February 1972 by Nixon's week-long visit. One of the key goals of the opening was to use China as a counterweight against the Soviet Union in an emerging triangular relationship between Washington, Moscow, and Beijing. In the excerpts below—taken from the memoranda of conversation from his

July 1971 trip to Beijing and his April 1972 trip to Moscow—Kissinger, the Chinese premier Zhou Enlai (Chou En-lai), and the Soviet leader Leonid Brezhnev each plays the triangular game in his own specific way.

A. Kissinger and Zhou Enlai on the Soviet Union, July 1971

ZHOU: When we talk about the tensions in South Asia, this is to say nothing about the Middle East, Europe, the Black Sea, the Mediterranean Sea, the Baltic Sea or the Atlantic. And what about this side of the Pacific, aren't there many military maneuvers in the Sea of Japan? On this very day joint U.S.–Japan maneuvers have taken place. Of course the Soviet Union is very tense about all this; there is mutual tension.

All this is to say, that due to the development of history in the past 25 years, powder kegs have been set up everywhere (…) Another aspect to be mentioned is the contention between the two superpowers. As a result, according to the objective facts the world is not moving toward relaxation of tensions, but on the contrary it continues in turmoil. This is precisely why we are digging air raid shelters here (…) You like to talk about philosophy. The worst would be that China would be carved up once again. You could unite, with the USSR occupying all areas north of the Yellow River, and you occupying all the areas south of the Yangtse River, and the eastern section between these two rivers could be left to Japan. In the past Japan has been interested in Shantung and Chingtao it also has been interested in Shanghai. It had been to all those places before when Japan committed aggression against China. You are familiar with that.

If such a large maneuver should occur, what would the Chinese Communist Party and Chairman Mao be prepared to do? We would be prepared to resist for a protracted period by people's warfare, engaging in a long-term struggle until final victory. This would take time and, of course, we would have to sacrifice lives, but this is something which we would have to contemplate.

Of course, you can say that such things will never happen. Friends from Europe say that the Soviets will not attack. We say that we will never provoke an attack, but once they enter our borders, we must be prepared (…)

Yesterday I also mentioned the USSR. The Soviet Union is following your suit, in stretching its hands all over the world. You said that you were triggered by the Soviet Union's probing throughout the world. No matter whether there is a case of contention or a case of being triggered anyway there is a situation of tension, of turmoil. This is the objective situation. If we look at the development of the objective world in a cool-headed manner, then we are called upon though our subjective efforts to attempt to undo some of the knots.

The sixth issue is arms control. You cited as an example of this question the proposal for a five-nation nuclear conference. I can answer Your Excellency now officially. The Chinese Government completely disapproves of the proposition of the Soviet government to hold a five-power nuclear conference. They are trying to lasso us. We didn't take part in the tripartite treaty on partial nuclear test bans in 1963 and we didn't take part in any later treaties or agreements on outer space, etc., because we do not believe that this is in accordance with the basic problem, which is the complete prohibition and thorough destruction of nuclear weapons which we advocate. Some people have asked us, since we have taken such a stand, why we are testing nuclear weapons. We must say very frankly that we do so to break the nuclear monopoly and to fight against the nuclear blackmail of certain great powers. All our nuclear tests have been held under the condition that they are necessary, and are limited. We do not engage in indiscriminate nuclear testing and every time we test, we make a statement that we will never be the first to use them. What we say counts. What we propose is that all nations of the world, whether large or small, should come together to discuss this problem and reach agreement on the complete prohibition and thorough destruction of nuclear weapons, and as a first step, should reach agreement on the non-use of nuclear weapons. It can't do to try to lasso us. The Soviet Union has such a scheme. That is our answer to the sixth question.

I would like to say a few words about the disarmament conference.

KISSINGER: Which one?

ZHOU: The Geneva Conference, which, of course, includes the SALT talks. We don't know the content in your SALT talks, and the only thing we know is that your defense budget rises every year and the result is that the more you talk about disarmament, the more armaments expand and that adds to the disquiet, the turmoil of the world. I am not prepared, I do not intend, to go into any more detail on that.

If there is no possibility of negotiations, we are opposed to any aggression, for example, as did the Soviets against Czechoslovakia (…) now, Soviet troops are in the Mongolian People's Republic. We are opposed. They pose a threat to us (…) if these troops pass through the territory of the MPR to invade even one inch of our territory, then we would immediately resist and fight back.

KISSINGER: Mr. Prime Minister, you discussed the issue of great power relations, specifically Japan and the Soviet Union, and you used the very striking phrase that there is chaos under the sky (…)

With respect to Soviet intentions, contrary to some of my American friends, I do not exclude the possibility of Soviet military adventurism. In fact, speaking personally and frankly, this is one of the new lessons I have learned in my present position. I had not believed it previously.

But that is a problem essentially between you and the USSR. As far as the U.S. is concerned, I can tell you flatly that there is no possibility, certainly in this Administration, nor probably in any other, of any cooperation such as you have described between the U. S., the Soviet Union and Japan to divide up China.

We are facing many potentially aggressive countries. How could it conceivably be in our interests, even for the most selfish motives, to encourage one super-power to destroy another country and even to cooperate with it? Particularly one with which, as the Prime Minister has himself pointed out, after the solution of the Taiwan issue, which will be in the relatively near future, we have no conflicting interests at all. If we are looking at the future in an historical context, and if we want to reduce some of the chaos in the world, then I believe that in relations among large countries the United States will be your supporter and not your opponent.

As I pointed out yesterday, we will not participate in efforts to lasso you.

So I repeat the offer I have made to you—that we attempt to discuss with you if we can find the means, any proposal made by any other large country which could affect your interests, and that we would take your views very seriously. Specifically, I am prepared to give you any information you may wish to know regarding any bilateral negotiations we are having with the Soviet Union on such issues as SALT, so as to alleviate any concerns you might have in this regard. So while these negotiations will continue, we will attempt to conduct them in such a way that they do not increase the opportunity for military pressures against you.

I think that is all I want to say on great power relations.

With respect to arms control, I have understood the Prime Minister's views. We understand that the People's Republic of China will not participate in the five power conference. Our own intention is to respond very slowly. Because of the pressure of other countries we may accept it in principle, but we will spend a lot of time on preparations, and we will conduct it in such a way that it offers no framework for pressures against the People's Republic of China.

In nuclear matters, we will put principal emphasis on negotiations which concern us and the USSR primarily, mainly the limitation of nuclear strategic arms. And on these, as I have pointed out, we are prepared to keep you informed, as we have attempted through the rather inadequate means of communication we now have.

ZHOU: As Your Excellency said in his analysis of developing events, we estimate the timing might be a bit later. That is after a number of matters have been thrashed out, and various things have occurred.

This raises the following questions.

For example, has your President ever considered the possibility of visiting the Soviet Union, or having leaders of the Soviet Union come to the United States, or to have the President and the leaders of the Soviet Union meet somewhere else?

If there is such a possibility, it would be best for President Nixon and the Soviet Union to meet before President Nixon visits China.

We are not afraid of a big turmoil. With the objective development of events, this might be possible. But we would not want to deliberately create tensions (...)

KISSINGER: I will be candid. This subject has been discussed. The President has received an invitation to visit Moscow.

As you know from your own dealings with the Soviet Union, there is a tendency on the part of Soviet leaders to attempt to squeeze every advantage out of any situation. (Zhou laughs.)

Therefore, after extending the invitation, certain conditions were attached which we can meet as a matter of fact, but as a question of principle it is now held in abeyance. It is not a question that we cannot meet them, but that we believe that if the President talks to the Head of State of another government it must be on its own merits. The same is true in your case.

But the principle of a meeting between the President and the Soviet leaders has been accepted. The visit has been extended by the Soviet leaders and a visit may still take place within the next 6 months.

ZHOU: In that case, we might set the date of the President's visit sometime in the summer of next year, say after May 1. That might be a more appropriate time for your President.

KISSINGER: One difficulty with this is that after May the political campaign begins in America. While it would be advantageous from a political point of view to have the visit during that season, I think, frankly, for our mutual interest, that we would not start our relationship under the suspicion that it has this short-term motivation.

So it should be somewhat earlier: a few months earlier would be better than in the summer. March or April.

ZHOU: Fine. I will report this to Chairman Mao and then give you a reply. But you do agree to the principle that it would be good for the President first to visit Moscow and then China? Would this be better for you?

KISSINGER: The problem in our relations with the Soviet Union is different from the problem of our relations with the People's Republic of China.

I understand your hesitation to begin with. In our relations with the Soviet Union we have a number of concrete issues but no overwhelming political issues.

ZHOU: Much more concrete issues.

KISSINGER: But no overwhelming philosophic issues. You have had your own experience in negotiations with the Soviet Union, so I need not describe it. They lend themselves less well to meetings at a very high level because they always get lost in a great amount of detail. And some very petty detail.

Our relations with the People's Republic of China are at an historic turning point which requires the intervention of top leaders who can set a basic direction and then let the details be worked out later.

So the problem is that with the Soviet Union we can do a lot of business in reg-

"THAT'S ONE SMALL STEP FOR A MAN— ONE GIANT LEAP FOR MANKIND !"

14. The opening to China: 'That's One Small step for a man, one giant leap for mankind!' (Nicholas Garland, *Daily Telegraph*, 21 February 1972). Reprinted by permission. Photo supplied by The Centre for the Study of Cartoons and Caricature, University of Kent.

ular ways, while with the People's Republic of China we can do the most important business really only between Chairman Mao and the President. That is the difference. (Zhou nods.)

But in principle, I repeat, there is a formal agreement that makes clear we are prepared to meet with the Soviet leaders, and they have expressed their willingness.

In all honesty, I cannot promise you it will happen no matter when we set a date. We shall try, but we will not meet prior conditions either with Moscow or with Peking; but you haven't made any prior conditions.

ZHOU: That's right. We agree.

B. Kissinger and Brezhnev on China and Nixon's visit, April 1972

BREZHNEV: I realize there are certain reasons and motives behind the President's visit to China, but I am certain he does not have the full picture.

KISSINGER: One related point. There have been rumors spread by Soviet personnel that there were discussions between us and the Chinese on military matters. I don't care about your propaganda, but I want to assure you that there were no military discussions.

BREZHNEV: There was only the one occasion when the Ambassador on instructions cited reports received from Chinese sources (...) It was related to that speech of the President's in Peking, when he made the remark that the U.S. and China were holding the fate of the world in their hands. This remark circled the world. It gave us concern.

KISSINGER: Let me give you our view. The People's Republic of China is very important in the Asian area, and in 10–15 years it will perhaps have a role in other regions. Peace in the world now depends on relations between the U.S. and the Soviet Union. We can settle things concretely; with others we can settle only theoretically.

BREZHNEV: The Chinese general tendency for world hegemony is an obsession with them. It is something they will not give up. It is important not to encourage it, but to localize it.

Once they made an enormous effort to gain hegemony in the world Communist movement (...)

This presents a very big question: What tendencies does one want to encourage? Although, as we have said, we believe it quite natural for two countries to improve relations, provided that it is not done in away that is harmful to third countries. Short-run considerations do not always yield benefits in the long run. Do you understand me?

KISSINGER: Yes I do.

BREZHNEV: I am just philosophizing. It may help us both to delve deeper into this matter.

KISSINGER: We have no interest in encouraging anti-Soviet policies on the part of the PRC.

BREZHNEV: There is enough of that already without you. If I am shot 150 times and buried with a cross on my grave, what more can you do?

15.9 The United States and the Soviet Union Agree on the 'Rules' of Détente, May 1972

At the May 1972 Moscow Summit—the culmination of the early road towards Soviet–American détente—the American and Soviet delegations signed a series of bilateral agreements. Perhaps the most significant of these were the ABM Treaty and the Interim Agreement on Offensive Weapons (SALT I). In addition, however, the two sides released a document entitled 'Basic Principles of Soviet–American Relations'. Many of the principles—some of which are extracted below—would be tested in the years following the first Soviet–American Summit.

The United States of America and the Union of Soviet Socialist Republics (…) have agreed as follows:

First: They will proceed from the common determination that in the nuclear age there is no alternative to conducting their mutual relations on the basis of peaceful coexistence (…)

Second: The USA and the USSR attach major importance to preventing the development of situations capable of causing a dangerous exacerbation of their relations. Therefore, they will do their utmost to avoid military confrontations and to prevent the outbreak of nuclear war. They will always exercise restraint in their mutual relations, and will be prepared to negotiate and settle differences by peaceful means (…) Both sides recognize that efforts to obtain unilateral advantages at the expense of the other (…) are inconsistent with these objectives (…)

Third: The USA and the USSR have a special responsibility (…) to do everything in their power so that conflicts or situations will not arise which would serve to increase international tensions. Accordingly, they will seek to promote conditions in which all countries will live in peace and security and will not be subject to outisde interference in their internal affairs.

Fourth: The USA and the USSR intend to widen the juridical basis of their mutual relations (…)

Fifth: The USA and the USSR reaffirm their readiness to continue the practice of exchanging views on problems of mutual interest (…)

Sixth: The parties will continue their efforts to limit armaments on a bilateral as well as on a multilateral basis. They will make special efforts to limit strategic armaments (…)

Seventh: The USA and the USSR regard commercial and economic ties as an important and necessary element in the strengthening of their bilateral relations and thus will actively promote the growth of such ties (…)

The development of US–Soviet relations is not directed against third countries and (…) do[es] not affect any obligations with respect to other countries earlier assumed by the USA and the USSR.

15.10 Kissinger on the Prospects of Soviet–American Relations, May 1973

By the spring of 1973 a certain optimism had set in regarding the future of Soviet–American relations. From the American perspective the signing of the January 1973

Paris Agreement that ended US overt involvement in Vietnam, and the apparent success of triangular diplomacy, seemed to provide Washington with growing leverage in negotiations with the USSR. Between 5 and 8 May 1973, as the Nixon administration prepared for the arrival of Leonid Brezhnev to the United States, Kissinger travelled to Moscow to iron out a number of agreements to be signed during the second summit. Among these was the Prevention of Nuclear War Agreement and a series of economic deals. Kissinger's upbeat mood is captured on this summary report to Nixon on the results of the preparatory trip.

Brezhnev (…) sees a trip to the United States and its political results as perhaps the crowning achievement of his political career (…)

P[revention of] N[uclear] W[ar Agreement]
Soviets wanted to limit the non-use clause to the US and USSR, thus giving them a free hand to use nuclear weapons against third parties (China or NATO) while binding the US not to use nuclear weapons against the USSR (…) we have succeeded in moving from a strictly bilateral non-aggression formula to a broad restraint on Soviet policy, which fully protects third countries (…)

Brezhnev (…) abandoned any claim to use consultation as the basis for intervention in a crisis that did not threaten the US or USSR (…)

We have now succeeded in building up clear provisions against Soviet use of nuclear weapons against third countries (…) [the] Soviets can't turn on NATO or China without violating the agreement (…) The increasingly complex relationship we are developing—in this agreement and in economics, in SALT, etc. will have to be a critical calculation in Brezhnev's decision-making (…) China will remain the unknown. And it is clear from this conversation that Brezhnev is obsessed with his China problem. Whether he decides to use force is the major question, but this current nuclear project with him could divert him from that course (…)

China thus remains a major variable in Soviet policy; it could lead to a major crisis in the next 12–18 months. But it is also a point of critical leverage for us. It may be that sometime late in the summer we might want to arrange with the Chinese for a visit by Zhou En-lai to the UN in the fall and a meeting with you in Washington. In any event, we must look at our contingency planning for the event of Soviet military actions against China (…)

[Economics is] our second point of leverage (…) a much broader economic arrangement with the USSR, one that would tie the USSR to the US as much as any factor, is possible (…) you will hold the high cards at the summit (…) your China policy and Soviet economic difficulties are your strong points (…)

Questions

Why did the Soviet Union install missiles in Cuba?

Why was the Kennedy administration unwilling to compromise on the withdrawal of the Soviet missiles in Cuba?

Did the Cuban Missile crisis prompt the beginning of Soviet–American détente?

What were the major proposals advanced by Kennedy in his June 1963 American University speech? How different were they from the Soviet position?

What similarities and differences can you detect between Adam Rapacki's recommendations and the Harmel Report?

Did Lyndon Johnson (and/or Dwight D. Eisenhower) believe that détente with the Soviets was possible in 1967?

What was the Chinese perspective on Soviet–American relations in the late 1960s?

What distinctions did Chinese leaders draw between the United States and the USSR's aims vis-à-vis China?

What were the points of agreement and disagreement between the United States and the Soviet Union according to Soviet ambassador Anatoly Dobrynin?

Compare and contrast Henry Kissinger's discussions with Zhou Enlai and Leonid Brezhnev. What are the main differences?

How did the Soviets view the Sino-American relationship?

What were the major achievements of Soviet–American détente by 1973?

What were the potential (or actual) pitfalls of détente?

16

The Fall of Détente

In the mid-1970s the policies of reducing military tension through negotiations and agreements came under increasing pressure in international affairs and within the superpowers themselves. Within a few years the optimistic climate of the early part of the decade had been replaced with what some scholars see as a second Cold War.

There were many reasons why US–Soviet détente collapsed as a political project. Some historians argue that the failure was inherent in the project itself: because Americans and Soviets had different notions of what détente consisted of, conflict would replace co-operation sooner or later. Others claim that superpower détente—different from détente in Europe—was less a policy of co-operation than an attempt, partially through covert means, to outmanoeuvre the other side and gain advantages in an ongoing Cold War.

It should also be remembered that neither of the superpowers was a unitary actor. In both countries there was considerable conflict over the aims and means of its foreign policy—in the United States much of this debate took place openly, while in the Soviet Union it was mostly carried out in secret within the top leadership. By 1973/4 many Americans felt that the Soviet Union gave too little in return for a more accomodating US attitude, and that President Richard Nixon and his main foreign policy adviser Henry Kissinger were bargaining away America's global superiority. After Nixon was forced to resign over the Watergate scandal some critics—both on the right and on the left—saw ominous links between the president's political behaviour at home and the secretiveness that surrounded the Republican administration's negotiations with the Soviets and the Chinese.

On the Soviet side, some leaders wanted to emphasize the opportunities offered through Moscow's military expansion—accepted by the United States within the generous ceilings of the SALT arms-control regime—and Third World left-wing revolutions. Their argument was that the world was moving—unstoppably—towards socialism, and that détente could only be *one* part of Soviet foreign policy. Another part should be to offer advice and assistance to 'progressive' movements and governments on a global scale.

While ideological arguments played a role on both sides in the collapse of détente, there were plenty of specific points of conflict that contributed to the process. While arms 'control' could be seen as being in the interest of both sides, arms 'reduction' was not necessarily easy to agree on. Because of their much lower level of technology, which made weapon dependability, precise delivery, and targeting more difficult, the Soviets were dependent on many and large missiles to preserve a credible strike capability. President Jimmy Carter, who replaced Nixon's hand-picked successor Gerald Ford in 1977, therefore got off to a difficult start with Moscow when he insisted on cuts in nuclear arsenals rather than on limiting their growth. On the other hand, both Americans and West Europeans were shocked when the Soviets in 1976/7 introduced new medium-range nuclear missiles in Europe—the SS20s—without any attempts at negotiating with the West. Carter's insistence on supporting human-rights activists in Eastern Europe and the Soviet Union also provoked Moscow's ire, and was seen by Soviet leader Leonid Brezhnev as an attempt at subverting Communist rule from within.

Still, it was conflict over developments in the Third World that brought the détente process to a halt. When the former Portuguese colony of Angola was getting its independence in 1975, three different liberation movements were battling for superiority. The Movimento Popular de Libertaçao de Angola (Popular Movement for the Liberation of Angola—MPLA), Marxist-oriented and supported by Moscow, soon got the upper hand, and the Ford administration decided to support foreign intervention. But unlike the Indonesian invasion of East Timor, the South African invasion of Angola broke down when Cuban forces came to the aid of the MPLA. Different from the Soviets, Cuban leader Fidel Castro was willing to intervene directly on the African continent. By 1976 a sceptical US Congress had ended most of the American covert support for the MPLA's rivals.

The Angolan war—which coincided with the Communist victory in Vietnam—symbolized a new pattern of Cold War interventions in the Third World. For the Soviet bloc, its main significance was that 'progressive forces' could now challenge the 'imperialists' and—with the support of 'socialist states'—win, even though confronted with considerable obstacles. For the American leaders, the Angolan war showed a new Soviet activism and assertiveness in the Third World that could undermine the foundations of détente and become a long-term threat to American security.

Rather remarkably, seen from today's perspective, the 1977/8 war between Ethiopia and Somalia over the Ogaden desert was also seen, both in Washington and Moscow, as a key conflict in Cold War terms. Jimmy Carter's national security adviser, Zbigniew Brzezinski, won support within the administration for viewing Soviet bloc aid to Ethiopia as a direct challenge to the United States. On the Soviet side, some leaders believed that through receiving Soviet advisers and Cuban troops, the leftist military regime in Ethiopia could become a star example of how socialism could triumph in Africa. Although no borders changed as a result of the Ethiopian victory in the war, many in Washington came to see the conflict in the Horn of Africa as an endpoint for superpower détente.

The final nail in the coffin of US–Soviet co-operation came with Moscow's invasion of Afghanistan in December 1979. While the documents show that the Soviet action was mainly intended to shore up the flagging Communist regime in Kabul, Carter understood it as being another step in a global Communist Third World challenge. As a reaction, his administration cut trade links with the Soviet Union, boycotted the 1980 Moscow Olympics, and intensified a renewed military build-up, which had begun the year before. The SALT II Treaty, intended to be the cornerstone of the détente relationship, was withdrawn from consideration in the US Senate. In this sense, it was the Afghanistan invasion that killed détente, although many experts would argue that even before the events of December 1979 it was unlikely that the Senate would have passed a new comprehensive arms-control agreement with the Soviet Union. That was the extent to which a new departure in international affairs—so well under way just a few years before—had come to a decisive halt by the turn of the decade.

Readings

O. A. Westad, *The Fall of Détente: Soviet–American Relations During the Carter Years* (1997). The first document-based overview of the 1977–80 period.

Henry S. Bradsher, *Afghan Communism and Soviet Intervention* (3rd edn., 1999). The best book on the circumstances surrounding the Soviet invasion of Afghanistan.

Zbigniew Brzezinski, *Power and Principle: The Memoirs of the National Security Adviser 1977–1981* (1983). A key memoir by a key participant.

Andrew Bennett, *Condemned to Repetition: The Rise, Fall, and Reprise of Soviet-Russian Military Interventionism, 1973–1996* (1999). Compares the Soviet interventions of the 1970s with the post-Soviet predicament at Russia's borders.

Raymond Garthoff, *Détente and Confrontation: Soviet–American Relations from Nixon to Reagan* (rev. edn., 1994). A first-rate survey of the rise and fall of détente.

16.1 The Angolan Revolution, 1975–1976

In April 1974 a left-wing military junta took power in Portugal and decided to free its African colonies the following year. In Angola, the Portuguese withdrawal led to a civil war between the main liberation movements, in which the United States supported the FNLA and UNITA, while the Soviets resumed their earlier support for the MPLA.

Document A is the minutes of a US National Security Council meeting, 27 June 1975. Document B is an excerpt from a book by John Stockwell, the CIA officer who headed the CIA operation in Angola. Assisted by the Soviet Union, Cuba sent troops to fight alongside the MPLA in Angola; document C is the report Raúl Díaz Argüelles, head of the first Cuban mission, sent to Cuban armed forces minister Raúl Castro, 11 August 1975, after his initial meetings with the Angolans. Document D is an excerpt from a speech celebrating the twenty-third anniversary of the start of the Cuban revolution, in which Cuban leader Fidel Castro explains his country's involvement in Africa.

A. US National Security Council on Angola, June 1975

THE PRESIDENT: Bill (to Colby), will you brief us on Angola and related problems.

MR COLBY: Yes, sir. (Briefed—as attached [not declassified])

THE PRESIDENT: Cabinda was a part of the Portuguese territories?

MR COLBY: Yes, sir.

THE PRESIDENT: What are the white areas within the borders of Angola?

MR COLBY: These are essentially tribal, not military, areas. These are additional tribes and I just chose (pointing on the chart) to mention those three. They have different languages and are different socially.

THE PRESIDENT: Did the Portuguese do much combating illiteracy? Are there many educated blacks?

MR COLBY: The Portuguese were not forceful in this area. The literacy rate is between 10–15 percent.

SECRETARY KISSINGER: Mr President, until the coup, the Portuguese had no intention of leaving their territories in Africa and didn't organize them for independence.

SECRETARY SCHLESINGER: Most of the educated classes are in Luanda and support the MPLA.

THE PRESIDENT: What is the white population?

MR COLBY: Three to four hundred thousand.

THE PRESIDENT: Out of a total of how many?

MR COLBY: About 5.7 million.

THE PRESIDENT: Are these mostly white Portuguese?

MR COLBY: Yes.

THE PRESIDENT: Now, Henry, can you give us the options?

SECRETARY KISSINGER: Mr President, I will be reasonably brief. This is an area where no one can be sure of the judgments. I do question the judgment that control of the capital is not of importance. The history of Africa has shown that a nation's only focal point is the capital, and whoever has the capital has a claim on international support. In the Congo civil war, the reason why we came out on top is because we never lost Leopoldville. If Neto can get Luanda, and drive the others out, he will have a power base, and gradually gain the support of other Africans.

MR COLBY: I agree, except to note the importance of the (Benguela) railway and Zaire and Zambia's need for it.

MR COLBY: Lobito. There is, of course, always the possibility for fragmentation.

SECRETARY KISSINGER: Soviet arms shipments have reversed the situation. Sheldon Vance has just come back from talking with Mobutu, who has stressed the change in the balance of power. Portugal is tilting towards Neto, and the Soviets are putting important equipment, such as armed personnel carriers, into Neto's hands.

Our understanding from Vance is that this is one reason Mobutu is moving away from Roberto and wants a coalition.

An interagency effort has developed options, none of which I am in wild agreement with. The first is neutrality—stay out and let nature take its course. This would enable us to avoid a costly involvement in a situation that may beyond our control; protect us from some international criticism; avoid tying us to any group; and avoid further antagonizing the MPLA. The probable outcome would be that Neto would establish a dominant position. Mobutu might try to go with Savimbi, or adjust to reality; Angola would go in a leftward direction; and Zaire would conclude we have disinterested ourselves in that part of the world and move towards anti-Americanism. As for the second course, my Department agrees, but I don't. It is recommended that we launch a diplomatic offensive to get the Soviets, the Yugoslavs, and others to lessen arms shipments to the MPLA, get Portugal to assert its authority, and encourage cooperation among the groups. We would have direct dealings with the Soviets or get African states to do it. If we appeal to the Soviets not to be active, it will be a sign of weakness; for us to police it next to impossible, and we would be bound to do nothing.

(SANITIZED)

THE PRESIDENT: Is there a specific proposal from the group on grants in the arms area? I don't want to make decision now, but I didn't see any proposals in the briefing papers.

SECRETARY KISSINGER: The Forty Committee has met twice to discuss the situation. The first meeting involved only money, but the second included some arms package. I recommend a working group make a more systematic study of this option and return to you.

(SANITIZED)

THE PRESIDENT: At dinner he was very forceful on this. He said that it was important to get his man in first. And then he will win the election. I asked him if there were not going to be elections, and he said yes, and that was why it was important to put Savimbi in first and then he would win.

SECRETARY KISSINGER: Kaunda was giving the President a lesson in political science.

(Laughter) (SANITIZED)

SECRETARY KISSINGER: But the reverse of that is that if we don't do something they would be suppressed.

THE PRESIDENT: Once the Popular Movement takes over you can write it off.

SECRETARY SCHLESINGER: We may wish to encourage the disintegration of Angola. Cabinda in the clutches of Mobutu would mean far greater security of the petroleum resources. Mr President, may I follow up—if we do something, we must have some confidence that we can win, or we should stay neutral. Roberto is not a strong horse. The fact that he stays in the Congo suggests he doesn't have the tenacity to win.

THE PRESIDENT: It seems to me that doing nothing is unacceptable. As for diplomatic efforts, it is naïve to think that's going to happen, and the proposals on Portugal sound amateurish.

(SANITIZED)

MR CLEMENTS: I agree with this. Doing something now and keeping the two parties afloat may well be encouraging Mobutu. Whatever happens in November is not final, and it is important to keep Roberto and Savimbi viable and keep the options open. Give Mobutu some help and let him channel it.

SECRETARY KISSINGER: In the first instance we could activate Mobutu and inform Kaunda.

THE PRESIDENT: He (Kaunda) was talking at dinner about getting together with someone. Who was that?

SECRETARY KISSINGER: With Savimbi and Mobutu.

THE PRESIDENT: Let's have some options prepared, Bill (to Colby). When can you have them?

MR COLBY: By mid-week.

(SANITIZED)

SECRETARY SCHLESINGER: (SANITIZED) The FNLA has a weak capacity to enforce discipline and we should see whether the Congolese (Zairians) can be used for instilling discipline. And then there is the question of the degree to which we can ring Roberto and Savimbi together.

THE PRESIDENT: Those are some of the things that have to be in the study. I think we need something for a week from Monday, so let's set something up.

B. US Intervention in Angola, 1975–1976

(…) we searched the world for allies who could provide qualified advisors to put into the conflict, or better yet, regular army units to crush the MPLA and deliver the country to Roberto and Savimbi. We canvassed moderate friends–Brazil, Morocco, South Korea, Belgium, Great Britain, France, and even Portugal, without success. South Africa eventually came to UNITA's rescue, but the Zairian commando battalions in northern Angola were only slightly better than the FNLA forces they joined.

Mercenaries seemed to be the answer, preferably Europeans with the requisite military skills and perhaps experience in Africa. As long as they were not Americans, the 40 Committee approved. We began an exhaustive search for suitable candidates, a search which brought me in conflict with my bosses and kept me at odds with them even into March 1976, months after the Senate had ordered a halt to the Angola program. The conduct of European and South African mercenaries in previous African civil wars had left them with a murderous reputation, and the use of white mercenaries at the crest of the era of black nationalism was a blunder, I felt, which could only damage United States credibility in the Third World. In addition, the mercenaries who have appeared in previous African wars have been a mixed bag, more often self-serving, ineffective, unmilitary. Potts, Bantam, Nelson, St. Martin, Foster—all lacked enough experience in Africa to know that. They tended to idealize mercenaries and exaggerate their capabilities. And they lacked sensitivity for the disgust the word 'mercenary' stirs in the hearts of black Africans. Nor did Colby know Africa, although perhaps he was in a class by himself. The mild, likable, church-going, master case officer who had commanded the PHOENIX program in Vietnam would hardly have qualms about a few mercenaries fighting blacks in Africa. I spoke out in staff meetings and in Potts's office every time the subject of mercenaries came up. Whenever a memo or buckslip or cable about mercenaries circulated the office I added my own critical comment in the margins, and I did have some effect. After several weeks of my pressure, the word 'mercenary' became taboo at headquarters. Potts forbade its use in cables, memoranda, and files, at headquarters and in the field. Thereafter the mercenaries who were hired and sent to Angola were to be called 'foreign military advisors.'

And so we proceeded to search the world for acceptable 'foreign military advisors.' We began the search with no leads whatsoever—astonishingly, we found that nowhere in the CIA, not even the Special Operations Group, with all its experiences in Southeast Asia, was there a file, reference list, or computer run of individuals who might be recruited as advisors. Anti-Castro Cubans, such as had been used in the Congo, the Bay of Pigs, and Watergate, were ruled out because they carried United States green resident alien cards and hence would fall under the 40 Committee's restrictions against using Americans. South Vietnamese refugees were approached, but they were busy rebuilding their lives in the new world, and were unanimously wary of a CIA adventure in black Africa. They too carried green cards. The British refused to help. South Koreans were excluded because of language and cultural problems. Biafrans and other Africans were rejected out of political considerations, and because they wouldn't have the impact of whites. Finally, five sources seemed to be available: Portuguese, French, Brazilians, Filipinos, and South Africans. Portuguese were already being recruited in small numbers by the FNLA, Colonel Castro, Captain Bento, and their men. We decided to expand this effort by recruiting three hundred Portuguese Angolans to support the FNLA. But for UNITA we needed two dozen technicians, and Savimbi wouldn't accept Portuguese.

France would not give us regular army troops, but it had no hesitation concerning mercenaries. The French intelligence service introduced CIA case officers to onetime Congo mercenary Bob Denard, and for $500,000 cash—paid in advance—he agreed to provide twenty French mercenaries who would 'advise' UNITA on short-term contracts. Denard was encrypted UNROBIN/I and this mercenary program was UNHOOD. To the waggish the twenty Frenchmen were 'Robin's Hoods' or the 'French Hoods' for the duration of the program (...)

South Africa was a different matter. It came into the conflict cautiously at first, watching the expanding U.S. program and timing their steps to the CIA's. In September the South Africans began to provide arms and training to UNITA and FNLA soldiers at Runtu on the Angolan/South-West African border. First two, then twelve, then forty advisors appeared with UNITA forces near Silva Porto. Eventually the South African armored column—regular soldiers, far better than mercenaries—teamed with UNITA to make the most effective military strike force ever seen in black Africa, exploding through the MPLA/Cuban ranks in a blitzkreig, which in November almost won the war (...)

The South African question led me into another confrontation with Potts. South African racial policies had of course become a hated symbol to blacks, civil libertarians, and world minorities—the focal point of centuries-old resentment of racism, colonialism, and white domination. Did Potts not see that the South Africans were attempting to draw closer to the United States, in preparation for future confrontations with the blacks in southern Africa? If he did, he was not troubled by the prospect. Potts viewed South Africa pragmatically, as a friend of the CIA and a potential ally of the United States. After all, twenty major American companies have interests in South Africa and the United States maintains a valuable NASA tracking station not far from Pretoria. Eventually Potts concluded, in one of our conversations, that blacks were 'irrational' on the subject of South Africa. This term caught on. It even crept into the cable traffic when the South African presence became known and the Nigerians, Tanzanians, and Ugandans reacted vigorously.

Escalation was a game the CIA and South Africa played very well together. In October the South Africans requested, through the CIA station chief in Pretoria, ammunition for their 155 mm. howitzers. It was not clear whether they intended to use this ammunition in Angola. At about the same time the CIA was seeking

15. Kissinger and Angola. (Nicholas Garland, *New Statesman*, 26 December 1975). Reprinted by permission. Photo supplied by The Centre for the Study of Cartoons and Caricature, University of Kent.

funds for another shipload of arms and worrying about how to get those arms into Angola efficiently. Our experience with the American Champion had us all dreading the thought of working another shipload of arms through the congested Matadi port and attempting to fly them into Angola with our ragtag little air force. The thought of putting the next shipload of arms into Walvis Bay in South-West Africa, where South African efficiency would rush them by C-130 to the fighting fronts, was irresistible to Jim Potts.

At the same time, Savimbi and Roberto were both running short of petrol. The South Africans had delivered small amounts in their C-130s, but they could not be expected to fuel the entire war, not with an Arab boycott on the sale of oil to South Africa. The MPLA's fuel problems had been solved when a tanker put into Luanda in September, and Potts, in frustration, began to consider having a tanker follow the second arms shipload to Walvis Bay.

When Potts proposed this to the working group, he met firm opposition: He was told by Ambassador Mulcahy that the sale or delivery of arms to South Africa was prohibited by a long-standing U.S. law. Never easily discouraged, Potts sent one of his aides to the CIA library, and in the next working group meeting triumphantly read to the working group the text of the thirteen-year-old 'law.'

'You see, gentlemen,' he concluded with obvious satisfaction. 'It isn't a law. It's a policy decision made under the Kennedy administration. Times have now changed and, given our present problems, we should have no difficulty modifying this policy.' He meant that a few technical strings could be pulled on the hill, Kissinger could wave his hand over a piece of paper, and a planeload of arms could leave for South Africa the next day.

C. Angola: The Cuban Intervention, 1975

1. We arrived at Luanda, Angola, on Sunday, August 3 and established contact with the MPLA. They immediately took us to a hotel. When President Neto heard about [our arrival], he sent for us and put some of us up in his house and the rest of the delegation in another compañero's house.

In our first conversation with Neto we greeted him on behalf of the Commander-in-Chief [Fidel Castro] and the Minister of the Armed Forces [Raúl Castro], we gave him the present and the note from the Commander-in-Chief and then we explained the purpose of our visit.

We based our explanation on the following points:

a) The request made by the MPLA when it was visited by a delegation from our party and our government in January [Cadelo and Pina] and the request made later in Mozambique by Cheito, the chief of staff of the FAPLA.

b) These requests were somewhat contradictory: during the January visit they asked for aid and the training of cadres in Cuba and in Angola, and later in Mozambique they asked only for the training of cadres in Cuba.

c) We were coming to clarify the aid we should offer, given the FNLA's and Mobutu's aggression against the MPLA and the possible course of events before independence in November. We knew that the forces of reaction and imperialism would try with all their might to prevent the MPLA from taking power, because it would mean a progressive government in Angola. Therefore we were bringing Neto the militant solidarity of our Commander-in-Chief, our party and our government, and we gave him the $100,000.

In the course of this conversation, the Angolans complained about the paucity of aid from the socialist camp, and they pointed out that if the socialist camp does not help them, no one will, since they are the most progressive forces [in the country], whereas the imperialists, Mobutu and [one word SANITIZED] are helping the FNLA in every way possible. They also complained that the Soviet Union stopped aiding them in 1972 and that although it is now sending them weapons, the amount of assistance is paltry, given the enormity of the need. In general, he [Neto] wants to portray the situation in Angola as a crucial struggle between the two systems—Imperialism and Socialism—in order to receive the assistance of the entire socialist camp. We believe that he is right in this, because at this time the two camps in Angola are well defined, the FNLA and UNITA represent reaction and world imperialism and the Portuguese reactionaries, and the MPLA represents the progressive and nationalist forces. We agreed that we would meet again the next day, because we needed to finalize the exact timetables, quantities and details etc. of the requests they had made.

[Half a page SANITIZED]

We believe that [the MPLA] enjoys the general support of the population; the population is organized and ready to fight, but lacks weapons, as well as food, clothing and basic gear. We believe that we must help them directly or indirectly to remedy this situation which is in essence the resistance of an entire people against the forces of reaction and imperialism.

D. Fidel Castro on Angola, July 1976

We are not being polite, we are not praising anyone, and we are not paying any compliments, but instead we are analyzing the facts and understanding their significance and we are expressing our most sincere feelings. Agostinho Neto is a man whose name will go down in history among the revolutionary leaders who have proven themselves to the people and to the revolutionary movement. At times history develops right before our eyes and we are unable to understand its full significance. We Cubans are able to understand it by referring to our own experiences above all. What was Cuba in the last century, if not a Spanish colony? What has Angola been until very recently, if not a Portuguese colony? Two nations of the same peninsula and two colonial systems, equally exploiting and cruel (...)

We had already triumphed in 1959, but Neto continued to be a victim of persecution and repression. Imprisoned in 1960 for the third time, he was imprisoned once more in 1961, around the time of the Bay of Pigs. A few weeks after the Bay of Pigs Agostinho Neto was being imprisoned for the fourth and last time. We had recently emerged from that difficult trial, after the Bay of Pigs victory, which became Yankee imperialism's first defeat in America. [applause] If in April of 1961 we had not defeated imperialism, then, at the end of 1975, we would not have been able to lend our collaboration to an invaded Angola. [applause] That is why when a people struggle for their rights and their just cause they are also struggling for the just causes of others. In their struggle against imperialism the Vietnamese also fought for us. In their struggle against imperialism the Angolans also fought for us. [applause] And, in our struggle against imperialism at the Bay of Pigs, Cubans were also creating the conditions so that some day Angolans and Cubans together could inflict on the imperialists an African Bay of Pigs. [rhythmic

applause and chanting] Because of this we can appreciate the profound significance and the extraordinary symbolism that Neto's presence at this event today
represents. To us, it is a living page in history that recalls the history of our own
fatherland. Because, who make up our nation, who made up our people, but—in
a very high proportion—Africans, and who struggled in our wars of independence of 1868 and in 1895, in a very high proportion, if not the African slaves of
the past or their descendents [applause] and, among them, who knows—how
many descendents of Angolans? (...)

We have fulfilled our basic internationalist duty with Angola. By fulfilling our
duty we are not only doing a favor. We are simply fulfilling a duty. We have
always believed that a man who is not ready to sacrifice himself for others will not
sacrifice himself for anything. [applause] A people who are not ready to sacrifice
themselves for another people will not make sacrifices even for themselves.
[applause] A people who are not ready to fight for others' freedom will never be
ready to fight for their own freedom. [applause] We have fulfilled our internationalist duty with our brothers of Angola and we are proud of it, [applause]
proud of our revolutionary people who were ready to enlist hundreds of thousands of fighters [applause], proud of our reserve troops and revolutionary soldiers who fought alongside Angolans with the same heroism and bravery that
they would fight in our own country. [applause] We are proud of those soldiers
who, 10,000 kms away, bearing aloft the slogan 'The Fight Continues, Victory Is
Certain' were able to proclaim their slogan 'Fatherland or Death, We will Win.'
[applause] They were completely justified, because when they fought beside their
Angolan brothers, it was as if they were fighting for their own country. [applause]
(...)

We will cooperate with Angolans in many other fields within our scope. Naturally, the assistance to Angola can be carried out only through the cooperation of
all socialist countries. And the socialist countries have expressed their willingness
to cooperate with Angola, some in one field and others in other fields. We have
analyzed cooperation between Cuba and Angola in the field of public health. We
have a group of doctors, medical aides, working in Angola and we intend to
increase this cooperation even more. This is a field in which we have experience
and in Angola the struggle against disease is a very big one, because colonialism
did absolutely nothing in matter of public health. Therefore, we will offer it
important cooperation in the field of public health. We will offer it our experience and cooperation in the field of construction. As you know, we have also
achieved great progress in this field and we can cooperate with them in that field
(...)

Angola is a country with vast natural resources; they have magnificent economic potential. The help they need now is the help that can be offered, manpower. It is the help of men and women trained for their tasks. That is why we expect from our people, our workers, and, especially, our youth, that in the same way in which hundreds of thousands were willing to go and fight in Angola there will now be tens of thousands willing to give Angola this civilian cooperation. [applause] This does not mean that we are going to send everyone who is willing to go. No. We will only be able to send a small number of those willing to go. What we are interested in is the spirit of solidarity, the spirit of cooperation. Let no one believe that a people loses anything when it helps another. When a people helps another it does not lose, it gains. A doctor, like the ones we have had practicing medicine in Algeria, Yemen, Somalia, or Angola, does not lose anything for our country. Our country gains. It gains a professional who becomes more conscientious, who becomes more revolutionary. [applause] Our country did not lose anything with the 900 construction workers that went to Vietnam. We gained with them. Today those workers make up magnificent and enthusiastic work cells in our construction sector. When they returned they were sent to the most important construction projects, the ones with the highest priority. The country does not lose anything when one of its technicians goes off to fulfill an internationalist mission. The country gains a lot. Our conscience, our political development gains. And it is a source of pride to any revolutionary party, it is a source of pride for any country. And this attitude of our country, willing to fight, to help, on one terrain or another, is a good way to measure its maturity and its revolutionary conscience. That is why the imperialists always make mistakes with Cuba; because they have no equipment to measure these moral attitudes. [applause] They have no way of measuring the spirit and morale of a people. [applause] They made a mistake at the Bay of Pigs. And now, when they planned the invasion of Angola, they again made a mistake. [applause] They could not conceive that, at a distance of 10,000 km, Cuba would be able to give Angola the cooperation that it did. At a distance of 10,000 km. [applause] Because they thought that the blockaded people, the people they have tried to sink and ruin, were not able to give this type of aid. And they made a mistake. Our combatants were there on the front line. Our sailors, the crews of our merchant marine were there. Our merchant marine ships were there. Our plans were there. [applause] And our aviation workers were there. And, between them, in a quick and efficient manner, they responded to the call of the MPLA and the People's Republic of Angola. [applause] The imperialists did not count on this. The most important thing about a country is not its wealth. The imperialists have a lot of wealth, but they do not have moral or spirit. The most important thing about a country, a society, is its morale and its spirit. [applause] [rhythmic applause and chanting]

16.2 The Indonesian Invasion of East Timor, December 1975

East Timor, another former Portuguese colony, was invaded by Indonesia in December 1975 to prevent a leftist takeover. In this excerpt US president Gerald Ford, Henry Kissinger, and Indonesian president Suharto discuss the background for the invasion.

FORD—My delegation is extremely grateful, Mr President, for the splendid arrangements for the visit. I regret that the time is short but after elections, I hope to come back again for a longer period. The opportunity for such face to face meetings is also highly important for me. The confidence established through such meetings is important to the development of our policies. I considered the meeting at Camp David to be most fruitful, and I am certain that this current visit will even further enhance our relationship. The United States intends to continue a strong interest in and influence in the Pacific, Southeast Asia and Asia. As a whole, we hope to expand this influence despite the severe setback of Vietnam. Our country-to-country relationships are very important to the development of these policies (…)

SUHARTO—What are your impressions of China's attitude towards Southeast Asia after Vietnam?

FORD —They will vigorously [resist] expansionism by others into Asia. In this they think particularly of the USSR. They don't appear to have ambitions of their own (…)

SUHARTO—(…) The local insurgencies represent a greater danger than would an overt physical threat. The ASEAN [Association of South East Asian Nations] leaders have now concluded that the insurgent elements have stepped up their activities. The ASEAN leaders will seek to consolidate their actions in the forthcoming ASEAN summit. The agenda will include economics as well as security. On the economic side the objective will be to strengthen national resilience. It is important to cooperate closely together so that no country is a weak link (…)

FORD—Do you consider the insurgency in Thailand and Malaysia your most immediate threat?

SUHARTO—Exactly. It is there that we are now trying to analyse what we should do. What we do must be closely related to our capabilities, to a determination of how strong we are. These capabilities are currently limited. It is important, therefore, that we consolidate the strength of the people's ideology, politically, economically, and militarily. All villages should become fortresses. This requires substantial small arms. Thailand and Indonesia are studying the means of providing such arms. Both Malaysia and Thailand are interested in small arms production but for security reasons would be prepared to see this production in Indonesia. We would like to build a plant to produce M-16 rifles. Would the United States consider assisting in the construction of such a plant?

KISSINGER—We would favor this as a government, because of its indication of wider cooperation.

FORD—We would be more than sympathetic, we would be enthusiastic about such a concept (...)

FORD—Is Thailand threatened by Vietnam?

SUHARTO—Yes. There is a long hatred between Thailand and Vietnam. I would like to speak to you Mr President about another problem, Timor. When it looked as if the Portuguese rule would end in Timor we sought to encourage the Portuguese to an orderly decolonization process. We had agreement with them on such a process and we recognized the authority of Portugal in carrying out of decolonization and in giving people the right to express their wishes. Indonesia has no territorial ambitions. We are concerned only about the security, tranquillity, and peace of Asia and the southern hemisphere. In the latest Rome agreement the Portuguese government wanted to invite all parties to negotiate. Similar efforts were made before, but FRETILIN [Revolutionary Front for an Independent East Timor] did not attend. After the FRETILIN forces occupied certain points and other forces were unable to consolidate, FRETILIN has declared its independence unilaterally. In consequence other parties declared their intention of integrating with Indonesia. Portugal reported the situation to the United Nations, but did not extend recognition to FRETILIN. Portugal, however, is unable to control the situation. If this continues it will prolong the suffering of the refugees and increase the instability in the area.

FORD—The four other parties have asked for integration?

SUHARTO—Yes. After the UDI [unilateral declaration of independence], Indonesia found itself facing a fait d'accompli. It is now important to determine what we can do to establish peace and order for the present and the future in the interest of security of the area and Indonesia. These are some of the considerations we are now contemplating. We want your understanding if we deem it necessary to take rapid or drastic action.

FORD—We will understand and will not press you on the issue. We understand the problem you have and the intentions you have.

KISSINGER—We appreciate that the use of US-made arms could create problems.

FORD—We could have technical and legal problems. You are familiar, Mr President, with the problems we had on Cyprus although this situation is different.

KISSINGER—It depends on how we construe it; whether it is self-defense or a foreign operation. It is important that whatever you do succeeds quickly. We would be able to influence the reaction in America if whatever happens happens after we return. This way there would be less chance of people talking in an un-authorized way. The President will be back on Monday at 2:00 PM Jakarta time. We understand your problem and the need to move quickly, but I am only saying that it would be better if it were done after we returned.

FORD—It would be more authoritative if we can do it in person.

KISSINGER—Whatever you do, however, we will try to handle in the best way possible.

FORD—We recognize that you have a time factor. We have merely expressed our view from our particular point of view.

KISSINGER—If you have made plans, we will do our best to keep everyone quiet until the President returns home. Do you anticipate a long guerrilla war there?

SUHARTO—There will probably be a small guerrilla war. The local kings are important, however, and they are on our side. The UDT [Timor's Democratic Union] represents former government officials and FRETILIN represents former soldiers. They are infected the same as is the Portuguese army with Communism.

16.3 Soviet Suppression of Dissidents, 1976

As a result of the Helsinki Agreements, which they had signed, the Soviet authorities faced an increasingly vocal opposition on human-rights issues at home. In this 15 November 1976 report to the Central Committee, the head of the KGB, Iurii Andropov, discusses the activities of the 'Group for the Surveillance of the Implementation of the Helsinki Accords'.

During the last years the special services and the propaganda organisations of the enemy have tried to promote the idea according to which an 'internal opposition' exists within the U.S.S.R. In order to do this, they have taken all measures in order to come to the help of the instigators of anti-social manifestations and have thus objectively contributed to the reunion of various anti-social tendencies.

Thus in 1969 anti-social elements, led by Iakir and Krassin, have created 'initiative groups' with the goal of tying together the groups of members of the so-called 'Movement for Democracy'.

In 1970, with the goal of multiplying the anti-social activities of hostile individuals, Chalidze has created a so-called 'Committee of the Defence of Human Rights' which counted among his members, apart from himself, the academics Sakharov and Chafarevitch from the Academy of Sciences.

In 1973 the so-called 'Russian section' of Amnesty International, directed by Tortchin and Tverdokhlebov, took on an organisational function in the regrouping of individuals sharing anti-Soviet views. The members of this organisation made contact with certain foreign anti-Soviet organisations. With the aim of discrediting the Soviet state and system they then undertook the collection and distribution of slanderous writings.

The initiatives taken by the K.G.B. have allowed for the total discrediting and the complete actual halt of the activities of the Committee of the Defence of Human Rights; the possibilities of the 'Russian section' were heavily curbed.

Nevertheless the enemy who does not take note of his failures constituting an 'internal opposition', continues to pursue his action in the same fashion.

On 12 March, on the initiative of Iuri Orlov, correspondent member of the Academy of Sciences of Armenia, unemployed, the anti-social elements have announced the creation of a 'group for the surveillance of the implementation of the Helsinki accords'.

This group reunites individuals that have already been condemned on various occasions: Ginzburg, born in 1936, Jewish, unemployed; Grigorenko, born in 1907, Ukrainian, retired; Martchenko, born in 1938, Russian, professional criminal currently serving a sentence of internal exile in the Irkutsk region; extremist Jews: (...) Shcharansky, born in 1948, Jewish, unemployed; participants of diverse hostile actions: the wife of Sakharov—Bonner, born in 1922, Jew, retired; Landan, born in 1918, retired Jew (...)

The above mentioned individuals have created this group for no other reason than provocation. Putting into doubt the efforts made by the U.S.S.R. to conform with the dispositions of the Final Act of the Conference for Security and Cooperation in Europe, they also try to put pressure onto the Soviet government concerning the implementation of the Helsinki accords, especially regarding questions concerning the 'third pillar'.

The members of this group organise the collection of material concerning alleged violations of the Final Act on the part of the Soviet government and particularly on the 'violation of fundamental rights of the Soviet citizens' and the 'persecutions for acts of dissidence' (...)

The accumulated material is passed on to the governments which have signed the Final Act through various channels.

The idea of the members of the group behind all this is to appeal to those countries so that they create international committees of investigation in some precise cases. Seen from this angle, the group counts on the pressure of the international public opinion to influence the Soviet government, and does not, as stated by Orlov, try to 'research the well-being of the [Soviet] people' (...)

The K.G.B. takes measures to discredit the members of that group and to suppress their hostile activities.

16.4 Ronald Reagan Attacks Détente, 1976

In the US election campaign of 1976 Ronald Reagan, campaigning for the Republican nomination, accused the Ford administration of giving in to the Soviets in areas of vital interest to American security, and of neglecting key American values. Here is an excerpt from one of Reagan's radio speeches, 31 March 1976.

Our nation is in danger, and the danger grows greater with each passing day (...)

'Wandering without aim' describes the United States' foreign policy. Angola is a case in point. We gave just enough support to one side to encourage it to fight and die, but too little to give them a chance of winning. And while we're disliked by the winner, distrusted by the loser, and viewed by the world as weak and unsure. If detente were the two-way street it's supposed to be, we could have told the Soviet Union to stop its trouble-making and leave Angola to the Angolans. But it didn't work out that way.

Now, we are told Washington is dropping the word 'detente,' but keeping the policy. But whatever it's called, the policy is what's at fault. What is our policy? Mr. Ford's new Ambassador to the United Nations attacks our longtime ally, Israel. In Asia, our new relationship with mainland China can have practical benefits for both sides. But that doesn't mean it should include yielding to demands by them, as the administration has, to reduce our military presence on Taiwan where we have a longtime friend and ally, the Republic of China.

And, it's also revealed now that we seek to establish friendly relations with Hanoi. To make it more palatable, we're told that this might help us learn the fate of the men still listed as Missing in Action. Well, there's no doubt our government has an obligation to end the agony of parents, wives and children who've lived so long with uncertainty. But, this should have been one of our first demands of Hanoi's patron saint, the Soviet Union, if detente had any meaning at all. To present it now as a reason for friendship with those who have already violated their promise to provide such information is hypocrisy.

In the last few days, Mr. Ford and Dr. Kissinger have taken us from hinting at invasion of Cuba, to laughing it off as a ridiculous idea. Except, that it was their ridiculous idea. No one else suggested it. Once again what is their policy? During this last year, they carried on a campaign to befriend Castro. They persuaded the Organization of American States to lift its trade embargo, lifted some of the U.S. trade restrictions. They engaged in cultural exchanges. And then, on the eve of the Florida primary election, Mr. Ford went to Florida, called Castro an outlaw and said he'd never recognize him. But he hasn't asked our Latin American neighbors to reimpose a single sanction, nor has he taken any action himself. Meanwhile, Castro continues to export revolution to Puerto Rico, to Angola, and who knows where else? (...)

Mr. Ford says detente will be replaced by 'peace through strength.' Well now, that slogan has a a nice ring to it, but neither Mr. Ford nor his new Secretary of Defense [Donald Rumsfeldt] will say that our strength is superior to all others. In one of the dark hours of the Great Depression, Franklin Delano Roosevelt said, 'It is time to speak the truth frankly and boldly.' Well, I believe former Secretary of Defense James Schlesinger was trying to speak the truth frankly and boldly to his fellow citizens. And that's why he is no longer Secretary of Defense.

The Soviet Army outnumbers ours more than two-to-one and in reserves four-to-one. They out-spend us on weapons by 50 percent. Their Navy outnumbers ours in surface ships and submarines two-to-one. We're outgunned in artillery three-to-one and their tanks outnumber ours four-to-one. Their strategic nuclear missiles are larger, more powerful and more numerous than ours. The evidence mounts that we are Number Two in a world where it's dangerous, if not fatal, to be second best. Is this why Mr. Ford refused to invite Alexander Solzhenitsyn to the White House? Or, why Mr. Ford traveled halfway 'round the world to sign the Helsinki Pact, putting our stamp of approval on Russia's enslavement of the captive nations? We gave away the freedom of millions of people, freedom that was not ours to give.

Now we must ask if someone is giving away our own freedom. Dr. Kissinger is quoted as saying that he thinks of the United States as Athens and the Soviet Union as Sparta. 'The day of the U.S. is past and today is the day of the Soviet Union.' And he added, '. . . My job as Secretary of State is to negotiate the most acceptable second-best position available.' [Quote disclaimed by Kissinger.] Well, I believe in the peace of which Mr. Ford spoke as much as any man. But peace does not come from weakness or from retreat. It comes from the restoration of American military superiority.

Ask the people of Latvia, Estonia, Lithuania, Czechoslovakia, Poland, Hungary [and] all the others: East Germany, Bulgaria, Romania ask them what it's like to live in a world where the Soviet Union is Number One. I don't want to live in that kind of world; and I don't think you do either. Now we learn that another high official of the State Department, Helmut Sonnenfeldt, whom Dr. Kissinger refers to as his 'Kissinger,' has expressed the belief that, in effect, the captive nations should give up any claim of national sovereignty and simply become a part of the Soviet Union. He says, 'their desire to break out of the Soviet straightjacket' threatens us with World War III. In other words, slaves should accept their fate.

Well, I don't believe the people I've met in almost every State of this Union are ready to consign this, the last island of freedom, to the dust bin of history, along with the bones of dead civilizations of the past. Call it mysticism, if you will, but I believe God had a divine purpose in placing this land between the two great oceans to be found by those who had a special love of freedom and the courage to leave the countries of their birth. From our forefathers to our modern-day immigrants, we've come from every corner of the earth, from every race and every ethnic background, and we've become a new breed in the world. We're Americans and we have a rendezvous with destiny. We spread across this land, building farms and towns and cities, and we did it without any federal land planning program or urban renewal.

16.5 Jimmy Carter's Soviet Policy, February 1977

In his first top-secret exchanges of letters with Soviet general secretary Leonid Brezhnev, the new US president Jimmy Carter attempted to extend the détente process, while making it clear that he expected Soviet co-operation in areas such as human rights. Here is an excerpt from Carter's 15 February 1977 letter.

Dear Mr. General Secretary,

I am very pleased to note that our first exchange of letters has brought us at once to consideration of the central questions of universal peace. Our two great countries share a special responsibility not only for doing everything possible for the lessening of tension, but also for working out a series of mutual understandings which can lead to a more reliable and less dangerous political climate in the world.

I know the history of your country and admire it. As a child I developed my literary taste reading your classics. I also know how much suffering your people endured very recently, during the last war. I know about your own role in this war and about the losses suffered by each Soviet family. That is why I believe that we both are sincere in our declarations about our devotion to peace, and that gives me hope for the future. The question is how we can turn this devotion into reality. How can we start a process which could widen our cooperation and simultaneously restrain and finally limit our rivalry. This rivalry—it is real, extremely expensive, and undeniable—can at any moment become very dangerous, which is why we must not allow it to develop without restraint. In my opinion, this demands, at least, first, work to widen where possible our coordinated efforts, especially in the area of limitation of nuclear weapons; and second, to demonstrate highly deliberate restraint towards those unstable regions of the world where direct confrontation could arise between us (...)

I agree that in our exchanges of opinion and in the conversations which Secretary of State Vance will have in Moscow at the end of March we must concentrate mainly on the question of achieving an agreement on the second stage of strategic arms limitation, possibly including some significant reductions of the level of forces. Maybe we could bring these negotiations to a successful conclusion if we agree that this is only the first step in the process which could lead to bigger reductions in our respective nuclear arsenals (…)

I can assure you that in the analysis of our arms control policy which I am carrying out at the present time, all applicable proposals will be considered. As I said during a conversation with your Ambassador, I hope that we can consider not only the question of possible sharp reductions of the total quantity of nuclear weapons, i.e. the question of the minimum number of missiles which would allow every country to feel secure from a first strike, but also the question of restrictions on throw weights, of the possibility of a ban on all mobile missiles, of refusal to take any long-term preparatory measures in the field of civil defense, and also of such additional confidence building measures as preliminary warning of all missile tests and achieving an agreement on the nonarming of satellites and an agreement to reject development of capability to destroy observation satellites. We also have to study practical means to satisfy our mutual desire that our agreements be observed. Such measures as on-site inspection and uninterrupted observation from space must be the subject of incorrect interpretation. These are the means, which can be used to achieve progress, and to win society's support and understanding of our efforts (…)

We expect cooperation in the realization of further steps toward the fulfillment of the agreements reached in Helsinki relating to human rights. As I said to Ambassador Dobrynin, we hope that all aspects of these agreements can be realized. It is not our intention to interfere in the internal affairs of other countries. We do not wish to create problems with the Soviet Union, but it will be necessary for our Administration from time to time to publicly express the sincere and deep feelings which our people and I feel. Our obligation to help promote human rights will not be expressed in an extreme form or by means not proportional to achieving reasonable results. We would also welcome, of course, personal, confidential exchanges of views on these delicate questions (…)

Permit me to say a few words about our efforts to improve the situation in other areas, where there exists disagreements and potential conflicts (…) In southern Africa, we believe that the Africans should solve their problems without outside interference. It is with this goal in mind that we support a peaceful solution, which corresponds to the will of the majority, and have limited actions which could increase the potential for violence.

16.6 The Beginning of Collapse, May 1978

During their conversations in Washington in May 1978 it was clear both to President Carter and to visiting Soviet foreign minister Andrei Gromyko that the détente process was in trouble. Here is an excerpt from their talks on 27 May.

Foreign Minister Gromyko said that yesterday he had deemed it necessary to express certain considerations from the rostrum of the U.N. General Assembly. He had said for all the world to hear that the Soviet Union, the Soviet leadership and L. I. Brezhnev personally had always been in favor and were now in favor of concluding a SALT TWO agreement. They had never wavered in this resolve and had conducted a policy that had been and remained consistent with that objective. They believed that the new agreement would be beneficial for the United States as well as the Soviet Union, indeed for the whole world. He wanted to take this opportunity to re-emphasize this thought to the President personally. He had been deeply gratified to hear the President's words to the effect that the United States, the Government of the United States and the President personally were also in favor of concluding the new agreement on the limitation of strategic offensive arms. He considered this to be of particular importance since various recent statement in the United States had raised some questions in this regard in the minds of the Soviet leadership (...)

Gromyko said that he had one more final question to address, one of an entirely different category. This was the question of the Soviet medium bomber TU-22-M, the Backfire, as it was called in the United States. He could only express regret over the fact that this issue was still being raised at the negotiations, although there was no justification whatsoever for that, neither *de facto* nor *de jure*. He had told Secretary Vance the other day that perhaps the Soviet side had been mistaken to discuss this airplane in the first place, because it was clearly not a strategic weapons system. However, the Soviet side had assumed that the questions raised about this bomber might be based on someone harbouring an honest misconception about it. Still, he would not rule out that at some point the Soviet side might simply refuse to discuss this airplane any further (...)

[Carter:] Soviet presence there [in Africa] had increased to alarming proportions. We knew that the Soviet Union was in a position to exert a strong influence on the Cubans. The Soviets usually claimed that Cuba was an independent country that made its own decisions; we knew, however, of the enormous economic support the Soviet Union was rendering Cuba and could not believe that the Cubans could put 40 or 50 or 60 thousand men into Africa without the Soviet Union's tacit approval or encouragement. Referring to Zaire and the Katangans' invasion into that country, the President said we did not believe it to have been possible without Cuban assistance (…)

Gromyko said that the Soviet leadership had certainly noted some of the President's recent statements on African matters, which, whether the President liked it or not, also somewhat exacerbated and heated up the atmosphere as regards relations between our two countries. In this connection he was now talk-ing about the specific matters the President had raised in connection with Africa. There was no increasing Soviet presence in Africa. The Soviet Union did not have a single soldier with a rifle in Africa and did not intend to send any to that area. The Soviet Union had indeed sent some quantities of arms to some African countries, as well as a very small number of experts who were helping the Africans master the use of the arms supplied. Not a single Soviet individual had fired a single shot in the course of the latest clashes in Africa, and not a single Soviet individual had taken part in any operation in that part of the world (…)

He called the presence of a Soviet general in Ethiopia a myth. Had the Soviet Union been invited to send a general there, it would have refused. There was no Soviet Napoleon in Africa. Evidently the President was being fed completely fan-tastic information.

16.7 The Soviet Politburo on Foreign Policy and Human Rights, June 1978

Among the issues that soured the US–Soviet relationship was the Carter administration's insistence that Moscow live up to its obligations under the Helsinki Accords. Here are two excerpts from Soviet Politburo discussions in June 1978.

8 June

BREZHNEV: Comrades, it is apparent from what Andrei Andreevich [Gromyko] has now told us, that Com. Gromyko has performed considerable and useful work during his time in America both in terms of participation in the special session of the General Assembly of the UN, as well as in the course of his ne-gotiations with Carter and Vance, and also at the time of bilateral meetings and discussions with representatives of many countries. I think that it is fitting to approve this work and to record this in our resolution.

But it would be, probably, incorrect to limit ourselves only to this. From the report of Com. Gromyko, and likewise from the extensive information, which has reached us recently through various channels, it is completely clearly appar-ent that we are experiencing a very complicated period in the development of international relations. A serious deterioration and exacerbation of the situation has occurred. And the primary source of this deterioration is the growing aggression of the foreign policy of the Carter government, the continually more sharply anti-Soviet character of the statements of the President himself and of his closest colleagues,—in the first instance those of Brzezinski.

Judging from appearances, Carter is not simply falling under the usual influence of the most shameless anti-Soviet types and ringleaders of the military-industrial complex of the United States, but is intent upon struggling for his election to a new term as President of the United States under the banner of anti-Soviet policy and a return to the 'cold war.' (…)

22 June

BREZHNEV. Comrade Andropov would like to inform the Politburo about the Shcharansky matter. Let's give him the floor.

ANDROPOV. I want to inform the Politburo that at the present time in the USSR 520 people are kept in prison, of these 110 people are held on charges that have political coloring. We will have to decide the question of Shcharansky's trial, the preparation of which is completed now. As is known, Carter made a speech to the effect that Shcharansky should not be brought to responsibility. But we can not satisfy such a request. Shcharansky committed crimes and has to take full responsibility for them. He will be put on trial. But what is the best time for the trial? May be it should be started on July 10, this seems to be better. The USSR Ambassador to the United States comrade Dobrynin also recommends this time.

We discussed all questions of organization of Shcharansky's trial together with comrades Rudenko and Smirnov. Shcharansky admits his guilt, we uncovered his spy activity and can provide appropriate materials. He is charged under two articles: under article 64 for espionage and under article 70 of the Criminal Code for betrayal of the Motherland. His trial will take place in the same court house as Orlov's. It is a good place, a club, a small audience will be appropriately prepared. Shcharansky refuses to take a lawyer. He can refuse the lawyer named by the court. If he names another lawyer, and he has right to do it in the trial, then we will have to take a break for 5 days. Besides, we meant to publish a short report about the beginning of Shcharansky's trial. I believe it is not expedient to allow any correspondents into the trial.

EVERYBODY. Right, don't let them in.

ANDROPOV. What Shcharansky's sentence be? Everything will depend on how he will behave himself. For example, Orlov was to be sentenced for three years according to the article of the Criminal Code, but he behaved in such a rude way during the trial that the court was obliged to sentence him for seven more years with further exile for five years. Shcharansky, of course, will not receive, say, the death sentence, but the court will give him a stern sentence of, say, 15 years (…)

16. Soviet prison guards to Andrei Sakharov: 'And if you should win the Nobel Peace Prize comrade, we're here to make sure you have somewhere peaceful to enjoy it!' (Emmwood, *Daily Mail*, 12 September 1973). Reprinted by permission. Photo supplied by The Centre for the Study of Cartoons and Caricature, University of Kent.

16.8 Ambassador Dobrynin on US–Soviet Relations, July 1978

Soviet Washington ambassador Anatolii Dobrynin gave his leaders in Moscow the following pessimistic report on Soviet–American relations on 11 July 1978. The report is excerpted.

Almost eighteen months ago—January 20, 1977—the new, 39th President of the United States, J. Carter, stepped across the threshold of the White House. Since that time, a definite policy has been conducted by his administration, the basic elements of which are the subject of the review in the present political letter.

As has already been noted by the Embassy, Soviet–American relations during the Carter Administration have been characterized by instability, major swings, which to a great extent are due to its calculations of the state of affairs in both its internal and external dimensions.

In the middle of April of this year, Carter, as is well known, conducted in his country residence, Camp David, a meeting of the members of his cabinet and closest advisors, at which was taken a decision to carry out a regular reevaluation of Soviet–American relations. The initiative for this affair came from Brzezinski and several Presidential advisors on domestic affairs, who convinced Carter that he would succeed in stopping the process of worsening of his position in the country if he would openly initiate a harsher course vis a vis the Soviet Union.

Africa (events on the Horn of Africa, and then in the Shaba Province of Zaire) was chosen as the pretext around which the Administration would begin earnestly to create tension in Soviet–American relations. In fact, in connection to these African events it was decided to attempt a review of the entire concept of the policy of detente, subordinating it to the needs of the Administration, not stopping even before publicly putting under threat the chances of concluding a new agreement on the limitation of offensive strategic weapons (by artificially linking it with other issues).

In the country, however, by the way pretty unexpectedly for Carter, this 'harsh' course, which had been firmly and clearly rejected by the Soviet Union, caused a reaction in which was evident a clear apprehension among broad strata of the American population regarding the long-term condition and fate of Soviet–American relations. There was expressed the depth of the American mood in support of the policy of detente, which had developed in the course of the last few years and which in the minds of the unsophisticated residents of this country is associated with a simple thesis: detente mitigates the threat of confrontation with the Soviet Union, and thus, of nuclear war with it. Characteristically, there were such apprehensions even in the Congress, the representatives of which began to demand explanations of the Administration, where anyway the matter of relations with the Soviet Union is heading and wasn't the Administration trying to bring about some sort of big changes in these relations without the consent of the Congress.

And so, Carter became convinced that detente is not a 'faucet' which he can turn on and off whenever he feels so disposed. The Administration was obliged to quickly make some adjustments in its position (particularly in light of the speech of L. I. Brezhnev, and also our answer in Pravda to Carter's speech in Annapolis, which he had found to be unexpectedly firm). The President, having let Vance go out front, decided to restrain Brzezinski a bit. Vance usually stresses the positive accomplishments in Soviet–American relations without leaving out, however, the negative things which are associated with Carter himself (for example, the notorious policy of 'defense of human rights' or 'dissidents').

(...) Consequently, in so far as it is possible to judge on the basis of information which the Embassy has at its disposal, the Carter Administration has come to its own variety of a selective, half-hearted conception of detente (of which

Brzezinski himself first accused us). Detente in its current concrete application by the White House is, as if, being partitioned. It is seen as important and necessary—in support of the national interests of the United States itself and the corresponding formation of public opinion—regarding problems associated with nuclear weapons, issues of war and peace (limitation of strategic weapons, a total ban on nuclear tests, certain other disarmament-related issues). As far as the majority of other questions is concerned, as in the past it is applied subject to the 'behavior' of the Soviet Union in Africa, in the Middle East, in relation to 'human rights,' and so on. T e reaction of the Administration to the recently-begun Shcharansky process is in this regard sufficiently instructive.

The Carter Administration variously denies that it is supporting a return to the 'Cold War.' It seems that it fears a decline of relations with the Soviet Union to a level when the threat of a serious, to say nothing of a military conflict with us would be interpreted by the American people, and also in other countries of the world, as something real. Carter, evidently has come to realize that this would cause deep alarm among the population of the country and would for him be a political loss, and maybe would represent a catastrophe in the 1980 presidential elections. In this regard the choice—'cooperation or confrontation'—which he tried to pose for us in his speech in Annapolis, seemed in its essence directed in the United States itself to him personally; the heartland is expecting from Carter himself an answer to that choice, and he—thanks to the adherence to principal in our position—has turned out to have not quite as free a choice as he tried to present it (…)

16.9 SCC Meeting on the Horn of Africa, March 1978

To many US leaders, the Soviet participation in the war between its new African ally Ethiopia and Somalia was an important issue in the breakdown of superpower détente. Here is an excerpt from a meeting of the Special Coordination Committee of the National Security Council, 2 March 1978.

C[YRUS] V[ANCE]: I want you to know what I said in hearings before Congress yesterday. I was asked, 'Is there linkage between what is going on in the Horn and SALT?' I replied, 'There is not.' I did have to recognize that what is happening could affect the political atmosphere. I made a speech for about two minutes on the importance of SALT.

Z[BIGNIEW] B[RZEZINSKI]: The President said in response to a question this noon that there is no linkage but Soviet actions may impose such linkage.

H[AROLD] B[ROWN] and CV: That is wrong.

CV: I think it is wrong to say that this is going to produce linkage, and it is of fundamental importance.

ZB: It is going to poison the atmosphere.

CV: We will end up losing SALT and that will be the worst thing that could happen. If we do not get a SALT treaty in the President's first four years, that will be a blemish on his record forever.

ZB: It will be a blemish on his record also if a treaty gets rejected by the Senate.

CV: Zbig, you yesterday and the President today said it may create linkage and I think it is wrong to say that.

V[ICE] P[RESIDENT WALTER MONDALE]: How would you see that playing out, Cy?

CV: It will toughen the Russians' position. What is more, we are getting ourselves in a problem here at home. The problem is that people will say that if the Russians are good, are we going to give in to them on something in SALT?

HB: There is going to be linkage—but we should not encourage it.

ZB: What we are saying is that if there is an aggravation of tensions because of what the Soviets are doing in the Horn, there is going to be linkage. That is a statement of fact.

HB: Not all statements of fact should be made.

ZB: The Soviets should be made aware of the fact that they are poisoning the atmosphere.

HB: We should find something else to beat the Soviets with.

CV: I do not think there is much leverage anyway on this issue (…)

ZB: Let's go to item no. 2: showing our displeasure to the Soviets. Frank Press has developed a memorandum on bilateral relationships—space, transportation and housing seem to be the areas in which we have the least interest (…)

HB: It most favors them and these are the ones we want to find.

ZB: I am convinced about the moondoggle.

HB: I think we should consider cancelling the meeting—not just postponing it.

VP: It is all pretty puny.

ZB: None of this amounts to much by itself except to convey displeasure on the Horn.

HB: The Salyut one they will feel. (…)

HB: I have an idea re China. The Chinese are less concerned about the aggressor. Why don't we get together with the Chinese in Warsaw and issue a joint statement of concern about the Horn and append to it a statement that we will consult on other areas where we have a joint interest? That would get the Soviets' attention.

CV: That would get their attention but we are at the point where we are on the brink of ending up with a real souring of relations between ourselves and the Soviet Union and it may take a helluva long while to change and may not be changed for years and I think that is a very important step to take—we should examine it carefully before we go down that road.

HB: It is an important step—it is not like postponing or cancelling a meeting on space. I am struck by the approach the Chinese ambassador made the other day to our ambassador in the Sudan. They want to be in close touch with us.

ZB: On this business of souring relations with the Soviets, the real question is why are they being soured? Do the Soviets want to sour these relations? If they can do what they want in the Horn without getting evidence of concern from us, we are going to have major problems with them in the south. We should communicate to the Soviets that they do not have a free hand and that what they do entails risks. Otherwise, what will they think? (…)

CV: I think the key still remains SALT. If we make progress on SALT, then a lot of things will fall into place that do not fall into place otherwise.

HB: I do not think a SALT treaty would make any difference—if we had it now, they would be reacting in the same way.

ZB: They must understand that there are consequences in their behavior. If we do not react, we are destroying our own posture—regionally and internationally and we are creating the conditions for domestic reaction.

CV: This is where you and I part. The consequences of doing something like this are very dangerous.

16.10 The Politburo Discusses Intervention in Afghanistan, March 1979

The 1978 Communist coup in Afghanistan brought to power a weak and isolated regime, which soon became dependent on Soviet aid to survive the attacks from the Islamist opposition. While providing civilian and military aid, the Soviets were at first reluctant to intervene directly, even with the opposition advancing on the major cities. Here is an excerpt from the Politburo's discussion on 18 March 1979.

KOSYGIN. I had the opportunity to speak with Comrade Taraki yesterday on two occasions. He says that everything there is falling apart and that we must send troops, that the situation is the same in all of Afghanistan as it is in Herat. He says that if we lose Herat, then everything will fall. Pakistan, in his opinion, is sending a large number of men, dressed in Afghan uniforms. According to his data, 4,000 such persons have been dispatched. There are 500 men situated on the airfield in Herat at this time. I asked him, who in Herat is on your side? Comrade Taraki responded that in essence the entire population there has fallen under the influ-

WELL, GROMYKO – WE RUSSIANS CAN BEGIN STRIVING FOR **INDIRECT** WHITE RULE SOMETIME AFTER DECEMBER 31sт..!

RUSSIAN INFLUENCE
RUSSIAN INFLUENCE PENDING

17. A cartoonist's view of Soviet policy in Africa after a date was set for Zimbabwe's independence (John Jensen, *Sunday Telegraph*, 5 March 1978). Reprinted by permission. Photo supplied by The Centre for the Study of Cartoons and Caricature, University of Kent.

ence of the religious fundamentalists. He said that there are 200–250 persons there who are organizing the entire thing. I asked him, are there any workers there? He said, that there are about two thousand workers. I asked him what, in your opinion, are the prospects for Herat? He said to me bluntly that Herat will fall tomorrow, but that it is holding on for the time being.

They are talking about forming new units and sending them to Herat. In the opinion of Comrade Taraki, all who have gathered from the ranks of those dissatisfied with the new regime will then unite and set out for Kabul, and that will be the end of his government. Again he requested assistance from our troops. I said that I could not answer his request at this time. I said that we were intensively studying the question, and that we would deliberate and then respond.

As you can see, the discussion with Comrade Taraki yielded no constructive results whatsoever. He spoke of the fall of Herat and requested a deployment of our troops. I asked him what was required from our side in order to combine political measures with those of a military character. Taraki then said to me, you should place Afghan insignias on your planes and tanks, and let them move on Herat from across the border. I then said that this would be direct aggression on the part of the U.S.S.R. against Afghanistan.

I asked him, can you muster soldiers and special drivers for tanks and armored cars from the ranks of the Afghans? He said that this could be done, but only a very few. I told him of our decision to render comprehensive assistance to Afghanistan, to send an additional number of advisors and specialists.

Naturally, we must preserve Afghanistan as an allied government. In addition, it would appear that we must appeal to Pakistan with a warning that intervention against Afghanistan is intolerable. The same measure must be taken in respect to Iran. The message must be directed to Khomeini and to Bazargan. We must also come out with a similar document in respect to Iran.

It would be good if the borders with Pakistan and Iran could be closed.

It seems to me that it would make sense to take the further step of sending a good ambassador to Afghanistan. From the discussion with Comrade Taraki I learned that he doesn't even know to whom the government should turn. A great political task is necessary there, and only in that event can we save Afghanistan as an ally.

BREZHNEV. Letters to Pakistan and Iran must be sent today.

USTINOV. Amin spoke with me yesterday morning. Having consulted beforehand with Leonid Ilych, I told him about the massive aid that we are turning out and will continue to render. Amin said that the Soviet Union is our closest and principal friend. He then started to lament about the fact that Pakistan and Iran are sending large numbers of saboteurs that are being trained on the territory of Pakistan by Chinese advisors, being equipped with Chinese arms, and are then being sent across the border into Afghanistan.

There is strong opposition in Afghanistan on the part of the feudal lords.

He then turned the discussion to Herat and, just like Taraki, asked us to send tanks. I told him about the aid that we had determined to give Afghanistan in the form of a supply of armaments. He said that such aid was helpful, but what they really need is for us to send tanks.

BREZHNEV. Their army is falling apart, and we are supposed to wage the war for them.

16.11 Reasons to Invade Afghanistan, December 1979

By late 1979, with détente in rapid decline on other issues, the Soviet leadership reversed their earlier decision not to intervene directly in Afghanistan. In this personal memorandum to Soviet leader Brezhnev from early December 1979, the head of the KGB, Iurii Andropov, sets out the key arguments for an invasion.

After the coup and the murder of Taraki in September of this year, the situation in Afghanistan began to undertake an undesirable turn for us. The situation in the party, the army and the government apparatus has become more acute, as they were essentially destroyed as a result of the mass repressions carried out by Amin. At the same time, alarming information started to arrive about Amin's secret activities, forewarning of a possible political shift to the West. [These included:] Contacts with an American agent about issues which are kept secret from us. Promises to tribal leaders to shift away from USSR and to adopt a 'policy of neutrality.' Closed meetings in which attacks were made against Soviet policy and the activities of our specialists. The practical removal of our headquarters in Kabul, etc. The diplomatic circles in Kabul are widely talking of Amin's differences with Moscow and his possible anti-Soviet steps.

All this has created, on the one hand, the danger of losing the gains made by the April [1978] revolution (the scale of insurgent attacks will increase by spring) within the country, while on the other hand—the threat to our positions in Afghanistan (right now there is no guarantee that Amin, in order to protect his personal power, will not shift to the West). [There has been] a growth of anti-Soviet sentiments within the population.

2. Recently we were contacted by group of Afghan communists abroad. In the course of our contact with Babrak [Karmal] and [Asadullah] Sarwari, it became clear (and they informed us of this) that they have worked out a plan for opposing Amin and creating new party and state organs. But Amin, as a preventive measure, has begun mass arrests of 'suspect persons' (300 people have been shot).

In these conditions, Babrak and Sarwari, without changing their plans of opposition, have raised the question of possible assistance, in case of need, including military. We have two battalions stationed in Kabul and there is the capability of rendering such assistance. It appears that this is entirely sufficient for a successful operation. But, as a precautionary measure in the event of unforeseen complications, it would be wise to have a military group close to the border. In case of the deployment of military forces we could at the same time decide various questions pertaining to the liquidation of gangs.

The implementation of the given operation would allow us to decide the question of defending the gains of the April revolution, establishing Leninist principles in the party and state leadership of Afghanistan, and securing our positions in this country.

16.12 Nato's Double-Track Decision, December 1979

Right before the invasion of Afghanistan took place, the NATO allies, at a special meeting of foreign and defence ministers in Brussels on 12 December 1979, had decided to

introduce the new American Pershing II and Cruise missiles in Western Europe. This
excerpt from the meeting's official communiqué explains the decision.

(...) 3. The Warsaw Pact has over the years developed a large and growing capability in nuclear systems that directly threaten Western Europe and have a strategic significance for the Alliance in Europe. This situation has been especially aggravated over the last few years by Soviet decisions to implement programmes modernising and expanding their long-range nuclear capability substantially. In particular, they have deployed the SS-20 missile, which offers significant improvements over previous systems in providing greater accuracy, more mobility, and greater range, as well as having multiple warheads, and the Backfire bomber, which has a much better performance than other Soviet aircraft deployed hitherto in a theatre role. During this period, while the Soviet Union has been reinforcing its superiority in Long-Range Theatre Nuclear Forces (LRTNF) both quantitatively and qualitatively, Western LRTNF capabilities have remained static. Indeed these forces are increasing in age and vulnerability and do not include land-based, long-range theatre nuclear missile systems.

4. At the same time, the Soviets have also undertaken a modernisation and expansion of their shorter-range TNF [Theatre Nuclear Forces] and greatly improved the overall quality of their conventional forces.

These developments took place against the background of increasing Soviet inter-continental capabilities and achievement of parity in inter-continental capability with the United States.

5. These trends have prompted serious concern within the Alliance, because, if they were to continue, Soviet superiority in theatre nuclear systems could undermine the stability achieved in inter-continental systems and cast doubt on the credibility of the Alliance's deterrent strategy by highlighting the gap in the spectrum of NATO's available nuclear response to aggression.

6. Ministers noted that these recent developments require concrete actions on the part of the Alliance if NATO's strategy of flexible response is to remain credible. After intensive consideration, including the merits of alternative approaches, and after taking note of the positions of certain members, Ministers concluded that the overall interest of the Alliance would best be served by pursuing two parallel and complementary approaches of TNF modernisation and arms control.

7. Accordingly Ministers have decided to modernise NATO's LRTNF by the deployment in Europe of US ground-launched systems comprising 108 Pershing II launchers, which would replace existing US Pershing I-A, and 464 Ground-Launched Cruise Missiles (GLCM), all with single warheads. All the nations currently participating in the integrated defence structure will participate in the

programme: the missiles will be stationed in selected countries and certain support costs will be met through NATO's existing common funding arrangements
(…)

Ministers fully support the decision taken by the United States following consultations within the Alliance to negotiate arms limitations on LRTNF and to propose to the USSR to begin negotiations as soon as possible along the following lines which have been elaborated in intensive consultations within the Alliance:

a. Any future limitations on US systems principally designed for theatre missions should be accompanied by appropriate limitations on Soviet theatre systems.

b. Limitations on US and Soviet long-range theatre nuclear systems should be negotiated bilaterally in the SALT II framework in a step-by-step approach.

c. The immediate objective of these negotiations should be the establishment of agreed limitations on US and Soviet land-based long-range theatre nuclear missile systems.

d. Any agreed limitations on these systems must be consistent with the principle of equality between the sides. Therefore, the limitations should take the form of de jure equality both in ceilings and in rights.

e. Any agreed limitations must be adequately verifiable (…)

11. The Ministers have decided to pursue these two parallel and complementary approaches in order to avert an arms race in Europe caused by the Soviet TNF buildup, yet preserve the viability of NATO's strategy of deterrence and defence and thus maintain the security of its member States.

a. A modernisation decision, including a commitment to deployments, is necessary to meet NATO's deterrence and defence needs, to provide a credible response to unilateral Soviet TNF deployments, and to provide the foundation for the pursuit of serious negotiations on TNF.

b. Success of arms control in constraining the Soviet buildup can enhance Alliance security, modify the scale of NATO's TNF requirements, and promote stability and détente in Europe in consonance with NATO's basic policy of deterrence, defence and détente as enunciated in the Harmel Report. NATO's TNF requirements will be examined in the light of concrete results reached through negotiations.

16.13 Brzezinski on the Soviet Afghan Intervention, December 1979

With the Soviet invasion of Afghanistan and the American Senate's refusal to ratify the SALT II agreement, détente was for all practical purposes dead. In this 26 December 1979 memorandum for the president, National Security Adviser Brzezinski sets up his views on US policies during the new conditions.

I will be sending you separately a proposed agenda for the NSC [National Security Council] meeting on Friday, and it will focus on both Afghanistan and Iran. In the meantime, you are receiving today's SCC [Special Coordination Committee] minutes on both subjects. This memorandum is meant merely to provide some stimulus to your thinking on this subject.

As I mentioned to you a week or so ago, we are now *facing a regional* crisis. Both Iran and Afghanistan are in turmoil, and Pakistan is both unstable internally and extremely apprehensive externally. If the Soviets succeed in Afghanistan [DELETION], and the age-long dream of Moscow to have direct [Indian] Ocean [access] will have been fulfilled.

Historically, the British provided the barrier to that drive and Afghanistan was their buffer state. We assumed that role in 1945, but the Iranian crisis has led to the collapse of the balance of power in Southwest Asia, and it could produce Soviet presence right down on the edge of the Arabian and Oman Gulfs.

Accordingly, the Soviet intervention in Afghanistan poses for us an extremely grave challenge, both internationally and domestically. While it could become a Soviet Vietnam, the initial effects of the intervention are likely to be adverse for us for the following domestic and international reasons:

Domestic

A. The Soviet intervention is likely to stimulate calls for more immediate U.S. military action in Iran. Soviet 'decisiveness' will be contrasted with our restraint, which will no longer be labeled as prudent but increasingly as timid;

B. At the same time, regional instability may make a resolution of the Iranian problem more difficult for us, and it could bring us into a head to head confrontation with the Soviets;

C. SALT is likely to be damaged, perhaps irreparably, because Soviet military aggressiveness will have been so naked;

D. More generally, our handling of Soviet affairs will be attacked by both the Right and the Left.

International

A. Pakistan, unless we somehow manage to project both confidence and power into the region, [DELETION]

B. With Iran destabilized, there will be no firm bulwark in Southwest Asia against the Soviet drive to the Indian Ocean;

C. The Chinese will certainly note that Soviet assertiveness in Afghanistan and in Cambodia is not effectively restrained by the United States.

Compensating Factors

There will be, to be sure, some compensating factors:

A. World public opinion may be outraged at the Soviet intervention. Certainly, Moslem countries will be concerned, and we might be in a position to exploit this.

B. There are already 300,000 refugees from Afghanistan in Pakistan, and we will be in a position to indict the Soviets for causing massive human suffering. That figure will certainly grow, and Soviet-sponsored actions in Cambodia have already taken their toll as well.

C. There will be greater awareness among our allies for the need to do more for their own defense.

A Soviet Vietnam?

However, we should not be too sanguine about Afghanistan becoming a Soviet Vietnam:

A. The guerrillas are badly organized and poorly led;

B. They have no sanctuary, no organized army, and no central government— all of which North Vietnam had;

C. They have limited foreign support, in contrast to the enormous amount of arms that flowed to the Vietnamese from both the Soviet Union and China;

D. The Soviets are likely to act decisively, unlike the U.S., which pursued in Vietnam a policy of 'inoculating' the enemy.

As a consequence, the Soviets might be able to assert themselves effectively, and in world politics nothing succeeds like success, whatever the moral aspects.

What is to be Done?

What follows are some preliminary thoughts, which need to be discussed more fully:

A. It is essential that Afghanistani resistance continues. This means more money as well as arms shipments to the rebels, and some technical advice;

B. To make the above possible we must both reassure Pakistan and encourage it to help the rebels. This will require a review of our policy toward Pakistan, more guarantees to it, more arms aid, and [DELETION]

C. We should encourage the Chinese to help the rebels also;

D. We should concert with Islamic countries both in a propaganda campaign and in a covert action campaign to help the rebels;

E. We should inform the Soviets that their actions are placing SALT in jeopardy and that will also influence the substance of the Brown visit to China, since the Chinese are doubtless going to be most concerned about implications for themselves of such Soviet assertiveness so close to their border. Unless we tell the Soviets directly and very clearly that our relations will suffer, I fear the Soviets will not take our 'expressions of concern' very seriously, with the effect that our *relations* will suffer, without the Soviets ever having been confronted with the need to ask the question whether such local adventurism is worth the long-term damage to the U.S.–Soviet relationship;

F. Finally, we should consider taking Soviet actions in Afghanistan to the UN as a threat to peace.

Questions

Why was the Angolan revolution a reason for the decline of the East–West détente process?

Why did the Cubans and the Soviet Union put such an emphasis on supporting the MPLA?

Why was the outcome of the Angolan civil war seen as a serious setback for the United States?

Did the United States encourage the Indonesian invasion of East Timor, or simply condone it?

Why was the human-rights issue such a difficult topic of discussion for the Soviet leaders?

What was the difference between Carter's and Reagan's approach to détente in 1976–7?

What are the main differences between Cyrus Vance's and Zbigniew Brzezinski's views of détente during the Horn of Africa crisis?

Why did the Soviet Union decide against invading Afghanistan in March and for in December 1979?

What were the main policy lines that Brzezinski recommended Carter to adopt regarding Afghanistan?

Challenges to the Cold War: The 1980s

Although there is disagreement among historians as to when the Cold War began to fade as an international system, most recent surveys point to the years around 1980 as the beginning of the end. In order to grasp that argument, one needs to look beyond the superpower conflict itself and see what broader changes took place that would make it unlikely for the Cold War to remain the main dividing-line in international politics. Some of the more fundamental changes were economic—the increase in international trade, the economic rise of East Asia, and the decline in prices for raw materials all stimulated the economies of the capitalist countries while impeding those of the Eastern Bloc and its Third World allies. Others were changes in technology, such as communications and computers, almost all of which were developed in the West and hardly implemented in the Soviet Union.

At the time, however, the political effects of the economic and technological changes were difficult to predict, and the challenges to the West were seen as being as big, if not bigger, than those facing the Soviet Bloc. In terms of productivity and economic management, many Americans viewed Japan as rapidly surpassing the United States and feared the long-term economic consequences of a less dominant US role in the global economy. The election of a right-wing Republican, Ronald Reagan, as US president in 1980 reflected, therefore, not only what were seen as political challenges internationally—the breakdown of détente, the Soviet invasion of Afghanistan, and the Iranian revolution—but also a general perception that America's position in the world was in decline and a stronger US response was needed. The Reagan Administration's policies came to reflect that mindset, with its willingness to intervene against revolutionary regimes and its massive build-up of American military power.

The Soviet leadership came into the 1980s hopeful that the global trends favoring socialism, which they believed to have observed in the previous decade, would continue. But soon it was clear to the ageing general secretary, Leonid Brezhnev, that that would not be the case. The Soviet economy seemed unable to keep up with the West, and the increased military spending in the late 1970s and early 1980s created severe shortages in the consumer industry. The war in Afghanistan was going badly for the Soviets, and the costs of assisting their Third World allies were mounting as Reagan's anti-revolutionary offensive took hold. For the ailing general secretaries who succeeded Brezhnev, Iurii Andropov (1982–4) and Konstantin Chernenko (1984–5), the world situation seemed bleak.

Even closer to home the Soviets had to accept changes they did not welcome. When Poland's workers again struck against the country's Communist leaders, Moscow was left with the decision of intervening to save the Polish regime. Coming on the heels of the unsuccessful intervention in Afghanistan, both the political and military leaders in the Soviet Union hesitated, preferring that the Polish Communists themselves should handle the situation, even if that meant a military takeover. The Solidarity movement, which represented the workers of Poland, meanwhile had more than a year to organize and prepare for the showdown with the Communists. When martial law was finally introduced and Solidarity outlawed in December 1981, the Polish Communist Party also seemed to be at its last gasp. The military crackdown was roundly condemned in Western Europe, including by the powerful Italian Communist Party, which made the Polish crisis the final step in its break with Soviet and East European Communism.

A major signal that the Cold War dichotomy was receding as the main ideological dividing-line was the growth, from the late 1970s, of political Islam or Islamism. Reading political doctrines—including a critique of both liberal democracy and Communism—into the Holy Koran, the Islamist groups began to organize against regimes that they saw as stooges of Western (i.e. US or Soviet) influence. The Iranian revolution in 1978–9, where Islamist groups were key in toppling the US-supported dictatorship of the shah, provided inspiration for young Muslims to join such movements elsewhere, even though both their political and religious messages would differ from that of the Imam Khomeini, leader of the mainly Shi'a Iran. The Soviet war in Afghanistan proved a fertile ground for radical Islamist groups, who organized the refugees and who—in spite of their anti-Western message—received strong support from the United States and the conservative Arab regimes because of their efficiency in fighting the Soviets.

Mikhail Gorbachev, elected general secretary of the Soviet Communist Party in 1985, understood that major initiatives would have to be taken to improve the position of the Communists at home and abroad, but had no ready plan to implement. Instead, he attempted to reduce tension with the United States and Western Europe in order to buy time for a reorganization of the Soviet economy. Gorbachev's initiatives led to a series of agreements in which the nuclear arms race was limited, even beyond the limitations envisaged during détente. Believing Soviet Communism to be in retreat internationally and under threat at home, Ronald Reagan had no hesitation in reducing the danger of nuclear war, since history, after all, was on the side of the United States. By 1987 the nuclear accident at Chernobyl and the resistance he had met within his own party forced Gorbachev to adopt more radical policies in his search for *perestroika* (restructuring)—including some form of freedom of speech (*glasnost*—openness). Towards the end of the decade both the Soviet Union and the Cold War seemed to be in rapid change.

Readings

Raymond Garthoff, *The Great Transition: American–Soviet Relations and the End of the Cold War* (1994). The best overview of the end of the Cold War.

Beth Fischer, *The Reagan Reversal: Foreign Policy and the End of the Cold War* (1997). An excellent study of the Reagan administration's changing policies towards the Soviet Union.

Archie Brown, *The Gorbachev Factor* (1996). A stimulating discussion of the significance of Mikhail Gorbachev as a leader.

Michael H. Bernhard, *The Origins of Democratization in Poland: Workers, Intellectuals, and Oppositional Politics, 1976–1980* (1993). Explains the reasons for the creation of the first independent trade unions in the Eastern Bloc.

John L. Esposito, *Islam and Politics* (4th edn., 1998). A good introduction to Islamist policies and their causes.

17.1 The Current Malaise

At the end of the 1970s many Western observers thought that the United States was in crisis—the country had lost the war in Vietnam, its economic prospects looked grim, and the Soviet Union seemed on the offensive. The influential social scientist Herman Kahn and his Hudson Institute produced the following gloomy outlook in 1976, in a book entitled The Next 200 Years. *The chapter is called 'The Current Malaise'.*

For the past several years many concerned, intelligent people have developed strongly pessimistic feelings about the evolution of economic, technological and industrial development. At first these feelings focused on glaring—and often growing—disparities in material well-being, not only between rich and poor nations, but within the rich nations themselves. More recently, rising concern about pollution and the possible exhaustion of many natural resources has increased the already serious doubts about the continuation of this 'disproportionate' consumption—doubts often expressed as questions about the moral right of the rich to use up so many 'non-renewable' or scarce resources and often at prices that are considered unfairly low.

On the other hand, concern is also growing about the possibility of a new economic order in which resource-rich nations of the Third World could combine in cartels to set high commodity prices. By thus pre-empting for themselves much of the surplus available in the production process, they might permanently diminish the prosperity of the wealthy nations and make life intolerable for the resource-poor nations or those unable to join a cartel.

Added to the feelings is a pervasive loss of confidence in the ability of national leaders in almost all developed countries to deal with the problems that beset the world today. Domestic political scandal and a decade of futile combat in Southeast Asia have eroded the leading position of the United States in international affairs, worldwide inflation, accompanied by a major downturn in economic growth, has called into question the major international economic institutions created in the wake of World War II. Bureaucracies have proliferated everywhere, while the services they offer have often declined as the number and cost of personnel have mounted alarmingly. To many it seems that the resources of the productive and fortunate are being increasingly drained without the lot of the less productive and less fortunate being measurable improved. Widely publicized ferment, agitation and so-called 'liberation' movements among young people, women, and minority groups have signaled to some the imminence of possible revolution. French President Giscard d'Estaing's remark that 'we can see that practically all these curves are leading us to disaster' accurately encapsulates this current mood of malaise.

Indeed, a consensus is emerging among many scholars and journalists that a turning point has been reached in world history, one that portends either a much more disciplined and austere—even bleak—future for mankind, or a dramatic and revolutionary change in domestic and international society, or perhaps both. These observers argue that contemporary trends—and the increasing threats that appear to accompany them—rule out any realistic possibility, through current or even reformed institutions, for continued worldwide economic development. Indeed, they tend to view further development as endangering the prospects for mankind, and they conclude that technological, economic, political and moral imperatives require a basic change in the emphasis of mankind's activities—from seeking growth to slowing growth, from affluence to austerity, from conspicuous consumption by the few to equitable distribution of a limited and finite product among all.

17.2 The Japanese Challenge

While the United States seemed to be heading downhill, many political observers and social scientist thought that Japan would gradually become the major economic player on the world stage. The Harvard sociologist Ezra F. Vogel entitled his 1979 book Japan as Number One: Lessons for America.

One of the best vantage points for looking at our institutions, for re-examining our assumptions and considering alternatives, is from another place that faces similar problems but finds different solutions. As world leadership is shared by more countries, we will have more to learn by studying their successes. Of these other countries, Japan, the world's second largest economy, a modern democratic nation with a free enterprise system similar to our own, offers us the best perspective.

Considering the nature and scope of Japan's successes, it is remarkable how little interest Americans have shown in profiting from the Japanese example. As Japanese institutions begin to function more effectively than foreign ones, many Japanese now return from foreign study tours discouraged that they found so little to learn, but they still scour the world for useful lessons or hints of lessons. While American institutions lag behind, America is still unprepared to learn from countries outside Europe. Japan is studied by some Americans as a fascinating culture with an interesting history, a subtle literature, intriguing customs, and profound religious thought. But those who seek to learn from Japan are from the world of culture, not from the world of affairs. It is perhaps understandable that the Japanese, in the habit of looking abroad for things to learn, continue studying, while the Americans in the world of affairs, in the habit of teaching the rest of the world, find it difficult to assume the posture of the student, even when such indifference to or casual dismissal of foreign success blinds us to useful lessons (...)

Until a few decades ago America's institutions, which grew out of the Western European experience, worked extraordinarily well. Doctrines of private enterprise, civil liberties, and states' rights allowed creative individuals and institutions to adapt to local situations. With its scientific and technological inventions, America was on the forefront of creativity. Laws developed in response to European tyranny gave individuals their highly prized personal freedom. Benevolent charities and academic institutions provided a level of humanity and decency lacking in many nations. When these institutions were at the height of their success, Americans were proud of and devoted to their country.

By the 1970s, however, institutions that once served our country effectively have often been found wanting and have been strained almost to breaking point. Organizations lost the power and flexibility to function effectively. In a loosely organized urban society, ordinary citizens are defenseless against crime and license. Government regulations have multiplied, creating endless litigation that burdens society financially and organizationally. Commitments made when resources were seemingly inexhaustible have created expectations that cannot be realized. Benevolent impulses and government programs have proliferated in a mass of confusion without adequate consideration of the financial burdens on the taxpayer and recipient, of the motivation of the low-paid worker, and of the self-deprecation of the recipient in an achievement-oriented society.

The pace of economic change has accelerated and foreign trade increased, but America's institutions are not strong enough to guide these developments or to respond effectively to the problems of its declining economic competitiveness. When sudden dislocation can cause enormous human misery, as in the excessive migration from the rural south to northern cities in recent decades, the United States has had no migration policy. Our institutional practices promote adversary relations and litigation at a time when the complexity of our organization requires greater consideration of overall goals and when divisiveness threatens to disrupt the society. As a result, judges are called upon to make complex rulings concerning social and economic situations, a task for which they are most often professionally unprepared.

Japan, with its greater sense of group orientation, more recent emergence from feudalism, and government-led modernization, has developed solutions for many of these problems that America, with its more individualistic and legalistic history, might never have invented. America's transition to industrialization did not require the central direction nor the high level of government and business cooperation required of a borrower. Now that postindustrial America, too, requires higher levels of cooperation and more central leadership oriented to a modern economic order, there is no reason why America could not borrow and adapt Japanese models which, with a different tradition, it could not have originally created.

17.3 The Chinese Capitalist Revolution

In the early 1980s China went through thorough reforms of its socialist policies. The purpose was to make the economy more efficient and productive. In some areas, the new policies amounted to a complete reversal of China's Maoist past. Here is the new leader Deng Xiaoping's remarks to his Central Committee colleagues in February 1984.

I gathered some impressions from my recent tour of three special economic zones in Guangdong and Fujian provinces and of the Baoshan Iron and Steel Complex in Shanghai. Today, I have invited you here today to discuss the best ways of running the special economic zones and the question of opening more cities to the outside world.

In establishing special economic zones and implementing an open policy, we must make it clear that our guideline is just that—to open and not to close.

I was impressed by the prosperity of the Shenzhen Special Economic Zone during my stay there. The pace of construction there is rapid. It doesn't take long to erect a tall building: the workers complete a storey in a couple of days. The

18. A cartoonist's view of Japan's export policy. (Nicholas Garland, *Spectator*, 12 December 1981). Reprinted by permission. Photo supplied by The Centre for the Study of Cartoons and Caricature, University of Kent.

construction workers are often from inland cities. Their high efficiency is due to the contracted responsibility system, under which they are paid according to their performance, and to a fair system of rewards and penalties. Construction is particularly fast in the Shekou industrial district, because the authorities there are permitted to make their own spending decisions up to a limit of US$5 million. Their slogan is 'Time is money, efficiency is life.'

A special economic zone is a medium for introducing technology, management and knowledge. It is also a window for our foreign policy. Through the special economic zones we can import foreign technology, obtain knowledge and learn management, which is also a kind of knowledge. At the base for our open policy, these zones will not only benefit our economy and train people but enhance our nation's influence in the world. Public order in Shenzhen is reportedly better than before, and people who slipped off to Hong Kong have begun to return. One reason is that there are more job opportunities and people's incomes and living standards are rising, all of which proves that, in the final analysis, ethical progress is based on material progress.

The Xiamen Special Economic Zone is too small. It should be expanded to cover all of Xiamen Island. If this is done, we shall be able to absorb a large amount of investment from overseas Chinese, from Hong Kong and Taiwan and from many foreigners and to stimulate surrounding areas, thus promoting the economic development of all the Fijian Province. The Xiamen Special Economic Zone will not be called a free port, although some free-port policies could be implemented there. There are precedents for this. With the free flow of funds, foreign business will invest there. I am sure that this endeavour will not fail and that, on the contrary, it will be very profitable.

In addition to existing special economic zones, we might consider opening more port cities, such as Dalian and Qingdao. We wouldn't call them special economic zones, but policies similar to those in the zones could be pursued there. We should also develop Hainan Island. Rapid economic development there would represent a substantial accomplishment.

Where shall we begin in developing China's economy? A Japanese friend has made two suggestions: first, that we begin with transport and communications, which are the starting points of economic development; second, that we encourage high wages and high consumption. Being in a different situation from other countries, we are not in a position to adopt the second suggestion as our policy nationwide. However, as we develop the coastal areas successfully, we shall be able to increase people's incomes, which accordingly will lead to higher consumption. This is in conformity with the laws of development. We shall allow some areas to become rich first; egalitarianism will not work. This is a cardinal policy, and I hope all of you will give it some thought.

[Note in original.] (...) During his tour [Deng] wrote inscriptions in visitors' books for the places he visited. The one he wrote in Shenzhen was, 'The development and experience of the Shenzhen Special Economic Zone prove that our policy of establishing such zones is correct.' In Zhuhai, he wrote, 'The Zhuhai Special Economic Zone is a success.' In Xiamen he wrote, 'Manage the special economic zones in such a way as to achieve better and faster results.' And for the Baoshan Iron and Steel Complex in Shanghai he wrote, 'Master new technologies and techniques, be good at learning and better at innovating.'

17.4 The Iranian Hostage Crisis, 1979

The Iranian revolution, which overthrew the US-supported Shah Reza Pahlavi, increased the American sense of a global challenge, especially after radical students took over the US embassy in Teheran and held more than fifty diplomats hostage. Gary Sick, who worked for the National Security Council at the time, gives the following account.

Sunday, November 4, was a working day at the embassy. Offices were open and manned, and the chargé d'affaires, Bruce Laingen, together with political counselor, Victor Tomseth, and the embassy security officer, Michael Howland, had gone to the Foreign Ministry to seek additional assistance and protection from the government. In mid-morning a crowd began to assemble around the embassy, shouting anti-American slogans. Then, at about ten-thirty, just as Laingen and his colleagues were leaving the Foreign Ministry, as many as three thousand demonstrators poured over the walls and forced their way into the basement and first floor of the chancery building. Laingen was notified of the attack on his car radio and returned immediately to the Foreign Ministry to seek help. Most of the embassy staff barricaded themselves behind the steel doors of the chancery, where they would hold out for more than two hours.

Prime Minister Bazargan and Foreign Minister Yazdi were on their way into Tehran from the airport at the time of the attack, having just returned from Algiers and their meeting with Zbigniew Brzezinski. In their absence, Bruce Laingen was offered the use of Yazdi's office upstairs, and from there he set up a direct telephone connection with the State Department Operations Center in Washington. His two colleagues remained on the first floor of the Foreign Ministry, where they could watch what was happening outside the building. They also established a direct telephone line to Washington. Other direct lines were established with approximately sixty embassy staff people trapped on the second floor of the chancery and with the U.S. Cultural Center some three miles from the compound.

These open telephone lines from four different locations provided Washington with more rapid and accurate information than was available to anyone in Tehran. The situation was not without its element of humor. At one point Michael Howland, on the first floor of the Foreign Ministry, saw a group of student guerrillas arrive at the entrance to the Foreign Ministry, apparently seeking the three missing Americans to add to their collection of hostages. Howland informed Washington immediately. Washington passed the word to Laingen and he in turn informed Yazdi, who by that time had arrived back at his office. Yazdi was dumfounded to be informed by Washington of what was happening only a few floors below him in his own ministry.

Kathryn Koob may have earned her way into some record book for what must have been the longest continuous telephone conversation in history between Tehran and Washington. From her location at the U.S. Cultural Center, she learned of the embassy takeover shortly after the initial attack. She immediately called Washington and she and her staff maintained unbroken telephone contact throughout all that day and most of the following day until she, too, was discovered and taken hostage. Many months later, as she languished in captivity, Kathryn Koob was presented by her captors, in all seriousness, with a staggering bill for her marathon telephone connection. She informed them, with equal seriousness, that she did not have that much cash, and they finally gave up. Presumably, good Islamic militants do not accept credit cards. The Iranian Foreign Ministry was obviously taken entirely by surprise by the attack on the embassy, and they did everything in their power during those first hours to attempt to resolve the problem as quickly as possible. Although Bruce Laingen had to evacuate Yazdi's office, he remained in the Foreign Ministry, with immediate access to government officials. From the very start, Laingen (and Washington) received Yazdi's assurances that the events at the embassy were comparable with a sit-in at a U.S. university and that the situation would be resolved 'within 48 hours.' Although the police protection of the embassy had melted away in the face of the mob, Yazdi was confident that once he succeeded in contacting the ayatollah and his retinue in Qom (the holy city some ninety miles south of Tehran), the religious leaders would be able to convince the students that they had made their point and should withdraw.

It was therefore with a considerable measure of relief that we learned that the ayatollah's son, Ahmed, was at last on his way to the embassy. What Yazdi (and we in Washington) had not expected was that Ahmed Khomeini would clamber excitedly over the embassy wall, losing his turban in the process, and congratulate the students for their action. As that fact gradually became known, the deadly seriousness of the situation became apparent for the first time. Prime Minister Bazargan submitted his resignation in protest, and it was accepted by Khomeini. Government operations were turned over to the radicals of the Revolutionary Council, and the siege began in earnest (...)

17.5 Ayatollah Khomeini's Message, 1980

The left wing and the Communists lost the struggle for power in Iran. Instead, groups that promoted a political version of Islam—often referred to as Islamism—took over the government. They were led by the 80-year-old Ayatollah Ruhollah Khomeini, who issued the following challenge in his message to pilgrims in September 1980.

Greetings to the visitors to God's Sacred House who have gathered at the local point of revelation, the place where God's angels alight. Greetings to the believers who have migrated from their own houses to the House of God (...) Greetings to those who have grasped the sense of God Almighty's summons and set out, in response, to His House.

Now it is necessary for me to bring certain matters to our attention, free Muslims who have gathered at the site of revelation in order to fulfill a duty that relates both to worship and politics, so that you may be made aware of what is happening in the Muslim countries; what plans are underway to subjugate, exploit, and dominate the Muslims; and what impure hands are engaged in kindling the fires of division.

At a time when all the Muslims in the world are about to join together and achieve mutual understanding between the different schools of thought in Islam, in order to deliver their nations from the foul grasp of the superpowers; at a time when the arms of the Eastern and Western oppressors are about to be foreshortened in Iran, by means of unity of purpose and reliance on God Almighty—precisely at this time, the Great Satan has summoned its agents and instructed them to sow dissension among the Muslims by every imaginable means, giving rise to hostility and dispute among brothers in faith who share the belief in *tauhid*, so that nothing will stand in the way of complete domination and plunder. Fearing the Islamic Revolution of Iran will spread to other countries, Muslim and non-Muslim alike, and thus compel it to remove its foul hands from the lands it dominates, the Great Satan is resorting to another stratagem now, after the failure of both the economic boycott and the military attack. It is attempting to distort the nature of our Islamic Revolution in the eyes of Muslims throughout the world in order to set the Muslims at each others' throats while it continues its exploitation and oppression of the Muslim countries. Thus it is that precisely at the time Iran is waging a determined struggle to ensure the unity of all Muslims in the world on the basis of *tauhid* and true Islam, the Great Satan gives its orders to one of the pawns in the region, one of the dead Shah's friends, to obtain decrees from Sunni *fuqaha* and *muftis* to the effect that the Iranians are unbelievers. These pawns of America say that the Islam of Iran is different from the Islam of those who support the pawns of America, like Sadat and Begin, who extend the hand of friendship to the enemies of Islam and flaunt the commands of God Almighty, and who leave no lie and calumny unuttered in their efforts to create disunity among the Muslims. The Muslims of the world must be aware of these people who are attempting to spread dissension, and must frustrate their foul conspiracy.

At a time when the superpowers are attacking Muslim countries like Afghanistan, inflicting pitiless and savage massacres on the Afghan Muslims who wish the destiny of their country to be free from foreign interference, at a time when America has a hand in every form of corruption; at a time when criminal

Israel is unleashing a comprehensive onslaught against the Muslims in its beloved Lebanon and Palestine, and is preparing to transfer its capital to Jerusalem and intensify and extend its crimes against the Muslims it has driven from their homelands; in short, at a time when the Muslims stand in greater need than ever of unity, Sadat, the traitor and servant of America, the friend and brother of Begin and the dead, deposed Shah, and Saddam, another humble servant of America, are trying to sow dissension among the Muslims and will not hesitate to commit any crime their masters enjoin upon them in order to achieve their goal. America is engaged in continuous attacks on Iran, sending spies in the hope of defeating our Islamic Revolution and conspiring with Sadat to diffuse (by way of Iraq) lies and false propaganda concerning the leaders of the Islamic government. The Muslims must beware of the treason to Islam and the Muslims that these agents of America engage in (…)

Muslims the world over who believe in the truth of Islam, arise and gather beneath the banner of *tauhid* and the teachings of Islam. Repel the treacherous superpowers from your countries and your abundant resources. Restore the glory of Islam, and abandon your selfish disputes and differences, for you possess everything! Rely on the culture of Islam, resist Western imitation, and stand on your own feet. Attack those intellectuals who are infatuated with the West and the East, and recover your true identity. Realize that intellectuals in the pay of foreigners have inflicted disaster upon their people and countries. As long as you remain disunited and fail to place your reliance in true Islam, you will continue to suffer what you have suffered already. We are now in an age when the masses act as the guides to the intellectuals and are rescuing them from abasement and humiliation by the East and the West. For today is the day that the masses of the people are on the move; they are the guides to those who previously sought to be the guides themselves (…)

Neutral countries, I call upon you to witness that America plans to destroy us, all of us. Come to your senses and help us achieve our common goal. We have turned our backs on the East and the West, on the Soviet Union and America, in order to run our country ourselves. Do we therefore deserve to be attacked by the East and the West? The position we have attained is an historical exception, given the present conditions in the world, but our goal will certainly not be lost if *we* are to die, martyred and defeated.

17.6 Islamism in Afghanistan

Islamism also became the major ideology in the resistance to the Soviet invasion of Afghanistan. The difference was that among the Afghans it was the United States and its allies who supported the Islamist movements. Here is Gulbuddin Hekmatyar, head of the Afghan Hezb-i-Islami (Islamic Party), addressing a conference in Pakistan in 1985.

The previous debaucherous and unrepresentative governments of Afghanistan by declaring war against the Mujahideen of the present Central Asian occupied Republics and forcing the refugees to go back to the Russian occupied land helped the Russians to invade Afghanistan, after more than half a century. Had they acted otherwise, Afghanistan today would not have been the victim of a similar invasion and aggression.

The Russians have not been able to make an Afghan Army in their six years of aggression in Afghanistan. What they call the Karmal troops are all those people between the age of 13 to 70, whom they round up from the village and send forcibly to the barracks. The number of these prisoner-cum-soldiers is hardly 40,000 men.

If you are not able to stop your enemies half-way—when they arrive at your gates—then you will have to fight them inside your house.

All those individuals and governments who in a servile manner indulged in the protection of Russian interests in Afghanistan faced their wicked destiny. Zahir Shah was opprobriously deposed, Daoud, Taraki and Amin were butchered at the Russians' hands and Karmal is counting down for the same fate.

Some people claim that the 'revolution' was necessitated by the prevalence of a feudal system in Afghanistan. We say all the leaders of the so-called revolution were aristocrats themselves. Daoud, the founder of the communist movement, owned thousands of acres of land all over the country and Karmal and his colleagues are famous aristocrats.

Those who claim that the Jihad in Afghanistan is a fight between the Americans and the Russians, are the people who are biding their time to take over, like Karmal, by dint of force of the Russian tanks and military hardware.

Some are justifying the naked aggression of the Russians in Afghanistan. We believe the worst form of slavery is the inability to call a spade before one's master.

Some people are proposing direct talks with the impotent Karmal regime, a regime which has no mandate or authority. We believe the Russians are desperately trying to get their puppet regime recognized by the world by advocating direct talks with Pakistan.

Some people think that the Russian military might is invincible, but is not the six year long resistance of the Afghan Mujahideen enough proof to the contrary? This was also said about Great Britain, the empire where the sun never set, but now it is a tiny country where the sun never rises and it is still facing the Irish problem.

Some people are worried about how long the Mujahideen will be able to fight.

We are not only not tired but are prepared for a long war and are confident of victory. Why do they not ask how long the Russians will be able to fight?

Some friends are purporting that Pakistan by supporting the Afghan Mujahideen is inviting the enmity of the Russians at the behest of another super power.

We do not know to which country of the world, no matter how big or small, the war in Afghanistan is of vital importance. I do not know whose security and territorial integrity is guaranteed by the Jihad in Afghanistan. I believe if this war is not fought behind the Hindukush mountains today, it will be being fought tomorrow on the Pakistani plains. The Russians did not become the enemies of Pakistan after the Jihad started but they have been the staunchest enemy of this country since its formation. Every knowledgeable Pakistani is, I am sure, aware of who is behind all the secessionist movements in this country.

If Pakistanis really want to have secure western borders and are not willing to see the Afghanistan catastrophe repeated here, they should support the Jihad in Afghanistan.

Some people are arguing that the resistance started because the regime was implementing 'progressive' policies. If they call mass-killings, destruction, bloodshed and holocaust a progressive policy we would surely agree to this contention. If we are to accept bombs as 'food', shrouds and coffins as 'clothes' and graves as 'shelters', then we have really seen the unmasked face of communism.

We are not prepared for negotiation as long as there is a single Russian soldier on Afghanistan soil. We would not settle for losing at the conference table what we have gained in the battlefield. Any movement that has gone to the conference table in the face of occupation of its territory has lost its gains. After the complete withdrawal of the Russian troops, of there is anything to discuss, it would be considered.

The Russians by proposing peace talks are intending to mitigate the sharp condemnation by world public opinion of their brutal invasion of Afghanistan and to create pseudo-hopes among our Mujahideen and to pit one Mujahideen group against the other.

If the Russians really want a solution, the key is with them; that is their immediate and total withdrawal from Afghanistan.

We guarantee that after the Russian's withdrawal, (a) Afghanistan will not be a military base of another power.

(b) Afghanistan will be a free, independent, Islamic and non-aligned country having independent judgement on all international issues.

Afghanistan will never be used against the Russians by other powers. Any misgivings about the above facts are misplaced and baseless, as we would need ages to reconstruct our devastated country and that is only possible in peace and active non-alignment.

The refugee problem will be instantly solved after the withdrawal of the Russian troops and all Afghans will go back with dignity and honor to their homes.

Pakistan for the first time will see a real friend on its western borders after the independence of Afghanistan.

17.7 The Soviet War in Afghanistan

It was soon clear to most Soviet soldiers arriving in Afghanistan that their war against the Afghan Islamists would be long and very difficult. Here is one Russian soldier's account of his first day in Kabul.

It had a rather banal beginning. In December 1979 Soviet troops entered Afghanistan. This wasn't anything unusual; our troops were already in East Germany, Poland, Czechoslovakia, Hungary; sometimes they dropped in on Africa, and even briefly on Egypt. So one country more or one country less—it didn't make much difference.

It's only now, after the Soviet government has officially declared *it was a mistake to bring Soviet troops into Afghanistan*, only now that the Soviet press has started to write *it was a mistake to bring Soviet troops into Afghanistan*. But at the time, *Soviet troops entered Afghanistan at the request of the Afghan people to bring comradely help to our Great Neighbor*, our government announced. *At the request of the Afghan people, in order to bring comradely help to or Great Neighbor, Soviet troops entered Afghanistan*, our newspapers said, and they printed pictures of smiling Soviet soldiers surrounded by laughing Afghan children.

On August 10, 1984, my plane landed in Kabul, the capital of Afghanistan. There were no skyscrapers there. The blue domes of the mosques and the faded mountains were the only things rising above the adobe *duvals* (the houses). The mosques came alive in the evening with multivoiced wailing: the mullahs were calling the faithful to evening prayer. It was such an unusual spectacle that, in the beginning, I used to leave the barracks to listen to the nightingales sing. For me, a nineteen-year-old boy who had lived his whole life in Leningrad, everything about Kabul was exotic: enormous skies—uncommonly starry—occasionally punctured by the blazing lines of tracers. And spread out before you, the mysterious Asian capital where strange people were bustling about like ants in an anthill: bearded men, faces darkened by the sun, in solid-colored wide cotton trousers and long shirts. Their modern jackets, worn over those outfits, looked completely unnatural. And women, hidden under plain dull garments that covered them from head to toe; only their hands visible, holding bulging shopping bags, and their feet, in worn-out shoes or sneakers, sticking out from under the hems.

And somewhere between this odd city and the deep black southern sky, the wailing, beautifully incomprehensible songs of the mullahs. The sounds didn't contradict each other, but rather, in a polyphonic echo, melted away among the narrow streets. The only thing missing was Scheherazade with her tales of *A Thousand and One Arabian Nights* . . . A few days later I saw my first missile attack on Kabul. This country was at war.

The war divided the Afghan people. Some were with us, and others were against us. On our side was the Afghan government, which had come to power in April 1978 (not without our help), and the Afghan Republican Army. This army, like any other, was made up of officers and soldiers. Most officers received special training at Afghan military colleges; some even studied in the Soviet Union. An 'amusing' example of this kind of training: an Afghan officer named Ahmad Shah. He had graduated from a Soviet military academy, returned to Afghanistan, and went over to the Mujahadeen in Panjsher, where he headed one of their largest groups and put his training to good use. Actually, the only thing an Afghan had to do to enter a military college was apply, and he was in. They chose the soldiers differently: troops went into a village and rounded up men of appropriate age. There were some volunteers, of course—a few.

The Afghan army often took part in combat missions together with Soviet troops. Frankly, they were lousy soldiers. They tried to stay behind us and were never in a hurry to overtake us. There was nothing surprising about this: many of them, like many of us, were not in this war of their own free will. We had nothing to lose but our lives, but they were fighting their *own* people on their *own* land. Our newspaper depicted them as brave and valiant warriors defending their revolution. There were some volunteers who fought on our side to avenge the deaths of their families murdered by the Mujahadeen, just as there were those who fought on the side of the Mujahadeen to avenge the death of families killed by our shelling. This is what a civil war is about; but the only question was, What were *we* doing there? And why were there more and more unmarked graves in *our* cemeteries?

17.8 Solidarity in Poland, 1980

The main challenge to Soviet positions inside the Eastern Bloc in the 1980s came—as often before—from Polish workers. Here are excerpts from the negotiations between striking workers in Gdansk, led by Lech Walesa, and officials from the Polish Communist Party in August 1980.

19. 'I've told you! From now on don't call them "killed and injured", call them "withdrawals".' (Mac (Stan McMurtry), *Daily Mail*, 24 June 1980). Reprinted by permission. Photo supplied by The Centre for the Study of Cartoons and Caricature, University of Kent.

First meeting (23 August)

WALESA: We welcome the delegation from the government. [*applause*]

   MIECZYSLAW JAGIELSKI: May I shake hands with the chairmen?

WALESA: Please do. As we agreed, the delegation will proceed to the back-room for discussions. Please make way. [*applause and cheering*] Can you hear me in the hall? Good. Since time is short, I propose we begin. Deputy Premier! We welcome you on behalf of the United Strike Committee representing about 370 factories in the Gdansk Region and some in Elblag. The fact that we represent hundreds of thousands of people makes us feel certain that the cause we are fighting for is just. Coming here may make you understand what a shipyard is like when the workers are governing themselves. You can see for yourself how orderly it all is. The serious matters we must settle require us to act with caution and without haste. We have been waiting patiently for nine days and we have plenty of patience left. So I suggest that we end today's negotiations no later than 10 p.m. I also suggest that by then you must have presented the government's general answer on our proposals, and replied to each one of them. We hope today's meeting will be the first step towards ending the strike.

JAGIELSKI: Thank you, Mr Chairman. I, too, on behalf of our Commission, the direction of which the Party and government leadership has entrusted to me, would like to greet all members of, as I understand it, the Presidium of the United Strike Committee. I would also like to state at the outset that it is my intention, as well as my duty and responsibility, to conduct these talks in a most straightforward and constructive manner. We wish to resolve basic and important problems of the greatest concern to workers here on the coast, together, between us, to the best of our ability. That is my clear aim.

Final meeting (31 August)

WALESA: Our meeting is open. We sincerely hope that everything we have begun to do will be settled today to everybody's satisfaction. I propose the Prime Minister presents his position on all issues remaining, including the arrests of activists. Points One and Two of our proposals are now clearly resolved. Those here in this hall already know how the remaining proposals were received in Warsaw. But we would like to have a brief summary so that everyone else can hear how they were resolved. After that, we plan to sign these things, for everything has in fact been dealt with. Then, three or four hours after we have signed the protocol, I will declare the strike over, by arrangement with the Prime Minister.

JAGIELSKI: I, too, express my satisfaction that we are able to continue talks and am convinced that we will conclude them today. I accept the procedure you suggest, Mr Chairman: we will regard the points agreed as settled (...)

WALESA: Point Three is agreed. Point Four is accepted, but some things in it are not clear and we would like to read them out. Simply to run through them very briefly. I also propose the Prime Minister give us his views on these arrests. I have a list of them here. It's not a question of names but of the Prime Minister telling us how he views the problem.

JAGIELSKI: I would prefer to do that at the end.

WALESA: At the end. It can be at the end.

LIS: So I will read out the proposals agreed with the United Strike Committee Presidium and ready for signature. These are, Point Three:

The government will submit a draft law to the *Sejm* [parliament] on the control of press and publications within three months. It will be based on the principles that censorship should protect: the state's interests, that is preservation of state and economic secrets which will be more closely defined by law; matters of state security and its major international interests; religious feelings and those of non-believers; and should prevent dissemination of morally damaging material. The draft law will also provide a right of appeal to the Supreme Administrative Court against decisions taken by bodies controlling press and publications. The right of appeal will also be incorporated into the Administrative Procedure Code.

Religious associations will be granted access to the mass media as part of their religious practice once various essential and technical questions have been resolved between the state organs and the religious associations. The government will allow the radio transmission of Sunday mass, in accordance with detailed arrangements to be made with the Episcopate.

Broadcasting, the press and publishing, should express a diversity of ideas, opinions and evaluations. They should be subject to social control.

The press, like members of society and their organisations, should have access to public documents such as administrative acts and social, economic or similar plans issued by the government and its departments. Exceptions to the principle of openness in administrative activity will be defined by the law in accordance with sub-point 1.

JAGIELSKI: Agreed. I accept this point. [*applause*] Are we to sign it? Here you are.

LIS: Point Four: '(a) To reinstate all those dismissed for participation in the strikes of 1970 and 1976 to their previous positions and those students expelled from studies for their beliefs or opinions; (b) To release all political prisoners, including Edmund Zadrozynski, Jan Kozlowski and Marek Kozlowski; (c) To cease repression people for their beliefs or opinions.'

17.9 Jaruzelski and Martial Law in Poland, 1981

On 12 December 1981 a faction in the Polish Communist Party, headed by the prime minister, General Vojciech Jaruzelski, took power by a coup d'état *and introduced martial law. They were supported by the Soviet Union, but—as this 11 December conversation between Jaruzelski's aide General Florian Siwicki and the head of the Warsaw Pact, Soviet Marshal Viktor Kulikov, shows—were not quite sure how much Soviet aid would be forthcoming. This extract is from the notebook of Kulikov's personal adjutant, Lieutenant-General Viktor Ivanovich Anoshkin.*

(…) Siwicki: The date of the Actions is set for the eve of Saturday–Sunday.
Until this decision is implemented, it will not be made known.
Only a narrow circle of people know about it.

The situation is getting complicated. A session of 'S[olidarity]' at the factory.
Roughly 200 young thugs gathered.
Per Jaruzelski's instruction, he reported:

(1) The Soviet side would send for consultations on political matters in the plan for the introduction of martial law.

(2) later—a request to consult on economic matters. The economic situation is dramatic. He thanked Baibakov. We understand the inconvenience in the USSR, but we are counting on the provision of aid in accordance with the decisions that were adopted

— we also viewed your [Kulikov's] arrival favorably.

For us this gives support in the matter of introducing martial law and struggling to overcome the crisis.

WW [Jaruzelski] is very worried that no one from the political leadership of the USSR has arrived to consult with us about large-scale economic and military aid.

Just 24 hours remains until the very painful moment. But we are not having political consultations on the part of the USSR.

At this stage there can be no consideration at all of sending troops.

In a conversation via secure telephone with Cde. Andropov, we understood that we could count on assistance at a 2nd stage of our operations.

But we don't know how the Soviet Union understands the 2nd stage.

WW raises this question because even though it was clear earlier, the situation recently has changed.

The adversary is supported from outside and is making the situation more *tense*. The *church* — whereas earlier it took a neutral position, it now is creating tension. It might join forces with 'S[olidarity]' and draw young people to its ranks, forcing a confrontation.

A week ago we appealed to the Sov[iet] leadership — but there is no answer.

Cde. Jaruz[elski] met yesterday with Aristov and raised questions of a political and economic nature. What is the reaction now of the USSR to our actions? But we received no answer (...)

Summing up these problems:
— have had no meeting at the level of the leadership. Consultations.
— the economic question

and we cannot embark on any adventurist actions if the Sov. comrades do not support us.

Whereas Gromyko, Andropov, and Ustinov earlier would come and see us, now no one is coming. We are not receiving an answer to our questions.
Econom. aid
Sending of troop
Politb[uro] memb. W Wlad [Jaruzelski] is very upset and nervous and put forth a request that while there is time they receive an answer by 10:00 a.m. on 12.12.

Otherwise we can extend the schedule for initiating it by one day, this is the most we can wait.

'We are soberly evaluating the situation, and if there will be no politic., econ., and mil. support from the USSR, our country !! might be lost' (for the W[arsaw] T[reaty] O[rganization])
Without the support of the USSR we cannot go forward or take this step.

Psychologically, WW's state of mind is very nervous.

With a heavy heart I report all of this to you.

— The leadership is resolute, but it's necessary to decide matters.

WW wanted to travel to the USSR. But the time wasn't suitable for us. I suggested traveling a bit earlier. But the situation did not permit it.

We transmitted the requests to the ambassador, but have received no answer.

With what sort of polit. slogan must we act against the adversary. 'The mechanism is operating; the bow is stretched tight.' — This is along military lines.

We can defer the schedule for starting by a day: from Sunday to Monday (13./14.12). But no later.

VG (Viktor Georgievich Kulikov): I am not fully informed about what you transmitted to the ambassador. I know what sort of work you carried out in preparing the introduction of martial law. It is very significant. You do have the forces. That much we know. If the church is stepping up its activity, that's because you did not give a rebuff to the enemy. And the church is continuing to exert pressure on the leadership. The leading officers for martial law are in good spirits, and there is no need to speak about any sort of adventurist action. You have real strength. You insisted that Poland is able to resolve its problems on its own. The friends spoke to you about this matter, and you remember it. We also spoke a lot about this at the Def[ence] Min[isters] Comm[ittee] meeting [of the Warsaw Pact]. It's now time to act. The date should not be postponed, and indeed a postponement is now impossible. I don't know what Andropov was saying. But friends remain friends.

I will report all the questions to my leadership, and you must act decisively.

17.10 The Reagan Challenge, 1982

Ronald Reagan took over as US president in 1981 and steered the country on a hard-right course—confrontational towards the Soviet Union and free-market oriented in domestic policies. Here is an excerpt from his speech to the British parliament in June 1982.

We're approaching the end of a bloody century plagued by a terrible political invention—totalitarianism. Optimism comes less easily today, not because democracy is less vigorous, but because democracy's enemies have refined their instruments of repression. Yet optimism is in order because day by day democracy is proving itself to be a not at all fragile flower. From Stettin on the Baltic to Varna on the Black Sea, the regimes planted by totalitarianism have had more than thirty years to establish their legitimacy. But none—not one regime—has yet been able to risk free elections. Regimes planted by bayonets do not take root.

The strength of the Solidarity movement in Poland demonstrates the truth told in an underground joke in the Soviet Union. It is that the Soviet Union would remain a one-party nation even if an opposition party were permitted because everyone would join the opposition party (...)

Historians looking back at our time will note the consistent restraint and peaceful intentions of the West. They will note that it was the democracies who refused to use the threat of their nuclear monopoly in the forties and early fifties for territorial or imperial gain. Had that nuclear monopoly been in the hands of the Communist world, the map of Europe—indeed, the world—would look very different today. And certainly they will note it was not the democracies that invaded Afghanistan or suppressed Polish Solidarity or used chemical and toxin warfare in Afghanistan and Southeast Asia.

If history teaches anything, it teaches self-delusion in the face of unpleasant facts is folly. We see around us today the marks of our terrible dilemma—predictions of doomsday, antinuclear demonstrations, an arms race in which the West must, for its own protection, be an unwilling participant. At the same time we see totalitarian forces in the world who seek subversion and conflict around the globe to further their barbarous assault on the human spirit. What, then, is our course? Must civilization perish in a hail of fiery atoms? Must freedom wither in a quiet, deadening accommodation with totalitarian evil? (...)

The hard evidence of totalitarian rule has caused in mankind an uprising of the intellect and will. Whether it is the growth of the new schools of economics in America or England or the appearance of the so-called new philosophers in France, there is one unifying thread running through the intellectual work of these groups—rejection of the arbitrary power of the state, the refusal to subordinate the rights of the individual to the superstate, the realization that collectivism stifles all the best human impulses (...)

Chairman Brezhnev repeatedly has stressed that the competition of ideas and systems must continue and that this is entirely consistent with relaxation of tensions and peace. Well, we ask only that these systems begin by living up to their own constitutions, abiding by their own laws, and complying with the international obligations they have undertaken. We ask only for a process, a direction, a basic code of decency, not for an instant transformation.

We cannot ignore the fact that even without our encouragement there has been and will continue to be repeated explosion against repression and dictatorships. The Soviet Union itself is not immune to this reality. Any system is inherently unstable that has no peaceful means to legitimize its leaders. In such cases, the very repressiveness of the state ultimately drives people to resist it, if necessary, by force.

While we must be cautious about forcing the pace of change, we must not hesitate to declare our ultimate objectives and to take concrete actions to move toward them. We must be staunch in our conviction that freedom is not the sole prerogative of a lucky few but the inalienable and universal right of all human beings. So states the United Nations Universal Declaration of Human Rights, which, among other things, guarantees free elections.

The objective I propose is quite simple to state: to foster the infrastructure of democracy, the system of a free press, unions, political parties, universities, which allows a people to choose their own way to develop their own culture, to reconcile their own differences through peaceful means (...)

I've often wondered about the shyness of some of us in the West about standing for these ideals that have done so much to ease the plight of man and the hardships of our imperfect world. This reluctance to use those vast resources at our command reminds me of the elderly lady whose home was bombed in the blitz. As the rescuers moved about, they found a bottle of brandy she'd stored behind the staircase, which was all that was left standing. And since she was barely conscious, one of the workers pulled the cork to give her a taste of it. She came around immediately and said, 'Here now—there now, put it back. That's for emergencies.'

Well, the emergency is upon us. Let us be shy no longer. Let us go to our strength. Let us offer hope. Let us tell the world that a new age is not only possible but probable.

17.11 The Soviet Union in Difficulties, May 1983

To the Soviet leadership, headed by the ailing Iurii Andropov, the world looked full of difficult and threatening problems. Here are some excerpts from the discussion at a meeting of the ruling Communist Party Politburo, 31 May 1983.

In the beginning of the session comrade Andropov expressed words of deep sadness about the death of comrade Arvid Ianovich Pelshe. Comrade Andropov informed that the funeral of comrade Pelshe, according to the decision of the CC is going to be held at 11 o'clock on the Red square by the Kremlin wall. The members of the funeral commission will come to the Dom Soiuzov at the time of carrying out the body; the rest of the members of Politburo, candidates to members of Politburo and the secretaries will come at 11 o'clock straight to the Mausoleum.

[ANDROPOV.] Now I would like to address an issue, which in my opinion deserves an exchange of opinions and suggestions.

Today I've talked with a number of members of the Politburo about our government's announcement of the response to the deployment of American missiles 'Pershing-2' and cruise missiles in Western European countries; and also concerning the resolution adopted by the 'Big Seven' countries [G7] in Williamsburg. It's important that we discuss this matter, exchange opinions, and express suggestions that should be developed.

If you look at the events that are taking place in the Western countries, you can say that an anti-Soviet coalition is being formed out there. Of course, that's not accidental, and its highly dangerous. At the session of the NATO countries that is going on in Williamsburg, very aggressive speeches are given; and the very resolution adopted by the 'Big Seven' is non-constructive, aggressive (…)

The actions of President Reagan, the bearer and creator of all anti-Soviet ideas, creator of all untrue insinuations regarding our country and the other countries of the Socialist Community, deserve very critical and harsh reactions from our side. [But] in the press, Mikhail Vasilyevich [Zimyanin], these actions do not find the full coverage and answers that they deseve. This, of course, is incorrect. The imperialist countries of the West want to put together a bloc against the USSR. They act together and, as you saw, Reagan managed, though with some pressure, to convince his partners in the 'Big Seven' to sign the resolution and express their opinions against the policies of the USSR (…)

We have to open up a wider network to win public opinion, to mobilize public opinion in the Western countries of Europe and America against the deployment of nuclear weapons in Europe and against a new arms race, that is being forced [upon us] by the American administration. The behavior of Japan, and especially of the president [Yasuhiro] Nakasone worries me. He completely took the side of the more aggressive part of the Western countries, and he completely supports Reagan's actions. Because of that we should consider some sort of compromise in our relations with Japan. For example: we could think about joint exploitation of those small islands [which] have no strategic importance. Maybe there will be other suggestions. I, personally, think that Japan could initiate more active cooperation with the Soviet Union in the economic sphere.

The next point concerns China. I think that the Chinese aren't going to move any further on their positions. But all our information shows that they could increase their trade with USSR. They did offer us a trade agreement this year, that substantially increases our goods exchange [compared to] the previous years of trading with China (…)

If you look at our propaganda, you could come to the conclusion that it's quite unconcerned when it comes to NATO's strategic preparations. It is true that we shouldn't scare people with war. But in our propaganda we should show more clerly and fully the military actions of the Reagan administration and its supporters in Western Europe, which in other words means disclosing the full scale aggressive character of the enemy. We need that, so we could use facts to mobilize the Soviet people for the fulfillment of social and economic plans for development of the country. We can't, comrades, in this situation forget the defense needs of our country (…)

Why don't we use our press to speak out against those lazy bums, those who abscond from work, the bad workers? I ask the comrades [here] to express their opinions about the questions brought up and maybe the comrades have other suggestions. Who would like to begin?

GROMYKO. I completely approve of the suggestions that were expressed by Yu. V. Andropov. First of all about calling a meeting of the leaders of socialist countries, the countries of the Warsaw Pact. That kind of meeting, to my opinion, we should gather. We should invite [Romanian leader Nicolae] Ceausescu to the meeting, I think. I would say, that is probably an advantage.

ANDROPOV. Right now they are asking for consultations.

GROMYKO. Especially since they were asking for that. The meeting of the leaders of the countries of the Warsaw Pact will show the unity of our Pact and prove our principal positions in the questions of nuclear weapons and reduction of the arms race. I think that we should adopt at the meeting a document, as rightly mentioned before by Yuri Vladimirovich [Andropov]. This document should be very clear. Not a long declaration, but sharp and concrete. This would be our collective action of the countries of Warsaw Pact. It is needed.

What to do with the talks? I fully support the suggestion of Yuri Vladimirovitch about uniting the talks on nuclear armament in Europe and strategic armaments as a whole. As you know, Reagan has got the goal, whatever it takes, to place the nuclear missiles 'Pershing-2' and cruise in the European countries. The question arises of what we should we do, whether we should continue the talks? As is known, many Western countries are ready for deployment. That's why we should bring in something new. And in connection with that, the suggestion about uniting the talks will serve our interests.

ANDROPOV. We should invite the English and French for these talks, let them participate, they are nuclear countries.

GROMYKO. I think the English and French for sure will refuse to hold such talks, but we should invite them, that's right (…)

GORBACHEV. You said it right, Yuri Vladimirovich, that the time now is calling us to increase our actions, taking the necessary steps to develop a broad program of counter-measures against the aggressive plans of the Western countries. And in our internal plan we have certain serious tasks. We can take some action towards the countries of CMEA [Council on Mutual Economic Assistance], the countries of the Warsaw Pact, and separate socialist countries. I completely support the suggestions about holding a meeting and other actions that were suggested here, including the military line. The United States is moving to Europe. Here we can't wait. We have to act (...)

17.12 Gorbachev on the Chernobyl Nuclear Accident, 1986

Mikhail Gorbachev became head of the Soviet Union in 1985 and soon moved towards reform of both its domestic and foreign policies. One of the events that increased his impatience was the accident at the Chernobyl nuclear plant—the worst nuclear accident of the Cold War era. This excerpt is from Gorbachev's memoirs.

The accident at the Chernobyl nuclear power station was graphic evidence, not only of how obsolete our technology was, but also of the failure of the old system. At the same time, and such is the irony of history, it severely affected our reforms by literally knocking the country off its tracks.

Today we know how great this tragedy really was and how much is still to be done for those who lost their health and home.

It happened on Saturday, 26 April, at 1.25 a.m., when the only people on duty were a standby crew and people conducting an experiment on the turbo-generator during a scheduled shutdown of the fourth reactor. News of the accident reached Moscow by on the morning of the 26th. It went via the Ministry of Medium Machine-Building, which was responsible for the 'nuclear complex', to Ryzhkov, who reported it to me.

I immediately called a meeting of the Politburo, where Dolgikh, who dealt with these matters, explained the situation. His information was quite vague and failed to give an idea of the scale of the disaster. It was decided to send to the site immediately a government commission headed by Boris Yevdokimovich Shcherbina, Deputy Chairman of the USSR Council of Ministers. The commission, which included specialists on nuclear power stations, doctors and radiologists, reached Chernobyl the same evening. Scientists from the USSR Academy of Sciences and the Ukrainian Academy of Sciences were also rushed in.

The commission began to send back reports the next day. These consisted mainly of preliminary fact-finding, with all kinds of cautious remarks but without any conclusions at all. The commission reported that there had been an explosion, two people had died, there was mass hospitalization for radiological observation, steps were being taken to localize the fire, the remaining three units had been shut down, etc. It also reported that the explosion had released radioactive material.

On 28 April Ryzhkov reported the first results of the commission's work to the Politburo. Based on that information, the public was informed on television that evening and in the newspapers next day, after which there were regular reports as new information came in. I absolutely reject the accusation that the Soviet leadership intentionally held back the truth about Chernobyl. We simply did not know the whole truth yet (…)

Steps were taken to keep radioactive substances from migrating through the soil to the Dnieper River. Chemical defence troops were sent in, the necessary equipment was procured, and decontamination work was begun. The members of the government commission worked without stopping, and then switched to a one-week rotating schedule. Shcherbina, Silayev, Voronin, Maslyukov, Gusev, Vedernikov, and then Shcherbina again, in turn chaired the commission. Scientific institutes in Moscow, Leningrad, Kiev and other cities were working around the clock to solve dozens of unusual problems. Practically the entire country was involved. The best qualities of our people were seen in those anxious days of 1986: selflessness, humanity, high moral virtues. Many asked to be sent to Chernobyl and offered help without thought for their own safety.

Eliminating the effects of the explosion cost initially 14 billion rubles, and then swallowed up several more billions. The organized efforts succeeded in limiting the number of victims and localizing the consequences of the accident. By July the idea of the 'sarcophagus' had been worked out and then this unique protective cover for the damaged reactor, with a permanent monitoring system, was built within a short time. The International Atomic Energy Authority (IAEA) observers were satisfied that everything possible and necessary was being done.

Nevertheless, it is necessary to say with all honesty that in the first days we just did not have a clear understanding that what had happened was not just a national catastrophe, but one that affected the whole world. We realized this as information came in. Both then and now there has been criticism of the actions of the leadership of Ukraine, Belorussia and the Soviet Union. Based on what I know, I would never suspect any of these individuals of having an irresponsible attitude towards the fate of the people. If something was not done in a timely manner, it was mainly because of a lack of information. Neither the politicians, nor even the scientists and specialists, were prepared to fully grasp what had happened.

The closed nature and secrecy of the nuclear power industry, which was burdened by bureaucracy and monopolism in science, had an extremely bad effect. I spoke of this at a meeting of the Politburo on 3 July 1986: 'For thirty years you scientists, specialists and ministers have been telling us that everything was safe. And you think that we will look on you as gods. But now we have ended up with a fiasco. The ministers and scientific centres have been working outside of any controls. Throughout the entire system there has reigned a spirit of servility, fawning, clannishness and persecution of independent thinkers, window dressing, and personal and clan ties between leaders.'

The Cold War and the mutual secrecy of the two military alliances had also been a factor. There had been 151 significant radiation leaks at nuclear power stations throughout the world, but almost nothing was known about them or their consequences. Academician V. A. Legasov said that the likelihood of nuclear accidents was believed to be very small, and that science and technology throughout the world were not particularly prepared for them. Complacency and even flippancy ruled. I still recall what Academicians A. P. Aleksandrov and Y. P. Slavsky told the Politburo immediately after the accident. These men had stood at the heart of our nuclear power industry and were our creators—people who were honoured and respected. But what we heard from them were arguments like this: 'Nothing terrible has occurred. These things happen at nuclear reactors. Just drink a little vodka, have a bite to eat, have a good night's sleep—forget it.' (…)

There were two opinions in the Politburo. One was that information should be given out gradually so as not to cause a panic and even greater harm. Even today we see attempts to hold back or even suppress information about problems at nuclear power stations. Nevertheless, a different point of view prevailed in the Politburo—information should be released completely, as it arrived, without limitation, so long as it was reliable. This was my view. Ryzhkov, Ligachev, Yakovlev, Medvedev, and Shevardnadze supported me. Chernobyl became a difficult test for glasnost, democracy and openness (…)

Chernobyl was a bell calling mankind to understand what kind of age we live in. It made people recognize the danger of careless or even criminally negligent attitudes towards the environment. Public opinion has now focused on the acute problems that the environmental movement had been pointing out.

Chernobyl shed light on many of the sicknesses of our system as a whole. Everything that had built up over the years converged in this drama: the concealing or hushing up of accidents and other bad news, irresponsibility and carelessness, slipshod work, wholesale drunkenness. This was one more convincing argument in favour of radical reforms.

17.13 The Gorbachev–Reagan Summit at Reykjavik, October 1986

In October 1986 in Reykjavik, Iceland, Mikhail Gorbachev and Ronald Reagan met for the second time to discuss issues such as SDI (the 'star wars' missile defence system) and the reduction in the number of nuclear weapons. While no agreement was signed in Reykjavik, both leaders felt that the meeting was a success and opened the way for further progress. Here is an excerpt from their talks on 11 October 1986.

PRESIDENT REAGAN: The apprehensions you voice fall into two categories.

First, you are concerned that defense could be used for offense. I can assure you that this is not the purpose of SDI. Yes, the concern was voiced that space-based weapons could be used to destroy targets on the ground. But there are no weapons that are more reliable, more effective and faster than ballistic missiles. We already have an agreement prohibiting deployment of mass destruction weapons in space. And if you have additional concerns in this connection, we can work together to ease them.

Second, you voiced the concern that the United States might obtain a possibility for carrying out a first strike, and then avoid retaliation owing to defense. I can say that we do not have the capability for carrying out a first strike, and that this is not our goal.

The concern you voiced encouraged me to suggest drawing up a treaty eliminating all offensive ballistic missiles. In this case the question as to the combinations of offensive and defensive systems that would allow one of the sides to make a first strike disappears automatically. I am convinced that owing to this the situation will become stabler, safer, and that all of this will cost us less. Armaments that reach their target in a few minutes and cannot be recalled would be eliminated, which would provide a guarantee against cheating and the actions of third countries. What we want most of all is to replace ballistic missiles by defense, transition to which would occur in stages, with stability ensured at each stage of the disarmament process (...)

SECRETARY GENERAL GORBACHEV: Before I respond, Mr. President, at least briefly to your statement, and the numerous issues you have touched upon, I would like to ask a few questions for the purposes of clarification. As I understand, you share our goal of reducing strategic offensive missiles by 50 percent.

PRESIDENT REAGAN: Yes.

SECRETARY GENERAL GORBACHEV: At the same time if I understood you correctly, the figures you cited reflect options that were discussed in Geneva and which foresee a 30 percent reduction.

PRESIDENT REAGAN: We proposed 6,000 units.

SECRETARY OF STATE SHULTZ: This level would include 4,500 ballistic missile warheads and 1,500 air-launched cruise missiles.

SECRETARY GENERAL GORBACHEV: Much has already been said about these options, and you know that the matter reached a dead end. Our diplomats in Geneva can go on discussing all of these figures, levels, sublevels, and so on forever. I have data here on American and Soviet strategic arms. I can give this table to you. And what I propose is this: Inasmuch as we agree that strategic missiles should be reduced by 50 percent, let's reduce all forms of armaments in our strategic arsenals by half—ground-launched missiles, submarine-launched missiles, and missiles carried by strategic bombers. Thus the strategic arsenals would be reduced by 50 percent across the entire spectrum. The structure of our strategic arms evolved historically, you see, and with such a reduction, not one form of armament would be wronged, and the level of strategic confrontation would be reduced by 50 percent. This is a simple, proportionate solution, one which everyone will understand. And then all of these debates, which have now been going on for so many years, about levels, sublevels, what counts or what doesn't count, and so on, will be resolved automatically, since a 50 percent reduction is a 50 percent reduction. And there will be nothing to debate. Do you agree with such an approach?

PRESIDENT REAGAN: But my proposal also includes all strategic weapons except freefall bombs carried by bombers. But even these are limited indirectly, since a limit is set on the number of bombers (…)

SECRETARY GENERAL GORBACHEV: But what I want to ask you, Mr. President, is this: If a solution is found for Asia, will you agree to the zero option?

PRESIDENT REAGAN: Yes. We stationed them there at the request of our allies, which my predecessor accepted and which I implemented in response to your SS-20 missiles. As far as your missiles in Asia are concerned, I have seen maps from which it follows that while they can't hit England, they can hit France, West Germany, Central Europe, Greece and Turkey. Plus, the fact that they are mobile.

All of this emphasizes everything I discussed back in Geneva. Before we can work things out in regard to armaments, we need to try to clarify the causes of mistrust. If we are able to eliminate it, it will be easier to resolve the problem of armaments.

SECRETARY GENERAL GORBACHEV: That's true. Which is why I am amazed that you dispute what I told you about our missiles in Asia. They cannot reach Europe. Specialists know this well, and therefore your position seems to be an obvious paradox. This is not to mention the fact that it could be stipulated precisely in an agreement that no missiles will be moved anywhere, and that everything will be subjected to the strictest inspection.

I think that we can instruct our experts to discuss your thoughts and my idea.

But do I understand correctly? If a solution is found regarding Asia, will you agree to the zero option in Europe.

PRESIDENT REAGAN: Yes. (...)

SECRETARY GENERAL GORBACHEV: As far as SDI is concerned, it is not evoking concern among us today in the military respect. We are not afraid of a three-echelon ABM system. If your laboratory research motivates you to create such a system, considering that obviously America has a great deal of money, our response will be different, asymmetrical. What actually troubles us is that it will be difficult for us to persuade our people and our allies as to the absence of the ABM treaty. There would be no logic in this, and nothing could be built on this basis.

PRESIDENT REAGAN: We have absolutely no desire to eliminate the ABM treaty. This treaty is defensive, but you capitalized on its provisions to create a powerful defensive potential. We did not do this.

In this situation all we can say to the Americans is this: If the other side destroys us, we will destroy it. But people are not sleeping any easier for this. We propose supplementing the ABM Treaty with provisions on specific defensive weapons being created not for a first strike or to obtain advantages. We want this to be available to all the world.

SECRETARY GENERAL GORBACHEV: We will not deploy SDI. We have another concept.

PRESIDENT REAGAN: We do not intend to eliminate the ABM Treaty (...)

PRESIDENT REAGAN: A couple of words in conclusion. You said that you don't need SDI, but then we would be able to carry out our programs in parallel, and if you find that you have something a little better, than perhaps you could share it with us.

SECRETARY GENERAL GORBACHEV: Excuse me, Mr. President, but I do not take your idea of sharing SDI seriously. You don't want to share even petroleum equipment, automatic machine tools or equipment for dairies, while sharing SDI would be a second American Revolution. And revolutions do not occur all that often. Let's be realistic and pragmatic. That's more reliable.

PRESIDENT REAGAN: If I thought that SDI could not be shared, I would have rejected it myself.

17.14 The Economic Collapse in East Germany, 1980s

Many of the East European regimes attempted to borrow their way out of the economic difficulties of the 1980s. Among these were East Germany, in which the precarious state of the economy and the effects of indebtedness became increasingly visible to the leadership in the latter half of the decade. In this excerpt, historian Charles S. Maier portrays their increasing desperation.

I am for trade with the nonsocialist economies, but not for dependence. We have come to a point where our room for maneuver has continually shrunk. . . . Increasing foreign trade means we increasingly confront the principles of the world market. We have to be careful about that in a country like ours, which can only live by value-added production. Increased indebtedness to the nonsocialist is not possible. We've gone as far as we can politically. Otherwise we'll get into a situation that is politically dangerous, and in that case our comrades in the Volkspolizei and the Ministry for State Security won't be any help at all. These are issues that have piled up for years, where we've chosen the path of least resistance, and the GDR will have to pay.

—Alfred Neumann in the Council of Ministers, October 19, 1989

'Ali' Neumann was a Politbüro old-timer and hardly one of its leading thinkers, but when the Council of Ministers convened for a session of collective breast-beating a day after Honecker agreed to retire, he put his finger on the economic dilemma of the GDR. Only as Communist rule was disintegrating could party leaders openly address the country's precarious situation. It was not foreordained that East German socialism had to collapse, but the financial pressures were becoming unrelenting. At the end, they culminated in a debt crisis, the extent of which astonished and demoralized party delegates. The GDR, so Gerhard Schürer, head of the Planning Commission, reported to Honecker's successor, Egon Krenz, at the end of October 1989, had accumulated a foreign debt of 49 billion 'valuta marks' ($26.5 billion), the currency unit used for foreign trade accounting and pegged at roughly the value of the West German deutsche mark. The deficit on current account would amount to over $12 billion for 1989, and debt service alone cost $4.5 billion or over 60 percent of yearly export earnings. Just to stabilize the debt by an austerity program would require a drop in living standards of 25 to 30 percent, and even such a sacrifice could not assure that the GDR would be able to sell the needed exports. As in all national credit crises, the looming East German disaster had its origins in the persistent failures to resolve contending claims on national income. In this case the defects arose from ideological commitments. To understand the terminal crisis that overtook the regime, one has to work back to long-term disabilities imposed by socialist production.

How far back, however? Was socialism doomed from the outset, or were there later fateful turning points? The SED Central Committee's chief finance expert, Günter Ehrensperger, dated the difficulties from November 1973, when

Honecker responded to his projections that foreign debt would rise from its still modest 2 billion valuta marks total to 20 billion by 1980. 'I was summoned to him on the same evening and he told me I was immediately to cease working on such calculations and studies. I was to receive no further material and I have to have all the statistical bases in the department destroyed. That was the beginning. That was the beginning.' When Schürer confessed to the Central Committee the extent of foreign indebtedness, he claimed that the difficulties originated with the Eighth Party Congress in 1971, which resolved that German communism must support a generous consumer society and welfare state. Their decision enshrined what became known as 'the unity of social and economic policy,' which Günter Mittag stubbornly defended as party orthodoxy for the next decade and a half. In practice it meant subsidizing consumer prices, vacations, social services so that the gap with West Germany did not undermine the acceptance of the regime. But it also limited the investment that East Germany required to produce goods that might be internationally competitive. As Schürer told the Central Committee, 'It was hardly visible then, but then was when the switches were set. From then on the train travelled millimeter by millimeter in the wrong direction. It travelled away from the realities of the GDR.' (...)

By November 1987, however, the accumulated deficit with the nonsocialist world had risen to 38.5 billion valuta marks. The finance minister was rebuked in the Politbüro (presumably by Mittag, though he did not specify) for his pessimism. He had supposedly argued that the deficit was no longer controllable. 'But if that were the case we would have to call it quits.' In late April and May 1988, Schürer made his 'most massive personal thrust' to push his ideas through the Politbüro. Honecker's support was critical but uncertain. Schürer pleaded with the general secretary for a special meeting to clarify the situation. 'It is hard for me to estimate how far you are able to support my "Reflections."' A few days later Mittag responded with a sharp attack. To accept Schürer's concepts, he argued, would be to place in question the decisions of the Eighth and Eleventh Party Congresses. The price rises that his program entailed were unacceptable; his complaints about the extensive construction program in Berlin focused too exclusively on the costs.

Although the president of the Council of Ministers, Willi Stoph, carried Schürer's proposal to the council level by early May, they were aborted in the Central Committee, which retained the more extensive decision-making power.

This dispute had major ramifications within the economic agencies of the regime. Schürer himself later confessed that he had not dared break party discipline. 'For several years I have lived with the conflict,' so he told the Central Committee, 'how far could I press the opinion I recognized as correct even if it did not correspond to the official party line?' Until the upheaval of 1989, however, he opted for fidelity to the SED. In any case he was always a 'candidate' member of the Politbüro, an expert in its service, and never fully credentialed in the SED ruling elite. The Stasi's own economic watchdog unit, Hauptabteilung XVIII, warned how demoralizing an effect Mittag's attack was exerting on economic debate within party ranks: 'The reproach that Comrade Schürer's ideas contradict the base lines of the Eighth and Eleventh Party Congresses of the SED is just not understood. . . . In this connection the opinion is expressed that in the future no leading functionary is likely to summon the courage to prepare proposals that aim at bringing production and distribution into a more favorable relation. If such "taboos" persist, it will be impossible to solve the problem of presenting a real, challenging plan for 1989.'

17.15 Gorbachev and Perestroika, 1987

What first inspired the course of reforms in Gorbachev's Soviet Union was not so much new ideas as the hope of returning to the Marxism-Leninism of Lenin's time. In this excerpt from a 1987 book, Gorbachev explains why he saw Lenin's thinking as vital to what he himself wanted to achieve.

The life-giving impetus of our great Revolution was too powerful for the Party and people to reconcile themselves to phenomena that were threatening to squander its gains. The works of Lenin and his ideals of socialism remained for us an inexhaustible source of dialectical creative thought, theoretical wealth and political sagacity. His very image is an undying example of lofty, moral strength, all-round spiritual culture and selfless devotion to the cause of the people and to socialism. Lenin lives on in the minds and hearts of millions of people. Breaking down all the barriers erected by scholastics and dogmatists, an interest in Lenin's legacy and a thirst to know him more extensively in the original grew as negative phenomena in society accumulated.

   Turning to Lenin has greatly stimulated the Party and society in their search to find explanations and answers to the questions that have arisen. Lenin's works in the last years of his life have drawn particular attention. I shall adduce my own experience to corroborate this point. In my report of 22 April 1983, at a gala session dedicated to the 113th anniversary of Lenin's birth, I referred to Lenin's tenets on the need for taking into account the requirements of objective economic laws, on planning and cost accounting, and intelligent use of commodity–money relations and material and moral incentives. The audience enthusiastically supported this reference to Lenin's ideas. I felt, once again, that my reflections coincided with the sentiments of my fellow Party members and the many people who were seriously concerned about our problems and sincerely wanted to rectify matters. Indeed, many of my fellow Party members felt an urgent need for the renewal of society, for changes. However, I should say that I also sensed that not everybody liked the report, but felt that it was not as optimistic as the time required.

Today we have a better understanding of Lenin's last works, which were in essence his political bequest, and we more clearly understand why these works appeared. Gravely ill, Lenin was deeply concerned for the new future of socialism. He perceived the lurking dangers for the new system. We, too, must understand this concern. He saw that socialism was encountering enormous problems and that it had to contend with a great deal of what the bourgeois revolution had failed to accomplish. Hence the utilization of methods which did not seem to be intrinsic to socialism itself or, at least, diverged in some respects from generally accepted classical notions of socialist development.

The Leninist period is indeed very important. It is instructive in that it proved the strength of Marxist-Leninist dialectics, the conclusions of which are based on an analysis of the actual historical situation. Many of us realized even long before the April Plenary Meeting that everything pertaining to the economy, culture, democracy, foreign policy—all spheres—had to be reappraised. The important thing was to translate it into the practical language of everyday life (…)

It is wrong, and even harmful, to see socialism as something rigid and unchangeable, to perceive its improvement as an effort to adapt complicated reality to concepts and formulas that have been established once and for all. The concepts of socialism keep on developing; they are being constantly enriched as historical experience and objective conditions are taken into consideration.

We have always learned, and continue to learn, from Lenin's creative approach to theory and practice of socialist construction. We are using his scientific methods and mastering his art of analysing concrete situations.

As perestroika continues, we again and again study Lenin's works, especially his last (…)

In the new conditions [after Lenin] the narrow democratic basis of the established system of management began to have a highly negative effect. Little room was left for Lenin's idea of the working people's self-management. Public property was gradually fenced off from its true owner—the working man. This property frequently suffered from departmentalism and localism, becoming a no man's land and free, deprived of a real owner. Ever increasing signs appeared of man's alienation from the property of the whole people, of lack of coordination between public interest and the personal interests of the working person. This was the major cause of what happened: at the new stage the old system of economic management began to turn from a factor of development into a brake that retarded socialism's advance.

Speaking of the political aspect of the braking mechanism, one cannot fail to see that a paradoxical situation developed: an educated and talented people committed to socialism could not make full use of the potentialities inherent in socialism, of their right to take a real part in the administration of state affairs. Of course, workers, farmers and intellectuals have always been represented in all bodies of authority and management, but they were not always drawn into the making and adoption of decisions to the extent required for the healthy development of socialist society. The masses had been prepared for more active political effort, but there was no room for this, although socialism grows stronger precisely because it involves ever greater numbers of people in political activity.

The braking mechanism in the economy, with all its social ideological consequences, led to bureaucracy-ridden public structures and to expansion at every level of bureaucracy. And this bureaucracy acquired too great an influence in all state, administrative and even public affairs.

It goes without saying that in these conditions, Lenin's valuable ideas on management and self-management, profit-and-loss accounting, and the linking of public and personal interests, failed to be applied and develop properly. This is only one example of ossified social thought that is divorced from reality (…)

I have mentioned several times, referring to Lenin, that if you take up particular issues without seeing the general perspective, you will keep bumping into the general perspective all the time. Taking this as our guideline, from the very start of perestroika, especially at the June 1987 Plenary Meeting of the CPSU Central Committee, we attached prime importance to a conceptual approach. Of course, we sought to make methods less chaotic. In order to make a substantial gain, it is not at all necessary to begin by turning everything upside down and then to start correcting all the mistakes.

New tasks have to be tackled, with no ready-made answers. Nor are there such answers today. Social scientists have not yet offered us anything cohesive. The political economy of socialism is stuck with outdated concepts and is no longer in tune with the dialectics of life. Philosophy and sociology, too, are lagging behind the requirements of practice. Historical science must undergo a major revision.

The 27th CPSU Congress and Plenary Meetings of the Central Committee have opened up new opportunities for creative thought and have given a powerful impulse to its development. No revolutionary movement is possible without a revolutionary theory—this Marxist precept is today more relevant than ever.

Questions

According to Kahn and Vogel, what was wrong with America at the end of the 1970s?

Why did Deng Xiaoping turn upside down previous Communist economic policies in China?

Why was the US embassy in Teheran taken over, and what was the American reaction?

What motivated the Islamist guerillas in their struggle against the Soviet occupation of Afghanistan? And what motivated the Soviet soldiers?

What were the main victories of the Solidarity movement in 1980?

Why did the Polish Communist regime introduce martial law in December 1981?

What did Ronald Reagan see as the main role for the United States in the world?

Why did the Soviet leaders feel that they were pushed on the defensive towards the mid-1980s?

What was Ronald Reagan's main aim at Reykjavik? What about Gorbachev's?

Why did East Germany get into serious economic difficulties in the 1980s?

How did Gorbachev want to respond to what he saw as 'stagnation' in the Soviet Union?

The End of the Cold War

The new challenges that both superpowers faced in the 1980s pointed in the direction of fundamental changes in international relations. By the late 1980s the Eastern Bloc economies were in crisis, and *perestroika* in the Soviet Union began to stall as increasing numbers of Soviet citizens lost faith in Gorbachev's ability to renew the system from within. And although the challenges to the West were of a less essential nature—primarily created by the crass ideological confrontations surrounding Reagan's and Thatcher's domestic neo-conservatism and, in the economy, by the massive American trade and budget deficits—they still made many people ask questions about the stability of the Cold War international system.

But while general trends condition change, it is people's actions that bring it about. The end of the Cold War was a consequence of the rebellion of those many in Eastern Europe who were tired of economic wants and political oppression, and who, gradually, came to believe that the Soviet Union under Gorbachev would not act, as the Soviets had done before, to defeat their political demands. As so many times previously, the changes started in Poland, where General Jaruzelski's government already in 1988 realized that some kind of settlement with the banned Solidarity trade union movement was a precondition for much-needed Western loans and economic progress. Encouraged by Gorbachev, Jaruzelski arranged for talks with Solidarity's leader Lech Walesa (the so-called round table negotiations), ending up with an agreement on *partially* free elections in June 1989. Although it was only allowed to contest a minority of seats in the *Sejm* (parliament), Solidarity received an overwhelming majority of votes cast, and Jaruzelski—fearful of the workers again taking to the streets—in August appointed Tadeusz Mazowiecki the first non-Communist prime minister in Eastern Europe since the beginning of the Cold War.

It was Gorbachev's acceptance of a non-Communist government in Poland that, more than anything, opened the floodgates for political change in Eastern Europe. Just as conflicts over Poland had signalled the beginning of the Cold War system in Europe, the resolution of those conflicts signalled its end. In the summer of 1989 round table negotiations on the Polish model began in Hungary, and the new Hungarian leadership—after having been promised a half-billion dollar West German loan—in September decided to open its borders with the West, giving the thousands of East Germans who had flocked to Hungary in the hope of emigrating to the FRG the chance to cross over freely. By late September the East German regime was coming under pressure from protesters who demanded reforms similar to those in Poland, Hungary, or even the USSR. On 18 October Erich Honecker was forced to resign, and the new Politburo began work on new liberal laws and instructions, especially for travel to the West. As the draft laws became known on 9 November, East Berliners began assembling at the Wall, demanding to be allowed to cross, and the demoralized GDR border guards opened the barriers. That weekend between 2 and 3 million East Germans visited West Berlin.

In Czechoslovakia the Communist Party leaders—fearful of having to face the consequences of their collaboration in 1968—at first tried using force to stop the demonstrators. After street battles in Prague on 17 November, the opposition responded by calling strikes and boycotts, and journalists took over control of most of the mass media, supporting the protesters. By the end of the month the party leaders had resigned, and in December the veteran dissident writer Vaclav Havel was elected president and Alexander Dubcek—the leader overturned by the Soviets in 1968—was made chairman of the Federal Assembly. Only in Romania, which long had been only half-connected to the Soviet bloc, were the changes accompanied by widespread violence. After demonstrations by the Hungarian minority in the western city of Timosoara were brutally crushed by the security police in mid-December, Romanians picked up information of what was going on through the mass media in the neighbouring countries and began small-scale protests elsewhere. On 21 December the Communist dictator Nicolae Ceaușescu made a televised address to a hand-picked crowd in Bucharest, but was interrupted by protesters. Over the week that followed armed protesters, gradually joined by the army, fought Ceaușescu loyalists in the streets. Ceaușescu and his wife were captured and executed on Christmas Day 1989.

While the events in Eastern Europe were unfolding, Gorbachev insisted on absolute Soviet non-intervention. As he explained to his Poliburo, the Soviet Union could not afford to intervene, financially or in terms of the cost in its relationship with the West. But most importantly, Gorbachev believed that it would not be *right* to intervene—just like the Soviets, the East Europeans should decide their own futures. He attempted to use his willingness to allow change as a bargaining card in his relationship with the new US administration of George Bush, but the cautious Bush was unwilling to give much in return, economically or politically. Steadily, though, the relationship between the two countries did improve, especially in terms of arms control, to the point that by 1990 both sides spoke of a partnership rather than a 'Cold War'.

The American hesitancy in providing tangible support for Gorbachev's reforms made the Soviet relationship with Western Europe, and especially with West Germany, even more essential to Moscow. At the same time, it was Helmut Kohl's government in Bonn that had more to gain than any other from a close relationship with Gorbachev—as the East German regime withered from within after the fall of the Berlin Wall, Kohl wanted Soviet support for a speedy process of German unification and was willing to offer significant economic aid in return. To the surprise of almost everyone, including many of his own advisers, Gorbachev in 1990 agreed to the Federal Republic absorbing East Germany, and that the new unified Germany could remain in NATO. Gorbachev's decision effectively sidelined those West European leaders, including French president François Mitterand and, especially, Britain's Margaret Thatcher, who feared the consequences of a quick German unification.

But German loans were not enough to stop the Soviet slide toward economic chaos and political instability. Encouraged by the events in Eastern Europe, the Baltic states that had been forcibly incorporated into the Soviet Union in 1939 began a campaign for independence. So, too, did Georgia, and a violent conflict broke out between the Soviet republics Armenia and Azerbaijian over the control of the Nagorno–Karabakh area. As Gorbachev in early 1991 began to apply the brakes on liberalization, he was challenged by Boris Yeltsin, who had been elected president of Russia, by far the biggest of the USSR's constituent republics. In August 1991 conservatives within the Soviet Communist Party attempted to grab power in order to turn the clock back, but their coup against Gorbachev was defeated by their own indecisiveness, the army's unwillingness to follow their orders, and Yeltsin's defence of the sovereignty of his Russian republic. The failed coup effectively meant the end of the Soviet Union—the Baltic states broke away immediately, and one after another all of the Soviet republics declared their independence, including Russia. Gorbachev remained in the Kremlin as president of a union that had ceased to exist, until he resigned on Christmas Day 1991. The Soviet Union, which for seventy-three years had created so much hope among its supporters and so much hatred among its enemies, was no more.

Just as the Cold War had many beginnings, it may be said to have had many endings, some of which are covered in this and the previous chapter. Still, most historians would agree that the collapse of the Soviet Union ended the Cold War as an international system, since it was the existence of the Soviet state and its entry into world politics after 1945 that had given rise to so many of the division-lines that created this system. But the story of why the Soviet Union collapsed is in itself intimately linked to many of the other stories of how people, in different places and in different ways, broke out of the stranglehold that they felt the ideas and practices of the Cold War represented. Perhaps, in the future, when we know more about the international history of the 1970s and 1980s, we will be able to tell these stories as one, in ways that give meaning to a multitude of developments that all contributed to ending the Cold War.

Readings

Timothy Garton Ash, *The Magic Lantern: The Revolution of 1989 Witnessed in Warsaw, Budapest, Berlin and Prague* (1990). An outstanding eyewitness account of the East European revolutions.

Charles S. Maier, *Dissolution: The Crisis of Communism and the End of East Germany* (1997). Explains the causes of the collapse of Communism in the GDR.

Jack F. Matlock, *Autopsy on an Empire: The American Ambassador's Account of the Collapse of the Soviet Union* (1995). Very informative, both on Gorbachev and on US policies.

Gale Stokes, *The Walls Came Tumbling Down: The Collapse of Communism in Eastern Europe* (1993). An excellent overview of the revolutions in Eastern Europe.

Jacques Lévesque, *The Enigma of 1989: The USSR and the Liberation of Eastern Europe*, trans. Keith Martin (1997). The best analysis so far of Soviet policies on Eastern Europe in 1989.

18.1 The Soviet Withdrawal from Afghanistan, February 1989

The Soviet withdrawal of its troops from Afghanistan came after an international agreement had been signed, just like the American withdrawal from Vietnam fifteen years before. Still, neither Washington not Moscow were in any doubt that they had lost the wars. Here is a report from the British newspaper the Independent's *correspondent on the then Soviet–Afghan border the day the last Soviet forces left.*

At 11.55 am local time yesterday General Boris Gromov walked out of Afghanistan across Friendship Bridge on the Oxus river into Soviet Uzbekistan. The final soldier had left and, after nine years and 50 days, Moscow's unwinnable Afghan war was over—at least on the battlefield. To the end, withdrawal was a model of military precision. Sixty armoured personnel carriers bearing the remaining 200 of what was once a 100,000-strong 'limited contingent' drive slowly across the bridge into the frontier town of Termez. Their commanding officer stepped down from the last vehicle and completed the passage on foot. On the Soviet side, 3,000 people were waiting for him. The familiar flowers were offered. Red flags fluttered and music played from loudspeakers in the chilly sunshine. 'As I left Afghanistan, I did not look back,' said the general, moved and close to tears. 'But I had many thoughts: above all for men who died in this war.' He leaves behind him not only 15,000 Soviet dead, but a raging civil war.

In his own country, he is returning to debate, wound-searching and a face-saving effort to resolve by diplomacy what force of arms could not.

Proclaiming it had kept its side of the Geneva bargain of April 1988, the government yesterday formally reiterated Mr Gorbachev's appeal at the United Nations for a ceasefire and an end to arms deliveries to both warring parties. Urging a central role for the UN in the peacemaking process, a Foreign Ministry statement urged the 'armed opposition groups' operating out of Pakistan and Iran to show 'responsibility and self-restraint', to help 'the rebirth of Afghanistan as a non-aligned and neutral state'. More realistically, Moscow is gambling on the enduring divisions between the guerrilla factions. Meanwhile, the Kremlin continues to provide military and economic aid to the Kabul government. Dozens of Il-76 cargo planes daily ferried in supplies, said Tass. The government newspaper *Izvestia* estimated the Soviet army had left behind military installations worth 570m pounds. Whatever their shaken pride, senior commanders, too, are putting a brave face on what amounts to the Soviet Union's first defeat since the Second World War.

'We did not seek a military victory,' General Nikolai Popov declared in Termez: 'Our soldiers have honourably fulfilled their task, and created all the necessary conditions for ending the bloodshed.' Withdrawal was 'a great victory for perestroika and new political thinking'. In technical terms perhaps the war did bring some benefits: 'We have learnt valuable lessons,' said General Gromov as he stepped off the bridge to be greeted by his 14-year-old son Maxim carrying flowers—a family reunion symbolic of many others since withdrawal began last May.

But the perfunctory ceremony and the blank, hollow expressions of his troops, which thin smiles could not mask, more closely caught the atmosphere. The mood of the country at large is sombre. Basically, everyone is relieved it is all over. Thoughts now are shifting to the dead and the 37,000 wounded, sacrifices which served no final purpose. The media are starting to probe the conduct of the war, from the very decision to invade in December 1979. Most painfully, the veil is being lifted on atrocities hidden from the public for a decade.

'When you send soldiers to fight on foreign soil, the public should be prepared for very unpleasant things: cruelty, bitterness and hatred,' wrote *Literaturnaya Gazeta* yesterday. 'Sooner or later you have to talk about this side of war, and not just in generalities.' The paper recounted one episode, when soldiers in an Afghan frontier zone opened fire on a car which refused to stop. Inside they found seven civilians, including three women and three young children. The driver was badly wounded, one of the women killed. The men sought instructions from headquarters. 'We don't need any prisoners,' came the reply. The soldiers killed the six survivors on the spot and buried them. The officer who gave the order received just a six-year jail sentence even though, the paper noted, 'this wasn't his only crime'.

Not a few who survived must take home similar memories. For those who did not, there is a different bitterness. *Komsomolskaya Pravda* quoted a mother who lost her son. 'They sent him off urging him to do his "internationalist duty". But what sort of duty was it, I often ask myself—and to whom?' Such are the thoughts now in everyone's mind.

18.2 US National Security Review 12, March 1989

In spite of improving relations with the Soviet Union, the new US administration of President George Bush was not sure if it could trust the process to continue. Here is an excerpt from Bush's instructions to his advisers in March 1989, two months after he came to office.

Throughout the post-war era, we have successfully provided for the security of the United States and for the furtherance of our security interests in the world by following a broad national defense strategy of containment. We have sought successfully, through the combined use of all elements of our national power, and in concert with our Allies, to prevent the Soviet Union from dominating the concentrations of industrial power and human capacity that are Western Europe and East Asia, and to protect our common security interests in other regions of the world. Central to this broad strategy have been the concepts of deterrence and flexible response. To deter potential adversaries, we have had to make clear that we, and our Allies, have the means and the will to respond effectively to coercion or aggression. But, our policy has been to avoid specifying exactly what our response would be, confronting potential adversaries instead with a broad range of potential responses. Within that range of responses, U.S. general purpose forces have provided the military capabilities that have made credible the conventional component of our national security strategy, and U.S. nuclear forces have served as the ultimate guarantors of our security.

Partly due to the success of this national security strategy, a new set of challenges and uncertainties confronts us. Our rebuilding of American military strength has served as an essential underpinning to our past success. We must preserve that strength as the underpinning for out future efforts. Changes in Soviet domestic and foreign policies, including some announced but not yet implemented, are hopeful signs. But it would be reckless to dismantle our military strength and the policies that have helped make the world less dangerous, and foolish to assume that all dangers have disappeared or that any apparent diminution is irreversible.

Therefore, I hereby direct a review of our basic national defense strategy. The review should produce a series of reports, as described below. These reports will be presented *seriatim* to the National Security Council for review and discussion. Following this discussion, I anticipate providing specific decisions and guidance that will better focus the remaining parts of the review, and, perhaps, identification of new issues for further study. The goal is a sound, thoughtful, iterative process that will constitute a careful, yet timely, review of our national defense strategy, of the principal forces that will be available to support that strategy, and of the contribution that can be made by arms control policy.

I do not expect this review to invent a new defense strategy for a new world. On the contrary, I believe that our fundamental purposes are enduring and that the broad elements of out current strategy—our Alliances, our military capabilities—remain sound. This defense review should assess how, with limited resources, we can best maintain our strength, preserve our Alliances, and meet our commitments in this changing but still dangerous world.

I. *Current U.S. Defense Posture and Key Trends and Uncertainties*: As a baseline for the review, this section should briefly describe current U.S. defense strategy and U.S. military forces. It should then analyze key trends and uncertainties that have affected and/or may in the next five to ten years affect the appropriateness and effectiveness of our national defense strategy. These trends and uncertainties should include but not be limited to the following:

Soviet Union
Do we expect major technological surprises in Soviet general purpose forces, strategic nuclear forces or in the area of strategic defense that could significantly reduce the effectiveness of the U.S. deterrent? Could we detect such developments? Could the Soviet Union compete effectively in a technological arms race in these areas, or offset U.S. technological advances by other means? (...)

II. *Force Posture Issues in a Constrained Resource Environment*: This section must begin with a recognition that our ability to meet our defense objectives and to pursue our defense strategy will be significantly affected by resources available for our military forces. Clearly, a dramatic increase in the projected threat would require additional resources, and a reduction in the threat (through unilateral action by adversaries or negotiated arms control arrangements) would enhance our ability to meet our objectives and pursue our strategy within existing resources. Under the budget guidance I have issued for the next four years, there will be difficult choices to make regarding priorities. Because constrained resources will demand that the U.S. take advantage of its traditional and enduring strengths while exploiting new opportunities, this section should also focus on how we can provide high value, competitive leverage from our defense investments in the 1990s.

This section of the study should address what combination of military assets within my 4-year budget guidance provides the most effective deterrent. It should also provide both a mid-term (5-year) and a longer-term perspective on the impact of specific force posture decisions on our relative ability, given those decisions, to respond to unanticipated changes in the projected threat. Specifically, we need to keep in mind what our defense capability will be at the end of the next five years vis-à-vis our national defense objectives and strategy. The analysis in this section should reflect the substantial uncertainties in the current international environment and the potential need at the end of five years' time to meet new and adverse trends in the threat. How reversible are any decisions we may make now to reduce force structure?

18.3 The Communist Crackdown in Beijing, June 1989

While some Communist regimes in Europe were preparing to negotiate with the opposition, the Chinese Communist leaders struck hard against its opponents. Here is a conversation within the ageing Chinese leadership on the eve of the crackdown on the student demonstrators in Tiananmen Square, Beijing, 4 June 1989.

DENG XIAOPING: 'Did you see that Zhao [Ziyang] went to Tiananmen and spoke? Did you hear what he said? Tears were streaming down his face, and he really tried to look mistreated. He's flouted Party principles here—very undisciplined.'

YANG SHANGKUN: 'Something seemed very wrong about the tone he assumed—as if he wanted to stop working or something. He said he was "old, and didn't matter any more." Doesn't this amount to dragging Party differences out into the open? He just got through asking for three day's leave from the Politburo Standing Committee, claiming to be ill, but I'm afraid he's getting more stubborn about his opinions.'

DENG XIAOPING: 'You know that I've taken a lot of heat inside the Party since this whole thing broke out (...) [Li] Xiannian told me this was the voice of a second headquarters inside the Party, and he wanted me to say something about it. Later Chen Yun, Xiannian, and others telephoned me with their views time and again. In their view, the students went to Tiananmen because the Center let it happen, and we should do something about it. But he [Zhao] was completely uncooperative—he didn't even show a sign of wanting to cooperate. I had to do what I did. He really was wandering farther and farther off.'

YANG SHANGKUN: 'I still think I should try to get him to come to the big meetings tonight. We shouldn't let things get set in stone.'

DENG XIAOPING: 'It's up to him. Our economy has improved a lot in recent years. The people have food to eat, and clothes to wear—as anybody can see. The economy is still the base; if we didn't have that economic base, the farmers would have risen in rebellion after only ten days of student protests—never mind a whole month. But as it is, the villages are stable all over the country, and the workers are basically stable too. This is the fruit of reform and opening. When economic reform reaches a certain point, you have to have political reform to accompany it. You know, I've never opposed political reform. But you have to consider the realities, you have to think about how many of the old comrades in the Party can accept it right now. You can't eat yourself fat in a day. It's not that easy. I'm old, and if somebody wants to say I'm senile, fine, confused, fine—but for somebody my age inside the Party, I don't think I'm conservative. Am I hanging on to power?'

YANG SHANGKUN: 'If that were true, you could have become Party chairman when Hua Guofeng lost power. You didn't have to name Hu Yaobang for the post.'

DENG XIAOPING: 'These last few days I've been thinking. I've never been formally number 1 in the Party, but everybody keeps hanging around me, showing me deference. I have to give the nod on every important decision. I carry too much weight, and that's not good for the Party or the state. I should think about retiring. But how can I, right now? With all this lying before us, how could I retire? Would Xiannian, Wang Zhen, and the others agree? Stepping down is not all that easy, but our Party does need new faces and new blood.'

YANG SHANGKUN: 'The people will remember your achievements, Comrade Xiaoping. I also think they will understand and accept your decision on martial law.'

DENG XIAOPING: 'How is the security guard work going?'

YANG SHANGKUN: 'We've already strengthened the guard around the Central state organs and the homes of the Central leading comrades. Some of the troops will enter Beijing this evening. Don't you think, for security, that you should move into Zhongnanhai for a while?'

DENG XIAOPING: 'I've never thought of going back ever since I moved out. I'm not going anywhere. It's fine here.'

YANG SHANGKUN: 'General Xu Haiding has a son named Xu Qinxian who is chief of the Thirty-Eighth Army. Yesterday, he got orders from the Central Military Commission, he said he wouldn't be able to carry them out. But Zhou Yibing and others from the Beijing Military District have just set this right.'

DENG XIAOPING: 'No military man can disobey orders, and Xu Haidong's son is no exception. You can take care of the military questions; just be sure discipline is strict and thinking is unified.'

18.4 Poland Gets a Non-Communist Prime Minister, August 1989

In August 1989 Eastern Europe got its first non-Communist prime minister since the late 1940s, when Tadeusz Mazowiecki took over the Polish government after an unsuccessful Communist attempt at manipulating the elections. While some Poles saw the change as the fulfillment of all they had fought for during more than two generations, others were impatient for better living conditions. Here is a report from the Independent *describing the new premier's first meeting with the workers of Gdansk on 21 August 1989.*

Tadeusz Mazowiecki, who will this week become the Soviet bloc's first non-Communist Prime Minister, yesterday chose an appropriate venue for his public debut as Poland's new leader. A crowd of around 2,000 cheered when he appeared with Solidarity's leader, Lech Walesa, in Gdansk, where the union was born nine years ago this month.

Mr Mazowiecki, the Catholic editor of the Solidarity weekly and a senior adviser to the Solidarity leader since the heady days of 1980, attended mass with Mr Walesa in the packed St Brygida's, effectively Solidarity's parish church. The congregation applauded the two as they arrived and waved the victory sign they had shown so defiantly throughout martial law. Now the v-sign seemed no longer for a victory still to be fought for, but for a victory achieved.

Mr Mazowiecki was in Gdansk for a meeting of the Solidarity leadership, which formally approved his nomination and discussed new strategy. General Wojciech Jaruzelski, Poland's President, had announced his support for Mr Mazowiecki's candidacy on Saturday. The irony escaped nobody: it was General Jaruzelski who was responsible for jailing his new prime minister for a year when the tanks first tried to crush Solidarity eight years ago. Parliament will vote on the candidacy on Wednesday. But, with the support of the Communists, their ex-allies and Solidarity, the vote is a foregone Conclusion—barring another of the extraordinary upsets which have become a regular feature of Polish politics in recent weeks.

Already there were hints of the trouble Mr Mazowiecki will face. He and Mr Walesa were cheered as they raised their hands in a joint victory salute, but members of the radical splinter group, Fighting Solidarity, protested against the deal that Solidarity has made. They shouted slogans such as: 'We don't want a prime minister, we want bread' and 'Down with price rises' Mr Walesa retorted: 'We can fight. We can shout. But will that give us bread?' Mr Mazowiecki, who described Mr Walesa as 'the creator of the historic event that has taken place', told the crowd: 'I know that Poland needs bread more than a prime minister. But we must get rid of the sense of hopelessness. We must believe that Poland could live better.'

Dissatisfaction at continued economic hardship is certain to damage Solidarity's popularity in coming months. Perhaps even more serious is the question of what the humiliated Communist Party will do. Its place-men still occupy Poland's main administrative posts and could make trouble for the new government. The weekend edition of the Communist Party daily, *Trybuna Ludu*, ran a front page story which accused Solidarity of breaking the round table agreement which led to the June elections.

Solidarity agreed to what was effectively a rigged election, with only 35 per cent of seats in the main parliamentary chamber freely contested. The Communists had not thought their allies—the traditionally tame Peasants Party and Democratic Party—could defect to Solidarity's side, permitting a coalition. Hence the present cries of betrayal: we made sure Solidarity would lose the election and now they have won, the hardliners say. After a plenary session of the Communist Party Central Committee on Saturday, one member, Slawomir Wiatr, said the two ministerial portfolios Solidarity had offered the Communists—Defence and Interior—were 'not enough' for a coalition. He insisted, however, there would be 'no bargaining'.

The crowd in Gdansk was optimistic. 'This is what we fought for. We're full of hope,' said one man. But there is still caution. 'If they've got the military—then what?' asked a woman. 'They can still go against the people.'

18.5 The Opening of Hungary's Borders, September 1989

In September 1989, after secret negotiations with West Germany, Hungary opened its borders, allowing East Germans who had come there in hope of reaching the West an opportunity to escape. Here is a report from the British newspaper the Financial Times *describing the situation at the border on 11 September.*

Thousands of East Germans this morning began flooding out of Hungary to start new lives in the West after Budapest lifted border restrictions on its frontier with Austria, writes Judy Dempsey in Vienna and Andrew Fisher in Frankfurt.

The first wave of more than 6,000 refugees left in battered cars from crowded camps in Hungary just after midnight.

Mr Gyula Horn, Hungarian Foreign Minister, said that any of an estimated 60,000 East German tourists in Hungary would also be allowed to leave. The decision followed an announcement last night by Hungary's reform-minded authorities that they would 'temporarily suspend' a bilateral agreement signed with East Germany 20 years ago, which committed the Hungarian authorities to return to East Germany those citizens who tried to cross to the West via Hungary without proper documents.

East Germany immediately denounced the decision as direct interference in its internal affairs. It accused Hungary of having broken valid treaties and agreements in letting the refugees go to Austria on their way to West Germany.

In a statement released through the official ADN news agency, the East Berlin Government said 'an organised trade in humanity' was now being carried out under the excuse of humanitarian considerations.

It added its regret that Hungarian officials had been misled into supporting 'this action prepared at arms' length by West Germany.'

In contrast Mr Hans-Dietrich Genscher, the West German Foreign Minister, called the Hungarian decision 'an act of humanity'. He said that no-one gave up their homeland lightly, adding that East Germans were not leaving mainly for material reasons.

'We, who have shared the anxiety of the (East) Germans in the camps in Hungary, will not forget this decision taken by Hungary on its own responsibility. It would be wrong to see material reasons as the main cause for people wanting to leave East Germany. Lack of perspective and of opportunities for self-development were much more important factors.' These problems could only be solved in and by East Germany, Mr Genscher said. In a Europe now characterised by reform, the refusal to reform led to self-isolation.

He emphasised that West Germany still wanted good and close co-operation with East Germany.

A Hungarian government statement released last night by MTI, the Hungarian news agency, stated that 'in the handling of the affairs of those wishing to resettle, the Government of the Hungarian People's Republic was all the time governed by the accepted principles of human rights and humanitarian aspects that are enforced in its policy'.

The Hungarian authorities had been reluctant to allow the East Germans to travel without hindrance to the West until Bonn and East Berlin resolved the issue of emigration.

'The talks between the Democratic Republic of Germany and the Federal Republic of Germany ended in failure,' the government statement said, adding, 'meanwhile the number of GDR citizens refusing to return home and seeking to leave for West Germany increased continuously in Hungary. An alarming situation has emerged on the Hungaro-Austrian border, involving an increasing number of illegal border crossings . . .'

Thousands of East Germans have tried to escape to the West through Hungary since May, when the authorities began to dismantle the barbed wire fence marking the border with neutral Austria.

During the summer months, more than 200,000 East Germans spent their holidays in Hungary. Hundreds crossed the border into Austria illegally and obtained travel documents from the West German embassy in Vienna. Those caught by Hungarian border guards could have been sent directly back to East Germany, where the likelihood that they would be free to travel in future to Hungary would be ruled out.

Instead, the Hungarian authorities, with the assistance of the West German Red Cross and Maltese Cross, set up special camps for at least 6,000 East Germans. Many of the refugees had been expected to be transported to West Germany a fortnight ago, but it appears the Hungarian authorities were under pressure from East Germany not to let them go.

'Both we and the authorities in East Berlin feared that Hungary would become a transit for thousands more East Germans and indeed other East Europeans,' a senior Hungarian official said earlier this week.

The Hungarian authorities last night instructed its police and border guards 'to let the GDR citizens staying in Hungary and wishing to leave for a third country to leave Hungary with East German documents.'

The Austrian authorities, with the assistance of the International Red Cross, will provide 30 buses to transport those East Germans staying at one of the camps in Zarna, on the edge of Lake Balaton in central Hungary. The Red Cross will send another 30 buses to Budapest, while other refugees will travel in their own cars.

But Hungarian officials yesterday privately admitted that although the problem had been 'temporarily resolved, real headaches lay ahead with our relations with our socialist neighbours.'

18.6 The Fall of the Berlin Wall, November 1989

After large demonstrations against the regime in many German cities, the new leaders of the East German Communist Party agreed to allow the people of East Berlin to visit across the Wall. But the East Berliners would not wait for an orderly transition. On 9 November tens of thousands forced their way to the Wall, and the border guards—demor-

20. Unstoppable reform. (Nicholas Garland, *The Independent*, 20 December 1989). Reprinted by permission. Photo supplied by The Centre for the Study of Cartoons and Caricature, University of Kent.

alized and with no clear orders—let them through. Here is an excerpt from the American historian Robert Darnton's diary for that week in November.

On the morning after, November 10, when both Berlins woke up wondering whether the first flood through the Wall had been a dream, the West Berlin tabloid *Volksblatt* ran two headlines, shoulder to shoulder, on its front page: 'The Wall is Gone' and 'Bonn Demands Destruction of the Wall.'

Both were right. The Wall is there and it is not there. On November 9, it cut through the heart of Berlin, a jagged wound in the middle of a great city, the Great Divide of the Cold War. On November 10, it had become a dance floor, a picture gallery, a bulletin board, a movie screen, a videocassette, a museum, and, as the woman who cleaned my office put it, 'nothing but a heap of stone.' The taking of the Wall, like the taking of the Bastille, transformed the world. No wonder that a day later, in Alexanderplatz, East Berlin, one conqueror of the Wall marched in a demonstration with a sign saying simply, '1789–1989.' He had helped dismantle the central symbol around which the postwar world had taken shape in the minds of millions.

To witness symbolic transformation on such a scale is a rare opportunity, and it raises many questions. To begin with the most concrete: What happened between November 9 and 12, and what does it mean?

The destruction of the Wall began in the early evening of Thursday, November 9, soon after the first wave of East Berliners, or *Ossis*, as they are called by the West Berliners here, burst upon the West, One Ossi, a young man with a knapsack on his back, somehow hoisted himself up on the Wall directly across from the Brandenburg Gate. He sauntered along the top of it, swinging his arms casually at his sides, a perfect target for the bullets that had felled many other wall jumpers, like Peter Fechter, an eighteen-year-old construction worker, who was shot and left to bleed to death a few feet in front of Checkpoint Charlie on August 17, 1962. Now, twenty-seven years later, a new generation of border guards took aim at a new kind of target and fired—but only with power hoses and without much conviction. The conqueror of the Wall continued his promenade, soaked to the skin, until at last the guards gave up. Then he opened his knapsack and poured the water toward the East, in a gesture that seemed to say, 'Good-bye to all that' (...)

Of course, it is very difficult for a visitor from the West to know what people are really thinking in the East. But at a time of popular uprising, voices are raised and they can be heard. Few East Germans have clamoured for reunification with the Federal Republic, despite the blandishments of Chancellor Kohl. The East Germans probably want what they say they want in the banners they carry in their demonstrations. Although the banners lend themselves to slogans, they provide a running commentary on the events as they have been since the 'fall' of the Wall from the East:

> 'Let the wall be painted on both sides.'
> 'We are the people, and we are millions.'
> 'No more wall in the head.'
> 'Travel, yes. Beg, no.'
> 'Change the border to a nature preserve:
> '1 national park and 2 states.'

Since the name of the new general secretary of the Communist Party, Egon Krenz, lends itself to punning with the word for border (*Grenze*), the signs show how the East Germans are playing with the notions of politics and boundaries:

> 'Reforms, but without limits [*Krenz*]' (*Reformen—aber unbekrenzt*).
> 'At last we see through' (an allusion to the cracks in the wall and also to Krenz, whose eyes appear above the lettering).

On the Western side, the wall carries its own commentary, because it has been covered with layers of graffiti for years. The bottom layers of the palimpsest contain some witticisms, but they lack the bite of the word play in the East:

'Tear along dotted line.'
'Make love not wall.'

The Western Wall has been taken over by tourists, who often treat it as a neutral surface for spray paint:

'Lisa ti amo'

Or whose high-mindedness says little about the divisions of Berlin:

'Essex University condemns all forms of political oppression.'

In places the palimpsest reads like a dialogue, in which the present answers the past with a comforting reflection: the Wall has fallen, even though it is standing before your eyes as a surface on which the writer sprays his assertion of its nonexistence:

'A pity that concrete doesn't burn.'
'It falls, though.'

'This wall will fall.'
'We saw it fall, Nov. '89.'

The graffiti sound triumphant, even when they joke, as in the message sprayed near Checkpoint Charlie:

'Charlie's retired. 10 Nov. 1989.'

18.7 The Trial of Ceauşescu, December 1989

Not everywhere in Eastern Europe was the fall of the Communist regimes peaceful and non-violent. In Romania, where the leader Nikolae Ceauşescu had combined independence from Moscow with increasingly dictatorial methods at home, the regime was overthrown by force, and some of its leaders executed. Here is an excerpt from the interrogation of Ceauşescu and his wife just before their execution by firing squad on Christmas Day 1989.

PROSECUTOR: For 25 years you humiliated the population. For 25 years all you did was talk.

CEAUŞESCU: I do not recognise any court. I recognise only the great National Assembly. This is a coup d'etat.

PROSECUTOR: We are judging you in accordance with the constitution of the country. This is not the time to give us lessons. We know very well what we have to do, and we know the law.

CEAUŞESCU: I will not reply to any question.

PROSECUTOR: The accused and his wife had luxurious personal arrangements, gave extravagant receptions and the people had only 200 grams of salami on presentation of an identity card. You pillaged the people and even today you deny it. He doesn't want to speak; he is a coward. We know everything. Representatives of the legal system, chairman of the court, members of the court, we are going to try Nicolae Ceauşescu and Elena Ceauşescu who carried out acts incompatible with human rights, who acted against the people. For the crimes which he perpetrated against his victims, I urge the death sentence. (The charges are read).

CEAUŞESCU: I won't sign anything.

PROSECUTOR: You are aware of the situation in the country—lack of medicines, of food, of electricity, of heating in homes. Who ordered genocide in Timisoara? Who gave orders to fire on the crowd in Bucharest? Even now innocent people are being fired on. Who are the fanatics who are shooting?

CEAUŞESCU: I will not reply. No one fired on the palace square. No one has been killed.

PROSECUTOR: Today there are more than 64,000 victims in all the towns. You have reduced the people to poverty. There are educated people, true geniuses, who have left the country to escape you. Who are the foreign mercenaries who are shooting? Who brought them here?

ELENA CEAUŞESCU: This is a provocation.

PROSECUTOR: Her, she is more talkative.

ELENA: Yes.

PROSECUTOR: Here we have the illiterate genius who didn't know how to speak, who didn't know how to read.

ELENA: I wonder what my intellectual colleagues in this country will say when they hear that.

CEAUŞESCU: I will speak only before the great National Assembly and before the working class. Before this coup d'etat I will not reply. It is you who brought in mercenaries. We have another organ of power. Nobody in the country recognises you. That is why the people are still fighting today. I accuse you for organising this coup d'etat with foreign help.

PROSECUTOR: You say that the coup d'etat was carried out by foreign agents?

CEAUŞESCU: I, simple citizen, with the hope that one day you will tell the truth (…)

PROSECUTOR: You know that you have been stripped, and her as well, of all your powers and functions of state and of government?

BOTH ACCUSED: Yes.

CEAUŞESCU: You must respect the process of law, I am the President of Romania and supreme commander of the army. I desire nothing, I am a simple citizen.

PROSECUTOR: Simple citizen or president?

ELENA: What a masquerade, those who organised the coup d'etat.

PROSECUTOR: Why did you humiliate the people? Peasants who made bread came into the towns to buy bread. Why did you starve the people?

CEAUŞESCU: I am not replying. But I want to say, as a simple citizen, that the people had 200 kilos of wheat per person and not per family.

PROSECUTOR: It is false, it is a lie.

CEAUŞESCU: Pardon?

PROSECUTOR: You wrote one thing on paper, but the reality was something else. You have thought of that? The plan for the destruction of villages, you have thought about that?

CEAUŞESCU: Never in the villages was there such wealth as today. I have built hospitals, schools—no country in the world has such things (…)

PROSECUTOR: For how long did the Romanian people have to put up with you, with the fear of being arrested at any time, with the fear of being drugged and taken into mental asylums? Your greatest fault was to organise a crowd, after the crimes of Timisoara. You took the ignoble decision to mass the crowd.

ELENA: They say that children were killed, it isn't true.

CEAUŞESCU: You are betraying the people, you are destroying the independence of Romania.

PROSECUTOR: It is not possible to discuss with you, we are going to deliberate. (The sound of chairs moving).

ELENA: No dear. Don't stand up. We are human beings.

CEAUŞESCU: I recognise neither defeat nor anything.

ELENA: No court. I sign nothing. I have struggled for the people since I was 14, and the people are our people.

PROSECUTOR: We consider that the accused, on the basis of articles 162, 163, 165 and 357 of the penal code are guilty, and the exceptional military court announces today, December 25, the sentence sought: confiscation of all property and capital punishment. (The camera switches to show two bodies on a pavement and a bullet hole in Ceauşescu's head).

18.8 The Malta Summit, December 1989

When presidents Bush and Gorbachev met at Malta towards the end of 1989, Europe had already changed beyond recognition. Here is an excerpt from their conversation on 2 December 1989.

GEORGE BUSH: (…) Since the idea of this summit was proposed many important events have been taking place in the international arena. I assume that during the forthcoming exchange we will be able to share our views of these changes, not only in Eastern Europe, but also in other regions, in order to improve our mutual understanding of where we stand. I am in favor of not only an exchange in the presence of our delegations, but only on eye-to-eye basis. I believe we should meet more often.

MIKHAIL GORBACHEV: I agree. I have a feeling that we have already talked, and this meeting is the continuation of our useful conversations.

GEORGE BUSH: Precisely (...) Concerning our attitude toward perestroika. I would like to say as clearly as possible that I agree completely with what you said in New York: The world would be better if perestroika succeeds. Not long ago there was considerable doubt about this in the United States. Back in New York [in December 1988] you said there were elements that did not wish for the success of perestroika. I cannot say that there are no such elements in the United States. But I can definitely say that serious, thinking people in the United States do not share such opinions. These shifts in public mood in the United States are affected by the changes in Eastern Europe, the whole process of perestroika (...) I would like now to lay out a number of positive initiatives that, in our opinion, could in general outline directions for our joint work to prepare an official summit in the United States (...)

[Bush also touched on regional issues, including the position of the United States with regard to the situation in Central America. Then he proposed to discuss the issues of disarmament.]

GEORGE BUSH: We would like to inquire if it is possible for the Soviet Union to publish roughly the same amount of data on the Soviet military budget as we do in the United States. I believe that our publications give a rather comprehensive impression about what kind of military activities are undertaken in our country. I am sure that your intelligence services can confirm this authoritatively.

MIKHAIL GORBACHEV: They report to me, on the contrary, that you do not publish everything.

GEORGE BUSH: I am convinced that the publication of more detailed data on military budgets, on a mutual basis, would encourage trust in this sphere (...)

MIKHAIL GORBACHEV: (...) I would like to share with you some of my thoughts of a philosophical nature. I believe it is important for us both to discuss which lessons should be drawn from past experience, from the Cold War (...)

Not everything that has taken place should be considered in a negative light. For 45 years we have been managing to avoid a big war. This single fact alone says that not everything was bad in the past. Nevertheless, one conclusion is obvious—the reliance on force, on military superiority and the arms race that stemmed from it, did not withstand the test. And our two countries seem to realize it better than anyone else. To no avail was the ideological confrontation which kept us busy maligning each other. We reached a dangerous brink. And it is good that we managed to stop. It is good that mutual trust emerged between our two countries (...)

Cold War methods, methods of confrontation suffered a strategic defeat. We have come to this realization. And common people have realized this, perhaps even better. I do not want to preach here. People simply interfere into policy making. Ecological problems, problems of preservation of natural resources, problems with regard to bad consequences of technological progress. And all this is understandable, essentially this is a question of survival. And this kind of public mood is strongly affecting us, politicians.

Therefore, we together—the U.S.S.R. and the U.S.—can do a lot on this stage to change radically our old approaches. We had already felt it in our contacts with the Reagan administration. And this process continues today. Look how we opened ourselves to each other (...)

18.9 Mitterrand and Thatcher on German Unification, December 1989

Both French and British leaders were privately still suspicious of Germany and wanted to postphone full unification between its two parts. Here are some statements by French president Franqis Mitterrand and excerpts from his conversation with British prime minister Margaret Thatcher at the end of 1989, excerpted from the diaries of Mitterrand's adviser Jacques Attali.

10 November 1989. While Michel Rocard, in Paris, greets the regained peace with enthusiasm, Mitterrand comments, acerbically, in private: 'Peace! How can he speak of peace? It is the opposite that awaits us! It is clear that he will never understand anything about foreign policy! Gorbachev will never accept going further. Or he will be replaced by a tougher [leader]. These people are playing with a world war, without seeing it.'

15 November 1989 [Mitterrand at the meeting of the French Defence Council, after being presented with current nuclear strategy] 'The present situation is perhaps more dangerous than before. It may lead to the reawakening of nationalities. The FRG, in the very long run, will it not take more than the GDR?'

28 November 1989 [Mitterrand, after receiving Kohl's proposals for the creation of a German confederation] 'But he did not tell me anything! Told me nothing! I will never forget it! Gorbachev will be furious; he will not let it happen, it is impossible. I do not need to oppose it, the Soviets will do it for me. Think about it, they will never accept this big Germany confronting them. In fact, Kohl agrees with the GDR: he does not want commissions to govern the common interests of the two Germanies. But he does not talk about modifying the political status of the Germanies. He will not get anything from me on this before European unity has progressed further. And in addition the GDR will not have it. It is the Prussians. They do not want to be under Bavarian control.'

8 December 1989 [EU summit in Strasbourg; private conversation between Mitterrand and British prime minister Margaret Thatcher]

M: In Kiev, Gorbachev seemed very tough to me, much tougher than I have just told the Germans.

T: The Four need to get together as soon as possible. In the GDR, people are increasingly calling for reunification. If that is what happens, it will present Gorbachev with a problem that he cannot control. This must be prevented by the actions of the CSCE [Conference on Security and Cooperation in Europe] and the Four Powers. The East Germans do not take the Four enough into consideration. They have forgot that it is thanks to us that Berlin is free. Kohl has no idea of what feelings come up in Europe on hearing about reunification. Germany is divided because it was the Germans who have imposed the most terrible of wars on us. Germany becomes more dominant in Europe from one day to the next. It is necessary for us to meet regularly to create a counterweight to Germany. One has make sure that she will not dominate, as Japan does. Douglas Hurd has spoken to Genscher about a meeting of the Four. He is very afraid that it will be about Berlin. Gorbachev must be very uneasy at the moment. If the crazy Germans attack the Soviet bases there will be terrible consequences.

M: When we spoke, Gorbachev was much tougher on Germany than he has been earlier. He recounted his conversation with Genscher. He talked about a German *diktat*. All of this must lead to excitement in the GDR where Soviet soldiers live with their families. The anger over the Germans has come back. But Gorbachev does not have any better means than we do; for psychological reasons, he can no longer use his divisions.

T: You are right. He can no longer, because of the recent developments in Poland. (She says this with a sense of regret.)

M: The Germans must think about this themselves if they are to move forward. The liberal party [FDP] has criticised Kohl's line, which is really easy to criticise. Willy Brandt has also expressed views close to ours. More reasonable forces are making themselves known in Germany. Kohl is speculating in the natural course of the German people, he wants to be the one who encourges it. Are there many Germans who will have enough character to resist these pressures? They have never found their borders, they have never had a destiny . . .

(The British Prime Minster opens her handbag and takes out two well-worn maps of Europe, cut out from a British magazine. The first one shows the the

European borders at the beginning of World War II, the second those that were drawn in Europe in 1945. She points to Silesia, Pomerania, East Prussia.) She says: They will take all of this, and Czechoslovakia.

M: Speeding up this process is really very dangerous.

T: Kohl will encourage it, he will inflame it! We have to place some limits on the Germans or that may really happen. They will make Berlin their capital again whatever happens.

M: Yes, and Gorbachev cannot prevent it any more than the United States [can].

T: The United States will not prevent it. There is a very strong pro-German lobby in America.

M: The American ambassador in Bonn, Vernon Walters, talks about reunification in five years. We do not have any means of power confronted with Germany. One is in the same situation as the French and British leaders before the war, who could not react to anything. We must not return to the situation at Munich!

T: The United States will do nothing, because they want to make major cuts in their defense budget and they adjust their foreign policy in accordance with that. Bush has said that if there is room for a second significant reduction of conventional forces in Europe, that is what counts. We have to look at his present policies. There is much instability at the moment. We must put together a communique from here that is very firm on the borders in the Europe. Genscher will be on our side.

M: I said to Genscher: 'We are friends and allies; but what is happening [is] that we are preparing a new alliance between France, Great Britain and the Soviet Union against Germany, just like in 1913. You have 90 million inhabitants, the USSR turns towards us, and you will be circled in.'

T: Gorbachev will no longer agree to arms reductions if Germany becomes to strong.

M: We must discuss with the Germans and respect the treaties.

T: First and foremost one must respect the borders. And then, when there has been fifteen years of democracy in the GDR, one may begin to talk of reunification.

M: We must create special relations between France and Great Britain just as in 1913 and 1938.

T: In 1914, we British could have remained outside the war, if there had not been such an agreement. A message from Gorbachev is on its way; in it, the Soviets propose a meeting of the Four. That is good. But the USSR may change. The USSR is now the only country in the East where there is not a multi-party system.

M: I am not so sure. The danger is that the USSR may be getting a nationalist and militarist multi-party regime.

T: There are too many issues that come up at the same time! It is not just a

German affair. If Germany controls events, she will get Eastern Europe in her power, just as Japan has done in the Pacific, and that wil be unacceptable from our point of view. The others must join together to avoid it.

18.10 James Baker and George Bush on US–Soviet Diplomacy, Spring 1990

In the spring of 1990 Bush and Baker grew increasingly concerned with the consequences the nationalist movements within the Soviet Union would have on Soviet-American relations and on Soviet foreign policy in general. Here are some snapshots of their inter-actions with the Soviet leaders, first from Baker's memoir and then from President Bush's (co-written with his National Security Adviser, Brent Scowcroft).

A. James Baker

My apprehensiveness grew with the arrival of Shevardnadze at Andrews Air Force Base on April 3 for a ministerial to finalize preparations for the summit. Upon his arrival, Shevardnadze compared the situation in Lithuania to an earth-quake, telling the press 'cataclysms happen not only in nature.' In three days of talks, Shevardnadze seemed utterly distracted. Even worse, he sometimes fell back on formalistic, ideological arguments or deferred to hard-liners such as Marshal Akhromeyev. Indeed, I had the image of a diplomat with a political gun to his head. Any step forward could lead to suicide.

'I have got to tell you that I am worried,' I told him in our first three-and-one-half-hour session, in which Lithuania was the only substantive topic covered. 'I am deeply and genuinely worried. We do not want to see this deteriorate, because it is going to have a direct effect on our relations. We have come so far in the last fourteen months. I do not want to see that undermined.' (…)

At one point, Shevardnadze tried to deflect me by pointing to the criticism Gorbachev was receiving. He tried to draw on our invasion of Panama to support his case. 'Of course,' he added dogmatically, 'the comparison between Panama and Lithuania is not necessarily appropriate—Panama was a different country, Lithuania is part of our country. But we still acted, and were able to act and speak with some restraint.' He hadn't raised Panama as a major problem in any of our conversations in the previous three months, yet now he was falling back on it. Moreover, he was worried about greater dangers. 'I have told U.S. reporters in the past,' he said, 'that there is no alternative to perestroika. Well, the truth is, that's a mistake. There is an alternative to perestroika. If perestroika doesn't suc-ceed, then you are going to have the destabilization of the Soviet Union. And if that happens, there will be a dictator.'

Dennis Ross interrupted to ask Shevardnadze, 'What in your eyes would it take right now to begin the process or a dialogue? What prevents it from starting now?'

'Well, speaking strictly or legally,' Shevardnadze answered, 'they will have to return to the status quo ante. Their decision has no legal force. On that basis, we will be able to discuss anything.' (...)

On Monday morning, April 23, I learned that Gorbachev's chief spokesman had said that Lithuania could keep its declaration of independence 'for history,' as long as Vilnius either rescinded the independence laws or froze them. However slight, Moscow's position was shifting. At an NSC meeting that evening, the President decided that a key goal must be to try and protect the continually improving overall relationship with the USSR. I had found little support among our European allies for stern measures to register our disapproval of Soviet coercive economic measures toward Lithuania, and hence any actions we would take would probably have to be unilateral. The President decided that 'any response should be proportional to the crime.' That meant that the U.S.–Soviet trade agreement we were finalizing would be put on hold—and the President wrote Gorbachev a letter to that effect on April 30.[2] (...)

Bonn, on a beautiful, sunny spring day in the first week of May [1990], was the site for the first ministerial meeting of Two-plus-Four [The two German states, plus the United States, the Soviet Union, Britain, and France]. (...)

Shevardnadze created the distinct impression that Moscow was more relaxed and confident that its strategy on Lithuania was working. He implied no sense of urgency, saying 'We must show patience.' Indeed, when I emphasized the importance of the Soviet's not simply talking about the need for dialogue, but actually taking steps to produce one, he said he thought one would be possible in time. He referred to the growing debate among the Lithuanian leadership over the need for compromise, and implied that they would come around. He repeated that the Soviets would be willing to start a dialogue if the Lithuanian leaders announced that they were freezing their declaration of independence and the laws that followed from it, and were willing to come to Moscow to begin talks. But he said the initiative, the first step, had to come from Vilnius.

'Sometimes I feel,' I said, 'that when I look at this situation in Lithuania, there are two ships that are passing in the night, that they are going right past each other. What I see is both you and the Lithuanians saying the right things about resolving the problem through peaceful dialogue, but I also don't see a dialogue beginning.' I asked if Landsbergis and the rest of the Lithuanian leadership clearly understood from the Soviets what they needed to do to get Moscow to lift its economic blockade, and what they would get in return—namely, a dialogue on independence. He said that he was confident that they did, 'but at this point, they haven't done anything. They talk, but they don't act.' He noted again that the

Kremlin would be patient and 'wait a little longer' as the Lithuanians debated the issue. I warned him that our room for maneuver was limited and raised the possibility that we might be pushed to economic sanctions. He said that wouldn't be a tragedy, but it would be unfortunate, as it would indicate where our relationship was headed. He also handed me a letter from Gorbachev to the President that made the same point: 'I wish to say quite frankly that the emerging retreat of the U.S. administration from its former reasonable position cannot possibly do a good turn either to the normalization of the situation in Lithuania or to Soviet–U.S. relations,' Gorbachev wrote, tellingly describing it as a problem that fell within the USSR's 'internal competence.'

B. George Bush

May 31 [1990] was a bright, hot day, and the arrival ceremony for Gorbachev was spectacular, set against the backdrop of the Washington Monument. The colourful ceremonial Revolutionary War uniforms of the Old Guard from Fort Meyer stood out against the new green grass and leaves. A military band played and honor guards from each of the services dipped their flags as Gorbachev and I reviewed them, always a moving experience for me.

Gorbachev looked well and seemed confident as he greeted me with a smile and a strong handshake, not at all tired. He was a bit tense at first, and spoke very softly. He relaxed once we got to the Oval Office, and was almost jovial as we sat down on the white armchairs near the fireplace, under the Gilbert Stuart portrait of George Washington.

Our talk that morning was largely philosophical, the kind each of us hoped to have at Malta. Gorbachev spoke of the need to free ourselves from old suspicions. We were at a watershed in history, he said. 'You may or may not agree, but the confrontation we got into after World War II wasted our time and energy, while others—the former vanquished—were moving ahead.' The world was changing in dramatic ways. The United States, despite its power, could not lead the world by playing itself and playing 'cards' (such as China) against each other was not the way to go. There was a 'regrouping' in the world, and U.S.–Soviet relations were vital in this process. 'The question is, can we cooperate?' he asked.

I listened carefully to his long and frank survey of the situation before us, writing notes to myself on each point. 'There is a significant change in US attitudes toward the Soviet Union, although there is an emerging suspicion,' I replied, keeping in my mind developments in Lithuania. I added that many Americans were probably not sufficiently sensitive, for example, to Soviet losses in World War II. 'As we wrestle with arms control, not only I have become more sensitive to that issue, but all my people have as well,' I continued. 'I wanted to get that comment on the table before we get, inevitably, to Germany . . . We do not want winners and losers.' Although the Soviets had problems, I wanted him to understand that as long as I was in office there would be no attempt to downgrade the position the Soviet Union rightly occupied. 'You must believe my sincerity on this point as we get into detailed issues.

'You gave me that map at Malta with the blue flags,' I continued. 'I asked the CIA to see how accurate your intelligence was. They gave you high marks . . . I told Brent that we have to convince you that these flags don't mean we are trying to surround you, to encircle the Soviet Union. Some of it we can do by words; some must be done by actions.' Germany headed the list of difficult questions before us. 'I understand you have hang-ups there which tie into the German problem. We don't want a Soviet Union that is threatened by any power. We may have very different ideas about the future of Germany. Will they return to their old ways, or have they learned and paid their dues? I am of the latter view.' After forty years, Germany was different. I didn't want to single it out in a way which threatened to make history repeat itself.

I could not ignore Lithuania. 'To the degree that we can see a commitment to your own principles of self-determination, we can cooperate,' I said. 'I have tried to conduct myself in a constrained way because I know you have big problems. But I am being hit both on my left and on my right by those who say that I am subordinating US dedication to principle.' (…)

'We are in favor of the American presence in Europe,' he said. 'But you seem to think your presence to NATO, that Germany going out of NATO will be NATO's destruction and thus the end of the US presence.' Perhaps a united Germany could have what he called 'two anchors'—that is, participate in both alliances, with the FRG in NATO and Soviet forces in the old GDR, and some kind of agreement between the two alliances (…)

I tried a new tack. I reminded Gorbachev that the Helsinki Final Act stated that all countries had the right to choose their alliances. To me, that meant Germany should be able to decide for itself what it wanted. Did he agree? To my astonishment, Gorbachev shrugged his shoulders and said, yes, that was correct.

The room became suddenly quiet. Akhromeyev and Valentin Falin looked at each other and squirmed in their seats. Bob Blackwill slipped me a note asking me whether I thought I could get Gorbachev to say that again. I nodded to him, 'I'm gratified that you and I seem to agree that nations can choose their own alliances,' I said.

'Do you and I agree that a united Germany has the right to be non-aligned, or a member of NATO, in a final document?' asked Gorbachev.

'I agree with that, but the German public wants to be in NATO,' I replied. 'But if they want out of NATO, we will respect that. They are a democracy.'

'I agree to say so publicly, that the United States and the USSR are in favor of seeing a united Germany, with a final settlement leading it up to where a united Germany can choose,' said Gorbachev.

'I would put it differently,' I said. 'We support a united Germany in NATO. If they don't want in, we will respect that.'

'I agree,' answered Gorbachev.

'With the second part?' I asked.

'With both parts,' responded Gorbachev.

'Good,' I said. 'Can we have the ministers work on it?'

'Let them work on a transition period,' said Gorbachev.

By this time, the dismay in the Soviet team was palpable. Akhromeyev's eyes flashed angrily as he gestured to Falin. They snapped back and forth in loud stage whispers in an agitated debate as Gorbachev spoke. It was an unbelievable scene, the likes of which none of us had ever seen before—virtually open rebellion against a Soviet leader. Then Shevardnadze tugged at Gorbachev's sleeve and whispered to him. Gorbachev indicated that he wanted Falin to make a presentation. Falin launched into a lengthy filibuster on why Germany in NATO was unacceptable to the Soviet people, during which Shevardnadze kept gesticulating and whispering heatedly to Gorbachev. After a few minutes of this fascinating display, Gorbachev reentered the discussion. He now tried to back away from his previous statements by calling again for a lengthy transition period, concluding with the suggestion, 'Let's let the foreign ministers pursue these issues.'

It was an obvious ploy to get out from under the controversy he had created— but then came another incredible moment. Shevardnadze refused. 'We can do that,' he said, 'but it is at the level of a President that such issues must be discussed.' Clearly, he wasn't going to be the fall guy. Gorbachev lamely continued the discussion, trying to back away from never completely repudiating his earlier statements. Appearing completely frustrated, he hit the transition period one more time and then called again for the foreign ministers to continue the discussions. This time Shevardnadze gave in.

I am not sure why Gorbachev did what he did. Perhaps he realized that our position would prevail and this was the best way to manage it within his own team. In any event, it was an amazing performance.

18.11 Kohl-Gorbachev Meetings, July 1990

In mid-July German chancellor Helmut Kohl met with Gorbachev to find a solution to the remaining problems of German reunification. For their final meeting Gorbachev invited Kohl to his birthplace in the Caucasus mountains. These are excerpts from their conversations.

15 July, Moscow

(...) [Kohl said that] he had told Foreign Minister [Eduard] Shevardnadze already yesterday on the way from the airport to the guest-house that these were historically significant years. Such years came and passed. The opportunities had to be used. If one did not act, they would be over. Bismarck once had said that you had to grab the mantle of history. PRESIDENT GORBACHEV agreed. [And said that] That statement by Bismarck was very interesting.

The CHANCELLOR continued by saying that the 1990s would be historically significant. This was particularly true for the first half of the decade that was lying ahead of us. He understood this as a special chance of the generation to which the President and he belonged, which had been too young in the Second World War to become personally guilty, but which, on the other hand, had been old enough to experience those years consciously. This was why he had once spoken of the 'mercy of late birth'. Now it was their task to use the existing chances. The generations that would follow them had had different experiences.

PRESIDENT GORBACHEV replied that he particularly wanted underline the Chancellor's thinking. He could detect similar things in the memory of the events in his own country. He, too, belonged to a generation that had experienced the war and could still remember it. He had been ten years old when the war began, and fifteen when it was over. He had committed everything to memory and he could remember these events very well. He [said that he] therefore agreed with the Chancellor's statement that their generation had a unique experience. Now great opportunities had opened up, and it was now the task of their generation to use and shape them. He [said that he] was particularly impressed by the fact that today there was less talk about who won or who lost. Together they took the notion of one world as the starting-point (...)

16 July, Archys [the Caucasus]

(...) PRESIDENT GORBACHEV continues by saying that some main principles would have to be established with the full sovereignty of Germany, namely, among others, the non-extension of NATO's military structures to the territory of the present GDR. A separate treaty should be concluded concerning the presence of the Soviet troops in the GDR.

F[OREIGN]M[INISTER] GENSCHER remarks that the concluding document had to pronounce that Germany had the right to join an alliance of its choice. It was obvious that this would be NATO.

PRESIDENT GORBACHEV desires that NATO should not be mentioned explicitly. Once Germany had full sovereignty, this was clear anyway.

The CHANCELLOR suggests to turn to the concrete issues. He once more states that according to the views of both sides the united Germany would have full sovereignty.

FM GENSCHER adds that they were also agreed that the united Germany had the right to be the member of an alliance and that this would be NATO, though that had not to be mentioned explicitly.

The CHANCELLOR summarises that the full sovereignty included the right to be a member of an alliance and that this membership meant NATO. An explicit mention in the document was therefore not necessary (…)

PRESIDENT GORBACHEV (…) calls the issue of a settlement of the Soviet troop presence on the territory of the GDR one of the most important points. It was related to the establishment of the non-extension of NATO structures to that territory. The commitment to the non-extension of NATO structures did not question the sovereignty of the united Germany. This was in the sphere of bilateral relations between the Soviet Union and Germany. A separate treaty about the troop presence had to be concluded for a certain duration.

FM GENSCHER recorded that the unified Germany had full sovereignty and that the stationing of Soviet forces on the territory of the present GDR was provided for a certain duration. The basis and pre-conditions of this stationing would be arranged in a bilateral treaty between the unified Germany and the Soviet Union.

The CHANCELLOR points out that the treaty has to worked out by November 1990. He repeats his suggestion to inform President Gorbachev of the treaty's content in a letter and to discuss and agree that content with the GDR beforehand. This bilateral agreement between the unified Germany and the Soviet Union had to be prepared already now.

PRESIDENT GORBACHEV raises as the next important point the assurance that NATO structures will not be extended to GDR territory as long as Soviet troops are stationed there. This will make it easier for him to make people in the Soviet Union understand that the unified Germany has a right to chose its alliance and that this would be NATO. It is understood that the unified Germany would remain in NATO. However, an extension of NATO territory should not take place as long as Soviet troops are in the GDR. President Gorbachev added that he needed arguments to explain the situation to the Soviet people. The suggested solution was linked to the restoration of the sovereignty of the unified Germany. The new sovereign Germany would declare that it understood the Soviet concerns and that no extension of NATO to the territory of the GDR would occur (…)

FM GENSCHER summarises: with the unification of Germany the unified Germany becomes fully sovereign. No extension of NATO structures to the territory of the present GDR would take place as long as Soviet armed forces stayed there. A bilateral treaty about the duration of the presence of those armed forces and other related issues would be concluded between the unified Germany and the Soviet Union. In addition to the Soviet armed forces on the present GDR territory, German armed forces would also be stationed there, but only such forces that were not integrated into NATO. As far as all of Berlin was concerned, the armed forces stationed there by the Four Powers should likewise remain there after the restoration of German sovereignty on the basis of bilateral agreements for the duration of the Soviet troop presence on the present GDR territory. The strength of the troops in Berlin should not be higher than before; the bilateral agreements should contain the same regulations concerning equipment and arming. The presence of the Four Power forces on the basis of bilateral agreements did not preclude the Berlin presence of German troops that were not integrated into NATO.

PRESIDENT GORBACHEV agrees to this summary. The Soviet troops would withdraw after a certain period; the unified Germany would already gain full sovereignty before. United Germany's NATO membership would not be written down explicitly. The stationing of the Federal Armed Forces was as before Germany's sovereign right. However, it had to be certain that NATO would not move into this area with nuclear weapons or NATO bases. The Soviet Union not only wanted to withdraw, it also wanted no extension of NATO territory (...)

18.12 Bush Speech in Kiev, August 1991

In August 1991 American president George Bush visited the Soviet Union. The following is an excerpt from the speech he gave to the Ukrainian Supreme Soviet (parliament) in Kiev on 1 August 1991, as the Ukrainians were debating full secession from the Soviet Union.

(...) Today, your people probe the promise of freedom. In cities and Republics, on farms, in businesses, around university campuses, you debate the fundamental questions of liberty, self-rule, and free enterprise. Americans, you see, have a deep commitment to these values. We follow your progress with a sense of fascination, excitement, and hope. This alone is historic. In the past, our nations engaged in duels of eloquent bluff and bravado. Now, the fireworks of super-power confrontation are giving way to the quieter and far more hopeful art of cooperation.

I come here to tell you: We support the struggle in this great country for democracy and economic reform. And I would like to talk to you today about how the United States views this complex and exciting period in your history, how we intend to relate to the Soviet central Government and the Republican governments.

In Moscow, I outlined our approach: We will support those in the center and the Republics who pursue freedom, democracy, and economic liberty. We will determine our support not on the basis of personalities but on the basis of principles. We cannot tell you how to reform your society. We will not try to pick winners and losers in political competitions between Republics or between Republics and the center. That is your business; that's not the business of the United States of America (…)

Some people have urged the United States to choose between supporting President Gorbachev and supporting independence-minded leaders throughout the U.S.S.R. I consider this a false choice. In fairness, President Gorbachev has achieved astonishing things, and his policies of glasnost, perestroika, and democratization point toward the goals of freedom, democracy, and economic liberty.

We will maintain the strongest possible relationship with the Soviet Government of President Gorbachev. But we also appreciate the new realities of life in the U.S.S.R. And therefore, as a federation ourselves, we want good relations— improved relations—with the Republics. So, let me build upon my comments in Moscow by describing in more detail what Americans mean when we talk about freedom, democracy, and economic liberty.

(…) freedom is not the same as independence. Americans will not support those who seek independence in order to replace a far-off tyranny with a local despotism. They will not aid those who promote a suicidal nationalism based upon ethnic hatred. We will support those who want to build democracy. By democracy, we mean a system of government in which people may vie openly for the hearts—and yes, the votes—of the public. We mean a system of government that derives its just power from the consent of the governed, that retains its legitimacy by controlling its appetite for power. For years, you had elections with ballots, but you did not enjoy democracy. And now, democracy has begun to set firm roots in Soviet soil.

(…) a free economy demands engagement in the economic mainstream. Adam Smith noted two centuries ago, trade enriches all who engage in it. Isolation and protectionism doom its practitioners to degradation and want.

I note this today because some Soviet cities, regions, and even Republics have engaged in ruinous trade wars. The Republics of this nation have extensive bonds of trade, which no one can repeal with the stroke of a pen or the passage of a law (…)

We understand that you cannot reform your system overnight. America's first system of government—the Continental Congress—failed because the States were too suspicious of one another and the central government too weak to protect commerce and individual rights. In 200 years, we have learned that freedom, democracy, and economic liberty are more than terms of inspiration. They're more than words. They are challenges.

18.13 The Soviet Coup Attempt, August 1991

Just a few weeks after Bush had left the Soviet Union, Mikhail Gorbachev was over-thrown in a Communist-led coup d'état. The first excerpt is from the confused press conference given by the new leadership on the evening of 19 August. The second is Russian leader Boris Yeltsin's defiant appeal to the army on the night of 20 August, as it was becoming clear that the coup was faltering.

A. The press conference of the State Committee for the State of Emergency

Yanaev: Ladies and gentlemen, friends and comrades: As you already know from media reports, because Mikhail Sergeevich Gorbachev is unable, owing to the state of his health, to discharge the duties of President of the USSR, the USSR Vice President has temporarily taken over the performance of the duties of the President on the basis of Article 127(7) of the USSR Constitution.

I address you today, ladies and gentlemen, at a moment that is crucial for destinies of the Soviet Union and the international situation throughout the world.

Having embarked on the path of profound reforms and having gone a considerable way in this direction, the Soviet Union has now reached a point at which it finds itself faced with a deep crisis, the further development of which could both place in question the course of reforms itself and lead to serious cataclysms in international life (…)

In many regions of the USSR, as a result of interethnic clashes, blood is being spilled, and the collapse of the USSR would have the most serious consequences, not only internally, but also internationally. In such conditions we have no alternative but to take decisive steps to stop the country from sliding into disaster (…)

Correspondent from *Pravda*: (…) The Russian Information Agency has broadcast today an appeal to the people of Russia from Yeltsin, Silaev, and Khasbulatov. In it, the events of the past night are defined as a right-wing, reactionary, anti-constitutional coup d'état. What is your reaction to this statement? (…)

Yanaev: (…) We have had contact with the leadership of many regions and territories of the Soviet Union. And I can state that, on the whole, they support the creation of the Emergency Committee and the Committee's attempts to enable the country to overcome the crisis we find ourselves in (…)

Nezavisimaia gazeta correspondent Tatiana Malkina: Could you please say whether or not you understand that last night you carried a coup d'état? Which comparison seems more apt to you—the comparison with 1917 or with 1964? [Khrushchev's removal] (…)

Yanaev: (…) As for your allegation that a coup d'état was staged last night, I would beg to disagree with you, inasmuch as we are following constitutional norms. And I assume that confirmation by the USSR Supreme Soviet of the deci-sions we have made will enable us to state that absolutely all the juridical and, so to speak, constitutional norms have been observed.

It does not seem to me correct to draw a comparison with either 1917 or 1964. I believe any analogy here is simply dangerous (…)

Associated Press: Can you please tell us whether your committee is prepared to order the use of force against civilians? And under what conditions would force be used against civilians?

Yanaev: First, I would like to do everything to ensure that the use of force against civilians is not required. We must do everything to prevent any excesses. And what we are envisaging now—some extraordinary measures—they are not at all linked with any attack on human rights. On the contrary, we want to protect human rights as much as possible. And I would like to hope very much that we will not be compelled, we will not be provoked, into using some kind of force against the civilian population.

B. Yeltsin's appeal to the army

Servicemen! Fellow countrymen! A coup d'etat has been attempted. The Presi-dent of the USSR, who is the Supreme Commander in Chief of the USSR Armed Forces, has been removed from his post. The Vice-President of the USSR, the Prime Minister of the USSR, the Chairman of the USSR State Security Com-mittee and the USSR Ministers of Defense and of Internal Affairs have become members of an unconstitutional body, thereby committing high treason—a very grave crime against the state.

The country is threatened with terror. The 'order' that the latter-day saviors of the fatherland are promising us will end in tragedy—the suppression of dissent, concentration camps, nighttime arrests. 'A better life' will remain a propaganda fraud.

Soldiers and officers of Russia! I appeal to you at this tragic moment for Russia and the whole country. Do not let yourself be caught in a web of false promises and demagogic talk about your military duty! Do not become a blind instrument of the criminal will of a group of adventurists who have flouted the Constitution and laws of USSR.

Soldiers! I appeal to you. Think about your loved ones, your friends, your people. At the difficult moment of choice, do not forget that you have taken an oath of loyalty to the people. The people against whom they are trying to turn your weapons.

You can build a throne out of bayonets, but you cannot sit on it for long. There is no return to the past, nor will there be. The conspirators' days are numbered.

Soldiers, officers and generals! An hour ago (4 P.M.) I appointed a Chairman of the RSFSR Committee of Defense Questions. He is your comrade-in-arms, Col. Gen. Konstantin Kobets. A decree has been issued according to which all territorial and other agencies of the Ministry of Defense on RSFSR territory are ordered to immediately carry out all orders of the President of the RSFSR, the RSFSR State Security Committee, the RSFSR Ministry of Internal Affairs and the RSFSR State Committee on Defense Questions.

Dark clouds of terror and dictatorship have gathered over Russia and the whole country, but they cannot become an eternal night. The law will triumph on our soil, and our long-suffering people will regain their freedom, this time once and for all.

Soldiers! I believe that in the tragic hour you will make the right choice, and that the honor and glory of Russian arms will not be stained with the blood of the people.

18.14 The Minsk Declaration, December 1991

After the collapse of the Moscow coup, all the republics of the Soviet Union moved towards independence, including Russia under Yeltsin's leadership. On 8 December 1991 the heads of state of Russia, Belarus, and Ukraine met in Minsk and declared the Soviet Union to have 'ceased to exist'. Here is their joint statement.

We, the Republic of Belarus, the Russian Federation and the Republic of Ukraine, as founder states of the Union of Soviet Socialist Republics (USSR), which signed the 1922 Union Treaty, further described as the high contracting parties, conclude that the USSR has ceased to exist as a subject of international law and a geopolitical reality. Taking as our basis the historic community of our peoples and the ties which have been established between them, taking into account the bilateral treaties concluded between the high contracting parties; striving to build democratic law-governed states; intending to develop our relations on the basis of mutual recognition and respect for state sovereignty, the inalienable right to self-determination, the principles of equality and non-interference in internal affairs, repudiation of the use of force and of economic or any other methods of coercion, settlement of contentious problems by means of mediation and other generally recognized principles and norms of international law; considering that further development and strengthening of relations of friendship, good-neighborliness and mutually beneficial co-operation between our states correspond to the vital national interests of their peoples and serve the cause of peace and security; confirming our adherence to the goals and principles of the United Nations Charter, the Helsinki Final Act and other documents of

the Conference on Security and Co-operation in Europe; and committing ourselves to observe the generally recognized internal norms on human rights and
the rights of peoples, we have agreed the following:

ARTICLE 1 The high contracting parties form the Commonwealth of Independent
States.

ARTICLE 2 The high contracting parties guarantee their citizens equal rights
and freedoms regardless of nationality or other distinctions. Each of the high
contracting parties guarantees the citizens of the other parties, and also persons
without citizenship that live on its territory, civil, political, social, economic
and cultural rights and freedoms in accordance with generally recognized international norms of human rights, regardless of national allegiance or other
distinctions.

ARTICLE 3 The high contracting parties, desiring to promote the expression,
preservation and development of the ethnic, cultural, linguistic and religious
individuality of the national minorities resident on their territories, and that of
the unique ethno-cultural regions that have come into being, take them under
their protection.

ARTICLE 4 The high contracting parties will develop the equal and mutually
beneficial co-operation of their peoples and states in the spheres of politics, the
economy, culture, education, public health, protection of the environment,
science and trade and in the humanitarian and other spheres, will promote the
broad exchange of information and will conscientiously and unconditionally
observe reciprocal obligations. The parties consider it a necessity to conclude
agreements on co-operation in the above spheres.

ARTICLE 5 The high contracting parties recognize and respect one another's territorial integrity and the inviolability of existing borders within the Commonwealth. They guarantee openness of borders, freedom of movement for citizens
and of transmission of information within the Commonwealth.

ARTICLE 6 The member-states of the Commonwealth will co-operate in safeguarding international peace and security and in implementing effective measures for reducing weapons and military spending. They seek the elimination of
all nuclear weapons and universal total disarmament under strict international
control. The parties will respect one another's aspiration to attain the status of
a non-nuclear zone and a neutral state. The member-states of the community
will preserve and maintain under united command a common military-strategic
space, including unified control over nuclear weapons, the procedure for implementing which is regulated by a special agreement. They also jointly guarantee

the necessary conditions for the stationing and functioning of and for material and social provision for the strategic armed forces. The parties contract to pursue a harmonized policy on questions of social protection and pension provision for members of the services and their families.

18.15 Gorbachev's Last Day in the Kremlin, December 1991

As result of the Minsk Declaration, Mikhail Gorbachev decided to resign as Soviet president, effecting the dissolution of the Soviet Union that the republics had decided on. Here is an excerpt from the memoirs of one of his key assistants, Andrei Grachev, describing Gorbachev's last day in office.

On December 25, the President arrived at the Kremlin later than usual and closeted himself in his office. His anteroom was strangely empty; not a single visitor was present. All the receptionists had come in at the same time (they normally alternated twenty-four-hour shifts) to sort out the books Gorbachev was taking with him and discard papers that were no longer needed (...)

Chernyaev and I had several pending matters to discuss with Gorbachev. Chernyaev needed him to sign some farewell letters that Gorbachev had decided to send to his foreign colleagues, and I was to brief him for the taping of his statement and the CNN interview that would follow.

When we went into his office at about three o'clock in the afternoon, the President wasn't there. We waited for a few minutes; then Chernyaev, anxious to send off the letters, knocked on the door of the resting room that was situated at the back of his office, behind the worktable. Gorbachev did not answer right away. Then, without opening the door, he asked what the problem was. 'Just a minute; I'll be right out.'

He appeared after about five minutes, fresh and looking fit despite a slight redness of the eyes caused by lack of sleep or the tension of the past few days. He began to sign the letters, first reading them over carefully, as he always did: to Andreotti, to Baker, and so on.

I showed him the front page of *Moscovsky Komsomolets*, whose headline was a quotation from Pushkin: 'No, I shall not die completely!'

'My soul, by the lyre, will survive me and escape corruption,' Gorbachev completed without emphasis, smiling.

Once the letters had been signed, Chernyaev left. The President and I stayed on alone. He took up the final version of his speech and, arming himself with a pen, began to read it aloud, asking me for my opinion wherever he had any doubts. He stopped at the phrase 'addressing you for the last time in the capacity of president of the USSR.'

'Chernyaev proposes that we delete "USSR,"' he said. (...)

The telephone rang. A very agitated Raisa Maximovna [Gorbachev] was calling from the dacha. Some of the new security men had come out to order her 'to remove her personal belongings from the premises of the governmental representative.' (This was Special Services jargon for the President's official residence.)

Gorbachev shoved the pages that he was annotating out of the way and immediately called the chief of security, Vladimir Redkoborody, who had been his own head of security a few days earlier. 'You're really out of line, and you'd better straighten up!' he exclaimed angrily. 'You're talking about somebody's home, here. Do I have to report all this to the press?' Redkoborody made excuses, citing orders from on high and excessive zeal from below, but in the end he promised to call off his people.

It took the President awhile to calm down. He said a few vehement words to me about 'those jerks.'

'You know, Andrei, the fact that they're acting this way makes me certain that I'm right,' he said suddenly, and with that thought, was able to regain his equanimity. He would need it that evening.

Around four o'clock, Yeltsin, in response to an inquiry from CNN, announces that he would come by Gorbachev's office at about 7:20 p.m. to take possession of the nuclear button. It had already been announced that Gorbachev would give his resignation speech at seven o'clock (...)

The studio, which was known in the Kremlin as 'room number 4,' was bustling with technicians, photographers and journalists from three television networks. Gorbachev entered the room at five minutes to seven and, greeting people he knew as he passed, made his way with some difficulty to the brightly lit table, where a microphone awaited him. He was carrying a briefcase containing his speech and the decree enacting his resignation from the post of commander in chief of the armed forces.

Gorbachev placed the decree in front of him and then asked suddenly, 'When should I sign it, before or after my statement?' He was speaking to Yakovlev and me, who were trying to manage all this chaos. Our opinions differed, and we each had our own set of reasons for one or the other approach. While we argued, Gorbachev asked me for a pen and tested it on a sheet of paper. 'I prefer a smoother-writing one,' he said. The head of the CNN crew, who was present at the taping, reached over my shoulder to offer his own pen. Gorbachev, satisfied with the instrument and paying no further attention to our discussion, placed the decree in front of him, signed it with a flourish, and set it aside. His abdication of nuclear power thus took place unnoticed by outside observers.

He gave the remaining three minutes to the photographers and reached for the text of his speech at seven o'clock on the dot. 'Dear compatriots, fellow citizens . . .' His voice sounded unnatural and hollow. It seemed on the verge of trembling, as did his chin. But as he continued to read one could see him gaining control of his emotions, aware that his words resonated with conviction and dignity.

'I leave office with anxiety,' he said at the end of his address. 'But also with hope and with faith in you, in your wisdom and your strength of mind. We are heirs to a great civilization, and it is now up to each and every one of us to ensure that this civilization is reborn to a modern, dignified new life.' He thanked all those who had struggled with him in 'a just and good cause' over the years and acknowledged that mistakes could have been avoided if better choices had been made.

I consider this one of his best speeches. When he deviated from his notes to add, 'I wish all of you the very best,' I think many people must have felt that an unpardonable and irreparable error was being made as the country and the world looked on. (...)

Gorbachev left the journalists in room number 4 and went back to his office, where Marshal Shaposhnikov was already waiting for him. Yeltsin, as promised, would arrive soon to pick up the nuclear codes. The ceremony of turning over control of the button was to be filmed by ABC, this time with Yeltsin's consent. But some bizarre news awaited Gorbachev and the film crew: Yeltsin, displeased with Gorbachev's speech, which he considered a political attack on the Russian leadership, had declared that he refused to enter the office of the former president of the Union. He proposed a meeting on neutral ground, in the Catherine Room (...)

This time it was Gorbachev's turn to be brusque: He rejected Yeltsin's proposal and announced that he would send everything that was necessary through Shaposhnikov. Two very ordinary-looking men in civilian clothes were sitting in the president's anteroom with an instrument that looked like a cellular phone. These two colonels, who accompanied the President wherever he went, were in fact the 'button,' or rather one of the elements in a complex network equipped with redundant security devices. They disappeared into the corridors in search of their new boss.

Questions

What were the feelings of Soviet soldiers on withdrawing from Afghanistan?

What were the main security concerns of the new Bush administration in early 1989?

Why did the Communist authorities in China crack down on the opposition in 1989?

Why was the new non-Communist premier of Poland met with mixed feelings by the workers in Gdansk?

Why did the opening of Hungary's borders undermine the East German regime?

What can the graffiti on the Berlin Wall tell us about those who destroyed it?

Why were the Ceauşescus executed?

Compare the Malta summit text with the text from Reykjavik. What has changed?

What was Mitterrand's main fear with regard to German reuification?

How much influence did Baker and Bush think that they could have with the Soviets?

What were their main concerns?

Why did Gorbachev accept Kohl's proposals on Germany?

What was Bush's main message to the Ukrainians?

What did the Moscow coup-makers hope to achieve? How did Yeltsin hope to stop them?

What would be the main differences between the Soviet Union and the Commonwealth of Independent States?

19

Cold War Legacies

The end of the Cold War, the collapse of the Soviet Union, and the reunification of Germany seemed to signal the dawn of a new era. Globalization, the watchword of the late twentieth and early twenty-first centuries, reflected the seemingly unstoppable spread of free markets, aided by rapidly expanding new information technology, and pushed on by the material benefits that would befall all those countries willing to join in this brave new world. As the key engine of globalization and the sole remaining superpower, the United States enjoyed what some called a 'unipolar moment', made clearer not only by the demise of the Soviet Union but also by the reduced economic challenges from Japan and Western Europe, and the fact that the United States was the only nation capable of projecting its military influence, if not always successfully, around the globe.

To most observers, the sense that capitalism had finally triumphed at the end of the twentieth century seemed irrefutable. Aside from the People's Republic of China, communism was the official ideology only in a handful of small states (such as Vietnam, Cuba, and North Korea). Moreover, even in these countries the appeal of the free market could not be held in check. China, in particular, continued on the road of economic reform. While political control remained in the hands of the Communist Party in China, the most populous country in the world was clearly being incorporated into the world economic system; the most evident signal of this was China's eventual entry into the World Trade Organization that was agreed—after a decade and a half of continuous negotiations—in the fall of 2001. Moreover, in the 1990s Vietnam, which had fought a number of wars with China since the late 1970s, adopted the Chinese model of economic liberalization (coupled with continued political control by the Communist Party). Cuba and, in particular, North Korea, became increasingly marginalized and isolated as vestiges of defunct totalitarian socialism.

But while such capitalist notions as 'free trade' were clearly on the march in the era of globalization, the Cold War had left behind many complicated legacies. In Europe the future of the former Soviet bloc and its relationship to NATO and European integration were a constant reminder of the difficulties in bridging the gaps—whether economic, cultural, or political—that had divided the continent for many decades. To be sure, integrating former Warsaw Pact countries like Poland, Hungary, and the Czech Republic (Czechoslovakia itself being divided into two parts) into NATO proved surprisingly painless, despite concerns by many that NATO enlargement would unduly alarm the Russians as an aggressive Western move. However, incorporating the same countries (as well as a number of other eager applicants) into the European Union has proved to be a far more complex venture. On the one hand, despite the enormous progress of some countries (such as the three that joined NATO) towards adopting a liberal economic and political system, the gap in living standards between East and West still remained wide ten years after the collapse of the Soviet bloc. On the other hand, within the EU countries themselves concerns over the 'corrosive' influence that further expansion would have on the efforts of building 'an ever closer union' has slowed down the process of EU expansion.

Nor did the end of the Cold War and the formation of the European Union lay to rest the nascent differences amongst Western European countries themselves. Britain, traditionally the 'reluctant European', has continued to express doubts over deeper integration and, along with Sweden and Denmark, opted not to join the common currency, the Euro, that was launched on 1 January 2002. The continued existence of NATO as the pillar of security policy and Britain's preference to maintain a strong 'special relationship' with the United States has further undermined the push for a federal Europe spearheaded, in particular, by the French and the Germans. In a Europe haunted by a series of destructive wars in the Balkans during the 1990s, the continued inability to forge a functional common foreign and security policy has, indeed, remained a constant hindrance to further integration as well as a potential block against expansion.

While European integration remains, despite its difficulties, one of the major positive legacies of the Cold War, there are many areas of the world that have continued to pay a bloody price for their—often involuntary—participation in the East–West confrontation. In the Balkans, the break-up of Yugoslavia into numerous states, following the delegitimation of the ideology that had helped to keep the ethnically fractured federal state together during Tito's long reign, led to tremendous bloodshed throughout the 1990s. In Africa, states that had only recently been Cold War battlegrounds—such as Somalia and Angola—saw few benefits from the West's triumph in the Cold War. In Afghanistan, a continued civil war followed the Soviet exit. In all of these countries the legacy of the Cold War contributed to the wreckage, either because the arms used to fight local wars were ones provided by the Soviets or the Americans in years past, or because the training that had made, say, the mujaheddin in Afghanistan into an effective fighting force had been at least partly provided by the superpowers (in that case the United States). Indeed, many of the Third World countries that had been the focus of excessive superpower interest in the 1970s and 1980s were dubbed 'failed states' in the 1990s as civil strife continued unabated and, often, with relatively little attention from the rest of the world.

In late 2001 one of these 'failed states', Afghanistan, became the focus of much of the world's attention. The 11 September 2001 terrorist attacks on the World Trade Center in New York and the Pentagon in Washington were quickly traced back to the Al Qaida organisation, headed by Saudi-born Islamic militant Osama Bin Laden. Afghanistan's ruling Taliban movement (an Islamic extremist group that had established control over most of the country in 1996 and introduced a strict Islamic code throughout the country) had provided Bin Laden and Al Qaida with a sanctuary for several years, and in the fall of 2001 became the target of an American-led military campaign that managed to dislodge the Taliban and resulted in the capture of hundreds of terrorist suspects (some of whom were sent, of all places, to the American base in Guantanamo Bay, Cuba).

The 11 September attacks had, however, fundamentally changed the outlook on the general issue of security. While earlier terrorist attacks had either been small in scale or relatively unsuccessful, the destruction of the twin towers of the World Trade Center revealed the potential reach of small but tightly organized terrorist groups. At least in the judgement of the Bush administration in the United States, the war on terrorism—the 'first war of the 21st century'—was to be a long-drawn-out struggle. Many even spoke of the 'war on terrorism' as a new Cold War; a struggle, in effect, between good and evil. The trouble was that, unlike during the Cold War, when the frontlines were relatively clear and the sources of danger and insecurity relatively easily (although sometimes mistaken-ly) identified, the new war was not only unpredictable but essentially borderless and global. While bombing the Taliban strongholds in Afghanistan was part of the initial campaign in the war on terrorism, the follow-up was far from clear. With dozens, if not hundreds, of different terrorist organizations around the world, the new millenium appeared suddenly far less stable and secure than many had been led to believe in the first decade after the Cold War.

Even with terrorism emerging as the new global threat and source of insecur-ity, some of the key security concerns of the Cold War continued to exist. No other threat commanded as much public interest as the proliferation of nuclear arms and other weapons of mass destruction. Yet, while the concern during the Cold War had been based on the possibility of nuclear annihilation spearheaded by the massive arsenals of the United States and the Soviet Union, the post-Cold War era threat was at the same time less total and more unpredictable. In the United States, the Bush administration chose December 2001 as the moment to withdraw from the 1972 Anti-Ballistic Missile Treaty with the Soviet Union, promising to build a new missile defence system capable of protecting the United States from threats arising from limited nuclear strikes by 'rogue states' (such as

Iran, Iraq, and North Korea—dubbed 'the axis of evil' by President George W. Bush in his 2002 State of the Union Address) or terrorist organizations.

In the end, the apparent success of free-market capitalism and the failure of state-controlled socialism had yet to produce a system—be it regional or global—that would have eliminated economic hardship as a source of political instability. Meanwhile, the interdependence of the globalized world meant that the impact of such hardships and instability was more difficult to contain than before. At the beginning of the new millenium the Cold War—as far as it was understood as a contest between two ways of life, between two economic systems, or even as a struggle for influence between the world's two most powerful nations—may well have been relegated to history. Yet its legacy continues to live on and influence the world of the twenty-first century.

Reading

David Calleo, *Rethinking Europe's Future* (2001). A stimulating study of Europe's prospects at the dawn of the twenty-first century.

Ian Clark, *Globalization and Fragmentation: International Relations in the Twentieth Century* (1997). As the title indicates, this study emphasizes one of the central dichotomies of the post-Cold War era.

David Remnick, *Resurrection: The Struggle for a New Russia* (1998). An insightful account of the troubled transition in post-Soviet Russia.

James Scott (ed.), *After the End: Making U.S. Foreign Policy in the Post-Cold War World* (1998). A collection of essays assessing the different factors that affect American foreign policy decision-making.

Strobe Talbott and Nayan Chanda (eds.), *The Age of Terror: America and the World After September 11* (2002). This early assessment of the impact of 11 September 2001 provides a series of contributions from leading academics.

19.1 Presidents Bush and Yeltsin on future Russian–American relations, February 1992

Soon after the dissolution of the Soviet Union in December 1991, the Russian president Boris Yeltsin visited the United States. In a meeting with President George Bush, he discussed the future of their countries' relationship. Excerpts from the joint news conference at the end of the Camp David meetings follow.

BUSH. Today, for the first time, an American President and the democratically elected President of an independent Russia have met, and we did so not as adversaries but as friends. This historic meeting is yet another confirmation of the end of the Cold War and the dawn of a new era. Russia and the United States are charting a new relationship. And it's based on trust; it's based on a commitment to economic and political freedom; it's based on a strong hope for true partnership. So, we agreed here that we're going to pull closer together economically and politically (...)

We agreed to cooperate in the safe handling of nuclear weapons, arms reductions, and a wide array of other subjects. So, from my standpoint and the standpoint of the United States, our first team here, we felt it was a very good visit (...)

YELTSIN. Mr. President Bush, ladies and gentlemen, I am very grateful to my friend George for the words which he has just spoken, in terms of our meeting and aimed at Russia and towards me (...)

We discussed a whole range of issues (...) economic reform in Russia, as well as cooperation and assistance so that this reform not die on the vine, and issues having to do with the Commonwealth of Independent Nations, economic issues having to do with the military condition now, the condition of the military.

(...) we talked about reduction of strategic and tactical arsenals down to the minimal of, say, two and a half thousand warheads for either side. And in this issue we will now begin very specific and concrete negotiations, the issue of arms sales, of nonproliferation of nuclear weapons (...) I'm very satisfied that today one might say that there has been written and drawn a new line, and crossed out all of the things that have been associated with the Cold War.

(...) From now on we do not consider ourselves to be potential enemies as it had been previously in our military doctrine. This is the historic value of this meeting (...)

Q. We see in the declaration that Russia and the United States do not regard each other as potential adversaries. Does it mean you followed President Yeltsin's example so that retargeting of American nuclear weapons are not targeted on Russian targets anymore?

BUSH. We agreed that all these matters will be discussed in Moscow. But certainly I agree with his objectives, and that is to turn former enemies not only into friends but allies. And it's that that we're starting down that road, and I'm quite optimistic about it. We both realize that there is some negotiation that has to take place in terms of the specifics.

Q.(...) if both sides are now friends, then why not call for a total elimination of nuclear weapons?

YELTSIN. The thing is that there are still adventurers, terrorists, and irresponsible politicians in some countries of the world against whom we have to have a certain arsenal of nuclear weapons for restraining them.

Q. Have you discussed with the President some sort of overall initiative?

YELTSIN. Yes, we did discuss this issue of a global shield, if you would. We consider that it's a very interesting topic, and George Bush confirmed that, yes, this is an exceptionally necessary topic. It would be interesting to utilize these systems on a mutual basis maybe even with the participation of some other nuclear-club countries. (…)

Q. President Bush, your thoughts on President Yeltsin's proposal for a global shield. Is this something that (…) you would philosophically be inclined towards?

BUSH. It's something that we talked about at lunch with Secretary Cheney. As I said, we reached no decision on these matters. The Soviet Union has a lot of expertise in space, for example. Perhaps one area of real cooperation can be in future space adventure; another could be in this area of defense. But we reached no conclusion except to say that we felt it was worth discussing it in much more detail (…)

Q. (…) What parts of economic assistance were discussed today, I mean assistance for economic reform, rather?

BUSH. Well, largely, today President Yeltsin had a chance to expand on the reforms he has undertaken (…) We feel it would be very important that they be full members in these international financial organizations. I pledged the United States' full efforts in support for early entry into the IMF [International Monetary Fund] and into the World Bank. We expanded a little bit on the programs we already have working. In terms of additional support for the Soviet Union, financial and food, Jim Baker had an opportunity to discuss to some degree the follow-on from the conference that we had, the cooperation conference that was held in Washington last week.

We didn't get into too many specifics on that, but (…) I did, in a general sense, say that the United States would like to assist in any way possible.

Q. President Yeltsin, in your opinion, do you consider that you are getting sufficient assistance from the United States, economic assistance? You heard a lot about it today.

YELTSIN. Well, I would somewhat differently approach this question. After all, what's important here is not just aid. We were looking at the question of support for the reform, cooperation in a lot of different areas, a lot of directions, accomplishing a whole series of programs in order to be supportive of reform.

I didn't come here just to stretch out my hand and ask for help, no. We're calling for cooperation, cooperation for the whole world. Because if the reform in Russia goes under, that means there will be a Cold War. The Cold War is going to turn into a hot war. This is again going to be an arms race. Again, this will be the same regime that we have just recently rid ourselves. We cannot allow this to happen because in this reform the whole world community has to participate, not just the United States, and not just some sort of financial help but political support, cooperation, and the accomplishment of overall programs by everybody in order to help.

Also, humanitarian aid, we have agreed on this. From February 10th there will be a massive assistance on the part of the United States and others, and I'm very appreciative to George Bush for this (...)

Q. Mr. President, are you convinced that President Yeltsin is committed to democratic and economic reform? And do you believe he will succeed?

BUSH. I am convinced that he is totally committed to democratic reform. And I'm convinced that the problems he faces are enormous, but I am also convinced that he will succeed if he gets the proper support from around the world for these worthy objectives (...) He laid his life on the line on top of a tank to make that message loud and clear, and the whole world rejoiced in it when they saw his courage. He's applying that same courage, and I'm not saying that just because he's standing here, he's applying that same courage now to this concept of economic reform. One certainly cannot doubt his full commitment to this subject (...)

Q. I'm just wondering if you gentlemen would care to share the personal relationship that you've developed . . .

BUSH. (...) I can only speak for myself, one half of the equation, but the visits that I have had with President Yeltsin before this have always been very pleasant. I think that we have a good understanding. I have a very warm feeling in my heart about what he has done and is trying to do. And I consider him my friend.

YELTSIN. I consider that I was very lucky in life, both as a political person and just as a man, to have met George Bush. We have contacted each other, have been in contact, oh, now about 2 years at least. And even in the days when I was in the opposition, we used to meet. And then, even then, I already felt his wide-ranging talent, his mind, and his qualities as a person. I'm just tremendously impressed by his wisdom. I think he has incredible qualities not only as a political person but also as a person, as a really great political figure of the United States.

Today our relations have now been formed up as friends, and we talk quite frequently to each other. We call each other on the telephone. We say 'Boris'; we say 'George.' And already this says a lot.

19.2 Report from Vietnam, January 1992

The end of the Cold War had a dramatic impact on a number of former client states of the Soviet Union. In Vietnam the country's leadership had adopted their version of peres-troika, the doi moi *policy. Already by the early 1990s the effects of* doi moi *were seen as the socialist republic saw an emergence of a small-scale private economic sector alongside continued Communist Party control. The following excerpts from journalist Philip Shenon's article for the* New York Times Magazine *provide an interesting glimpse at the daily life in post-Cold War Vietnam.*

Lam Van lives the Vietnamese good life selling shiny new Dreams. Honda Dreams—8.5-horsepower, $2,000 motorbikes manufactured in Thailand—are the most coveted status symbol on the streets of Saigon, the bustling, hustling Vietnamese metropolis that almost no one calls by its still-official name, Ho Chi Minh City.

'Everyone calls it Saigon,' says Van, who owns a small motorbike shop. 'We never stopped calling it Saigon.' Business has been so good that the 31-year-old entrepreneur can afford to smoke black-market English-made John Player cigarettes, wear a gold Longines watch and join his friends most nights at the city's neon-flooded Superstar disco, where he rocks to bootleg recordings from Guns 'n' Roses and Madonna, his 'No. 1 favorite' recording star.

North Vietnamese troops overran Saigon in 1975, humiliating the United States just as they had humiliated France two decades earlier. But if the North won the Vietnam War, it is the South that is finally winning the peace. The old men who run the Vietnamese Communist Party, most of them dour Northerners, still hold tightly to power. But it is the freewheeling Southern spirit—one that is pro-Western and avidly capitalistic—that is taking hold in the North and South, city and countryside, and transforming a nation of 66 million people.

The city of Vinh, 600 miles north of Saigon, is the Vietnamese Dresden, leveled by American B-52 bombers during the war and rebuilt by the East Germans in the late 1970's. The city's nondescript five-story apartment buildings, representing the worst of East Bloc architecture and construction, were a gift from the regime of Erich Honecker.

Vinh is cursed by location (as one of the southernmost major cities in North Vietnam, it was a natural target for American bombers) and by red gritty soil and typhoons that make agriculture a perennial gamble. It is the capital of Nghe Tinh, one of the poorest provinces of Vietnam and, perhaps because of its endemic poverty, the birthplace of several of the nation's best-known revolutionaries. Ho Chi Minh, the legendary North Vietnamese leader, was born 101 years ago in a thatch-roof hut a few miles northwest of Vinh. Even today, running water and electricity are a dream to most farm families in the province, and malaria has reached epidemic proportions.

Yet even in Vinh, a city that sacrificed as much as any to unify Vietnam as a Communist state, the concept of free markets has begun to take root under the five-year-old policy known as doi moi, or 'renovation.' It is the Vietnamese version of perestroika (…)

Doi moi has encouraged the creation of private businesses, provided one of the most liberal foreign investment codes in Asia, ended price controls on major commodities and forced the devaluation of the Vietnamese currency, the dong, to bring it closer to its black-market exchange rate. American dollars and gold can now be traded legally. In its most recent annual report, the World Bank described doi moi as 'dramatic' and 'far-reaching' and said the reforms had created a 'fast-growing but still small-scale private sector.'

(...) Vietnam today is not the unrelievedly grim and gray country of the mid-1980's, but neither is it like Thailand or Taiwan or the other economic tigers of Southeast Asia. Vietnam is still among the poorest nations on earth, in large part because of the American trade embargo that has been in place since April 30, 1975, when the last American troops evacuated from Saigon. The embargo has isolated the country economically, cutting Hanoi off from international development aid—specifically that of the World Bank and the International Monetary Fund—and keeping away billions of dollars in foreign investment. The per capita income is estimated at $195 a year (53 cents a day). Malnutrition and disease are widespread.

Vietnam's economic troubles have been worsened by the cutoff of more than $1 billion a year in aid from the former Soviet Union, long Vietnam's closest ally. Although official figures are unreliable, the unemployment rate is believed to be as high as 20 percent. In the first three quarters of 1991, inflation ran as high as 7 percent a month, or nearly 125 percent a year (...)

Last year, Japan replaced the Soviet Union as Vietnam's largest trading partner, and the Japanese already buy 80 percent of Vietnam's crude-oil output. Japanese firms have opened scores of trading offices in Saigon and, for the better part of a decade, have been scouting out business and Government contacts. When the American trade embargo is lifted, Japanese investment is expected to explode. 'It may soon be too late for American investors,' says Ninh Van Mien, senior manager of the Hanoi Electronic Corporation, which manufactures Japanese JVC-brand television sets at a newly built factory in the Vietnamese capital. 'The Japanese have been in Vietnam for years, and it may be difficult for the Americans to catch up unless they come to Vietnam soon. In Vietnam we have a saying: the buffalo that is too slow to reach the watering hole must drink from the muddy water.'

(...) Foreign investors and Vietnamese business people alike complain that they are often caught in turf battles between the local and central governments, and between different agencies within the central Government—each offering a different interpretation of Vietnames laws and regulations, each seeking to take its own cut of a lucrative investment contract.

Last fall, an official newspaper reported that corruption involving senior officials had cost Vietnam more than $2 billion since 1989, and that more than 10,000 government and business officials—including seven deputy ministers and hundreds of company and factory managers—had recently been disciplined for corruption (...)

Even as Communism self-destructs elsewhere, the Communist Party of the Socialist Republic of Vietnam retains largely unchallenged control over the

Government and economic policy, and its influence extends throughout the military and the educational system. As of 1990, the party had about two million members, and government bureaucrats at virtually all levels and in all parts of the country must be members of the party or must have demonstrated unquestioning loyalty to its policies (…)

Although the Government tolerates some dissent from a handful of intellectuals, dozens of others—prominent academics, theologians and journalists—have been imprisoned. Scores of former officials of the old South Vietnamese regime are believed to be held in hard-labor 're-education camps.'

(…) The disintegration of the Soviet Union has horrified Vietnamese leaders, pushing them to do what only a few years ago would have been unthinkable—embrace their traditional enemy, China. Last year, Hanoi announced it would restore full diplomatic relations with Beijing after decades of hostility and sporadic warfare. Some Vietnamese officials have even begun citing China as an example of a nation that has successfully promoted free enterprise while holding on to a hardline political stance. They see serious flaws in the Chinese model, including rampant corruption and mounting public anger against Beijing's septuagenarian leaders, but the Chinese economy is booming, its gross national product up 6 percent in the first three quarters of 1991, an advance credited entirely to the private sector.

(…) Whatever path the Vietnamese decide to take, that decision will have to be made in Hanoi. The capital is a storybook vision of Asia, its quiet streets lined with tall, gently swaying tamarind trees that give it a slow-paced innocence entirely missing from Saigon. The air is scented by the inviting aroma of the noodle-and-beef soup called pho, sold from large steel pots at open-air street stands, and by the yeasty smell of freshly baked baguettes, the great contribution of France, Vietnam's former colonizer (…)

There is almost nothing to remind a visitor that Hanoi was for much of this century a city at war—nothing, that is, except for the charred wreckage of an American F-111 fighter on display at the Vietnamese Army Museum and the air-raid siren that blares across the city each day at noon as a reminder of the need for Vietnamese vigilance. Hanoi is under the spell of the free-market reforms born in the South, and the results can be seen everywhere in the city, although they are displayed without Saigon's hard-edged glitz.

Vietnam's new obsession with making money goes hand in hand with its obsession for all things American. It is rare for an American visitor to encounter rancor, even in the North, where virtually every family lost someone in the war. Instead, there is a fascination among the Vietnamese about what the former enemy is really like.

North Vietnamese television opened a recent Sunday evening broadcast with the show 'Learning English,' followed by the television series 'Highway to

Heaven,' dubbed in Vietnamese and starring the late Michael Landon, who has something of a cult following in Vietnam.

At Hanoi University—the university of choice both for the North's most gifted students and the offspring of the nation's most powerful leaders—a large sign in the overgrown courtyard reads 'Do as Uncle Ho Would Do.' It is unlikely, however, that Uncle Ho would have chosen the music heard in the hallway early one morning from a Japanese-made tape player: 'Hound Dog' by Elvis Presley, who is almost as popular here as his Vietnamese counterpart, Elvis Phuong.

In one classroom, a group of fourth-year English students reading Arthur Miller's 'Death of a Salesman' struggle with the concept that American capitalism might have contributed to Willy Loman's doom. They find the play confusing and difficult to follow (...)

As he shines the chrome grill of one of the Honda Dreams at his motorbike shop, Lam Van says that even though his beloved eldest brother died as a soldier defending the Saigon regime, he harbors no bitterness.

'Why should I hate Ho?' he says. 'It is time to forget hatred. We all want to forget the war and to live better lives—more happiness, money, more motorbikes, too—and we want the Americans to come back to help us to accomplish that.' He grins as he points to another of the Honda motorbikes whizzing by outside his shop. Dreams, he says, are filling the streets of Saigon.

19.3 Samuel P. Huntington, on the Coming 'Clash of Civilizations'

Not everyone was overtly optimistic about the future of the post-Cold War world. In his widely read 1997 book The Clash of Civilizations, *Harvard University Professor Samuel Huntington explained his concerns regarding the future:*

In the post-Cold War world, for the first time in history, global politics has become multipolar and multicivilizational. During most of human existence, contacts between civilizations were intermittent or nonexistent. Then, with the beginning of the modern era, about A.D. 1500, global politics assumed two dimensions. For over four hundred years, the nation states of the West—Britain, France, Spain, Austria, Prussia, Germany, the United States, and others—constituted a multipolar international system within Western civilization and interacted, competed, and fought wars with each other. At the same time, Western nations also expanded, conquered, colonized, or decisively influenced every other civilization. During the Cold War global politics became bipolar and the world was divided into three parts. A group of mostly wealthy and democratic societies, led by the United States, was engaged in a pervasive, ideological, political, economic, and, at times, military competition with a group of somewhat poorer communist societies associated with and led by the Soviet Union. Much of this conflict occurred in the Third World outside these two camps, composed of countries which often were poor, lacked political stability, were recently independent, and claimed to be nonaligned.

In the late 1980s the communist world collapsed, and the Cold War international system became history. In the post-Cold War world, the most important distinctions among peoples are not ideological, political, or economic. They are cultural. Peoples and nations are attempting to answer the most basic question humans can face: Who are we? And they are answering that question in the traditional way human beings have answered it, by reference to the things that mean most to them. People define themselves in terms of ancestry, religion, language, history, values, customs, and institutions. They identify with cultural groups: tribes, ethnic groups, religious communities, nations, and, at the broadest level, civilizations. People use politics not just to advance their interests but also to define their identity. We know who we are only when we know who we are not and often only when we know whom we are against.

Nation states remain the principal actors in world affairs. Their behavior is shaped as in the past by the pursuit of power and wealth, but it is also shaped by cultural preferences, commonalities, and differences. The most important groupings of states are no longer the three blocs of the Cold War but rather the world's seven or eight major civilizations. Non-Western societies, particularly in East Asia, are developing their economic wealth and creating the basis for enhanced military power and political influence. As their power and self-confidence increase, non-Western societies increasingly assert their own cultural values and reject those 'imposed' on them by the West. The 'international system of the twenty-first century,' Henry Kissinger has noted, 'will contain at least six major powers—the United States, Europe, China, Japan, Russia, and probably India—as well as a multiplicity of medium-sized and smaller countries.' Kissinger's six major powers belong to five very different civilizations, and in addition there are important Islamic states whose strategic locations, large populations, and/or oil resources make them influential in world affairs. In this new world, local politics is the politics of ethnicity; global politics is the politics of civilizations. The rivalry of the superpowers is replaced by the clash of civilizations.

In this new world the most pervasive, important, and dangerous conflicts will not be between social classes, rich and poor, or other economically defined groups, but between peoples belonging to different cultural entities. Tribal wars and ethnic conflicts will occur within civilizations. Violence between states and groups from different civilizations, however, carries with it the potential for escalation as other states and groups from these civilizations rally to the support of their 'kin countries.' The bloody clash of clans in Somalia poses no threat of broader conflict. The bloody clash of tribes in Rwanda has consequences for Uganda, Zaire, and Burundi but not much further. The bloody clashes of civilizations in Bosnia, the Caucasus, Central Asia, or Kashmir could become bigger wars. In the Yugoslav conflicts, Russia provided diplomatic support to the Serbs, and Saudi Arabia, Turkey, Iran, and Libya provided funds and arms to the Bosnians, not for reasons of ideology or power politics or economic interest but because of cultural kinship (...)

In the post-Cold War world, culture is both a divisive and a unifying force. People separated by ideology but united by culture come together, as the two Germanys did and as the two Koreas and the several Chinas are beginning to. Societies united by ideology or historical circumstance but divided by civilization either come apart, as did the Soviet Union, Yugoslavia, and Bosnia, or are subjected to intense strain, as is the case with Ukraine, Nigeria, Sudan, India, Sri Lanka, and many others. Countries with cultural affinities cooperate economically and politically. International organizations based on states with cultural commonality, such as the European Union, are far more successful than those that attempt to transcend cultures. For forty-five years the Iron Curtain was the central dividing line in Europe. That line has moved several hundred miles east. It is now the line separating the peoples of Western Christianity, on the one hand, from Muslim and Orthodox peoples on the other (...)

The West is and will remain for years to come the most powerful civilization. Yet its power relative to that of other civilizations is declining. As the West attempts to assert its values and to protect its interests, non-Western societies confront a choice. Some attempt to emulate the West and to join or to 'bandwagon' with the West. Other Confucian and Islamic societies attempt to expand their own economic and military power to resist and to 'balance' against the West. A central axis of post-Cold War world politics is thus the interaction of Western power and culture with the power and culture of non-Western civilizations.

In sum, the post-Cold War world is a world of seven or eight major civilizations. Cultural commonalities and differences shape the interests, antagonisms, and associations of states. The most important countries in the world come overwhelmingly from different civilizations. The local conflicts most likely to escalate into broader wars are those between groups and states from different civilizations. The predominant patterns of political and economic development differ from civilization to civilization. The key issues on the international agenda involve differences among civilizations. Power is shifting from the long predominant West to non-Western civilizations. Global politics has become multipolar and multicivilizational.

19.4 Margaret Thatcher and Helmut Kohl on European Union, January–February 1996

The 1992 Maastricht Treaty established the European Union that came into being on 1 January 1995. Now consisting of fifteen countries (Austria, Finland, and Sweden were the newest members), the EU greatly expanded the powers of the various European institutions and signalled a major step towards deeper integration. Among other things, the EU began to move towards the establishment of a single currency (the Euro was finally launched in twelve countries on 1 January 2002) and called for the member states to establish a Common Foreign and Security Policy. But the establishment of the EU was not uniformly popular. One of the foremost critics was former British prime minister Margaret Thatcher, whose early 1996 speech provides the excerpts in the first document. The second document gives excerpts from an address by one of the foremost supporters of further integration, Germany's chancellor Helmut Kohl.

A. Margaret Thatcher, January 1996

(…) today the main challenge to limited government comes not from within these shores, but rather beyond them—from the European Union. There is, of course, also a challenge to self-government—and the two are closely connected. The activity of the European Court, which can only ultimately be checked by amending the European Communities Act itself, is increasingly undermining our judicial system and the sovereignty of our Parliament. Proposals are being made for common European defence—proposals which Michael Portillo has roundly and rightly attacked. They are a threat to national independence. But most important, of course, is the proposed single European currency which, as John Redwood has argued, 'would be a major step on the way to a single European nation'. The Prime Minister [John Major] will have the support of all of us who wish to see these dangerous and damaging proposals resisted, and the present trends reversed, as he argues Britain's case at the forthcoming intergovernmental council. And we look forward to a successful outcome. But vital as the issue of self-government is, it is limited government that concerns me today. For the European Union not only wishes to take away our powers; it wishes to increase its own. It wants to regulate our industries and labour markets, pontificate over our tastes, in short to determine our lives. The Maastricht Treaty, which established a common European citizenship and greatly expanded the remit of the European Commission, shows the outlines of the bureaucratic superstate which is envisaged. And Maastricht is the beginning, not the end of that process (…) Self-government, limited government, our laws, our Parliament, our freedom. These things were not easily won. And if we Conservatives explain that they are now in peril, they will not be lightly surrendered.

B. Helmut Kohl, February 1996

(...) there is no reasonable alternative to ever closer integration among the European peoples. We all need a united Europe. I would like to single out three reasons for this here:

First, the policy of European integration is in reality a question of war and peace in the 21st century. My deceased friend François Mitterrand shared this view. He stated before the European Parliament in Strasbourg on 17 January 1995 that nationalism is war. I know that some people do not like to hear this. My warnings may come as an unpleasant truth. However, it is no use burying one's head in the sand. If there is no momentum for continued integration this will not only lead to standstill but also to retrogression. But we have no desire to return to the nation state of old. It cannot solve the great problems of the 21st century. Nationalism has brought great suffering to our continent—just think of the first fifty years of this century.

Second, we need Europe to ensure that our common views count in the world. We can only protect our common interests if we speak with one voice and pool our resources.

Third, we all need Europe in order to remain competitive on the world markets. Only together can we hold our own in international competition with the other major economic areas of East Asia and North America. Latin America, too, is entering into this competition with the Mercosur Pact (...)

Economic and monetary union is certainly one of the greatest challenges facing us in the European Union at the present. The current preparatory phase is a period of uncertainty, a period in which the very continuation of European integration is being questioned. Have the Europeans become tired of Europe again?

I do not believe that this really is the case. However, the road mapped out at Maastricht not only signifies great progress but also calls for considerable efforts on everybody's part to achieve a major step forward (...)

No one wants a centralized superstate. It does not and never will exist (...) I would regard it as a disastrous development if Europe's strength were to diminish with its enlargement. However, I would find it equally disastrous if Europe were only able to derive its strength from keeping others out.

During the next few years we will have to prove that a viable Europe can be built with 15 and more states. At the same time, however, the slowest ship in the convoy should not be allowed to determine its speed. If individual partners are not prepared or able to participate in certain steps towards integration the others should not be denied the opportunity to move forward and develop increased cooperation in which all partners are welcome to take part.

19. 5 Legacies of the Angolan War, January 1997

In many parts of Africa the end of the Cold War did not translate into a happier future. In Angola the civil war of the mid-1970s had been followed by ongoing civil strife that continued to wreak havoc in the West African nation throughout the 1990s. Below, the journalist Santos Virgilio describes life in Luanda in 1997.

Guilherme Sebastiao's story reflects the main factors that have forced thousands of children onto the streets of Angola's capital: war, poverty and violence.

Just over five years ago, his mother left Guilherme, his elder brother and two older sisters in Luanda to go on a trip up country. That was during a one-and-a-half year lull in the rebel war that had wracked Angola since independence in 1975.

The war resumed in October 1992 while Guilherme's mother, who was the head of the household, was still away. She never came back even after a shaky peace agreement signed in 1994, broken on occasion by the two sides, and reaffirmed last year.

Before leaving Luanda, she had paid six month's rent up front. When that period elapsed the landlord evicted them and they went to live with their maternal uncle. However, he kicked them out shortly afterwards, accusing them of being sorcerers.

'Even in the street, my uncle used to pursue me with a pistol to kill me,' recalls 12-year-old Guilherme. 'All these years, I had to run whenever I came across him.' The CIES, an Italian non-governmental organisation, came to his rescue, filing a complaint against the uncle, who was made by a Luanda court to promise to leave the youngster alone or face a prison term.

Guilherme now lives in the basement of a building with four other youths, the oldest—and leader—is 16 years old. 'The residents of the building help us with food, clothes, and registered us in a school,' says the fifth-grader.

In the meantime, his family has disintegrated. His brother is teaching somewhere. One of his sisters is somewhere in South Africa and the other is reportedly in London.

A street child comes across many obstacles in life and matures quickly. Guilherme is no exception. He thinks carefully before uttering a word. He thinks 'the government has to help all children in difficult situations (...)'. How? 'Shelters ought to be built,' he suggests, 'more schools, hospitals have to be built (...) so as to end these problems.'

He feels all this is possible 'if the government collaborates with the children'. If it doesn't, 'what are we going to do?' he wonders.

Children like Guilherme face an uncertain future on the streets of Luanda even though NGOs have been trying to alleviate their situation. Some have provided food, others have given medical help or social assistance when in a position to do so.

Stories like Guilherme's can be heard in most of Angola's cities. 'The latest statistics, compiled in 1995, indicate that there are 10,000 street children countrywide and 4,000 here in the capital,' says Afonso Ngonda, a teacher at the National Institute for Children (NAC) here.

However, Graziela Mancini, coordinator of the CIES's Street Children Support Project says no one knows for sure how many they are. Moreover, not all actually live on the street, she says.

According to Mancini, 'there must be about five hundred street children in Luanda'. The rest, she says, are children of the street, who survive by begging and doing odd jobs during the day then retire to their homes in the evening. Much of the time, the war is blamed for their being there, but it is not the only factor. 'The problem which characterises these children is poverty,' says Mancini. 'It may have begun with the war but today it is poverty and domestic violence.'

Ngonda agrees that poverty is widespread. 'Nearly 70 percent of families in our country live in almost absolute poverty,' he says. But he adds that 'before the 1992 war there were no street children'.

Mancini's work with the children does not involve the distribution of food and clothes: she feels such projects are not sustainable: at some point they come to an end and it's back to square one. 'We give them classes,' she explains, 'we teach them about the role of state institutions so that they can know their rights as children and citizens and decide for themselves when and how to get off the street.'

She feels a street child is 'in most cases a child with many dreams, full of imagination and creativity; a child who really wants to study'.

Many do not get that chance, especially some of the girls, who are lured or forced into prostitution. 'Child prostitutes are a bigger and much more serious problem,' says Mancini. 'We are working with the government and UNICEF (U.N. Children's Fund) to try and minimise it because we know that eliminating it is already impossible.'

'Our biggest difficulty with child prostitutes is that we do not manage to find them jobs or other occupations in which they can earn as much as they do in prostitution,' adds Mancini.

Ngonda confirms that 'the sexual exploitation of minors is increasing dangerously.' He adds that children are being allowed entry into nightclubs, where anything can happen and, in some cases, relatives or supposed guardians fetch girls aged as young as 10 from the country and force them into prostitution.

A national meeting on the sexual exploitation of minors, promoted by INAC, has resulted in a draft project for future action that has been submitted to the cabinet, he says.

The experts feel the solution has to be a global one: making society aware of the problem, then tackling the issue of consolidating peace and 'paying more attention to assisting families instead of investing in defence,' according to Mancini.

For the children, such attention would come none too soon. They feel it's time the government did its bit and they have been trying to find an opportunity to discuss their concerns with the decision-makers.

'We are organising with the help of NGOs so that we can speak with ministers and, or parliamentarians,' said Guilherme. 'Then we are going to know what they are thinking of our life.'

In the meantime, he still hopes that his mother will come back sometime soon.

19.6 Poland Joins NATO, December 1997

One of the key changes after the end of the Cold War was NATO's expansion eastwards. Poland became one of three countries to join NATO in late 1997. Below, Poland's foreign minister, Bronislaw Geremek, speaks at the accession ceremony in Brussels.

For over two hundred years, when foreign leaders put their signatures under documents concerning Poland, disasters were sure to follow. Today, I am to witness Poland's friends sign a document which is a source of joy, pride and hope for me and my compatriots. In this great moment, I wish to salute all those, in Poland and abroad, who have helped this to happen. (…)

History has been an unforgiving teacher to us. But we have learned our lesson well. Eight years ago we undertook to unlive the past, to restore Poland as a free, democratic and truly sovereign nation. We have since spared no effort to return to the roots of our culture and statehood, to join the Euro-Atlantic family of democratic nations. We will not rest until Poland is safely anchored in Western economic, political and military structures. This is the essence of our aspirations to join NATO.

I wish to stress that we are not trying to draw a new line between the West and the East. On the contrary, by joining the Alliance, we wish to help reduce these notions to their purely geographic meaning. We wish to partake in the great endeavor to build an undivided Europe, whole and free.

We would prefer to live in a Europe with no arms and no alliances. But we do live in a world where military power remains the ultimate guarantor of security. We know that NATO is not a discussion club for idealists. We have chosen to join it because it is an alliance which has managed to put its immense military might in service of fundamental values and principles that we share. NATO can make

Europe safe for democracy. No other organization can replace the Alliance in this role. We know many Central and Eastern European nations share our beliefs and aspirations. Not all of them have yet been invited to join NATO. To those nations I address today our assurances of understanding and support. We believe there is a room in the Alliance for all peace-loving, democratic states, wishing and able to further its goals.

On this occasion I also wish to reiterate our unaltered desire to maintain and develop close, good-neighborly relations with Russia, based on confidence and mutual respect. We want our membership of NATO to serve as a catalyst for Polish–Russian cooperation on political and security issues. We look forward to working with Russia and our Allies in the framework of the Permanent Joint Council.

A skeptic could say that promises are easy to make and difficult to keep. I would respond by noting that it is not our declarations that have paved the way to this ceremony. It is the success of the political and economic transformation of Poland, the unquestionable achievements of our foreign policy, and our determination in preparing our defense system for integration within NATO. Our actions have spoken louder than our words—and they will in the future. We will make no mistakes while charting the course for our country into the 21st century.

19.7 The Proliferation of Weapons of Mass Destruction, May 1998

Nuclear weapons have remained a key security concern after the end of the Cold War. In particular, the concern over nuclear proliferation and the possibility of nuclear terrorism have been at the top of the agenda of the post-Cold War American administrations. In this 1998 article journalist Michael R. Gordon describes a number of the new threat scenarios.

(…) At the advent of the nuclear age, the fight against proliferation seemed to be a stark struggle between the haves and the have-nots. The nations that had the bomb belonged to an exclusive club. Those that did not had to reconcile themselves with being second-class powers. But that simple dichotomy is gone. Technology and the post-Cold War arms market have made it easier for third-world countries to acquire the means to wage war with terror weapons—a category no longer limited to nuclear bombs.

The new watchwords for those who would slow the proliferation of arms are containment and playing for time. Missiles, poison gas and germs, for example, have become the poor man's nukes. Those technologies are so pervasive and hard to control that countering the spread of weapons of mass destruction is not like turning off the spigot. It is more like plugging a gaping leak with chewing gum—again and again.

Though those systems are not nearly as destructive as a nuclear bomb, the newly available combination of a fast-flying missile and a chemical warhead is by itself a dangerous threat, especially given the fact that nations like Iraq have breached the old taboos against the use of poison gas.

And while end of the Cold War brought an end of the spiraling arms race between Moscow and Washington a decade ago, the countries that made up the Soviet state have now become a potential supermarket for shady middlemen and third world arms merchants.

Missile technology, for example, has been seeping out of what was a vast archipelago of military research institutes and defense plants in the Soviet Union. Starved for cash, the enterprises have increasingly turned to exports to survive and they have not been picky about their customers.

In this new world, the key is to delay the emergence of new hardware or expertise that could destabilize an already volatile region or erode the American military's edge. Playing for time can be an eminently sensible strategy, especially if efforts to talk would-be proliferators out of seeking weapons of mass destruction fail. Diplomats need time to try their hand at negotiations or for implacable regimes to fall. A quick survey shows how complex the task of containing arms proliferation has become.

The leakage of Russian missile technology to Iran is a major worry because it will help Iran speed the development of the Shahab-3. That missile will have the range to strike Israel on short notice. Coupled with Iran's chemical and biological weapons programs, and Teheran's continuing effort to develop nuclear arms, the Shahab-3 will only tighten the hair trigger in the Middle East.

The flow of foreign technology has also fueled the missile race between Pakistan and India, an ominous development given that the two antagonists have already crossed the nuclear threshold. Pakistan recently test fired the Ghauri, a medium-range ballistic missile based on smuggled North Korean technology. India has been on the receiving end of Russian missile technology, though Washington has yet to decide if Moscow's new assistance has violated international export guidelines.

Third world nations are nowhere near the point where they could develop an ocean-spanning missile that could strike the United States. But short and medium range rockets pose a threat to American troops posted overseas (…)

To be sure, the weapons busters in the West have had some important victories, particularly on the nuclear front. As it passed from being an apartheid regime to being a multiracial state, South Africa voluntarily gave up its bombs. Argentina and Brazil, which never obtained the bomb, have forsworn nuclear weapons.

American officials shut down Taiwan's clandestine nuclear program and brought the nuclear material back to the United States. South Korea was persuaded not to go nuclear. And North Korea's nuclear bomb program has also been frozen, though the CIA has concluded that the North Koreans probably already have a bomb or two in their basement.

Caches of nuclear material spread throughout the former Soviet Union remain a big headache, though headway has been made in assuring their security. American transport planes spirited a small supply of highly enriched uranium and spent fuel from the Caucasian nation of Georgia to Britain last month.

There have been some notable setbacks. Several American Administrations were unable to pursuade Pakistan to abandon its nuclear efforts.

Russia wants to sell as many as four nuclear power reactors to Iran. And Russia's ministry for atomic energy wants to broaden the sale to include a new research reactor.

Those plans are a concern for American officials, who fear that the sales enable Tehran build up its nuclear expertise and mask a clandestine nuclear weapons program.

Israel also has a small but potent nuclear arsenal, which nobody expects it to relinquish. But the Middle East has learned to live with Israel's nuclear capability and the Israeli government has been careful not to flaunt it.

Containing the proliferation of missiles and chemical and biological weapons is trickier. An international treaty banning chemical weapons has been negotiated, but key Arab countries, citing Israel's nuclear arsenal, have not joined.

The threat of germ weapons is a more remote danger, in part because no one is quite sure about their utility on the battlefield. But biological agents might yet form a potent weapon in the hands of a terrorist and defending against them is problematic.

International controls have been established on the sale of missile technology. But the technology for making single-stage liquid fueled missiles is already well within the grasp of many third world states.

There are two basic ways to deal with proliferation challenges: persuading the recipients it is not worth the effort and trying to squelch the exports if the recipients do not listen.

Persuasion can work. The West's decision to provide North Korea with fuel oil and light water reactors, which are suitable for producing power and unsuitable for making weapons material, was instrumental in convincing Pyongyang to freeze its nuclear bomb program.

'It's important to offer incentives and not just think in terms of sanctions,' said Leon Sigal, the author of 'Disarming Strangers,' a study of the nuclear diplomacy with North Korea.

But it is also necessary to go to the source, such as China and Russia. 'Russia is the biggest problem in terms of the sources of technology and material,' an American official said.

19.8 Korean Family Reunion, August 2000

Unlike Germany, Korea remained divided after the end of the Cold War. Indeed, only in 2000 were the tensions between North and South Korea sufficiently low to allow the first small steps towards reconciliation. In the Korean context this meant a series of reunions that brought together small groups of family members that had been separated during the Korean War some fifty years earlier. In this report the journalist Damian Grammaticas describes one of these emotional reunions.

In room number 1406 of the Sheraton Walker Hill hotel in Seoul, a family have come together. But this is no ordinary meeting. The three brothers sitting here haven't met like this in half a century.

Dr Paek Nam-bok left his family when the Korean War began in 1950. He's spent his life in North Korea; now he's face-to-face with his flesh and blood.

'I can't explain my feelings in words,' says the 72-year-old man. Asked how he feels about being in South Korea after so many years, his answer is simple. 'Peaceful'.

There are no tears, no anguish, no hugs. Those all came when the family were reunited for the first time 24 hours earlier.

His brothers believed he had perished—there had been no word for 50 years, nothing until a few days before the reunion.

'We thought he was dead,' one says. 'It was a long forgotten world. He just appeared from nowhere. I don't have any memories of him.'

Now Dr Paek appears a little overwhelmed by the occasion. His breath is heavy, he blinks nervously at the television cameras eager to catch every moment of his reunion, the reporters poised for his every word.

Dr Paek was one of seven brothers; the eldest four have died, just the three gathered in room 1406 are left alive.

When the conflict engulfed the Korean peninsula, Paek Nam-bok, then in his early twenties, left to join the armies of the Communist North.

The decision was voluntary but it determined the course of his life and split his family for half a century.

'There were bombs and everyone was busy fleeing,' explains his younger brother Paek Nam-hyuk.

'I don't recall anything about the separation. I was 16 then, I was busy fleeing like the others. Later, when I realised that my brother was gone, that was when I got sad.'

Paek Nam-hyuk is now 67-years-old. He's a little overweight and has the air of a successful man. The contrast with his brother who's spent his lifetime in a Stalinist state is stark.

Dr Paek Nam-bok is thin and drawn, his face carved with deep lines. The difference between the brothers looks much greater than the five years that separate them.

Dr Paek is a man of note in North Korea. He is a physician, smartly dressed in a short-sleeved suit. On one lapel he wears a badge with a picture of his grinning leader, Kim Jong-il.

Just to be picked to be one of the 100 lucky people allowed to travel to South Korea and meet his relatives is a sign he is trusted by the state, and loyal to his leader.

'I have worked very hard to be on the list,' he says, but doesn't explain what he means.

In case he's tempted to say anything out of line there's a minder on hand to hear every word. Twice the North Korean official tells Dr Paek: 'Be open, say anything you wish to say.'

But it doesn't seem to calm the doctor. His brothers produce presents for him to take back home. There's a watch, a calculator, clothes, and photographs in a special album. The pictures will be his only link with his family once he's flown across the impenetrable border between North and South Korea.

It's a moment his youngest brother doesn't want to see, but which will come after they've had just a few days together.

'It is sad that we will be separating after four days,' says Paek Nam hyuk. 'But I believe with this reunion there is a possibility for North Koreans and South Koreans to reunite.'

19.9 China Joins the World Trade Organisation, September–November 2001

One of the remarkable events of the early twenty-first century was China's (and Taiwan's) accession to the Geneva-based World Trade Organisation. In these speeches Long Yongtu, head of the Chinese Delegation to the WTO, and the director-general of WTO, Mike Moore, give their assessments of the significance of China's membership.

A. Long Yongtu, September 2001

Today is a memorable day of importance. It marks the final conclusion of negotiations on China's WTO accession, and the Working Party that has been established for 14 and half years will complete its historical mission (...) we are part of a historical event, an event which will bring a country with one-fourth of the world population into the multilateral trading system which takes the promotion of the world trade and economic development as its major goal (...)

Just as President Jiang Zemin pointed out recently, WTO accession is a strategic decision made by the Chinese Government under economic globalization and is in line with China's reform and opening-up policy and the goal of establishing a socialist market economic system. The achievements made in China's reform and opening-up process have provided conditions and possibilities for China's participation into the multilateral trading system. And on the other hand, the efforts made by China for its WTO accession have greatly accelerated the reform and opening-up process in China.

The history of the past 15 years is the history of China's advancing toward market economic system and of China's gradually adopting international rules. It is the history of China's continuous effort to accelerate its opening to the outside world. It is the history of China's gradually deepening its participation into the process of economic globalization. China has substantially reduced its tariff levels for many times, eliminated over-whelming majority of its non-tariff measures, gradually opened its service sectors, abolished the mandatory plan for imports and exports, eliminated export subsidies, established its market-based pricing mechanism, unified the exchange system, realized the convertibility of RMB [Chinese currency] under current account in international transactions, unified taxation system and provided national treatment to imported product (...)

As for the rest of world, after China's accession, the great potential of China's market will be gradually translated into actual purchasing power, so as to provide a huge open market to all countries and regions in the world. This would be an important contribution to be made by China to the mankind. As for China, it will further improve the market economic system to be in line with the current international rules and the principles of the WTO (...)

B. Mike Moore, November 2001

(...) the meeting at Doha will be remembered as a turning-point in the history of the WTO and the trading system and in relations between developed and developing countries within that system.

(...) it is worthwhile to reflect on the value of the multilateral trading system, indeed what mankind has done over the past 50 years to advance the human condition. I do this because 'alarmists' have painted a picture of a world gone backwards over the past fifty years and I think the opposite.

The capacity of the human species to learn, adapt and improve marks us out as different to other species. This observation may seem a little hollow given a new type of war being fought on every front against terrorism when so many people are asking; why war? Will we ever learn? Yes, we have learnt, that's why the war. We make mistakes but we correct them.

That's why the Marshall Plan, the mirror opposite of the vicious Versailles Treaty, was implemented—the first case in history when the victors refinanced the vanquished. The great depression was made more lethal and deeper by protectionism which helped produce a second world war and gave life to the twin tyrannies of last century, fascism and Marxism, both of which have been destroyed and discredited. We suffered and learnt. That's why the GATT/WTO was created to build stable open trading rules, the UN and its agencies to promote political peace and to alleviate the problems and poverty that allow political hate to fester. Imperfect mechanisms, but the world would be a more dangerous place without them.

More has been done to reduce poverty in the past 50 years than the previous 500 years, yet many protest 'not enough' and have created a myth about globalization. Globalization is not new, historians argue we had about the same level of trade 100 years ago as today. Certainly more people were on the move then than now. We should not reject criticism and scrutiny, nor should we be smug (…) Open societies, open economies do better. Development means security, means peace, means higher living standards and better outcomes in terms of the human condition and human rights improve (…)

The accession of China and Chinese Taipei to the organization (…) was a massive achievement. Indeed it was enough in itself to make this conference a defining moment in the development of the trading system. These two countries alone, accounted for half of world trade which until now remained outside of WTO rules. Their integration into the WTO is an event of major political and economic importance.

On 10 November [2001] in Doha, Minister Shi signed China's accession treaty, a document of around 1,000 pages, the product of fifteen years of complex and arduous negotiations. It brings one of the world's most important trading nations into the rules-based multilateral trading system. WTO membership will provide the 1.3 billion Chinese people with secure, predictable and non-discriminatory access to the markets of 142 trading partners. It will commit China to implement legal and domestic policy reform. For other WTO Members, China's accession will cement and accelerate the benefits of the dramatic liberalization undertaken in China over the last 20 years (…) Now that

China has a seat at the table, the WTO has a more legitimate claim to be a truly universal organization (...)

19.10 Interview with Osama Bin Laden, 1999

One of the broadly debated dangers of the post-Cold War world was the apparent prolif-eration of international terrorism. While a number of the hundreds of terrorist groups in existence by the late 1990s had a specifically regional character, some, such as the Saudi-born Osama Bin Laden's Al-Qaida network, took on a much more 'global' (and clearly religious) character. In 1999, two years prior to the attacks on New York's World Trade Center and the Pentagon (see below), the reporter John Miller caught up with Osama Bin Laden in the Afghan mountains where he was provided with sanctuary by the Taliban, the ruling Islamic extremist movement that had taken control over most of the country by 1996.

Osama bin Muhammad bin Awad bin Laden was born forty-one years ago in Saudi Arabia, one of twenty sons of wealthy construction magnate Muhammad bin Laden. The kingdom's Bin Laden Group is a $5 billion concern. The family's close ties to the Saudi royal family made it easy to get huge government contracts to build roads through the cities and deserts. It is likely that Osama bin Laden would have gone to school, settled in London, and focused on living comfort-ably—if history hadn't intervened.

On December 25, 1979, the Soviet Union invaded Afghanistan. Bin Laden, then twenty-two, left for the fighting immediately. When he arrived, he wasted no time. Spending his money, he financed the recruitment, transportation, and arming of thousands of Palestinians, Tunisians, Somalians, Egyptians, Saudis, and Pakistanis to fight the Russians.

Bin Laden brought in his own bulldozers and dump trucks. Grizzled mujahideen fighters still tell of the young man who rode the bulldozers himself, digging trenches on the front lines. The men who follow bin Laden have all heard the stories, and they pass them on to the younger men. By his own account, he was in the thick of the action. He says he got the rifle he carries now in hand-to-hand combat.

'We went through vicious battles with the Russians,' bin Laden told me. 'The Russians are known for their brutality. They used poison gases against us. I was subjected to this. We lost many fighters. But we were able to deter many com-mando attacks, unlike anything before.'

I asked him why a man of wealth, from a powerful family, had gone to Afghanistan to live in trenches and fight the Russian invaders on the front lines.

'It is hard for one to understand if the person does not understand Islam,' he said, patiently explaining his interpretation of Islam for a citizen of his sworn enemy. 'During the days of jihad, thousands of young men who were well-off financially left the Arabian Peninsula and other areas and joined the fighting. Hundreds of them were killed in Afghanistan, Bosnia, and Chechnya.'

Of course, by the time of our meeting, the enemy had shifted. The Soviet Union no longer existed. The enemy was us. And when I asked bin Laden if he was worried about being captured in an American raid, he quickly dismissed the possibility, turning instead to the reasons he hates the United States.

'The American imposes himself on everyone. Americans accuse our children in Palestine of being terrorists—those children, who have no weapons and have not even reached maturity. At the same time, Americans defend a country, the state of the Jews, that has a policy to destroy the future of these children.

'We are sure of our victory against the Americans and the Jews as promised by the Prophet: Judgment day shall not come until the Muslim fights the Jew, where the Jew will hide behind trees and stones, and the tree and the stone will speak and say, "Muslim, behind me is a Jew. Come and kill him."'

Bin Laden never raises his voice, and to listen to his untranslated answers, one could imagine that he was talking about something that did not much concern him. Nonchalant. He does not smile. He continued, looking down at his hands as if he were reading invisible notes. 'Your situation with Muslims in Palestine is shameful—if there is any shame left in America. Houses were demolished over the heads of children. Also, by the testimony of relief workers in Iraq, the American-led sanctions resulted in the death of more than one million Iraqi children. All of this is done in the name of American interests. We believe that the biggest thieves in the world and the terrorists are the Americans. The only way for us to fend off these assaults is to use similar means. We do not worry about American opinion or the fact that they place prices on our heads. We as Muslims believe our fate is set.'

(...) Bin Laden believes that the United States, which was so heavily involved in supporting the Afghan rebels, misses the profound point of that exercise: Through sheer will, even superpowers can be defeated.

'There is a lesson to learn from this for he who wishes to learn,' he said. 'The Soviet Union entered Afghanistan in the last week of 1979, and with Allah's help their flag was folded a few years later and thrown in the trash, and there was nothing left to call the Soviet Union.'

The war changed bin Laden. 'It cleared from Muslim minds the myth of superpowers,' he said. He was blooded, a hero among militant Muslims, with perhaps three thousand men waiting to follow him. But follow him where, into what battle? Many of these men had not been home for years. By then, fighting was all some of them knew. And there were huge stockpiles of weapons and grenades and rocket launchers, many of them bought for the mujahideen rebels by the CIA.

In December 1992, bin Laden found the battle he'd been waiting for. The United States was leading a UN-sanctioned rescue mission into Somalia. In the midst of a famine, the country's government had completely broken down, and warring tribes—largely Muslim—had cut off relief efforts by humanitarian groups. Somalians were starving to death in cities and villages, and the U.S., which had moved quickly to rescue oil-rich Kuwait, had come under mounting criticism for doing nothing. When the Marines landed in the last days of 1992, bin Laden sent in his own soldiers, armed with AK-47's and rocket launchers. Soon, using the techniques they had perfected against the Russians, they were shooting down American helicopters. The gruesome pictures of the body of a young army ranger being dragged naked through the streets by cheering crowds flashed around the world. The yearlong American rescue mission for starving Somalians went from humanitarian effort to quagmire in just three weeks. Another superpower humiliated. Another bin Laden victory.

'After leaving Afghanistan, the Muslim fighters headed for Somalia and prepared for a long battle, thinking that the Americans were like the Russians,' bin Laden said. 'The youth were surprised at the low morale of the American soldiers and realized more than before that the American soldier was a paper tiger and after a few blows ran in defeat. And America forgot all the hoopla and media propaganda (…) about being the world leader and the leader of the New World Order, and after a few blows they forgot about this title and left, dragging their corpses and their shameful defeat.'

(…) The Somalia operation, in some ways, made bin Laden. During the Afghan war, the CIA had been very aware of him (although the agency now insists it never 'controlled' him), but in Somalia, bin Laden had taken a swing at the biggest kid in the school yard and given him a black eye. The next fight, a few weeks later, would begin with a sucker punch.

It was snowing in New York on February 26, 1993, when a massive truck bomb exploded at the World Trade Center, tearing through three levels of the building's underground garage, basement, and foundation (…) Six people were killed, and more than a thousand were injured. It was the first major international terrorist attack on U.S. soil. Within weeks, the FBI had tracked down four of the bombers, a collection of militant Muslims, most of whom had fought in Afghanistan and had become followers of a blind sheik in Jersey City named Omar Abdel Rahman. The organizer of the bombing plot, Ramzi Yousef, boarded a plane at Kennedy airport a few hours after the explosion and escaped (…) investigators have since uncovered a series of connections between Yousef and groups funded by an individual, Osama bin Laden.

But bin Laden denied to me that he was behind the bombing and claimed he didn't know Ramzi Yousef. 'Unfortunately,' he said with a wave of his hand, 'I did not know him before the incident.' (...)

Sitting in the hut on bin Laden's mountain in Afghanistan, I asked bin Laden if he had tried to kill Clinton. 'As I said, every action elicits a similar reaction,' he explained. 'What does Clinton expect from those that he killed, assaulting their children and mothers?' But he was quick to sidestep the question of his culpability, very careful not to implicate himself. He wasn't in Somalia, but he liked what he saw. He didn't blow up American bases in Saudi Arabia, but those who did are martyrs. He didn't pay for the World Trade Center bombing or the plot to kill Clinton, but they were good ideas.

For the future, bin Laden told me his first priority is to get the American military out of Saudi Arabia, the holiest of lands in Islam. 'Every day the Americans delay their departure, they will receive a new corpse.'

Already, U.S. forces have been dealt devastating blows there. Nineteen servicemen were killed in the 1996 bombing of the airforce barracks in Dhahran, and five U.S. military personnel were killed in a similar bombing in Riyadh in 1995. Investigators believe bin Laden is tied at some level to both attacks. Bin Laden said that the American military would leave Saudi Arabia, regardless of the fact that the Saudi royal family welcomes the American presence (...)

'We do not differentiate between those dressed in military uniforms and civilians; they are all targets in this fatwa.' Bin Laden argued that American outrage at attacks on American civilians constitutes a great double standard.

'American history does not distinguish between civilians and military, not even women and children. They are the ones who used bombs against Nagasaki. Can these bombs distinguish between infants and military? America does not have a religion that will prevent it from destroying all people.'

Bin Laden believes that what we consider to be terrorism is just the amount of violence required to get the attention of the American people. His aim is to get Americans to consider whether continued support of Israel is worth the bloodshed he promises.

'So we tell the Americans as people,' bin Laden said softly, 'and we tell the mothers of soldiers and American mothers in general that if they value their lives and the lives of their children, to find a nationalistic government that will look after their interests and not the interests of the Jews. The continuation of tyranny will bring the fight to America, as Ramzi Yousef and others did. This is my message to the American people: to look for a serious government that looks out for their interests and does not attack others, their lands, or their honor. And my word to American journalists is not to ask why we did that but ask what their government has done that forced us to defend ourselves.'

His last words to the camera were, 'It is our duty to lead people to the light.'

(...) we had our little story, and a few weeks later, in a few minutes of footage,

Osama bin Laden would say hi to America. Not many people would pay attention. Just another Arab terrorist . . .

19.11 The War on Terrorism and the Lessons of the Cold War

On 11 September 2001 the unimaginable became reality as three hijacked planes hit the twin towers of the World Trade Center in New York and the Pentagon building in Washington, DC (a fourth hijacked plane went down in Pennsylvania). Within hours the WTC towers collapsed, and the estimated number of casualties reached as high as 5,000 (later it was confirmed to be around 3,000). The attacks were quickly identified as the work of Osama Bin Laden's Al Qaida network. The following month the United States, with the assistance of a number of other countries, launched strikes on Afghanistan's ruling Taliban regime, which had provided sanctuary for Bin-Laden and refused to hand him over. By November 2001 Kabul was in the hands of the opposition and the United States was actively spearheading a war on terrorism both at home and abroad. In the extract below, Stanley A. Weiss, founder and chairman of Business Executives for National Security, compares the new war to the Cold War.

The war on terrorism, we are told, is a new kind of war. The scale and scope of terrorism's targeting of innocent civilians across borders and the stateless nature of the organizers represent a security challenge the likes of which the West has never seen before.

True, some of the specific threats have changed, in remarkable ways. But this first war of the 21st century looks much like the last war of the 20th—the Cold War against communism. As the long battle against global terrorism begins, we should look at the lessons of that long and ultimately victorious struggle.

Communist leaders from Lenin and Stalin to Mao to Castro had worldwide ambitions that were hostile to Western values, particularly freedom, tolerance and prosperity. Like Osama bin Laden, they were willing to resort to mass violence and were expert in the use of propaganda to attract the poor and uneducated to their cause.

It took more than 70 years, but the West ultimately beat back the challenge posed by communism. How did we do it? Part of the answer, of course, was military. We fought two large-scale wars in Asia against communism and provided military equipment to dozens of anti-Communist insurgencies, including one that became the Taliban in Afghanistan.

But in the end it was not only military prowess that proved decisive but also the ability to win the hearts, minds and wallets of billions worldwide. The West's economic success, and particularly its ability to extend the promise of market economies to developing nations of Latin America, Southern and Eastern Europe and the Pacific Rim countries of Asia, helped suck the lifeblood out of communism's global appeal. Eventually the inability of communism to meet the yearning for a better life spelled its doom.

The same could be the case in the war against global terrorism. The military effort must be coupled with a revival of some of the programs and initiatives that proved so effective during the Cold War. In some cases, these programs should take precedence over purely military tactics.

Development aid. During the Cold War the United States provided billions of dollars in economic aid, much of which was used to build infrastructure and to feed and educate the people. The most spectacular successes were the Marshall Plan for Europe and rebuilding Japan and Germany.

Building market economies. Insistence on open and free trade was instrumental in allowing many developing countries to build stable and prosperous economies. The 20th century proved the axiom that good economics builds good politics—not the other way around. Authoritarian countries and regions that embraced capitalism, such as Taiwan, South Korea, Thailand and Latin America eventually produced a middle class that saw democracy take root.

Public diplomacy. To counter bin Laden's appeal to disenfranchised young Muslims, we will have to articulate a better vision of the future. We must become a beacon not just to the privileged classes in the Islamic world but to the Muslim 'street.'

Western leaders have indicated at least a token understanding of this broader agenda. The decision to couple bombing with food delivery is a step in the right direction, as is the decision to minimize civilian casualties. The United States and Britain should now agree to curtail the bombing even more and work with Pakistan, Iran and Afghanistan's other neighbors to ensure stability in the region after the Taliban are gone.

The West should announce a Marshall-like plan for those moderate regimes in the Muslim world willing to commit to the war against fanaticism. In the long run the only way to win this war is to encourage economic growth and market capitalism (...)

Spreading the wealth leads to greater stability and a middle class that will demand a political voice (...) Those North African and Middle Eastern states, such as Jordan, Morocco and Tunisia, that are developing their economies before pushing democracy are now more enlightened than states such as Syria, Iraq and Sudan, where instant democracy descended into military tyranny. The West must offer a stake in the modern capitalist economic system to all who are now disadvantaged.

19.12 American–Russian Relations in Late 2001

One of the countries that the United States was keen on co-operating with in the war on terrorism was Russia. Facing the problem of Islamic militants within his own borders, Russia's president Vladimir Putin was a willing participant in an anti-terrorist coalition; the first extract is drawn from a joint US–Russian statement to this end. However, while the events of 11 September 2001 commanded most of the attention of the Bush administration, the president did follow up on his earlier pledge to cancel the 1972 Soviet–American ABM Treaty. The Bush administration did this in order to focus upon the development of a new Missile Defense System that would ideally protect the United States agains any incoming missiles. The ABM Treaty had restricted the number of antiballistic missile sites to two. Along with the 'war on terrorism', this decision heralded the clear emergence of new priorities for the US administration.

A. George W. Bush and Vladimir Putin, October 2001

The President of the United States and the President of Russia categorically reject and resolutely condemn terrorism in all its forms and manifestations, regardless of motive. The Presidents stress that the barbaric act of terrorism committed in the United States on September 11, 2001 represents a crime against all humanity.

The Presidents note that terrorism threatens not only the security of the United States and Russia, but also that of the entire international community, as well as international peace and security. They believe that terrorism poses a direct threat to the rule of law and to human rights and democratic values. It has no foundation in any religion, national or cultural traditions, and it only uses them as a cover for its criminal goals (...)

The Presidents call for all states to join a sustained global coalition to defeat international terrorism. Nations must make use of diplomatic, political, law enforcement, financial, intelligence, and military means to root out terrorists and their sponsors and bring them to justice.

The Presidents emphasize that the current situation in Afghanistan is a direct consequence of the policies pursued by the Taliban, which turned that country into an international center of terrorism and extremism. They reaffirm that the United States and Russia are ready to cooperate closely with the United Nations to promote a post-conflict settlement in Afghanistan that would provide for the formation of a representative, broad-based government capable of ensuring the restoration of a peaceful Afghanistan that maintains good relations with countries of the region and beyond it.

The leaders of the two countries view U.S.–Russian cooperation as a critical element in the global effort against terrorism. They reaffirm their personal commitment and that of their two countries to fight this deadly challenge through active cooperation and coordination, both bilaterally and within the framework of international institutions (…)

The Presidents agree that the financial, communications, and logistics networks of terrorist organizations must be destroyed. They call upon all nations without exception to take measures to block access of terrorist organizations to financial resources, to enhance law enforcement tools to combat terrorism, and to strengthen procedures to stop the transit of terrorists and their material within and between countries. They stress the importance of speedy ratification and implementation of existing international counterterrorism conventions.

The two Presidents are resolved to advance cooperation in combating new terrorist threats: nuclear, chemical and biological, as well as those in cyberspace. They agreed to enhance bilateral and multilateral action to stem the export and proliferation of nuclear, chemical and biological materials, related technologies, and delivery systems as a critical component of the battle to defeat international terrorism.

B. George W. Bush on the United States Leaving the 1972 ABM TREATY, December 2001

(…) I've just concluded a meeting of my National Security Council. We reviewed what I discussed with my friend, President Vladimir Putin, over the course of many meetings, many months. And that is the need for America to move beyond the 1972 Anti Ballistic Missile treaty.

Today, I have given formal notice to Russia, in accordance with the treaty, that the United States of America is withdrawing from this almost 30 year old treaty. I have concluded the ABM treaty hinders our government's ability to develop ways to protect our people from future terrorist or rogue state missile attacks.

The 1972 ABM treaty was signed by the United States and the Soviet Union at a much different time, in a vastly different world. One of the signatories, the Soviet Union, no longer exists. And neither does the hostility that once led both our countries to keep thousands of nuclear weapons on hair-trigger alert, pointed at each other. The grim theory was that neither side would launch a nuclear attack because it knew the other would respond, thereby destroying both.

Today, as the events of September the 11th made all too clear, the greatest threats to both our countries come not from each other, or other big powers in the world, but from terrorists who strike without warning, or rogue states who seek weapons of mass destruction.

We know that the terrorists, and some of those who support them, seek the ability to deliver death and destruction to our doorstep via missile. And we must have the freedom and the flexibility to develop effective defenses against those attacks. Defending the American people is my highest priority as Commander in Chief, and I cannot and will not allow the United States to remain in a treaty that prevents us from developing effective defenses.

At the same time, the United States and Russia have developed a new, much more hopeful and constructive relationship. We are moving to replace mutually assured destruction with mutual cooperation. Beginning in Ljubljana, and continuing in meetings in Genoa, Shanghai, Washington and Crawford, President Putin and I developed common ground for a new strategic relationship. Russia is in the midst of a transition to free markets and democracy. We are committed to forging strong economic ties between Russia and the United States, and new bonds between Russia and our partners in NATO (...)

We're already working closely together as the world rallies in the war against terrorism. I appreciate so much President Putin's important advice and cooperation as we fight to dismantle the al Qaeda network in Afghanistan. I appreciate his commitment to reduce Russia's offensive nuclear weapons. I reiterate our pledge to reduce our own nuclear arsenal between 1,700 and 2,200 operationally deployed strategic nuclear weapons. President Putin and I have also agreed that my decision to withdraw from the treaty will not, in any way, undermine our new relationship or Russian security.

As President Putin said in Crawford, we are on the path to a fundamentally different relationship. The Cold War is long gone. Today we leave behind one of its last vestiges.

Questions

What were the key issues in the new Russian–American relationship of the early 1990s?

How deep had capitalism penetrated in Vietnam by the early 1990s?

Was Samuel P. Huntington too pessimistic in his 1996 prognosis of the future 'clash of civilizations'?

What were the key points of disagreement between German chancellor Helmut Kohl and British prime minister Margaret Thatcher on the question of European integration?

What accounts for the different post-Cold War fates of Poland and Angola?

How different were the concerns over nuclear weapons in 1998 as opposed to various stages during the Cold War (see also documents in Chapter 9)?

Are Long Yongtu's and Mike Moore's descriptions of the significance of China's WTO accession identical?

What are the links between the Cold War and Osama bin Laden's 'programme'?

Do you agree with the parallels that Stanley A. Weiss draws between the war on terrorism and the Cold War?

What points of agreement and disagreement between Russia and the United States can be detected from the last two documents (Vladimir Putin and George W. Bush)?

Sources

The editors endeavored to contact all copyright holders and would be happy to rectify any possible omissions.

Abbreviations Used in Sources

AFPRF	Archive of the Foreign Policy of the Russian Federation, Moscow
AJBT	Archive of Josip Broz Tito, Belgrade
ANR	Archive of New Records, Warsaw
APRF	Archive of the President of the Russian Federation, Moscow
CCA	Chinese Central Archives, Beijing
CWIHP	Cold War International History Project, Woodrow Wilson Center, Washington, DC
DBPO	*Documents on British Policy Overseas*
DOIA	*Documents on International Affairs*
DOSB	Department of State Bulletin
DPRK	Democratic People's Republic of Korea
FDRL	Franklin D. Roosevelt Presidential Library, Hyde Park, New York
FRUS	*Foreign Relations of the United States*
GFL	Gerald Ford Presidential Library, Ann Arbor, Michigan
HSTL	Harry S. Truman Presidential Library, Independence, Missouri
JFKL	John F. Kennedy Presidential Library, Boston, Massachusetts
NA	US National Archives, College Park, Maryland
NPMP	Nixon Presidential Materials Project, US National Archives
NSecA	National Security Archives, Washington, DC
PPP	Public Papers of the President
PRO	Public Record Office, Kew, Surrey
RSACH	Russian State Archive for Contemporary History, Moscow

Chapter 1

1. V. I. Lenin, 'Letter to Workers in America', 1918. V. I. Lenin, *Collected Works*, vol. 28 (Moscow: Progress Publishers, 1966), 62–75.
2. A. Mitchell Palmer, 'The Case Against the "Reds"', *Forum*, 63 (1920), 173–85.
3. Bainbridge Colby to Woodrow Wilson, Aug. 1920. *FRUS 1920*, vol. III, pp. 463–8.
4. J. V. Stalin, 'The International Situation and the Tasks of the Communist Parties', 22 Mar. 1925. J. V. Stalin, *Works*, vol. 7 (Moscow: Foreign Languages Publishing House, 1954), 51–7.

5. Mao Zedong, 'Report on Hunan', 1927. *Selected Works of Mao Tse-tung*, vol. I (3rd printing; Beijing: Foreign Languages Press, 1975), 23–9.
6. FRUS. *The Soviet Union 1933–1939*, 14–17.
7. John Scott, *Behind the Urals* (Bloomington, Ind.: Indiana University Press, 1976 [1942]), 3–6, 264–6. Reprinted by permission from Indiana University Press.
8A. Molotov Speech on the Nazi–Soviet Pact, Aug. 1939. *DOIA 1939–1946*, 437–42.
8B. Secret Protocols of the Nazi–Soviet Pact, Aug. 1939. *Nazi–Soviet Relations 1939–1941. Documents from the Archives of the German Foreign Office* (Washington DC: Government Printing Office, 1948), 78–81.
9A. Memorandum of conversation, Harry Hopkins–Joseph Stalin, 30 July 1941. *FRUS 1941*, volume I, pp. 802–4.
9B. Joint Message of Churchill and Roosevelt to Stalin, 15 Aug. 1941. *DOSB*, 8 Nov. 1941, pp. 9–10.
10. Memorandum of conversation between Churchill, Stalin, and Roosevelt, 30 Nov. 1943. *FRUS 1943. Conferences at Cairo and Teheran*, pp. 596–600.
11. PRO.
12. HSTL. First published on the Truman Library website: www.whistlestop.org/study_collection

Chapter 2

1. Winston Churchill, *The Second World War*: Vol. 6: *Triumph and Tragedy* (London: Cassell & Co. Ltd., 1954), 196–7. Copyright 1953 by Houghton Mifflin Co., © renewed 1981 by The Hon. Lady Sarah Audley and The Hon. Lady Soames. Reprinted by permission of Houghton Mifflin Co. All rights reserved.
2A. *FRUS. Conferences at Malta and Yalta*, pp. 221–3.
2B. Ibid. 667–71.
2C. FDRL. First published at the CWIHP website: http://cwihp.si.edu
3. APRF. First published on the CWIHP website, http://cwihp.si.edu. Trans. Daniel Rozas.
4A. *Winston S. Churchill: His Complete Speeches 1897–1963*, ed. Robert Rhodes James, Vol. VII, *1943–1949* (New York and London: Chelsea House Publishers, 1974), 7285–93.
4B. 'Stalin's Reply to Churchill', *New York Times*, 14 Mar. 1946. Originally published in *Pravda*.
5. Archives of the Institute for Political History, Budapest, Hungary. First published in the CWIHP Bulletin, 10. Trans. David Evans.
6. 'A. Zhdanov, at the Founding of the Cominform, September 1947', *DOIA 1947–1948*, pp. 122–37.
7. AJBT, Belgrade, Yugoslavia. First published in the *CWIHP Bulletin*, 10. Trans. Vladislav Zubok.
8A. Einar Gerhardsen, *Samarbeid og strid. Erindringer 1945–55* (Oslo: Tiden Norsk Forlag, 1971), 195–6. ©. Trans. the editors.

8B. J. K. Paasikivi. *Paasikiven päiväkirjat, 1944–1956*, vol. I (Helsinki: WSOY, 1985), 625–6. Reprinted by permission from WSOY, Juhani Paasikivi, and Sinikka Couchman. Trans. the editors.

9. Amelie Pose, *När järnridån föll över Prag* (Stockholm: Natur och kultur, 1968), 150–5. Trans. the editors.

10. *The Cominform: Minutes of the Three Conferences 1947/1948/1949*, ed. Giuliano Procacci (Milan: Fondazione Giangiacomo Feltrinelli, 1994), 641 (appendix B).

11. The indictment of Laszlo Rajk, September 1949, *DOIA, 1949–1950*, pp. 390–6.

12. *FRUS 1952–54*, vol. VII, pp. 110–16.

Chapter 3

1. *FRUS. Conferences at Malta and Yalta*, p. 155.

2. *The Testament of Adolf Hitler: The Hitler–Bormann Documents, February–April, 1945*, ed. François Genoud, trans. R. H. Stevens (London: Cassell, 1961), 103–9.

3. Studs Terkel, *'The Good War': An Oral History of World War II* (New York: Random House, 1984), 444–8, 450–3. Reprinted by permission of Donaldio & Olson Inc. Copyright © 1980 by Studs Terkel.

4. Norman Naimark, *The Russians in Germany: A History of the Soviet Zone of Occupation, 1945–1949* (Cambridge, Mass.: The Belknap Press of Harvard University Press, 1995), 78–83. Copyright © by the President and Fellows of Harvard College. Reprinted by permission.

5. *FRUS. 1945*, volume II, pp. 520–4.

6. APRF. First published on the CWIHP website: http://cwihp.si.edu

7. RSACH. First published in *CWIHP Bulletin*, 4.

8. *The Papers of General Lucius D. Clay*: vol. 1, *Germany, 1945–1949*, ed. Jean Edward Smith (Bloomington, Ind.: Indiana University Press, 1974), 279–84. Reprinted by permission.

9. PRO.

10. Willy Brandt, *My Road to Berlin* (London: Doubleday, 1960), 184–98.

11. AFPRF. First published on the CWIHP website: http://cwihp.si.edu

12A. *FRUS 1952–54*, vol. VII: 2, pp. 169–72.

12B. Ibid. 194–9.

12C. RSACH. First published in *CWIHP Bulletin*, 4.

Chapter 4

1. *FRUS 1946*, vol. VI, pp. 696–709.

2. AFPRF. Published at the CWIHP website: http://cwihp.si.edu

3. *FRUS 1947*, vol. V, pp. 32–5.

4. *DOIA 1947–1948*, pp. 2–7.

5. Janet Flanner (Genet), *Paris Journal 1944–1965*, ed. William Shawn (London: Victor Gollancz, 1966), 51–4, 82–3.

6. George Marshall's address at the commencement ceremonies of Harvard University, 12 June 1947. *DOSB*, June 15, 1947, pp. 1159–60.
7. Vincent Auriol, *Mon Septennat, 1947–1954* (Paris: Gallimard, 1970), 52–6. Trans. Jerome Elie.
8. *DOIA 1947–48*, pp. 58–9.
9. *FRUS 1948*, vol. III, pp. 153–8.
10. *DOIA 1949–50*, pp. 254–6.
11. *FRUS 1949*, vol. IV, pp. 261–5.

Chapter 5

1. Tatsuichiro Akaizuki, *Nagasaki 1945: The First Full-Length Eyewitness Account of the Atomic Bomb Attack on Nagasaki*, trans. Keiichi Nagata, ed. and with an Introduction by Gordon Honeycombe (London: Quartet Books, 1981), 22–31.
2. Transmitted by Domei and recorded by the US Federal Communications Commission, 14 Aug. 1945.
3. 'Basic Initial Post-Surrender Directive'. *Political Reorientation of Japan: Report of the Government Section, Supreme Commander for the Allied Powers*, vol. 2 (Washington, DC: US Government Printing Office, 1949), Appendix A, pp. 423–6.
4. John Dower, *Embracing Defeat: Japan in the Wake of World War II* (New York: Norton, 1999), 126–32. Copyright © 1999 by John W. Dower. Used by permission of W. W. Norton & Company, Inc.
5. Mark Gayn, *Japan Diary* (New York: William Sloan Associates, 1948), 226–32.
6. *FRUS 1948*, vol. VI.
7. *FRUS 1952–1954*, vol. XIV.
10. *FRUS 1955–1957*, vol. XXIII: *Japan*, pp. 53–62.
11. *FRUS 1958–1960*, vol. XVIII: *Japan*, pp. 344–9.
12. Ibid. 329–31, 394–7.
13. Based on the English-language version of the Income-Doubling Plan issued by the Japanese Economic Planning Agency in 1960. Quoted from Gary D. Allinson (ed.), *The Columbia Guide to Modern Japanese History* (New York: Columbia University Press, 1999).
14. NA.

Chapter 6

1. Mikoyan to Stalin, 4 Feb. 1949. APRF. Trans. Tamara Karganova.
2. Record of conversation, Stalin–Kim Il Sung, 5 Mar. 1949. AFPRF. First published in *CWIHP Bulletin*, 5. Trans. Kathryn Weathersby.
3. Record of conversation, Stalin–Mao Zedong, 16 Dec. 1949. APRF. First published in *CWIHP Bulletin*, 6–7. Trans. Danny Rozas.
4. Quoted from *The DPRK Report* (Moscow), no. 23 (Mar.–Apr. 2000).
5. Shtykov to Stalin, 26 June 1950. Collection of Soviet military documents obtained in 1994 by the BBC. First published in *CWIHP Bulletin*, 6–7.

6. Statement by the President on the Situation in Korea. PPP. Harry S Truman. 1950. P. 172.

7A. Marguerite Higgins, 'Reds in Seoul Forcing G.I.s to Blast City Apart', *New York Herald-Tribune*, 25 Sept. 1950.

7B. Marguerite Higgins. 'Inside Seoul: Marines Gain Inch by Inch', *New York Herald-Tribune*, 27 Sept. 1950.

8. Donald Knox, *The Korean War, Pusan to Chosin: An Oral History* (San Diego, Calif.: Harcourt, Brace, Jovanovich, 1985), 439–40.

9. Jim G. Lucas, 'One Misstep Spells Death in Korea', *New York World-Telegram*, 7 Jan. 1953.

10. *Major Speeches and Debates of Senator Joseph McCarthy Delivered in the United States Senate 1950–1951* (New York: Garden Press, 1975), 157–60.

11. Record of conversation, Stalin–Zhou Enlai, 19 Sept. 1952. APRF. Trans. Danny Rozas with Kathryn Weathersby. First published in *CWIHP Bulletin*, 6–7.

12. Speech by Mao Zedong at a CCP Conference, 27 Jan. 1957. CCA. First published in *Mao Zedong waijiao wenxuan* [Selected Diplomatic Papers of Mao Zedong] (Beijing: Zhongyang wenxian, 1993), 280–3. Trans. Shu Guang Zhang and Chen Jian.

13. Record of conversation, Mao Zedong–Pavel Yudin, 22 July 1958. CCA. First published in *Mao Zedong waijiao wenxuan*, 322–33. Trans. Shu Guang Zhang and Chen Jian.

14. Incomplete notes by Mao Zedong. CCA. First published in *Jianguo yilai Mao Zedong wengao* [Mao Zedong's Writings after the Founding of the PRC], vol. 8 (Beijing: Zhongyang wenxian, 1991) (marked 'internal publication'), 559–603. Trans. the editors.

15. Record of conversation, Zhou Enlai–Stephan Chervonenko, 25 June 1961. AFPRF. First published in OA Westad (ed.), *Brothers in Arms: The Rise and Fall of the Sino-Soviet Alliance, 1945–1963* (Stanford, Calif.: Stanford University Press, 1998). Trans. Olga Baeva.

16. Record of conversation, Soviet and Chinese Delegations, Moscow, 8–10 July 1963. Archival Fond of Parties and Mass Organizations in the Former German Democratic Republic, German Federal Archive, Berlin. Obtained by Vladislav Zubok; trans. Benjamin Aldrich-Moodie. First published in *CWIHP Bulletin*, 10.

Chapter 7

1. Ho Chi Minh's declaration of Vietnamese independence, August 1945, http://home.vnn.vn/english/government/declar_of_indep.html

2. *FRUS 1952–54*, vol. XVI, pp. 1325–7.

3. *FRUS 1961–63*, vol. II: *Vietnam 1961*, pp. 591–4.

4. *FRUS 1961–1963*, vol. IV: *Vietnam 1963*, pp. 472–3.

5. Michael Beschloss (ed.), *Taking Charge: The Johnson White House Tapes,*

1963–1964 (New York: Simon & Schuster, 1998), 401–3. Reprinted with the permission of Simon & Schuster. Copyright © 1998 by Michael Beschloss.

6. http://students.vassar.edu/~vietnam/doc18.html. Trans. Robert K. Brigham and Le Phuong Anh.

7. Michael Herr, *Dispatches* (New York: Knopf, 1977), 86–7. Reprinted by permission of Donaldio & Olson Inc. and Alfred A. Knopf, a division of Random House, Inc. Copyright © 1977 by Michael Herr.

8. Bao Ninh, *The Sorrow of War: A Novel of North Vietnam*, trans. from the Vietnamese by Phan Thanh Hao, ed. Frank Palmos (New York: Riverhead Books, 1995), 2–4. Copyright © 1995 by Bao Ninh. Used by permission of Pantheon Books, a division of Random House, Inc.

9. Norman Mailer, *Armies of the Night: History as a Novel, The Novel as History* (London, Weidenfeld & Nicolson, 1968), 258–63. ©

10. Record of conversation, Mao Zedong–Le Duan, May 1970. Odd Arne Westad *et al.* (eds.), *77 Conversations Between Chinese and Foreign Leaders on the Wars in Indochina* (1964–1977), CWIHP Working Paper 22, pp. 163–9.

11A. NPMP.

11B. Ibid.

12A. H. R. Haldeman, *The Haldeman Diaries: Inside the Nixon White House* (New York: Berkeley Books, 1994), 692–3, 696–7. Copyright © 1994 by The Haldeman Family Trust. Used by permission of G. P. Putnam's Sons, a division of Penguin Putnam Inc.

12B. NPMP.

13. Ibid.

14. John Pilger, *Heroes* (London: J. Cape, 1986), 228–9. Reprinted by permission.

Chapter 8

1A. Torsten Diedrich, *Der 17. Juni 1953 in der DDR* [17 June 1953 in the GDR] (Berlin: Dietz, 1991), 227–8. Trans. Laura Schmidt.

1B. Ibid. 282–7. Trans. Laura Schmidt.

2. *Khrushchev Speaks: Selected Speeches, Articles, and Press Conferences, 1949–1961*, ed., with Commentary, by Thomas P. Whitney (Ann Arbor, Mich.: University of Michigan Press, 1963), 259–65.

3. Carl and Shelley Mydans, *The Violent Peace* (New York: Atheneum, 1968), 189–94.

4A. Thomas Scholze and Falk Blash, *Halt! Grenzgebiet! Leben im Schatten der Mauer* [Stop! Border Zone! Living in the Shadow of the Wall] (Berlin: BasisDruck, 1992), 79–83, 199–207. Trans. Laura Schmidt.

4B. Gerda Szepansky, *Die Stille Emanzipation: Frauen in der DDR* [The Quiet Emancipation: Women in the GDR] (Frankfurt a.M.: Fischer, 1995), 126–40. Trans. Laura Schmidt.

5. János Kádár, Speech at the IKARUS Cultural Centre, February 1968. Published

in *János Kádár: First Secretary of the Hungarian Socialist Workers' Party. Selected Speeches and Interviews* (Oxford: Pergamon, 1985), 317–19.

6A–B. *The Prague Spring 1968. A National Security Archive Documents Reader*, compiled and edited by Jaromir Navratil *et al.* (New York: Central University Press, 1998).

  6C. *FRUS 1964–1968*, vol. XVII, pp. 236–41.

   7. Adam Bromke and John Strong, *Gierek's Poland* (New York: Praeger, 1973), 213–15; originally in Ewa Wacowska (ed.), *Rewolta szczecińska i jej znaczenie* (Paris: Instytut Literacki, 1971).

  8A. Roderick MacFarquhar, Tomothy Cheek, and Eugene Wu, *The Secret Speeches of Chairman Mao: From the Hundred Flowers to the Great Leap* (Cambridge, Mass.: Harvard University Press, 1989), 406–11. Reprinted by permission of the publisher.

  8B. Michael Schoenhals (ed.), *China's Cultural Revolution, 1966–1969: NOT a Dinner Party* (Armonk, NY: M. E. Sharpe, 1996), 101–16.

Chapter 9

   1. Stephen I. Schwartz (ed.), *Atomic Audit: The Costs and Consequences of US Nuclear Weapons Since 1940* (Washington, DC: Brookings Institution Press, 1998), 6. Reprinted by permission of the publisher.

   2. Andrei Sakharov, *Memoirs*, trans. Richard Courie (London: Hutchinson, 1990), 173–5. Used by permission of the Random House Group Ltd.

   3. *DOSB*, 25 January 1962, pp. 107–10.

   4. NA. First published in *International Security*, 6: 3 (Winter 1981/2), 3–38.

   5. Otto Nathan and Heinz Norden (eds.), *Einstein on Peace* (London: Methuen & Co., 1963), 632–6.

  6A. Thomas Watson, Jr. and Peter Petre, *Father and Son & Co.: My Life at IBM and Beyond* (London: Bantam, 1990), 230–3. Copyright © 1990 by Thomas J. Watson, Jr. Used by permission of Bantam Books, a division of Random House, Inc.

  6B. Roald Sagdeev, *The Making of a Soviet Scientist* (New York: John Wiley & Sons, 1994), 119–23. Used by permission of John Wiley & Sons, Inc.

   7. *New York Times*, 6 Oct. 1957.

  8A. PPP. Dwight D. Eisenhower, 1960. Pp. 1036–9.

  8B. US Senate, 86th Congress Hearings (Missiles, Space and Other Defense Matters—1960).

   9. NA.

  10. SIOP-62. JFKL. First published in *International Security*, 12: 1 (Summer 1987), 41–51.

  13. Schwartz (ed.), *Atomic Audit*, 408–11. Reprinted by permission of the publisher.

  14. Aleksandr G. Saveliyev and Nikolay N. Detinov, *The Big Five: Arms Control Decision-Making in the Soviet Union*, trans. Dimitryi Trenin, ed., Gregory Vorhall (Westport, Conn.: Praeger, 1995), 3–8.

15. Congress of the United States. Office of Technology Assessment. The Effects of Nuclear War. Washington: OTA, May 1979. Pp. 27–35.

16A. PPP. Ronald Reagan, 1985. Pp. 917–19.

16B. Mikhail Gorbachev, *Perestroika: New Thinking for Our Country and the World* (London: Collins, 1987), 218–20.

Chapter 10

1. *Jean Monnet–Robert Schuman Correspondance 1947–1953* (Lausanne, Switzerland: Fondation Jean Monnet pour l'Europe, 1986), 35–8. Reprinted by permission of Fondation Jean Monnet pour l'Europe.

2A. From the History of European integration website: http://www.let.leidenuniv.nl/history/rtg/res1/pleven.htm

2B. From the European Union website: http://europa.eu.int/abc/obj/treaties/en/entoc29.htm

3A. *DBPO*, series II, vol. I, *1950–1952*, pp. 462–5.

3B. Ibid. 787–8.

4. From the History of European Integration website: http://www.let.leidenuniv.nl/history/rtg/res1/messina.htm

5A. *FRUS 1955–57*, vol. IV, pp. 363–4.

5B. Ibid. 66–70.

6. PRO.

7A. RSACH. First published in *CWIHP Bulletin*, 3. Trans. Vladislav Zubok.

7B. *DOSB*, 4 September 1961, pp. 397–400.

7C. PPP. John F. Kennedy, 1963. Pp. 524–5.

8. PRO.

9A. PRO.

9B. American Foreign Policy, Current Documents, 1967, pp. 328–31.

10A. *A Retrospective View of the Political Year in Europe, 1969* (Paris: WEU, 1970), 127–31.

10B. NPMP.

11. *The Times*, 22 May 1971.

12. *DBPO*, series III, vol. II, *The Conference on Security and Cooperation in Europe, 1972–1975*, pp. 474–9.

13. *DOSB*, 8 December 1975, pp. 805–7.

14. PPP. Ronald Reagan, 1986, vol. I. Pp. 502–7.

Chapter 11

1. Originally published in *Let a New Asia and a New Africa Be Born!* (Jakarta: Ministry of Foreign Affairs, Republic of Indonesia, [1955]). Reprinted in George McT. Kahin, *The Asian–African Conference, Bandung, Indonesia, April 1955* (Port Washington, NY: Kennikat Press, 1956), Appendix, pp. 39–51.

2. Max F. Millikan and W. W. Rostow, *A Proposal: Key to an Effective Foreign Policy*

(New York: Harper & Row, 1957), 2–8. Copyright © 1957 by Massachusetts Institute of Technology. Copyright renewed © 1985 by Massachusetts Institute of Technology. Reprinted by permission of HarperCollins Publishers, Inc.

3. Kwame Nkrumah, *I Speak of Freedom: A Statement of African Ideology* (London: Heinemann, 1961), 142–5.

4. Harold Macmillan, *Pointing the Way: 1959–1961* (London: Macmillan, 1972). Reprinted by permission of the publisher.

5. RSACH.

6. PPP. John F. Kennedy, 1961. Pp. 204–6.

7A. *La Pensée politique de Patrice Lumumba* [The Political Thought of Patrice Lumumba], collected and introduced by Jean van Lierde; preface by Jean-Paul Sartre (Paris: Présence africaine, 1964), 394–8. Trans. Laura Schmidt.

7B. Mydans, *The Violent Peace*, 313.

8. *FRUS 1961–1963*, vol. XX, pp. 858–63.

9. Frantz Fanon, *The Wretched of the Earth*, trans. Constance Farrington (Harmondsworth: Penguin, 1983), 73–84. Reprinted by permission of HarperCollins Publisher, Ltd. © Frantz Fanon 1983.

10. *Russia in Asia and Africa: Documents 1946–1971*, ed. J. A. Naik (Kalhapur: Avinash Reference Publications, 1979), 489–509.

11. *FRUS 1964–1968*, vol. XXVI, pp. 361–3.

12. Ernesto 'Che' Guevara, *The African Dream: The Diaries of the Revolutionary War in the Congo*, with an Introduction by Richard Gott and a Foreword by Alida Guevara March (London: Harvill Press, 2000), 232–44. © Archivo Personal del Che, 1999. English trans. © Patrick Camillier, 2000. Reprinted by permission of the Harvill Press.

13. *Sacred Hope: Poems by Agostinho Neto*, trans. Marga Holness, Foreword by Basil Davidson (London: Journeyman, 1988), 129–31.

Chapter 12

1. *FRUS 1950*, vol. II, pp. 598–624.

2. Juan Jose Arevalo, *The Shark and the Sardines*, trans. from the Spanish by June Cobb and Raul Osegueda (New York: L. Stuart, 1961 [1956]), 9–13. Reprinted in *Latin America and the United States: A Documentary History*, ed. Robert H. Holden and Eric Zolov (Oxford: Oxford University Press, 2000), 235–7.

3. *FRUS 1958–1960*, vol. V, pp. 239–46.

4. NA. Copy obtained via the NSecA.

5. *Soviet News*, no. 4304 (11 July 1960), 28–9.

6A. PPP. John F. Kennedy, 1961. Pp. 170–5.

6B. Eduardo Frei, 'The Lost Alliance', *Foreign Affairs*, 45: 3 (1967), 437–48. Reprinted by permission of The *New York Times* Syndicate.

7. NSecA.

8A. Ernesto 'Che' Guevara, 'Guerrilla Warfare: A Method', *CHE: Selected Works of Ernesto Guevara*, ed. Rolando E. Bonache and Nelson P. Valdes

(Cambridge, Mass.: MIT Press, 1969), 89–103. Reprinted by permission of MIT Press.

8B. NSecA.

9A. NPMP.

9B. Samuel Chackin, *Storm Approaching: The Junta Under Siege* (Westport, Conn.: Greenwood Press, 1985), 158–61.

10A. RSACH. First published in *CWIHP Bulletin*, 8–9.

10B. O'Donnell to State Department 20 July 1979. Document 986 in *Nicaragua: The Making of U.S. Policy, 1978–1990*. Microform collection. Washington, DC: NSecA, 1991.

11A. PPP. Ronald Reagan, 1983. Pp. 601–7.

11B. Richard Aregood, 'Dangers', *Philadelphia Daily News*, 1 Oct. 1984.

Chapter 13

1. George Orwell, *Nineteen Eighty-Four* (London: Everyman, 1992 [1949]), 312–26.

2. Arthur Koestler, *Bricks To Babel: Selected Writings with Comments by the Author* (London: Hutchinson, 1980), 252–8. Reprinted by permission of PFD on behalf of the Estate of Arthur Koestler. © ORIGINAL

3. Pablo Neruda, *Canto General*, trans. Jack Smith (Berkeley: University of California Press, 1991), 332–3. Copyright © 1991 Fundacion Pablo Neruda. Reprinted by permission. Pablo Neruda, *Twenty Poems*, trans. James Wright and Robert Bly (London: Rapp and Whiting, 1968), 63–5. Bertolt Brecht, *Poems 1913–1956*, ed. by John Willett and Ralph Manheim (London: Methuen Drama, 1976), 437–8, 440. © First published by Eyre Methuen Ltd. in 1976 and in the USA by Methuen Inc. in 1979, by arrangement with Suhrkamp Verlag, Frankfurt am Main.

4B. Carlton Lake, *The Atlantic Monthly*, July 1957.

5. See website http://www.cnn.com/SPECIALS/cold.war/episodes/06/documents/huac/disney.html

6. *Pravda*, 13 Jan. 1953. Trans. for CNN Cold War webpage.

7. Alexander Solzhenitsyn, *One Day in the Life of Ivan Denisovitch*, trans. by H. T. Willetts (London: Everyman, 1962). Reprinted by permission of the publisher.

8. http://www.turnerlearning.com/cnn/coldwar/sputnik/sput_re4.html

9. Diane Solway, *Nureyev: His Life* (New York: William Morrow, 1998). Copyright © 1998 by Diane Solway. Reprinted by permission of HarperCollins Publisher, Inc.

10. Vice-Chairman of the KGB Piotr Ivashutin to the Central Committee of the CPSU, 7 June 1962. Strictly confidential. (On the document it can be read: Comrade Kozlov has communicated orally to the presidium of the Central Committee. 10 June 1962.)

11. *Malcolm X Speaks* (New York: Pathfinder Press, 1965). Copyright © 1970 1992 Betty Shabazz and Pathfinder Press. Reprinted by permission.

12. Julie Frederikse, *South Africa: A Different Kind of War* (Gweru: Mambo Press, 1986), 43.

13. Günter Grass, *Denkzettel: Politische Reden und Aufsätze* [Memos: Political Speeches and Articles] (Darmstadt: Luchterhand, 1978), 83–8. Trans. Laura Schmidt.

14. Olof Palme, *En levande vilja* [A Living Determination] (Stockholm: Tidens, 1987), 24–5. Trans. the editors.

15. Peter George, *Dr Strangelove* [original title: *Red Alert*] (Oxford: Oxford University Press, 1988 [1963]), 18–22.

Chapter 14

1. 'On the Origins of the Soviet Atomic Project: Role of the Intelligence Service 1941–1946', ed. V. P. Visgin, *Voprosy istorii estestvoznaniia i tekhniki* [Problems in the History of Science and Technology], 3 (1992), 97–134.

2. David Greenglass's testimony at the Rosenberg trial, March 1951: www.foia.ucia.gov.

3. RSACH. First published on 11 June 1993 in *Izvestiia*. First published in English in the *CWIHP Bulletin*, 10. Trans. Natasha Shur.

4A. Joint CIA–SIS 'TPAJAX' plan for the overthrow of Prime Minister Mossadeq, June 1953. NSecA.

4B. Nicholas Cullather, *Operation PBSUCCESS: The United States and Guatemala, 1952–1954* (Washington DC: Center for the Study of Intelligence, 1994), 1–9.

5. David E. Murphy, Sergei A. Kondrashev, and George Bailey (eds.), *Battleground Berlin: CIA vs. KGB in the Cold War* (New Haven: Yale University Press, 1997), 423–8. © Yale University Press. Reprinted by permission.

6. Paul Lashamar, *Spyflights of the Cold War* (Annapolis, Md.: Naval Institute Press, 1996), 117–20. Reprinted by permission of Sutton Publishing and Naval Institute Press.

7. RSACH. First published in *CWIHP Bulletin*, 4. Trans. Vladislav Zubok.

8. *FRUS 1961–1963*, vol. X: *Cuba, 1961–1962*, pp. 213–16.

9. Jerrold L. Schecter and Peter S. Deriabin, *The Spy Who Saved the World: How a Soviet Colonel Changed the Course of the Cold War* (New York: C. Scribner's Sons, 1992), 429–33.

10A. RSACH. First published in *CWIHP Bulletin*, 4. Trans. Mark Kramer.

10B. Christopher Andrew and Vasili Mitrokhin, *The Mitrokhin Archive: The KGB in Europe and the West* (New York and London: Penguin Books, 1999), 420–2. Copyright © Christopher Andrew & Vasili Mitrokhin, 1999. Reprinted by permission.

11. Memorandum of Conversation between Gerald Ford and Richard Helms, 4 Jan. 1975. GFL.

12. CNN interview with Aldrich Ames, March 1998: www2.cnn.com/SPECIALS/coldwarexperience/spies/interviews/ames/

Chapter 15

1A. Original source unidentified. First published in *CWIHP Bulletin*, 11. Trans. Raymond Garthoff.

1B. *FRUS 1961–1963*, vol. XI, pp. 104–6.

1C. *DOSB*, 12 November 1962, pp. 737–40.

1D. Original source unidentified. First published in *CWIHP Bulletin*, 11. Trans. Raymond Garthoff.

 2. *FRUS 1961–1963*, vol. VI, pp. 190–8.

 3. PPP. John F. Kennedy, 1963. Pp. 459–64.

4A. Archiwum Akt Nowych, Warsaw. First published in *CWIHP Bulletin*, 11. Trans. Jan Chowaniec.

4B. *American Foreign Policy: Current Documents, 1967*, pp. 320–3.

 5. *FRUS 1964–1968*, vol. XIV, pp. 558–64.

 6. *Zhonggong dangshi zilao* [Chinese Communist Party History Materials], no. 42 (June 1992). First published in English in *CWIHP Bulletin*, 11. Trans. Chen Jian and Li Di.

 7. RSACH. First published in *CWIHP Bulletin*, 3. Trans. Mark Doctoroff.

8A. NPMP.

8B. NPMP.

 9. *DOSB*, 26 June 1972, pp. 898–9.

 10. NPMP.

Chapter 16

1A. GFL.

1B. John Stockwell, *In Search of Enemies: A CIA Story* (New York: Norton, 1978). Copyright © 1978 by John Stockwell. Used by permission of W. W. Norton & Company, Inc.

1C. Center for Defense Information, Revolutionary Armed Forces, Havana. Published in *CWIHP Bulletin*, 8–9. Trans. Piero Gleijeses.

1D. Havana Domestic Radio/Television Services in Spanish 2305 GMT 26 July 1976; speech by Cuban Prime Minister Fidel Castro marking the 23rd anniversary of the assault on the Moncada Barracks in Pinar del Rio City—live. Trans. at http://www.lanic.utexas.edu/la/cb/cuba/castro.html

 2. GFL. Published in '*East Timor Revisited: Ford, Kissinger, and the Indonesian Invasion, 1975–76*,' ed. William Burr and Michael L. Evans: NSecA Electronic Briefing Book No. 62 (Dec. 2001).

 3. RSACH. Published in Nicholas Wert and Gaël Moullec (eds.), *Raports secrets Soviétiques: la société dans les documents confidentiels 1921–1991* (Paris: Gallimard, 1994), 513–14. Trans. Laura Schmidt.

 4. http://reagan.com/plate.main/ronald/speeches/rrspeech07.html

 5. AFPRF.

6. Carter–Brezhnev Collection, NSecA.
7. RSACH.
8. RSACH.
9. Carter–Brezhnev Collection, NSecA.
10. RSACH.
11. APRF.
12. Carter–Brezhnev Collection, NSecA.
13. Ibid.

Chapter 17

1. Herman Kahn, William Brown, and Leon Martel, with the assistance of the Staff of the Hudson Institute, *The Next 200 Years* (New York: Morrow, 1976), 2–3. Copyright © 1976 by the Hudson Institute. Reprinted by permission of HarperCollins Publishers Inc.
2. Ezra F. Vogel, *Japan as Number One: Lessons for America* (Cambridge, Mass.: Harvard University Press, 1979), 4–5, 253–4. Copyright © 1979 by the President and Fellows of Harvard College. Reprinted by permission of the publisher.
3. *Selected Works of Deng Xiaoping*, vol. III, *1982–1992* (Beijing: Foreign Languages Press, 1994), 61–2. Reprinted by permission.
4. Gary Sick, *All Fall Down: America's Tragic Encounter with Iran* (New York: Random House, 1985), 195–7. Reprinted by permission.
5. Ruhollah Khomeini, *Islam and Revolution: Writings and Declarations*, trans. and annotated by Hamid Algar (London: KPI, 1981), 300–6.
6. *The Mujahideen Monthly* (Jan. 1986), 14–15.
7. Vladimir Tamarov, *Afghanistan: Soviet Vietnam* (San Francisco: Mercury House, 1996), 3–5. Copyright © 2001 by Vladimir Tamarov, Tan Speed Press, Burberry, California, USA.
8. ANR, Warsaw.
9. 'The Anoshkin Notebook on the Polish Crisis, December 1981', trans. and annotated by Mark Kramer, *CWIHP Bulletin*, 11.
10. PPP. Ronald Reagan, 1982.
11. Draft transcript of session of Politburo of CC CPSU, 31 May 1983. RSACH. First published in *CWIHP Bulletin*, 4; trans. Lena Milman.
12. Mikhail Gorbachev, *Memoirs* (New York: Doubleday, 1996), 189–93. Copyright © 1995 by Mikhail Gorbachev, English translation © by Wolf Jobst Siedler Verlag Gmbh, Berlin. Used by permission of Doubleday, a division of Random House, Inc.
13. NSecA.
14. Charles S. Maier, *Dissolution: The Crisis of Communism and the End of East Germany* (Princeton: Princeton University Press, 1997), 59–60, 71–2. Copyright © 1997 by Princeton University Press. Reprinted by permission.
15. Gorbacher, *Perestroika: New Thinking for Our Country and the World*, 25–6, 45–9.

Chapter 18

1. Rupert Cornwell, 'Moscow Leaves Afghanistan to the Afghans', *The Independent*, 16 Feb. 1989.
2. The President [George Bush], Review of National Defense Strategy, 3 March 1989. NA.
3. Zhang Li (comp.), *The Tiananmen Papers*, ed. Andrew J. Nathan and Perry Link (New York: Public Affairs, 2001).
4. Steve Crawshaw. '"We want bread" cry greets the new premier', *The Independent*, 21 Aug. 1989.
5. Judy Dempsey and Andrew Fisher, 'East Germans flood to West after Hungary opens its border', *Financial Times*, 11 Sept. 1989.
6. Robert Darnton, *Berlin Journal, 1989–1990* (New York: Norton, 1991), 74–81. Copyright © Robert Darnton. Used by permission of W. W. Norton & Company, Inc.
7. *The Independent*, 28 Dec. 1989.
8. NSecA.
9. Jacques Attali, *Verbatim*: vol. III, *1988–1991* (Paris: Fayard: 1995), 337. Trans. the editors. Reprinted by permission of the publisher.
10A. 'Spring of Tumult', from James A. Baker, III, *The Politics of Diplomacy: Revolution, War, and Peace* (New York: G. P. Putnam's Sons, 1995), 239–54. Copyright © 1995 by James A. Baker, III. Used by permission of G. P. Putnam's Sons, a division of Penguin Putnam Inc.
10B. George Bush and Brent Scowcroft, *A World Transformed* (New York: Alfred A. Knopf, 1998), 279–83. Copyright © 1998 by George Bush and Brent Scowcroft. Used by permission of Alfred A. Knopf, a division of Random House, Inc.
11. Record of conversation, Kohl–Gorbachev, 15 July 1990. Archive of the Office of the German Federal Chancellor, Berlin. First published in *Dokumente zur Deutschlandpolitik. Deutsche Einheit. Sonderedition aus den Akten des Bundeskanzleramtes 1989/90*, ed, Hans Jürgen Küsters and Daniel Hofmann. (Munich: Oldenbourg, 1998), 1340–8. Trans. Arne Hofmann.
12. PPP. George Bush. 1991, vol. 2. Pp. 1005–8.
13A. *Russia at the Barricades: Eyewitness Accounts of the August 1991 Coup*, ed. Victoria E. Bonnell et al. (Armonk, NY: M. E. Sharpe, 1994), 42–54.
13B. *Kuranty* (Moscow). Special edn. no. 3 (20 Aug. 1991). English trans. from *Current Digest of the Soviet Press*, vol. 43, no. 33.
14. Andrei Grachev, *Final Days: The Inside Story of the Collapse of the Soviet Union* (Boulder, Col.: Westview, 1995), 185–90.

Chapter 19

1. Joint Press Conference by Presidents Bush and Yeltsin, 1 Feb. 1992. PPP. George Bush, 1992–93. Pp. 177–81.

2. Philip Shenon, 'Reaching for the Good Life in Vietnam', *The New York Times Magazine*, 5 Jan. 1992.

3. Samuel Huntington, *The Clash of Civilizations and the Remaking of World Order* (New York and London: Simon & Schuster, 1997), 28–9. Reprinted by permission. Copyright © Samuel Huntington, 1997.

4A. The Keith Joseph Memorial Lecture, delivered by Baroness Thatcher on 11 Jan. 1996. In *Britain and European Integration 1945–1998: A Documentary History*, ed. David Gowland and Arthur Turner (London: Routledge, 2000), 203–4.

4B. Address by Helmut Kohl on receiving an honorary doctorate from the University of Louvain, 2 Feb. 1996. Ibid. 199–200.

5. Santos Virgilio, 'Angola—Children Hounded by Poverty and the Effects of War', 8 Jan. 1997. From the Inter Press Service Website: http://www.oneworld.org/ips2/jan98/angola.html

6. Address by Foreign Minister Bronislaw Geremek of Poland, Brussels, 16 Dec. 1997. From the 'Polishworld' website: http://www.polishworld.com/polemb/nato/speech/address1.html

7. Michael R. Gordon, 'A Whole New World of Arms Races to Contain', *New York Times*, 3 May 1998.

8. Damian Grammaticas, 'A Family Affair: Age Old Barriers Come Down for Family Reunion,' 16 Aug. 2000. From BBC World website: http://news.bbc.co.uk/hi/english/world/asia-pacific/newsid_883000/883349.stm Reprinted by permission of BBC World Service.

9A. From the WTO website: http://docsonline.wto.org/

9B. Ibid.

10. John Miller, 'Greetings America, My Name is Osama Bin Laden', excerpts from an interview conducted in May 1998. From the PBS website: http://www.pbs.org/wgbh/pages/frontline/shows/binladen/who/miller.html. ©

11. Stanley A. Weiss, 'As in the Cold War, the West Can Win in the End', *International Herald Tribune*, 19 Oct. 2001.

12A. A Joint Statement by Presidents Bush and Putin, 21 Oct. 2001. http://www.whitehouse.gov

12B. President Bush's Statement to the Press, 13 Dec. 2001. http://www.whitehouse.gov

Index and glossary

Brief identifications have been added to all entries in the index. For further information see Michael Kort, *The Columbia Guide to the Cold War* or Joseph Smith, *Historical Dictionary of the Cold War*.